UNIONISTS IN THE HEART OF DIXIE

1ST ALABAMA CAVALRY, USV

VOLUME I: SURNAMES A–G

BY

GLENDA MCWHIRTER TODD

HERITAGE BOOKS
2012

HERITAGE BOOKS
AN IMPRINT OF HERITAGE BOOKS, INC.

Books, CDs, and more—Worldwide

For our listing of thousands of titles see our website
at
www.HeritageBooks.com

Published 2012 by
HERITAGE BOOKS, INC.
Publishing Division
100 Railroad Ave. #104
Westminster, Maryland 21157

International Standard Book Numbers
Paperbound: 978-0-7884-5404-2
Clothbound: 978-0-7884-9323-2

UNIONISTS IN THE HEART OF DIXIE

1ST ALABAMA CAVALRY, USV

By

Glenda McWhirter Todd

Heritage Books, Inc.

Copyright 2012
Glenda McWhirter Todd

DEDICATION

**This book is dedicated to my ancestors,
Andrew Ferrier McWhirter and
Andrew Jackson McWhirter,
Who gave me my name and my
Interest in the Civil War and
Especially the 1ˢᵗ Alabama Cavalry, US Volunteers**

**Andrew Jackson McWhirter & wife,
Nancy Jane Whitehead McWhirter**

DISMANTLING AND BURNING THE WEST POINT RAILROAD TRACKS

Sketch by Joe Harper, descendant of Private Joseph Harper

UNIONISTS IN THE HEART OF DIXIE
TABLE OF CONTENTS

Volume I

Private Joseph Harper
Sketch by Descendant Joe Harper

ILLUSTRATIONS

The wonderful sketches in this book were drawn by Joe Harper and used with his permission. He is a descendant of Private Joseph Harper, who served in the 1st Alabama Cavalry, USV. Thanks, Joe, for sharing your talent with us.

Sketch by Joe Harper, Descendant of Private Joseph Harper

The Coldwater Covered Bridge is a locally owned covered bridge that spans the inlet to Oxford Lake in Calhoun County, Alabama. It is located at Oxford Lake Park off State Route 21 in the city of Oxford, about 4 miles south of Anniston, Alabama. Coldwater Creek Bridge is listed on the National Register of Historic Places. It was originally built around 1839-1850 over Coldwater Creek but has since been restored and moved to Oxford Lake Park.

PREFACE

When I began writing *Unionists in the Heart of Dixie*, it never occurred to me it would be any longer than the one book. However, word spread fast among the descendants of the soldiers who served in this regiment, and they generously began submitting stories on their ancestors and their families, some 45 pages long, which regretfully had to be condensed. By the time the military records of all of the soldiers had been transcribed and the wonderful family stories had been added, the one proposed book had turned into four or five volumes due to the fact the book can only contain a certain number of pages, which made it impossible to include it all in one book. These descendants of the loyal Union soldiers are extremely passionate about the regiment and their ancestors who served in the 1st Alabama Cavalry, USV, and it has been a pleasure working with them all of these years. It is my hope that each word in these books will be a treasure to descendants for years to come. My thanks to all who took the time to write and submit these family stories, they are very much appreciated.

Glenda McWhirter Todd

Sketch by Joe Harper, descendant of Joseph Harper

ACKNOWLEDGMENTS

As usual, I would like to express my thanks to some very special people whose talented collaboration brought this project to fruition.

My dear friend, L. Kent Henson, who put up with my questions and whose guidance was immeasurable throughout the writing of this and other books. He also designs the beautiful covers. It would be difficult to complete a book without his help.

Many of the descendants of these soldiers who have generously shared stories of their ancestors who fought in the 1st Alabama Cavalry, USV.

Editor, Barbara Kois, whose work is appreciated immensely. "Thanks again Barbara". If errors are found it was in something added after she edited the book.

Joe Harper of Alabama, the artist who drew the wonderful Civil War sketches for the book.

"Aunt Ethel" Terrill, who sat down with her grandnephew, Reid Bruton, and told her life story while he taped each word, transcribed the story, and submitted it to the author for publication in this book. Ms. Waldrop celebrated her 100th birthday on April 2, 2012. A belated Happy Birthday, "Aunt Ethel", and thanks for sharing your wonderful life story with us. Ms. Waldrop is a great granddaughter of Corporal Thomas P. Kirkman and great, great granddaughter of his father, William F. Kirkman, who both served as corporals in the 1st Alabama Cavalry, USV.

Robin Sterling has been enormously helpful and generous in sharing information on people from Winston County, Alabama.

Peter Gossett has generously given permission for use of his Civil War stories.

Janie Spencer, who has supplied an enormous amount of Guin information and tried to keep me straight on the family names.

Johnny L.T.N. Potter, author of *First Tennessee & Alabama Independent Vidette Cavalry,* for his help with information on soldiers who not only served in the 1st Alabama Cavalry, USV, but also served in the First Tennessee and Alabama Cavalry, Independent Vidette Cavalry.

Ryan Dupree, 1st Alabama Cavalry Webmaster, who helped me decipher some of the military records.

Robert E. "Bob" Hurst, whose insight and writings have been extremely helpful.

My apologies to anyone whose name I failed to mention.

By Joe Harper, Descendant of Joseph Harper

INTRODUCTION

When I first began the quest for my heritage and surprisingly found that several of my ancestors fought for the Union during the Civil War, I began looking for information on the 1st Alabama Cavalry, USV. As did other descendants of soldiers who served in this regiment, I wondered why so many men from Alabama, Mississippi, Tennessee, Georgia and South Carolina, would fight for the Union. What I found was, a few books written by Confederate sympathizers, who had not been kind to the Union cause. I decided it was time someone told their story as it happened.

After writing two previous books on the Civil War and 1st Alabama Cavalry, USV, I keep locating many captivating and terrifying stories on the struggles of these loyal Unionists who left their families to fend for themselves while they went off to fight in this horrendous war. Also, descendants of the soldiers who served in this regiment have submitted an enormous amount of information about their ancestors and their families. I'm sure there are still stories out there which have not been found. It stands to reason that everyone affected by the war has a story to tell.

UNIONISTS IN THE HEART OF DIXIE
Volume I

PRELUDE TO WAR

The following is a narrative essay composed of ancestral incidents and experiences related by descendants of some of the bravest soldiers who ever fought on American soil. Their love for their country far exceeded any notion they might have had to secede from the Union. They refused to fire on Old Glory; the Flag for which their ancestors before them had fought and died. Many of these same ancestors had to fight their way out of Scotland and Ireland and sail to America seeking a more peaceful place where they could worship as they desired. Not long after many of them arrived, they were in yet another fight with the British over control of America in the Revolutionary War. Not many years later they had to fight the British again in the War of 1812. Their ancestors considered these wars an inconvenience but were ready to do what was required of them to save their country. These Unionists did not take this legacy of battle for freedom lightly; they were prepared to give their all for their country. They carved their way through the howling wilderness, cleared land, built cabins and churches, and planted their crops, all of which involved incredible hardships for them and their families. These men loved their country enough to leave their families and seek refuge in the rugged mountains of northwest Alabama for months in all types of inclement weather, sometimes hungry and sick, to keep from being conscripted into the Confederate Army where they would have to fight against their beloved country.

Many of these early settlers of Northwest Alabama had previously fought in the War of 1812 with Andrew Jackson who later became President of the United States. One of these settlers, Solomon Curtis, felt very strongly for the Union, as did many of those who fought with Andrew Jackson. They did not want to see the Union that they worked so hard for "divided against itself." On his deathbed in 1860, Solomon asked that his children stay with the Union. Jackson was a staunch Unionist and already had experience fighting against individual states rights when South Carolina passed the Nullification Act which said they could ignore Federal legislation if they wanted to. South Carolina backed off of that, of course, but it cemented Jackson's reputation as a Unionist and all the men who followed him during the Indian Wars in the South of 1813 - 1815 and later settled in the Hill Country still tended to support his policies. These same men also did not want to fight against their southern neighbors who wanted to secede from the Union. However, some of those neighbors who wished to secede from the Union formed a band of Home Guard and Partisan Rangers to search for the Unionists. As they combed the mountains looking for these men, the Union Loyalists were running out of food and were in dire need of medical treatment. The ones who were caught were forced into the Confederate Army, but would later desert, make their way to the Union lines and join the 1st Alabama Cavalry, USV. These Alabama Unionists deserve a place in Alabama history.

When the Confederate Congress passed the Conscription Act on April 16, 1862, requiring every able-bodied man between the ages of 18 and 35 to be subject to military service, the loyalists found themselves in a quandary. Unwilling to fight for the Confederacy and unable to remain neutral, many took to the hills and caves and caverns to hide from conscription patrols. These unionist evaders along with Confederate deserters hiding in the hills became known as "mossbacks." Many of the unionists tried to hide their political views in order not to draw attention to themselves. It worked to a point.

Steve Ross, in his *History of the 1st Alabama Cavalry, USV, Knights of the Free State of Nickajack*, stated the following: In war it's helpful if soldiers learn to hate the enemy, something the citizens of a democracy aren't normally brought up to do. In the case of the 1st Alabama Cavalry, United States Volunteers, however, hatred for their enemy wasn't something learned under fire. Soldiers of the regiment brought their hatred for secession, and secessionists with them to the battlefield. Their blue uniforms clothed a red fury at the state government and its citizens that sought to coerce them into the Confederate army. These minions harassed and brutalized their families, drove them from their homes into the Alabama hills, then into Union lines, and at last into the ranks of the U.S. Army. . .

Christopher Sheats, the leader of the Unionists, spoke to a large group of Unionists and urged the following action: "The time has come to fight side by side for a cause we believe in, and put down the rebellion. The time has come to either fight in an army for which we have no sympathy and in a cause for which we hate, or join the army of the United States for a cause we love, and put down the rebellion so peace can again prevail. Tomorrow morning I am going to the Union Army, I am going to expose this fiendish villainy before the world. They shall hear from me. I have slept in mountains, in caves and caverns, till I am become musty, my health and manhood are failing me, I will stay here no longer till I am enabled to dwell in quiet at home." The Unionists took a stand and risked their lives traveling, in some cases, hundreds of miles to the Union lines to join their forces in the quest for freedom to live in peace.

Sheats had been to college and was highly loved and respected by all of the Unionists; however, he was hated just as much by the secessionists. He returned home after college and became a school teacher. The Alabama Governor, A.B. Moore, called a meeting to decide if Alabama would secede from the Union. Chris Sheats was selected to represent Winston County in this convention because the Unionists knew he would vote against secession first, last, and always. After arriving in Montgomery, Alabama to cast his vote not to secede, he read several stories in newspapers and became dismayed that these stories in southern newspapers were all in favor of secession. It appeared he would be the only person voting not to secede from the Union. He talked to several of his friends explaining how important it was not to secede but his words fell on deaf ears. While the convention was going on, news arrived that Mississippi and Florida had seceded from the United States and he feared Alabama was going to be next. When he thought things couldn't get any worse, they were told that those who dared to oppose the secession would be considered as traitors and delt with as such. After casting his "Nay" vote the results to secede and become an independent state were read, Chris began to make his way out of the court room when he was pushed, beaten, and shoved into a corner, drug into the street, thrown into a carriage, and thrown into jail, where he would remain a prisoner throughout the war. Although Christopher Sheats never served in the Union Army, he was able to draw Pension No. 1285004 of $30 per month by Special Act of Congress, (HR4008) Special Act (SC1044447), dated May 3, 1902. He filed for the pension on May 12, 1902.

Chris Sheats stated the following about the men he recruited for the 1st Alabama Cavalry, USV: "I wish to say a word in relation to the condition of these people. They are mostly poor, though many of them are, or rather were, in comfortable circumstances. They outnumber nearly 3 to 1 the secessionists in portions of Morgan, Blount, Winston, Marion, Walker, Fayette, and Jefferson Counties; but situated as they are, surrounded by a most relentless foe, mostly unarmed and destitute of ammunition, they are persecuted in every conceivable way, yet up to this time most of them have kept out of the way sufficiently to avoid being dragged off by the gangs that infest the country for the purpose of plunder and enforcing the provisions of the rebel Conscription Act. Their horses and cattle are driven off in vast numbers. Every public road is patrolled by guerilla bands, and the Union men have been compelled to seek protection in the fastnesses of the mountainous wilderness. They cannot hold out much longer. This state of things has so disturbed them that but very little attention was paid to farming; consequently many of them are now destitute of food of their own and are living off their more fortunate neighbors. Such examples of patriotism as these people have set are worthy of being followed. When it is taken into consideration that these people were sparsely settled, this case is without a parallel in American history. I have never witnessed such an outpouring of devoted and determined patriotism among any other people.

In a letter George Meade wrote to his wife, April 13, 1865, he stated: "MY GOD, WHAT MISERY THIS DREADFUL WAR HAS PRODUCED, AND HOW IT COMES HOME TO THE DOORS OF ALMOST EVERYONE!"

Truer words were never spoken! It did indeed come home to the doors of everyone, but nowhere in this country were the ravages of war as insufferable or the vengeance as brutal as it was in Northwest Alabama and on up into east Tennessee, between the secessionists of the Confederacy and the staunch Unionists including the First Alabama Cavalry, USV.

Information coming out of Covington in Tipton County, Tennessee and other areas of east Tennessee, tells horrible stories about the atrocities committed on the Unionists by the Confederate guerrillas in those and other areas of the state.

The narratives of the Civil War have always revolved around the metaphor of brother against brother, and father against son, in some cases. However, in the counties of Northwest Alabama, and areas in Tennessee, this was no metaphor. States, counties, towns, neighbors, and many close families were divided between the two sides and they fought with gruesome fury in one of the bloodiest, deadliest, least understood, and most talked about wars in history.

Most people are surprised to learn there were Union regiments in Alabama during the Civil War. They assume anyone from Alabama would have automatically joined the Confederacy and they immediately ask "Why, why did they fight for the Union?" These Unionists were not going to betray the love their ancestors had for America by fighting against it, and there was no way they could bring themselves to fire on Old Glory, the Flag of their forefathers. These loyal Unionists refused to cast a vote to break asunder the ties which held them together as a mighty nation of free and happy people. They refused to give their hands and hearts to secession which would have separated their magnificent government whose benign laws had nurtured them since birth. The Union men believed in their country even though they were afraid to express their opinions less they were beheaded. They were threatened and hunted down like wild animals. They continued to secrete themselves for months in the dreary damp caves and coves of the mountainous region of northwest Alabama in their efforts to elude the grasp of the Confederate guerrillas and Home Guard.

Union Soldiers hiding out in the Rock House, a name given to one of the caves in the Northwest Alabama Mountains

As more and more of these Unionists were basically living in the caves and other areas of the mountains, their wives would slip food to them when they thought they weren't being watched. They would also hang a certain color cloth on the clothes line to let them know when no one was around.

The Union Home Guard was formed which was made up of elderly men and others not able to be in the regular service. They would also look out for not only the men in the mountains, but their wives and families. This was a very dangerous service as they took their lives in their own hands should they be caught aiding these Unionists. Many of the poor Union ladies were threatened; they were often cursed and hundreds of them were forced to watch the foul murder of their husbands, sons and brothers. Many of the sweet young babes were made orphans by the unpardonable miscreants who enlisted in the Confederacy. Some of the wives of the men hiding in the mountains had to hold off some

3

of the bands of Confederate guerrillas who approached their house, by having their rifle aimed at them when they rode up in her yard. The women always had to be on the lookout for them.

There was no honor in this war, the Unionists were fighting in a noble cause, the holy laws, the sacred institutions which made us a free and happy nation, and defending the land that gave them birth, the land on which their forefathers settled before them. They wanted to preserve the government, the sacred liberties bequeathed to them by their revolutionary ancestors.

The Confederates had what they called "The Slaughter Pen", and if they caught Unionists who refused to join the Confederacy, they threw them in the slaughter pen and shot them. Most of them were shot in the back. Byrd Norris was married to Loduska Dorthula Frances Ingle, who was the granddaughter of Peter Ingle. He was one of those who refused to enlist at gun point, so he was tied to a tree, north of Jasper and given 5 days to join the Confederacy or die. He died with 7 bullets "at the cross of his back."

During the Civil War, A school teacher in east Tennessee commented on the hardships they were suffering and she told the following story: One cold winter day a company of rebel soldiers went to the house of Richard Smith's a very old man some 80 years of age, and after cursing him as much as they liked, they tore down his door, broke open his trunk, containing his valuable papers, and utterly demolished his trunk, papers and everything they thought would be of any value to the poor old man. Still not being satisfied they broke his clock and took the old man's hat off his grey head. The rebels then went off and laughed about how they made this old man suffer, they swore "no damned old rascal who had as many Lincolnite sons and grandsons as old Dick Smith should have anything, and that they would just as soon put lead in him as any other way." She went on to talk about the many martyrs to their government and how the bravest and best sons had fought the tyrant rebel foe, and many of their precious bones now lie bleaching on the battle fields at Stone's River, Knoxville, Chickamauga, as well as Atlanta, South and North Carolina.

There are numerous stories of Union families being murdered, of having their houses, barns and crops burned while the wives, widows, and sometimes children, of Union soldiers were raped and others were run out of their homes. (See "Heartbreak of a Civil War Widow" by Todd.) Their cattle, corn, meat, and anything the Confederate sympathizers could eat or sell, were taken. Some of these stories appeared in newspapers as far away as Nashville, Tennessee, in the *Nashville Daily Union*. These guerrillas were not the average hard working, run-of-the-mill citizens; they were homegrown terrorists turned loose to settle old scores. They robbed and pillaged the countryside and murdered any Unionists they encountered, with the popular support of local Confederates. The Confederate guerrilla, Champ Ferguson was convicted and hung for killing 53 men in the Tipton County, Tennessee area. He said himself that was a low figure; he knew for certain that he killed well over a hundred Unionists. In the book, *Confederate Outlaw* by Brian Dallas McKnight, the author states that Captain James W. McHenry gave a knife to Champ Ferguson telling him to "take it and gut the Yankees." J.A. Brents also wrote that Ferguson never took prisoners, rather he "ordered his satellites to hold them by the arms while he deliberately ripped them open with a huge knife, their bowels dropping upon the ground." Ferguson had killed several men, "cut one in twain", removed the man's entrails, and threw them on a log near by." Several days afterward, the news of the raid and the revelations that followed was also printed in *The Nashville Daily Union*. It was reported that Ferguson had taken "a promising little boy 12 years old by the name of Zachary out of his sick bed and while being held by two guerrillas, a third cut his abdomen wide open." While these are stories told in Tipton County, Tennessee, these same horrors were going on in northwest Alabama.

It should be made clear that the Confederates did not have a monopoly on acts of violence in Alabama or Tennessee during the Civil War. It should also be known that the fighting did not end just because the Civil War had ended. Both sides were guilty of atrocities that preceded, ran throughout, and continued into the years following the Civil War. Being a minority in the deep South, however, made Unionists easy targets for brutal attacks including robbery, harassment, burning of houses, and murder by the Confederate Home Guard, dog cavalry, and guerrillas. And as tempers flared and desperation took hold of the South when it seemed as if their cause was lost, these incidents against anyone suspected of having Unionist sympathies escalated in their number and graphic nature. Also, although it happened on both sides, documentation suggests that the treatment of the Confederates by

4

the Unionists was not as horrific or prevalent as that perpetrated by the Confederates toward the Unionists.

Gilbert Guin was the son of Levi Guin, the elder, who along with his wife, Nancy, had four sons who served in the 1st Alabama Cavalry Union Army. These boys had a cousin, Michael Guin, who also served in the 1st Alabama Union Army.

Gilbert was murdered by a Confederate Army Troop called the Dog Cavalry during the Civil War. This troop was led by an officer known as "Old Dog John Wilson." One story is that Gilbert was plowing in the field of his farm when he was abducted by the Home Guard and drug into the woods. Another is that he was on his way to Columbus to take supplies to the soldiers when he was caught by one of the worst gangs that roamed the area. Gilbert had met up with "Old Dog Wilson" and given him a thrashing just a few days prior to this.

Gilbert's mutilated body was found hanging from the limb of a dogwood tree, about six miles west of his home, near the old McGee Graveyard in Lamar County, Alabama. He was found by his wife who was accompanied by female neighbors, all of whom were on horseback. They had been roaming the woods and swamps for several days looking for him. He was located, as most dead carcasses were in those days, by the flight of buzzards. He had been dis-emboweled, his throat cut and an iron wedge was driven down his throat. What was left by the buzzards was buried in the old McGee Graveyard which was near by. Gilbert was opposed to secession and he and his brothers, being Irish frontiersmen, were ready to die fighting against any measure they thought unjust or tyrannical towards themselves and their neighbors. "Old Dog John Wilson" had been an officer of a Confederate Home Guard company, and he and his command turned guerilla. In all northwesterly Alabama, all the way from Tuscaloosa to the Tennessee River, where the Union Army held a line during most of the Civil War, the habit of Confederate Home Guard companies to turn guerillas and outlaw was not particularly unusual. The inspiration for such an action grew out of the situation itself."

Murder or political assassination was a constant threat for Alabama Unionists who chose to remain at home. Three sons of Solomon Curtis were all killed in Winston County.

Joel Jackson Curtis was killed in 1862 for refusing to join the Confederate Army.

George Washington Curtis, home on leave from the Union Army, was killed by the Home Guard in his yard while his wife and three children watched.

Thomas Pink Curtis, the probate judge of Winston County, was arrested near Houston by Confederate authorities in 1864 and taken to a bluff on Clear Creek where he was summarily executed with two shots to the right eye.

It has been difficult for people in later years to believe just how horrendous this reign of terror in northwest Alabama and Tennessee was. Some of them tend to believe the stories are embellished, but many of the stories were documented and published in the newspapers. These hostilities were not only carried out by the Confederates but by the Unionists as well. However, it appears the Confederates were more aggressive in what they did, and caused more deaths, harm and destruction to the Unionists and their families. In June 1863 the US Army escorted many of the Unionists' families to Illinois for their protection. Some of these included the wives, widows and children of Union soldiers and the infirm and elderly men known to be Union sympathizers. After the war, many of the soldiers whose families went to Illinois for protection, joined them there where they remained and are buried. Others finally moved back to their former homes and in many cases, found them burned.

Transcribed below is an excerpt from *A Civil War Diary*, written by Mary Katherine "Miss Molly" Sproul. She and her family were staunch Union supporters in Covington, Tipton County, Tennessee. Miss Molly was an extremely intelligent lady who had a college education, something almost unheard of for women in those days. She was eloquent in her thoughts, speech, patriotism and unwavering support for the Union families caught in the suffering nightmare of the war. She taught school in a little log cabin until the Confederate sympathizers pulled their children from her class room at which time the funds were not sufficient to continue operating the school and it was closed. The Confederate sympathizers were willing to deny their children an education solely because their teacher, Miss Molly, loved her country and believed in the Union cause.

From A *Civil War Diary*, by Mary Katherine Sproul

"No one must ever insinuate to me, that there were no loyalists in Tennessee. The very idea is absurd. Too often I have prayed to Almighty God to preserve our government, the sacred liberties bequeathed to us by our revolutionary ancestors; too often have I witnessed scenes of barbarity perpetrated by the rebels, too often has the heart of the writer been made to bleed at the nefarious crimes of rebel soldiers, to ever utter a disloyal word, harbor a disloyal thought, or commit a disloyal act. Thousands in this state as well as myself have spurned the idea of secession, have repudiated the doctrine with indignation and as I before remarked have sealed their faith with their own precious blood. Our state has been overrun, its buildings defaced and many of them have been burned. Numbers of loyal families have been driven from their homes, with no covering for their honest heads save the deep blue vault of heaven. Many a heart broken mother that once rolled in affluence has heard her prattling babes cry for bread and gazed with tearful eyes upon their tattered garments. I have known hundreds of Union ladies whose feeble strength forbade laborious exercise, but through sheer necessity, have been compelled to plow and hoe to make bread for the little sufferers around her and ere she reaped the fruits of her toil she must see it dragged away from her by the defenders of "southern rights." Such my dear readers is the case in Middle and East Tennessee. I could tell you of a multitude of circumstances that would also cause the coldest heart to throb with emotions of sorrow. I know it does not look reasonable that men who had been reared upon the same soil, bred at the same schools, ate and drank at the same festive board would commit such ignoble deeds, but nevertheless they have and are committing crimes of blackest atrocity every day. I do candidly believe they have become so habituated to deeds of horror until murdering inoffensive Union men has become a feast to their remorseless souls, and the screams of broken hearted women is music in their ears. I heard a rebel soldier say myself that he believed he would go to killing women and children."

This type of torture, abuse, and murder was no different in Alabama. Sarah Harper McWhirter, the author's great-great-grandmother, watched her husband, three sons, one barely 15 years of age, and three brothers go off to war with the 1st Alabama Cavalry, USV, while three other brothers joined the Confederacy. She was abused and molested by the Confederate Home Guard due to the fact her husband and three sons were in the Union Army. [More can be read about this in *Heartbreak of a Civil War Widow* by the author.]

Sarah's brother, Josiah Houston Harper was a Scout for the 1st Alabama Cavalry, USV, and the scouts were not endeared by the Confederacy as they did not like being spied upon. Civil War scouts operated on the fringes of an army with the purpose of obtaining information about enemy locations, movements, and strengths. They often operated behind enemy lines. Josiah was said to have made shoes for the army.

Josiah Harper had served his time in the 1st Alabama Cavalry, USV, had been honorably discharged and went home to his wife and children. However, during a visit to see John Lyon, the Confederate Home Guard caught him, brutally tortured and hung him. The following is the testimony of John Lyon who found him still hanging: (sic) "40 out of 80 men in my beat went to the Union army. I aided their wives and family all I could. I cut and hauled wood for them. I went to the salt works and got salt for them. This was done during the war. Josiah Harper, a Union soldier, went to the war, served out his time and came home. While here I protected him from being caught by the Confederates all I could without being found out at it. They at last caught him and hanged him. Myself and family looked for him after he was hanged until found. I hauled him to the graveyard and helped bury him, and other like favors I done for the Union cause and its defenders." This is the type of brutality these people were subjected to before, during and after the Civil War, only because their families loved their country, wanted to protect it and refused to fire on the flag of their Revolutionary forefathers. John Lyon explained this when he filed his Southern Claim.

THE WAR

General Sherman stated, "TRUE IT IS, PIERCE THE SHELL OF THE C.S.A. AND IT'S ALL HOLLOW INSIDE." He knew the Union not only had to defeat the Confederacy, but had to break the will of the Southern people to resist Federal authority. He stated they were not only fighting hostile armies but a hostile people, and they must make old and young, rich and poor, feel the hard hand of war, as well as their organized armies. This he did. Robert E. Lee stated: "WHAT A CRUEL THING IS WAR: TO SEPARATE AND DESTROY FAMILIES AND FRIENDS, AND MAR THE PUREST JOYS AND HAPPINESS GOD HAS GRANTED US IN THIS WORLD; TO FILL OUR HEARTS WITH HATRED INSTEAD OF LOVE FOR OUR NEIGHBORS, AND TO DEVASTATE THE FAIR FACE OF THIS BEAUTIFUL WORLD." You will read about just how much hate there was in Northwest Alabama and how much hatred was in their hearts to torture men to death and throw their bodies over the bluffs never to be seen again. These Unionist did not believe in secession, but they did strongly believe in liberty and they vowed to fight to the death to defend their liberty.

The war definitely destroyed many families and friendships, some never to speak again after the war. Some of the soldiers and their families moved as far west as California and others as far north as Illinois and Indiana.

Corporal Horatio D. Chapman, who served in Company C, 20th Connecticut Volunteers, US, stated the following in his *Civil War Diary of a Forty-niner*: "July 3, 1863 - We built fires all over the battle field and the dead of the blue and gray were being buried all night, and the wounded carried to the hospital. We made no distinction between our own and the Confederate wounded, but treated them both alike, and although we had been engaged in fierce and deadly combat all day and weary and all begrimed with smoke and powder and dust, many of us went around among the wounded and gave cooling water or hot coffee to drink. The confederates were surprised and so expressed themselves that they received such kind treatment at our hands, and some of the slightly wounded were glad they were wounded and our prisoners.

But in front of our breastworks, where the Confederates were massed in large numbers, the sight was truly awful and appalling. The shells from our batteries had told with fearful and terrible effect upon them and the dead in some places were piled upon each other, and the groans and moans of the wounded were truly saddening to hear. Some were just alive and gasping, but unconscious. Others were mortally wounded and were conscious of the fact that they could not live long; and there were others wounded, how bad they could not tell, whether mortal or otherwise, and so it was they would linger on some longer and some for a shorter time-without the sight or consolation of wife, mother, sister or friend. I saw a letter sticking out of the breast pocket of one of the Confederate dead, a young man apparently about twenty-four. Curiosity prompted me to read it. It was from his young wife away down in the state of Louisiana. She was hoping and longing that this cruel war would end and he could come home, and she says, "Our little boy gets into my lap and says, `Now, Mama, I will give you a kiss for Papa. But oh how I wish you could come home and kiss me for yourself."

In an 1861 letter to his son, Curtis, Robert E. Lee stated the following: "I CAN ANTICIPATE NO GREATER CALAMITY FOR THE COUNTRY THAN THE DISSOLUTION OF THE UNION. IT WOULD BE AN ACCUMULATION OF ALL THE EVILS WE COMPLAIN OF, AND I AM WILLING TO SACRIFICE EVERYTHING BUT HONOR FOR ITS PRESERVATION."

One-hundred fifty years later, people still debate the cause of the Civil War. In CSA Major General John B. Gordon's Book, *Reminiscences of the Civil War*, he stated the following: "People still debate the reason for the Civil War and some maintain it was fought over slavery, but slavery was far from being the sole cause of the prolonged conflict. Neither its destruction on the one hand, nor its defense on the other, was the energizing force that held the contending armies to four years of bloody work. I apprehend that if all living Union soldiers were summoned to the witness-stand, every one of them would testify that it was the preservation of the American Union and not the destruction of Southern slavery that induced him to volunteer at the call of his country. As for the South, it is enough to say that perhaps eighty per cent, of her armies were neither slave-holders, nor had the remotest interest in the institution. No other proof, however, is needed than the undeniable fact that at any period of the war from its beginning to near its close, the South could have saved slavery by simply laying down its arms and returning to the Union."

We must therefore, look beyond the institution of slavery for the fundamental issues which dominated and inspired all classes of the contending sections. It is not difficult to find them. The "Old Man Eloquent," William E. Gladstone, who was perhaps England's foremost statesman of the century, believed that the Government formed by our fathers was the noblest political fabric ever devised by the brain of man. This undoubtedly is true; and yet before these inspired builders were dead, controversy arose as to the nature and powers of their free constitutional government. Indeed, in the very convention that framed the Constitution the clashing theories and bristling arguments of 1787 presaged the glistening bayonets of 1861."

Showing Colonel Abel D. Streight the way to Davis Gap
Sketch by Joe Harper, Descendant of Private Joseph Harper

8

IMPORTANT FROM NORTHERN ALABAMA
UNION MEN RALLY AROUND THE OLD FLAG
Published: August 2, 1862 in the *New York Times*

A few days ago a citizen of Alabama, residing among the mountains south of Decatur, distant some thirty or forty miles, found his way to the camp of the Twentieth Brigade, and made known the fact, that in the vicinity of his home there were many men who were anxious to enlist and fight for the Union, under the good old flag.

The representations made resulted in sending Colonel Streight, with the 51st Regiment Indiana Volunteers, down into the region named, with a view of offering protection to any who might desire to enlist. After an absence of four days, Colonel Streight returned to camp, bringing with him nearly two hundred able-bodied and earnest men. When Colonel Streight first reached their homes in the hill country, not a man could be found at his house, all of them being obliged to conceal themselves in the forests or among the hiding-places of the mountains, lest they be obliged to enter the rebel army by the hated conscript law, or be shot down like wild beasts for being Union men. As soon, however, as the Colonel made known his mission to the wives and daughters of these hardy mountaineers they were on the move to communicate with the fugitives; and within forty-eight hours, the Colonel was ready to return with the recruits.

In his official report, which is dated near Morrisville [Mooresville], Alabama, July 14, Colonel Streight says: "I wish to say a word relative to the condition of these people. They are mostly poor, though many of them are, or rather have been in good circumstances. They outnumber nearly three to one the Secessionists, in portions of Morgan, Blount, Winston, Marion, Walker, Fayette and Jefferson Counties, but situated as they are, surrounded by a most relentless foe, mostly unarmed and destitute of ammunition, they are persecuted in every conceivable way, yet up to this time most of them have kept out of the way sufficiently to avoid being dragged off by the gangs that infest the country for the purpose of plunder, and enforcing the provisions of the rebel Conscription Act, but their horses and cattle are driven off in vast numbers. Each public road is patrolled by guerrilla bands, and the Union men have been compelled to seek protection in the fastnesses of the mountainous wilderness. They cannot hold out much longer. This state of things has so much disturbed them that but very little attention has been paid to farming; consequently many of them are now destitute of food of their own, and are living off their more fortunate neighbors.

Such examples of patriotism as these people have set are worthy of being followed. One elderly lady, Mrs. Anna Campbell, volunteered to ride thirty-five miles and return, making seventy miles, with about thirty recruits, inside of thirty-six hours. WHEN IT IS TAKEN INTO CONSIDERATION THAT THESE PEOPLE WERE ALL HID AWAY TO AVOID BEING TAKEN BY THE REBELS, AND THAT THE COUNTRY IS BUT SPARSELY SETTLED, THIS CASE IS WITHOUT A PARALLEL IN AMERICAN HISTORY. There are many cases of a similar nature that came under my observation, but I do not desire to weary your patience with them. Suffice it to say that I have never witnessed such an outpouring of devoted and determined patriotism among any other people. And I am now of the opinion that if there could be a sufficient force in that portion of the country to protect these people, there could be at least two full regiments raised of as good and true men as ever defended the American flag. So confident am I that my views are correct, that if the Commanding-General will grant me permission to do so, I will take my regiment (the boys all want to go) and two weeks' rations of bread, salt, sugar and coffee, (meat we can get there,) and five hundred extra stand of arms, with a sufficient supply of ammunition, and locate at least thirty miles south of Decatur, where I will rally around me a sufficient number of the brave mountaineers to protect the country effectually against anything except the regular rebel army, who, by the way, would find it a difficult country to operate in. NEVER DID PEOPLE STAND IN GREATER NEED OF PROTECTION. THEY HAVE BATTLED MANFULLY AGAINST THE MOST UNSCRUPULOUS FOE THAT CIVILIZED WELFARE HAS EVER WITNESSED. THEY HAVE BEEN SHUT OUT FROM ALL COMMUNICATION WITHOUT ANYTHING BUT THEIR ENEMIES FOR A YEAR AND A HALF, AND YET THEY STAND FIRM AND TRUE. IF SUCH MERIT IS NOT TO BE REWARDED; IF SUCH CITIZENS ARE NOT TO RECEIVE PROTECTION, THEN IS THEIR CASE A DEPLORABLE ONE INDEED."

On the night of July 14, 1862, Streight, who was intent on organizing the Alabamians into a fighting force, spoke to a gathering of Unionists before introducing Chris Sheats to them.

Sheats apparently gave a stem-winder of a speech, telling his fellow Alabamians that the time had come join the army of the United States and fight the Confederacy "to hell and back again."

The *Encyclopedia of Alabama* states, "Although Winston County's Unionists wanted to be left alone, the governments of the Confederacy and of Alabama did not oblige. The hill-country Unionists soon faced Confederate conscription beginning in 1862 and many fled their homes, seeking refuge from conscription agents in the county's rugged forests and canyons. The Natural Bridge in western Winston County was said to have been a major gathering point for Unionists avoiding the draft or who had deserted from the Confederate Army. From Winston County, many of these Unionists eventually made their way north to the Tennessee River valley and joined the Union Army, most commonly enlisting in the First Alabama Cavalry, USA. A few of the county's residents, including Bill Looney, served the Union Army by helping Unionists escape to the safety of Union lines. In July 1862, Colonel Abel D. Streight led a detachment of Union troops into the hills to gather more recruits for the Union Army. The Unionist farmers who fled into the woods and to the Union Army to avoid the Confederate draft could not work on their farms. Hence, the county's residents had difficulty growing enough food. Confederate impressment agents worsened matters by taking food and livestock from the county to feed the Confederate army."

No matter how careful they were, traveling the back roads, woods and other out of the way places, there were many Union soldiers who were caught by the Confederates, Confederate Home Guard, or the dog cavalry, who killed them on the spot and threw their bodies over the cliff, never to be found. There was an infinite number of distressed parents, wives and children who would not learn the fate of their loved ones until years after the war when someone in their later guilt-filled years, finally broke their silence and told what happened to some of the soldiers.

When the Confederate Congress passed the Conscription Act on April 16, 1862, requiring every able-bodied man between the ages of 18 and 35 to be subject to military service, the hill people found themselves in a quandary. Unwilling to fight for the Confederacy and unable to remain neutral, many took to the hills, caves, and caverns to hide from conscription patrols. These unionist evaders along with Confederate deserters hiding in the hills became known as "mossbacks."

Many of the unionists tried to hide their political views in order not to draw attention to themselves. It worked to a point.

"IT WAS FIRMLY IN MY MIND THAT I WOULD NEVER GO BACK ON "OLD GLORY", WROTE MARION COUNTY RESIDENT JOHN PHILLIPS AFTER THE WAR. "I HAD HEARD TOO MUCH FROM MY OLD GRANDPARENTS ABOUT THE SUFFERINGS AND PRIVATIONS THEY HAD TO ENDURE DURING THE REVOLUTIONARY WAR TO EVER ENGAGE AGAINST THE STARS AND STRIPES. HOWEVER, I WENT SLOW AND TALKED BUT LITTLE AND THOUGHT BY NOT TALKING EITHER FOR OR AGAINST IT AND GIVING THEM ALL THEY ASKED FOR AND TREATING THEM KINDLY, THEY WOULD LET ME ALONE."

It is unclear how many Alabamians wore the blue, because many, after secreting themselves to federal lines, simply joined other state regiments. Perhaps as many as 5,000 served in federal units. We do know that about 400 joined Abel D. Streight's 51st Indiana in July 1862. We know that many Alabama unionists served in 4th Indiana Cavalry; the 12th Tennessee Cavalry; the 7th Illinois Cavalry; the 1st Middle Tennessee Cavalry; the 10th Missouri Cavalry; the 5th Tennessee Cavalry; the 14th Michigan Infantry; the 41st New York Infantry; the 56th Illinois Infantry and the 11th Wisconsin Infantry.

More than 2,000 served in the 1st Alabama Cavalry, 239 from Winston County alone.

Eventually, John Phillips would be found out and the Home Guard would come calling on him. "They commenced robbing my family of the support I had left for them; they drove off my cattle and took my horses and mules, also my corn. They went so far as to pour what meal my family had out in the floor and fill the sacks with meat. They took our cups, saucers and plates, not leaving anything for their sustenance."

The severe treatment to his family by the Home Guard pushed John Phillips to making his way to federal lines and joining the 1st Alabama Cavalry, United States Volunteers.

"We all enlisted in the U.S. Army without any medical examination as we all wanted to enlist. I told them the Rebs had conscripted me and would claim me as a deserter and I never would suffer myself to be captured by them alive. The head officer said he would appoint me the Company Sergeant, and that would relieve me from guard duty, and place me in a position that would shield me from the chance of being captured as much as possible."

Most of the men and women who supported the Union after Alabama's secession faced great difficulties. Many were ostracized and ridiculed by neighbors, called before community vigilance committees for questioning and intimidation, or actually harmed for endorsing the Union. Such treatment was most commonly meted out to those who publicly asserted their views; those who kept quiet and did not interfere with volunteering were often left alone during the first year of the war. After Confederate conscription began in April 1862, however, community tolerance of Unionists waned. Individuals who resisted the draft, for whatever reason, were subject to arrest and imprisonment. Family members who supported resisters were frequently threatened with violence or exile by conscript cavalry who hoped to pressure men to come in from the woods or mountains and surrender. In addition, it was not at all uncommon for the families of Unionists to be targeted for punitive foraging or arson by Confederate forces or local conscript cavalry.

It wasn't only men who served in the Union army who were threatened during and after the war, as was the case with William Holland Wright of DeKalb County, Alabama. William Holland Wright was a staunch Unionists. He was born December 17, 1812, in Tennessee, and therefore his age and or debility possibly prevented him from joining the Union Army during the Civil War, However, he suffered just the same at the hands of the Confederate Home Guard, as did many of the other Unionists of northwest Alabama. Not serving in the Union Army did not exempt him from the atrocities these Unionists suffered at the hands of the Confederate Home Guard. He hid out in the mountains and caves of Northwest Alabama with hundreds of the other Unionists trying to keep from being conscripted into the Confederate Army, or killed because he didn't believe in secession. One of these members of the Confederate Home Guard was a Captain Freeman who had threatened William on different occasions, causing him to constantly be frightened for his life, or the life of his family members.

Wright stated Captain George F. Allen of the 1st Tennessee & Alabama Independent Vidette Cavalry, USV confiscated a black mare for the 15th Army Corps. The Union Army also confiscated several horses, hogs, food, hay, corn, cotton, potatoes, etc. for their use for which they finally compensated him with $1,128.00. The Union, as well as the Confederacy, were forced to live off the land as they could not carry enough rations. He stated he was in favor of the old government and the Union, and that he did all he could do for the Union and Union citizens.

William told of his horrifying story when he applied for a Southern Claim. He stated there were times when thirty or forty of the Confederates would stand over him snapping their pistols and guns on him, cursing and abusing him all the while. They kept him in fear of them all the time because he said they would come like a passel of wild men and he did not know at any time but that they would come and kill him.

William Holland Wright's Southern Claim was 149 pages long and much of it was written in pencil and extremely faded, making most of it illegible.

One of William's sons had joined an Arkansas Regiment of the Confederate Army, and William used a $60 gold piece as an incentive for his son to join the Union Army when it passed through where he was. When soldiers escaped from the Confederate Army or became separated from their units, William welcomed them into his home, fed them and hid them out. In the summer of 1864, he supposedly fed five prisoners who had escaped from the Confederate Army and stated they had not eaten in two days. William also furnished them with rations and directed them as to which way to go to escape the Confederate soldiers. They told William that several black men told them the county was occupied by Rebels and had directed them to his house and told them William Wright was a man who could be trusted.

After the Union Army invaded Alabama in early 1862, Unionists had more opportunities to flee behind Union lines for safety and the possibility of employment as soldiers, spies, or laborers. Most well known of Alabama's Union troops was the First Alabama Cavalry, USA, organized in late 1862 by Brig. General Grenville M. Dodge, stationed at Corinth, Mississippi. In some cases, they collaborated

11

with local African Americans to aid and abet the Union Army or pro-Union men in their neighborhoods. Moreover, African Americans from Alabama also crossed the Union lines to serve as laborers and soldiers. There were 5 regiments of African Americans in Alabama: 1st Regiment (Siege) Heavy Artillery, 1st Regiment Infantry, 2nd Regiment Infantry, 3rd Regiment Infantry, and 4th Regiment Infantry, all of African Descent.

Almost 5,000 African Americans, or 6 percent of Alabama's black male population between the ages of 18 and 45, volunteered in the Union ranks. As was the case throughout the South, by the midpoint of the war, Alabama's original Unionists were increasingly joined in their dissent by deserters from the Confederate Army, mostly men whose families were struggling at home without their labor. Disillusioned by the realities of warfare, angered by the inequities of service under laws exempting slave-owners and selected professionals, such Alabamians generally wanted the war to end more than they desired Union victory, though some did cross lines and join the Union army rather than desert and avoid service altogether. A small peace movement also emerged at this time among men who had originally opposed secession but later supported the state.

After the war, Unionists continued to struggle politically and socially, for their wartime activities had alienated them from their now-defeated neighbors. Most eagerly joined the Union League and the Republican Party. Some wartime Unionists helped reintroduce the Methodist-Episcopal Church (as contrasted with the Methodist-Episcopal Church, South) to northern Alabama, finding there a more hospitable environment for worship. Many campaigned strenuously to convince the president and Congress to limit the political rights of former Confederates. They also sought positions of local and state authority for others who had supported the Union during the war. At this point, a number of men who had originally opposed secession but supported the state in 1861, as well as citizens who had become disillusioned with the war, also moved to the fore of political life in Alabama. These moderates were, in general, encouraged by President Andrew Johnson, who appointed such men to positions of political authority in the immediate post-war provisional governments he established. The Republican Party in Alabama was populated by such individuals, as well as core Unionists who had served in the Union Army or otherwise actively resisted the Confederacy. Both groups were referred to by their Democratic opponents as scalawags.

Many of the soldiers in the 1st Alabama Cavalry, USV suffered legally, politically and socially for their loyalty to their country, and they were indeed loyal.

MURDER IN THE SOLOMON CURTIS FAMILY

Solomon Curtis was born in Buncombe County, North Carolina, in 1797. Not much is known of his early life. We know that at some time in his early life he moved to Humphreys County, Tennessee. No information is available on his extended family. What we do know is that he joined Andrew Jackson's Army of the 1st West Tennessee Militia, Peter Searcy's Unit, at Fayetteville, Lincoln County, Tennessee in 1814. He marched with General Jackson through Alabama to Fort Jackson and participated in the Battle of Fort Jackson. Solomon Curtis stayed in Alabama after his military service.

He married Charlotta Heaton in Clarke County, Alabama on February 18, 1819. To this union, ten children were born. There were nine boys and one girl. George Washington Curtis, Joel Jackson Curtis, William Verpo Curtis, Thomas Pinkney Curtis, James G. Curtis, Benjamin Franklin Curtis, Darrell Hollis Curtis, Louisa Jane Curtis (Taylor), John Wesley Curtis, and Jasper Newton Curtis.

Solomon and Charlotta moved frequently during their early years. Some of the early places they lived were Fayette County, Alabama 1830; Lamar County, Alabama 1838; Marion County, Alabama 1840; Tippah County, Mississippi 1850; and Winston County, Alabama about 1855.

Solomon was a merchant and land owner. He owned a store in Littleville, Alabama. At his death in 1860 the value of his estate was estimated to be around $20,000.00. Fast horses and horse racing was a pastime for him.

One thing that made Solomon stand out so uniquely in the history of Winston County was his stand on the War Between the States. On his death bed in 1860 he called all of his children to his bedside and asked them to remain loyal to the Union. The story goes that his father fought in the Revolutionary War and he did not want his family to go against the government of the United States. All of his children remained loyal to this promise and because of this; three of them lost their lives. George Washington Curtis was murdered in his own front yard by the (Confederate) Home Guard; Thomas Pinkney, then Probate Judge, was murdered by the (Confederate) Home Guard for refusing to hand over the County's money. Joel Jackson was captured and carried to the Jasper, Alabama jail. He was shot and killed there. We know that James G. Curtis and Darrell Hollis Curtis fought for the Union. John Wesley Curtis was a member of the 10th Missouri Cavalry Company B. Many hardships and atrocities were inflicted on the Curtis family during the War because of their belief and stand on issues of the War.

As stated, Solomon Curtis died in 1860 leaving his beloved Charlotta, who died in 1893 and is buried at the Curtis Cemetery near Double Springs, Alabama. Inclement weather and impassable road conditions prevented Charlotta from being buried by Solomon in the Union Grove Cemetery.

Solomon Curtis was a man of mystery. He was a man that appeared to live life at its fullest. He staunchly adhered to his beliefs no matter what the cost. He was a man that believed in justice for all. Written by 4th great-granddaughter, Joann Holdbrooks

Death of the Curtis Brothers

The event that turned Winston extremely bitter against the Confederacy was the murder of George Washington "Wash" Curtis, son of Solomon Curtis and brother to the probate judge. Wash was the first of three of Solomon Curtis' children to die at the hands of the Confederates. Probate Judge John Bennett Weaver, early historian, has the following account: Wash Curtis had gone north hunting turkeys before dawn the morning of June 8, 1862. He realized that the Confederate Home Guard wanted to kill the brothers of Tom Pink Curtis, and knew that Stoke Roberts and his guerrillas would come looking for him. However, he, also, knew that they were likely to appear any day, and that he would be captured or killed unless he could elude them. Due to the fact that his daughter, Nancy, had a baby 3 weeks old that he had not seen, he wanted to see it before he went back into hiding and knew she would be at his house that day. Shortly after Wash reached the door and greeted his daughter with a kiss, his wife returned with two buckets of water from the spring. Her given name as shown by the U.S. Census in 1860 was Nancy, her daughter being named for her mother. 'Wash Curtis, Dear, I have got a plenty of food prepared for you to do you a couple of days, there in that sack. You should lose no time in getting it, and getting away from here. Strange men have been slipping around here. Two groups have been in sight at two different times in the last half hour. They are surely

Confederates, for they didn't look right. Wash, I beg you, believe your dear wife, you had better get your sack of food, and get away from here, or it will be too late. We will all be in trouble, unless you hurry. Go now!' Wash replied to his wife, 'Dear, I have not seen my grandchild, as it is on the bed asleep. I will have to hug and kiss my grandbaby this morning, for I may never see it again. Just as Wash was making the foregoing reply, his daughter ran into the house, grabbed her sleeping baby in her arms and ran back to her father, who hastily took it into his arms, hugged and kissed it, while tears were streaming down his cheeks. While this was taking place, Wash's wife screamed out: 'Wash, yonder they come! Be in a hurry, or they will get you. They are just now in sight. Not more than fifty yards up the road. It looks like an Army. They are coming in a hurry. Hurry Wash or it will be too late. Wash grabbed his sack, ran, unhitched and mounted his horse. It was too late. Just as he got balanced in his saddle, he applied his heel spurs to his horse a little too hard. This excited the horse, and caused him to stand on his rear feet. Without any orders to halt, or any warning whatever to the victim, Wash Curtis was shot by several of the invaders led by Stoke Roberts. Wash died in less than a minute. When Roberts saw that Wash Curtis was dead, he immediately turned and fled up the road, down which they came. They fled in great haste. Wash's body lay on the ground drenched in blood, and his grief-stricken, sobbing wife and daughter, stood in shock and Wash's wife fainted.

The Home Guard captured Joel Curtis and carried him to Jasper and put him in jail. He was given five days to sign up with the Confederate Army. Joel refused and they carried him to what they called the Slaughter Pen and shot him in the back. He was buried in a shallow grave. At the time of Joel's death he was married to Lucinda Barker. When Lucinda heard of Joel's death she went to Jasper, dug him up, and brought him to Union Grove. Some of the neighbors helped to bury him next to Wash and Solomon. Lucinda made this trip in a steer wagon, which was a slow way to travel. She had to make this trip herself. The men knew if they went to help her they would be put in jail. On her way back some of the people along the way tried to get her to spend the night with them. She refused due to the condition of Joel's body as he was already stinking."

The third child of Solomon Curtis to die was Thomas Pinkney Curtis, Probate Judge of Winston County. The following account is taken from the papers of Judge John Bennett Weaver: "On January 19, 1864, six or seven cavalry men came from South Walker, East Fayette, and North Tuscaloosa Counties...to the County Seat [then Houston], took Thomas P. Curtis, the Probate Judge...and told him that he would be released if he could pay them as much as $2,000.00. Judge Curtis was mad and expressed himself freely but finally decided that they meant to kill him, so he went to his home, where his wife and children were, and told his wife to get his pocket book, and when he counted out the $2,000.00 he had about $1,500.00 more, and when the cavalrymen saw it they took the pocket book with its contents above the $2,000.00. There were no banks here in those days. Judge Curtis was already mad, of course, and when that happened he expressed himself to the extent that the cavalrymen were provoked." Apparently, Judge Curtis did not want to give up the money; in other accounts, it states that he was persuaded with a red-hot poker, which severed his spine. "The next day, on January 20th, pretty early, about nine O'clock A.M., the friends of Judge Curtis found him shot to death down under a bluff about 30 feet high, with his head leaning back against a tree and his feet down in a branch. The branch was frozen over." He had been shot once in his right eye and once above his right eye.

In August of 1864, Jim Curtis, another brother to those killed and was also, at one time, tax collector of Winston County, learned about the deaths of his brothers and got a furlough from the Union Army; he worked in a hospital. While he was at home, he was captured by Southern Raiders and put in jail in Jasper. Either on the way to the jail or during his stay in the jail, he learned the names of the men who took part in the killing of his brothers. A brother to Jim, Frank Curtis asked a man by the name of Sam Ellenburg to make a saw that would cut through iron, and of course Sam made the saw. Someone smuggled it in to Jim, and he was free in no time. On the way back to Winston County, or shortly thereafter, Jim Curtis, along with Bennett Jones, Jack Revis, Bill Farley, Tom Barker, Bill Barker, Bal Brown, and a Mr. Williams stopped by Dr. Andrew Kaeiser's plantation in southwest Winston County, shot, and killed him on September 2, 1864. He was instrumental in the deaths of his brothers. A daughter of Andrew Kaeiser, Mattie Moody, later in life, wrote a biography that included what happened when Dr. Kaeiser was killed: "September 2nd was a miserable day for us all...late in the afternoon my Mother called my sister and me to walk to a graveyard out in front of the house, where baby sister who had died in infancy from whooping cough was buried. As we reached the front gate, I looked up and saw 2 men standing beside little sister's grave. I called Mother's attention to this so she went back and sat down in a chair near the front door. About that time my Father walked out into the front yard. The men at the grave had evidently been waiting to make sure he was about the house, and must have given a signal, for immediately six men came riding down the road to the front gate...the man in front who had his gun raised and cocked, asked, "Who are you?" Pa answered. "Dr. Kaeiser." He took aim and shot him through the heart. The bullet went through his body and was buried deep in a plank of the house. Pa fell and Mother sprang to him and took his head in her lap. He opened his eyes once and that was the last. He could not speak. My sister and I, supposing they were coming to rob the house again [as happened the night before], had run upstairs and began putting on extra clothing. As soon as we heard the shot we knew instinctively what had happened, so we ran downstairs, out the back door to the kitchen where the cook had started supper. The men who killed him met some of the Negroes coming home from the field and said to them, "We have killed your old Master, so dig a hole and put him in it." They did not intend that he should have a decent burial. Mother called on the Masons to bury him, and although most of them were friends and probably some relatives of the men who fired the shot, they did not dare refuse that call. My Father, a Mason was Royal Arch and even higher orders. He had several suits of regalia. These Tories had sent word to all the neighbors that any of them who went to Mother's assistance, should share the same fate. One old man...said he was an old man and did not have long to live anyway, so he was going to Mrs. Kaeiser, even if they killed him. His wife went with him. Mother and I went up into the loft to get burial clothes, linen sheets, etc. Mother with the help of this old man and his wife and the Negroes prepared him for burial. The man who fired the shot was Jim Curtis. My Father was killed Friday evening, September 2, 1864. Saturday some of the Negroes made a wooden coffin and covered it with some black cloth Mother had. They covered the inside with cotton batting and a white linen sheet. Into this they put my Father's body and on Sunday afternoon, September 4th he was buried with Masonic honors on the hill beside my little sister."

Jim Curtis continued his "manhunt" of those who took part in the killing of his brothers. He killed two of them in Walker County, shooting them in the dogtrot of their home. He also killed two in Texas and two in Mississippi. His wife, Priscilla Spain, tried to get him to forget about it and told him that if he continued, to not come back home. After he was through with his manhunt, he moved to Wayne County, Tennessee and became a doctor. Although Priscilla never remarried, Jim did. While picking cotton one day, a lightening storm came up, and he put the cotton basket over his head. When the storm was over, the people there found him dead. The Confederacy lost the war.

Several people still living in Winston County, descendants of these families related here, still have strong Union sentiments that will continue forever in the hills of Winston. The war will likely not ever be over for the people in that area.

"THE CIVIL WAR IN SONG AND STORY" (sic)

Ryan Dupree wrote the following about the First Alabama Cavalry, US Volunteers, which was originally published in *The Civil War in Song and Story,* by Frank Moore, in 1889.

The Union Men of Alabama. - The following account of the condition and persecutions of the Union men of North Alabama, and of the efforts of our troops, particularly of the Fifty-first Indiana regiment, commanded by Colonel Abel D. Streight, to relieve them, is from the pen of the chaplain of that regiment.

In Camp near Decatur, July 16.

The subject, on which I wish to write, is the condition and suffering of the mountaineers in Northern and Central Alabama. There is a vast valley of rich soil extending from beyond Tuscumbia west of Huntsville in the east. In this valley the great planters live. Here is their great cotton-growing region and the wealth of the state.

These mountains are peopled with quite another class of inhabitants, short of highfalutin aristocracy, a plain, candid, industrious people. Now these poor classes, deprived of culture, as they climb the mountains, pass through the gorges, and roam over the plains, think for themselves.

It came to pass in the course of human events, when Jefferson Davis wished these honest-hearted men to assist him and carrying out his great, grand, and overwhelming scheme of unnatural rebellion against the government they cherished, they said no. Things went on without opposition only as they opposed its course to destruction at the ballot box. Here they met the enemies of their country every time, and almost with a unanimous voice did they declare against secession in every form. When the affairs of the state had assumed a malignant form, and were far on the road to ruin in wild desperation, they only expostulated; but when the abominable, uncivil, anti-republican conscript act passed, and was being enforced by an unfeeling, heartless band of ruffians; when confusion, dire confusion, had come up on them, turning brotherhood against brother, and father and against son; when squalid poverty stared them in the face and depression was ensuing, caused by their being driven from home to seek a place of safety in the mountains, in caverns, and dens, they opened their eyes to gaze upon the painful site of liberty gone, constitution prostrated, home gone, and with it quietude and honor. To escape despotism and these heartless ruffians, men left their homes and fled to the mountains. Some made for the Union army, coming through the mountain pathways for twenty, forty, sixty, and some even ninety miles, having a complete line of friends to help them extending from Decatur, [Alabama] to near Montgomery, [Alabama] the best underground railroad ever heard of or ever established.

All old men and young men came asking and praying the army to assist them, demanding protection from the old flag, and asking to live and to fight under the old Constitution, declaring they only owed allegiance to the old government, and it was the only one they would fight for.

Their piteous cries moved our colonel, A. D. Streight, who asked for a leave of absence for four days, that his regiment might visit the mountains, prying into the caverns, and ascertained more positively the true condition of those loyal persecuted men. Accordingly, early Saturday morning, July 12th, with the Fourteenth Cavalry, and a sufficient number of our Alabamians for pilots, the Fifty-first crossed the river, and set out for the mountain regions. On we moved across the valley, while the sun poured its rays upon us, not in Indiana sun, but the sun away down in Alabama. Now this sun was shining much hotter than the sun shines any day in Indiana. Col. Streight steered us for Col. Davis's, who lived twenty-five miles out from Decatur, at a pass in the mountains called Davis's Gap.

We arrived at Colonel Davis's at dark and merciful heavens, what did we there behold! An elderly lady came to the door, who was between sixty and seventy years old. She was asked does Col. Davis live here. She answered he did. Is he home? She answered he is not. Said Colonel Streight, "we are Union troops; have heard of your suffering, and have come to relieve you." She still hesitated. "Do you believe me?" She said she would dislike to dispute his word, but a young lady came to the door and asked, "have you any of the Alabama boys with you?" They were called up from the rear. While coming, the young lady remarked, "We have been so often deceived by guerrillas, that we "- The boys came." Is that you, John?" Instantly she sprang into his arms, threw her arms around him, while she exclaimed: "Thank God, we are safe." "Now," answered the elderly lady, "I can have the old man here in a few minutes." "Where is he?" "Just back in the mountains." What! An old man of seventy-three

16

years, resident of the same farm for more than forty-four years, known by all man is a quiet, peaceable, and pious man-to be driven from his home, to have to seek refuge in the mountains, in the caverns, and dismal, secluded retreats, where the eyes of only the wild beasts had gazed! Yes, it is this old gentleman who had been driven from his home, simply because he loved his country.

The night passed away without any strange occurrence and morning came on. We started out, three companies strong, to scour the country round to, if possible, find the wounded man, but after searching, inquiring after, and tracing until he abandoned his horse, we came to the conclusion that further search would be fruitless, fearing the rascals had pursued and murdered him. He may, there is a slight possibility he will, come up yet. They stole his horse and accoutrements. While this search was going on, companies were sent out in almost every direction to scour the surrounding country. When we all met, in the evening, some have arrested prominent secessionists, who have saddles; some have pantaloons taken from artillerymen they had previously murdered several miles away, and other horses. Sunday evening found us with over fifty recruits. They came to us all day Monday like doves to the window. Monday evening we had speaking exercises, in which Col. Streight, Adjutant Ramsay, and Chris Sheats took part. The speeches of the colonel and adjutant were such as they should have delivered, but that of Sheats was a strange tune coming from an Alabamian. Sheats represented Winston County in the convention when Alabama is said to have seceded. He was prominent among the very few in that convention who would not and did not sign the ordnance of secession.

Tuesday morning came, the morning we had set, and were compelled by our time being out to return to camp, thirty-one or thirty-two miles away. At about seven o'clock a company of about twenty men were seen approaching our lines, being led by a woman. They entered amid great applause. She told her story in her peculiar way, with her own peculiar gestures, the tears streaming from her eyes. She said, "I knew I could pass those guerrillas, and find my husband and son," who had fled for their lives some thirty-four miles back in the mountains. The lady, not in good health, and fifty-five years old, had ridden a poor old horse over the mountains, tracing the mountain pathways through the gorges and around the precipices, sixty-four miles, counting the distance to and from her friends, and had made the trip in thirty hours, hunting her friends and cooking their breakfast in the time. These acts (for there are many such) should be known. Such heroines from the mountains have manifested more devotion for their country and friends than any of our Revolutionary mothers, whose acts of patriotism are held an everlasting remembrance. When the historian tells of noble deeds of daring and devotion to country, Anna Campbell, of Morgan County, Alabama, should stand first on the scroll of fame. It is no use to talk-when this old lady related her simple tale, there were but a few were not affected. Adjutant Ramsay wept, and it is said that even Colonel Streight shed tears. I know I did. I felt it was noble to weep on such occasions.

I visited an old patriot of eighty-four years. He was blind, so that he had not left his home in seven years, a peaceful, quiet old man, ripening for a better land, for he was devotedly pious. Now, simply because this old gentleman had raised his family well, so that they were all for the Union, and none of them in the Southern army, these friends incarnate were thirsting for his blood, and had threatened him with hanging; for they had taken one of his neighbors not less virtuous, and only ten years younger.

The 51st Indiana was one of the first Northern regiments to land in Alabama. The chaplain was deeply moved when the recruits had to leave.

Time came for us to leave, and our boys, having divided the rations with the Alabama recruits, were on less than half rations. This was the hottest day of the season, and there were no ambulances in which to carry the weak. But there could be no falling out, for we must pass through a hostile country. The men were formed into a long line, for we had about one hundred and fifty recruits from the mountains. And now comes the most touching scene of the expedition. We had left our families when it was heart-rending to part with loved ones; but what was that to the parting here? We left our wives in the bosom of a sympathizing community; but these poor men must now leave their families in the midst of an unfeeling, heartless set, a community who would turn their wives out, or burn their houses over their heads, or destroy their scanty means of substance, and, may be, as they have done several times before, outrage their persons. The wives bade their husbands farewell, bidding them go, and they would take care of themselves as best they could. Mothers wept when they bade their sons good by,

17

with their blessings on them. Forward! was the command - a wild shriek - and we moved from scenes of sufferings such as we have never before seen.

Who were the Alabama Unionists, why did these southerners fight for the Union, where did they come from, and what happened to them during and after the war?

These are all logical questions that can be answered after decades of research.

They certainly didn't join the army to get rich, because privates only drew $14 per month until June 20, 1864, when their pay was increased to $16 per month. However, some of the soldiers devised a plan to make more money and they were called "Bounty Jumpers". These were the bully boys engaged in the fine art of repeated desertions. All you had to do was sign up in a high bounty district, take whatever portion of the total bounties that were paid out on enlistment, and, at first opportunity "skeedaddle", then show up at a distant, prosperous recruiting area to sign up and repeat the process. Gangs, usually consisting of 20 to 25 or so, banded together. About one half of them would volunteer and the other half would arrange the escape, usually as the so-called recruits were on the trains to boot camps - train jumping. Of some 268,000 desertions, a fair percentage were these bounty jumpers.

Wash Day

Sketch by Joe Harper, Descendant of Joseph Harper

SOUTHERNERS WEARING THE BLUE IN DIXIE

Walter Lynwood Fleming, in his Book, *Civil War and Reconstruction in Alabama*, has mendaciously referred to the soldiers in the 1st Alabama Cavalry as being "of the lowest class of the population…shut off from the world…mountain whites…knew scarcely anything of the Union or of the questions at issue…" and he goes on to talk about the blind antagonism to the "slave holder…secluded and ignorant…"

The author of this book has researched the 1st Alabama Cavalry, USV and its soldiers for over forty-five years and can truthfully say these words do not portray the majority of these brave, patriotic soldiers of the 1st Alabama Cavalry Union Army and there are many records to prove this.

<u>Poor?</u> Some of them were indeed poor as one might find in any community in the 1860's.

<u>Ignorant?</u> A few of them were unable to sign their name but there were probably more of them who could read and write. Many of them went on to become Senators, State Representatives, Mayors, Probate Clerks, County Court Clerks, and other positions of distinction, and held other jobs that could not have been held by the type of men Fleming portrayed them to be.

<u>Knew scarcely anything of the Union or questions at issue?</u> Absolutely untrue, these men held secret meetings, one being at Looney's Tavern and another at a Mr. Taylor's house, to discuss these issues, the secession, the reasons they could not fight against their country, and other issues facing them and their families. All of these men knew their ancestors came to this country looking for a place to worship as they pleased without fear of persecution, and knew America embraced them and allowed them that privilege. Some of their ancestors helped form this country and write the laws. Some of their grandfathers fought and died for this country in the Revolutionary War and these soldiers were well aware of that fact. The fathers of some of these soldiers fought with Andrew Jackson in the War of 1812, and they were not only aware of that, but knew it was all about their beloved country. They knew exactly what the Union was about and they intended to fight to preserve the same Union for which their ancestors fought and died. When they stated they would not go against the "Old Flag" of their forefathers, they meant it. They had no intentions of firing on Old Glory. They knew exactly what they were doing and most importantly, why they were doing it!

<u>Slave holders?</u> The majority of them did not believe in slavery, and there were less than 5% of slaves in the northwest Alabama area where most of these men lived. To show how proud these loyalists were of the Union and their leaders, hundreds of them named their children after their Union Generals and Colonels. The census records will show many of them named their children "Sherman", "Ulysses", and other names after famous Union Generals and other officers.

As a matter of fact, until the past several years most descendants of soldiers who served in the 1st Alabama Cavalry, Union Army were not aware their ancestors fought with the Union, but there was a reason for this. In Larry Linley's Article "Why? He was a Yankee!" He tells about a story his ancestors passed down to him, which went like this; "During high school in an Alabama history class, I developed a desire to learn more about the American Civil War and my ancestral involvement. SO I began asking questions of my granddad, and learned through him that my great-great granddad, Jonathan Lindley was a soldier of the Civil War. Strangely, that was all he would tell me, commenting that "It's best to leave those stones unturned." At age thirteen, I really couldn't understand why. It took me years to find an answer, and it turned out to be one of surprise and sadness.

Many descendants state they are surprised to find out their ancestor served in the Union Army during the Civil War, while many others state although they were aware they had an ancestor in the Union Army, they were not allowed to discuss the war or their ancestors who served in the war.

The times were so difficult and atrocities so many that the people living through the war refused to discuss it. Terry Thornton, a dear friend of the author's, wrote one of the most enlightening stories on this subject. It is about his ancestors in the Union Army always being told, "Shhhhhhhh. Let's not talk about this!" This wonderful story will be in one of the last 2 volumes of this book.

When genealogists found records showing where their Union ancestors also served in the Confederacy, they could not believe it and the ones who refused to believe they had southern ancestors in the Union army, firmly denied it at this point. What they didn't know was, these Alabama Unionists were so adamant about not helping the Confederacy bring down the country they loved, they became known as the "Leave Aloners", they wanted to be left alone to their own fate because while they did not want to fight against their neighbors, they certainly were not going to fight against the country that embraced their persecuted ancestors and the country their ancestors helped to form. Also, many of their grandfathers fought for this country during the Revolutionary War, and they refused to fire on Old Glory, the flag of their forefathers.

Union Soldiers hiding out in the Rock House, a name given to one of the caves in the Northwest Alabama Mountains. Sketch by Joe Harper, descendant of Private Joseph Harper.

They hid out in the coves and caves of Northwest Alabama, one prominent cave they called, the "Rock House", a cave on the border of Winston and Marion Counties near Natural Bridge in Alabama, trying to avoid being conscripted into the Confederate Army. Some of them could be compared with the Movie, *Shenandoah* where Jimmy Stewart wanted him and his boys to be left alone, but that was not to happen. Within few months, they were found by the Confederate Home Guard and ordered to join the Confederacy or be shot where they stood. Many escaped and either hid out in the woods or made their way to the Union lines and joined the 1st Alabama Cavalry, USV while many others joined the Confederacy just long enough to escape and make their way to the Union lines where they joined the Union Army. They tried to remain neutral but were not given that choice. Therefore, many of the soldiers in the 1st Alabama Cavalry, USV also have records showing where they also served in the Confederacy. This confused many descendants, especially the ones who refuse to believe their ancestor from Alabama, Mississippi, Tennessee, or other southern states ever fought for the Union. Some see their ancestor listed among the 1st Alabama Cavalry, US Soldiers on the 1st Alabama Website and write wanting to have their ancestor's name removed because they have proof they fought for the Confederate. It is difficult trying to prove to them that their ancestors galvanized and actually have records on both sides.

Descendant Larry Linley stated that anytime the Civil War was brought up in his family, his grandfather would say it was best to leave those stones unturned. In an article Linley wrote for "The American Digger" Magazine, he stated, "During a family reunion in Marion County, Alabama, a first cousin stated that through his research, he learned of their great-great grandfather; Jonathan "Jot" Lindley's involvement in the Civil War was with the Union army. The family could not believe their ancestor was a "Yankee"!

Linley knew right then what his grandfather meant when he said it was best to leave those stones unturned. "What a surprise", Linley stated. "Even to this day the emotions run high in Northwest Alabama toward the Union sympathizers that could border on mawkishness."

The 1st Alabama Cavalry, USV is a story that is largely unknown. It certainly is not taught in the schools and their story is never told. It is a story of courage, conviction, patriotism, persecution, retribution, and even atrocity. It has been forgotten as generations passed and denied by families who were too proud of the myth that all Alabama men fought for the Confederacy. Some could not see the truth. Above all, it is a great American history story worth telling and preserving. Those descendants who had ancestors who served in this regiment can well be proud of their southern Union ancestors who stood up and fought for what they believed. They fought the Confederate factions in the area even before the war began.

Not much has been written about the 1st Alabama Cavalry and its soldiers and most of what has been written was done so by Confederate sympathizers who falsely portrayed the Union soldiers. It is past time for someone to tell their story and tell it as it actually was.

Time has taken a toll on their story, but today, there is a new movement. Family histories have come alive, and descendants have begun to dive into the past to find the truth, a past that they did not talk about and once abandoned. Researchers and authors have begun to write about the sacrifices of the men and families who held true to "The Old Flag". These descendants have a thirst for knowledge into their ancestor's past and why they remained true to the Union. They want to know the truth and not just what they have heard or read that was written by someone who either didn't know what the truth was or distorted the truth for their own purposes.

Also generally unknown today, all eleven states of the old Confederacy had sons who fought in Union blue and all Confederate states, with the exception of South Carolina, had at least one Union regiment formed in their state. For a total of 55 regiments. Strong ties to the "Old Flag" existed in the South, mostly in the hill country where few owned slaves. They had no wish to fight what they saw as a planters' war to preserve slavery and the economic power that went with it.

In *The Southern Loyalists*, Robert Hurst stated the following, in part: "So you think that just because you come from the south, your ancestors must have been Confederates? Richard Nelson Current, author of *Lincoln's Loyalists*, estimates that as many as 100,000 white, Southern males wore the Blue instead of the Gray as regular soldiers or local militia.

Were these men patriots or were they, as some Southern historians such as William Stanley Hoole maintained, traitors to the Cause? Who were these men who risked so much to remain loyal to "the Old Flag, sealed with the blood of our forefathers?" Were they uneducated hill folk, or were they sophisticated anti-slavery and anti-plantation visionaries? These loyal Unionists stood up and fought for what they felt in their hearts was right, even though many had their houses, barns and crops burned, their cattle, meat and corn stolen, and many paid the ultimate cost with their lives. Some lost their families while the wives and children of others were abused and molested. These Union soldiers knew they would pay a price but were determined to stand up and fight for the country they loved and the country for which their forefathers fought, and in many cases died.

From the perspective of the present, we must deal with the Myth of the Lost Cause rather than the reality. With time, the Myth has grown to epic proportions; a solid Confederacy of people standing firm against the tyranny of the strong central government of agriculturalism and Jeffersonian Democracy against the factory and the political machine. From the very beginning, division haunted the Confederacy. In Alabama, for example, of 52 counties, 23 voted to remain within the Union. These counties lay mostly within the Appalachian Highlands of northern Alabama, and this division was one that was repeated everywhere within the South. The people of the uplands were pro-Union, and the people of the Plantation areas represented the fire-eaters of the Confederacy. Where plantations ruled, slavery held sway, and the Confederacy was strong. Where free men tilled the soil, slavery, slaves, the Confederacy, and most particularly the Planters, were not popular. On the coastal lowlands of North Carolina, where the people earned their living by fishing and commerce, lumbering and other enterprises that were inimical to the slave labor economy, the people tended to remain loyal to the nation their forefathers had fought to build.

Sadly, the war that was fought among Southerners was never civil, and in a war characterized by grand gestures among the principal armies, viciousness seemed to prevail. We're all familiar with

Grant stopping the war to present his friend Pickett with a silver tea set on the occasion of the birth of his child. But how many know that the same George Pickett faced prosecution as a war criminal for hanging 22 men of the First North Carolina. Hostage taking and murder were common, and the Confederates so feared the Unionists within their midst that they used brutal tactics to suppress them.

The Unionists were a thorn in the side of the Confederacy from the beginning, and Abe Lincoln, that wily old Politician, sought to exploit this advantage. East Tennessee and West Virginia were hotbeds of outrage against the rebellion. The only problem for Lincoln was to get access for recruiters and arms.

Tennessee was a bitterly divided state and considerable efforts were expended by both sides either to deny the military resources to the enemy or to tap them. East Tennessee, particularly, was a hotbed of Union sentiment, and no one was more vigorous in the cause than Andrew Johnson. Johnson had campaigned vigorously in East Tennessee prior to the secession vote. A friend of Johnson's, James T.T. Carter, an Annapolis graduate and lieutenant in the US Navy, was detailed from the Navy to drill troops in East Tennessee. Carter, incidentally, was the only American to hold the ranks of Major General and Rear Admiral.

The problem with East Tennessee was its inaccessibility to the Federals. Guarded by the Cumberland Mountains, and cut only by three passes, the region was denied to the Union. The trip to Union territory was arduous, and the Rebels managed to interdict the passes. A New Market physician and Mexican War veteran, John W. Thornburgh, organized a cavalry company and was ambushed in Baptist Gap. Only about a third managed to get through to Barbourville, Kentucky. Thornburgh, himself, and eight men were captured. The remainder retreated to their homes. Nonetheless, some two thousand men managed to escape and became the First and Second East Tennessee.

Reaching the loyalists was a source of contention between Lincoln and his generals. Buell saw only the military difficulties and was less than enthusiastic. George Thomas, one of his division commanders, was even less enthusiastic. Buell's refusal to move on east Tennessee was one of the main reasons Lincoln replaced him.

Another Carter brother, William B., looked to organize a bolder stroke. On the night of November 8, loyal men burned a number of bridges on the east Tennessee and Virginia Railroad, one of the few steel arteries of the South. The Confederates reacted with a savagery that belied their talk about "rights". Isham G. Harris, the fire-eating governor of Tennessee, wrote to Jefferson Davis, "The burning of railroad bridges in East Tennessee shows a deep-seated spirit of rebellion in that section. Union men are organizing. This rebellion must be crushed out instantly, the leaders arrested, and summarily punished."

Confederate troops began scouring the hills, and slowly the numbers of captives increased, reaching the hundreds. Secretary of War, Judah Benjamin sent the following instructions for dealing with the "traitors".

1st. All such as can be identified as having been engaged in bridge-burning are to be tried summarily by drum-head court-martial, and, if found guilty, executed on the spot by hanging. It would be well to leave their bodies hanging in the vicinity of the burned bridges.

2nd. All such as have not been so engaged area to be treated as prisoners of war, and sent with an armed guard to Tuscaloosa, Alabama, there to be kept imprisoned…till the end of the war.

P.S. Judge Patterson, Colonel Pickens, and other ringleaders of the same class must be sent at once to Tuscaloosa to jail as prisoners of war.

SEVERAL PRISONERS WERE HANGED AND LEFT NEAR THE RAILROAD, WHERE PASSENGERS WERE ENCOURAGED TO FLOG THEIR DEAD BODIES WITH CANES AS THE TRAIN PASSED. The weather being somewhat warm, the corpses were cut down after only thirty-six hours. This barbarous treatment was justified by Jefferson Davis' proclamation, "stating that all those who did not fully recognize their allegiance to the Government should remove from its limits, with their effects before October, 1861. Those persons who remained tacitly recognized the Government and are amenable to the laws."

Not everyone supported such high-handed practices and recognized the resulting calm was more apparent than real. Meanwhile, the disaffected continued to trickle through the passes. Finally, after Grant opened the way by taking Forts Donelson and Henry, Nashville fell in February, 1862, and East Tennessee was available for recruiting. Andrew Johnson was appointed military governor, but he and his subordinates botched the recruiting job by bickering among themselves. Besides, some of the ardor had been cooled by the Emancipation Proclamation.

The differences between the northern and southern states over the question of slavery and states rights had been festering for years. However, it came to a head in 1860 when the Republican Party adopted what was known as the "Black Platform" and nominated Abraham Lincoln. Many southern politicians warned that Lincoln's election would result in secession of some states. These states had joined the Union voluntarily and many felt they had every right to withdraw from the Union. Lincoln was elected and before he was inaugurated as president, Governor Shorter of Alabama called a state convention to meet January 7, 1861 for the purpose of a decision on secession. The delegates were to be elected on the prior December 24th. After four days of debate, the secessionists won over the cooperationists by a vote of 61 to 39 with practically all of the opposition to secession coming from North Alabama.

The situation in North Alabama was vastly different from that in Central and South Alabama. The slave population was lower, and in the counties stretching across the state in the area of Sand Mountain was sparse. Possibly overriding this was the allegiance to and dependence upon Tennessee, which was not thought, would secede. There was no railroad between Montgomery and the area of North Alabama. North Alabama depended on the Tennessee River which led to Chattanooga on the East and through Nashville and Memphis, Tennessee to market their goods. Therefore the section of Alabama opposing secession ultimately became the one to suffer most from the resulting war. It just so happened there was pillaging by vigilante groups in North Alabama which sprang up quite frequently.

Unionist feeling in Alabama was strongest in the northern half of the state and, while centered in Winston County, was heavy throughout the region. Winston County itself was referred to as "The Free State of Winston," and the 1st Alabama Cavalry, US Volunteers was the military result of that anti-secession feeling.

Robert E. "Bob" Hurst, descendant of Private Billington Sanders Hurst, wrote the following article.

THE SOUTHERN LOYALISTS

So you think that just because you come from the south, your ancestors must have been Confederates? Richard Nelson Current, author of "Lincoln's Loyalists," estimates that as many as 100,000 white, Southern males wore the Blue instead of the Gray as regular soldiers or local militia. Did you know every state in the Confederacy except for South Carolina raised at least one unit for the Federal Army, for a total of 55 regiments?

Were these men patriots or were they, as some Southern historians such as William Stanley Hoole maintained, traitors to the Cause? Who were these men who risked so much to remain loyal to "the Old Flag, sealed with the blood of our forefathers?" Were they uneducated hill folk, or were they sophisticated anti-slavery and anti-plantation visionaries? I want to address the Southern Unionist, specifically,

1. The facts of their numbers and demography.

2. An assessment of their impact on the conduct of the war.

3. Some history of one of the most valiant of these units, the First Alabama Cavalry, US Volunteers and one soldier in it, the 50-year old Pvt. Billington Sanders Hurst.

4. The fate of these men after the war.

From the perspective of the present, we must deal with the Myth of the Lost Cause rather than the reality. With time, the myth has grown to epic proportions; a solid Confederacy of people standing firm against the tyranny of the strong central government, of agriculturalism and Jeffersonian Democracy against the factory and the political machine. From the very beginning, division haunted the Confederacy. In Alabama, for example, of 52 counties, 23 voted to remain within the Union. These counties lay mostly within the Appalachian Highlands of northern Alabama, and this division was one that was repeated everywhere within the South. The people of the uplands were pro-Union, and the people of the plantation areas represented the fire-eaters of the Confederacy. Where plantations ruled, slavery held sway, and the Confederacy was strong. Where free men tilled the soil, slavery, slaves, the Confederacy, and most particularly the Planters, were not popular. On the coastal lowlands of North Carolina, where the people earned their living by fishing and commerce, lumbering and other enterprises that were inimical to the slave labor economy, the people tended to remain loyal to the nation their forefathers had fought to build.

Consider Alabama, the only state for which I have the figures handy. A Deep South state, the location of the first capitol of the Confederacy, yet 23 counties voted the "Cooperationist" ticket. IN WINSTON COUNTY, NOT A SINGLE VOTE WAS CAST FOR SECESSION. In the 23 loyalist counties, the vote was 21,665 to 12,042. However, the plantation states wielded the power, and in the slave-holding plantation counties, 24,865 voted to secede and 6,965 voted to remain. The totals for the state were 28,630 to remain in the Union and 36,907 for secession. Barbour, Bibb, Butler, Henry, Lowndes, Marengo, Pike and Russell Counties tallied no Cooperationist votes. Thus, 43.7% of the voters of the ostensibly solid Confederate state voted to remain within the Union.

The vote for secession followed closely the distribution of slaves or the number of bales of cotton produced in Alabama. Winston County held only 122 slaves, or 3.41% of the population, and in most of the loyal counties, the proportion of slaves was less than 20%. However, substantial Unionist sentiment was found even in the plantation counties. In Green County, with 76.5% of the population being African slaves, nearly 40% of voters wished to remain within the Union. It must be pointed out that these figures overestimate Unionist support because many Southerners voted Cooperationist and then enlisted in Confederate forces. Nonetheless, I think we can conclude that at the beginning, the South was far from united in its rebellion, and substantial minorities still held the Old Flag in high regard, while in some areas the loyalists comprised a majority. This represented a worrisome threat that drained substantial Confederate resources throughout the entire war.

The mountain area in western Virginia and eastern Tennessee was one of the major hotbeds of Unionism. Virginia, arguably the very heart of the Confederacy, was split along lines similar to those seen in Alabama. The people of the mountain counties of Virginia remained so solidly Union that they petitioned to be admitted as a separate state in 1863. Tennessee was perhaps the most split of the states voting to secede and sent approximately equal numbers to each Army. As mentioned by Sam Watkins, the First Tennessee, the regiment that stood Sherman's assaults on the Dead Line at Kennesaw Mountain all alone and saying they needed no help, had Union sympathizers in its ranks.

Lincoln immediately authorized a number of individuals to raise regiments of loyal Virginians. Normally the governor of the state was responsible for enrolling the state militia into the Federal Army, and clearly none of the Southern governors would be any help. William Burton, the governor of Delaware refused to cooperate, but Lincoln found a way to enroll the Delawareans through Robert Patterson, then commanding the Pennsylvania troops. The First Delaware enrolled through Pennsylvania, and at first, Lincoln used this mechanism to enroll Virginians. Ohio served as a major recruiting ground for Virginians.

Early Federal military movements revolved around protecting the Virginia Unionists and maintaining access to these military resources. McClellan moved on Grafton in May of 1961, partly to protect the B&O Highway and partly to protect the Unionists. Cox moved up the Kanawha toward Charleston, then held by Gen. Henry Wise, a rabid secessionist and ex-governor of Virginia. Wise reported to Lee he was surrounded by hostile people. "They invite the enemy, feed him, and he arms and drills them. A spy is on every hill top, at every cabin, and from Charleston to Point Pleasant they swarm." On the retreat "the State volunteers under my command lost from three to five hundred men by desertion. The Kanawha Valley is wholly disaffected and traitorous." Well, not entirely. Thomas Jackson called the Kanawha home.

The government of the State of Virginia moved its military forces to attempt to stem the hemorrhage of potential manpower and moved some 5000 men to Mill Creek, near Martinsburg, which slowed recruiting across the Ohio considerably.

A few men even were raised in the heart of the Tidewater. In spite of hopes to raise an entire regiment of Loyal East Virginians, only a single company, the First Loyal East Virginia Infantry rallied to the Old Flag. Other men joined the Accotink Home Guard. Both units spent most of their time patrolling telegraph lines. But when the total was added up, 31,872 white Virginia men, including those who joined before West Virginia was admitted as a separate state, wore the Blue. This figure did not count militia who did not enter Federal service. When it was said that on July 3, 1863, as the troops lined up for their ill-fated assault, that "All Virginia was there," it just wasn't true.

The Confederates tried to recruit in East Tennessee, finally resorting to the draft. Many wondered whether the results were worth the effort. East Tennesseans were notoriously unreliable, often surrendering at the first opportunity, or simply deserting. Worse, the more conscription was enforced, the more men went North.

The deserters presented problems to both sides. The Confederates felt justified in executing men who had left the Confederate Cause to join the Union. Yet, these men claimed the only reason they wore the Gray was because of the draft, and had they been given a choice, they would have worn the Blue in the first place. The Federal authorities recognized that they were asking a lot of men to doubly risk their lives by serving against the Confederacy. Many of the "galvanized Yankees" were placed in units that guarded the frontiers and fought Indians.

All over the South, the pattern of Tennessee was repeated. In North Carolina, a number of regiments were raised on the coast and in the highlands. Even Georgia sent a regiment near the end of the war. In Alabama, my great-great grandfather, Billington Sanders Hurst managed to elude Confederate patrols and, at age 50, rode 210 miles from his home in St. Clair County, Alabama, to enlist as a private in the First Alabama Cavalry, US Volunteers. More about the proud Fighting First later.

In Arkansas, the main problem was with equipping volunteers. Surprisingly, Louisiana was also a hotbed of loyalist sentiment. The Cajun population, particularly, held no love for the planters and enlisted in Union units in considerable numbers. The Irish, German and Yankees of New Orleans saw the Confederate cause as treason, and when Butler and Farragut steamed up the Mississippi in April, 1862, the dragooned men holding Ft. Jackson were such unwilling conscripts that they spiked their guns and shot the officers who wouldn't agree to surrender. The fort fell without a Union shot being fired.

If a brigade of Federals could have worked their way through Indian Territory to West Texas and the Hill Country, Texas would undoubtedly have returned to the Union. Sam Houston, the governor at the time of the secession vote, had done everything legal and illegal he could manage to keep Texas in the Union. The German immigrants saw no advantages to the Confederacy. Even today, few of the courthouses in areas settled by Germans display the ubiquitous Confederate infantryman on the square. The Hispanic population in Texas was solidly Unionist, and a number of irregular units were formed. These units were most unreliable, however, because Mexico started its own civil war about that time, and these men had the bad habit of taking their equipment further South. The situation in Texas was particularly bitter. MORE THAN 100 UNIONISTS WERE HANGED FOR THEIR LOYALTY TO THEIR COUNTRY. Every state of the Confederacy except for South Carolina sent at least one regiment of white men to the Union Army. Mississippi contributed the First Mississippi Mounted Rifles, though the unit never filled completely. Florida contributed the First and Second Florida Cavalry. Georgia contributed the First Georgia Battalion. Many other Georgia men enlisted in Tennessee units or the First Alabama Cavalry, USV, as did nearly 100 South Carolinians and 300 Mississippi men.

PART II. Who Were These Men

Why were some men of the South vehement supporters of the Union, while other Southerners rallied to the Stars and Bars? William Stanley Hoole, author of a monograph on the First Alabama, characterized them as a "poor, often underprivileged people who had long been isolated on their rocky highlands, suspicious of intruders and generally antisocial. Blindly hating the affluent slave-holder and his slave alike, they had first refused to support the cause of secession and, afterwards, ignored all Confederate civilians and military conscription laws." The descendants of the men of the First have charged Hoole, better known for his Confederate histories, with slander. In fact, Hoole was only reporting what the Myth of the Lost Cause needed to claim. To validate the Great Rebellion, the loyalists needed to be discounted.

Very few Unionists owned slaves, but, then, very few ordinary Confederate soldiers were slave-holders, either. Throughout the South, only one family in three owned as much as a single slave. Examination of the 1860 census for Washington County, North Carolina, which furnished roughly equal numbers of men to each army, showed the average Union soldier owned only $269 in personal property. The average Confederate soldier owned $3,759, but is this an example of the fallacy of the mean? None of the Unionist heads of household reported more than $1000 in family income, while a couple of dozen Confederates did. All but one of the Unionists was a landowner, while 19 of the Confederates were landless. After all, the mean of one million dollars and one hundred dollars is $500,050.

Close examination showed the Confederates of Washington County to be large planters and their dependents, their sons, the merchants with whom they dealt, the lawyers and clergymen they patronized, and the poor white men who worked as day laborers, an alliance of the very rich and the very poor. The division between Unionist and Secessionist was not simply between rich and poor. The middle class that had no economic interest in the slave economy tended to be solidly Unionist, and why not? These Middle-class folk themselves were oppressed economically by the system. Moreover, they tended to be mightily offended by the airs put on by the planters, who tended to see themselves as a privileged aristocracy. In the case of the Hurst family, Billington owned 160 acres of land in St. Clair County, Alabama. I've seen his property, and it is good bottom land, rich and productive, and I doubt if he were a hillbilly. Interestingly, the geographic division of politics remains still in Alabama, where politics in the northern part of the state still has a much stronger populist flavor than in the old plantation counties.

PART III. The Fighting Southern Federals

What was the impact of the Southern Loyalists? Three factors need to be considered; the direct contribution of the men as soldiers to the Union cause, the resources expended by the Confederacy to counter the threat, and finally, the loss of manpower to the Southern cause. Taking these in reverse order, the loss of manpower to the South was probably fatal to its cause. While estimates of the

26

numbers differ. Current estimates that as many as 100,000 white men of the South served the Union cause as Federal forces and local defense forces. This was more men than Lee or any other Southern commander ever had under arms at any time. In addition, thousands of other troops were diverted from the main armies to control the loyalists. Cavalry patrols. How much difference would the cavalry patrols that tried to interdict the flow of manpower have made to the cavalry-poor army of Johnston? Consider the impact of the 30,000 East Tennesseans who joined the Union. Had they joined the Confederate forces, this would have amounted to a swing of 60,000 men, and when the 10,000 Confederates who were required to keep East Tennessee in subjugation are added in, a difference of 70,000 men results.

Finally, there is the direct contribution. There is no question that some of the southern units were hard-fighting, crack units, while others were of questionable value. The Tennessee Unionists units were of solid quality, as were most of the Virginia units, who saw fighting almost from the beginning at Philippi and Romney under McClellan. The First Mississippi Mounted Infantry rode with Grierson in his famous raid through the heart of Mississippi. In the movie "The Horse Soldiers" with John Wayne and William Holden, the Southern-speaking men (Ken Curtis) were authentic and represented the First Mississippi. It is true that when Pickett executed 22 men of the First North Carolina USV, he did, in fact, cut the heart out of some units, particularly those containing "galvanized Yankees." Still, these men could, and did, perform valuable duty in less exposed positions.

Other Unionists such as the First Alabama were dependable units, just as hard-fighting as any Ohio, Maine, or Pennsylvania troops. The Myth of the Lost Cause demands the loyalists be branded as poor soldiers. Interestingly, many of the Unionists served in cavalry units, and early in the war, the quality of the Union cavalry in general was very poor. But by 1864, the Federal cavalry were, in general, at least equal to the Confederates. The hard-riding Blue troopers of Phil Sheridan scattered Jeb Stuart's plumed cavaliers and killed the famed cavalryman. While they never tamed "that devil Forrest", the Union cavalry in general, and the First Alabama did humble Joe Wheeler and Wade Hampton.

The First Alabama began humbly. Poorly trained and equipped, and sent against superior numbers of Confederate cavalrymen in 1862, they fared poorly early. But by the time Sherman began his Red Clay Minuet with Johnston, the First was a solid, invaluable unit. The regiment was formed in 1862 in Huntsville and Memphis and mustered into Federal service that December in Corinth, Mississippi. Company officers were chosen from among the men, and Captain George E. Spencer was later named Colonel and given overall command.

During most of its operational life, the First Alabama was part of the 16th Corps, Army of the Tennessee. As a cavalry unit, its missions were scouting, raiding, reconnaissance, flank guard and screening the army on the march The names on its battle flag, like most cavalry actions, are mostly forgotten; Nickajack Creek, Vincent's Crossroads and Cherokee Station among others. Better known names are there, too; Streight's Raid through north Alabama; and battles at Dalton, Resaca and Kennesaw Mountain in the Atlanta Campaign.

One general characterized the Alabama troops "invaluable...equal in zeal to anything we discovered in Tennessee." And Major General John Logan, commanding the 15th Army Corps in Sherman's forces, praised the troopers as "the best scouts I ever saw, and (they) know the country well from here to Montgomery." General Sherman, knowing the value of his Alabama troops as soldiers and symbols of the loyal South, honored the First by his selecting it to be his escort on the march from Atlanta to the sea.

The First, part of Kilpatrick's Third Cavalry Brigade (with the Fifth Kentucky and Fifth Ohio) rode over 700 miles in 55 days during the winter of 1864. In February, they routed a brigade of Wheeler's cavalry at Williston, SC, taking 5 battle flags and scattering the Confederates over miles of countryside. On March 10, surprised in camp by 5,000 of Wade Hampton's and Joe Wheeler's cavalry, the 800 men of the Third Brigade killed 103 of their attackers with the loss of 18 men and officers at Monroe's Crossroad (also known as the Battle of Kilpatrick's Pants). The official report said that "a bloody hand-to-hand conflict" followed, lasting more than three hours. Brave Lieutenant Stetson managed to turn the tide when he crept to one of his guns and delivered a barrage of canisters into the ranks of the attackers.

The First displayed a darker side, also and was "zealous in its chastisement of Rebels". They took seriously their role as foragers, and it was charged the First, knowing where a Southerner was likely to stash his food, never went hungry. This is not entirely true because they often went hungry and their horses starved for lack of forage. They relished their job as incendiaries, too and "laid Barnwell in ashes" despite Kilpatrick's efforts to stop them. These actions are more understandable when one learns the fates of their families. Many had their homes burned or their families abused, and some saw their kin lynched by vindictive Confederates. So badly were many of their innocent families treated that a "Refugee House" was established in Nashville for those who were able to escape Rebel persecution. Our family fared well, probably because Billington's son, my great grandfather, served in the 19th Louisiana Infantry, CSA.

PART IV. The Fate of the Southern Unionists During Reconstruction

The fate of the Southern Unionists began to be clear with the massacre at Ft. Pillow, where Forrest's men massacred a number of white soldiers of the 13th Tennessee Cavalry. The commanding officer, Maj. Bradford, was shot after he had surrendered and was being taken to Forrest's headquarters at Jackson, Tennessee. Yet, Ft. Pillow is remembered mainly for the massacre of black soldiers. Both Congress and Lincoln were forgetting the Tennessee loyalists, and forgotten they are today. Yet, these men risked more for their nation than did the men of the North, for they risked execution on capture and consigned their families to the often not-so-tender mercies of their often unforgiving neighbors.

In part, they fell into obscurity because Lincoln saw the African-American population as representing a larger manpower resource, and after the war, the Radical Republicans sought to consolidate their power through the freed slaves rather than the Southern Unionists. There were some exceptions. Col. Spencer, commander of the First Alabama, was elected governor and then Senator, and was the only Republican re-elected to the Senate. Nonetheless, he ended up his years in Nevada, leaving Alabama for a variety of reasons.

The end of the war did not end the private grudges that the division of the Southern whites had produced. Victorious Union veterans sought retribution for the depravations their families had suffered during the war. Yet, the government failed to reimburse them for their losses, or even to provide effective protection in many areas. Andrew Johnson was extremely generous in pardoning ex-Confederates, and in many areas these pardoned men established governments that were inimical to the Union veterans. Some were murdered, many left and went West, while others, such as Billington Sanders Hurst moved away from their homes. On his return, he gathered his goods and left. Our family never spoke of him again and I was the one who discovered his Union service. He moved to Jefferson County, Alabama, where he married again. In 1881 he was apparently destitute and applied for a disability pension.

Reconstruction under the Act of 1867 brought temporary relief, but the loyalists, like all Southerners, had been impoverished by the War. The Southern economy was in shambles, and the industrial powers of the North quickly established their economic hegemony. Until the late 1940's Southern goods moving north paid a higher price on the railroads than Northern goods moving South or Southern raw materials moving north. Moreover, the white loyalists felt alienated in the Republican Party, which tended to give more emphasis to the needs of the freed slaves than to the loyal whites. One of the tenets of Northern industry was to divide and conquer, and by setting black against white, a reservoir of cheap labor could be guaranteed. Additionally, the often corrupt and inefficient "Carpetbagger-Scalawag" governments did little to help Southerners of any color or loyalty, preferring to line their own pockets. Finally, as racial divisions emerged in the South, the loyalists saw how they finally would have to decide their political loyalties, and so they submerged into the white culture virtually without a trace. Only in the last decade have most descendants of men who served with the First Alabama learned the truth about their ancestors.

Horror of the War in South Carolina in 1865 (sic)
By Sgt. Josiah Wilson

The Union soldiers bore a particular grudge against the state of South Carolina and its citizens, who they blamed for starting the war. One of Sherman's men declared, THIS IS WHERE SECESSION BEGAN, AND BY GOD, HERE IS WHERE IT WILL END." Poverty would mark the state for generations to come.

The following story, Horror of the war in South Carolina in 1865, was written at the end of Josiah Wilson's Civil War Diary. He was an Orderly Sergeant in Company D of the 1st Alabama Cavalry, USV. The diary was submitted by descendant Ed Wilson.

Very little that people know who have not witnessed of the distresses and troubles that follow the Army in pursuit of the enemy. While the roar of the cannon can be heard clocking through the valleys and thundering through the mountains which serves to tell to all the nation that pain and death is in the land. Oh what horror it is to witness this scene. While heavy colonnades are advancing on the enemy which lies concealed behind some enclosure. And the death shots of their muskets lay many beneath the foot of their comrade to be trampled on as stones of the earth and the cries of the wounded and dying seem to mingle with the boom of the cannon and to descent away to the ears of all the country. While men are rushing on in the greatest of fury and confusion right into the mouths of cannon and the points of the bayonet. Oh to hear them. Bitter oaths that come from the mouths of pursuing men mixed in with groans of the dying. But distress does not stop here. Oh no. But turn your attention to the citizens of South Carolina while this expedition was ensuing while the rebel army was retreating through their midst in fury and confusion destroying and mislaying as they went and the federal in pursuit of them burning all out houses and cotton and cotton gins: thrashers and mills, factories and foundry, all government works together with nearly all the towns and a vast quantity of dwellings. The eye could not be turned anyway but it could see the vast columns of smoke ascending towards the sky. It would rise to an extensive height and then it would seem to turn and bend over the land, to behold the scene that ensued from its descendents…and the cries and shouts of the women and children seemed to mingle with the roar of the fire and ascend to the sky. Oh horror stricken country often my heart has been made to sink within me to behold these sights.

REUNION OF 1ˢᵗ ALABAMA CAVALRY, USV SOLDIERS
From *The Double Springs Observer*, September 5, 1895

Grand Reunion of Federal Veteran Soldiers At Lynn, Alabama. On August 22nd and 23rd, 44 of the First Regiment Alabama Union Veteran Soldiers met at Lynn, Winston county, Alabama, Lieutenant Jerry Files of Townley, Alabama, and Sergeant William Wilson, of Lucky, Alabama being all the officers present. The forenoon of the 22nd was consumed in organizing, where a free dinner was served in which all partook and enjoyed very much. After dinner all the old Union and Confederate veterans present formed in line and marched to a small grove near by where Mr. W.R. Long, our principal merchant and one of our most influential citizens, welcomed the old veterans among us offering them our hospitality and sympathy in a very neat and entertaining little speech, after which he introduced Mr. A.P. Van Fleet, who opened the meeting with prayer and gave them a short talk. After this Lieutenant Files made a few remarks. There being no other speakers the veterans held a consultation and announced their proffer the following day. Then the meeting was dismissed for the day and veterans and citizens dispersed for the homes of their friends and entertainers, where they enjoyed themselves, as only old soldiers can relating incidents of the war, in fighting old battles over and in talking with their Confederate brothers of occasions where they had engaged in deadly combat with each other.

Friday morning, the 23rd, and second day of the reunion, was a beautiful morning and the old veterans with their friends were on the grounds at an early hour. The principal part of the forenoon was consumed with a business meeting, after which the old veterans formed in line and marched to the grove, with the choir marching in front singing "Am I soldier of the cross?" This being the request of Mr. Simeon Tucker, who is 78 years old and one of the oldest veterans. He was 45 years old when he enlisted. It is his request that his brother soldiers sing this hymn when he joins that great reunion beyond the grave. After reaching the grove they formed around the table, where a bounteous dinner had been spread, and was served to all present. After dinner they again formed in line and marched to the place of meeting. The meeting was opened with prayer by Mr. Van Fleet and the singing of several appropriate places by the choir. Mr. Van Fleet then gave them a short address and was followed by Lieutenant Files who spoke at some length, returning thanks to the choir for their valuable services and thanking the people of Lynn and vicinity for their kind hospitality to them during the meeting. He then requested the veterans to form in line where all who wished could take them by the hand and bid them farewell before they dispersed. The ladies first marched by and grasped the hands of these sturdy defenders of our county. Then followed the Confederate veterans--it would have melted a heart of stone to see these grey headed members of opposing armies clasp each other's hands, with tears streaming down their cheeks, and bid farewell. With many this must be the last farewell on earth for the heads of the youngest are blossoming for the grave. But few dry eyes were to be seen among the large assembly of people during this touching scene.

The place of the next meeting was then announced for September 1896, to be held at Poplar Springs Church, Marion County, Alabama. This place is located on what is known as the Russellville and Tuscaloosa road about seven miles northeast from Glen Allen. The meeting was then dismissed with prayer and the people dispersed to their homes feeling they had profitably spent two days. The writer of this article never witnessed a more harmonious meeting of any kind. Every one present seemed determined on pleasing and being pleased. May the old heroes enjoy many more reunions is the writer's wish. One of the People.

ETHEL WALDROP TERRELL BIOGRAPHY (sic)

The following is a transcription by Reid Bruton of an interview he taped with his Aunt Ethel Waldrop Terrell, who was 98 years of age at the time of the interview, and her reminisces of her life and her ancestors, Thomas and William Kirkman, who served in the 1st Alabama Cavalry, USV. She celebrated her 100th Birthday on April 2, 2012. Happy Birthday, "Aunt Ethel", and thanks for sharing your wonderful story.

Did I ever think I'd live to be a hundred years old? Well, I'm 2 years shy of it at present and to be honest… I never gave it much thought. But I will say this: I've always felt that I would live to see the day when Jesus comes again. Until then I've lived life to the fullest. I've read quite a few romance novels in my time. You might say I'm having a romance with life in general. I get up every morning and get dressed and ready for anything or anyone who might come my way that day. And generally speaking there will be a knock at the door or an unexpected phone call from a distant relative a thousand miles away. Or I'll get in the car (yes, I still drive!) and go visitin' with others, go to church or to the grocery store. Or do something completely out of the ordinary like attending the local spelling bee contest recently at the Caruthersville library. I've had, and continue to have, a wonderful time living this life and I'm looking forward to the life hereafter.

To know me, and my history with Pemiscot County, is to know the people who came before me. My Grandfather, John Garfield Waldrop moved to the newly created Pemiscot County in the 1850's… before the town of Caruthersville had been formed. Given the times, this move would have required a covered wagon holding all their belongings with livestock in tow. He settled and cleared land for farming in an area known as "Blow Ridge" – a couple of miles south east of the newly founded township of Braggadocio. Clearing the land would have been an enormous undertaking at that time for it was heavily wooded, swampy and uneven due to the earthquakes of 1812. He built a cabin on the highest portion of the land which was still standing when I was a young girl. The lowest of his land served as a water-way or a "slough" when the Mississippi river was high. My Papa remembered going from Blow Ridge to Caruthersville for supplies in a canoe via the slough. This was before S.P. Reynolds headed the construction of the Mississippi River levee and drainage ditches throughout Pemiscot County. That old slough is now Number 6 Ditch.

Grandpa Waldrop married my Grandmother, Malissa Jane Harris on February 26, 1866. We've always been told that we are part American Indian and part Black Dutch. Judging by the old photograph of my Grandma Waldrop it seems this must be true. Many of my cousins and me and my siblings look part Indian especially my sister, Tommie Waldrop Bruton… she had a fair amount of color and the smoothest complexion. This trait most certainly came from our Grandmother. Malissa Jane was a charter member of the Braggadocio Baptist Church where I am a member and have served as Sunday School Secretary for 60 years (and they haven't fired me yet!).

My maternal grandparents, Thomas Pharoah Kirkman and Nancy Evelina Mayfield moved from Tennessee to Pemiscot County around 1874. They settled in a small community known as "Cow Skin" near the bayou north west of Steele. But before moving to Missouri both Thomas Pharoah and his father, William Fields Kirkman served, side-by-side in the Civil War. Their involvement in the Civil War was unique among southern men. He and his father joined with approximately 2,500 other "Southrons" whose goal was "to hold true to the Old Flag" – the Union. In other words, they took up arms against their neighbors, the Confederates. They were both Corporals in Company "F" of 1st Alabama Cavalry UNION Army, enlisting on June 29, 1863 in Corinth, Mississippi. Thomas was only 18 years of age.

My Grandma Kirkman was a registered "mid-wife". In the rural areas the doctor couldn't be there when the time came and a mid-wife would bring the baby into the world. I'd love to know how many children my Grandmother helped deliver. She died in 1890 at age 45. After her death, Grandpa Kirkman remarried and moved to a small community south of Kennett called "Shady Grove". My father would take Mama and us kids in a wagon to the station at Micola to board the train for the long trip to Grandpa Kirkman's – my only grandparent living when I was born. In those days you'd put on your Sunday best to go on a trip like this. The train had to go south through Blytheville, Arkansas then north again into Missouri before reaching Shady Grove - a trip that would take 20 minutes via paved roads today. We'd stay several days with Grandpa Kirkman before returning. Grandpa Kirkman was a member of the Shady Grove Baptist Church which is still in existence today.

Land was so different back then. Even I can remember when there was nothing but impenetrable woods between Pemiscot and Dunklin Counties. Uncle Bob, a brother of my Grandpa Kirkman who also lived over on Shady Grove, found a way to meet up with some of the men-folk from Blow Ridge in the middle of the woods between the two counties. They'd camp and hunt for a few days.

Land was so different back then. Even I can remember when there was nothing but impenetrable woods between Pemiscot and Dunklin Counties. Uncle Bob, a brother of my Grandpa Kirkman who also lived over on Shady Grove, found a way to meet up with some of the men-folk from Blow Ridge in the middle of the woods between the two counties. They'd camp and hunt for a few days.

There was a lot more wildlife in Pemiscot County when my grandfathers settled here. We have a rack of antlers from a deer that my father shot not far from Blow Ridge. Papa said they also had bears in the area as well as beaver, wild turkey and pheasants. I remember the first time I ever saw a red fox. Papa took us down to Clarence Bruton's where he had caught one and had it in a cage. You might say this was the country version of a zoo!

There were no grocery stores or butchers… at least not near where we lived. So we had to rely on the native animals, as well as our domesticated cattle, hogs and fowl for food. My family has been known to hunt and cook 'coon, possum, squirrel, rabbit, black bird, pigeons, turkey and doves. Years later, my husband Fred, a great bird hunter, would hunt quail every Christmas and take them to the Mehrle's, the owners of Globe Clothing Store, for them to have for Christmas breakfast. Mr. Mehrle paid 25 cents per bird.

My father, John Thomas Waldrop born in 1868, lived 75 years of his life at the Blow Ridge farm on which he was born. His last 9 years he lived with my sister Tommie. He never attended school but Papa always said his life-long friend, Chip Franklin, Sr., taught him to "read, write and figure while sittin' on a log". This life-long friend later became Sheriff of Pemiscot County. When Sheriff Franklin became ill and was dying, Papa stayed by his side for over a week, only going home to change clothes.

Papa married my mother, Rosalie Kirkman in 1890 "by consent of her parents at the home of Thomas Pharoah Kirkman" – according to their marriage record. Mama was 17. Papa was 22. We all like to think our parents were beautiful at this young age. Well mine really were. An elderly lady used to tell me how all the girls were jealous of Mama for she'd gotten the "handsomest man around".

Papa was known for being able to cure babies of the thrush. For as long as I can remember people would come from miles around on wagons bringing their sick babies to "Uncle Tom" and he would blow in their mouth and cure them. The cure was a secret which he said he "could only share with one other person". I do not know "the secret" for he shared it with my sister Tommie.

Mama always said her people were French. To look at a formal, seated photograph from about 1900 of my parents and their young family you'd think she just got off the boat from Paris. But don't be fooled by the pretty picture for she knew how to use a tree switch *real* good. Papa never whipped us… Mama was the disciplinarian. One time, as a young girl, I slipped off and went down to my eldest sisters' house without permission. When I got back to the gate of our house I hollered out for Papa to "come get me, come get me Papa!"… I needed him to escort me into the house to keep Mama from whippin' me. Just as Papa was coming out of the house to get me here came Mama right behind him switchin' him instead of me… for trying to save me from punishment. We've laughed about that for 90 years now and it's still just as funny!

Mama and Papa lived in a little log house with a dirt floor and tiny 12x12 inch windows when first married in 1890. The home was situated on the 40 acres given to my Papa from his father. By the time I was born in 1912 they had moved into a 3-room home each room being rather large but not very private. There was a kitchen, a living room and a bedroom. Plus an L-shaped porch that wrapped around the side. We had 3 beds total, one being in the living room. In those days everybody had a bed in the living room.

I never felt we were poor for there were others who had less than us… much less. Papa had a cousin who died young leaving behind a helpless wife and children. We had a house full so we set our cousin's family up in the corner of our yard in a make-shift tent with a dirt floor and a wood burning cook stove. They used wooden kegs for chairs. I well remember them living there for quite some time.

Our family made headline news in 1913 - the year after I was born. The news reached all the way to Kansas City. This story was told to me by my Aunt Matt in hushed, whispered tones. We never spoke of it in my house nor did we ever speak to the person in question about the incident even though we knew her quite well. I will quote an article from the Kansas City Star dated August 6, 1913. The headline read:

THREATENED WIFE SHOT FIRST

Missouri Planter Killed Before He Could Kill Woman. With her baby in her arms and carrying the revolver with which she shot and killed her husband, Mrs. Anderson Waldrop, wife of a prosperous planter, walked two miles to a neighboring farm house yesterday to telephone to the sheriff here. Waldrop's body was found in his farm dwelling. Mrs. Waldrop is in jail here. According to her statement Waldrop had threatened to kill her. She claims she shot him while he was preparing to carry out his threat."

The woman in question was my father's sister, Susie Ann Waldrop. She was not convicted of murder for she acted in self-defense. Her husband was known to be mean to her. It must have been a tough decision to make... but made it she did!

In the summer of 1917 us kids were playing outside when we heard "it"! We'd heard about it. Our parents had read about it. But none of us had ever seen it. All the adults came runnin' out of the house to catch a glimpse of it. An aunt of mine, who was very proud of her son, said "David'l spot it". Sure 'nough he did for there it was in the direction he was pointing... an airplane! It was unbelievable that someone was that high in the sky in a machine that could fly. My first time seeing an airplane. The Wright Brothers had taken their first flight the year after my sister Beulah was born – 1903.

We lived across the way from the cow stomp. Some of the old folks will know what that is. I'll explain it for the others. Cows were branded for identification of owner then allowed to roam the countryside freely - "free range cattle". There were no fences. At night all the cows would come together to the cow stomp where there was water. And let me tell you, if you live across the way from a cow stomp you're gonna get an early education about the birds and the bees!

Papa and another man would cut wood together for each of our families. They had a very long 2-man saw with large teeth and a handle on each end and would take down a tree in no time. Then they'd chop the wood into 2 different sizes. One size was for the cook stove the other size for heat.

I had my first car ride in 1917. I was 5 years old. A cousin, John Acuff bought a car and came by our house and said "Rosie, you and the girls wanna go for a ride?" About half a mile up the road and back is all we went but I well remember sittin' in that back seat of that car with my little sister Tommie – our first car ride! Later my father bought a "T Model" car. I learned how to drive on a T Model but not on Papa's. He wouldn't let us drive. I sure couldn't drive a T Model today.... the brake was different, it had 2 pedals and a rod... suffice to say it was complicated!

Also in 1917 I had the thrill of seeing my first moving picture show. I don't remember the name of the movie but it was about a little girl who got chased up a tree by a bear. They'd constructed a large tent in Braggadocio near where the Coppage Gin used to be and would project the movie onto a sheet. A man would read aloud the words of this silent movie for those who were unable to read. They continued showing movies in this manner for quite some time.

We were all in the field on November 11, 1918. The adults were pickin' cotton. At about noontime the gin whistle up at "Braggy" started blowing. The adults thought that it might be because the war had ended so some of the men got in a car and went up to the gin to find the good news that yes indeed, World War I had ended – Armistice Day.

We had to pump our water to be carried inside for cooking and cleaning. To take a bath was quite a chore. We'd have to bring the tub into the kitchen (it would usually be hanging off the outside of the house), carry in buckets of water from the pump which was about 50 yards away, heat up the water in pots and kettles on the wood burning stove then fill the tub. In the summer we'd fill the tub up outside during the day and let the sun heat up the water then take our bath outside in the dark. We used this method of heating bath water even after I got married. It sounds rather crude now but everybody we knew had to bathe in this manner.

Of course we had no electricity throughout my entire childhood and my early married life. We had oil lamps for lighting. I believe it wasn't until the early 40's when electricity made it's way to where my husband and I lived. I did all my washing on a washboard and ironed with a flat iron heated on the cook stove. I'm known for my heavy starched and ironed shirts. Until recently I always made a little cash-on-the-side ironing. But I was never able to iron as well with an electric iron as I was with a good ol' flat iron.

We raised and butchered our own meat. In my childhood and early adult life we raised everything from chickens, ducks, guineas, cows, pigs and domesticated turkeys although we mostly hunted wild turkey. At the first hog slaughter of the season Fred would spread open the hog and take the heart, the "light" (the lungs) and the "melt" (the spleen) and I'd make a stew with sage and other seasonings. It was an annual tradition. The first of fall was the time to butcher a cow for meat. In the early years if a neighbor killed his cow he'd put it in a big tub covered with a cloth. Then go around from house to house with a mule pulled wagon selling off pieces of this fresh meat. He'd call out from the road and Mama would go to his wagon and pick out which piece she wanted. We'd cook what she'd bought that day for there was no icebox, no ice deliveryman and certainly no refrigerator!

Before we had an icebox we'd buy a 50 pound block of ice and kept it wrapped real good with towels in a tub. It'd last almost 2 days. I didn't have an icebox until after I'd been married several years. The ice deliveryman would come every other day to fill up the icebox. I got into a habit of makin' him a chicken and biscuit breakfast from time to time. You'd do things like that for folks who came into your home on a regular basis.

When I was a kid we didn't know what "an allowance" was. But Papa always kept a 50 gallon barrel of kerosene and sacks of tobacco and me and my sister Tommie would be the salesmen of these things to the neighbors. The money from the sales was our allowance. Also, as far back as I can remember we farmed a plot of land called "the Curtner Farm". There were several pecan trees on that farm which we'd pick in the fall. Papa would sell them to a store in Caruthersville and Tommie and I would get all the money from the pecan sales as well. That was quite generous of our Papa… considering the times. Another little money making deal: a man would come around peddlin' apples in our area. He'd get to our house about sundown and spend the night. My sister and I would count his money for him and he'd give us a nickel for doing so. And Mama and Papa were given a bushel of apples for his lodging.

Papa would take us to Caruthersville almost every week and we'd always go down to see the river. When we'd finished picking up all we'd come to town for we'd go by the fish dock located about where 1st State Bank is now, and buy some fresh fish. There was an ice cream stand next to the fish salesman. I'd always get a strawberry shake. To this day I cannot go to Caruthersville without driving by to see the river – some habits are hard to break. If that ice cream stand was still there today I'd be as big as the side of a barn!

I attended a 2 room school at a nearby community called Shake Rag. One room was 1st - 4th grade and the other was 5th – 8th. We sat 2 to a seat. We had recess but no basketball or football. We did play softball in the summertime though. Girls and boys played together. I was always on 3rd base. Sometimes we'd play against other little country schools like "Midway". And we had spelling bee contests with the "Gibson Bayou School". A bread wagon from Caruthersville would come by the schoolyard twice a week. You could get 2 cinnamon rolls for a nickel. We'd raise and take down the American Flag every day at school except when it rained. It was a very formal affair requiring 2 children to do the task – a boy and a girl. By the time I reached 8th grade I had a heavy load to carry - geography, reading, writing, science… about 6 books total. After 8th grade graduation my sister and I stayed home. Some kids went on to high school at Braggadocio but not us. There were no busses at that time and to be honest I don't know if Mama and Papa would have let us go on to high school anyway. We'll just say they didn't push it. Then came my courtin' years!

After crops were laid out in the summer the men around our community would build a brush arbor near the school at Shake Rag. They'd take the largest limbs of trees and construct a structure for us to have church services under. We'd have Sunday morning Sunday School and services at night as well. One preacher would preach one week, next week another preacher. Everybody in the community went to the brush arbor for it was not only a place to worship but also a place to socialize, especially for us younger kids… as I said, it was courtin' season!

I was introduced to Fred Terrell by his sister in the middle of the road one night in 1925 but we didn't start dating until '27 for Fred was a bit older that I was. After our first date his sister brought me a letter he'd written… I guess you could say it was a love letter. It read: "you are one person I could spend the rest of my life with". I still have the letter to this day. We were married in July of 1929 in Blytheville, Arkansas with Papa, Mamma, sister Tommie and a cousin in attendance. After the marriage was performed the Clerk of the Judge asked for $6.10 – the fee for the Marriage License. Fred handed the clerk the $6 and started feelin' around in his pocket for a dime. The clerk said something I'll never forget: "it'll be easier to find that dime now than it will a year from now". And she was right for the Great Depression hit one year later and Fred didn't have a dime to his name.

Fred's father gave us 5 acres of cotton that year. It was a good crop – 2 ½ bails to an acre. With the money from the cotton we bought furniture and rented some farmland that included a 4-room house. Back then every farmhouse had a smaller tenement house right at the backyard. Our farm hand lived there. We had something we thought was rather fancy for a young married couple: our wood-burning cook stove had an extra compartment to keep things warm before suppertime – a "morning oven". My dowry or trousseau from Mama and Papa consisted of a dozen hens, 1 rooster, a feather bed, 2 pillows and a bolster. Sister Wisey gave several household goods for the kitchen.

Papa helped build homes for my three older siblings. They were all within hollerin' distance from each other and all located near my father's childhood home on Blow Ridge. Across from the old Blow Ridge slough or Number 6 Ditch, there's a little dirt road or lane affectionately called "Waldrop Lane" for the obvious reason.

I churned butter the same way my Mama did until well after I was married. Depending on the temperature of the milk it would take anywhere from 15 to 40 minutes of churning to make the milk clabber. I sold milk and butter to neighbors for a little extra spending money. It didn't take long before a lot of people wanted some of the Terrell's milk and butter and Fred, who did all the milking, became my deliveryman as well. We had a nice little side-gig making money from fresh milk and hand-churned butter well into the 1940's.

Mama and I both cooked on wood burning cook stoves. Later we upgraded to kerosene then to gas. To keep warm during my childhood we used a wood burning heat stove. But when Fred and I first married all we had was a fireplace in the living room… the only room with heat. I liked to froze to death… burned my shins while wrapped up in a blanket with my feet in the heat box in front of that fireplace. At night we'd get in that feather bed with all the quilts in the house. Later on we got two coal-burning potbelly stoves and then later upgraded to gas heat. Our only means of keeping cool during the humid summer months was with a cardboard "funeral fan" – the older folks will get that one!

We didn't have a telephone growing up. You'd get your phone messages from Burt Skinner's store in Braggadocio. "Braggy" sure looked different back in the old days. There were raised wooden sidewalks, 2 drug stores, a bowling alley, movie theater, pool hall, 2 barber shops, 3 churches, 3 doctors and 5 general stores.

For entertainment Fred and I would play poker at night with matches instead of chips. Later on people would come by and we'd play cards, make popcorn, roast pecans or peanuts. Many people in Pemiscot County are familiar with the concrete remains of a building that once stood at Shake Rag. The man who built that building said he built it to last for a hundred years. Well, he was right! I've heard a lot of stories about what went on in that building but from my own personal experience I only knew it as a general store by day and a "nightclub" by night! I never went there at night but Fred and I would go down to the store during the day and I'd play the Victrolla. The store owners' son and I would dance. Fred wouldn't dance much. He was more into visiting with the store owner.

No one in our family drank much but during prohibition Fred, my brother "Bud" and brother-in-law Sheb thought they'd try to make some "home-brew". They hid their illegal contraption out in the off-season garden… after it had growed up. As fate would have it the thing blew up like a bomb, and POP, POP, POP… you could hear it all over the County! Those boys were shakin' in their boots…. worried that my mother would be mad for "Ms. Rosie" would certainly not go for anything like "home-brew"!

Farming was done on a much smaller scale than now. You'd live on the land where you worked… with the crop you were growing. The countryside was peppered with farmhouses. There was a house about every 1/8th of a mile… most with a barn. It's all farmland now. I didn't work much in the field as a child but I certainly did after I was married. Fred and I worked side-by-side choppin' and pickin' cotton. I'd where a bonnet and a full dress with long sleeves to keep the sun off me…. not because I was worried about a suntan. I was already dark. But the clothes helped to keep you cool. We farmed in the same manner my Papa and his father had farmed… with a pair of mules and a 1-row plow. After pickin' the cotton I'd ride the mule-pulled stalk cutter which would cut the remaining plant down. Fred used to take his mule, plow and wagon over to the nearby Morgan farm and prep their land for planting. They gave him $2.50 per day and fed him and his mule their supper. My Papa grew corn and cotton. Fred added soybeans to our list some time later.

The first tractor Fred bought was a used red Farmall. Next year we rented some more land and got a John Deere. Later on we rented even more land and upgraded for another tractor. Then in the 50's we got a 1-row picker. The tractor and picker sure made farming easier but it came with a price. In 1957 Fred was working on the edge of a ditch on Blow Ridge when the tractor turned over on him. The wheel broke his pelvis in two. He was bedridden for 6 months and had to learn how to walk again.

First radio we bought was a battery powered Philco in 1937… remember, no electricity in those days. In the summer time we'd put the radio near the window and sit out on the porch to listen. Fred and some of the other men were listenin' to a big Joe Louis boxing match one evenin' when a black man walked by our house. The man stopped at the edge of our yard to listen for a minute. Now this was when segregation was a very big issue. "Colored folks" or "negros" were not allowed to co-mingle with white folks in public areas. Fred, realizing how important this Joe Louis fight must have been to the man, asked him to come up and sit on the porch to listen with us. At first he said "that's alright, I'll just listen from here". But eventually he came up to the porch and we all listened as Joe Louis won the title in 1937.

People would come from other states to help during cotton pickin' season. In 1939 a woman came for work and she's the one who introduced me to the pressure cooker. From then on I canned *everything* from the garden for us to have in the winter. Before the pressure cooker we would only have canned pickles or tomatoes and dried peas or butter beans in the winter months. Also in 1939 a man came all the way from Kansas City in a car that had a rumble seat in the back. He was writing a book about rural life and wanted to learn how to pick cotton. We let him sleep in the barn and he picked with us during the day. He was nice enough… but the city slicker wasn't a good picker!

The Ladies Extension Club was a government run deal for farm wives to help us better our living situation. They would come every other week to Braggadocio and give classes. My good friend, Ms. Pickens and I would walk to "Braggy" for the bi-weekly meetings. One time a truck driver picked us up and carried us the rest of the way. After that we never walked to an Extension Club meeting again… he picked us up every time. You wouldn't trust a stranger today the way we did back then! Ms. Pickens and I would also go sit-up with the sick. When a neighbor was sick and needed help we'd stay 'til midnight or sometimes the entire night… helping tend to their needs. This was all on a voluntary basis. Others would have done the same for me and my family if needed.

WWII changed our lives. Sister Wisey moved up to St. Louis with her children to work in a factory. Tommie and I took a train up to visit her a few times. On one of our trips we took our seats up in the front of the train cabin. The Conductor came by and looked us up and down real good and said "alright, I guess it's OK for you to sit up here". This was during the middle of the segregation debate… we're part American Indian… he wasn't sure *what* race we were. For a minute we thought we'd have to hitch a ride back home.

Funny story: We were always "Fred and Ethel", just like on the "I Love Lucy" show. And this Ethel was beginning to look more and more like the one on TV. I'd gained weight and wanted to take it off. A friend told me about a pill you could get from the doctor that would "burn the fat away". I got a prescription for this pill which is now, I believe, out-lawed!! Basically, it's what the young folks today call "speed". Little did we know of the addictive nature of this medicine or it's side-effects. But let me tell you one thing: I NEVER PICKED SO MUCH COTTON IN ALL MY LIFE!!

1952 was a big year for us. Fred and I moved into our second home. Yep, you guessed it… on Blow Ridge! Finally, we had indoor plumbing, a refrigerator and an automatic clothes washer. But no indoor bathroom until 1954 - the same year we got our first television. I stopped choppin' cotton when we moved to the Ridge. I'd done my share in the fields.

I was unable to have children. I used to *wish* that someone would leave a baby on my doorstep. Due to very unfortunate circumstances, in a way, my wish came true in 1961. My sister Beulah's grown daughter died of cancer leaving her bewildered husband and young children behind. Sister Beulah took her granddaughter, little Brenda to live with her. Fred and I took in the boy, Danny to live with us. Both Brenda and Danny are like my own children today. I love them both dearly.

My Fred was diagnosed with cancer in 1971 and died 4 years later. After he passed away I kept active with Nurses Aid and Red Cross classes and my church activities. At one time we had over 100 in regular attendance at Braggadocio Baptist and during revivals we'd have many more than that. We also had a good size choir which I sang in for 62 years. I've seen that old church through four different buildings, a tornado and a decline in attendance. But I'm there every time the door's open. I've also done a little traveling in my later years. I've been to almost all of the 50 United States, Nova Scotia, Canada and Mexico.

All my life my sister Tommie and I were inseparable. We'd played together, went to school together, worked together, courted at the same time, married around the same time and both widowed within two years of each other. Tommie didn't like to sleep in a house all by herself so right after her Edwin passed away I'd spend the nights with her. I'd get my nightgown and head over to Tommie's every night and we'd knit and crochet, watch Johnny Carson, eat a bowl of ice cream or popcorn and share a lot of laughs. I wore down a good path from my house to hers for we continued this nightly ritual for over 20 years!

After a few years of being single again we started going to the senior citizens' dances with groups of other widowed women whom we'd known all of our lives. It's embarrassing to say but it was a bit like bein' a teenager again. We had such a good time going to those dances. Even met a new boyfriend or two… just someone to pass the time with. My "late-in-life friend" was George Walker. He was a great dance partner!

A grandnephew of mine is a psychologist out in California. He says I'm a "text book example" for what they call a "Hardy Personality". Supposedly this type of person has a longer life-span. All I know is I enjoy life, I laugh a lot, sing for my own enjoyment, I stay busy, I get up and get *dressed up* every day… and I have an unending faith in God. I've lived thru 2 World Wars, the Great Depression, a double tornado, the death of everyone I grew up with (some quite tragic deaths)… and… it ain't got me down yet! So maybe the psychologist out in California is right.

One last thing: my singing voice is gone now but I've sung all my life. I would wake up singing and continue singing all day long while doing my chores. I HIGHLY recommend it!

Much Thanks, Ethel Waldrop Terrell

(These words were transcribed by Reid Bruton in the summer of 2010 from his Great Aunt Ethel Terrell - GREAT being the operative word. Please do not copy without consent of Ms. Terrell, a family member or the Pemiscot County Historical Society.) Submitted to author with permission to print in *Unionists in the Heart of Dixie*.

The following is information on "Aunt Ethel's" grandfather, Thomas P. Kirkman and great grandfather, William F. Kirkman, who served in the 1st Alabama Cavalry, USV.

According to Thomas P. Kirkman's Death Certificate, his address was listed as R.F.D. Kennett, MO, born Dec. 7, 1845 in Mifflin, Tennessee to William F. and Amy E. Kirkman. He was buried August 5, 1936 in Oak Ridge Cemetery in Kennett, MO by Baldwin Funeral Home. Information was given by C.F. Kirkman. Dr. George Gilmore, D.O., of Kennett, MO, stated he died of decompensation of the heart, which is described as fatigue, stress, illness, or old age. It also stated he had hypotrophy of the prostrate gland, (which just means enlarged prostrate.)

Thomas Pharoah Kirkman was born about December 7, 1845, in Henderson County, Tennessee and died April 3, 1871, probably in Henderson County, Tennessee. He married Nancy Evelina Mayfield on December 21, 1868, in Gibson County, Tennessee Nancy Evelina was born in 1845 and died in 1890. Their children were: William S., born April 26, 1870, died April 3, 1871; John T., born August 25 1871; Rosalie V., born March 2, 1873, died April 24, 1941; Robert Charley, born June 26, 1875, died November 3, 1884; Landon (Landrum) Washington, born September 30, 1877 in Missouri, died December 18, 1953; James Clinton, born October 3, 1880, died May 8, 1882; Martha Elizabeth, born

October 29, 1883; and Nancy Evelina Kirkman Baker, born August 7, 1887 and died September 21, 1974.

Given the location of Thomas and Evelina's children's births we can assume that he moved his family from Tennessee to Pemiscot County, Missouri sometime between May 1873 and June 1875. Thomas Pharoah served in the Civil War as a Corporal in Company F of 1st Alabama Cavalry UNION Army, enlisting on June 29, 1863, in Corinth, Mississippi at age 18 and mustered out July 27, 1864 in Rome, GA. His involvement in the Civil War was unique among southern men. He and his father joined with a small minority whose goal was "to hold true to the Old Flag" – the Union. He took up arms against his neighbors, the Confederates.

His wife, Nancy Evelina Mayfield, also known as "Mandy", is listed as being a "mid-wife" in the Pemiscot County local birth records between August 24,1883 and January 29, 1885. Nancy was born in Tennessee and according to census records, it shows that both of her parents were born in Illinois on or around 1820. Her mother's name was Martha, possibly Ervin. Nancy died at age 45. She and their young son John T. Kirkman are buried on "Blow Ridge". It is unclear if they lived on Blow Ridge (the Waldrop's land) at the time. Their grave "markers" were moved and lost. The land is now farmed. But I have an older map of the land which indicates where their graves are located.

After Nancy Evelina's death in 1890, Thomas Pharoah remarried and moved to a small community south of Kennett, Missouri called "Shady Grove". His granddaughter, Ethel Waldrop Terrell remembers her father taking the family in a "wagon pulled by a mule" to the station at Micola, Missouri to board a train for the long trip to go visit "Grandpa Kirkman". The train had to go south through Blytheville Arkansas and north again into Missouri before reaching "Shady Grove" in Dunklin County where Grandpa Kirkman lived (a trip that would take 20 minutes via paved roads today). They would stay several days before returning. Thomas Pharoah was a founding member of "Shady Grove Baptist Church" which is still in existence today. He is buried in a Cemetery just north of Kennett, Missouri. Thomas Pharoah's second wife was Mary Elizabeth Hale. They had the following children: Betty Kirkman Stroup, Samuel Kirkman, Hattie Kirkman Floyd. (Information submitted by Linda Rochelle.)

William Fields Kirkman, father of soldier Thomas Pharoah Kirkman, enlisted as a Private in the 1st Alabama Cavalry, USV on June 29, 1863, in Corinth, Mississippi and was discharged as a Corporal on July 27, 1864, in Rome, Georgia. He filed for a pension # 912.412 on October 18, 1890, listing his address as Mifflin, Tennessee. In one of the affidavits he filed dated August 4, 1898, it gave his Certificate No. as 767.236, and he stated he was married to Elizabeth Stout in 1886 in Chester County, Tennessee by H.H. Fry, Esq. but the records were destroyed by fire in 1891. He also stated he had previously been married to Amey Wooley (Vestal). He listed the names of his living children as: Thomas Kirkman, born December 7, 1845; Mary (Brewer), born April 2, 1847; Judia (Carpenter), born April 2, 1849; Eliza (Whitwell) born March 3, 1851; Martha, born August 21, 1853; R.L. (Robert Lemuel), born April 27, 1856; John, born August 24, 1862; Andrew, born August 15, 1888; and Annie Kirkman, born May 3, 1893.

His pension of $12 per month began October 18, 1890, listing his disability as "Complete, double inguinal hernia. William stated he thought the cause of the hernia was due to his service as a soldier although it didn't appear until 1882 or 1883.

J.H. Fry, age 56, of Chester County, Tennessee signed an affidavit stating he had known William F. Kirkman for about 56 years and knew he was a farmer and suffered with a rupture. A.J. Vestal, age 55, also signed an affidavit stating he knew William Kirkman was a farmer and suffered with a rupture. W.C. Brown, M.D. signed a Physician's Certificate stating he had been practicing medicine for 13 years and had been intimately acquainted with the claimant as his family physician all that time. He stated his disability was a rupture, complete double inguinal hernia – total, and that the disability was permanent and was not the result of his vicious habits. He stated claimant was advanced in life and his disability is therefore permanent.

On June 3, 1891, William F. Kirkman signed an affidavit in Mifflin, Henderson County, Tennessee stating the following, "In 1883 while hoeing cotton was ruptured on right side and hernia following was ruptured on left side. On the same affidavit, W.C. Brown, M.D. stated he examined Kirkman and found his pulse rate was 100, respiration 20, temperature 98.5, height 5' 8 ½", weight 139

38

pounds and age 65 years. He stated he found a double inguinal hernia and the tumors were 4 inches long and 2 inches in diameter each and he did find that a disability existed.

The United States Pension Agency stated on September 24, 1907, that pension certificate No. 767.230 of Pensioner William F. Kirkman, Company F, 1st Alabama Volunteer Cavalry was last paid to May 4, 1907, and had been dropped because of death on September 20, 1907. On October 22, 1907, in Chester County, Tennessee, J.T. Kirkman went to the Chester County Court Clerk asking for a letter of administration of William F. Kirkman's estate since he died intestate. The clerk signed an affidavit naming him as Administrator and authorizing him to take into his possession and control all the goods, chattels, claims, and papers of the said intestate, and return a true and perfect inventory thereof to their next County Court, or within ninety days from that date, to collect and pay all debts, and to do and transact all the duties in relation to said estate which lawfully devolve on him as Administrator; and after having settled up said estate, to deliver the residue thereof to those who have a right thereto by law. Signed J.W. Stewart, Clerk of said Court, in the 132 year of American Independence.

BATTLE OF VINCENT'S CROSSROADS - October 26, 1863 (sic)

In the Civil War Diary of Francis Wayland Dunn, he wrote about the Battle of Vincent's Crossroads stating the following: Started about six in the morning. Heard that there were plenty of Rebels, 5,000 or them ahead of us at Vinson's (Vincent's) Crossroads. We kept on however and heard that there was only Morelans (Moreland's) Battery and so pushed forward. At the crossroads did not find any tracks and thought the thing was a hoax. Four or five miles from there we found a squad of six out in the field. They all run. Fed our horses at Patterson. His wife was a rough woman. Spencer told her we were the children of Israel bringing the plague on them. Colonel left me to guard the cotton. Barker came down to burn it. We went about two miles. I had not got to the front when several shots were fired. I pushed ahead and found the two guns on a little rise of ground and the gunners loading. Companies F, B, & G had been deployed to the left of the road, E & A to the right and H was just going in. The road runs north and south. On the right was a narrow field 30-40 rods wide for almost half a mile, only broken by a strip of underbrush about 20 rods through. Companies L & D were put into the open field on the right, at first facing to the east and then L faced to the north. I & K were in a similar position on the west of the road. C was rear guard. Pack mules and refugees were also to the rear. Their line was also longer than ours and they were outflanking us. The two guns were brought back to the house in the middle of the field.

1st Alabama Cavalry, USV soldiers killed during this battle or dying from wounds soon afterwards were: Marshal H. Byrd, Erasmus D. Chandler, James K. Morphus, James Perry, Phillip A. Sternberg, and William T. Tyler, all killed in action October 26, 1863. James Mack Cooper was wounded and died December 15, 1863, from wounds received in the battle. James C. Swift died November 2, 1863, from wounds received in the battle.

This battle was fought over such a long, wooded area, that some of the bodies were not located for some period of time, and a few were later buried on the grounds where the battle was fought. Several of the troopers were captured and sent to Andersonville, Prison in Georgia where many later died in the horrendous prison.

Larry E. Linley writes the following story about the battle: Colonel Spencer, Commander of the 1st Alabama received word from his forward scouts that a Confederate force of 5,000 cavalry awaited him at Vincent's Cross Roads, Alabama, (present day Red Bay, Alabama). Upon arrival no Confederate force was seen, therefore the command continued it's northwesterly march. Suddenly, out of nowhere, Confederate artillery was spotted on a ridge to their front. It was immediately ascertained the cannons were primed and ready for firing. Spencer ordered his companies into action. Companies F, B and G to were deployed immediately to the left of the road, Companies E and A immediately to the right. He ordered Company H to move forward and remain on the road, while Companies D and L (L being my great, great granddad's company) were deployed in the most forward position to the right of the road in a large field. Companies I and K were to do the same on the left side of the road.

The Confederate cannons boomed with deadly accuracy from canister and grape shot in the direction of Company L and several soldiers fell. The Rebels began yelling and charged with infantry and cavalry. Several hundred rifles were firing in both directions and Company L was taking the brunt of the attack. Orders were given to fall back and mount horses. All companies were scattered and disorganized with a loss of two officers and twenty enlisted . The sadness was my great, great, granddad was one of the twenty causalities.

The remaining companies were so badly scattered and disorganized that it became every man for himself. Some stragglers were captured, some made their way back to the camps in northern Mississippi near Iuka and to Camp Davies.. Stragglers continued to report to camp for several days following the defeat. There had been so much confusion, the Commanders had no way of knowing what actually happened to many of the First Alabama members who were killed, captured or deserted. It is a believed that local residents buried the dead and they were later removed and interned at the Corinth National Cemetery. My great, great granddad, Jonathan "Jot" Lindley, was believed to have been one of those buried at Corinth.

Battle of Day's Gap

The Battle of Day's Gap, fought on April 30, 1863, was the first in a series of American Civil War skirmishes in Cullman County, Alabama, that lasted until May 2nd, known as Streight's Raid. Commanding the Union forces was Colonel Abel D. Streight; Brigadier General Nathan Bedford Forrest led the Confederate forces.

The goal of Streight's raid was to cut off the Western & Atlantic Railroad, which supplied General Braxton Bragg's Confederate army in Middle Tennessee. Starting in Nashville, Tennessee, Streight and his men first traveled to Eastport, Mississippi, and then eastward to Tuscumbia, Alabama. On April 26, 1863, Streight left Tuscumbia and marched southeastward. Streight's initial movements were screened by Union Brig. Gen. Grenville Dodge's troops.

On April 30 at Day's Gap on Sand Mountain, Forrest caught up with Streight's expedition and attacked his rear guard. Streight's men managed to repulse this attack and as a result they continued their march to avoid any further delays and envelopments caused by the Confederate troops.

This battle set off a chain of skirmishes and engagements at Crooked Creek on April 30th, Hog Mountain April 30th, Blountsville May 1st, Black Creek/Gadsden May 2nd, and Blount's Plantation May 2nd, and finally, on May 3rd, Forrest surrounded Streight's exhausted men 3 miles east of Cedar Bluff, Alabama, and forced their surrender. They were sent to Libby Prison in Richmond, Virginia. Streight and some of his men escaped on February 9, 1864.

Principal Commanders were Colonel Abel Streight, US; Brig. Gen. Nathan Bedford Forrest, CS.

Forces Engaged were troopers from the 51st Indiana Infantry, 73rd Indiana Infantry, 3rd Ohio Infantry, 80th Illinois Infantry, and 1st Middle Tennessee Cavalry, which included some of the men from the 1st Alabama Cavalry, US, and three CS regiments.

Estimated Casualties were 88 total - US 23 and CS 65.

Description: Union Colonel Abel D. Streight led a provisional brigade on a raid to cut the Western & Atlantic Railroad that supplied General Braxton Bragg's Confederate army in Middle Tennessee. From Nashville, Tennessee, Streight's command traveled to Eastport, Mississippi, and then proceeded east to Tuscumbia, Alabama, in conjunction with another Union force commanded by Brigadier General Grenville Dodge. On April 26, 1863, Streight's men left Tuscumbia and marched southeast, their initial movements screened by Dodge's troops. The Results of this battle were: Union victory, although the raid ultimately failed.

Chronology of events of Streight's Raid in April and May 1863

Nashville, Tennessee, April 7-10 — proceeded by river
Palmyra, Tennessee, April 11-13 — proceeded on foot
Yellow Creek, Tennessee, April 13-14 — proceeded on foot
Fort Henry, Tennessee, April 15-17 — proceeded by river
Eastport, Mississippi, April 19-21 — proceeded either by foot or river
Bear Creek/River, Mississippi, April 22 — proceeded on foot the rest of the way
Tuscumbia, Alabama, April 24-26
Mount Hope, Alabama, April 27-28
Moulton, Alabama, April 28
Day's Gap, Alabama, April 29-30
Battle of Day's Gap, April 30
Skirmish at Crooked Creek, April 30
Skirmish at Hog Mountain, April 30
Arrival at Blountsville, May 1
Skirmishes at Blountsville, May 1
Skirmishes at the East Branch of the Black Warrior River, May 1
Skirmishes at the crossing of Black Creek, near Gadsden, May 2
Damaged ammunition while crossing Will's Creek, near Gadsden, May 2
Gadsden, Alabama, May 2
Blount's plantation, about 15 miles from Gadsden, May 2

Skirmishes at/near Blount's Plantation, Cherokee County, May 2-3
Centre, Alabama, May 3

ORGANIZATION & PATH OF 1ST ALABAMA CAVALRY, USV

Organized at Huntsville, Alabama, and Memphis, Tennessee, October, 1862. Attached to Cavalry Brigade, District of Corinth, 16th Army Corps, Department of Tennessee, January to March, 1863. Cavalry Brigade, District of Corinth, 2nd Division, 16th Army Corps, to June, 1863. 3rd Brigade, 1st Cavalry Division, 16th Army Corps, to August, 1863. 1st Brigade, 1st Division, 16th Army Corps, to April, 1864. Cavalry 4th Division, 16th Army Corps, to May, 1864. Headquarters 16th Army Corps to September, 1864. Unattached 15th Army Corps to November, 1864. Unattached 3rd Division, Cavalry Corps, Military Division Mississippi, to January, 1865. 3rd Brigade, Kilpatrick's 3rd Cavalry Division, Cavalry Corps, Military Division Mississippi, to June, 1865. District of Northern Alabama, Department of the Cumberland, to October, 1865.

SERVICE - Duty in District of Corinth, Mississippi, until June, 1863. Action at Cherokee Station, Alabama, December 12, 1862. Chewalla, Tennessee, January 20, 1863. Tuscumbia, Alabama, February 22. Bear Creek March 3. Carroll County (Companies "H" and "L") April 4. Glendale, Mississippi April 14. Dodge's Expedition to North Alabama April 15-May 8. Barton's Station April 16-17. Dickson, Great Bear Creek, Cherokee Station and Lundy's Lane April 17. Rock Cut, near Tuscumbia, Alabama April 22. Tuscumbia April 23. Town Creek April 28. Expedition to Tupelo, Mississippi, May 2-8. King's Creek, near Tupelo, Mississippi May 5. Burnsville, Mississippi, June 11. Ripley August 3. Vincent's Cross Roads and Bay Springs, Alabama, October 26. Operations on Memphis & Charleston Railroad November 3-5. Colliersville, Tennessee, November 3. Moscow, Mississippi, November 4. Camp Davies, Mississippi, November 22 (Detachment). Operations on Memphis & Charleston Railroad against Lee's attack November 28-December 10. Molino November 28. Wolf River Bridge December 4. Expedition toward Tuscumbia, Alabama, December 9-24. Jack's Creek December 24. Expedition from Memphis to Wyatt's, Mississippi, February 6-18, 1864 (Detachment). Coldwater Ferry February 8. Near Senatobia February 8-9. Wyatt's February 13. Operations against Forrest, in West Tennessee and Kentucky, February 16-April 14. Reconnaissance down Tennessee River to Triana, Alabama April 12-16 (Detachment). Decatur, Alabama, April 17. Atlanta Campaign May to September. Movements on Dalton May 5-9. Snake Creek Gap May 10-12. Battle of Resaca May 13-15. Rome Cross Roads May 16. Battles about Dallas May 25-June 5. Operations about Marietta, Georgia and against Kennesaw Mountain, Georgia June 10-July 2. Nickajack Creek July 2-5. Chattahoochee River July 6-17. Cove Springs July 8. Expedition to Centre, Alabama, July 11-13. Decatur, Alabama July 19-22. Battle of Atlanta, Georgia July 22. Siege of Atlanta July 22-August 25. Scout to Cedar Bluff, Alabama, July 28-29. Expedition from Rome, Georgia to Jacksonville, Alabama, August 11-15. Buchanan August 15. Coreysville August 20. Flank movement on Jonesboro August 25-30. Battle of Jonesboro August 31-September 1. Bolensville September 3. Rome, Georgia September 6. Reconnaissance from Rome on Cave Springs Road October 12-13. March to the sea November 15-December 10. Ball's Ferry, Oconee River, November 24-25. Waynesboro November 27-29. Briar Creek December 4. Little Ogeechee River December 4. Siege of Savannah, Georgia December 10-21. Campaign of the Carolinas January to April, 1865. River's Bridge, South Carolina, February 7. Williston February 8. Near White Post February 8. Aiken, North Carolina February 11. Gunther's Bridge February 14. Rockingham, North Carolina, March 7. Monroe's Cross Roads, North Carolina March 10. Taylor's Hole Creek, March 16. Battle of Bentonville March 19-21. Faison's Depot, North Carolina March 30-31. Roachland, North Carolina April 1. Mt. Pleasant April 11. Occupation of Raleigh April 13. Bennett's House April 26. Surrender of Johnston and his Army. Ordered to Department of the Cumberland May. Duty in District of Northern Alabama and at Huntsville, Alabama, until October. Mustered out October 20, 1865.

MILITARY STRUCTURE
By Dave Frederick

FORMATION OF REGIMENTS

Here are the "basics" of how regiments were formed and what they did in the Civil War.

On the Union side of the Civil War, the first calls for regiments of volunteers were in the early spring of 1862. Congress passed "enabling acts" calling upon the states named in the act to create and fill regiments. Typically there might be a call for four regiments included in one state portion of one enabling act. The purpose of each regiment was specified, being either:

1. Infantry: The walking/marching soldiers
2. Cavalry: Soldiers on horseback with swords
3. Artillery: Soldiers firing cannons
4. Heavy Artillery: Usually ended up as an infantry regiment
5. Light artillery or Mounted Infantry: A slower, heavier cavalry
6. Grenadiers, Fusiliers, Zouaves, etc.: Usually Infantry
7. Sharpshooters: A single company of a larger regiment of Infantry. Crack shots with a rifle used primarily to protect cavalry charges. It was a very honorable and very dangerous position to fill.

CHAIN OF COMMAND

The governor of the state would formally ask his legislature for a state bill creating the regiments called for by Congress, but would immediately start jawboning local political men to start recruiting enlisted men, on the promise that the recruiters would be appointed as officers of the company by the Governor. The most typical regimental organization was:

One Colonel Commanding the regiment.

One Lieutenant Colonel: Second in command of the regiment, and commanding a brigade or wing of the regiment.

One Major: Commanding another brigade or wing of the regiment.

One Regimental Surgeon: A medical doctor, equal to a captain, Assistant Surgeon(s): Usually more like a physician's assistant (number, pay and importance varied).

Ten Captains: Commanding one of ten companies (usually A,B,C,D,E,F,G,H,J & K).

Ten Lieutenants or 1st Lieutenants: Second in command of the company.

Ten Second Lieutenants: Third in command of the company.

The companies were usually authorized at a strength of sixty enlisted men, but rarely were that large. In general a company was considered full at forty or so men. Typically it was divided into five squads, each with: One Sergeant, One Corporal, and Ten Privates.

ROSTER OF 1st ALABAMA CAVALRY, USV SOLDIERS

The family information on the following soldiers was submitted by descendants and is included as submitted.

- A -

Abbott, David D. - David D. Abbott, sometimes spelled Abbitt, enlisted in Company M of the 1st Alabama Cavalry, USV on December 16, 1863 at Camp Davies, Mississippi, as a private for a period of 3 years. He was enlisted by Captain Trammel and another muster roll stated he enlisted for a period of one year. He was mustered in December 29, 1863 at Corinth, Mississippi. On his January and February 1864 Muster Roll, it stated he had not been paid any bounty and was due $302 for bounty. On his May and June 1864 Muster Roll it stated he was to be charged with one lost Remington Revolver. His March and April 1865 Muster Roll showed him to be absent, taken prisoner of war March 10, 1865, which was the day of the Battle of Monroe's Crossroads in North Carolina. He was discharged June 12, 1865 at Camp Chase, Ohio by reason of General Order No. 77, War Department, dated April 23, 1865. He was shown as having mustered out October 20, 1865 in Huntsville, Alabama. A note on the Detachment Muster-Out Roll from Camp Chase, Ohio stated: Due the US for transportation, $9.16. Three months extra pay due the above enlisted man by order of the Secretary of War dated Washington, D.C. May 31, 1865. David D. Abbott's name appeared on a Muster Roll of a detachment of Paroled Prisoners at Camp Chase, Ohio January and February 1865, dated April 10, 1865, stated he was present, captured March 10, 1865 at Solomon Grove, North Carolina. His name appeared on the Returns under Companies L and M as follows: December 1863, enlisted in regiment December 16, 1863 at Camp Davies, Mississippi. March 1865 to May 1865, absent, prison of war since March 10, 1865. June 1865, discharged June 16, 1865 at Camp Chase, Ohio by reason of General Orders No. 77, War Department, April 1865. The Company Descriptive Book showed David D. Abbott to have been 34 years of age, 5'-7" tall, having a dark complexion, blue eyes, light hair, born in Wayne County, Kentucky, and a farmer by occupation. David D. Abbott's POW Record stated he was confined at Richmond, Virginia on March 28, 1865, paroled at Boulware and Cox's Wharf in Virginia on March 30, 1865, reported at Camp Parole, Maryland March 27th, to 31st, 1865, sent to Camp Chase, Ohio on April 2, 1865, reported April 5, 1865, furloughed April 9, 1865 for 30 days, returned May 3, 1865, mustered out of service June 13, 1865. On some rolls, he was listed as David D. Abbitt, Private, Company M, 1st Alabama Cavalry.

David D. Abbott was born about 1829 in Wayne County, Kentucky to William Absalom Abbott and Elizabeth Snude, who were married February 19, 1812, in Wake County, North Carolina. Other children of William and Elizabeth were: Tobias, Henry Marion, William, Abner, and Mary Ann Abbott, who was born January 12, 1832, in Wayne County, Kentucky and died February 6, 1913, in Columbus, Cherokee County, Kansas. David was shown in the home of his parents in the 1850 Dade County, Georgia Census, and in the 1860 Marion County, Alabama Census, he and his wife, Elizabeth were living in the Eastern District, Allen's Factory area of Marion County, Alabama with five children, John J.; Bennet S.S.; Sarah; Isaac; and Mary Abbott.

On July 26, 1887, David D. Abbott, or Abbitt, filed a Declaration for an Original Invalid Pension stating that while a member of the 1st Alabama Cavalry, USV, in the line of duty at Whites Crossroads in North Carolina on or about March 10, 1865, he received a saber wound in his head. He stated he was struck by a Rebel soldier while in action, that he was struck with a saber to his head while in action, which said wound disabled him and prevented him from working. He was taken prisoner at the same time and carried to Richmond, Virginia. He stated that after leaving the military service he had resided in Marion and Franklin Counties in Alabama and was disabled to work about one-half of the time. The affidavit was witnessed by John F. Tuck and R.J. Moody. Benjamin F. Tidwell filed an Officer's or Comrade's Testimony stating he was a resident of Allen's Factory in Franklin County, Alabama and that he was a former private of Company A of the 1st Alabama Cavalry, USV and the said D.D. Abbott was in sound health, but while in the military service, on or about March 10, 1864, at White's Crossroads, North Carolina, a fight wherein he was present, said Abbott was captured by the enemy and received a saber cut across the head. He stated he was not there at the time and did not see him until he was discharged and came to the company at Huntsville, when he was. He stated that the fact of Abbott's having been so wounded was known to the whole company at the time because John Blackwell, H. Granger, and J. Medlin were with them at the time and had been with Abbott in prison and assured them of the fact of his having been so wounded.

R.S. Kennedy, a resident of Hackleburg in Marion County, Alabama also filed an Officer's or Comrade's Testimony Form on August 15, 1887, stating he was a Private of Company M of the 1st Alabama Cavalry, USV and that at the time of David D. Abbott's enlistment, he was an able-bodied man. He stated that on or about March 10, 1865, while in battle received a wound on the head by a blow with a saber and fell into the hands of the enemy. He stated he was informed by David D. Abbott that he never received any medical treatment until he was discharged from the service. The affidavit was witnessed by S.M. Hall and William Frederick.

A Neighbor's Affidavit was completed by William Frederick, stating he was fifty-one years of age, a resident of Chalkbluff in Marion County, Alabama, and S.M. Hall, fifty-four years of age, also from Hackleburg, Marion County, Alabama, stated they had known David D. Abbott for thirty-five and twenty-five years respectively, and had worked with and seen Abbott work before the war and had hired him to work with them about ten years ago to work on the farm and he was not able to work over two-thirds of his time. They stated he had lived in the neighborhood with them until about two years ago when he moved to an adjoining county, but they had seen him frequently since then and his disability had been growing worse ever since the war. They stated the last six months Abbott had not been able to do anything, and that his symptoms were difficult for them to describe as he was dull in spirit and complained with a severe pain in his head, supposed to be the stroke he received in his head. S.M. Hall stated he knew David D. Abbott before the war and he was sound as a silver dollar.

A letter from David D. Abbott dated August 7, 1889, stated: In regard to my application for a pension in consequence of a saber wound received at the time I was Captain on the 10th day of March 1864, I upon oath depose and say: The direct evidence of the wound can only be furnished by comrades who were captured with me at the time. I have made the most diligent search for some of them and applied through the Bureau for aid in tracing them, but never by my own efforts, nor by the aid of the Bureau have I been able to find any of them. After I was released from prison I was discharged but returned to my company in Huntsville and remained some time. There it was well known by the report of my fellow prisoners, that I had been sabered; and I send the affidavit of Ben F. Tidwell in consideration of that fact, herewith. I have furthermore written to 1st Lieutenant C.J. Cobleigh in Missouri Valley, Iowa; Joseph D. Morris, Ramer, Tennessee; Lieutenant George C. Jenkins, Washington, Ohio; for further evidence of this kind and received no answer. Thus it is evident that I have done all that lies in my power to present the fullest evidence before the bureau. I have no means to prosecute the search in person but have furnished the department with all the names of my comrades who knew of my wounds, and it is evident that I am honest and sincere in this matter. Now I am old and poor and dying of my wound. I trust the case may be decided upon the evidence without further delay. D.D. Abbott. John G. Blackwell signed an affidavit stating he was a resident of Huntsville, Madison County, Alabama, a former 2nd M. Sergeant of Company M of the 1st Alabama Cavalry, USV and at the time of enlistment David D. Abbott was a sound and able bodied man. He stated that on or about March 10, 1864, at White's Crossroads, North Carolina, David D. Abbott was wounded by a saber in the head and he knew he had never been a sound healthy man since. He stated he was well acquainted with Abbott. William R. Carnes, a Justice of the Peace, signed an affidavit dated February 23, 1891, stating he solemnized the marriage of David D. Abbott and Rebecca Purser in May 1866 in Marion County, Alabama. Carnes stated he was 60 years old in 1891. An affidavit filed by Mary E. Purser on February 23, 1891, stated she was 46 years of age, a resident of near Hamilton, Marion County, Alabama and that Rebecca Abbott was very poor and was solely dependent on her own labor for support. She stated that Rebecca had not remarried since the death of her husband and she was the lawful widow of David D. Abbott. M.E. Britnell signed an affidavit on August 10, 1891, stating he was 49 years of age, and a resident of Chalkbluff in Marion County, Alabama. He stated the following: David Abbott's first wife (Elizabeth) left this country in or about the year of 1863, and they say she has not been heard of in this country since the date above given, and that it is unknown what went with her. I have been living in this county ever since the date above given (1863) and that my relationship with her and acquaintance with other relations and friends of her has been such that if anything had been heard of her I would have heard of it. The law of the state has considered Rebecca Abbott the only living wife of David Abbott for 20 years.

A.M. Mitchell signed an affidavit on December 3, 1891, stating: I have been acquainted with Mr. David Abbott and his wife, Elizabeth Abbott from the year 1860. A short while after he went in the army Mrs. Elizabeth Abbott said she was going to her husband, and left this country and has never been heard from since she left. It was reported that she was drowned with her family in the Tennessee River. It is generally believed by friends and relations that she is dead or they would have heard of her. The relationship between Mr. Abbott and his wife was good so far as I ever heard. I am now and have been living in the same neighborhood that Mr. Abbott and his wife live in since 1860. Signed A.M. Mitchell.

E.B. Faard, aged eighty-six of Chalkbluff, Marion County, Alabama signed an affidavit on December 3, 1891, stating he had moved to Illinois about the year 1862, and that after the war David D. Abbott came to his house in Illinois on the hunt for his wife and was making close inquiry of her and asked him and other neighbors to make all the inquiries they could, and that he seemed very anxious to hear from her. Abbott stated his wife had left Alabama after he joined the army and went north and that he had not heard anything from her after that.

Rebecca Abbott filed a Deposition for Number 459.504, on June 2, 1893, stating she lived at Price's Mill in Marion County, Alabama. She stated she was 72 years of age and was the widow of David D. Abbott. She stated her husband died May 22, 1890, at Spruce Pine, in Franklin County, Alabama. She stated they were married May 15, 1866, by W.R. Carnes, Justice of the Peace, and that the her only living witnesses were Mary Purser of Hamilton, Alabama; Sarah Ann Sullins, Price's Mill, Alabama; and John Purser of Knowle, Alabama. She stated her name before she married was Rebecca Purser and that she had not remarried since the death of her husband. In talking about David D. Abbott's first wife, she says: His first wife was a widow and her name was Betsy Frederick. While he was in the army she started to go to him and was never heard from again except a man by the name of Dazel Duncan, her cousin, said he saw her on the bank of the Tennessee River and the refugees were crossing as fast as possible. He started away from the river, when he heard that a boat was sinking. He did not go back to see about it and she had never been heard from since. David Duncan is dead, I think his family lives somewhere in Mississippi. He stated the children of David and Rebecca were with her when she was lost. After David was out of the army, he went to Illinois to look for his wife and children. He went into the place where the refugees were to cross the river, searching for them and every where else he could think of but he could not hear anything. Rebecca stated she and David never had any children. David Abbott died of dropsy of the heart and his head was wounded which helped kill him. Dr. Swaving of Mobil, Alabama was treating him when he died.

John A. Purser filed a Deposition on June 3, 1893, stating he was thirty-eight years old, a farmer, address near Hackleburg in Marion County, Alabama. He stated Rebecca Purser Abbott was his father's sister, and that he had heard David complain of dropsy some six years previous to his death. He had a wound on his head which he said had been made by a saber, his feet and hands swelled up every once in a while. He stated he was present at the marriage of David Abbott and his aunt, Rebecca Purser, at her father's place on William's Creek in Marion County, Alabama. He remembered his father writing letters to different people for David inquiring about his wife.

M.M. Mitchell filed a Deposition on June 3, 1893, stating he was forty years old and that he knew Rebecca Abbott before she married David Abbott and knew David before the war. His wife left here saying she was going to her husband which was the last heard of her. She was going toward Eastport, Mississippi and had their three children with her. As soon as David got home he left looking for his wife and children and was gone nearly a year and when he came back, he stated he could not find them. He stated he had been in Tennessee, Kentucky, Illinois and Mississippi looking for them.

Rebecca Abbott received a pension of $8 per month beginning October 11, 1890, but she was dropped from the rolls on January 7, 1897, due to her death. A letter from the US Pension Agency stated she was last paid to May 4, 1896.

The 1860 Marion County, Alabama Census showed David and Elizabeth J. Abbott as having five children in the household, John J., age seventeen; Bennett S.S., age twelve; Sarah M., age five; Isaac M., age two; and Mary L.C. Abbott, age eight months. The first two children were shown to have been born in Tennessee and the other three were shown to have been born in Alabama.

Abbott, Israel Pickens - Israel P. Abbott enlisted in Company L of the 1st Alabama Cavalry, USV on April 7, 1865, at Stevenson, Alabama, and mustered in April 18, 1865, at Nashville, Tennessee. He was enrolled by James B. McGoughey for a period of 3 years. The Muster and Descriptive Roll shows Israel to have been 18 years of age, 5'-11" tall, having a fair complexion, gray eyes, light hair, born Walker County, Alabama, and a farmer by occupation. Israel P. Abbott died in the Post Hospital No. 297 at Huntsville, Madison County, Alabama on June 18, 1865, of chronic diarrhea. He was originally buried in Grave 219 of the Huntsville Cemetery, which is the present Glenwood Cemetery, but later disinterred and reinterred in the Chattanooga National Cemetery. Israel's Inventory of Effects showed him to have had one pair of cotton drawers, one cotton shirt, one pair of shoes, one rubber blanket and one vest.

According to descendants, Israel Pickens Abbott, sometimes spelled Esrel, was born about 1846 in Walker County, Alabama to James Heil Abbott and his wife, Jane Mills "Cricket" Key, who were both born in North Carolina. Israel died during the war on June 18, 1865, in Huntsville, Madison County, Alabama due to chronic diarrhea. He is buried in the Chattanooga National Cemetery with a Union tombstone.

Abbott, Lewis W. - Lewis W. Abbott enlisted in Company C of the 1st Alabama Cavalry, USV on January 1, 1863 at Corinth, Mississippi for a period of one year, and was mustered in on January 20, 1863, at Corinth. He was enrolled by John Latty. He was appointed Corporal on December 19, 1863. His name appeared on the returns dated September 1863, stating he was detailed at hospital September 31, 1863. The Regimental Descriptive Book shows him to have been 23 years of age, 5'-10" inches tall, having a dark complexion, hazel eyes, dark hair, born in Spartanburg, South Carolina and a Shoemaker by occupation.

Abernathy, John - John Abernathy enlisted as a private in Company A of the 1st Alabama Cavalry, USV on October 1, 1864, at Rome, Georgia for a period of 3 years. Another Muster Roll stated he enlisted January 5, 1865, at Savannah, Georgia. He was enrolled by Captain Hinds. For some reason, he wasn't mustered in until July 19, 1865, at Huntsville, Alabama. From March and April 1865, he was shown as an orderly Brig. Headquarters. The Muster and Descriptive Roll recorded him as 45 years of age, 5'-9" tall, having a fair complexion, blue eyes, auburn hair, born in Lawrence District, South Carolina, and a farmer by occupation. It stated he was due a bounty of $300. He was transferred to Company L on July 19, 1865, by Special Order Number 30, Headquarters, 1st Alabama Cavalry. He was mustered out October 20, 1865, in Huntsville, Alabama.

John was born about 1820 in Laurens County, South Carolina to George Abernathy and Abigail Lindsay. George was born about 1786 in Newberry District, South Carolina and died May 2, 1836, in Newberry County. Abigail was born 1790 in Newberry and died 1851 in Gadsden, Etowah County, Alabama. John Abernathy was married to Sibella Lindsay on October 12, 1858, in Floyd County, Georgia. Sibella was born November 24, 1838, in South Carolina and died March 31, 1867, in Cave Springs, Floyd County, Georgia. Children of John and Sibella were: Martha, Mary, Moses Clarence, Margaret, Newton, and Marion R. Abernathy. John Abernathy died August 20, 1870, and was buried in the Providence Baptist Church Cemetery, Highway 411 in Forney, Cherokee County, Alabama.

Able, Thomas M. - Thomas M. Able was born June 16, 1838, in Blount County, Tennessee to John B. Able and Rhoda Johnston. John B. Able was born December 22, 1793, in Abbeville, South Carolina and died sometime before 1870 in Alabama. Rhoda Johnston Able was born about 1801 in South Carolina and died before 1867 in Randolph County, Alabama. Thomas M. Able married Lucinda E. Ray about 1862. Their children were Mary J.; Nancy J.; John; Missouri; Silas; Sarah Elizabeth; Rose E.; and Mark Able. Lucinda E. Ray was the daughter of Solomon Ray and Jane Church who married March 1, 1829, in Henry County, Georgia.

Thomas M. Abel signed a Declaration for Invalid Pension on December 9, 1890, stating he was a resident of Elk, Winston County, Alabama. He stated he enrolled in company B of the 1st Alabama Cavalry, USV on or about March 15, 1864, that Colonel Spencer was in command and his Lieutenant was named Bolton. He stated he was in the company with Joel Williams, Dick Holley, Pink Holley and a

Salter. He stated he was discharged at Salt Creek, Alabama near Decatur, Alabama. Thomas Abel went on to state he was unable to earn a support by manual labor by reason of rheumatism, breast and lung diseases and severe pains in his head. He signed his name as Thomas M. Abel and it was witnessed by E. O'Rear and L.N. Richardson.

An undated Memorandum stated Thomas W. Abel was enlisted in 1st Alabama Cavalry Regiment, USV. His health was wrecked in camp at Salt Creek near Decatur, Alabama. He enlisted Spring 1864 for 3 years and was discharged by a board of 3 doctors. Don't know any of their names. Never received any discharge papers. After discharge from regular duty he remained on Government farm near Decatur and worked under a man named Harris. He managed and kept Government horses and mules until close of war. While in camp he contracted a cold and ever since has suffered with lung disease deep seated and pain in breast. He suffered eight or ten years from Rheumatism in knees. He is not able to do but very little manual labor since the war. When he enlisted at age 27 or 28 years old he had black hair, blue eyes, sandy beard, and was about 5' 9" tall. He stated in the Memorandum that his Post Office Address was Elk, Alabama, and his present age was 58.

Someone stated his mind was very weak and he could hardly remember anything about the details of enlistment and did not even remember names of officers in his company. He said his Colonel or General was Spencer, and that he was in the same company as Joel Williams, Dick Holley, Pink Holley and a Salter. He may have been talking about William W. Salyers as he was in Company B.

A letter from the Department of the Interior, Bureau of Pensions in Washington, DC, dated August 24, 1891, about Thomas M. Abel and his request for pension #1026.991, stated: Sir, In the claim of the above named claimant alleged late a private Company B, 1 Regiment Alabama Cavalry further action cannot be taken by this Bureau until his proper service shall have been furnished. The records on file in the War Department fail to show his name in connection with the service named in the application. If possible his discharge certificate should be furnished; if not, the correct letter of the company, number of the regiment, names of all vessels, or designation of the organization in which service was rendered, should be given, together with the names of commanding officers and dates of enlistment and discharge; also the nature of the duties performed and the correct name under which he enlisted and served. Very respectfully, Green G. Raum, Commissioner.

Another letter from Attorney William H. Lamar, dated August 28, 1891, stated: Sir, In response to your letter of the 24th instant (enclosed herewith) calling for "proper services" in the pension claim of Thomas M. Abel, supposed to have been a private in Co. B, 1st Alabama Cavalry, I enclose herewith a memorandum which was furnished me by my correspondent after a conversation by him with the claimant. I respectfully request that it be referred by you to the War Department to be used by the proper officials there in connection with a further examination of the records for the purpose of ascertaining the actual service which the claimant rendered. This course is made necessary on account of the present weak condition of the claimant's mind. His memory is said to be very poor. Very Respectfully, W.H. Lamar

Abner, John - John Abner enlisted and mustered into Company A of the 1st Alabama Cavalry, USV on October 6, 1864, at Rome, Georgia for a period of 3 years, with his brother William. The Muster and Descriptive Roll recorded him as 21 years of age, 6'-2" tall, having a fair complexion, blue eyes, red hair, born in Cobb County, Georgia, and was a farmer by occupation. John Abner was killed in action April 1, 1865, at Faison's Station, North Carolina. The Muster-Out Roll stated he was killed in action on April 9, 1865, at Faison's Depot, North Carolina. His Final Statement showed he died April 10, 1865. G.W. Benson, 2nd Lieutenant, showed John Abner was killed in action by gun-shot wounds on April 10, 1865 at Faison's Station, North Carolina, which is the date of the Battle of Monroe's Crossroads.

Abner, William J. - William J. Abner enlisted and was mustered into Company A of the 1st Alabama Cavalry, USV on October 6, 1864 in Cobb County, Georgia for a period of 3 years, with his brother, John. The Muster and Descriptive Roll recorded him as 23 years of age, 6'-2"tall, having a fair complexion, blue eyes, red hair, born in Cobb County, Georgia, and a farmer by occupation. William was shown to have deserted on November 10, 1864, from Rome, Georgia with complete pistol and belt. His name appeared on the Muster-Out Roll dated October 20, 1865, as owing the US Government

$17.15 for one pistol, saber belt and accoutrements complete. A Notation from the War Department of the Pension and Record Department was in his records which stated: Application for the removal of the charge of desertion and for an honorable discharge is denied. His name was also listed as William T. Abner.

Adair, Francis O. - Francis O. Adair enlisted and was mustered into Company H of the 1st Alabama Cavalry, USV on October 10, 1863, at Glendale, Mississippi for a period of 3 years. He was 18 years of age at enlistment. On the September and October 1863 Muster Roll, he was listed as Corporal. He was mustered out October 24, 1864, at Rome, Georgia because of expiration of term of service. Remarks on his Muster-Out Roll stated: Stop for one thong and brush wiper, and one haversack. Earlier in the year it stated: Stop for one Remington Revolver. Francis O. Adair was also in Company B, 5th US Cavalry. On February 1, 1898, he filed a Declaration for Invalid Pension while in a Soldiers Home in Los Angeles County, California. He stated he had been married May 17, 1863, in Winston County, Alabama by Perry Shipman but was a widower with no children. In 1898, Adair was listed as living in the US National Homes for Volunteer Soldiers in Mountain Branch at Johnson County, Tennessee. He was listed on the 1900 and 1910 Los Angeles, California Census in the National Home for Disabled Volunteer Soldiers as age 54. It listed him as being born in January 1846 in Georgia, both parents born in Georgia, and stated he was able to read and write. At the time he was there, he was drawing $12 per month pension with a disability of catarrh and a shoulder injury. Francis O. and Jasper N. Adair were brothers and sons of Nathan M. Adair and Telitha (or Tabitha) Elizabeth Raper who married March 24, 1844, in Paulding County, Georgia. Other siblings of Francis and Jasper were John; Mary; Joseph; and Sarah Adair.

Adair, Jasper Newton - Jasper Newton Adair enlisted and mustered into Company H of the 1st Alabama Cavalry, USV on December 18, 1863, as a Private for a period of one year. He was 18 years of age at enlistment. Remarks on his March and April 1864 Muster Roll stated: Stop for one Remington Revolver. He was mustered out November 23, 1864, in Nashville, Tennessee. A Remark on his Muster-Out Roll stated: Owing to the exigencies of the service could not be mustered out of service until the present date November 23, 1864. There was another Muster-Out Roll dated February 7, 1865, which stating he owed $12 for one Remington Revolver lost through neglect. Jasper died September 10, 1914. Jasper Newton Adair and Francis O. Adair were brothers. Jasper Newton Adair died September 10, 1914, and is thought to be buried in the East Fairview Cemetery in Cromwell, Ohio County, Kentucky.

Jasper Newton "James" Adair was born in December 1848 in Paulding County, Georgia to Nathanial M. "Nathan" Adair and his wife, Telitha or Tabitha Elizabeth Raper, daughter of Joseph Thomas Raper and Rachael Mahala Box, who were married January 16, 1823, in Hall County, Georgia. Jasper "James" supposedly married Mary J. Millican on March 2, 1873, but apparently she died and he married Mary Elizabeth Carter in 1887. Children of Jasper Newton Adair and his wife, Mary Elizabeth, were: Ada, born July 1888; Jesse Milton, born January 18, 1890, died March 29, 1966; Bertha, born September 19, 1891, died May 11, 1970; Henry Claude, born January 23, 1893, died December 2, 1862; and Augustus N. "Gussie" Adair, born September 11, 1897, died February 1, 1968. Descendants state Jasper died September 10, 1914, however, there was a J.N. Adair listed in the household of Bertha and Robert E. Lee, as the father-in-law of the head of household. Jasper had a daughter name Bertha but it states this J.N. Adair was born in Tennessee, and his military records state he was born in Georgia. If this J.N. Adair was Jasper Newton Adair, then he was still living in 1920, in Hopkins County, Texas, but it is unclear at this point if it was him.

Adair, Nathan - Nathan Adair was a Unionists and tried to join the Union Army December 20, 1863, at Camp Davies, Mississippi, but he was rejected by the surgeon for a "broken down constitution". He was 46 years of age, born in Madison County, Georgia, and was a Wagon Maker by occupation.

Adams, James M. - James M. Adams enlisted and mustered into Company C of the 1st Alabama Cavalry, USV December 22, 1862, at Corinth, Mississippi. He was enrolled by D.R. Adams. The March and April 1863 Muster Roll stated he enrolled December 1, 1862, and mustered in December 22, 1862.

In June and July 1863, James was on daily duty at Regimental Headquarters as Dispatch Carrier since May 20, 1863. The November and December 1863 Muster Roll stated he died of wounds received in action and was shot by accident. A Notation from the War Department of the Adjutant General's Office dated August 23, 1866, stated that James M. Adams died of an accidental gunshot wound November 28, 1863, in Camp Davies, Mississippi. The Regimental and Descriptive Book showed James to have been 17 years of age, 5'-7" inches tall, having a fair complexion, blue eyes, light hair, born Tishomingo County, Mississippi, and a farmer by occupation. His Casualty Sheet shows him to have been killed in action December 15, 1863. Two Casualty Sheats stated James was killed in action December 15, 1863, while a Casualty Sheet of Wounded, stated he died November 28, 1863. However, it stated he was in Company E.

Adams, James M. - James M. Adams enlisted in Company G of the 1st Alabama Cavalry, USV on April 10, 1864, at Decatur, Alabama for a period of 3 years. He was mustered in from date of enlistment in Rome, Georgia. He was enrolled by Lieutenant D.A. Pease. The Muster and Descriptive Roll recorded him as 21 years of age, 5'-9" tall, having a fair complexion, blue eyes, sandy hair, born in Carroll County, Georgia, and a farmer by occupation. It stated he was due a bounty of $100. James was promoted from Private to Corporal in May 1864. The March and April 1865 Muster Roll recorded him as absent, a prisoner of war since March 10, 1865, which was the date of the Battle of Monroe's Crossroads. The May and June 1865 Muster Roll stated he was absent, in confinement in Huntsville, Alabama since June 29, 1865. He was shown as present on the July and August 1865 Muster Roll. His name appeared on the Returns as being in confinement in Decatur, Alabama June 29, 1865, and in confinement in Nashville, Tennessee June 29, 1865. (One date could be in error, or they could have moved him from Decatur to Nashville.) James M. Adams was mustered out on October 20, 1865, in Huntsville, Alabama. A Notation from the Adjutant General's Office of the War Department dated May 14, 1880, stated: Captured at Solemn (Solomon's) Grove, North Carolina on March 10, 1865, paroled at Aikens Landing, Virginia on March 30, 1865, reported at College Green Barracks, Maryland March 31, 1865; sent to Camp Chase, Ohio April 2, 1865, reported there April 5, 1865, furloughed April 9, 1865, date reported to regiment not given. Company Muster Report dated June 30, 1865, reports him put in confinement August 24, 1865. (Dates possibly mixed up.) Released from arrest, cause of confinement not stated. A Muster Roll of a Detachment of Paroled Prisoners at Camp Chase, Ohio, dated January and February 1865, stated: Present, captured March 10, 1865, at Solomon Grove, North Carolina. James was able to sign his name to his enlistment records. A letter from the Assistant Quartermaster's Office, Railroad Transportation Office, Louisville, Kentucky, dated April 13, 1865, stated: I have the honor of notifying you that I have furnished James M. Adams, G Company, 1st Regiment Alabama Cavalry, with transportation from this city to Nashville, Tennessee, cost $3.80, to be deducted from his pay. Very Respectfully, Your Obedient Servant, (signature not legible). A letter or note of charges from: Near Decatur, Alabama June 29, 1865, Charges and Specifications against James M. Adams, Corp. of Co. G, 1st Regt. Ala. Cav. Vols. Charge I, Violation of the Sixth Article of War. Specification to Charge I. In this that the said James M. Adams, Corporal of Co. G, 1st Regiment Ala. Cav. Vols, did publicly and in the presence of his company refuse to obey his company commander, when ordered to take care of a horse. This on or about the 28th Day of June 1865, at Decatur, Alabama. Charge II. Violation of the twenty first article of War Specification to Charge II. In this that the said James M. Adams, Corporal of Co. G, 1st Regt. Ala. Cav. Vols; did absent himself from his troop or company without leave or consent from his commanding officer, either written or verbal, and has after been put in arrest. This on or about the 28th Day of June 1865, at or near Decatur, Alabama. Charge III, Violation of the 42nd Article of Specifications to Charge III, In this that the said James M. Adams Corporal of Co. G, 1st Regt. Ala. Cav. did lie out of his quarters over night without any leave or permit whatever from his commander. This at or near Decatur, Alabama on or about the night of the 28th of June 1865. Witnesses to Charge I: William J. Elkins, Sgt. Co. G, 1st Regt. Alabama Cav. Vol.; William B. Fagans, Private, Co. G, 1st Regt. Ala. Cav. Vol. Witnesses to Charge II: James M. Blaylock, 2nd Lt. Co. G, 1st Regt. Ala. Cav. Vol.; Joseph P. Byers, Sgt. Co. G, 1st Regt. Ala. Cav. Vol.; Witnesses to charge III: James M. Blaylock, 2nd Lt. Co. G, 1st Regt. Alabama Cav. Vol. Wm. J. Elkins, Sgt. Co. G, 1st Regt. Alabama Cav. Vol. Accusing Witnesses: E.J. Cobleigh, 1st Lt., 1st Ala. Cav. Vol., Commanding Company G.

James M. Adams first enlisted in Company G of the 40th Georgia Infantry, Confederate Army on May 10, 1862, as a Private. However, as the Battle of Vicksburg, Mississippi, fell to the Union troops he was captured on July 4, 1863, and on July 6, 1863, he was paroled. His brother, William Washington Adams, served in the 18th Alabama Infantry Regiment, CSA. James M. Adams is buried in the Mt. Tabor Methodist Church Cemetery in Westover, Shelby County, Alabama

Adams, John Quincy "Jack" - John Quincy "Jack" Adams enlisted in Company C of the 1st Alabama Cavalry, USV on December 22, 186,2 for a period of one year, and mustered in December 27, 1862, at Corinth, Mississippi. He was appointed Corporal April 10, 1863. John Q. Adams died June 18, 1863, at the regimental hospital in Glendale, Forrest County, Mississippi. The Regimental Descriptive Book recorded John as 28 years of age, 5'-7" tall, having a fair complexion, blue eyes, dark hair, born in Fayette, Tennessee (Fayette County, Tennessee), and a farmer by occupation.

John Quincy "Jack" Adams was born about 1834 in Fayette County, Tennessee to John Squire "Jack" Adams and his wife, Elizabeth Boyd. John was married to Candace Elizabeth Brooks on January 8, 1851, near Bay Springs, in Tishomingo County, Mississippi. Candace was the daughter of Thomas and Mary Brooks. Children of John and Candace Adams were: John Thomas, born March 30, 1852, died May 4, 1931; David Andrew, born September 29, 1853, died June 24, 1924; Samuel Houston, born December 29, 1855, died March 11, 1871; Alfred Leroy, born September 9, 1858, died April 5, 1919; and Mary K. Adams, born September 20, 1861, and died January 12, 1863. John's wife, Candace, was born May 16, 1833, in Rutherford County, Tennessee and died in 1883 in Iuka, Tishomingo County, Mississippi. John died while in service on June 18, 1863, at Glendale, Forrest County, Mississippi.

Adams, Levi - Levi Adams enlisted and was mustered into Company K of the 1st Alabama Cavalry, USV on June 26, 1862, in Limestone County, Alabama, for a period of 3 years. He was enrolled by Captain Canfield. Levi was with the early enlistees who immediately shipped to Nashville, Tennessee and merged with the 1st Middle Tennessee Cavalry, US. He was in Company E of this regiment. The Regimental Descriptive Book recorded him as 20 years of age, 5'-7" tall, having a dark complexion, black eyes, black hair, born in Johnson County, North Carolina, and a farmer by occupation. He was transferred from Company K, 21st Regiment Ohio Volunteers to the 1st Alabama Cavalry, USV by Special Order of Headquarters, Army of the Ohio, July 18, 1862. Levi was appointed Sergeant on October 1, 1862, by Colonel Spencer, 1st Alabama Cavalry, USV. The Company Muster Roll dated June 30, 1863 to October 31, 1863, stated Levi Adams was reduced from Sergeant to ranks by order of Colonel Pickens, 3rd East Tennessee Cavalry, September 15, 1863. Levi died of pneumonia on February 2, 1864, in the hospital at Memphis, Tennessee. The May and June 1864 Company Muster Roll stated Levi Adams was promoted from Private to Sergeant on January 1, 1864. His name appeared on the Returns as follows: January and February 1863, he was on detached service January on Courier Post; January 1864, sick in hospital in Memphis, Tennessee; February 1864, died in Overton USA General Hospital in Memphis February 2, 1864, of pneumonia. There were two Prisoner of War Records in Levi's file. Inventory of Effects of Deceased Soldier stated he left the following effects: 1 hat, 1 great coat, 1 uniform jacket, 1 pair trousers, 2 pair of flannel drawers, 1 pair of boots, 1 pair of shoes, 1 flannel shirt, 2 blankets and 1 oil blanket. A letter in Levi Adams' Military Records dated September 16, 1863, from Headquarters, 3rd East Tennessee Cavalry, Camp near Nashville, Tennessee, Special Orders: Sergeant Levi Adams, Company E, 1st Alabama Cavalry, for conduct unbecoming a non-commissioned officer is hereby reduced to the ranks. This to take effect from the 15th of September 1863. By Order of Lt. Col. D.G. Thornburgh, Commanding 3rd East Tennessee Cavalry, and detachment 1st Alabama Cavalry, John B. Minnis, 1st Lieutenant and Adjutant. Levi's Prisoner of War Record stated he was sent from Knoxville, Tennessee to Richmond, Virginia for exchange May 8, 1863. He had been captured at Blountsville, Tennessee May 1, 1863, confined at Richmond, Virginia on May 9, 1863, paroled at City Point, Virginia May 14, 1863, reported at Camp Parole, Maryland, May 16, 1863, sent to Camp Chase, Ohio May 19, 1863, reported at Camp Chase May 22, 1863, sent from Camp Chase to regiment June 9, 1863. Lieutenant Joseph H. Hornback signed an affidavit stating: I do certify, on honor, that Levi Adams, a Sergeant of Captain David D. Smith's Company K of the 1st Regiment Cavalry Volunteers of the State of Alabama, born in Johnson County,

North Carolina, aged 20 years, 5'-7" high, dark complexion, black eyes, black hair, and by occupation a farmer, having joining the company on its original organization at Limestone County, Alabama, and enrolled in it at the muster into the service at Huntsville, Alabama on July 24, 1862. Levi Adams is buried in Section B Site 1342 of the Memphis National Cemetery in Memphis, Tennessee.

Adams, William C. - William C. Adams, age 29, enlisted in Company G of the 1st Alabama Cavalry, USV as a private on March 5, 1863, at Chewalla, Tennessee for a period of one year. He was shown as having deserted April 30, 1863, from Chewalla. (It is unclear if these two William C. Adams are the same person, or what happened to them.)

Adams, William C. - William C. Adams enlisted in Company C of the 1st Alabama Cavalry, USV as a private on December 22, 1862, at Corinth, Mississippi for a period of one year. He was enrolled by D.R. Adams. He was mustered in December 27, 1862, at Corinth. He was listed as being absent without leave February 1, 1863. The Regimental Descriptive Book recorded him as 24 years of age, 6'-2" tall, having a fair complexion, blue eyes, dark hair, born in Itawamba County, Mississippi, and a farmer by occupation. He was still listed as being absent without leave on the March and April 1863 Muster Roll. The May and June 1863 Muster Roll stated William C. Adams was absent, and was a prisoner of war in the hands of the enemy. In November and December 1863, he was still listed as being a prisoner of war, in the hands of the enemy. This was the last Muster Roll in his file. However, there was another William C. Adams listed as being 29 years of age, enlisted in the 1st Alabama Cavalry, USV on March 5, 1863, at Chewalla, Tennessee, for a period of one year, shown on a Descriptive List of Deserters dated September 1, 1863, at Glendale, Mississippi, stating he deserted April 30, 1863, from Chewalla, Tennessee. His name appeared on the Company Muster-Out Roll dated January 3, 1864, with pay due from enlistment. This is most likely the same soldier as above but may not have been.

Aikins, James B. - James B. Aikens, also spelled Eakins, enlisted and was mustered into Company D of the 1st Alabama Cavalry, USV as a private on June 1, 1863, in Glendale, Mississippi for a period of 1 year. He was enrolled by J.H. Shurtliff. His name appeared on the Returns as follows: October 1863, on daily duty as company cook; February 1864, on detached service at Refugee Camp in Memphis, Tennessee. The Regimental Descriptive Book recorded him as 23 years of age, 5'-8" tall, having a light complexion, blue eyes, sandy hair, born in Marshall County, Alabama, and a farmer by occupation. One of the muster rolls recorded him as being 28 years of age. He was discharged June 16, 1864, in Decatur, Alabama due to expiration of term of service. He was probably a brother of John C. and William T. Aikins, who were born in the same place and enlisted the same day. See John, below, for family information.

Aikins, John C. - John C. Aikins, also spelled Aikens and Eakins, enlisted and mustered into Company D of the 1st Alabama Cavalry, USV as a private on June 1, 1863, at Glendale, Mississippi for a period of 1 year. He was enrolled by J.H. Shurtliff. The Regimental Descriptive Book recorded him as 30 years of age, 5'-11" tall, having a light complexion, blue eyes, sandy hair, born in Marshall County, Alabama and a farmer by occupation. He was discharged June 16, 1864, in Decatur, Alabama due to expiration of term of service.

John Aikens was born September 24, 1836, in Marshall County, Alabama to Joseph and Mary Wedgewoath Aikens, or Eakins. Is it thought all four of the Aikens soldiers were brothers and sons of Joseph and Mary. John died July 25, 1880, in Florence, Lauderdale County, Alabama, and was buried in Plot M section M1-03 of the Florence City Cemetery in Lauderdale County, Alabama.

Aikins, Robert - Robert Aikens, also listed as Eakins and Aikens, enlisted and mustered into Company D of the 1st Alabama Cavalry, USV as a private on August 24, 1863, in Glendale, Mississippi for a period of 1 year. The Company Descriptive Book recorded him as 30 years of age, 5'-10" tall, having a light complexion, blue eyes, light hair, born in Marshall County, Alabama, and a farmer by occupation. He was enrolled by Major Shurtliff. His name appeared on the Returns as follows: January to March 1864, on detached service at Refugee Camp in Memphis, Tennessee; July 1864, absent, sick in hospital. He was mustered out September 28, 1864, in Rome, Georgia due to expiration of term of service. His pay was stopped due to owing the U.S. Government $3.47 for losing one haversack, 1 canteen, and 1 rubber blanket. A note in his file stated his transportation would be furnished to Nashville, Tennessee by the Quartermaster Department.

Robert was born in 1834 in Marshall County, Alabama and died in 1879, in Crab Orchard, Williamson County, Illinois. He is buried in the McKinney Hill Cemetery in Williamson County, Illinois under the name of Robert Akens. One descendant stated the parents of Robert were James M. Aiken and Nancy Yates.

Aikins, William T. - William T. Eakins, also spelled Aikens and Eakins, enlisted and mustered into Company D on June 1, 1863, in Glendale, Mississippi as a private for a period of 1 year. He was enrolled by Major Shurtliff. The Regimental Descriptive Book recorded him as 25 years of age, 5'-11" tall, having a dark complexion, blue eyes, dark hair, born in Marshall County, Alabama, and was a farmer by occupation. In April 1864, he was on daily duty as company cook. He was discharged June 16, 1864, in Decatur, Alabama due to expiration of term of service. It is thought William T. was a brother to James B. and John C. Aikins as they were born in the same place and enlisted the same day. See John C. Aikins, above, for family information.

Aldridge, Henry - Henry Aldridge enlisted in Company A of the 1st Alabama Cavalry, USV as a private on December 25, 1863, at Camp Davies, Mississippi for a period of 3 years. He was enrolled by Lieutenant Hinds, and was mustered in February 5, 1864, at Memphis, Tennessee. The Muster and Descriptive Roll recorded him as 21 years of age, 5'-8" tall, having a fair complexion, blue eyes, light hair, born in Walker County, Alabama, and a farmer by occupation. Henry Aldridge's name appeared on a Descriptive List of Deserters dated November 30, 1864, in the field in Georgia, stating he deserted November 3, 1864, from Rome, Georgia with 1 belt and 2 pistols, complete. The Company Muster Roll for November and December 1864 stated Henry deserted with 2 Remington Revolvers, 1 belt and accoutrements complete and 1 cavalry saddle and bridle complete. The May and June 1865 Muster Roll stated Henry Aldridge was present and reported for duty May 1, 1865. Taken up on rolls under president's proclamation. The July and August 1865 Muster Roll recorded him as present and stated he reported to detachment commander at Stevenson, Alabama on May 1, 1865, and was taken up on rolls under president's proclamation pardoning deserters. Arms were made good. He was mustered out October 20, 1865, at Huntsville, Alabama. A Notation from the War Department, Adjutant General's Office, dated September 1, 1887, stated the following: This man deserted on or about November 3, 1864, but as he returned to the service on or about May 1, 1865, under the president's proclamation dated March 11, 1865, and appears to have complied with the conditions thereof, the charge of desertion no longer stands against him. The record of the fact that he was absent in desertion from on or about November 3, 1864, to on or about May 1, 1865, cannot, however, be expunged.

Henry Aldridge was born in November 1844 in Walker County, Alabama to James and Sarah Aldridge. He was married about 1862 to Mickey Jane Simmons, daughter of Giles Adams Simmons and Caroline Elizabeth Taylor. Children of Henry and Mickey were: John W.; Lucinda; Sarah L.; Nancy E.; Feaby C.; Celia C.; George W.; Henry J.; Irvin; Francis Marion; William A.; Andrew; and James J. Aldridge.

Alford, Jackson - Jackson Alford enlisted in Company L of the 1st Alabama Cavalry, USV as a private on September 1, 1864, and was mustered in October 17, 1864, at Rome, Georgia for a period of 3 years. The Muster and Descriptive Roll recorded him as 35 years of age, 5'-6" tall, having a fair complexion, blue eyes, dark hair, born in St. Clair County, Alabama, and a farmer by occupation. His enlistment was credited to Cherokee County, Alabama. It stated he was due a bounty of $300. Jackson was mustered out on October 20, 1865, at Huntsville, Alabama. His Muster-Out Roll stated he deserted November 10, 1864, at Rome, Georgia.

Allison, Jasper M.C. - Jasper M.C. Allison, also listed as Jasper McAllison, enlisted and mustered into Company D of the 1st Alabama Cavalry, USV as a private on June 10, 1863, at Glendale, Mississippi for a period of 1 year. He was enrolled by Captain Shurtleff. The Company Descriptive Book recorded him as 27 years of age, 5'-6" tall, having a dark complexion, blue eyes, dark hair, born

Morgan County, Alabama, and a farmer by occupation. In July 1863, he was on daily duty as company cook. The September and October 1863 Muster Roll listed him as absent, missing in action October 26, 1863, which is when the Battle of Vincent's Crossroads near Bay Springs, Mississippi was fought. However, he was listed as present on the November and December Muster Roll. In April 1864, Jasper was on daily duty as a teamster. He was discharged June 27, 1864, by reason of expiration of term of service.

Jasper M.C. Allison was born in November 1832 in Morgan County, Alabama to Elijah M. Allison and Catherine Pate, who were married March 21, 1826, in Morgan County, Alabama. Jasper married Letha Elizabeth Osborn and had at least two children: Perry A. and Henry N. Allison. Jasper's wife, Letha Osborn, was the sister of Fountain W.S., George W.L., Chesley F.M., and Newton H. Osborn, or Ozbirn, which was the old family spelling, who all served in the 1st Alabama Cavalry, USV.

Allison, Jonathan Kinard - Jonathan Kinard Allison enlisted in Company H of the 1st Alabama Cavalry, USV on May 25, 1865, in Huntsville, Alabama for a period of 3 years, and was mustered in October 16, 1865, in Huntsville. He was enrolled by Captain James W. DeVaney. The Muster and Descriptive Roll recorded him as 18 years of age, 5'-10" tall, having a dark complexion, blue eyes, black hair, born in St. Clair County, Alabama, and a farmer by occupation. He was mustered out October 20, 1865, at Huntsville, Alabama.

Jonathan K. Allison was born April 7, 1844, in St. Clair County, Alabama, according to his military records. His parents were Jonathan Baugh Allison and Lucinda Elizabeth "Eliza" Moody, who were married July 12, 1832, in Moody, St. Clair County, Alabama. Jonathan Kinard Allison was married in 1867 to Sarah Angeline Hagwood, who was born September 8, 1847, and died December 18, 1936. She was the daughter of M.W. Hagwood, and Trudie Chaney. Children of Jonathan K. and Sarah Allison were: Alonzo Lafayette, born May 2, 1868, died January 16, 1955; James Thomas, born May 11, 1869, died October 26, 1939; Sarah Francis, born December 15, 1870, died April 26, 1947; Lucinda Eliza, born March 20, 1872, died August 15, 1957; William Daniel, born August 27, 1873, died April 21, 1967; Andrew Jackson, born March 12, 1875, died October 3, 1899; Lydia Angeline, born June 30, 1876, died July 6, 1906; George Leroy, born December 17, 1880, died June 17, 1977; Mary Ester, born November 4, 1881, died April 23, 1978; and Robert Glen Allison, born December 29, 1883, and died July 7, 1971. Jonathan Kinard Allison died June 21, 1906, in St. Clair County, Alabama and was buried in the Bethel Baptist Church Cemetery in Branchville, St. Clair County, Alabama.

Alvis, David H. - David H. Alvis enlisted in Company B of the 1st Alabama Cavalry, USV on March 16, 1864, in Decatur, Alabama for a period of 3 years. He was enrolled by Lt. Judy. He was mustered in March 27, 1864, in Decatur. The Company Muster and Descriptive Roll recorded him as 18 years of age, 5'-6" tall, having a dark complexion, gray eyes, dark hair, born in Jackson County, Alabama and a farmer by occupation. The November and December Muster Roll stated David was absent, wounded in action March 23, 1864, and sent to the hospital. The March and April 1864 Muster Roll recorded him as present. The November and December 1864 Hospital Muster Roll for U.S.A. General Hospital in Hilton Head, South Carolina stated David H. Alvis was present, having been admitted on December 20, 1864. He was still a patient in this hospital in January and February 1865. He was returned to duty March 7, 1865, and was mustered out October 20, 1865 in Huntsville, Alabama owing the U.S. Government $1.06 for a bridle he had lost.

David H. Alvis was born August 3, 1848, in Jackson or Madison County, Alabama. His military records state he was born in Jackson County, Alabama, while some descendants state he was born in Madison County, Alabama. His parents were Henry S. Alvis and Margaret Catherine Maynard. His father, Henry, also served in the 1st Alabama Cavalry, USV. See Henry Alvis, below, for more family information. David married Mary Catherine McGlatheny on December 19, 1866, in Blount County, Alabama, and they had the following children: Margaret M.; Andrew Bent; George Columbus; and Walter Scott Alvis. David H. Alvis died July 26, 1906, in Cullman County, Alabama and was buried in the Mt. Zion Cemetery in Cullman, Alabama.

Alvis, Franklin Newton - Franklin Newton Alvis enlisted and mustered into Company L of the

1st Alabama Cavalry, USV on September 25, 1863, in Fayette County, Alabama as a Private for a period of 1 year. He was 18 years old at time of enlistment. On October 26, 1863, he was reported missing in action from the Battle of Vincent's Crossroads near Bay Springs, Mississippi. A Muster Roll dated September 25 to October 31, 1863, stated he was absent with leave October 21, 1863. The November and December 1863 Muster Roll stated he was absent with leave since October 20, 1863 by order of Colonel Spencer. The January and February 1864 Muster Roll stated Alvis was missing in action from Vincent's Crossroads since October 26, 1863. The December 31, 1863 through April 30, 1864 Muster Roll stated he was missing in action since October 26, 1863. He was listed as present on the September 25, 1863 Muster Roll. Franklin N. Alvis was mustered out by reason of expiration of term of service on September 25, 1864, at Rome, Georgia, and was paid in full by Major Holt.

Franklin Alvis was born April 5, 1843, in Alabama to Abner Alvis and Elizabeth Stovall, who had married September 7, 1835. Elizabeth was the daughter of Thomas Stovall and Mary Carroll who married September 30, 1815 in Wilkes County, Georgia. Other children of Abner and Elizabeth were: Thomas G., born 1842; William John, born April 5, 1843; Nancy Elizabeth, born 1844; Mary E., born 1848; James Houston, born October 1849; Abner, Jr., born December 1854, died July 1931; Margaret Sarah, born June 26, 1855, died April 1, 1898; and Caroline Alvis, born March 2, 1859, died February 10, 1878. (Note: Some of these dates may differ as they were submitted by two different descendants along with the pension records and they were not always the same.)

On December 1863, Franklin Newton Alvis was arrested by Lieutenant Bibb of the Rebel army in Walker County, Alabama while on scout but managed to escape from the Confederate Home Guard 12 days later minus 1 mare, bridle and saddle.

During September 1863, the First Regiment Cavalry of the Alabama Volunteers (Union) were in and around Glendale, Mississippi. This regiment was under the control of Colonel George E. Spencer, later to become a senator. A Mr. Dewes (or Davis) and a Mr. Pat Lawson ventured into Alabama trying to recruit boys for the regiment. Near a town called Holly Grove in Walker County, Alabama, these recruiters came to know a very highly respected woman…Elizabeth Alvis…She lived there with her sickly husband, Abner Alvis. At times he was barely able to sit up. (He was suffering from consumption, from which he later died, on February 19, 1871, at the age of 58.) Elizabeth, 42 years old, would tell boys where to go in the woods to meet up with Lawson and join the army. One of which was her son F.N. (Franklin Newton Alvis) 19 years of age. A brother of Elizabeth joined around this time also. His name was James F. Stovall. A Mr. J.F. Files traveled with F.N. (and others probably) through the night for 140 miles to Glendale, Mississippi. F.N. enlisted into Company L on September 1, 1863. James was in Company E. There was another Stovall brother in the Union Army, but his name or company is unknown at this time. Elizabeth had to be careful with whom she talked concerning the Union, but as careful as she was, a group of Rebel soldiers calling themselves Texian Rangers (that is spelled correctly-Texian) came to her house threatening to burn everything and hang "the old man". They were going to kill her son if she didn't give him up. (F.N. was home at the time – October of 1863) F.N. managed to stay away and the Texians left after their searching left them empty handed. F.N. felt if he had been caught "no doubt they would have hanged me." He was probably having the same feelings when he was arrested in December 1863 by Lieutenant Bibb of the Rebel army in Walker County, Alabama while on a scout. Luckily, he escaped by running away from the guards, 12 days after his capture, minus 1 mare, bridle and saddle. Elizabeth continued to aid Union soldiers as J.L. Romine remembered: "While I was out in the woods to keep away from the Rebels, and she knew where I was, she had a signal, which was a white cloth, that she hung out if there was any danger. If the cloth was not at a certain place I could venture to the house and get something to eat and all the information she had to give me.

She was frequently heard to say: "I have two sons in the Union Army and wished I had a dozen sons to put in the Union Army." With a remark like this it makes you wonder how she felt about her son, Thomas G. Alvis who joined the Rebel army under Captain John Morast in 1862. After joining, he went to Mobil and died within three months after enlisting. The other son (besides F.N.) that joined the Union Army was William John Alvis. He enlisted into the First Alabama Cavalry on April 2, 1864. You can almost picture him – 21 years old having lived in Jasper, Walker County, Alabama for the past 15 years, 5'-11" having a fair complexion, light hair, grey eyes – ready to go out and win the war. On

55

August 1, 1864, he was appointed to Corporal. F.N. served his time and was discharged September 25, 1864, at Rome, Georgia, but stayed on with the army doing "army service."

Wilson's Cavalry was going through Walker County and camped near Jasper. On March 27, 1865, about noon, James Huston Alvis was driving the family oxen and cart over to Mrs. Williams's house to get a load of corn. James is a 17 year old son of Elizabeth. On the way, about eleven miles from the army camp, some of the Yankees came to him. James states: "They said to me that they had to have the oxen and cart to haul their provisions. I told them that I hoped they would not take them for it was all the team we had to do our work with. They ordered me to get out of the cart. They said that they wanted it to haul provisions. They loaded it with bacon and drove off towards Jasper."

Robert Guttery, serving in the First Alabama Cavalry saw the cart and oxen in possession of the U.S. Army and having lived within a quarter of a mile of the Alvis' before the war, knew it was their cart and oxen. At that time, the army was very short of stock to do the hauling and Robert testified later that they were used for that purpose only and not taken or used for beef. The oxen were "a good smart yoke of steers, five years old, well broke and over the average size. Well matched in color and size, in good condition and first class work cattle." The cart was "nearly new with a good bed on it." Elizabeth filed a claim in 1871 for reimbursement for these items. She wanted $75.00 for the yoke of oxen and $20.00 for a "rifle gun". She did not claim the cart yet it was estimated at $30.00. She was awarded $75.00 for the oxen.

Also at the end of March 1865, in Durham Station, North Carolina, F.N. turned his horse over to Quartermaster McWorkman of the First Alabama Cavalry. McWorkman said he had been on a long march and he was in great need of stock and that he would pay for one of F.N.'s best horses. And as his younger brother, James Huston, had done – no voucher was asked for or given.

F.N.'s horse was 7 years old, 16 hands high, well proportioned, sound and in good order, "a good saddle horse" worth $150.00. His claim filed in 1873 was not allowed for the following reasons, as stated by the Claims Commission: "The kind of Army Service being rendered is not apparent and the witness Smith has a similar claim for two horses which is disallowed and the claimant Alvis is a witness for him. The probabilities are all against this being a just claim.

F.N. gave his discharge papers to a Mr. Granger, a claim agent, for the purpose of getting his bounty and never heard another word.

J.L. Romine talked with Elizabeth and her family during the war and remarked: "I think I can say truthfully that a more loyal and true union woman did not live in the United States and her husband and her sons were just as loyal as she. She had two brothers in the Union Army also. She did not do anything to aid the confederacy, but she done all she could to aid the Union cause. No such people as she and her family could have lived in this country if the rebels had succeeded in establishing a separate government." Franklin Newton Alvis is buried in the Pocahontas Cemetery in Townley, Walker County, Alabama. William John Alvis is buried in Red Hill Cemetery, Henderson County, Texas.

Alvis, Gabriel Alexander - Gabriel Alexander Alvis enlisted in Company B of the 1st Alabama Cavalry, USV as G.A. Alvis, on March 16, 1864, in Decatur, Alabama by Lieutenant Judy, for a period of 3 years, and was mustered in March 27, 1864, in Decatur. His enlistment was credited to Pulaski, Giles County, Tennessee. The Company Muster and Descriptive Roll recorded Gabriel as being 38 years of age, 5'-11" tall, having a fair complexion, blue eyes, dark hair, born in Madison County, Alabama, and a farmer by occupation. The April 13, to June 30, 1864, Muster Roll listed Gabriel as being absent, left sick in U.S.A. General Hospital in Decatur, Alabama on April 17, 1864. Gabriel was shown as being absent, left in the hospital in Decatur, Alabama from April 17, 1864, all through the war until his name was listed on the Muster-Out Roll of the Organization on October 20, 1865, in Huntsville, Alabama where it stated he was due pay from enlistment, and stated he had not been paid any bounty. In April 1865, he was recorded as being on detached service in North Alabama. A Notation from the War Department of the Adjutant General's Office in Washington, DC dated July 15, 1869, stated the following: Investigation fails to elicit any further information relative to this soldier. Gabriel A. Alvis was a brother to the below Henry S. Alvis, who also served in the 1st Alabama Cavalry, USV.

Gabriel Alexander Alvis was born about 1830 in Morgan County, Alabama to David Alvis and Elizabeth Degourie who were married June 17, 1807, in Fluvanna County, Virginia. Gabriel married

Mary A. Vanzant April 9, 1851, in Wilhite Mountain, Morgan County, Alabama and had the following children: Mary Ann Elizabeth, born October 17, 1854, died April 14, 1914; Margaret C., born July 4, 1856; Charles Henry Alvis, born February 15, 1858, died February 12, 1942; John P.D. Alvis, born 1859, died before 1866; and Gabriel Alexander Alvis, born October 21, 1861, and died September 23, 1927. Gabriel Alexander Alvis died May 20, 1864, in Decatur, Morgan County, Alabama.

<u>Alvis, Henry S.</u> – Henry Alvis enlisted in Company B of the 1st Alabama Cavalry, USV on March 20, 1864, in Decatur, Alabama for a period of 3 years. He was enrolled by Lieutenant Judy, and was mustered in March 27, 1864 in Decatur. The Company Descriptive Book recorded Henry as 43 years of age, 5'-10" tall, having a dark complexion, gray eyes, dark hair, born Winston County, Alabama, and a farmer by occupation. The Muster Roll for September and October 1864, recorded him as absent, left sick in the U.S. General Hospital at Decatur, Alabama since April 17, 1864. April 30, 1864, he was recorded as being on furlough from April 17, 1864, to May 1, 1864, to settle his family in Pulaski, Tennessee. From April 17, 1864, until July 1865, he was sick in the hospital in Decatur, Alabama. Another muster roll stated he returned from sick in hospital in Chattanooga, Tennessee on August 13, 1865. He was mustered out October 20, 1865, in Huntsville, Alabama with pay due from enlistment. He was due a bounty of $300. When Alvis mustered out, he owed the US Government $21.27 due to losing 1 saddle and 1 halter and bridle.

Henry S. Alvis was born about 1823, probably in Madison County, Alabama. He was the 10th child of David Alvis III and Elizabeth Degourie of Virginia. Henry married Margaret Catherine Maynard about 1847. Before the war, Henry farmed near a settlement called Gandy's Cove in Morgan County. Henry enlisted relatively late in the Civil War. Before he saw service in the 1st Alabama Cavalry, Henry hired himself out as an independent scout and guide. Family legend holds that he worked for both Union and Confederate officials depending on who paid the most at any one particular time. It is also rumored he would lure Confederate sympathizers to Union lines under the pretense of going into Confederate lines.

Henry S. Alvis enlisted as a Union soldier in Decatur, Alabama on March 20, 1864 and was mustered into service March 27, 1864, in Decatur. He spent part of the summer of 1864 sick in the Union Army field hospital at Decatur. His service record mentions he was hospitalized for a time in a field hospital near Chattanooga in the summer of 1865, where he was stationed. Henry was discharged from the Army on October 20, 1865, in Huntsville, Alabama. On this date, the First Alabama Cavalry disbanded and most of the soldiers went home. Henry went back home to live with his wife in Morgan County, Alabama. On December 18, 1888, when Henry was 66-years-old, he applied for a Union pension as an invalid. By then, Henry and his family had moved to near Jones Chapel in Cullman County. In the application he says that he contracted "heart disease and piles" as a result of his service in the military. He also states "I was never treated by no one except our company doctor. I was detached and was kept patched up by Dr. Maten [Martin?] who is now dead." Based on this application, the Federal Government saw fit to award Henry a pension.

On December 3, 1890, Henry's wife Margaret died. Margaret was buried in the historic Shady Grove Cemetery near Logan in Cullman County. At the time of Margaret's death, she and Henry Alvis were living near the farm of the widow Emily Echols. Emily had moved with her two sons and an invalid daughter to Cullman County from Georgia in the late 1870s. Emily, born October 21, 1834, was a daughter of George and Elizabeth Duncan. She married William J. Echols August 7, 1852, in Coweta County, Georgia. About 1858, the Echols family moved to southern Arkansas and entered land in Ouachita County. The family is listed there in the 1860 Federal Census. About the time the war began, the family moved back to near Newnan, Georgia and William Echols enlisted in the Confederacy. William died in service in October 1863. After the war, the widow Emily moved to Texas for a time with her brother, and then went back to live with her father in Georgia by 1870, and eventually moved to Logan where she lived near the residence of Henry and Margaret Alvis. On July 26, 1887, Emily applied for a Confederate pension through Cullman County on the service of her husband William J. Echols. Unfortunately, after 25 years or so, she could not remember his unit and company. As a result of the lack of documentation, she never received a Confederate widow's pension.

Henry and Emily became acquainted with each other while they lived in the Shady Grove and Jones Chapel area. About six months after Margaret died, Henry Alvis married the widow Emily

Echols June 8, 1891, in Cullman County. Not long after that, they moved up to near Westpoint in Lawrence County, Tennessee. There, they rented a farm from S.W. Mabry, son of James P Mabry, one of Henry's comrades from the 1st Alabama Cavalry. Henry had a history of heart problems and died a little over three years later on October 3, 1894. The exact circumstances surrounding Henry's last few years are a mystery. Emily had accumulated a good deal of land in Cullman County and some say after they married, Henry sold off the land to the exclusion of Emily's two sons and pocketed the money before he moved away to Tennessee. One story is the two sons never forgave Henry for that and in league with the Klan, caught up with Henry and hung him near Westpoint. In other words, his existing heart trouble was exacerbated by the rope around his neck. Another story, also involving the Klan, reported he was murdered for his Unionist leanings during the war. Whether Henry died of natural causes or was helped along to an untimely end will continue to be a source of speculation. No grave marker has been located for Henry S. Alvis in Lawrence County, Tennessee. In an affidavit, S.W. Mabry said, ...[Henry] was a renter on my place at the time of his death. I was with him during his last sickness and was present at his death. This affidavit is made for the purpose of assisting the widow of the said Henry S. Alvis (deceased) to secure a pension from the United States.

Another affidavit was submitted by John W. Alvis, Henry's son: I, John W. Alvis do certify that I am a son of Henry S. Alvis and Margaret M. Alvis and I lived at home with my parents up to 1893. My mother died in 1890 on the 3rd day of December. My father, Henry S. Alvis never had been married until he was married to my mother, Margaret M. Maynard. After the death of my mother, my father married Emily C. Echols on the 8th day of June 1891 and they never was divorced from each other. My father died October 2, 1894. I lived at home with them for two years and they live together as man and wife. I know these facts from being with them and a part of the family.

Emily C. Duncan Echols Alvis finally collected her widow's pension, but from her second husband, a Unionist, not her Confederate first husband. Emily moved from Lawrence County, Tennessee back to Cullman County, Alabama in late 1894 or early 1895 and lived near her two sons and invalid daughter until her death February 11, 1909. Emily Alvis is buried near her children in the Emeus Cemetery near Logan in Cullman County.

Henry S. Alvis' son David H. Alvis also served in the 1st Alabama Cavalry. Other family members serving in the 1st included Henry's brother Gabriel Alexander Alvis, and nephews Franklin Newton Alvis, and William John Alvis. Submitted by Robin Sterling who is a descendant of William and Emily Echols. He is indebted to Alvis Hancock, a descendant of Henry S. and Margaret Alvis, for some of the details of this article. The Alvis family history can be studied in Alvis Family Heritage, 1998, compiled in part by Alvis Hancock.

Alvis, William John "Billy" - William John Alvis enlisted in Company B of the 1st Alabama Cavalry, USV as a private on April 2, 1864, at Decatur, Alabama.. He was enrolled by Lieutenant Judy for a period of 3 years. The Muster and Descriptive Roll recorded him 21 years of age, 5'-11" tall, having a fair complexion, gray eyes, light hair, born in Tuscaloosa County, Alabama, and a farmer by occupation. He was mustered in on April 13, 1864, at Decatur, Alabama. He was appointed Corporal on August 1, 1864. However, another muster roll stated he was a private until March 28, 1864, and then a Corporal until he mustered out. W.J. Alvis was mustered out on October 20, 1865, at Huntsville, Alabama. See Franklin N. Alvis, above, for family information. William John Alvis died July 28, 1920, in Henderson County, Texas, and was buried in the Red Hill Cemetery in Henderson County, Texas. Conflicting dates of birth have been given for Billy Alvis, one being April 5, 1843, and the other May 4, 1844.

William John Alvis went home in August of 1865 and married Sarah Francis Leonard on August 15, 1865. Before he returned to the army, Sarah took his measurements and while he was away, she picked the cotton, wove the thread, and made him a suit and even the underwear. She received no letters from him or any information on his well being. One day Sarah and her mom, Hettie, were talking. Hettie said, "He isn't coming back." Sarah said "Yes he will. He said he would be back and Billy is good for his word." They then heard the screen door open and there was Billy. He was carrying his shoes because his feet and legs were swollen and they had large knots on them. These knots were to give him trouble in later years.

Billy had stayed until the Company B had been disbanded at Huntsville, Alabama on October 20, 1865. Conflicting stories arise here concerning Billy's service. The military papers show him home in August and discharged in October. Family story says he joined the Confederates, in August and returned to the Union. There was no word received because he had changed sides.

<u>Amerson, William M.C., alias John Amerson</u>, William M.C. Amerson, alias John W. Amason, enlisted in Company B of the 1st Alabama Cavalry, USV as a Private on March 9, 1864, in Decatur, Alabama for a period of 3 years. He was enrolled by Lieutenant Judy. He was mustered in March 27, 1864, at Decatur, and his enlistment was credited to Pulaski, Giles County, Tennessee. The Company Descriptive Roll recorded William as 37 years of age, 5'-5" tall, having a fair complexion, gray eyes, red hair, born in Blount County, Alabama, and a farmer by occupation. A Descriptive List of Deserters, dated October 3, 1864, at Rome, Georgia, stated W.M.C. Amason deserted September 30, 1864, from Rome, Georgia. A Company Muster-Out Roll dated October 20, 1865, Huntsville, Alabama, stated John W. Anderson, age 37, of Company B, had deserted. A Notation from the War Department of the Adjutant General's Office in Washington, D.C. dated September 18, 1888, stated the following: The Charges of desertion of September 29 and 30, 1864, against this man are removed. He is discharged to date September 29, 1864, to complete his military record, by reason of disability, nature and reason unknown. Discharge certificate furnished by A.G.O. September 26, 1888. Muster Roll also shows he was discharged February 29, 1864, due to disability, nature and reason unknown. One POW Record was in his file.

There are conflicting records in Julia Amerson's pension about Amerson's discharge. On one record it states he died July 24, 1865, while in service, while another record states he was discharged February 29, 1864, due to a disability.

The reason he was listed as "William M.D. Amerson" on some documents was because the Amerson name was originally spelled "McAmerson". He signed his clothing book as "William M.C. Amerson".

An Affidavit to Origin of Disability which was not dated stated Julia A. Green, widow of William M. Amerson was 44 years old and that on or about September 15, 1864, while in the line of duty, and without fault of improper conduct on his part, at or near Rome, Georgia said soldier incurred an injury in his arm and shoulder that disabled him for duty. It was caused by a jerk from an unruly horse that he was trying to control while out on special duty with a foraging wagon by order of Colonel Spencer. The affidavit was signed by W.W. Salyers of Tishomingo, Mississippi. He stated he was not an eye witness to the facts but saw him shortly after it happened and was in the same company at the time of the disability.

There are also conflicting records on when William and Julia Hawkins Amerson married. One record stated they married November 6, 1845, while another one stated November 6, 1849. They were married by John Anderton at the home of Dennis Hawkins. Julia listed the names of their children under the age of 16 as Harvey Poe, born November 14, 1853; Sarah Eliza, born February 6, 1855; Lucinda Tina, born February 18, 1857; and Benjamin Horton Amerson, born May 16, 1861. She stated William M. Amerson was born William McAmason and the name changed to Amerson through the years. Julia signed the affidavit by making her mark, and it was witnessed by Henson D. Harbin and Dennis Hawkins. (sic)

The State of Alabama, Blount County, To any Judge, minister of the Gospel or Justice, lawfully authorized to celebrate the rites of Matrimony between Wm. M. Amison and Julian (Julia Ann) Hawkins, and for so doing this shall be your warrant. Given under my hand and seal of office this 9th Day of November in the year of our Lord One thousand eight hundred and forty nine. Signed John C. Gillespie, Clerk. In virtue of a License from the Clerk of the County Court of said County, I have this day celebrated the rites of Matrimony between William M. Amerson and Julian Hawkins. Given under my hand this 9th day of November 1849. Signed John Anderton, Justice of the Peace. The State of Alabama, Blount County. I Jesse W. Ellis, Judge of the Probate Court and Custodian of Marriage Records and Licenses, do hereby certify that the foregoing is a true copy of the Marriage License and the return there on of Solemnization, as appears from original on file in this office of the Marriage of Wm. M. Amison to Julian Hawkins. Witness my hand and…. (Second page of document is missing from pension records.)

An undated General Affidavit states: State of Alabama, County of Blount, In the matter of claim for pension, Julia A. Green, late widow of Wm. M. Amasen, Co. B, 1st Alabama Cavalry, Personally came before me, a Justice of the Peace in and for aforesaid County and State, J.L. Moss of Little Warrior, Alabama and W.W. Salyers, Tidmore, Blount County Alabama who being persons of lawful age, who, being duly sworn, declare in relation to the aforesaid case as follows: We know that there was but the one Amason or Amerson or any name of the kind that enlisted at Decatur or anywhere in Co. B, First Alabama Cavalry and if the name is on the Roll, John W. Amerson it was a mistake on the part of the recruiting officer when Amason enlisted. We are positive they are the one and same individual person. His name correct was William M.C. Amason. Signed Joseph (illegible) and W.W. Salyers.

Another undated General Affidavit stated: State of Alabama, Blount County, In the matter of claim for pension of Julia A. Green, former widower of William M. Amason, Co. B. 1st Alabama Cavalry Vols. Personally came before me, a Justice of the Peace in and for aforesaid County and State, Daniel Y. Hawkins, 44 years of age. P.B. Anderton, Blount County, Alabama and E.W. Hawkins, age 58 years. P.O. Chepulte___ Blount County, Alabama, persons of lawful age, who, being duly sworn, declare in relation to the aforesaid case as follows: That we have known the said Julia A. Green 40 years and that we saw her married to the said William M. Amason November 8th 1849, and that we have reason to believe the children whose names are as follows are: His by herself, Harvey Poe Amason, born November 14' 1853; Sarah Eliz Amason, born February 5, 1855; Lucinda Tina Amason, born February 18, 1857; Benjamin Horton Amason, born May 16, 1861, and that we further declare that to the best of our knowledge, all those that were present at their birth are dead or gone from the county and there is no church record of their baptism. We further declare that we have no interest in said case, and that we are not concerned in its prosecution. Signed Isaac Standridge, H.M. Tidmore, Daniel Y. Hawkins and E.W. Hawkins.

A Marriage License found in the pension records stated Julia A. Hawkins Amerson married A.J. Green at her residence on January 2, 1881. They were married by Isaac Standridge, M.G.

An affidavit from the Adjutant General's Office, dated November 1, 1883, stated: "Respectfully returned to the Commissioner of Pensions. John W. Amason, a Private Of Company B, 1st Regiment Alabama Cavalry Volunteers was enrolled on March 9, 1864, at Decatur, Alabama by Lieutenant Judy for 3 years and mustered into service March 27, 1864, at Decatur, Alabama. Muster Rolls of Company from date of muster in to August 31, 1864, report him present. September and October 1864, John W. Amason was recorded as having deserted September 29th from Rome, Georgia. Muster-Out Roll of Company dated October 20, 1865, reports him, John W. Anderson, under head of deserted without remark. Muster rolls of Company show him to have been enrolled March 20, 1864. Personal description in case of the above man is as follows. Born in Blount Company, Alabama, 37 years of age, 5-5" tall, having a fair complexion, gray eyes, red hair, born in Blount County, Alabama and a farmer by occupation. The name W.M.C. Amason is borne on Company B. description, of Clothing Books, 1st Alabama Cavalry He signs Clothing Book as W.M.C. Amason. This man's description as shown by Company B. Descriptive Book agrees in every particular way with that given above in case of John W. Amason. The names William M. Amerson or William McAmerson are not borne on any rolls of the above Company on file in this office. E.B. West was Captain of Company B.

A letter from the Adjutant General's Office of the War Department dated October 15, 1888, stated: Respectfully returned to the Commissioner of Pensions. John W. Amason, a Private Of Company B, 1st Regiment Alabama Cavalry Volunteers. "The charges of desertion of September 29th and 30th, 1864, against this man are removed. He is discharged to date September 29, 1964, he completed his military record, by reason of disability, nature and origin unknown." Signed R.C. Drum. Claim Number 188.546

A letter dated April 20, 1889, from Tidmore, Alabama, addressed to the Commissioner of Pensions, stated: "Dear Sir, Will you please inform me if there is the name of William McAmason on the list of Soldier's names in Co. B. 1 Alabama Cavalry or is there any other Amason in that Company. William McAmason was my father who died while in the army and I believe we are entitled to a pension now. Please let me hear from you as soon as possible and you will very much oblige. Yours Respectfully, Ben Amason, Tidmore, Blount County, Alabama." It appears Julia Ann Hawkins

Amerson's pension was denied because William's death was the result of Bilious Fever and not connected to his military service or disability.

Anders, William P. - William P. Anders enlisted in Company G of the 1st Alabama Cavalry, USV on April 10, 1864, at Decatur, Alabama. He was enrolled by Lieutenant David A. Pease for a period of 3 years. The July and August 1864 Muster Roll listed him as having deserted July 11, 1864, from Rome, Georgia with arms, horse, and accoutrements. The Company Muster-Out Roll stated he was 25 years of age, mustered out October 20, 1865, with pay due from enrollment, but he deserted with saddle, bridle, halter and blanket. The Company Descriptive Book showed William to have been 26 years of age, 5'-11" tall, having a sandy complexion, gray eyes, sandy hair, born Shelby County, Alabama, and a farmer by occupation.

Anderson, Charles - Charles Anderson enlisted in Company H of the 1st Alabama Cavalry, USV as a private on March 1, 1865, in Stevenson, Alabama for a period of 3 years. He was enrolled by Sergeant James W. DeVaney. He was mustered in April 5, 1865, in Nashville, Tennessee. The Muster and Descriptive Roll recorded Charles as being 18 years of age, 5'-3" tall, having a fair complexion, blue eyes, light hair, born in Dade County, Georgia and a farmer by occupation. The May and June 1865 Muster Roll recorded Charles Anderson as absent without leave since May 8, 1865. The July and August 1865 Muster Roll stated he was absent and had deserted May 8, 1865, from Huntsville, Alabama. Charles was able to signed his name to his Volunteer Enlistment.

Anderson, John W. - See William M.C. Amerson, alias John Amerson.

Anderson, Lee M. - Lee M. Anderson enlisted in Company G of the 1st Alabama Cavalry, USV as a private on March 31, 1863, at Chewalla, Tennessee for a period of one year. His name appeared on the Descriptive List of Deserters as Lee H. Anderson, and stated he deserted from Chewalla on April 30, 1863. Other Muster Roll showing he deserted listed him as Lee M. Anderson.

Anditon, Samuel - Samuel Anditon enlisted in Company F of the 1st Alabama Cavalry, USV on October 25, 1863, at Camp Davies, Mississippi for a period of one year. He was enrolled by W.H. Cheney. He was discharged January 15, 1864, at Camp Davies for a disability. The Company Descriptive Book recorded Samuel to have been 28 years of age, 6' tall, having a fair complexion, gray eyes, red hair, born in Marion County, Alabama, and a farmer by occupation.

Andous, William A. - See John Wesley Evans, below. Evans used the alias of William A. Andous and various spellings.

Anglin, George Washington - George Washington Anglin was a Bugler in Company E of the 1st Alabama Cavalry, USV having enlisted as a private on April 1, 1863, at Glendale, Mississippi for a period of 1 year. He was mustered in April 15, 1863, at Corinth, Mississippi. The July and August 1863 Muster Roll listed him as a Bugler. George was discharged March 18, 1864, at Memphis, Tennessee due to expiration of term of service. George W. Anglin also served in Company E of the 14th Mississippi Infantry Regiment.

George Washington Anglin was born in February 1844, in Monroe County, Mississippi to John Sheppard Anglin and Rebecca Riddings. He married Kate Anne "Katie" Boone, daughter of Thomas and Melinda Boone, on January 21, 1872, in Chickasaw County, Mississippi. Children of George W. and Katie Anglin were: Malinda B. "Minnie", born August 1876; Kate Ann, "Katie", born January 1879; Georgia, born August 1880; James, "Jim", born August 1881, and died June 10, 1940; Belton Cleon, born August 10, 1883, died December 1950; Rebecca "Rebbie", born October 1886, died February 24, 1950; and Hal Green Anglin, born January 27, 1888, and died April 18, 1959. George Washington Anglin died March 11, 1913, in Okolona, Chickasaw County, Mississippi, and is buried in the Odd Fellows Cemetery, formerly the IOFF Cemetery in Okolona.

Anthony, John C. - John C. Anthony, alias William H. Anthony, enlisted in Company K of the 1st Alabama Cavalry, USV on December 25, 1863, at Camp Davies, Mississippi by Lieutenant Hornback, for a period of 3 years. The Company Descriptive Book shows him to have been 44 years of age, 5'-10" tall, having a light complexion, gray eyes, brown hair, born in St. Clair County, Alabama, and a farmer by occupation. He traveled 100 miles on horseback from Marion County, Alabama to Camp Davies, Mississippi to enlist in the Union Army. The name William H. Anthony, a private in Company K, appeared on the Descriptive List of Deserters stating he deserted February 21, 1864, from Memphis, Tennessee, and it was filed with John C. Anthony. The Company Muster Roll for January and February 1864 for John C. Anthony reported him to have deserted February 21, 1864, from camp in Memphis, Tennessee. He was on guard at the time and was missed at Midnight. No other records were in his file.

John C. Anthony was born in 1825 in St. Clair County, Alabama, according to his military records. Some descendants state he was born in Fayette County, Alabama. He married Cynthia McMinn, daughter of Robert and Sarah Kuykendall McMinn. Cynthia's father, Robert, served in Company B of the 28th Texas Cavalry, CSA. John C. Anthony was the son of William Anthony, II and Jane "Jenny" McMinn, who were married about 1814 in Marion County, Alabama. Children of John and Jenny Anthony were: Robert Valentine, born August 16, 1851, died February 13, 1933 in Marion County, Alabama; Sarah Affa, born 1853, died November 11, 1927; John Carroll, born November 28, 1863, died October 25, 1936; and James Sherman Anthony, born June 8, 1868, died August 9, 1950. John C. Anthony died in 1895 and was buried in the Greenbriar Cemetery in Becker, Monroe County, Mississippi in an unmarked grave.

Anthony, William H. - See John C. Anthony, above. Two muster rolls with the name William H. Anthony were in John C. Anthony's file. Apparently he used both names while in service.

Armor, William Lively - William L. Armor enlisted in Company C of the 1st Alabama Cavalry, USV as a private on December 1, 1863, in Corinth, Mississippi for a period of 1 year. He was enrolled by D.R. Adams. He was mustered in on December 22, 1863, at Corinth. He had first enlisted in Company H of the 32nd Mississippi Volunteers. He enlisted as a private on March 19, 1862, at Iuka, Mississippi for a period of 3 years. On December 23, 1862, he was recorded as being deserted in consequence of long absence. He then joined the 1st Alabama Cavalry where on August 20, 1863, he was on duty as company cook. The Detachment Muster-Out Roll stated he mustered out December 17, 1863, due to expiration of term of service. The Regimental Descriptive Book recorded William L. Armor as 40 years of age, 5'-11" tall, having a fair complexion, brown eyes, dark hair, born in Giles County, Tennessee and a farmer by occupation. William's brother, John Davis Armor enlisted in the 32nd Mississippi.

William Lively Armor was born March 1, 1823, in Giles County, Tennessee to Davis Wiley Armor and his wife, Elizabeth Lively, who were married August 10, 1815. They were among the founding members of the Ripley Presbyterian Church in Tippah County, Mississippi. Elizabeth's parents were William Lively and Teresa Livers, who were married April 18, 1797, in Frederick County, Virginia. William married Elizabeth "Eliza" Jane Hallmark, daughter of Jesse Hallmark and Mary Frances Wright, on July 22, 1849, in Tishomingo County, Mississippi. Children of William and Eliza Armor were: Robert J., born and died April 18, 1850; Mary E., born July 19, 1851; Amanda E., born April 24, 1853, died March 22, 1910: Matilda Jane, born March 12, 1855; Nancy K., born February 13, 1857: Leanah, born August 17, 1859, died May 1, 1880; Martha A., born March 4, 1862, died June 25, 1862; Marshall T., born February 9, 1865, (stillborn); Clarinda Rhoda, born September 2, 1866, died November 14, 1920; Laura, born about 1859; Susan M., born January 18, 1870; Ernest Frank, born October 26, 1873; Robert, born about 1875; and Ada/Ader Armor, born October 26, 1873.

Siblings of William Lively Armor, and other children of his parents, Davis Wiley Armor and Elizabeth Lively, were: Mahala Jane, James Brooks, Margaret Amanda, Nancy Isabella, Newton Monroe, Thomas Jefferson, Mary Elizabeth, Joseph Jasper, John Davis, and Marshall Blackburn Armor. William's mother, Eliza Hallmark Armor died December 22, 1891, in Union County, Illinois. William L. Armor died December 21, 1879, and was buried in the Toledo Christian Church Cemetery in Cobden, Union County, Illinois.

Armstrong, Charles - Charles Armstrong enlisted in Company A of the 1st Alabama Cavalry, USV as a private on January 12, 1864 at Camp Davies, Mississippi, for a period of 3 years. He was enrolled by Lieutenant Hinds. He was mustered in February 6, 1864, at Memphis, Tennessee. The Muster and Descriptive Roll recorded him as 22 years of age, 5'-10" tall, having a dark complexion, black eyes, black hair, born in Bibb County, Alabama and a farmer by occupation. The July and August 1864 Muster Roll showed Charles to have been absent, sick in hospital at Larkinsville, Alabama. He died August 5, 1864, in the U.S. General Hospital in Larkinsville, Alabama from typhoid fever and dysentery. He had been admitted to the hospital on May 1, 1864. Charles signed his name on his Enlistment Form as Charles H. Armstrong. A note from the Surgeon General's Office of the Record and Pension Bureau, dated October 10, 1866, stated: It appeared from the records of this office that Charles Armstrong of Company A, 1st Alabama Cavalry died in Regimental Hospital in Rome, Georgia August 5, 1864, of typhoid fever. The records of the hospital are not on file in this office and it is not proven what disposition has been made of them. There was an investigation into this but no records to state for sure if he died in Alabama or Georgia,

Charles Armstrong was born about 1842 in Bibb County, Alabama to Joseph Armstrong and Mary Carr, who had married 22 Nov 1832 in Bibb County, Alabama. Charles married Jincy M. Green, daughter of Absalom and Mary Green, on November 16, 1859. Known children of Charles and Jincy were: Joseph A., born September 1860, died 1926; and Charles W. Armstrong, born June 22, 1864, died March 16, 1916.

Armstrong, James M. - James M. Armstrong enlisted in Company C of the 1st Alabama Cavalry, USV as a Private on December 21, 1862 at Corinth, Mississippi, by John Latty for a period of 1 year. The September and October 1863 Muster Roll recorded him as being absent, sick in hospital in Memphis, Tennessee, first having been sick in Glendale, Mississippi on October 16, 1863. The November and December 1863 Muster Roll stated James died December 9, 1863, in the hospital at Memphis. The Regimental Descriptive Book recorded James as being 21 years of age, 5'-7" tall, having a fair complexion, dark eyes, dark hair, born in Marshall County, Mississippi, and a farmer by occupation. The Casualty Sheet for James M. Armstrong stated he died of Pneumonia, and was certified by A.T. Cameron, Captain of Company C. James M. Armstrong is buried in the Memphis National Cemetery.

Armstrong, William - Enlisted as Private in Company C, no date or place given, sent to hospital in Memphis, Tennessee October 16, 1863. Could possibly have been a brother to Charles Armstrong as Charles had a brother named William. No other information could be located on this trooper.*

Arnold, Asbury B. - Asbury B. Arnold enlisted in Company H of the 1st Alabama Cavalry, USV as a private on October 17, 1863, at Glendale, Mississippi for a period of 1 year. He was enlisted by Captain Ford. The January and February 1864 Company Muster Roll recorded him as being absent, sick in the General Hospital in Memphis, Tennessee. On March 26, 1864, Asbury was discharged due to a disability. A Hospital Muster Roll from Adams U.S.A. General Hospital in Memphis recorded him as present as a patient on January 20, 1864, however, his name appeared on the Returns as having been a patient in the hospital since November 10, 1863. The March and April 1864 Hospital Muster Roll listed him as still a patient stating: Discharged March 29, 1864. Final statement given. The Return also stated Asbury's name also appeared as A.W. Arnold. The Certificate of Disability of Discharge for Asbury B. Arnold from Headquarters in Memphis dated March 26, 1864, stated he was to be discharged in pursuance of General Orders No. 36, A.G.O. since 1862. His Certificate of Disability for Discharge recorded Asbury as 26 years of age, 5'8" tall, having a light complexion, black eyes, dark hair, born in Marion County, Illinois, and a farmer by occupation. The Certificate of Disability for Discharge stated the following: I certify that I have carefully examined the said Asbury B. Arnold of Sergeant Peek's Company and find him incapable of performing the duties of a soldier because of phthisis pulmonalis contracted before enlistment. He has had a cough for five years, has had frequent attacks of known _____ _____ from the lungs and is very much debilitated and emaciated and will never be fit for military duty of any kind whatever. He has a cough with copious phthisis pulmonalis and frequent attacks of haematemesis. He is emaciated. He is unfit for Invalid Corps. Degree of disability is three-fourth.

<u>Arthur, James</u> - James Arthur enlisted in Company A of the 1st Alabama Cavalry, USV as a private on February 4, 1864, at Memphis, Tennessee for a period of 3 years, and was mustered-in February 5, 1864, at Memphis. He was enrolled by Captain Hinds. The Company Muster in and Descriptive Roll showed James as being 25 years of age, 5'-11" tall, having a fair complexion, blue eyes, dark hair, born New York City, New York, and a farmer by occupation. His name appeared on the Descriptive List of Deserters stating he deserted March 25, 1864, from Memphis, Tennessee with arms, mule and equipment. A Company Muster Roll for March and April 1864, stated James had never received any bounty, and deserted with 1 horse, 1 saddle, complete, 1 carbine and equipment, 1 pair of spurs and straps, 1 bridle, 1 halter, and 1 single blanket. He deserted owing the U.S. Government $167 for the horse and equipment. James Arthur was able to sign his name to his Volunteer Enlistment Form.

<u>Atkerson, John R.</u> - See John R. Atkinson, see below.

<u>Atkins, Martin</u> - Martin Atkins and his brother, William C., enlisted in Company H of the 1st Alabama Cavalry, USV on October 17, 1863, at Glendale, Mississippi as a private for a period of 1 year. He was recorded as being 44 years of age at the time of enlistment. The September and October 1863 Muster Roll recorded him as being absent, supposed prisoner in the hands of the enemy. However, the November and December 1863 Muster Roll recorded him as present. He was mustered out October 24, 1864, in Rome, Georgia due to expiration of term of service. His Muster-Out Roll stated he owed the U.S. Government thirty-five cents for losing one thong and brush wiper. Martin was apparently captured October 26, 1863, during the Battle of Vincent's Crossroads, but he either escaped or was released and was back in camp in November.

Martin Atkins was born about 1820 in Lowndes County, Mississippi to Spencer Atkins and Millie Franks who were married about 1815 in Laurens County, South Carolina. Martin married Nancy P. Kemp and they had the following children: Nancy Jane, born August 1848, died 1937; William Jefferson, born January 3, 1852, died July 27, 1915; Sarah F., born 1847; Thomas S., born September 8, 1850, died April 29, 1938; John Henry, born March 4, 1855, died January 16, 1917; Mary Ann, born May 8, 1858, died April 7, 1947; Robert F., born May 1860, died 1949; and Cordelia Paralee Atkins, born in 1863. Siblings of Martin Atkins, and children of Spencer and Millie Franks Atkins were: Martha Ann, Matilda, Joseph, Thomas Jefferson, Mary Ann, William Clark, Alexander, and James Spencer Atkins. Martin Atkins died in March 1868 in Jones County, Mississippi.

<u>Atkins, William C.</u> - William C. Atkins, and his brother, Martin, enlisted in Company H of the 1st Alabama Cavalry, USV on October 17, 1863, in Glendale, Mississippi, for a period of 1 year at age 35. William enlisted as a private but in September he was shown as 4th Sergeant. The March and April 1864 Muster Roll recorded him as absent, sick in hospital in Memphis, Tennessee. In July and August 1864, he was shown as Sergeant. William was mustered out October 24, 1864, in Rome, Georgia due to expiration of term of service. He owed the U.S. Government $2.45 for losing one thong and brush wiper and one painted blanket. See Martin Atkins, above, for family information.

<u>Atkinson, John R.</u> - John R. Atkinson enlisted in Company B of the 1st Alabama Cavalry, USV as a private on February 6, 1864, at Pulaski, Tennessee for a period of 3 years. He was enrolled by Lieutenant Judy. He was mustered in March 27, 1864 at Decatur, Alabama. The Company Muster and Descriptive Roll recorded John as being 28 years of age, 6' tall, having a fair complexion, blue eyes, dark hair, born in Walker County, Alabama, and a wood-corder by occupation. His enlistment was credited to Pulaski, in Giles County, Tennessee. The Company Muster Roll for April 30, 1864, recorded him as being absent, on sick furlough to Pulaski for 20 days, from April 10, 1864. The April 13th to June 30, 1864, Muster Roll listed him as present. The name John R. Atkerson appeared on a Descriptive List of Deserters dated July 31, 1864, at Rome, Georgia stating he deserted on July 10, 1864, from Rome, Georgia with arms and accoutrements. The July and August 1864 Muster Roll stated John deserted

from Rome, Georgia on July 16, 1864, with 1 Smith Carbine, 1 sling, 1 swivel, 1 cartridge box, 1 cap pouch, and 1 waist belt and plate. Another Company Descriptive Book recorded John as having been born in Winston County, Alabama. He deserted owing the U.S. Government $46.77 for all of the equipment he either lost or took with him.

Austin, Bryant - Bryant Austin, also listed as Bryan Austin, enlisted in Company D of the 1ˢᵗ Alabama Cavalry, USV as a private on April 19, 1864, at Decatur, Alabama for a period of 3 years. He was enrolled by Lieutenant David A. Pease and was mustered in June 16, 1864, at Decatur. The Muster and Descriptive Roll listed him as being 21 years of age, 6'-½" tall, having a light complexion, blue eyes, brown hair, born in Franklin County, Alabama, and a farmer by occupation. The July and August 1864 Muster Roll stated Bryant owed the U.S. Government $20 for losing one Remington Revolver. The same muster roll listed him as a Corporal. Bryant Austin was mustered out on October 20, 1865, at Huntsville, Alabama. The Muster-Out Roll stated he was appointed Corporal on July 1, 1864, by Order Number 70. He then owed the U.S. Government $1.80 for losing one surcingle and one curry comb.

Austin, Jasper - Jasper Austin enlisted into Company E of the 1ˢᵗ Alabama Cavalry, USV on December 16, 1862, at Chewalla, Tennessee as a 3ʳᵈ Corporal, for a period of 1 year. The May and June 1863 Muster Roll showed him to be a Corporal. He was mustered out December 17, 1863, at Memphis, Tennessee at age 23, for reason of expiration of term of service. The November and December 1863 Muster Roll showed Jasper Austin to have been a Sergeant.

Austin, Jesse W. – Jesse W. Austin enlisted in Company L of the 1ˢᵗ Alabama Cavalry, USV as a private on September 25, 1863, at Fayette County, Alabama for a period of 1 year. He was enrolled by Captain Tramel. Another muster roll stated he enlisted in Glendale, Mississippi. There was a note in his file that stated the following: Jesse W. Austin, L-1ˢᵗ Alabama Cavalry. For report for Returns, March 1864, see Jesse Files, Co. L. Jesse W. Austin enlisted in Company L of the 1ˢᵗ Alabama Cavalry, USV as a private on September 25, 1863, at Fayette County, Alabama for a period of 1 year. He was enrolled by Captain Trammel. Another muster roll stated he enlisted in Glendale, Mississippi. There was a note in his file that stated the following: Jesse W. Austin, L-1ˢᵗ Alabama Cavalry For report for Returns, March 1864, see Jesse Files, Company L. The January and February 1864 Muster Roll listed Jesse as being absent, sick in the hospital in Memphis, Tennessee since February 19, 1864. Jesse W. Austin died of measles March 13, 1864, in Overton U.S.A. General Military Hospital in Memphis, Shelby County, Tennessee. Another muster roll stated he died March 15, 1864, while a note dated July 22, 1867 stated he died March 3, 1864. The Company Descriptive Book recorded Jesse as having been 19 years of age, 5'-7" tall, having a dark complexion, dark eyes, dark hair, born in Fayette County, Alabama, and a farmer by occupation. The Final Statement of Jesse W. Austin stated he died March 3, 1864, and that he had been enlisted by Lieutenant Hoffman. The Statement of Effects showed Jesse with the following items: 1 great coat, 1 uniform jacket, 1 flannel sack coat, 2 pairs of trowsers, 1 pair of books, 1 blanket, and 1 oil blanket, totaling $19.00. A note with the Statement of Effects stated: $19, received at Memphis, Tennessee January 20, 1865, of Assistant Surgeon, J.C.G. Hoppensett, U.S. Army, Nineteen dollars in Treasury Notes, the property of the late Private J.A. Austin, Company L, 1ˢᵗ Alabama Cavalry, who died in Overton General Hospital, Memphis, Tennessee, March 3, 1864. Signed H.V. Sullivan, Paymaster, U.S. Army. This is probably the Austin buried in Grave 1-14 in the Memphis National Cemetery.

Austin, John R. - John R. Austin enlisted in Company D of the 1ˢᵗ Alabama Cavalry, USV on April 19, 1864, in Decatur, Alabama as a private for a period of 3 years, and mustered in June 16, 1864, in Decatur. He was enrolled by Lieutenant David A. Pease. The Muster and Descriptive Roll recorded John as being 19 years of age, 5'-7" tall, having a light complexion, blue eyes, brown hair, born in Walker County, Alabama, and a farmer by occupation. He was mustered out October 20, 1865, in Huntsville, Alabama.

Austin, Sanders - Cards filed with Austin Sanders. Sanders Austin, enlisted in Company C of the 1ˢᵗ Alabama Cavalry, USV on December 21, 1862, at Corinth, Mississippi as a private, and was mustered in December 22, 1862 at Corinth for a period of 1 year. He was enrolled by John Latty. Sanders Austin's name appeared on the Returns on September 26, 1863, as being absent with leave. The Regimental Descriptive Book recorded him as 25 years of age, 5'-9" tall, having a fair complexion, blue eyes, dark hair, born in Anson County, North Carolina, and a farmer by occupation. He was mustered out December 27, 1863 at Camp Davies, Mississippi on account of expiration of term of service.

Sanders and his family remained in Mississippi until about 1870. During that time his brother, Wyatt, was listed as missing in action during the Battle of Harrisburg (Tupelo) in 1864. Wyatt had enlisted (or was conscripted) into the Confederate Army and served in the 1st Tennessee Cavalry under the command of General Nathan Bedford Forrest. He had been serving for less than six months when he was missing. He also had fought in the Battle of Brice's Cross Roads in Mississippi. After the loss of Wyatt, Easter Emma and her three children went to live with Sanders and his family. Easter Emma died from cancer prior to 1870, and when Sanders died in 1871, Elizabeth was left with 10 children, including infant, Sannie, to care for. Economic hardship plagued the family for years. Elizabeth died in 1892 and is buried beside her husband in the Cedar Creek Cemetery in Scott County, Arkansas. Their son, Elijah, and his first wife, Roxie, with their daughter, Dessie, are also buried in Cedar Creek Cemetery. Roxie died at age 19 after giving birth to Henry Doyle Austin in 1898, and Dessie in 1897. Roxie and Dessie died in 1899, both as the result of measles. After Elijah's death in 1905, of unknown cause, Henry Doyle went to live with his maternal grandparents. Family information submitted by Richard Austin

Autry, William Thomas - Notation stating, "probably belonged to scout or guide not mustered into the service, in Cumberland USA Hospital at Nashville, Tennessee on May 1, 1864.

William T. Autry was born 1846 in Tippah County, Mississippi, and died in 1910 in Yell County, Arkansas. He was the son of George Washington Autry and Lucretia N. Vest. He was a brother to Mary Lovina Autry, who married James H. Kimbrough, who served in Company B of the 1st Alabama Cavalry, USV.

- B -

Baggett, Andrew Jackson - Andrew Jackson Baggett enlisted in Company E of the 1st Alabama Cavalry, USV as a private on March 1, 1863 at Glendale, Mississippi, for a period of one year. He was mustered in the same day at Corinth, Mississippi. The July and August 1863 Muster Roll listed him as having deserted, however, the September and October 1863 Muster Roll listed him as absent, missing in late action, which would have been the Battle of Vincent's Crossroads in Red Bay, Alabama on October 26, 1863. He was shown as a prisoner in the hands of the enemy. On November 26, 1863, he was shown as gained from missing in action. The November and December 1863 Muster Roll showed him to have been present. On January 25, 1864, Baggett was listed as being absent, on detached service as Teamster in Quartermaster Department at Vicksburg, Mississippi. He was mustered out March 18, 1864 at expiration of term of service. Andrew Jackson Baggett was the son of Abraham Baggett and the brother of James W. Baggett. He was also the nephew of Drury Baggett. Andrew J. Baggett enlisted on September 5, 1862, in Cherokee County, Alabama and was mustered in September 15, 1862, in Mountain Springs, Alabama. He was enrolled by Captain Clark at age 19 for the duration of the war. This was known as Captain Clark's Company, Warren's Battalion of Cavalry It is believed that Andrew and James were conscripted and eventually deserted the Confederate cavalry to join the Union Army. Since they enlisted in the CSA in September 1862, and the 1st Alabama Cavalry, USV in March 1863, this must be true as they didn't serve in the Confederate Army long.

Andrew J. Baggett was born about 1817 and was married first to Catherine about 1840. Catherine was born about 1822 in Alabama. They were listed in the 1850 Macon County, Alabama Federal Census. His second wife was Elizabeth, who was from Tennessee. They were married sometime between 1868 and 1870, when they appear on the Giles County, Tennessee Census. He apparently died in 1878 in Haywood County, Tennessee, where his second wife, Elizabeth, is listed as "widow" in the administrative bonds of Haywood County on March 7, 1878.

Children of Andrew and Catharine Baggett were: James Wesley, born 1841; William Brittian, born 1842, no known information, probably died at an early age; Andrew Jackson, born 1843; Elizabeth, born 1844; Thomas Jefferson, born 1846, great grandfather of Geoff Baggett; Margaret J., born 1849; Bradford, born 1854, from Arkansas, adopted by the family during a relocation to and from Texas in the late 1860s and early 1870s; Mary F., born 1855; Lunsford, born 1856; Louis, born 1858; Emily Catherine, born 1861; Annie, born 1863; and Charley Baggett, born 1867. Nassau Baggett was born 1875 to Andrew Jackson Baggett and his second wife, Elizabeth. All were born in Alabama except for Nassau, who was born in Tennessee. It is thought that Catharine possibly died in childbirth or from complications of the childbirth of Charley in 1867. By 1878 the family relocated to Giles County, Tennessee early in the next decade. (Geoff, I don't understand this sentence.)

<u>Baggett, Drury Blake</u> - Drury Blake Baggett enlisted in Company E of the 1st Alabama Cavalry, USV on March 1, 1863 at Glendale, Mississippi as a private for a period of one year, and was mustered in the same day at Corinth, Mississippi. He enlisted in the 1st Alabama with his nephews Andrew Jackson Baggett and James William Baggett. Andrew and James were the sons of Abraham Baggett, Drury's older brother. On May 1, 1863, Drury was listed as being absent without leave, supposed to have deserted. The Descriptive List of Deserters reported him to have deserted on July 3, 1863, at Glendale, He was also listed as being absent without leave on June 2, 1863, but he returned to Glendale, Mississippi on July 6, 1863. He was mustered out March 3, 1864 at Memphis, Tennessee at age 40 due to expiration of term of service.

Drury B. Baggett was born March 1, 1823 in Lauderdale County, Alabama to Burrell or Burl Baggett and Elizabeth McLemore in Lauderdale County, Alabama. Drury married Nancy Delilah McLemore in 1850 in Franklin County, Alabama. Drury and Delilah had three children, William Mary and John. During the war, Drury lost his wife and two children to illness. After the war, Drury left Alabama with William, his only surviving son, for Tennessee and Kentucky. He married Matilda Ann Songer on January 20, 1867 in Pikeville, Tennessee, and they had ten children. From about 1869 to 1879, Drury lived in Huntsville, Kentucky working as a farmer and timbering. He moved back to Bledsoe County, Tennessee around 1879.

Drury died at home on September 18, 1907 at the age of 84. Matilda was granted a widow's pension of $12 a month for Drury's service in the Civil War. Drury and Matilda are buried at the Rollins Cemetery in Bledsoe County, Tennessee near land that they owned.

Drury Blake Baggett and Matilda Ann Songer were basket weavers. They had Cherokee mothers who knew and taught them this skill. The rib type baskets made by the Baggett Family were the same type made by the Cherokee Indians in North Carolina. Cherokees still make rib baskets of white oak splits. The Rib Baskets made by the Baggett family were always made from white oak strips called "splints". They were made from young white oak trees between 6" and 8" in diameter. The oak trunks were split at right angles to the rings, and the sides of the sections were shaved to smooth them. After starting them with a knife, thin strips were split off by hand from the edge, following the growth rings. Two flat oak strips were formed into rings and fastened together at right angles to form the handle and the rim of the basket. Additional ribs were added, and then thin splints were woven between them. The splits were soaked in water before use. Depending on size and shape, the baskets were called egg baskets, fruit baskets, magazine baskets and were even made in bushel size for storing corn. The North Carolina Cherokees used natural dyes to color their baskets. The only tools used by the Baggett Basket makers were a wedge and mallet for splitting, an awl, and a knife. It took about 8 hours for them to weave a single basket, not including the time spent to prepare the oak splints.

<u>Baggett, James William</u> - James W. Baggett enlisted in Company E of the 1st Alabama Cavalry, USV on March 1, 1863 at Glendale, Mississippi for a period of one year, and was mustered in the same day at Corinth, Mississippi. However, his name appeared on the Returns as enrolling April 1, 1863, at Glendale, Mississippi and was absent with leave, at Corinth. In May 1863, he was absent without leave to be dropped as deserter after date. June 1863, he was shown as absent, sick April 20, 1863. The March and April 1863 Muster Roll listed James as absent, sick in the hospital at Corinth, Mississippi. July and August 1863 Muster Roll listed him as having deserted July 9th. The September and October 1863 Muster Roll listed him as absent, missing in action during late action, which would have been at

the Battle of Vincent's Crossroads in Red Bay, Alabama, prisoner of war in the hands of the enemy. He was back in camp in November and December 1863, gained from missing in action. The January and February 1864 Muster Roll listed James as being absent, on detached service as Teamster in Quartermaster Department at Vicksburg, Mississippi since January 25, 1864. He was mustered out March 18, 1864, at Memphis, Tennessee.

James William Baggett was the son of Abraham Baggett and the brother of Andrew Baggett. He is also the nephew of Drury Baggett. Andrew and James are previously shown on the muster rolls of Company E of the 5th Alabama Cavalry, CSA. James W. enlisted on September 5, 1862, in Cherokee County, Alabama and was mustered in September 15, 1862, in Mountain Springs, Alabama. He was enrolled by Captain Clark at age 24 for the duration of the war. This was known as Captain Clark's Company, Warren's Battalion of Cavalry It is believed that Andrew and James were conscripted and eventually deserted the Confederate cavalry. Since they enlisted in the CSA in September 1862, and the 1st Alabama Cavalry, USV in March 1863, this must be true as they didn't stay in the Confederate Army long.

Baggett, William F. - William F. Baggett enlisted in Company F of the 1st Alabama Cavalry, USV as a private. The date was not shown, however, a muster roll in his file dated April 30, 1864, stated he was sick in the hospital at Louisville, Kentucky. No other military records were found for him.

Bailey, George M. - George M. Bailey enlisted in Company D of the 1st Alabama Cavalry, USV on May 23, 1863 at Corinth, Mississippi for a period of one year. He was appointed 1st Lieutenant by Special Order of Brigadier General Dodge. He was mustered in as 1st Lieutenant on May 23, 1863. The July and August 1863 Muster Roll listed him as being absent, on detached service by order of Brigadier General Dodge on July 14, 1863, until the January and February 1864 Muster Roll which listed him as being absent, on detached service as aide de camp by order of Brigadier General G.M. Dodge. Another January and February 1864 Muster Roll from Pulaski, Tennessee listed George as being absent with leave per Special Order 39, Headquarters D & A, Tennessee, February 19, 1864. His name appeared on the Returns for August 1863, stating he was detached for admission at West Point in Special Orders, Headquarters, Left Wing, 16th Army Corps dated August 29, 1863. George M. Bailey's name appeared on a Muster Roll of General and Staff and Detached Men on Duty at Headquarters, Left Wing, 16th Army Corps, stated he was absent with leave for 20 days from February 20, 1864. An Individual Muster Roll dated May 30, 1864, at Pulaski, Tennessee stated: Joined the regiment as 1st Lieutenant acting adjutant for most of the time until July 12, 1863, when I was detailed as A.D.C. to Brigadier General G.M. Dodge and have acted in that capacity up to date when mustered out by reason of expiration of term of service from May 30, 1864. This officer's account not settled with Government. A U.S. Military Telegraph dated February 19, 1864, Pulaski, Tennessee, stated the following: Lt. G.M. Bailey, A.D.C. on my staff has received notice that his father is sick and not expected to live. I respectfully request that a leave of absence be granted . His company reenlisted as veterans but he did not accompany it. Signed G.M. Dodge, Maj. Gen. with a note, See S.O. 39. A Note from Cairo, Illinois dated September 23, 1863, Order 210 or 216, stated: Requisition of George M. Bailey of the 1st Alabama Cavalry, from Cairo, Illinois to Memphis, Tennessee, Nature of Service, Joining Regiment by Order of Secretary of War, S.O. 406. The Muster and Descriptive Roll showed George as having been 20 years of age, 5'-9" tall, having a light complexion, blue eyes, light hair, and born in Illinois. A letter from Headquarters, Left Wing 16th Army Corps, Corinth, Mississippi, July 14, 1863, stated: General Order Number 8, 1st Lieutenant George M. Bailey, 1st Alabama Cavalry, is hereby announced as aide-de-camp. He will be obeyed and respected accordingly. By Order of Brigadier General G.M. Dodge. A Special Order Number 52, from Headquarters, Left Wing, Sixteenth Army Corps, Corinth, Mississippi, dated August 29, 1863, stated: 1st Lieutenant George M. Bailey, 1st Alabama Cavalry, will proceed without delay to Memphis, Tennessee, reporting to Lieutenant Henry Brimmore (?), Apt. Adjutant General, 16th Army Corps preparatory to proceeding to West Point for examination. By Order of Colonel Mersy, J.W. Barnes, Lieutenant and A.A.A. Gen. An Officers Casualty Sheet stated George M. Bailey resigned September 2, 1864.

According to descendants, George M. Bailey was born August 12, 1843, in Illinois to G. Burton Bailey and Manerva A. Brown, who were married October 20, 1842, in Lee County, Illinois. He died

August 30, 1909, and was buried in the Walnut Hill Cemetery in Council Bluffs, Pottawattamie County, Iowa. He was a member of the Nebraska GAR, Grand Army of the Republic, Post 174, Valley, Nebraska.

<u>Bailey, William B.</u> - A muster roll dated October 6, 1863, Glendale, Mississippi, stated William B. Baley, enlisted in Company E of the 1st Alabama Cavalry, USV at age 32 on June 24, 1863 as a Private at Glendale, Mississippi for a period of one year. However, another muster roll dated May and June 1863, listed him as being present and in Company D. His name was listed on the Returns for August 1863 as being absent and was reported to have deserted July 9, 1863.

<u>Bain, Alfred A.D.</u> - Alfred A.D. Bain, also spelled Baine, enlisted in Company I of the 1st Alabama Cavalry, USV as a Corporal on July 21, 1862 in Huntsville, Alabama for a period of 3 years. His brother, John D.H. Bain, also enlisted at the same time. He was shown as being 25 years of age. He was enrolled by Captain Bankhead. The Company Descriptive Book only shows him to have had a dark complexion, nothing else was answered on the form. Alfred Baine was among the first enlistees who were immediately shipped to Nashville, Tennessee and assigned to the 1st Middle Tennessee Cavalry and the 5th Tennessee Cavalry, US. He was assigned to Company D of the 1st Middle Tennessee Cavalry, which is what his Casualty Sheet shows. A note in his file stated: He died of disease on November 8, 1862, in Nashville, Tennessee, and that the books of the organization show no further information regarding his death.

Alfred A.D. and John D.H. Bain were brothers and sons of James E. Bain and Margaret Holmes, who were married May 30, 1829, in Limestone County, Alabama. Alfred married Mary Margaret Mabry and they had a son, James W. Bain. On the 1900 Lawrence County, Tennessee Census, Mary Margaret Bain was shown as widowed and stated she had had two children, with only one still living.

<u>Bain, John D.H.</u> - John D.H. Bain, also spelled Baine, enlisted in Company D of the 1st Alabama Cavalry, USV as a private on July 21, 1862 at Huntsville, Alabama. He was enrolled by Captain Bankhead for a period of 3years. His brother, Alfred A.D. Bain, also enlisted the same day and in the same company. John was shown as being 21 years of age. John died December 20, 1862 in Nashville, Davidson County, Tennessee, only about three weeks after his brother, Alfred, died. Another muster roll stated he died December 30, 1862. John, as was Alfred, above, one of the first enlistees who were immediately shipped to Nashville, Tennessee where they were merged with the 1st Middle Tennessee Cavalry, and the 5th Tennessee Cavalry. John was assigned to Company D of the 1st Middle Tennessee. The Company Descriptive Book shows John D.H. Bain to have been 21 years of age, 5'-9" tall, having a light complexion, blue eyes, light hair, born in Morgan County, Alabama, and a farmer by occupation.

<u>Baker, Henry Melvin</u> - Henry M. Baker enlisted in Company A of the 1st Alabama Cavalry, USV as a private on January 13, 1864, at Camp Davies, Mississippi, and was mustered in February 5, 1864, at Memphis, Tennessee. He was enrolled by Captain Shurtliff for a period of 3 years. The Company Muster and Descriptive Roll listed Henry as having been 33 years of age, 5'-10" tall, having a fair complexion, blue eyes, black hair, born in Ashe County, North Carolina, and a farmer by occupation. He was shown as having deserted on May 10, 1865, from Huntsville, Alabama. The January and February 1864 Muster Roll stated Henry had been assigned to duty with Company D from Company H by Regimental Order Number 47. The May and June 1864 Muster Roll stated he was absent on recruiting service. The July and August 1864 Muster Roll stated Henry was still absent, recruiting by order of Colonel Spencer, transferred from Company A, 1st Alabama Cavalry. The September and October 1864 Muster Roll stated he was absent, on recruiting service by order of Major Fairfield. Henry was listed as recruiting through December 1864, and in January and February 1865, he was on detached service in Decatur, Alabama. The May and June 1865 Muster Roll reported him to have deserted on June 1, 1865, at Huntsville, Alabama with one Remington Revolver and accoutrements. The Company Muster-Out Roll dated October 20, 1865, in Huntsville, Alabama stated Henry had been transferred August 1, 1864, in Rome, Georgia, per Regimental Order Number 69, to Company D for promotion. A Notation from the Record and Pension Division of the War Department

in Washington, DC, dated March 27, 1890, stated the following: Application for removal of the charge of desertion and for an honorable discharge has been denied. Another Notation from The Adjutant General's Office of the War Department in Washington, DC dated January 10, 1927, stated: Henry M. Baker, Private, Company D, 1st Alabama Cavalry, Book Mark A.G. 2201, stated: The charge of desertion of May 10, 1865, against the above named soldier has been removed and he is discharged to date May 10, 1865, under the provisions of the act of Congress approved March 2, 1889. So much of the records as show this soldier deserted any other date is erroneous. Discharge Certificate prepared in the War Department January 27, 1927, and filed. By authority of the Secretary of war.

Henry Melvin Baker was born August 20, 1840, in Ashe County, North Carolina to Hiram Baker and Nancy B. Saunders. On December 19, 1871, Henry married Martha J. Long, daughter of Charles R. and Rutha Katherine Hunnicutt. Martha was born September 12, 1839, and died August 17, 1894. Some descendants have stated that Martha Jane Long had previously married John Pickney Lunsford in Georgia but as they removed from Georgia to Alabama by oxen and wagons, John took pneumonia and died in Mississippi. Martha was going to try to make it back to Georgia with her two small sons, William Thomas and Charles Pinkney, but met Henry Baker, a widower, somewhere west of Hackleburg, in Marion County, Alabama and they were married. Henry M. Baker died June 28, 1929, and was buried in the Lindsey Cemetery outside of Hackleburg, Marion County, Alabama.

Baker, Peter - Peter Baker, also spelled Becker, enlisted in Company K of the 1st Alabama Cavalry, USV on July 24, 1862, as a private in Huntsville, Alabama. He was enrolled by Captain Bankhead for a period of 3 years. The Regimental Descriptive Book showed him to have been 44 years of age, 6' tall, having a light complexion, blue eyes, light hair, born in Jackson County, Tennessee, and a farmer by occupation. (Peter apparently gave his age as 44 in order to be accepted in the Union Army.) The Company Descriptive Book and the Company Muster-In Roll showed Peter to have been 57 years of age. Another Peter was among the first enlistees who were immediately shipped to Nashville, Tennessee and merged with the 1st Middle Tennessee Cavalry, and the 5th Tennessee Cavalry. Peter was assigned to the 5th Tennessee. In October 1862, Peter was listed as being on extra or daily duty as a company cook. A Company Muster Roll dated January 1, to June 30, 1863, showed him to have been absent, sent to hospital in Nashville, Tennessee January 6, 1863. His name appeared on the returns as follows: January and February 1863, showed him to have been on detached service January 14, as a nurse in a hospital in Nashville, Tennessee. August 1863 to February 1864, he was shown as being absent, sick in hospital in Nashville since January 6, 1863. April 1864, showed him to be sick in the hospital in Nashville, and in February 1863, he was dropped from the rolls, supposed to be dead. A Hospital Muster Roll from U.S.A. General Hospital Number 12, in Nashville showed Peter to have been present May and June 1863. It showed him as having been attached to Company E of the 1st Middle Tennessee Cavalry. The July and August 1863 Hospital Muster Roll for U.S.A. General Hospital Number 19, in Nashville listed Peter as a patient. His name appeared on the Muster Out-Roll dated July 19, 1865, as being discharged on Surgeon's Certificate of Disability. No official notice furnished the company commander at Nashville, 1863, date unknown. A Certificate of Disability of Discharge was issued to Peter Baker of the 1st Middle Tennessee Cavalry, Department of the Cumberland, Nashville, Tennessee, September 20, 1863, to be discharged by Major General Rosecrans. His Certificate of Disability Discharged stated: I certify that I have examined the said Peter Baker of Lt. Hornback's Company and find him incapable of performing the duties of a soldier because of a Ventral Hernia and old age (59 years) prior to enlistment, unfit for Invalid Corps, dated September 21, 1863 at Nashville, Tennessee

Baker, R. - The only record shown on this R. Baker was that he was in Company E and was shown as being absent, sick in July 1863.*

Baker, William H. - William H. Baker was shown as being a private in Company E, and being on detached service as a teamster in Vicksburg, Mississippi on January 25, 1864. The last entry in his records stated he was taken a prisoner of war in February 1865.*

Baker, William J. - William J. Baker enlisted in Company D of the 1st Alabama Cavalry, USV as a private on March 15, 1863 in Glendale, Mississippi for a period of one year. He was mustered in March 26, 1863 at Corinth, Mississippi The May and June 1863 Muster Roll listed him as being absent, on detailed duty as a secret scout. The July and August 1863 Muster Roll listed him as being absent, supposed to have been captured by the enemy, June 3, 1863. William was listed as being present on the September and October 1863 Muster Roll. He was mustered out March 25, 1864, in Decatur, Alabama due to expiration of term of service.

William J. Baker was born about 1834 in Georgia to James Thomas Baker and Mary Grogan or Cook, who married March 18, 1806, in Cabarrus County, North Carolina. William married Martha Rachael Chafin, sister to John H. and William Marion Chafin, who both served in the 1st Alabama Cavalry, USV. William and Martha were married November 1, 1854, in Cobb County, Georgia and had the following children: Sarah Ann, born May 22, 1855, died September 16, 1936; Mary Jane, born November 3, 1858; and James W. Chafin, born about 1859. William died April 30, 1864, and is buried in the Chattanooga National Cemetery, according to the descendants. Martha Rachel Chaffin Baker died November 17, 1863, in Marion County, Alabama.

Bakerstaff, John W. - Cards filed under John W. Bickerstaff, below.

Baley, William B. - Cards filed under William B. Bailey.

Ballard, Albert J. - Albert J. Ballard enlisted in Company M of the 1st Alabama Cavalry, USV as a private on December 9, 1863, at Camp Davies, Mississippi. He was enrolled by Capt. Lomax for a period of one year. He was mustered in the same day in Corinth. The January and February 1864 Muster Roll listed him as having deserted January 20, 1864 from Camp Davies. He was still shown as being deserted on the May and June 1864 Muster Roll with one Remington Revolver. The Descriptive List of Deserters states he lived in Marion County, Alabama and was supposed to have gone home. His name appeared on the Company Muster-Out Roll October 20, 1865 stating he owed the U.S. Government $43.56 for the revolver and possibly other equipment. The Company Descriptive Book showed Albert to have been 20 years of age, 5'-7" tall, having a light complexion, blue eyes, light hair, born in Pontotoc County, Mississippi, and a farmer by occupation.

Ballard, George W. - George W. Ballard enlisted in Company G of the 1st Alabama Cavalry, USV on May 16, 1863 in Chewalla, Tennessee for a period of one year at 17 years of age. He was mustered out November 26, 1863 from Memphis, Tennessee. No other records found.

Ballard, Levi, G. - Levi G. Ballard enlisted in Company A of the 1st Alabama Cavalry, USV on December 3, 1863 at Camp Davies, Mississippi for a period of 3 years. He was enrolled by J.S. DeVaney. Levi was mustered in February 5, 1864, at Memphis, Tennessee. His enlistment   was recorded as having been credited to Ripley, Chautauqua County, 31st Congressional District, in New York. Apparently he reenlisted on January 12, 1865 in Huntsville, Alabama and mustered in the same day at Nashville, Tennessee. He was paid $100 bounty. On July 30, 1865, he was reported to have deserted from Blountsville, Alabama. The Company Muster and Descriptive Roll listed Levi G. Ballard as having been 18 years of age, 5'-6" inches tall, having a fair complexion, blue eyes, light hair, born in Marion County, Alabama, and a farmer by occupation. On July 30, 1865, Levi was reported to have deserted from Blountsville, Alabama. The March and April 1865 Muster Roll listed Levi as being in Company H of the 1st Alabama Cavalry, USV, having been mustered in February 13, 1865, in Nashville, Tennessee. From June 1865 to August 1865, he was listed as being extra or daily duty as a regimental teamster. The July and August 1865 Muster Roll listed Levi as being absent without leave since August 1, 1865. He was listed on the Company Muster Roll of October 20, 1865, at 18 years of age. Levi was shown as owing the U.S. Government $70.46 for losing one Colt Revolver, one saber, one S Carbine, one G Sling, one belt and plate, one pistol cartridge box, one sling and wiper, one pistol holster, two spurs and thongs, one shelter tent. A note in his file stated Levi was not issued a discharge furnished at muster out of organization. A Notation from The Military Secretary's Office of the War Department dated December 16, 1904, stated: It has this Day, December 16, 1904, been determined from the War Department from the records from the above named man was not in the military service of the United States in this organization. A File, called File No. 2, stated Levi G. Ballard Volunteered at Huntsville, Alabama January 12, 1865, by J.W. DeVaney, Sergeant Major, 50th Regiment Illinois Infantry, $100 U.S. Bounty paid.

Ballew, William H. - William H. Ballew enlisted and was mustered into Company I of the 1st Alabama Cavalry, USV on July 21, 1862 at Huntsville, Alabama. He was enrolled by Captain Bankhead for a period of 3 years or the duration of the war. The Company Descriptive Book shows him to have been 20 years of age, 6' tall, having a light complexion, blue eyes, black hair, born in Polk County, Tennessee, and a blacksmith by occupation. William was one of the first enlistees who was shipped to Nashville, Tennessee and merged with the 1st Middle Tennessee Cavalry, US and the 1st Tennessee Cavalry, US. He was a Corporal in Company D of the 1st Middle Tennessee Cavalry. The Company Muster Roll for December 31, 1862 to June 30, 1863 stated William was missing in action April 28, 1863 from Day's Gap, Alabama. His name appeared on the Returns dated February 1863, as absent, on Courier Post. His name also appeared on the Returns dated June and July 1863, stating a loss, May 3, 1863, missing in action. He was listed on the Company Muster-Out Roll dated July 19, 1865 in Nashville and with Company D of the 1st Alabama Cavalry, USV. He was still missing in action April 28, 1863 from action at Day's Gap, Alabama.

Balton, Hugh L. - Cards filed under Hugh L. Bolton.

Bangers, I.M. - I. M. Bangers served in Company L and was on detached service in October 1864. No further information relative to this soldier was found, he may have been in a Northern regiment.*

Bardon, Michael - Michael Bardon, also spelled Barden, enlisted in Company C of the 1st Alabama Cavalry, USV on December 6, 1862, at Corinth, Mississippi for a period of one year, and was mustered in December 22, 1862 at Corinth. He was enrolled by D.R. Adams. The September and October 1863 Muster Roll stated Michael was a Corporal. He was mustered out December 17, 1863, at Memphis, Tennessee due to expiration of term of service. The Regimental Descriptive Book shows Michael Barden to have been 38 years of age, 5'-8" tall, having a fair complexion, dark eyes, dark hair, born in Longford, Ireland, and was a farmer by occupation.

Michael was born about 1824 in Longford, Ireland to John Bardon and Ann Flannigan. He married Kisiah Gallop, who was born about 1842 in Columbus, Lowndes County, Mississippi. Children of Michael and Kisiah Bardon were: Mary B., Frances M., Amanda, Sarah L., John A., James H., Bleecher Littleton, and Katie Bardon. Michael Bardon died August 14, 1889, and was buried in the Old Asbury Cemetery in Lamar County, Alabama. Kisiah died August 18, 1895.

Barker, Charles F. - Charles F. Barker enlisted and was mustered into Company I of the 1st Alabama Cavalry, USV on February 1, 1863, at Corinth, Mississippi for a period of one year. The Muster-In Roll listed him as a Sergeant. From April 1863 to August 1863, Charles F. Barker was on extra or daily duty as a Regimental Bugler. September 1863 to January 1864, he was on extra or daily duty as a wagon master. The September and October 1863 Muster Roll showed him to have been a 1st Duty Sergeant. He was discharged February 5, 1864 at Memphis, Tennessee at age 25 due to expiration of term of service. There was a Notation in his military records Record and Pension Division of the War Department, dated March 1, 1890, stating the following: Previously served in Company A of the 1st Kansas Volunteers under the name of Benjamin P. Curtis.

Charles Edward Barker, alias Benjamin Patton Curtis, was born April 4, 1842, in Fulton County, Illinois to John Barker and Eleanor Ellen Rutledge. He married Mary Elizabeth Pontius, daughter of Andrew Pontius and Anna Maria Baer, on April 19, 1866, in Macomb, Fulton County, Illinois. Children of Charles and Mary were: Nora E., born March 15, 1867, died February 17, 1870; Leonard W., born January 24, 1869, died June 8, 1927; Ira C., born May 19, 1871, died April 19, 1950; William Lee, born June 27, 1873, died January 1, 1951; Harry E., born September 17, 1875, died May 7, 1953; and Perry Barker, born March 8, 1878, died January 10, 1863. Charles E. Barker died October

21, 1920 in Effingham, Atchison County, Kansas and is buried in the Mount Olive Cemetery, Troy, Doniphan County, Kansas. Mary Elizabeth Barker died December 6, 1928 in Muscotah, Atchison County, Kansas

Barker, Thomas J. - Thomas J. Barker enlisted in Company D of the 1st Alabama Cavalry, USV on March 5, 1863, at Glendale, Mississippi, and was mustered in March 26, 1863, in Corinth, Mississippi. He was enrolled by W. Williams. The May and June 1863 Muster Roll listed him as being a 3rd Sergeant. The November and December 1863 Muster Roll stated he was promoted to 1st Sergeant on November 2, 1863. Thomas was mustered out March 25, 1863, at expiration of term of service on April 18, 1864. The Regimental Descriptive Book shows Thomas to have been 33 years of age, 6'-¾" tall, having a light complexion, blue eyes, sandy hair, born in Fayette County, Alabama, and a farmer by occupation. Thomas J. Barker's name appeared on the Returns as supposed prisoner in the hands of the enemy on October 26, 1863.

Thomas J Barker was born August 14, 1831, in Marion County, Alabama, to Ira and Nancy Barker. Ira Barker was a millwright who came to Marion County, Alabama from his birthplace in Massachusetts. He was murdered by his employer when Thomas was about 21. Thomas was the fourth of eleven children of Ira and Nancy Barker.

Thomas J Barker married Elizabeth McClung in Marion County, Alabama. In 1861 he acquired 240 acres of land in Walker and Winston Counties, which he farmed.

He enlisted in the 1st Alabama Cavalry March 5, 1863 at Glendale, Mississippi.

Other members of Thomas J Barker's family were involved in the Civil War:

(1) His sister Lucinda Barker's husband, Joel Jackson Curtis, was killed by the Confederate Home Guard at or near Jasper, Alabama for his refusal to join the Confederate Army.

(2) His brother William Barker enlisted in the 1st Alabama Cavalry on January 20, 1864, but was never mustered in and later was reported as "deserted". He was captured by the Confederate Home Guard and was eventually killed in Jasper, Alabama September 12, 1864.

(3) His brother Joseph Franklin Barker served in the Confederate Army, 16th Alabama Infantry. He was born November 29, 1843, and died July 26, 1909.

After 12 months service in the 1st Alabama Cavalry, Thomas J Barker was mustered out and returned to his home. He died January 25, 1906, in Winston County, Alabama. He is interred in the Barker Family Cemetery near Haleyville. (Family information written and submitted by Craig Burton Jr. Military records transcribed by the author.)

Barker, William M. - William M. Barker enlisted in Company C of the 1st Alabama Cavalry, USV as a private on January 20, 1864 at Corinth, Mississippi, the Company Descriptive Book stated he enlisted at Camp Davies, which was just out of Corinth, for a period of 3 years. He was enrolled by Captain Latty, but never mustered in. He was reported to have deserted March 3, 1864, from Memphis, Tennessee with one Remington Revolver, one Smith Carbine and accoutrements, Inft. Belt, pistol cartridge and cap box and pistol holder. William M. Barker's name appeared on the Company Muster-Out Roll dated October 20, 1865, stating he deserted at Memphis, Tennessee March 3, 1864, owing the U.S. Government $30.38 for one revolver, one Smith Carbine, and accoutrements. There was a Notation in the Record and Pension Office of the War Department June 9, 1897, stating the following: In the absence of any record evidence of this man's muster into service, he is not regarded by this Department as having been in the military service of the United States in this organization. The Company Descriptive Book showed Barker to have been 36 years of age, 5'-10" tall, having a fair complexion, blue eyes, sandy hair, born in Marion County, Alabama, and a farmer by occupation.

William M Barker was born about 1836, in Marion County, Alabama, to Ira and Nancy Barker. Ira Barker was a millwright who came to Marion County, Alabama from his birthplace in Massachusetts. He was murdered by his employer when William was about 17. William was the sixth of eleven children of Ira and Nancy Barker.

William Barker married Katherine Angeline Taylor, born 1839, daughter of Mathias Taylor, in Marion County, Alabama, on March 9, 1859. In 1859 he acquired 80 acres of land in Marion County which he farmed. Their children were: (1) James, born January 4, 1860, married Josephine Brown, died June 28, 1891; (2) John, born January 31, 1862, married Mamie Lear Trentham, died June 30, 1927; and (3) William, born May 23, 1864, married Millie Alice Tucker, died February 23, 1943.

The records of the 1st Alabama Cavalry indicate that William M Barker enlisted January 20, 1854, at Corinth, Mississippi. The record further indicates he was never "mustered in" and that he "deserted" March 3, 1864, at Memphis, Tennessee.

Other members of William Barker's family were involved in the Civil War:

(1) His sister Lucinda Barker's husband, Joel Jackson Curtis, was killed by the Confederate Home Guard at or near Jasper, Alabama for his refusal to join the Confederate Army.

(2) His brother Thomas J Barker enlisted in the 1st Alabama Cavalry on March 5, 1863, and served 12 months. He was born August 14, 1841, and died January 25, 1906.

(3) His brother Joseph Franklin Barker served in the Confederate Army, 16th Alabama Infantry. He was born November 29, 1843, and died July 26, 1909.

There are conflicting accounts of the events leading to the death of William Barker, but the end result was that he died September 12, 1864, in Jasper, Alabama.

In May, 1875 an Application for Pension on behalf of William M Barker was filed in Marion County, Alabama, by his widow, Angeline Barker. It stated her maiden name and age, her husband's name, their marriage date and place, the names and birth dates of their three children, and a statement that William M Barker died in Jasper, Alabama, "by being shot by the rebels". Affidavits filed with the pension application included statements that William Barker was brought to the Jasper, Alabama jail by the Confederate Home Guard, and later was taken from the jail by a detachment of Confederate soldiers, led off and never returned.

Angeline's claim was eventually completely denied, the reason given was that "the man deserted before muster-in and is not considered as an enlisted soldier".

William Barker's widow, Angeline, married Elias Chaffin September 15, 1876, in Marion County, Alabama. Their two children were Elias Posey Chaffin and Elijah Allen Chaffin. She died March 3, 1911, in Lamar County, Alabama. The burial place of William Barker remains unknown. (Family information written and submitted by Craig Burton Jr. Military records transcribed by the author.)

Barnes, Morgan C. - Morgan Cleveland Barnes enlisted in Company D of the 1st Alabama Cavalry, USV as a private on June 26, 1863, at Glendale, Mississippi at age 18. He was enrolled by Jude H. Shurtleff for a period of one year. The March and April 1864 Muster Roll listed Morgan as having been absent, sick in the hospital at Nashville, Tennessee. He was mustered out July 27, 1864. at Rome, Georgia at expiration of term of service. A Notation from the Adjutant General's Office of the War Department dated July 3, 1888, stated: Application of certificate in lieu of lost discharge. Bookmark noted for reference only. Morgan C. Barnes' name appeared on the Returns dated October 1863, supposed prisoner of war in the hands of the enemy October 26, 1863, which would have been the Battle of Vincent's Crossroads, Alabama; March 1864, absent, sick in hospital in Memphis, Tennessee; April 1, 1864, absent, on detached service; July 1864, discharged, term of service expired July 28, 1864. at Rome, Georgia. The Regimental Descriptive Book listed Morgan C. Barns as having been 18 years of age, 5'-10" tall, having a light complexion, blue eyes, light hair, born in Cleveland, North Carolina, and a farmer by occupation.

Morgan Cleveland Barnes was born September 30, 1844, in Cleveland, North Carolina to Miles Reeves Barnes and Margaret Lucretia Ford. On July 20, 1866, Morgan Barnes was married to Martha Adelia Beaver in Itawamba County, Mississippi. Children from this marriage were: Florence B., Lucy E., Ida P., Ada S., Ollie F., Noonan B., and Clarence Eric Barnes. Morgan Cleveland Barnes died June 2, 1929 in Rara Avis, Itawamba County, Mississippi and was buried at the Providence Baptist Church Cemetery in Itawamba County. His wife, Martha, died August 10, 1930 in Red Bay, Franklin County, Alabama

On May 29, 1912, in a Declaration for Pension, he stated he was 67 years old and besides his fourteen-months' service in the 1st AL Cav., USV, after he mustered out of the US Army, he joined the US Navy in Cairo, Illinois on or about Feb. 15, 1865, was discharged Aug. 5, 1865, and served for six months on the "Great Western" Receiving Ship. He was discharged August 5, 1865, at Mound City, Illinois. His Descriptive File states he was 5'-10" tall, had a light complexion, blue eyes, light hair, and his occupation was a farmer. His Pension Certificate was No. 22,175, and he was able to sign his name to the affidavits.

(The Great Western Receiving Ship had previously been used as a side-wheel steamer. It was built at Cincinnati, Ohio, in 1857 and was purchased by the War Department February 10, 1862. She was transferred to the Navy September 30, 1862, but had been used since her purchase by the Western Flotilla. In July 1864 she was sent to Cairo, Illinois, the great Union naval base in the west, to act as a receiving ship. The Great Western was transferred as a receiving ship in Mound City, Illinois, in March 1865, and was subsequently sold at auction there in November 29, 1865.)

On July 16, 1812, Barnes filed another Declaration for Pension stating he enlisted in Company D of the 1st Alabama Cavalry, USV on June 23, 1863, at Rome, Georgia and discharged August 1, 1864, War Department states he mustered out July 27, 1864, in Rome, Georgia. The affidavit was witnessed by R.C.(or G.) Douglas. (sic)

On January 12, 1921, his disability was listed as V.H.D. (Valvular heart disease) Mitral Valve Insufficiency Varicose Veins in feet and legs. This affidavit was witnessed by C. Barnes and Noonan B. Barnes of Red Bay, AL. Morgan's address was shown as R.F.D. No. 2, Red Bay, Alabama. (sic)

Morgan C. Barnes, in an undated affidavit, although it was stamped received by the US Pension Office, stated the following: (sic) "I Morgan C. Barnes vol. entered in the First Ala. Cav. June 23 -1863 for twelve months near Corinth, Miss. And served until July the last 1864 and was discharged. And then I joined the U.S. Navy and shipped aboard of the Great Western Receiving Ship in Cairo, Illinois about Feb between 15 and the first of March 1865 and was transferred to the Fort Hindman and served until August the 5th 1865 and was discharged at Mounds City Illinois. I never done any service in the Civil War only between those dates mentioned above. Those dates are as I recollect as it has bin along time since the Civil War."

On November 13, 1897, Joshua D. Creel signed a Deposition in Salem, Fulton County, Arkansas for Morgan C. Barnes concerning Barnes' request for pension. The Deposition stated the following: (sic)

"I was a Private in Company D. 1st Alabama Cavalry - I remember Cleve Barnes well - Don't remember of any sickness, injury or wound he may have incurred while in the service. As I recollect him he was nearly always on duty.

Yes, I was with that scouting party that cold New Year - Jan 1, 1864. We were out some four or five days through Collierville, Tennessee a day or so later and returned to camp at Camp Davis, near Corinth, Miss. I don't remember of any thing happening to Barnes on that said Frostbitten feet: Well if he says so I don't doubt it but I don't remember it myself and hearing his statement does not refresh my memory - either as to the frost bitten feet, varicose veins or some wound. Barnes was a good and honorable man and if he claims he contracted said ailments I don't doubt it in the least. I have read this and it is correct." Signed - Joshua D. Creel

B.Z. (or Y.) Stone to Hiram Smith stated the following: "Bexar PO Marion Co., AL, January 9, 1890, Dear Sir, I take pleasure in writing. Myself and M.C. Barnes was in the 1st regiment of Alabama Cavalry, Co. D in the US. We was on a scout for some time the latter part of December 1863 and the first of January 1864 and when we returned to camp, M.C. Barnes had his feet frosted badly and ever since that his feet frets and burns in hot weather. The veins are very large in both feet and legs. He is disabled about one third from manual labor." Yours Truly, B.Z. or Y. Stone

I forgot we was camped at Camp Davis (Davies) Miss. We went south west for 3 days around in black land then back in Tennessee close to Jackson then back through Purdy to Corinth then to LaGrange at the cars and then south and west for some time the weather got so cold and bad we had to go to camp, back near Corinth, Miss. We was after Gen. Forest. (This was not typed sic as it was too difficult to read)

On May 19, 1897, John A. Snelling of Slacking Precinct, Saunders County, Nebraska, signed a Deposition for Morgan C. Barnes stating the following: "I am 65 years old, Farmer, my post office address is Wahoo Nebraska. I served as a 2nd Lieutenant of Company "D" 1st Alabama Cavalry from March 1863 to March 1864. I served to July 1864. I helped to recruit the regiment. I first knew the claimant in spring of 1863. I wrote you all that I can remember about him (Barnes)- I think that he is the man that we had wounded at a place between Glendale and Burnsville Mississippi About June or

July of 1863. We had a man wounded in the leg there but I am not good in remembering names. This Barnes was a brave young fellow, but I cant make sure that I have the name of the man right."

Question: Have you any remembrance of the claimant having had his feet frosted or of having the measles or throat or lung trouble in service?

Answer: "No, I have no knowledge of any of that. There was but one instance of any of our boys being frosted – that was the cold New Years – we had some who were frosted on that day, and we had a few cases of measles, but I can't remember that he is one of the men who had the measles. The day before the cold New Year- Januray 1, 1864, we were out on a raid trying to cut off a train that some of Forest forces had gathered up in Tenn. And were trying to get south – and we had been out 4 or 5 days trying to recapture that train when the cold snap overtook us, but my horse gave out Dec. 31, 1863 and I started back to Corinth by train. I was in camp when the boys got back and a good many had their ears and fingers frosted and had suffered terribly from the cold. I can't recall that Morgan C. Barnes was on that raid. No I don't recall that he suffered from varicose veins, and can't recall that he had a cough or lung trouble, although that was a prevalent trouble with our men. I don't remember that he had any sore mouth in the army. I see I am mistaken about it being Morgan C. Barnes, that was wounded. I can't remember the claimant's condition at discharge. I have heard you read the claimants statement and while I believe his statements I don't remember any of his disabilities in service. I am not related and not interested (in his pension). I have understood your questions and my answers are _____ recorded." Signed - John A. Snelling, Special Examiner, W.W. Macy.

An Affidavit dated January 12, 1921, on stationary of the American Red Cross US General Hospital No. 6 at Fort McPherson, GA stated the following: "This is to certify that I am the attendant of the said Morgan C. Barnes. I see regular to his wants each and every day. That is to his fire wood, milling, and all out door work which requires about ¼ to ½ of my time, approximately." Signed Noonan B. Barnes

PS - My relation to claimant is son. Sworn to before me this 12th day of Jan. 1921 GS Almerson, J.P.

There were two other long Depositions signed by James Edgar Railsback and Elizabeth Mitchell stating almost the same thing as the other affiants.

Barnes stated since leaving the service he had lived in Rara Avis, in Itawamba Co., MS.

Zadoc L. Weatherford, M.D. signed Barnes Death Certificate stating he died of Apoplexy (Cerebral) and contributed "Old Age". His date of death was listed as June 2, 1929.

An Affidavit from the Navy Department, Bureau of Navigation in Washington, DC stated on 15 October 1929 that the records show that Morgan C. Barnes enlisted in the navy February 26, 1865 at Cairo, Ill., served in the "Great Western," "Tennessee", and "Fort Hindman" to August 5, 1865, when discharged, as landsman. The termination of his service was of honorable nature. Signed - R.H. Leigh, Chief of Bureau.

An Affidavit Supporting Burial Claim, dated July 30, 1929, stated Morgan C. Barnes was 84 years old, lived in Red Bay, Alabama, buried June 3, 1929, at Providence Cemetery and the citizens (neighbors) took care of his body. It was signed by Martha Barnes' mark and Witnessed by J.T. Beasley and Z.L. Weatherford of Red Bay, Alabama.

Morgan C. Barnes' wife, Martha, filed for a Widow's Pension July 1, 1929 and was allowed $40 per month. She was shown as over 75 years of age at the time. Her pension was suspended when Check #16583501 was returned on August 31, 1836, due to her death.

Ruben S. Gray, age 50, Marion F. Wright, age 66, Wm. M. Chaffin, age 78, and Christopher Lee Pate, age 82, all stated they had known Martha Barnes for a number of years. Zadoc L. Weatherford, M.D. stated he was a regular practicing physician, age 41, address Red Bay, Alabama and he attended Morgan C. Barnes during his last illness and that he died June 2, 1929. He stated he graduated from University of Tennessee Medical Department on June 6, 1914.

A letter to the U.S. Veteran's Bureau from Martha Barnes dated September 23, 1929, stated there were no funeral directors in the town of Red Bay, Alabama and that the robe in which this old soldier was buried was purchased from McPeters Home, Corinth, Mississippi, bill of which had already been properly rendered. The casket was purchased from Red Bay Hardware Company and the bill for the casket had also been rendered. Bill for robe was $15 and Casket $85, making a total of $100. They also stated the citizens (neighbors) buried the soldier and there was no bill for that service or the services of the Minister.

Morgan C. Barnes is buried at Providence Baptist Church Cemetery in Itawamba County, Mississippi....between Fulton, Mississippi and Red Bay, Alabama.

Barnes, William - William Barnes enlisted in Company C of the 1st Alabama Cavalry, USV on December 10, 1863, at Corinth, Mississippi for a period of one year. He was enrolled by D.R. Adams. One of the muster rolls stated he was absent without leave since February 20, 1863, but wasn't dated. The March and April 1863 Muster Roll stated he had been absent without leave since February 20, 1863. The January and February 1864 Hospital Muster Roll from Overton U.S.A. General Hospital in Memphis, Tennessee listed him as being present, but did not say if it was a patient or working. He was still listed as present in same hospital through June 1864. William's name appeared on the Returns as follows: March and April 1863, absent without leave; May 1863, returned to his command May 18th; August to December 1863, on extra duty as nurse in hospital August 1, 1863. The Regimental Descriptive Book listed William as having been 22 years of age, 5'-7" tall, having a fair complexion, blue eyes, light hair, born in Bibb County, Alabama, and a farmer by occupation. William Barnes mustered out February 1, 1864, at Memphis, Tennessee on account of expiration of term of service.

Barnett, James - Only one card was found for James Barnett which was filed at the end of the last roll of microfilm of the 1st Alabama Cavalry, USV records. It recorded him as enlisting in Company F of the 1st Alabama Cavalry, USV and stated he was on detached secret service in August 1863. No further information relative to this soldier was found.*

Barnett, James W. - James W. Barnett enlisted in Company H of the 1st Alabama Cavalry, USV on April 1, 1865, in Stevenson, Alabama for a period of three years. He was enrolled by J.W. DeVaney, and was mustered in April 5, 1865, in Nashville, Tennessee. The Muster and Descriptive Roll showed James as being 19 years of age, 6' tall, having a fair complexion, blue eyes, light hair, born in Marshall County, Alabama, and a farmer by occupation. The May and June 1865 Muster Roll stated he was absent without leave since May 8, 1865. The July and August 1865 Muster Roll reported him as having deserted May 8, 1865, from Huntsville, Alabama. No discharge was furnished to James Barnett upon muster out of regiment on October 20, 1865.

Barnett, Jobe - Jobe Barnett enlisted in Company F of the 1st Alabama Cavalry, USV on June 27, 1863, at Corinth, Mississippi, as a corporal for a period of one year. He was enrolled by Captain L.W. Pierce and was mustered in August 13, 1863, at Corinth. In July and August 1863, he was shown as being absent with leave at home near Adamsville, Tennessee. Job was listed as being absent sick in Winston County, Alabama from October 24, 1863, through August 1865, left on raid by order of Surgeon Steward, assigned to duty from one-year of organization of 1st Alabama Cavalry by order of Colonel Spencer July 25, 1864. No discharge was issued on muster out of organization. Jobe Barnett died of disease on March 18, 1864, in prison hospital in Richmond, Virginia while a prisoner of war. (Apparently Jobe Barnett was captured during the Battle of Vincent's Crossroads in Red Bay, Alabama.) The Company Descriptive Book shows Job to have been 35 years of age, 6' tall, having a fair complexion, blue eyes, light hair, born in Marshall County, Alabama, and a shoemaker by occupation. He was admitted to Hospital Number 21, in Richmond, Virginia on March 3, 1864, where he died March 18, 1864, of chronic bronchitis. Jobe Barnett was buried in the Richmond National Cemetery, in Virginia.

Barnett, Lewis - Lewis Barnett enlisted in Company E of the 1st Alabama Cavalry, USV on February 2, 1863, at Sulphur Springs, probably in Alabama, for a period of one year. He was mustered in March 1, 1863, at Corinth, Mississippi. The May and June 1863 Muster Roll states Lewis was absent, taken prisoner of war, between Glendale and Burnsville, Mississippi on June 11, 1863. The September and October 1863 Muster Roll stated Lewis Barnett had died. He was paroled at City Point, Virginia July 2, 1863, reported at Camp Parole July 3, 1863, and died at Camp Parole, Maryland on July 11, 1863, of acute diarrhea at age 18. The Record of Death and Interment states Lewis Barnett was buried in Grave Number 131 in Ashgrove Cemetery. He had been in Ward Number 1, Bed Number 1l. His residence before enlistment was listed as Hardin County, Tennessee, married, widow living in Monticello, Hardin County, Tennessee. He was buried July 12, 1863. He was re-interred in the Annapolis National Cemetery, Annapolis, Maryland.

Barnett, Robert - Robert Barnett enlisted in Company F, and was recorded as being absent a prisoner of war in April 1865. No further information relative to this soldier was found.*

Barnett, Thomas - Thomas Barnett enlisted in Company B of the 1st Alabama Cavalry, USV on January 10, 1863, at Glendale, Mississippi. He was enrolled by P.A. Sternberg, for a period of one year. He was mustered in January 22, 1863, at Corinth, Mississippi. The July and August 1863 Muster Roll stated Thomas was absent, transferred to Company A by Major Micajah J. Fairfield on October 6, 1863. From February 1863 to April 1863, Thomas was shown as extra or daily duty as a scout per order of Lieutenant Colonel Morrell. Thomas Barnett's name appeared on the Returns as having been in arrest at Corinth, on November 24, 1863. The Regimental Descriptive Book listed Thomas as having been 18 years of age, 6' tall, having light complexion, black eyes, light hair, born in Lawrence County, Alabama, and a farmer by occupation. Charges and specifications against Thomas Barnett, Private, Company A, 1st Regiment Alabama Cavalry – 1st Charge, Robbery, 1st Specification, In this that Thomas Barnett Private of Company A of 1st Regiment of Alabama Cavalry did on or about the 11th day of November 1863, with several others, (said Barnett being the leader) entered the houses of citizens Burcham Larkin Carthey and Isaac Richardson and did in a very boisterous manner demand their money and other valuables, broke open a safe bureau drawers and took them from Handkerchief pieces of ribbon ___. The said Barnett also did enter the housing of Short Graves and Ga___ and take five sides of leather , all this about five-miles from Camp Davies, Mississippi. Charge 2nd, Conduct presidential to good order and military discipline. Specification 2nd – in this that the said Thomas Barnett , Private of Company A of the 1st Regiment Alabama Cavalry, did on or about the 11th Day of November 1863, entered the houses of Burcham S. Carthey and Isaac Richardson and did while in said houses, curse and abuse and kick over furniture, and otherwise behaving very rude and noisy, all this about five miles from Camp Davies, Mississippi. Signed Frank G. Burdick, Captain, Company A, 1st Alabama Cavalry, USV, November 16, 1863. Court proceedings and depositions on microfilm. Thomas was mustered out on December 22, 1863 at Memphis, Tennessee.

The 1880 Tishomingo County, Mississippi shows Thomas "Tom" W. and Mary Bennett to have the following children: Marshal S., age 16; William, age 14; Thomas, age 13; George, age 11; Sallie, age 8, and Tabitha Barnett, age 4, all born in Mississippi, and Tom and Mary were born in Alabama. It showed Thomas to be a Com. and Forwarding Agent

Barnet, William - William Barnet enlisted in Company F, and was recorded as being absent, a prisoner of war taken by enemy. No further information relative to this soldier was found.*

Barny, Francis A. - Francis A. Barny, also spelled Burney, enlisted in Company B as a private. See Francis A. Burney.

Barren, Joseph M. - Joseph M. Barren enlisted in Company K of the 1st Alabama Cavalry, USV on November 28, 1862, at Glendale, Mississippi for a period of one year. He was mustered in December 31, 1862, in Corinth, Mississippi. On December 18, 1862, he was promoted to 3rd Sergeant of Company A. He was mustered out November 7, 1863, at Memphis, Tennessee due to expiration of term of service at age 20.

Barraun, George L. - George L. Barraun died of smallpox on November 6, 1863, in a post hospital in Corinth, Mississippi. No further information relative to this soldier was found.*

Barren, Thomas A. J. - Thomas A.J. Barren enlisted in Company K of the 1st Alabama Cavalry, USV on November 15, 1862, at Corinth, Mississippi for a period of one year. He was mustered in December 31, 1862, at Corinth. The January and February 1863 Muster Roll showed him to have been

4th Corporal in Company A. Thomas Barren died June 29, 1863, at Glendale, Mississippi. The Inventory of Effects showed Thomas A.J. Barren to have been 47 years of age, 5'-7" tall, having a dark complexion, gray eyes, dark hair, born in Jasper County, Georgia, and a farmer by occupation. He died in the regimental hospital at Glendale, Mississippi of dysentery. His effects included one hat, one great coat, one pair of trowsers, one pair of boots, and one blanket. The form was signed by Captain Frank C. Burdick.

Testimony of Thomas A.J. Barren as published in the *Nashville Daily Union* in Nashville, Tennessee on March 4, 1863, under "Reign of Terror in the South" stated, "I live in Marion County, Alabama. The rebels have burned my house with furniture, beds, bedding, clothing, and etc; Also, 3 bales of cotton, two-hundred bushels of corn, fodder, etc." Sworn to and subscribed before me at Glendale, Mississippi, this 24th day of January, 1863 and signed by J.W. Stewart.

Barren, Wiley J. - Wiley J. Barren, also spelled Barron, enlisted in Company K of the 1st Alabama Cavalry, USV on November 28, 1862, at Glendale, Mississippi for a period of one year. He was mustered in December 24, 1862, in Corinth, Mississippi and later transferred to Company A. The March and April 1863 Muster Roll listed him as being absent with leave. He was mustered out December 22, 1863, at Glendale, Mississippi. Barren's name appeared on the Returns for March 1863 as being with the Refugees at Purdy, Tennessee for 20 days from March 7, 1863. In April and May 1863, he was shown as being absent with leave at Jackson, Tennessee. The Returns stated he was discharged November 7, 1863 from Glendale for expiration of term of service. Barron was court martialed for horse stealing and larceny on or about September 14, 1863, from Glendale, Mississippi.

Charge 1 – Specification in this that the said Wiley J. Barren, Private, Company A of the 1st Alabama Cavalry Volunteers, did feloniously steal, take and carry away one horse, the property of the United States with intent to appropriate the same to his own use. All this at Glendale, Mississippi on or about September 14, 1863.

Charge II – Specification in this that the said Wiley J. Barren, Private, Company A of the 1st Alabama Cavalry Volunteers did steal and carry away one halter, the property of the United States with intent to appropriate the same to his own use. All this at Glendale, Mississippi on or about September 14, 1863. Signed P.A. Sternberg, Commander Company B, 1st Alabama Cavalry. Witnessed by Harper Lewis and William Jones.

Barren, William - William Barren enlisted in Company K of the 1st Alabama Cavalry, USV on December 5, 1862, at Glendale, Mississippi for a period of one year. He was mustered in December 31, 1862, at Corinth, Mississippi. He also served in Company A. The January and February 1863 Muster Roll stated he was absent, sick in hospital at Corinth, Mississippi, but was present for the March and April 1863 Muster Roll. Barren was mustered out December 22, 1863. A Notation in his file from the Adjutant General's Office of the War Department dated December 29, 1883, stated "Application for certificate in lieu of Discharge was furnished.

Barrett, George W. - George W. Barrett enlisted in Company A of the 1st Alabama Cavalry, USV on January 4, 1864, at Camp Davies, Mississippi for a period of 3 years. The Company Muster Roll dated February 29, 1864, reported him as having deserted from Camp Davies on January 24, 1864. He was shown on the Descriptive List of Deserters stating he deserted with his horse, equipment and arms. His name was listed on the Company Muster-Out Roll dated October 20 1865, as owing the U.S. Government $34.98 for one horse, saddle, bridle, carbine belt and accoutrements complete. The Company Descriptive Book shows Barrett to have been 18 years of age, 5'-2" tall, having a fair complexion, black eyes, dark hair, born Lawrence County, Alabama, and a farmer by occupation.

Bartholomew, Rion - The only thing known about Rion Bartholomew is that he was a Private in Company I of the 1st Alabama Cavalry, USV and was discharged June 28, 1865, due to a disability.*

Bartlett, John - John Bartlett enlisted in Company F of the 1st Alabama Cavalry, USV as a private on April 3, 1863, in Corinth, Mississippi for a period of one year. He was enrolled by Captain Pierce. He was reported to have deserted from Glendale, Mississippi on September 10, 1863. The

Company Descriptive Book shows him to have been 24 years of age, 5'-9" tall, having a light complexion, blue eyes, red hair, born in Wayne County, Illinois, and a farmer by occupation. The Company Descriptive Book also shows Bartlett to have been captured and taken prisoner by the enemy on September 11, 1863, near Burnsville.

Barton Brothers, Gilford, James, Jonathan, Madison & William

There were five Barton brothers who served in the 1st Alabama Cavalry, USV, and they were sons of Willis Barton and Margaret Nancy Martin, who were married about 1824 in Douglas, Georgia . Willis Barton was born September 22, 1803, in South Carolina and died September 4, 1891, in Winston County, Alabama. It was said that Willis Barton never knew that his wife, Margaret, died and that Margaret never knew that Willis had died, since they died within two days of each other. Margaret was born March 11, 1806, in Georgia and died September 6, 1891, in Winston County, Alabama. Children of Willis and Margaret were: James Alexander, born December 26, 1825, died April 6, 1914; Jonathan Marion, born December 26, 1830, died April 17, 1910; Gilford M., born January 26, 1840, died August 1, 1915; James Alexander, born December 7, 1826, died April 6, 1914; Madison Matthew, born August 26, 1837, died in 1905; William H., born March 15, 1835, died September 1, 1864; Sarah Jarome, born September 30, 1828, died June 28, 1879; Delilah M., born January 6, 1833, died March 2, 1897; Nancy, born June 23, 1842, died in 1862; Joseph, born January 20, 1849, died March 19, 1907; Margaret J., born June 7, 1851, died May 19, 1928; and Julia Ann Barton, born April 8, 1855, died August 27, 1928.

Barton and Hyde: The Move West
By Peter J. Gossett

It was turning cold over in Hall County, Georgia, in late 1859 when our Barton's decided to take a long trip west. No one knows what pressed them to leave during the cold months, but they sometimes woke up in the morning with frost in their hair! Their destination was Northwest Alabama, mainly Winston County, where the land was poor, rocky, and sold cheap. There is no doubt that our Barton clan traveled with a wagon train, for there were many that settled in Winston County from Hall County, GA, at the same time. According to Timber Ridge Baptist Church records, Willis, "Margrete," and Delilah Barton were granted letters of dismission in October of 1859. The main group of family members arrived in Winston County on Christmas Eve day in 1859. The reason they waited until so late was because one of Willis' daughters, Sarah, was due to deliver a baby so they waited until Alfred Marion Hyde was born on October 7, 1859. They had a little dog who walked all the way from Hall County, GA to Winston County, AL with them. Another daughter, Delilah Barton, was being courted by young Francis Harris. The two parted unhappily. Francis waited around a few days and couldn't stand being away from Delilah any longer so he packed a few belongings, left family and friends, and rode after them. The Bartons could see a cloud of dust in the far distance and hear the thundering of hooves. It made them uneasy. Finally Francis showed up at camp. He continued on to Winston with them. When they arrived in Winston County, there was no place for them to stay so they immediately had to start building shelters. (Sources for this story include Debby Black and her book Barton Quest)

The five sons who served in the 1st Alabama Cavalry, USV were Jonathan, Gilford, James, Madison and William H. All five served in Company L under Captain Sanford Tramel and then Captain Edwards. They had three brothers-in-law: F.C. Harris, Jesse D. Hyde and Thomas H. Blackstock who also served in this regiment.

Barton, Gilford M. - Enlisted in Company L as a Private at age twenty-five on September 25, 1863, in Fayette County, Alabama for a period of 3 years. He was enrolled by Captain Trammel. He was mustered in the same day at Glendale, Mississippi. The Muster Roll dated September 30 through October 31, 1863, stated he was absent with leave. Another muster roll stated he enrolled for one year. In November 1863, Gilford was listed as being absent, left sick in Alabama by order of Colonel George E. Spencer. Barton was mustered out on September 28, 1864, in Rome, Georgia due to expiration of term of service. The Company Descriptive Book showed Gilford M. Barton to have been 25 years of age, 6' tall, having a fair complexion, blue eyes, dark hair, born in Hall County, Georgia, and a farmer by occupation.

Gilford was born January 26, 1840, in Hall County, Georgia and died August 1, 1915, in Tuscaloosa County, Alabama. He married Nancy Jane Weaver about 1858 in Hall County, Georgia, and they had the following children: General Bewell, born July 12, 1862, and died February 6, 1951; John Mace, born January 1864, died 1918; Joseph H., born August 10, 1865, died February 26, 1936; William Harrison, born 1868, died 1869; Sennie Jane (or June), born 1870, died 1898; Willis Andrew "Andy", born December 9, 1872, died January 17, 1963; James Harrison, born October 1873, died 1967; Alonzo Irving, born March, 1876, died December 25, 1969; Martha Caroline, born June 8, 1878; and Virgin M. "Virgie Barton, born July 1883 and died June 1967. Gilford is buried in the Sardis Baptist Church Cemetery in Winston County, Alabama. (See additional family information above)

<u>Barton, James Alexander</u> – James Alexander Barton enlisted in Company L of the 1st Alabama Cavalry, USV, on September 25, 1863, in Fayette County, Alabama, for a period of one year. He was enrolled by Captain Trammel. He mustered in the same day in Glendale, Mississippi. James was a blacksmith for the Union and was discharged September 28, 1864, in Rome Georgia due to expiration of term of service. He was paid in full in Nashville, Tennessee by Major Holt. The Company Descriptive Book listed James as having been 37 years of age, 6'-1" tall, having a fair complexion, blue eyes, dark hair, born in Hall County, Georgia and a blacksmith by occupation.

James A. Barton was born December 7, 1825 in Hall County, Georgia and on June 5, 1848, he married Martha Jane Garrard, daughter of James Garrard and Rebecca Pinnon. Children of James and Martha Barton were: Willis Monroe, born May 4, 1849, died March 18, 1936; Sunnah M., born September 13, 1852, died October 22, 1921; James Marion "Dee", born January 1, 1854; died May 2, 1937; Rebecca Ann "Becky", born July 4, 1856, died April 25, 1942; Margurite; Mary Melissa, born May 22, 1862, died April 26, 1946; Sarah Drucilla, born February 16, 1866, died February 6, 1914; Eva Marion, born August 31, 1868, died May 11, 1932; Martha Savannah, born March 11, 1870, died January 14, 1923; and Noah J. Barton, born December 19, 1873, died December 1, 1956; James A. Barton died April 6, 1914 in Franklin County, Alabama and was buried in the Mount Zion Cemetery, 6 miles from Red Bay, Alabama. (See additional family information above)

<u>Barton, Jonathan Marion</u> - Jonathan Marion Barton enlisted as a Sergeant in Company L on September 25, 1863, in Fayette County, Alabama, at the age of 33. He was mustered in the same day at Glendale, Mississippi, a camp about ten miles outside of Corinth, Mississippi. He mustered out September 28, 1864, in Rome Georgia. He was married to Hannah Ann Blackstock and had three brothers and two brothers-in-law who served in this regiment. He was a Sheriff, while William J. Barton was a Sheriff's Deputy. William had arrested a criminal, apparently around Jonathan's house. While Jonathan was outside, his wife, Hannah Barton, heard a commotion in the living room. She rushed in to see what was going on and found William J. Barton dead on the floor and the criminal had escaped. Jonathan is buried in the Sardis #1 Baptist Church Cemetery in Winston County, Alabama. In a claim filed by Jonathan Barton with the Southern Claims Commission after the war, he stated, "I was threatened, shot at, and molested by the rebel soldiers on account of my union principals or sentiments. They burned my still, took one mare, two mules, and a buggy, knocked the heads out of my whiskey barrels after taking what they wanted, and turned out the balance. They threatened to kill me and burn my dwelling if I did not come in and give up to them. The still house was burned and the mare and two mules and buggy taken by the rebels on the 15th March 1863, at my house..."

Francis C. Harris stated, "The Rebels threatened to burn him out and did burn his still house, took his whisky what they wanted and poured out the balance. The Rebels took from claimant a mare, two mules, a good buggy and other plunder, and used and destroyed his meat and corn, and tried to kill him by shooting at him. I was in hearing of the guns when they were firing at him.

His sympathies were for the Union and by feeding Union men and soldiers. I knew he done all he could for the Union cause. He piloted men through to the Union lines, done all he could in recruiting the Union army with good and true soldiers.

Jonathan stated in his Southern Claim that he turned over five head of horses to QM Gray of the 1st Alabama Cavalry volunteers and saw him take them in charge. I furnished the pork and rations to U.S. soldiers on detached service. Roan mare, corn, fodder, bacon, lard, meal, flour, syrup, potatoes, pork, peas and honey was taken by General Wilson's command.

The five horses turned over to Quartermaster Gray would average from five to seven years of age, in height from fourteen to fifteen hands high. They were turned over at Camp Davis, Mississippi; the horses of good quality, good saddle horses, and were used in the regiment as cavalry horses. They were at that time worth one hundred and fifty dollars each in United States money to the best of my knowledge. The horses were turned over to Quartermaster Gray in November 1863 to best of my recollection. The horses was turned over and used in 1st Regiment Alabama Cavalry Volunteers commanded by Colonel George E. Spencer. I taken the horses from my own home voluntarily and turned them over as I have said before, with expectation of receiving some pay at some time, and to prevent them Rebels from taking them and using them against the Union army. Captain J.J. Hinds and Lieutenant George Emerick were with me when I carried my horses and turned them over. Captain Hinds and Lieutenant Emerick advised me that it would be best to turn over the horses, to keep the Rebels from getting them and that I would receive pay some day for them. I know my horses were of great necessity and use to the army as many soldiers and recruits were without horses, and horses were greatly needed there then. He further stated he also turned over the following: The four hundred and fifty pounds of pork was from fat hogs furnished by me at my residence in Winston County, Alabama. The quantity was four hundred and fifty pounds, which was ascertained by weighing. The pork was worth at that time forty-five dollars, to best of my knowledge, in United States money. This pork was furnished about latter part of December 1863 or first January 1864, and was used for a detachment of the 1st Alabama Cavalry Volunteers under Lieutenant George Emerick. The pork was carried to the camp in the vicinity and there used. Lieutenant George Emerick of my own regiment was present. The taking or furnishing of the pork was authorized by Lieutenant George Emerick, and was necessary for the soldiers as they were not in reach of the Government supplies.

The rations furnished for which one hundred dollars is claimed, was furnished to detachments of the 1st Alabama Cavalry Volunteers in my presence at different times, and consisted in bread, meat and other eatables, mostly cooked by my wife, at my residence in Winston County, Alabama. Hardly know the quantity, but it was for twenty-five to thirty men and some times as many as forty men at a time. These rations were furnished at different times to those detachments and for from three or four days to ten days at a time. These rations were furnished at about five different times. Then rations were worth one hundred dollars in United States money, and was furnished at different times from first part of September 1863 to about March 1864; was furnished to detachments of the 1st Alabama Cavalry Volunteers. The rations were actually used by the said detachments and were necessary as they could get no other rations conveniently at the time.

The roan mare taken by General Wilson's command was in good condition for service, was a good qualified animal, about 14 hands high, six years old, and was worth at that time one hundred and fifty dollars in United States money, and was taken by General Wilson's command about 24th day of March 1865. I don't know names of any of the officers in General Wilson's command. The soldiers taken my mare from her stable and rode her off. A great many of the soldiers were at my house and about the premises. They moved the property southward. I don't know how long they kept the mare. I never saw the mare again. A captain was present at the taking of the mare. I asked him to have my mare left with me, he replied that the soldiers were compelled to have horses to ride. I knew him to be a captain from his dress and the authority he exercised among the soldiers. I believe the property was authorized to be taken by the proper officers, from the fact they were on a raid south, horses giving out all along and fresh ones had to be taken from citizens and for this reason the mare was for the necessary use of General Wilson's army.

The condition of the corn was that about two hundred bushels of it was husked and in my crib; about fifty bushels of it was shelled and in barrels and boxes, some of it in my house. Three barrels of it at back end of my house. It was all at my residence in Winston County, Alabama, about two hundred and fifty bushels. I know the quantity by knowing the size of my crib, which had been gauged and formed to hold 300 bushels. The crib was at least two-thirds full, and they taken all the corn in it. The other fifty bushels I had measured when put into the barrels and boxes. It was good sound corn, was worth at that time two dollars per bushel in United States money, and could not be bought for less price here. This corn was taken from me about the 24th of March 1865. The corn was taken by General

Wilson's command. The troops put the corn in sacks and carried it and fed their horses and used it up about my premises and in the vicinity. A captain ordered the soldiers to take the corn. I suppose they could get nothing else to feed their horses on.

Four thousand pounds fodder in good condition in stacks and some in stable loft. I know that there was fully four thousand pounds of it by the size of the binds; was worth forty dollars in United States money. Bacon hanging, and boxed, in my meat house at my residence, the quantity of the bacon was 2000 pounds. I had weighed the hogs, from which I estimate the amount of bacon. The bacon was good and was worth at that time five hundred dollars in United States money.

Lard at my place, in my meat house, at my residence, quantity 100 pounds. My wife so estimated it. It was good lard and worth twenty-five dollars in United States money.

Meal taken from my cook room at my residence; the quantity was an ordinary flour barrel full. It was good corn meal and worth at least five dollars in United States money.

Flour taken from my cook room at my residence; the quantity was the ordinary flour barrel full, good flour, worth at least ten dollars in United States money at that time. Syrup taken out of my meat house at my residence; quantity thirty gallons, measured syrup, worth at that time thirty dollars in United States money. Sweet potatoes, taken from my cellar at my residence; quantity ten bushels, the potatoes were measured and put in the cellar, and were worth ten dollars in United States money at that time. Pork, taken on my premises; the soldiers killed, cleaned, cooked and eat six fat shoats or hogs at my residence. The shoats were supposed by myself and neighbors to weigh something near one hundred pounds each, and was worth at that time fifty-five dollars in United States money. Peas, taken from my meat house where they were stored in barrels, quantity fifteen bushels, had been measured, and were worth at that time fifteen dollars in United States money. Honey, taken out of my bee stands at my residence, quantity about 25 pounds or more, so supposed to be; worth twelve dollars in United States money, all of the above mentioned property except as stated, was taken by General Wilson's command on or about the 24th day of March 1865. I know no names of officers that were in the command except General Wilson. The property was taken by orders of the officers, and was used by the soldiers there. The command camped all about my premises and in the vicinity for only one night, about the 24th of March 1865, then moved onward south. Some officers were present. I knew them by their uniforms and dress. They said that they were obliged to take my property for the use of the army. I don't know the names of officers. I believe the property taken was actually needed by the soldiers as they were on a raid and out of reach of Government rations and necessaries. [signed] Jonathan Barton. Attest: A.B. Hays, Special Commissioner.   John N. Baughn witnessed this.

The Commissioners of claims stated the following about Jonathan Barton: "At the beginning of the war, Claimant was a man past 30 years old and well-to-do farmer near Larissa in North Alabama. He talked and voted against secession and had a universal reputation as a Union man. In the earliest part of the war, he did the only thing that a loyal man in his neighborhood could do - harbor and pass along Union men who were making their way to the Federal lines. He was much abused and threatened by the Confederates civil and military and was often a refugee from his home. Much property belonging to him was also taken and destroyed because of his position as a loyalist. When Spencer organized the First Alabama Federal Cavalry in 1863, claimant made his way, with four brothers and three brothers-in-law, to the Union lines and served one year till honorably discharged. Jonathan was a true and notorious Union man from the beginning of secession until the end of the war. His claim for his property was approved.

Barton, Madison Matthew - Madison M. Barton enlisted in Company L at age 26 in Fayette County, Alabama as a Private and mustered in the same day at Glendale, Mississippi, a Camp about ten miles from Corinth. He was born in Hall County, Georgia and was a farmer. He was mustered out on September 28, 1864, at Rome, Georgia. He reenlisted November 1, 1864, in Stevenson, Alabama, was appointed Sergeant July 1, 1865, and mustered in July 19, 1865. He mustered out October 20, 1865 with the rest of the regiment, in Huntsville, Alabama. Madison married 1st, Sarah Jane Dodd on November 24, 1859 in Hall County, Georgia and married 2nd Mariah Duke. He is buried at Dodd (Cap Baughn) Cemetery near Lynn in Winston County, Alabama. (Some information submitted by James E. Gilbert.)

Barton, William H. - William H. Barton enlisted as a Private in Company L at age 27, on

September 25, 1863, in Fayette County, Alabama. He mustered in the same day at Glendale, Mississippi, which was a camp about ten miles out of Corinth. His muster rolls stated he was born in Georgia, and was captured October 26, 1863, at the Battle of Vincent's Crossroads, and held as a prisoner of war at Andersonville Prison in Andersonville, Georgia. He died September 1, 1864, while still a POW at Andersonville, and is buried in the Andersonville National Cemetery in Andersonville, Georgia. (Some information submitted by James E. Gilbert.

Barton, John - John Barton enlisted in Company C of the 1st Alabama Cavalry, USV as a private on December 21, 1862 at Corinth, Mississippi, and was mustered in at the same place. He was mustered out at Camp Davies, Mississippi on December 27, 1863, by reason of expiration of term of service. From March to November 1863, John was with the Regimental Quartermaster as teamster. The Regimental Descriptive Book showed John to have been 35 years of age, 5'-9½" tall, having a fair complexion, blue eyes, light hair, born in Tishomingo County, Mississippi, and a farmer by occupation.

Barton, John - This John Barton enlisted in Company L of the 1st Alabama Cavalry, USV. He was listed as missing in action after the Battle of Vincent's Crossroads, but then he was listed as being sick in the hospital in Nashville, Tennessee. He was next listed as being on detached service recruiting in Decatur, Alabama on August 4, 1864.*

Baswell, Andrew G. "Andy" - Andrew G. Baswell, also spelled Basnell, enlisted in Company E of the 1st Alabama Cavalry, USV as a private on March 1, 1863, in Glendale, Mississippi, for a period of one year and was mustered in the same day in Corinth, Mississippi. The next muster roll listed him absent without leave. His name was listed on the Descriptive List of Deserters showing him as having deserted May 20, 1863. However, the January and February 1864 Muster Roll stated Andrew was absent, on detached service as teamster since January 25, 1864. He was shown to have been discharged, mustered out on March 18, 1863, at expiration of term of service at Memphis, Tennessee. There was a Notation from the Adjutant General's Office of the War Department dated July 30, 1869, which stated there had been an investigation but they were not able to elicit additional information. It did not divulge the type of investigation it was. His name appeared on the Returns in March 1863, stating Basnell supposedly joined another company March 14, 1863, absent without leave, absconded April 1, 1863. May 1863, Absent without leave, to be dropped as deserter after date. June 1863, deserted April 1, 1863, supposed as per numerical column. October 1863, returned from desertion June 10, 1863. January and February 1864, on detached service as teamster in Quartermaster Department at Vicksburg, Mississippi since January 25, 1864. March 1864, term of service expired March 1, 1864 in Memphis, Tennessee. There was a Prisoner of War Record in Andrew G. Basnell's military records but it stated there was no record of capture in 1863, nothing more to show capture.

Bates, Hamilton Stinson - Hamilton S. Bates enlisted in Company K of the 1st Alabama Cavalry, USV as a private on November 1, 1862 at Corinth, Mississippi for a period of one year. He was mustered on December 1, 1862 at Corinth. He was later reassigned to Company A. He was mustered out November 28, 1863, at Memphis, Tennessee due to expiration of term of service at age 17. Another muster roll stated he mustered out at age 18.

Hamilton S. Bates was born June 7, 1846, in Marion County, Alabama to William Carroll Bates and Sarah Ann Kennedy, who were married September 7, 1838, in Marion County, Alabama. His father, William, also served in the 1st Alabama Cavalry, USV. Hamilton married Ellen Hurst, daughter of Wiley and Millie Hurst, and was born November 28, 1869, died June 7, 1927. They had the following children: Franklin T., born February 10, 1871, died 1892; Commodore Charles, born January 21, 1873, died November 26, 1943; Nora Edith, born July 3, 1875, died May 25, 1926; Nona, born 1876; Homer S., born August 3, 1878, died November 20, 1935; Ader, born November 28, 1880; Clara, born June 30, 1882, died July 8, 1953; Lee C., born December 10, 1885, died 1886; Julia M., born December 9, 1887, died March 1901; Lelar, born July 8, 1890, died 1891; Clinton Earl, born July 8, 1892; and Luther Ray Bates, born June 28, 1895, died July 20, 1971. The 1900 Sebastian County, Arkansas Census stated Hamilton's mother, Sara, had 11 children with only 4 still living. The 1910 Sebastian County, Arkansas Census showed Hamilton's wife, Ellen, to have had 11 children with only 7 still living. Hamilton Stinson

Bates died January 18, 1939 in Sebastian County, Arkansas and is buried in the White Cemetery on the Fort Chaffee Military Reservation.

Bates, John - John Bates enlisted in Company I of the 1st Alabama Cavalry, USV as a private on October 1, 1863, at Glendale, Mississippi for a period of 3 years. From December 1863 through February 1864, he was on extra or daily duty as a nurse in the hospital. On March 25, 1864, he was absent, sick in the hospital in Memphis, Tennessee. November 1864 through May 1865, he was on extra duty as a saddler. The Company Descriptive Book showed John to have been 36 years of age, 5'-5"tall, having a light complexion, gray eyes and dark hair, born in Georgia and a farmer by occupation. John Bates was mustered out July 19, 1865 at Nashville, Tennessee.

Bates, Stephen - Stephen Decatur Bates enlisted in Company I of the 1st Alabama Cavalry, USV on September 30, 1863, in Glendale, Mississippi, for a period of 3 years. He was enrolled by Lieutenant Snelling. The Company Descriptive Book shows Stephen to have been 34 years of age, 5'-7" tall, having a light complexion, gray eyes, dark hair, born in Georgia and a farmer by occupation. From November 1863 through March 1864, he was on extra or daily duty as a company cook. In April 1864, he was absent, sick in hospital in Nashville, Tennessee since April 15, 1864. He was mustered out July 19, 1865, in Nashville, Davidson County, Tennessee.

Stephen Decatur Bates was born September 29, 1829, in Georgia to Fleming Bates and Elizabeth Echols. On June 30, 1861, Stephen married Mary Jane Cleghorn in Paulding County, Georgia, and had a son, Fleming Bates about 1862. On January 24, 1877, he married Barbara A. Hutson in Dyer County, Tennessee, and they had the following children: William Ryle Bates, John E. Bates, and Melvina Bates. On October 6, 1885, he married Mary L. Freeman in Cullman County, Alabama. Stephen may have had more children but these were the only ones furnished by descendants. Stephen Decatur Bates died September 12, 1904, in Winston County, Alabama and was buried in the Bates Cemetery. Robin Sterling gave the following directions to the cemetery February 28, 2010. The cemetery is near Helicon, Winston County, Alabama, Township- 11S, Range- 6W, Section-3. From Addison go South on County Road 41, go 8 miles to Arley, turn left on County Road 77, go 5.1 miles. Just pass intersection of County Road22, on the right, look for a dirt drive. The drive goes up a steep hill half finished with concrete. The Woodard residence is at the top of the hill. A barbed wire fence is a few yards in front of the house. The grave site is about 150 feet to the West, just inside and along the fence and behind shed. The monument has fallen and the site has suffered destruction by livestock.

Bates, William Carroll - William Carroll Bates, father of trooper, Hamilton Stinson Bates, enlisted in Company K of the 1st Alabama Cavalry, USV on November 1, 1862, at Corinth, Mississippi for a period of one year, and was mustered in December 31, 1862, at Corinth. The November and December 1862, Muster Roll listed him as being absent with leave. The January and February 1863 Muster Roll listed him as still being absent, sick with leave. The March and April 1863 Muster Roll stated William was still home sick in Corinth, Mississippi, however, the Returns stated he was sick in the hospital at Corinth. The May and June 1863 Muster Roll stated he had been discharged at Glendale, Mississippi June 18, 1863, and final statement was given. He was shown as being in Company A when he was discharged. William's Disability Discharge listed him as being 46 years of age, 5'9" tall, having a light complexion, gray eyes, dark hair, born in Marion County, Alabama and was a farmer by occupation. It stated that William C. Bates was totally unfit for the duties of a soldier the result of premature old age, broken down constitution, and general debility of the whole system. He had chronic rheumatism, a partially dislocated ankle, and toes on the same foot were drawn back upon the dorsalis (dorsal artery of foot) before entering the service. It was signed by Frank C. Burdick, Commanding Company. This was ordered by Brigadier General G.M. Dodge.

William Carroll Bates was born About 1817 in Marion County, Alabama to William Bates and Frances "Fanny" Proctor. William Carroll married Sarah Ann Kennedy September 7, 1838, in Marion County, Alabama and had the following children: James, Micajah C., Hamilton Stinson, Elizabeth, William David, George W., Lucinda, John Elbert, and Ann Belle Bates. Sarah Ann Kennedy Bates was born in January 1822, and died in 1901 in Sebastian County, Arkansas. William Carroll Bates died September 16, 1867, and was supposedly killed by the Confederate Home Guard because of having served in the Union Army. (Some information submitted by Becky Davenport)

Batey, William T. - William T. Battey, also spelled Baty, enlisted in Company C of the 1st Alabama Cavalry, USV as a private on April 25, 1864, at Decatur, Alabama for a period of three years, and mustered in April 29, 1864, in Decatur. Another muster roll stated he enlisted at Mooresville, Alabama. He was enrolled by Captain John Latty and was listed as being single. The Muster and Descriptive Book listed William as having been 18 years of age, 5'-6" tall, having a fair complexion, blue eyes, light hair, born in Rome, Floyd County, Georgia, and a farmer by occupation. His residence was listed as Morgan County, Alabama. The March and April 1865 Muster Roll listed William as being absent, a prisoner of war near Fayetteville, North Carolina since March 1865. (This was probably from the Battle of Monroe's Crossroads on march 10, 1865. His discharge was not issued but he was mustered out of service April 28, 1865 according to General Order #77 of the War Department. He was shown as being mustered out on October 20, 1865, and owing the U.S. Government $16.82 for losing one belt, one plate, one cartridge and cap box. He also owed the U.S. Government $2.46 for transportation. A note in his file stated "Extra pay due this enlisted man by order of the Secretary of War dated Washington, D.C. May 31, 1865." William Battey was paroled at Camp Chase, Ohio on April 10, 1865, from being captured March 10, 1865, from Solomon Grove, North Carolina. He was discharged June 12, 1865, from Camp Chase, Ohio. A Notation in his file stated he was single. A Prisoner of War Records stated he was paroled at Boulware's and Cox's Wharf on March 30, 1865. (This was located on the James River in Virginia.)

Baty, John A. - John A. Baty enlisted in Company G of the 1st Alabama Cavalry, USV as a private on April 24, 1864, at Mooresville, Alabama for a period of 3 years. He was enrolled by Lieutenant E.J. Cobleigh. He was mustered in the same day at Rome, Georgia. The Muster and Descriptive Roll showed him to have been 18 years of age, 5'-9½" tall, having a fair complexion, blue eyes, dark hair, born in Paulding County, Georgia, and a farmer by occupation. Another Descriptive Roll stated he was 5'-4½" tall. His name appeared on the Returns stating he was absent, sick at Rome, Georgia since July 8, 1864. John Mustered out October 20, 1865, in Huntsville, Alabama owing the U.S. Government $25.61 for losing one wiper and thong, one screw driver, one Surcingle, two spurs, nine straps, one curry comb, and one mess pan.

Baugh, James P. - James P. Baugh enlisted in Company G of the 1st Alabama Cavalry, USV on March 10, 1864, at Decatur, Alabama as a private for a period of 3 years, and was mustered in April 13, 1864, at Decatur, Alabama. The Muster and Descriptive Roll listed James as having been 19 years of age, 5'-7" tall, having a fair complexion, blue eyes, light hair, born in Carroll County, Georgia, and a farmer by occupation. In September and October 1864, James was on extra or daily duty as company cook. James was mustered out October 20, 1865 in Huntsville, Alabama owing the U.S. Government $29.45 for losing one Carbine retained under General Order 101, War Department: one thong, one wiper, one screw driver, one Carbine cartridge box, and one saber belt and plate.

Baughn, John N. – (Bugler) John N. Baughn enlisted in Company L of the 1st Alabama Cavalry, USV on September 25, 1863, as a Bugler in Fayette County, Alabama for a period of one year He was shown as age 24. He was mustered in the same day in Glendale, Mississippi. A Company Muster Roll dated September 25 to October 31, 1863, he was listed as being absent with leave. The December 31, 1863, through April 30, 1864, Muster Roll shows John to have been absent, in Alabama recruiting by order of Colonel George Spencer, April 15, 1864. The May 1864 through February 1865 Muster Rolls show him to have been absent, recruiting in Alabama since April 3, 1865. The May and June 1865 Muster Roll showed John N. Baughn to have been absent in Nashville, Tennessee to be mustered out June 29, 1865. He was mustered out June 30, 1865, at Nashville, Davidson County, Tennessee due to expiration of term of service.

John was born September 9, 1838, in Pike County, Georgia and died April 26, 1891, in Winston County, Alabama. He was buried in the Ingle-Wakefield Cemetery, South of Lynn, in Winston County, Alabama. John N. Baughn and his brother, Frederick below, were the sons of Peyton Baughn and Nancy Hicks. John N. Baughn homesteaded land adjoining the land of both William Baughn and

Frederick "Cap" Baughn. The John Baughn homestead was just west of that of Frederick "Cap" Baughn and south of the home of William Baughn, the two lower homesteads on Black Water Creek, about two miles or less from where Lynn, Alabama now stands. He is buried in Ingle-Wakefield Cemetery, South of Lynn in Winston County, Alabama.

Fredrick Hicks "Cap" Baughn was born December 24, 1833, in Harris County, Georgia and died November 16, 1916, in Winston County, Alabama. He was the brother to John N. Baughn, above, and son of Peyton Baughn and Nancy Hicks. He is buried in the Baughn Cemetery in Winston County, Alabama.

Cap Baughn came to Alabama with his father, Payton Baughn, in the year 1849 when he was sixteen years old and lived with his father until he married Margaret "Peggy" Hold on August 16, 1856. They homesteaded land and built their home where they lived the remainder of their lives. Margaret was born August 17, 1835, and died June 14, 1925. She was the daughter of G.W. Holt and Caroline Morris.

Cap & Margaret lost one child in infancy and raised seven children. The boys were William J. Baughn, George P. Baughn, Frederick Jackson Baughn and Joseph H. Baughn; the girls, Nancy Carolyn, Sarah Jane, and Martha Anne. Cap Baughn was eighty-three years old when he died and Margaret (Peggy) was near ninety.

In his early life, Cap Baughn took up the trade of tanning leather and making shoes and became a very accomplished shoemaker. He tanned leather for years, hauled it off to market and tried to learn as much as he could about the leather and shoemaking business. In 1882, he was robbed of about twelve hundred dollars. The robbery was supposed to have been done by Sanford Wafford and his brother-in-law, Thomas Arnold, but at that time, they did not have positive proof.

According to Frederick Baughn's death certificate, he principal disease causing his death was Senility with the contributory disease causing death being Systitis (or Cystitis). It also states he was buried in the Baughn Cemetery.

Peyton Baughn, father of John N. Baughn of the 1st Alabama Cavalry, USV, was shown as a school teacher in the 1850 Winston County, Alabama Census. It may have been later in life that he became a crippled man who had to use a crutch and a walking stick to walk. He served in Winston County as Tax Assessor and Tax Collector both. While there was not enough money to pay two men to do the work he got twenty-five dollars a month for doing the Assessing and Collecting and had three months in the year to do the work making seventy-five dollars per year. This was around the end of the Civil War.

Just after this date he was elected Probate Judge of Winston County and served there for a while and was killed in his office by a drunken man. Paul Garrison stabbed him with a knife. Garrison skipped bond and got away. While a bond of $1000.00 was made detectives looked for him but never found him. He was in Arkansas but got word of the reward and skipped from there.

"Peyton Baughn was born in Oglethorpe County, Georgia in 1804, married Nancy Hicks March 27, 1827, in Pike County, Georgia, and moved to Talladega County, Alabama about 1849. According to the 1850 Census, he was a teacher at that time. In the 1860 census, he was shown as a tax assessor and tax collector (using initials), which is confirmed by Joseph H. Baughn's recollection.

In Wesley Thompson, The Free State of Winston, it is reported that Thomas Curtis was probate judge until killed January 19, 1864, by Confederate forces. Peyton Baughn was appointed to complete Curtis's term and then elected in his own right in 1868. (See death of Thomas "Tom Pink" Curtis else where in book.) The Baughn family information is a compilation of information from several people, including Joyce Farris, Elisa Sanford, and the author.

Baulch, Joseph Bruce - Joseph Bruce Baulch enlisted in Company C of the 1st Alabama Cavalry, USV as a private on January 1, 1864, at Camp Davies or Corinth, Mississippi for a period of 3 years. He was mustered in March 10, 1864, at Memphis, Tennessee, but was reported to have deserted April 24, 1864, from Mooresville, Alabama owing the U.S. Government $11.33 for losing one Remington revolver, saber belt, pistol holster, and a cartridge and cap box. The Muster and Descriptive Roll shows Joseph to have been 18 years of age, 5'3" tall, having a fair complexion, blue eyes, light hair, born in Lawrence County, Tennessee, and a farmer by occupation. Joseph B. Balch was listed as being single.

Joseph B. Balch was born January 15, 1846, in Lawrence County, Tennessee to James Washington Baulch and his wife, Martha Powell who were married November 19, 1838, in Giles County, Tennessee. Joseph married Melinda "Manda" Catherine Owens on November 19, 1882, in Lawrence County, Tennessee. Melinda was born July 4, 1861, in Lawrence County, Tennessee and died February 12, 1957, in Lauderdale County, Alabama. Joseph B. Baulch died January 20, 1892, and was buried in the Owen Cemetery in Lawrence County, Tennessee.

Baxter, Richard - Only one card was found for Richard Baxter which was filed at the end of the last roll of microfilm of the 1st Alabama Cavalry, USV records. It recorded him as a private in Company L. The card was a Return which recorded him as being on daily duty as a blacksmith in November 1863.   No further information relative to this soldier was found.*

Baxter, William R. - William R. Baxter enlisted in Company L of the 1st Alabama Cavalry, USV as a private on August 8, 1864, in Rome, Georgia, for a period of three years. He was mustered in October 17, 1864, in Rome, Georgia. The Muster and Descriptive Roll listed William as having been 18 years of age, 5'-7" tall, having a fair complexion, blue eyes, light hair, born in Cherokee County, Alabama, and a farmer by occupation. The Company Descriptive Book showed William to have been 28 years of age, however, he was only 18 years old. The November and December 1864 Muster Roll showed him to be in Company F and instructed them to stop his pay for one Colt revolver, one sabre belt and plate, one pistol belt and holster, one pistol cartridge pouch, he owed the U.S. Government $23.30 for the revolver and equipment. The January and February 1865, Muster Roll instructed them to stop William R. Baxter's pay for two Colt revolvers, a sabre belt and plate, one pistol belt and holster, one pistol cartridge pouch and pick. The March and April Muster Roll stated he had been captured from Solomon Grove, North Carolina on March 10, 1865, and held prisoner of war. The May and June 1865 Muster Roll stated he owed the U.S. Government $43.30 for the loss of two Colt revolvers, one saber belt and plate, belt, holster, pistol cartridge pouch and pick. William was discharged at Camp Chase, Ohio June 12, 1865, by reason of General Order #77. He was transferred to Company L on April 7, 1865, by Special Regimental Order. The Company Muster-Out Roll stated William R. Baxter had been a prisoner of war since March 10, 1865, was not mustered out, and not discharge was given at muster out of the organization. One muster roll stated William was 18 years of age, while another stated he was 26 years of age. There was a notation in his file that stated: Three months extra pay due this enlisted man by order of Secretary of War, dated Washington, D.C. May 31, 1865. The Prisoner of War Record stated William was captured near Fayetteville, North Carolina, paroled from Boulware and Cox's Wharf in Virginia on March 30, 1865, and furloughed for 30 days on April 9, 1865.
William R. Baxter was the son of William A. and Rachel Baxter of Georgia. He married Martha A. (last name unknown), who was born about 1849 in Georgia.

Bayne, Thomas C. - Thomas C. Bayne was shown as being in Company F of the 1st Alabama Cavalry, USV. The only other record showed him to have been absent, sick in Memphis, Tennessee in December 1863.*

Beach, John - John Beach was a private in Company D of the 1st Alabama Cavalry, USV. The only record listed for him showed him to have died April 19, 1863, of pneumonia.*

Beacham, Hugh L. - Hugh Lawson Beacham, also spelled Beachum, enlisted in Company C of the 1st Alabama Cavalry, USV as a private on January 1, 1864, for a period of three years in Camp Davies, Mississippi. He was enrolled by Captain John Latty. He was mustered in March 10, 1864, in Memphis, Tennessee. The July and August 1864 Muster Roll stated he was absent, on furlough since August 7, 1864, due to the fact that his family living near Decatur, Alabama was without the means of procuring the necessities of life, and part of them were very sick. George E. Spencer approved Hugh's furlough stating it would be an act of humanity to allow the man to go and visit his family for a short time. The September and October 1864 Muster Roll stated he was absent, on recruiting service in Alabama, and had received no bounty. The November and December 1864 Muster Roll stated he was absent, recruiting in Alabama since September 3, 1864. He was still on detached service in Decatur, Alabama through April 1865. Hugh L. Beacham was mustered out October 20, 1865, in Huntsville, Alabama owing the U.S. Government $7.10 for losing a screw driver, one wiper and one bridle, one pair of spurs, one cap pouch, and one curry comb. He was paid $180 bounty and still owed $120 bounty by the U.S. Government. The Company Descriptive Book listed Hugh as being 25 years old, 5'-8" tall, having a fair complexion, hazel eyes, light hair, born in Marshal County, Mississippi, a farmer by occupation, and was shown as being married. Hugh L. Beacham died August 27, 1867.

In the pension records for Hugh Lawson Beacham, James Lowry signed an affidavit stating "I was well acquainted with Dr. Frank Rogers who attended Hugh L. Beachum after his return from the war, have talked with him about the case and before his death heard him say that Hugh L. Beachum's death was caused by exposure during the service in the Army. Mr. Beachum was in good health when he enlisted but his health was ruined when he returned home at the close of the war."

Margaret Tabler stated, "I knew the said Hugh L. Beachum before the Civil War and was at his bed side when he died August 27, 1867 and I heard the doctor say who attended him that he had consumption caused by exposure during his services in the Federal Army." She lived a neighbor to him for several years.

There was a Notation from the Pension Office dated August 3, 1864, which stated: On furlough since August 7, 1864. October 31, 1864, on recruiting service in Alabama December 31, 1864, Same to April 30, 1865.

Lula J. Mincey signed an affidavit in Clay County, North Carolina stating she was a minor child of Hugh Lawson Beachum. She stated: My Mother's maiden name was Nancy Tabler, died December 14, 1873. I have never made claim for pension prior to the one first filed. She stated her mother and father married April 16, 1862, but a descendant stated they married April 14, 1861.

William Beck filed an affidavit from Ben Lomand, Arkansas stating, "I was personally acquainted with Hugh L. Beachum and that he entered the service a hole and healthy man and on his return he was suffering with lung trouble caused, so Doctor Jim Rodgers said, from exposure on camp life while in service in the federal army during Civil War." He was a neighbor and waiting on him during his illness.

M.J. Tabler stated, "I was personally acquainted with Hugh Beacham and I know that he came home from the U.S. Army sick and was present when he died. The physician said he died of consumption and it was commonly known as having been contracted during his service in the army by exposure."

March 7, 1836,"Several years ago a lawyer in Washington City, A.B. Webb, was working on a pension for my mother and had everything proved except her being the only heir and she was discouraged and didn't prove it as she thought she would have to go back to Mississippi to prove that and she wasn't able to go. My grandfather, Hugh Lawson Beachum, was discharged from Federal Army - was wounded and later died. He never drew any money due him. Do you think you could help her in the matter. She needs it so much. My father is almost helpless and her health is very poor." Signed Mrs. O.L. Sims, and at the time her mother was living in Gainesville, Texas.

On 26 March 1936, the Widows and Descendants Claims Services wrote a letter stating the claim for pension had been rejected because not enough proof had been submitted that his death was caused by his time in the service. Pension Records were submitted by Janette Maddux.

<u>Beard, Alfred</u> – Alfred Beard enlisted in Company C of the 1st Alabama Cavalry, USV on January 1, 1864, in Corinth, Mississippi for a period of three years, and was mustered in March 10, 1864, at Memphis, Tennessee. The Muster and Descriptive Book shows Alfred to have been 18 years of age, 5'-9" tall, having a fair complexion, blue eyes, light complexion, born in Lincoln County, Tennessee, and a farmer by occupation. He was reported to have deserted May 30, 1864, near Dallas, Georgia with one Remington revolver and accoutrements, Smith's Carbine and accoutrements, saddle and equipment, and horse and equipment. He was later listed as having been captured by the enemy June 1, 1864, near Dallas, Georgia. No discharge was furnished on muster out of organization. A Notation in Alfred Beard's file from the Adjutant General's Office of the War Department dated April 16, 1864, stated: Charges of desertion of May 30, 1864, are removed, he was captured by the enemy near Dalton, Georgia May 30, 1864, and taken to Andersonville Prison in Andersonville, Georgia where

he died on or about December 1, 1864. He was also reported to have been captured March 10, 1865, which would have been during the Battle of Monroe's Crossroads near Fayetteville, North Carolina. The Company Descriptive Book shows Alfred Beard to have been single and showed him to have died of disease (Scurvy) in the hospital at Annapolis, Maryland. The Prisoner of War Records show Alfred to have died in prison at Andersonville, Georgia on or about December 1, 1864.

Alfred Beard was born about 1843 according to the 1850 Lincoln County, Tennessee Federal Census which states his age as 7 years old. This same census says that Alfred is the son of Thomas Beard who was born about 1804 in South Carolina and his wife Susan who was born about 1820. Alfred's sisters are Mary Jane, age 13, Nancy, age 3, and Martha, age 10 months old as listed on the same 1850 census. Alfred's family is living next door to Francis M. Beard who is the father of Leander Pinckney Beard, my Great Grandfather. I believe Thomas Y. Beard and Francis M. Beard are brothers and the sons of Francis A. Beard who was born about 1765 in South Carolina.

Alfred is listed on the 1860 Itawamba County, Mississippi Federal Census with his mother, Susan, and his sisters Nancy and Martha. Alfred's father, Thomas, passed away in 1857 leaving Alfred as the only male in the household to take care of his mother and sisters. The piece of land Thomas had chosen to raise his family on was small and not very fertile according to neighbors. Alfred worked the land after his father's death and tried to raise a few head of livestock to support his mother and sisters. When Alfred was not working in his own fields, his mother would hire him out to other neighbors to work their fields just to make enough money to meet their needs. Alfred's older sister, Mary Jane, was probably married at this time since she was not listed in her mother's household in 1860.

January 1, 1864, Alfred joined the Federal Army, the Union. Can you imagine living in the DEEP South and being brave enough to enlist to fight for the North? Think about it for a moment. Think of how strong this young man's convictions had to have been to go against his neighbors and "YES" relatives who joined the Confederacy either by choice or from extreme pressure. Alfred lived in Mississippi, the "HEART" of the South. The War had been going on for two to three years and the whole area was crawling with Confederate Soldiers. There were recruitment meetings everywhere in the different neighborhoods. There were men assigned to go out and find all the young men who were old enough or "big" enough to join, but had not done so; and then force them to enlist or kill them or at least threaten to kill them if they did not join.

Alfred's sister, Mary Jane, wrote "my brother had to keep himself hidden from the Rebels being of Conscript (Draft) size and may have been of Conscript or Draft age. The family records were lost in the War (which means the family birth records were lost). My brother left home at night with Hugh L. Beacham to find the nearest Federal Soldiers which was near Corinth, Mississippi, a distance of 35-40 miles from home. The country was infested with Rebels. The next morning I followed my brother and Beacham to see if they were able to get through to the Federal Camp at Camp Davies, Mississippi.. I overtook them within a few miles of the Camp. I went with my brother and Beacham inside the Federal lines at Camp Davies and remained there long enough to know that my brother and Beacham both enlisted in Company C of the 1st Alabama Cavalry, USV. I saw them wearing Federal uniforms, holding their weapons, and heard Alfred answer to Roll Call".

Susan, Alfred's mother, had received word of Alfred's capture and death so she began filing for his pension on May 7, 1866. The war was over and she and her daughters were struggling to make a living for themselves. Susan stated over and over to the War Department that Alfred was her main support before the war and she had depended wholly or in part upon him. Alfred left no widow and no children under the age of sixteen. He had never married. His mother was the next of kin to receive his pension. Susan wrote letter after letter and was able to get neighbors, Alfred's fellow soldiers, their family Doctor, their minister and others to help her receive her son's pension.

John M. Sweat wrote in a Deposition in November, 1887: "I was personally acquainted with Alfred Beard, who was a Private in Company "C" Commanded by Captain John Latty of the 1st Regiment of Alabama, United States Volunteers. I was a Private in the same Company and Regiment with Alfred Beard. I was a prisoner before Alfred arrived at the prison. We were in different detachments of prisoners. Alfred was on one side of the hollow and I was on the other. James Chastain, Blakely Jones, and Louis VanHoos were also prisoners from our regiment. I can't remember when I first saw Beard in prison, but think it was late in the winter of 1864 and then saw him everyday. I went to visit him while he was sick and I was able to travel. Alfred had what I called Scurvy. He was weak and thin. He could shake his teeth about. I have seen him lying on the ground when he could not get up; on the cold wet ground; don't remember shoes being on him. I escaped the 20th of January, 1865 and never saw Beard again. Alfred Beard, while in confinement, and in said Prison contracted Scurvy of which he died while in the said prison in the month of January 1865 and on or about the 20th day of the month".

Susan continued appealing her case as late as April 1889. In July 1888, Susan received a check from the Office of Depot Commissary of Subsistence an Assistant Treasurer of the United States for $41.85. This money is designated as "payment of your claim for commutation of rations while your son was prisoner of war, as settled by Certificate of Second Comptroller, No 8848".

Joseph D. Morris wrote a Deposition in October 1887 giving a written account of Alfred Beard's capture in order to help Susan receive her son's pension. Joseph says, "I have known Alfred Beard, son of Susan Beard from the time he was a boy. I remember that it was about June of 1864 when we were on a march to Rome, Georgia and got there about the first of July. The capture was not long before we got to Rome. There were four men captured, I believe a Corporal or a Sergeant was with them. I do not know that they were ordered to go out, but it was my understanding at the time that they were ordered to do so. I made special inquiry at the time, as he was only a boy and one I had always known, and his mother had asked me to look out for him. Alfred was a prime good soldier – not a boy to do anything against orders".

Susan Beard gave her account of what happened the night her son was captured by the Rebels. She says that her son and three or four others left the camp for the purpose of obtaining milk for a sick comrade and was captured through the intrigue of a woman who led him to believe that she would supply him with milk for his comrade. Instead, she turned him and his comrades over to the Rebels. Susan must have heard this from someone who was with Alfred or at least one of his fellow soldiers.

Susan applied for a "Declaration For Dependent Mother's Pension" on the 15 day of July, 1890 at the age of 72 and a resident of McNairy County, Tennessee. This new law was put into place on June 27, 1890. Susan's application was denied, again, on March 9, 1892, saying Alfred's capture was not in the line of duty since he did not have permission to leave the camp.

Alfred's file that I received did not contain papers from the Government removing the charges of desertion dated April 14, 1884, or papers indicating that his mother, Susan, ever received Alfred's pension. In my opinion, Alfred Beard is a hero and deserves to have his story told. If anyone is interested in knowing more, I suggest you read about the horrible conditions of the Andersonville Prison Camp and the brave men who served in the 1st Alabama Cavalry. (Submitted by Janette Beard Maddux, A proud cousin)

Beard, George R. - George R. Beard enlisted in Company L of the 1st Alabama Cavalry, USV on April 7, 1865 in Stevenson, Alabama as a private for a period of 3 years. He was mustered in April 18, 1865, in Nashville, Tennessee. The Muster and Descriptive Roll listed him as being 21 years of age, 5'-10" tall, having a fair complexion, blue eyes, light hair, born in Lincoln County, Tennessee, and a farmer by occupation. He was mustered out October 20, 1865, at Huntsville, Alabama with the U.S. Government owing him $100 bounty. For some reason not stated, he owed the Government $12.26. George Beard was the brother of John Beard, below.

George Beard filed for a pension and on December 30, 1897, he stated he had been married to Martha Wilbanks on March 24, 1870, by Rev. William Beard in Winston County, Alabama. He stated Martha Beard was born May 20, 182,2 at Spartanburg, South Carolina.

In a 16 page Deposition on legal size paper, given by George R. Beard on July 9, 1906, in Bear Creek, Searcy County, Arkansas, he stated the following: (sic) I am 62 years of age; I was born January 26, 1844; post office address, Bear Creek, Arkansas; residence four miles south; occupation farmer.

I served during the War of the Rebellion in Co. L 1st Alabama Vol. Cav., United States Troops. I enlisted at Decatur, Ala. April 7, 1865, and was discharged at Huntsville, ala. on October 20, 1865.

I am a pensioner of the United States on account of my above service at the rate of $8.00 per month under the Act of June 27, 1890, my certificate is numbered 1,011,954. I have an application on file for increase of my pension. I filed the same last Fall sometime. I was never in the military or Naval Service of the United States other than above service.

I was born in Tennessee and my father moved to Alabama when I was about 10 years of age. I loved within 5 miles of Nauvoo, Walker Co., Ala. from the time I went into that country up until I enlisted in the above named organization, I lived south of Nauvoo. Joe Jackson, Bill Norris, Rick McGough, Ike Cagle, Ben Williams, George Davis, Bob King, were neighbors of mine during the war. The first three named were in Co. L, 1st Ala. Cav. Davis was in the Confederate Service. Pete McGough, a brother-in-law of mine, now lives near Carbon Hill and although he was young during the war, he can probably give the names of old settlers there, the same can be said of Jones Beard, a nephew, who lives near Nauvoo. Van Davis was a neighbor that was in the Confederate service, also, Wiley Johnson and Nat Johnson. The Kings and Millers who lived on Lost Creek, towards Jasper, Rasp Miller was one of the boys, were Confederates. All the persons I have named, if they are living, now live in the same old vicinity as far as I know. I have two brothers, and one sister living. Sam lives at Cleveland, Conway Co., Ark., he is perhaps ten years younger than I. William lives about Nauvoo, Ala. and is two years older than Sam. My sister, the wife of Pete McGough, named above is the youngest in the family now. Sam, Ike, and Jerry Roberts were old neighbors, also. They were not with either side.

Question: Now, Mr. Beard, tell me your entire connection with the Confederate Troops, and remember that you are under oath in answering, to tell the whole truth.

Answer: Well, my father was a northern sympathizer, and I was always of that sentiment also. I was too young at the early part of the war to think of going in the service. The southern people had lots of big gatherings around, and musters, before the Conscript Act was passed, but I never attended any of them. After that act was passed, I heard of a big speaking that was going to take place on Mill Creek near Kelly's Mill about two miles from home. I went to it to see what was going on after I got there, one of the speakers said that they were going to conscript on the day following, every man who did not enlist in the Confederate Service, and take them to Talladega, Ala., I think they said. I heard it whispered around that I was old enough and would have to go. I enlisted there that day, and took the oath of enlistment to support the Confederacy, I suppose. I did it to prevent being conscripted as I knew I would be. On the day of this meeting after we had taken the oath, we were permitted to go home with the promise that we would come immediately to Tuscaloosa, Ala. for service. I went on home, and the next day, or the day after, started with several others for Tuscaloosa, a distance of about 60 miles, walking. It seems to one, that some of the others in the party were Jim and John, Tom and Bill McGough, and Elias Abbott. Jim and John remained with the Confederates. They were living in the vicinity of Nauvoo the last I heard of them. Bill and Tom are dead. Don't know what became of Abbott. After I got to Tuscaloosa, things didn't suit me, and as my sympathy was with the Union side, I decided to leave. Tom McGough, the Abbott fellow, and several others that I do not now remember as I did not know them very well, left them by night, after a day or two. I am positive that I did not stay at Tuscaloosa over a week. I returned home, and it seems to me, now, that I was around home and lying out in the brush for about one year. At the end of that time, I was captured in the house, where I was sleeping one rainy night. Madison Johnson, Lal Kelly and Green Tesney were in the company that captured me, I think Esom Kelly was the Captain. They took me to Shelbyville, Tenn. And kept me in prison there about 10 or 12 days and then a day or so at several other places. No it was these other places that they had me on my way to Shelbyville. After I had been in prison at Shelbyville about ten or twelve days, they came and questioned me there about the Confederate Company that I had joined. It was the intention of the men that captured me to take me to the regiment I had joined and had left at Tuscaloosa. It was the 43rd Ala. Inf., I think. Don't remember whose company, or the name of any of its officers. Well at Shelbyville, they told me that that regiment was too far off, and it would cost too much to send me there, so they would just turn me over to one of the other regiments there at Shelbyville. So they just took me over to some Captain and turned me over for service. They had not asked me anything about putting me in the service. I did not volunteer to go in, in order to get out of prison. They did ask me what company I had rather go in, and I told them I had no choice, as I did not know any of the men there. I was put in the 16th Alabama, I think it was. I left them that night. Don't know what was the letter of the company, or the name of any officers or men in the regiment. I went on back home and laid out around in hiding. Six or eight months after I got home, a recruiting officer for the Union Troops came around and a number of us boys just enlisted and went back with him.

Question: When you were at home for the year after you left the Confederates at Tuscaloosa, did you make any effort to get with the Union Troops?

Answer: Well, I just saw no good chance to get through to the Union lines. I had no pilot. Yes, the Union men made one raid into our vicinity during that time, but they were gone before I heard of it. On my way back from Shelbyville, I saw no chance to get to the Union Troops. Yes, My father died in 1863, and I thought that my services were needed at home, and when I was lying out, I took every opportunity to work around the farm. My father died soon after I got back from Tuscaloosa. Yes, brother John was in the Confederate Service for about a year. He was in the 43rd Ala., I think. I enlisted in Co. L, 1st Ala. Cav. because I thought that side would win and was right. I joined for three years.

I was not a member of any Confederate Organization other than the two mentioned by me herein. The 43rd and 16th Alabama Inf.

Question: Why did you take oath sometime back that you had never served in the Confederate Army:

Answer: Well, I did not consider that enlisting and joining with them for only a day or two was service. I do not desire to be present or represented by attorney during the further examination of my case either here, or elsewhere. My father died about June 1863, it was just before this that I had joined the Confederates. Not it may have been 1862 that father died, but I am most sure it was 1863. Now to the best of my belief it was the 43rd and 16th Alabama Confederate Troops that I was in. I do not remember of taking any oath when I was put in the 16th. I positively do not remember the name of any officer of either company or regiment of Confederate Troops that I was in.

I have heard this statement read carefully by you. I have understood all your questions, and you have correctly recorded my answers herein.

I contracted no wound or injury while I was in the Union service. The only sickness I had while in the Union Army was scurvy. I had my first touch of this just a short time after I enlisted just after I had got through the lines. I never had the slightest touch of it that I knew of before that time.

I have never been married but once. I am living with my only wife. Her maiden name was Martha Wilbanks. She was never previously married. We have had no children. We were married in Winston Co., Ala. by W.H. Beard, my uncle, a minister of the Southern Methodist Church. We were married March 24, 1870. I suppose the certificate is of record in Winston Co., we have none at home. We were licensed. This further statement has been read me, and is correct. Signed George R. Beard, Deponent.

Additional statement of claimant: Since you were at my house a few days ago, I have thought of two other Confederate Companies that I belonged to and I came in town today for the purpose of making affidavit to that fact and of submitting the same to the Bureau. I unexpectedly met you and desire to make such additional statements under oath to you. After I returned from Tuscaloosa, I believe that it was as much as a year thereafter, I heard it reported that Jeff Davis had issued a proclamation that all who did not enlist who were fit for service, would be hunted out and killed. This must have been in the Fall of 1863. There was a guerilla company in the country commanded by Capt. Inman I think, or Enman. I was hiding out and was afraid of being captured and killed. At that time, I heard of a Confederate officer who was enlisting men at Old Uncle Red Davis'. Can't say whether he was a regular recruiting officer or was simply getting up a company of his own. I there went over to Red Davis' house where such officer was and gave him my name as a volunteer. Can't say whether I took another oath or not, don't think I did. I staid there at Davis' house with the men for a few days until the company was completed. We were then marched off towards the Miss. River. I left them that night, I think, because I had not intended to stay with them. I made my way back to the vicinity of home again, and went in hiding again. I don't remember the designation of the company, or the name of any officer that was with them. The only one of the men I remember is Pete Ingle one of the men of the neighborhood boys. I may be mistaken about him being with that company. I laid out there six, eight, or ten months and because they were hunting me so close, and threatening to kill me if I was caught, I again came out and went voluntarily and joined Capt. Watley's Company which was attached to Roddey's Command, Confederate States Army. Ben Jackson, I think, went along with me and joined at the same time. I believe he went into the same company, but won't be certain. Can't name any of the other officers or men. I staid with them about ten days and left them about 40 miles north of home. They got orders to move West, and had started, I left them, and went on back in the vicinity of home, and staid around in hiding until I enlisted in the Union Army in April 1865. Now, it seems to one that, it was before I enlisted in the company at Red Davis' house that I was captured and taken to Shelbyville,

93

Tenn. By Kelly's men, as I told you in my first statement. It was in the Spring of 1863, it seems to me, that I was taken prisoner. Then it must have been in the Spring of 1862 that I enlisted the first time and went to Tuscaloosa, Ala. I know that I must have been home from that place nearly a year before I was captured by Kelly's men.

George Davis, named by me, was a son of old Red Davis, but he was not in any of the companies that I joined, although some of his brothers may have been, there was John Ransom, and Billie. The last two were hardly old enough to have been in the service.

This is a complete history of my service in the Confederate Army, I do positively swear, to the best of my present knowledge.

Question: Why die you not mention your service in the two companies named to me when you were under oath the other day? Answer: Although you named Capt. Watley to me the other day, I did not remember having enlisted in his company or the other company, either. I have heard you read this statement carefully to me, I have understood fully all your questions, and you have correctly recorded my answers herein. Signed George R. Beard

In a Declaration for Pension dated March 25, 1907, George R. Beard stated he was 63 years of age and lived at Bear Creek in Searcy County, Arkansas.

On March 4, 1926, he filed a Declaration for Pension stating he lived at Conway County, Arkansas. He required the regular personal aid and attendance of another person on account of the following disabilities: Old age and run down condition, kidney trouble, rheumatism of legs, lumbago and old age which make it necessary for me to have the assistance of someone to care for me. He stated since leaving the service he had resided at Bear Creek and Cleveland, Arkansas. He signed his name to the document and it was witnessed by Thetus Horne and M.C. Knighten of Cleveland, Arkansas.

Affidavit dated July 27, 1927, at Cleveland, Conway County, Arkansas: Before me, E.P. Curley, Inspector of the Bureau of Pensions, personally appeared George R. Beard, who being by me first duly sworn to answer truly all interrogatories propounded to him during this special examination of aforesaid claim for pension, deposes and says:

My age is 83 years, being born in 1844; no occupation at the present time; residence and post office address, Cleveland, Ark. I am the same George R. Beard who served in the Civil War in Co. L 1st Alabama Cavalry. That was the only service I had in the United States. I am now receiving a pension at the rate of $65 per month under the act of July 3, 1926, but have filed for the $72 rate. No sir, I have not filed a claim for the $90 rate on account of total helplessness or blindness.

Q: How is your eyesight? A: It is getting bad.

Q: You can tell daylight from dark: A: O yes. Q: You can see different objects at several feet distance? A: Yes, if the object is in the shade. I cannot see well in the sun light.

Q: You can see Well enough to read the newspapers and other printed matter? A: Oh yes, I read the newspaper alright.

Q: Can you dress and undress yourself? A: Some of the time, yes. Part of the time I am unable to get into my shirt because I cannot move my arms freely enough. In the morning when I awake and attempt to get up I will try to put on my clothes and I can get them on sometimes, but other times I have to have someone help me. Last Winter I had a pretty bad spell of sickness and I was in bed for a good long while. Then when Spring came on I seemed to get better, but still I am weak and feeble. I can put my clothes on right now, because I am feeling alright, but n the mornings, when I awake I have a swimming in my head and I feel so weak that I will just have to get my sister-in-law to help with my clothes. Yes sir, she will have to help me take them off at night, too.

Q: You can walk about the house and the yard without the aid or assistance of another person; can you not? A: Yes sir, when I am feeling alright I can. Some days, you must remember, I am not feeling as good as I am right now, and of course I cannot leave the house. I do not leave the house very much but just sit down nearly the entire day. Yes, it is as much on account of the hot sun as anything else.

Q: You can prepare your food on the plate and eat without the assistance of another; can you not? A: Yes sir, I can, and have so far. Of course when I am so sick in bed that I cannot get up my sister-in-law just brings my meals to me.

Q: You can attend to your personal wants and attend the calls of nature without assistance? A: Yes sir, most of the time, I can. There are times, you must remember, that I cannot do those things, but will have to have someone help me.

Q: How frequently do you need the aid and assistance of another person? A: Well, last November or December I had the sick spell, and when I was so sick I had to have an attendant every day to do for me, but after I got well enough to get up I could do those things myself, except at times when I felt weak. My sister-in-law will have to help me to dress and undress about two thirds of the time, and that is on account of me being unable to straighten out my hands and arms like I should.

Q: From what date have you needed the regular aid and assistance of another person? A: From the first of December 1926. Well I took sick in November, but it was the latter part. December 1st would be sure enough so I will put in that date from which I first needed the aid and assistance of another person. I needed the almost constant aid and assistance of another person from the time I was sick until this past Spring. Since then I have received the regular aid and assistance of another person about two or three times a week.

A Drop Report for Pensioner stated George R. Beard of Cleveland, Arkansas was last paid at the rate of $95 per month to July 31, 1934 and had been dropped from the roll because of his death on August 2, 1934.

Q: Who has treated you during the past year? A: Dr. John Coley of Cleveland has been treating me during the past year, or since I had that sick spell last November. He is the only doctor who has treated me. I depend a whole lot on the drug store Medicines.

Q: How many times have you been married? A: I was married only once. I was married to Martha Wilbanks in Winston Co., Ala. in March, 1870. Neither she nor I had been previously married. We never had any children. Martha and I lived together from the time of our marriage until she died. We were never separated and neither she nor I ever applied for a divorce from the other. We were living near Bear Creek, Searcy Co., Ark., when she died. She has been dead about fifteen years, and she is buried on top of the mountain about a mile from Bear Creek. Yes Sir, we were living together when she died. Since her death I have resided in Searcy County, and here at Cleveland, Ark. I have not remarried since the death of my wife, Martha. Signed George R. Beard. (His signature continuously becomes shakier.)

An affidavit dated July 27, 1927 at Cleveland, Conway County, Arkansas by Mary L. Beard states the following: My age is 51 years; widow of Sam Beard; residence and post office address, Cleveland, Arkansas.

The pensioner, George R. Beard, is my brother-in-law. My husband, Sam Beard, was his brother. I married Sam Beard in October 1925, and have known the pensioner since then. No Sir, I never knew him before then. The pensioner has lived with us all the time since then. Well he was living with us before my husband died, and since his death I have taken care of the old man. My husband died in December, 1926. The pensioner is very weak and feeble. He is unable to dress and undress himself all the time, but other things he generally does himself. Last November, the pensioner took sick, and had an awful bad spell. We thought he was going into pneumonia. He was laid up all winter. Yes sir, he was sick in bed when my husband died, and he was in bed for a couple of months afterward. He did not get over his sick spell until the past Spring. Since then he has felt better, but not near as well as before he took sick. The old man gets about the house and the yard and once in a while he will fiddle around in the yard in the early morning or late in the evening when the sun goes down. He does not stay out very long, but maybe just for about fifteen minutes or a half hour. He does it mostly to get out of the house and for a little exercise. No sir, he is not able to work very long, and he is nearly helpless so that I have to help him dress and undress at times. Well no sir, I do not help him on and off with his clothes all the time, but fully two thirds of the time. He is weak, alright, and he cannot straighten out his arms or hands to get into his clothes, and I will have to come to his assistance and then have to help him into his clothes, and it is the same way at night. Yes sir, he can get about the house and the yard alright by himself, and he can attend the calls of nature without aid or assistance of another, and he can also eat without any help. But he does need me to help him on and off with his clothes regularly. Well no, I do not mean every day and night, but nearly every day and night. Yes sir, at least three or four times a week. Q: How long has he needed this assistance? A: Well ever since the first of last December. He was in bed then, and remained in bed most of the time until this Spring when we sent in the affidavits in his

95

pension claim. Since that time he has needed me to look after him in general fully three fourths of the time. I have no financial interest in this claim. I have heard this, my deposition, read, and it is correct. Signed, Mary L. Beard, Deponent.

A Deposition dated July 27, 1927, at Cleveland, Conway County, Arkansas, by E.P. Curley states the following: My age is 18 years; occupation, farmer; residence and post office address, Cleveland, Arkansas. I know the pensioner, George R. Beard, and have known him for about seven years. I did not live close to him until about two years ago. Since then I have been intimately acquainted with him, and know him real well. The old man is very weak and feeble and needs someone to look after him all the time. I know his widow sister-in-law cannot leave him alone for a minute. Someone has to be around him all the time to look out for him. He is so weak that he is liable to fall anytime. I remember a couple of times the old man was walking out in the yard and he did fall, and I helped pick him up. I know the old man needs someone to help him on and off with his clothes, and help him up and down in bed. He says he has dizzy spells, and whenever he gets up out of a chair or bed someone will have to hold onto him for a moment. He walks about the house and yard alright but he should not do it because as I have said he is liable to fall any time, and I know he did fall a couple of times. Yes sir, I have personal knowledge of the fact that he needs someone to help him on and off with his clothes, because I stayed here with him when his sister-in-law was visiting her folds sometime ago. Last week she went away on a visit and I stayed here and tended to the old man, and about two months ago she went away and I stayed here that time, too. I had to help the old man on and off with his clothes, and watch after him like he was a child. The pensioner is very weak, and I know he needs the regular aid and assistance of another person. He has been in that condition now since last December when his brother, Sam Beard, died. The pensioner was sick in bed at that time, and ever since then he has been gradually been getting worse. Before he took that sick spell he was apparently alright for one of his age, but since then he has needed or required the aid and assistance of another person regularly. I have no financial interest in this claim, and am not related. I have heard this, my deposition, and it is correct. Signed: W.E. Poteet, Deponent

Beard, John - John Beard, younger brother of George R. Beard, enlisted in Company L of the 1st Alabama Cavalry, USV on April 7, 1865, at Stevenson, Alabama as a private for a period of 3 years. He was mustered in April 18, 1865, in Nashville, Tennessee. The Muster and Descriptive Roll showed him to be 19 years of age, being 5'-6" tall, having a fair complexion, blue eyes, auburn hair, born in Lincoln County, Tennessee and a farmer by occupation. John was mustered out October 20, 1865, in Huntsville, Alabama. While he was shown as owing the U.S. Government $10.85, it stated the U.S. Government owed him $100 bounty.

Beard, Robert Elisha - Robert E. Beard enlisted in Company H of the 1st Alabama Cavalry, USV on April 1, 1865, at Stevenson, Alabama for a period of 3 years by J.W. DeVaney. Robert was mustered in April 18, 1865, in Nashville, Tennessee. The Muster and Descriptive Roll showed Robert as being 26 years of age, 5'-7" tall, having a fair complexion, black eyes, black hair, born Abbeville District, South Carolina, and a farmer by occupation. He was mustered out October 20, 1865, in Huntsville, Alabama, being paid $100 bounty.

Robert Elisha Beard was born October 1836 in Abbeville District, South Carolina to Thomas Young and Mary Beard. On February 7, 1861, Robert married Mary Ann Cothron in Talladega County, Alabama and they had the following children: William Thomas, born 14 May 1866; James F., born October 6, 1869; Joseph H., born November 7, 1871; Robert E., born October 10, 1875; Zella Ada (or Ada Zella), born February 23, 1878; John Benjamin, born September 27, 1880; David M., born January 10, 1885, and Susan Beard, born June 2, 1888. These were the only children mentioned in Robert's Application for Civil War Pension but another descendant stated they had one other child, Flora Ann Beard, born November 18, 1891. Mary A. Cothron Beard died December 9, 1905 in Carbon Hill, Walker County, Alabama.

Robert E. Beard enlisted as a Private in Company H, 1st Alabama Cavalry, USV on April 1, 1865 in Stevenson, Alabama at age 26. He mustered in April 18, 1865 in Nashville, Davidson County, Tennessee and was reassigned to Company H. He was mustered out October 20, 1865 in Huntsville,

Alabama with the rest of what was left of the regiment. He apparently was forced to join the Confederacy in 1862. In his Application for Pension, Robert stated the following: (sic)

"Regarding my service in the Confederate Army I submit the following. In the winter of 1861-62 I enlisted in Pellams Battery CSA and five or six days after was sent to hospital with fever and then furloughed home where I remained until the fall of 1862 and being pressed by neighbors and officers to return to the army and avoid being taken up as a deserter I returned to the Battery it being then commanded by Captain Henry of Stuart's Light Artillery and although they had no record of my original enlistment I was forced to remain with the Battery until August 1863 when I escaped to the Federal lines and immediately entered the Union Army and remained in it until after the termination of the war.

When I enlisted in the Confederate service I was in jail under indictment accused of a crime of which I was innocent and owing to the war excitement I could not secure a trial and interested partys offered to secure bond for me provided I would enlist in Pellams Battery and believing that if I refused to enlist and remained in jail that my life would be in danger. I enlisted, not voluntary but to save my life."

He stated he enlisted in Company F, 27th Pennsylvania Volunteers in 1863 remaining until March or April 1865 when he again enlisted in Company H, 1st Alabama Cavalry, USV from which he was discharged in October 1865.

In January 1904 he gave this statement from Pocahontis, Walker County, Alabama and stated that he suffered from piles, chronic rheumatism, ..., injury to head, general debility, kidney disease, spine and diabetes. Robert died December 22, 1911 in Walker County, Alabama. On 19 September 19, 1912, John Benjamin Beard wrote a letter on Oak Leaf Coal Company Stationary asking for burial expenses for his father, Robert E. Beard. The letterhead stated the Coal Company was "Miners and Shippers of "Bituminous, Steam and Domestic Coal, Cordova, Alabama. According to the 1900 Walker County, Alabama Census, Robert had three sons who were Coal Miners, Joseph, John & David Beard. Most information from Military and Pension Records of Robert E. Beard.

Beasley, Thomas F. - Thomas F. Beasley enlisted and mustered into Company L of the 1st Alabama Cavalry, USV as a private on August 18, 1862, in Huntsville, Alabama at age 19. He was one of the fires enlistees who were immediately shipped to Nashville, Tennessee and merged with the 1st Middle Tennessee and 5th Tennessee. Thomas was with Company D of the 1st Middle Tennessee Cavalry. On November 30, 1862, he was shown as being absent, sick in Hospital #14 in Nashville. On April 28, 1863, he was reported as missing in action from the battle at Day's Gap, Alabama, however, he returned to his company at Glendale, Mississippi on October 2, 1863. On January 1, 1864, Thomas was appointed Corporal by Lieutenant Colonel Dodds. On October 1, 1864, he was reduced to private by Colonel Spencer. He was mustered out July 19, 1865 in Nashville, Tennessee owing the U.S. Government $28.24. The Company Descriptive Book showed Thomas to have been 18 years of age, having a dark complexion, black eyes, light hair, born in Shelby County, Alabama, and a farmer by occupation.

Thomas F. Beasley was the son of Samuel Lemuel Beasley and Martha Hitchcock. Known children other than Thomas were: Samuel Lemuel, Jr., William, Edmund, and Josephine Beasley.

Beasley, William - William Beasley enlisted in Company A of the 1st Alabama, USV as a private on January 1, 1864, at Camp Davies, Mississippi for a period of 3 years. He was enrolled by Lieutenant Hinds and was mustered in February 5, at Memphis. The Muster and Descriptive Roll listed him as having been 50 years old, 5'-10" tall, having a fair complexion, blue eyes, light hair, born in Abbeville District, South Carolina, and a farmer by occupation. The March and April 1864 Muster Roll reported him to have deserted from Mooresville, Alabama on April 11, 1864, with 1 Carbine and Carbine accoutrements complete, 1 saber belt, and 1 Remington Revolver complete. William was mustered out October 20, 1865, in Huntsville, Alabama owing the U.S. Government $33.15 for the arms and equipment.

Beasley, William M. – William M. Beasley enlisted in Company I of the 1st Alabama Cavalry, USV as a 1st Lieutenant on July 21, 1865, in Huntsville, Alabama for the duration of the war. He was one of the early enlistees who was shipped to Nashville, Tennessee and merged with Company D of the 1st Middle Tennessee Cavalry, US. On November 30, 1862, William was shown as being absent, resigned October 8, 1862, in Nashville. His name appeared on the Company Muster-Out Roll July 19, 1865, stating he had resigned. A letter in Beasley's file dated October 5, 1862, in Nashville, Tennessee, stated: The following communication was received from the Medical Director: Lieut. Beasley is sick in bed in General Hospital No. 14, therefore unable to present himself and purposes to send in his resignation. Signed Eben Swift, Surgeon U.S. Army, Medical Director. The examination was then closed and the board proceeded to deliberate the case. Finding: The board after due deliberation said that 1st Lieut. William M. Beasley, 1st Tennessee Cavalry is physically unable to present himself for examination by this board, and they do therefore respectively refer to the matter addressed in the examination of the witnesses, and the report of the Medical Director and recommend his resignation be accepted. Respectfully submitted, Col. George W. Roberts. A note in his file stated: 2nd Lieut. John R. Henry, 1st Tennessee Cavalry, was called and made the following statement: Lieut. Beasley was mustered in as a private in a company of infantry men on or about the 21st Day of July 1862 in Huntsville, Alabama, and for a while drilled squads in the infantry. The company was transferred to the 1st Tennessee Cavalry on or about the 8th Day of September 1862. He has never drilled in cavalry tactics, he has not been really on duty, he has been apparently unwilling to command the company in the absence of the captain and he obliged me to receipt for the company property. I do not think he has been sick much of the time, he is indisposed to act, is not an active man, and is continually complaining of pain in his back, or something of the sort, he has no business qualifications. He is an intelligent man but is not the style of man to make an officer. He is deformed and is slovenly in his appearance and ways, is however temperate in his habits and is a religious man. He desired me to state to the board that he intended to send in his resignation. Col. Tilson moved the following resolution and the motion was accepted: That the Medical Director of the department be directed to examine William M. Beasley, 1st Tennessee Cavalry, and as to his physical condition, and report the result of his examination to the board. On motion, the board adjourned to meet Wednesday, October 16, 1862. Signed Col. George W. Roberts, 42nd Illinois Infantry. Another letter dated October 14, 1862, from Hospital No. 14, Nashville, Tennessee stated: I hereby certify that I have carefully examined William M. Beasley, 1st Lieut., Co. D, 1st Tennessee Cavalry, and find him incapable of performing the duties of a soldier on account of a tendency to phthisis pulmonalis (consumption of the lungs). He has a very bad cough, and has done no duty for the past 60 days. Approved, A.C. Wedge, Assistant Surgeon, 3rd Reg. Min. Vols. William M. Beasley was honorable discharged on October 16, 1862, in Nashville, Tennessee. A letter from Headquarters District of Ohio, Nashville, Tennessee, October 16, 1862, Official Order No. 185, In accordance with the recommendation of the Board of Examiners and the report of the Medical Director, the resignation of 1st Lieut. William M. Beasley, 1st Tennessee Cavalry is hereby accepted and he is accordingly discharged the service this date. By Command of Major General Buell, signed W.H. Sidell, May 15th U.S. Infantry A.A.A.G.

William Beasley was born in 1827, most likely in North Carolina, where he spent most of his childhood. His father was Silas Mercer Beasley and his mother was Sarah Elizabeth (Reese) Beasley. They were God-fearing people who were strict, but loving in raising their children. William had six brothers and five sisters. The family moved often – usually every year. They lived mostly in abandoned Indian villages, which they would clear, plant then sell and move on. The children grew up playing with Indian children and learned many of their ways.

On February 5th, 1852, William married Almeda L. Hamrick in Gilmer County, Georgia. The "story" passed down in our family was that Almeda was a Cherokee Indian. We haven't been able to prove or disprove this. This was the time when the government was "relocating" the Cherokees, so perhaps William married Almeda to keep her from being moved. Since William grew up playing with Indian children, it's certainly possible. Although we've spent a great deal of time looking for her in the many of the censuses prior to her marriage, we haven't been able to find her anywhere. She may have been living on a reservation and later "passed" for white. It's still a "mystery".

Children of William and Almeda were: Henry Philford Beasley, born December 6, 1852, in Pickens County, Georgia, died October 8, 1890, in Licking, Missouri; Jesse J. Beasley, born May 12, 1854, died June 22, 1925, buried in Boone Creek Cemetery, Licking, Missouri; Rachel Elizabeth Beasley born April 11, 1856, in Pickens County, Georgia, died in October 1881, buried in Bethel

Cemetery, Summersville, Missouri; Martha Winiford Beasley born November 11, 1857, in Winston County, Alabama, died July 27, 1865; William Byrd Beasley born May 16, 1859, in Winston County, Alabama; John Silas Patrick Beasley, born January 15, 1861, in Winston County, Alabama, died September 10, 1909, in Summersville, Missouri, buried in Bethel Cemetery, Summersville.

William and Almeda lived in Georgia and later Alabama. He owned 40 acres in Alabama and worked as a farmer and a carpenter.

William, his father and brothers did not agree with the South's position in the Civil War. They felt that it was "not their war", so eventually when the war broke out, William and three of his brothers joined the Union Army. William served as 1st Lieutenant in the 1st Alabama Cavalry, USV. While in the Army, William initially trained and drilled squads. Various documents list different diseases that he contracted – among them are measles (which the family always said was the cause of his death), consumption and a bad cough, plus a few others. He became ill within a few months of mustering in, and eventually had to resign his commission and ultimately passed away in Nashville Hospital #14 on January 23, 1863. He is buried in Nashville National Cemetery. Family information written and submitted by Susan (Valentine) McWilliam & Janet (Beasley) Keagy, great, great granddaughters of William Beasley.

Beaver, William - William Beaver was shown as serving in Company F of the 1st Alabama Cavalry, USV. The only other information about him showed him absent sick in USA Hospital in March 1865.*

Belcher, Charles W. - Charles W. Belcher enlisted in Company D of the 1st Alabama Cavalry, USV as a private on May 20, 1864, in Decatur, Alabama for a period of 3 years. He was enrolled by Lieutenant Pease, and was mustered in June 16, 1864, in Decatur. The Muster and Descriptive Roll showed him to have been 23 years of age, 6'-1" tall, having a light complexion, blue eyes, light hair, born in Jefferson County, Alabama, and a farmer by occupation. The July and August 1864 Muster Roll showed him to have been a Corporal. The May and June 1865 Muster Roll listed him as having been a Sergeant. He was mustered out October 20, 1865 in Huntsville, Alabama owing the U.S. Government $2.70 for losing 1 halter and 1 curry comb. Charles W. Belcher was appointed Corporal July 1, 1864, by Regimental Order Number 70, and was appointed Sergeant from Corporal on September 1, 1864, by order of Colonel Spencer.

Belford, S. - There was only one record for this S. Belford, which showed him being in Company H of the 1st Alabama Cavalry, USV and being absent sick in Post Hospital at Huntsville, Alabama June 5, 1865.*

Story of the Bell Family – Brother Against Brother

The following is an example of divided families during the Civil War, and how strongly the Unionist felt toward family members who chose to fight for the Confederacy. Mr. James B. Bell of Winston County, Alabama was a staunch Unionist who loved his country and wanted his sons to join the 1st AL Cavalry, US Volunteers to fight and help protect the country he loved. While three of them did indeed fight for the Union, he had one son who wasn't convinced that was the right thing to do, so he went off with a cousin and joined the Confederacy, which astounded his father and brothers. His father writes letters to Henry expressing his displeasure for his choice and actions. (See military service of sons in the Union after these letters.)

James B. Bell had six children (Robert, John, Henry, Eliza Jane, Francis, and James T.), all Union Loyalists except for one son, Henry. He joined the Confederacy with his cousin, Andrew Lowrimore, and moved to Mississippi. James B. and wife Elizabeth Lowrimore raised their children in Winston County. Henry's brothers, sister, and father all tried to convince Henry to rethink his feelings to no avail. There are seven known letters sent to Henry, who turned them in to the authorities in his community. They were then sent to Governor Moore on July 10, 1861 with a letter signed by A.W. Irvin from Lodi, MS. They are now on file in Montgomery.

"Dear Sir, Enclosed please find a treasonable correspondence from Kansas P.O. Walker Co., Ala. to a citizen of our community, Mr. Henry Bell signed by James B. Bell, John Bell, and Robert Bell which the undersigned regard as dangerous and forward the same to Your Excellency in order that you may be advised of the existence of such sentiment in your State and to enable you to investigate or take such cause in the premises as your judgment and duty may dictate. Mr. Henry Bell to whom the ___ documents were written ___ ___ these individuals reside in Black Swamp Beat in Winston Co. Ala but the Kansas Walker Co. is their P.O."

Robert died in Andersonville on August 3, 1864 (Prisoner of War), John died on August 17, 1864 in Rome, GA, Henry died March 24, 1863, James T. died on July 24, 1864, and James B., their father, died September 15, 1862, all of their deaths occurring during the Civil War. Francis was the only male who survived, and his descendants can still be found in Winston County. These letters have little punctuation, gaps, and blanks, and were written to Henry trying to convince him to come home and change his ways.

John Bell is writing to Henry in Choctaw County, Mississippi - Letter One (sic)

This April the 11th 1860 (1861?) - State of Ala winston county

Dear brother and sister i this day i take my pin in hand to draf you a few lines in ancer to our leter we are all well and i hope when these few lines cumes to hand tha may find you all well and a doing well times is hard hear and there is such a dis steer bene hear a bout our union that there is no chances to sell eny thing henry you never Sed nothing in your liter a bout what you was whether you was youning or diSuning we are uning here and we are are far linkern we are no dis uning hear we are wil ling to be a gavernd by a man that will do as linkern ses he will do he ses that he was elected for the united States and he is a going to be a presidennt for all or nun and i say huraw far lindern henry i want you to doo all you can for mee about that lnd if you can fix eny way to Satisfy oliver and take the land your self try do So and it will all be _____ so no more at this time Joh Bell to henry write.

James B. Bell is writing to son, Henry - Letter Two (sic)

Kansas P.O. C Ala. - April 21st 1861

My dear affectionate son I hav just Recsived a letter from you which gave me great satisfaction to hear from you. but Alas to my sorrow you have priverd to be a cesessionest which I hoped you would be as far from as the north from the south. O my God would that you could see where you stand and turn to the sure and just that Blaced good old Union which our fore fathers fought bled and died to Establ our liberty peace and comfort. 'O would we then soon trample that sacred peace and union under our feet. God forbid my son.

My son dont be angry with me for I truly fear that our peace is done here on this earth. suffer me to adrs you in a fatherly good manner as I have Been living Along time and have Been a close abserver in my time I can see what is coming up just as fast as the ____ of time can Roll it on but I have not the language to Express it. O, that I had so that I could convince you where you stand and what you are doing.

Consider my son what you are doing consult your own judgment and dont listen to the persuasions of others. those large negro holder that just gives one side of the question they will speak to you as what glories would be in the South if you will just help us and Blaspheme the union that sacred union to the lowest degnade, view it my son.

O my son I am sooner to think that you are sorrow that I am a union man would to God my son that you were unionist for you are the only disunion son that I have In Existance and I hope you will take all things Into consideration & turn with me for I belive that I am Right.

My son you stated in your letter & seemed to Indicat that we were all I a land of heathern where we did not no anything and could not get the news. suffer me to Inform you that we are not & I thank God for it though If times keep on we will be as might just a will be if the South cares her disigns into Executions which I hope she will never be able to do. I get the general new from all quarters of the East and am tolerably well inlighten. but is the South Inevensile turn! for this reason I will tell you – enly! For I dont think It is right.

The next statement was that you had been __Terated on I wish you had told me In what way & manner the northhad Ever Intruded on you & what time & what was the case of this I believe I know you say that the north has taking your Negros when has Ala. or Mip ever ___arg negros just tell me of one It is the fronteer states that has suffered by them states if any has why did they seat. ___ick up you did not hear them hollow out for the Southernors ____ no, they pled for the South to hold on and fly off to stay and see If them states wouldnt rescind that law, why Dident those southern sister cut then states off. They could have done it if they unconstitutional law. no, that wasent the Idie with them I till you my son It is office seekers that has caused the hole of this. thy must fly off hav a southern confedracy and have a presedent In the south to rule over us In ____ ____ what they have already done we the south has to pay what the united states had to pay. how are you going to stop all this, where is your force to do it where are your arms where are your B____ of war and In fact I dont see any chance for you. The north has them all & all the materials to work with & the men to ____ so I think the chance of the south is but slim but 7 states and half of them is for the union & a great portion has got to crave for the war to ____ommence as there is no chanc for peace & as Ala has ceseded there is about 1 half of the Counties a going to cesede from the state for they have the same Right as the state had to secede from the untied states they will go Back to to Tennessee! not Back (haverwill) to be cut off to Tenn! For it is not come off nor has (haverwill) The States that have seceded. S.C. Ala Missp g. A. L. A. & florida. It is doubtful any Being off for they cannot come out only In the same way that they went In by petition. I am sure there is not one done that just one or two said it was off and it is slaves that why did they not let the people have the vote on it. cant you see that the few ruled the hole state They dont let us have nothing to say In public concerns state and If ____ ____ ____ have that they will take more & press a little harder as we could ____ it that is the way they are working the thing. what is the Reason they not let us have vote on it. Because they ____ the union would carry and the be –nonsintes- in there Designs. and for my heart I believe lincoln will make a fair president, give him a trial and see what he does and if he dont administration right then I say take him out hang him as high as negro swing him between ____ the heavens and Earth; he has no power on things. Congress congress has to Empower him before he can do anything. he can only veto and 2 thirds of the house will take the power away from him Then. what has Davis done why they in 15,0000.00 millions of Bonds to be sole and our childrens children will be taxed to pay off the Bonds. 29 millions of debt hanging over Ala cant more than pay the intrest on it, lincon has never done that yet. he hasent put the tarf on us yet nor taxet but still he is the object of scorn & for the ____ he is just as fair blood as any. If he is negro It looks like the south Exceptly as they are ____ of negros. I am not a avolitaineast you ____ to cencer me. I don't care for the negros [the last page of this letter is missing.]

Eliza Jane Bell writes to her brother Henry - Letter Three (sic)

The State of Alabama Winston County - April 21, 1861

Dear brother If you could but Simpathise with me after hearing that you have Rebeled against the government that you have been bornd and Raised under it is a hart rending thing to me I did not think I had a brother in the world that would done to Do sutch a thing I can but hope that you will Return as the prodigal son did when he was prest with hunger So I hope that you will come back before you are prest Back but if you dont it wont be long before you will be prest back by force with Shame I wrote to you to pick out me a Sooter before I got there but if there is none but disunion men there for God Sake let them alone for I would disdain to keep company with a disuinist for if he will cecede from the government that has allways sustaned his Rights he would Cecede from his family he would not Claim a union with them he would say after while I am a cecede God forbid that I Should ever get such a Sooter or that for I Can but put my Centements here for the world to see.

May the time hasten to Roll a Round when all the true men of America may be bound together in one Soled band of Republic and all the Cecessionist that can se and wont see may tha fall to the ground as a fig tree casteth his untimely fruit to the ground when Shaken by a mity wind.

Please Read my Centiments to those young gentlemen that claim them Selves to be disunionist I can State futher that it would not be worth while for you to pick me a Sooter in that in lighted land where tha are old So intelagent for tha would not have a Sooter that came from this hethern land when people Cant hear any thing nor know any thing.

Brother dont think Hard of me when you Read my letter. But change back that opinon of yours to the Rite one. I have to wrighte my sentiment as they are but dont let sucession do a way the love between Brother and sister so non But remain your Sister Elizza Bell.

P.S. write me as soon as you get this & let me hear from you so farewell

[At the bottom of this letter is written: "Henry Bell is my name and fight I will before I will submit to black republican princible my i will first." A.L. Lowrimore signed his name three

times.|James Bell is writing to his nephew, Andrew Lowrimore in Choctaw County - Letter Four (sic)
April the 22 1861

My Dear nephew, a few words to you & I will close you wante me to give your love to all your friends & you wanted to no what they all are in Regard to their pricipals they are all union to A man & full Booded union at that so you have no friends here if your principal In disunion I mean, your father is as strong a union man as ever was so he is not a friend to your principal although he loves you dearly he cannot bid you God speed In that one thing. We are all union men. Andrew you Requested me to give your love to your friends you give my love to all Relalationns In that vicinity & if any I have any union friends there tell them howdy for me. & I will do so for you here But I want you to think for a moment where and what you are doing See if you aint wrong Who are you going to fight. Your own Born Kin your relations It is just like it was in 1775 Read the history about the stamp act & see if you cant foretell what is coming Mr Davis has to hav 1/8 of your cotton now beside the taft they have put on us. no more But Remains your Uncle until Death. James Bell

P.S. write me & let us hear from you as quick as posably. that all now and if you are not satisfied tell me so in your next letter.

James Bell is writing to son, Henry Bell - Letter Five (sic)

Kansas Ala - April 22, 1861

My Dear afectionate son it is with pleasure that I right a few more lines to you. my love and affection is not grown cold to toward you, I love you Dearly. but suffer me to Reason with you I cant see nor find any place in the Bible says any thing about negroes It only speaks about slaves and they were not treated like negroes & Beasts. But like humanes If you would take up the history of the united states & Read that and see how that liberty came that you disdain uneto to live under that you have Been Born & Raised under & which ought to Be sweeter to you than honey come see how it was established & what hardships our forefathers has to undergo before obtained. It is a shame to this America, now this quick after tare up things in such a manner. Deslove that union which our forefathers gained us they knew that they could not live long to Enjoy that freedon. But ____ bring one another up that their children would Enjoy it & be free from tyranny,s yoke, & when they had gained freedon & went In to a union and compact of treaties. They had no though that their children would be so near of baring that yoke on their necks in 1861, about 84 years freedon & before 10 years we will Be In bondage if you keep on. In that course no other chance under heaven, unless the God of heaven assist I pray He will hear in our behalf, take up the History of the world henry & look at the instances in that & in evry place where a nation devided if you Exmine you will see that they did not Remain so long for another nation would come In and capture them & take them off Into Bondage & there never has been many nations stood as long as America has but the time is close by when it will fall. I fear it is any how! to this thing has Been a working up for the last 20 years look at the changes they made In it for you look at the History you cannot be decieved, but there is a liability of your being decieved if you lisen to the persuasions of them grandis & not believe the History, you Read nothing bus disunion papers and I have never heard a word of truth In it yet, they dont Bring themselves to the South But put statements In them that are not so. nor never, can be so, I have ____ both sides of the question carefully & without any partiality I was bound to be on thee Rite cause & if every man in the south was a ceader I would remain a union man all the time I am unmoveable in that I dond change with the Majority I go in for the sondness of the thing and not to be Ruled by unnatureal beings who will make you believe that you are wrong if you do go with them, & after they get there plans ____ then you may go to Ruin for, O, they care [a page possibly missing at this point.] they will be able to buy some of those Bonds & then you may be taxt to to pay them off, we wont get shed of them fifty years we cant pay the interest on them let alone the principal.

Henry read my letter and dont get vent at me for writing you such a letter and think for a while & see if you are not wrong & see if you cant view it the same way I do. I would be glad if I could see you now and converse with you on this subject I could show you planer than I can handwrite, so no more at this time bit everby Remain you affectionate Father until Death James Bell.

N.B. this leaves us all well with the Exception foof Bad colds & I hope it will find you all well and doing well. James Bell L.S. Give my love to all Relations in that part & tell them I would like to see them & tell all the union Boys howddy foor me. Write as soon as you get this & let us hear from you

James Bell to Henry Bell. [At the bottom of this page is "A.L. Lowrimore is my name" the message is not readable.]

James B. Bell is writing to son, Henry Bell - Letter Six (sic)

Ethridge, Alabama, April 27th 1861

Dear Son, it is with pleasure that I seat my self this morning to let you know that we are all well at present hoping when these few lines comes to hand that they may find you all well and doing well. I received A letter from you and Andrew Lowirmore this morning and was glad to hear that you are well but it was disgusting to me to think that I had Raised A Child that woud Cecede from under the government that he was bornd and Raised under it is Something Strane to me that people Can forget the grones and crys of our fourfathers in the Revoloutin So quick. Henry just think back to the time when our forefatherse walked over the frozened ground bare foot leaving ther blood on the ground when fighting for the liberties that you have enjoyed ever Since you hav had a being in the world God forbid that I ever Should even be Cald a Cecessionist. I had jest as Soon be Cald a tory, as to Comit treson ganst the government that was Sealed with the blood of my fathers. the Scripture informs us that a House Devided against its Self Cannot stand. The Scriptures informs us that the Isralites divided in to Northism & Souhisn's and She was in bondage in less than ten years. Henry you are out in a Ceceding Country and tha have got you puft up with Cecessionism as tight as a tode. I dont see what you nede to care for you hant got no Slaves. All tha want is to get you puft up and go to fight for their infurnerl negroes and after you do there fighting you may kiss ther hine parts for a tha ceare. Henry you wrote that if we was in a inlighten Country that we could see better. I want you to understand that we ant in a hethen Land or wasent until Ala went out of the union and this ant any nigher a hethern Land than that. Thare is as Smart men in this Country as thare is in Mississippi and as intellagent gentlemen as lives anywhere. henry may time hasten to Roll around when you can se your own intrest and turn your Back upon the Cursed question Caled Cecessionism and Return like the prodigal Son and then Come over and we will kill the fated Calf. So I will Close my few Remarks hoping when you se these few lines that you will no longer a Cecessionist. J.B. Bell to Henry Bell.

Robert Bell is writing to his brother, Henry Bell in Choctaw County Mississippi

Letter Seven (sic)

June 10th 1861

State of Alabama Winston County Dear brother it is this one time more that I take my pin in hand to try to right you a few lines to let you no that I am tolebral well and I hope that when this Comes to hand that it may findes you all well and that you aught to bee when I say what you aught to bee is to not bee and rebel nor a fool the way you hair bin righting hear you air one or the other and you cant deniy it nor you nead not to try to deniy it to mee your side has not got a foundaution that is eney sounder than a soft bull tied in the spring of the year you have not I suppose from the way you have bin riting seen nor heard nothing but disunion secession confederate confederated and confederation and you all haive Swollode it down like Sweet milk and Softe peaches I say hurrow for lincol [Lincoln] it has ben Said that lincol [Lincoln] was a going to free the negros that is a ly I will say that it seames to me like congress has something to say aboute it first it has bin said that the union men was traitors that I say is a ly again I am a heap freader of the disunions with their helish principals than I am of lincol. he has not said that he was a going to free the negros he has bin beging far peas ever since he was elected he has offered the south more than I wood have dun he has offerd the south eney thing they wood ask for if they would stay in [One full line is unreadable because of fold.] bee as it was with Joseph and his brothers if the south will not do eney thing that is right and fair it is said by you or some of you dis union party that lincol was elected by a large negro vote that is not so and you now it two when I say you I mean you all on the dis union side and all hoo the shoe may fit Can ware it. theair was something said a bout a company being sent out here to do something with the union men Send them on when you git redy and it will bee a too hand again I am not afeard in to it my self come on and you will mete with your uncle feddys theair is no dainger of you a coming or sending on that bysness there is too mutch meanness at the bottom of the disunion party to soot me one man in this county said that he wood live fat among the (women) if the war cum on and he has left the County and I heard of a nother one being shot or shot at for trying to force a woman to it.

I am a union man my self and a union principal and all the rest of the connection here there is not ceding 15 rebels in our beat and I say hurrow for lincon and the union party the dis union party has committed treason You say that lincon was elected by a large negro vot that will not do if that bee the case why did not you brake the election at the start it looks to me like he was lawfully elected when he beat the others all to gether you all had better try to keep your negros as for mine they may go I do not like to smell them so will Rebel is one who opposis lawful authority. Rebel to rise in opposition against lawful authority Rebellion insurrection against lawful authority Secede to withdraw from fellowship secession the act of with draw ing from union the act of joining concord.

This is what I am in for I was bornd and Raised in the union and I exspect to dy with the union principal in mee I will Dy before I will take an oath to support the Southern confedersa when ever lincoln dus eney thing Contray to the Constitution I am then ready and willing to help put him a way from their so i ad no more. Robert Bell

Bell, Francis - Francis Bell (3rd great-grandfather of P.J. Gossett) entered the Union army as a private in 1862 and was discharged in 1863 for disability. It's probably lucky that he did get discharged, since he had two brothers to die in the Union army, both within two weeks of each other and one of those being at Andersonville prison. Another brother died in the Confederate army, and their father, James B. Bell, wrote letters to his son in the Confederate army trying to convince him to come home. James died, himself, in 1862 while caring for his sons in Tennessee. Imagine how James' wife, Elizabeth, felt! My favorite quotes from the letters are where he was glad to hear his son was doing well (sic) "but it was disgusting to me to think that I had Raised A Child that would secede from under the government that he was born and Raised under..." and you haven't "seen nor heard nothing but disunion secession confederate confederated and confederation and you all have Swollode it down like Sweet milk and Soft peaches..." After the Rebellion, Francis started a church that is still organized today: Old Union. (Written by P.J. Gossett)

Francis Bell enlisted in Company K of the 1st Alabama Cavalry, USV as a private on July 24, 1862, for a period of 3 years. He was enrolled by Captain Bankhead and mustered in the same day in Huntsville, Alabama. The Muster and Descriptive Roll shows Francis to have been 19 years of age, 5'-11¾" tall, having a light complexion, blue eyes, auburn hair, born in Marshall County, Alabama and a farmer by occupation. He was among the first enlistees who were immediately ordered to Nashville where they were merged with the 1st Middle Tennessee Cavalry, and the 5th Tennessee Cavalry. Bell was with the 5th Tennessee Cavalry. The Company Muster Roll dated October 31, 1862, shows Francis Bell to have been absent, sent to hospital in Nashville, Tennessee on October 9, 1862. At this time he was shown as being with Company E of the 1st Middle Tennessee Cavalry. He was still in the hospital in Nashville December 26, 1862. The Company Muster Roll dated January 1, to June 31, 1863, stated Bell had been discharged by reason of surgeon's certificate of disability March 14, 1863, and notice had been furnished the company commander. A Notation in his file from the Adjutant General's Office of the War Department stated Francis Bell was discharged March 12, 1863. The Certificate of Disability dated March 12, 1863, stated: I certify I have carefully examined Francis Bell of Captain David H. Smith's Company and find him incapable of performing the duties of a soldier because of Chronic Diarrhea of 4 months standing and with decided tendency to organic pulmonary disease. He is much emaciated and entirely disabled for service. Signed G.L. Gown, Surgeon, U.S.A. A letter in his file from U.S. General Hospital No. 4, Nashville, Tennessee, dated March 21, 1863, to the Commander of Company E of the 1st Tennessee Cavalry, stated: Sir, a private from your company, was discharged from service March 14, 1863, by reason of Surgeon's Certificate of Disability. Very Respectfully, Your obedient servant, F.L. Town, Assistant Surgeon in charge.

Francis Bell was born November 8, 1842, and died September 4, 1925. He is buried in the Old Union Baptist Church Cemetery in Winston County, Alabama. Tombstone states he served in Company E of the 1st Middle Tennessee Cavalry, which is the regiment in which the men in the 1st Alabama were merged when they arrived in Tennessee.

Bell, James T. - James T. Bell enlisted in Company K as a Private on October 23, 1863, in Marion County, Alabama at age 17 for three years. He was mustered in October 23, 1863, at Camp Davies, Mississippi. In January and February 1864, he was listed as being absent, on detached service as teamster in Vicksburg, Mississippi, in General Sherman's expedition, since January 24, 1864 by order of General Grierson. On March 1, 1864, he was listed as having been taken prisoner by the enemy in Arkansas, near Memphis, Tennessee. In May and June 1864, he was shown as being absent, sick at Decatur, Alabama. James T. Bell died in the U.S.A. Post Hospital in Decatur, Alabama July 24, 1864, of phthisis (pulmonary tuberculosis). He was listed on the Company Muster-Out Roll July 19, 1865, in Nashville, Tennessee, as pay due from enrollment, and $100 Bounty due him. The Company Descriptive Book shows James T. Bell to have been 17 years old, 5'-11" tall, having a light complexion, gray eyes, light hair, born in Marshall County, Alabama, and a farmer by occupation.

A letter from the Post Hospital in Decatur, Alabama dated July 24, 1864, to the commanding officer of Company K of the 1st Alabama Cavalry, USV stated: Sir, It becomes my duty to notify you of the death of James T. Bell, late, a member of our company. He died in this Hospital on the 24th Day of July 1864, from phthisis. Very Respectively I.M. Evans, Surgeon 13th Wis. Vol. Infantry, Surgeon in Charge. Inventory of the effects of James T. Bell stated he had one hat, one great coat, one woolen uniform jacket, one pair of cotton drawers, one flannel shirt, one pair of shoes and one pair of socks. Signed by Lt. J.H. Hornback.

Bell, John - Sergeant & Private John Bell enlisted in Company K on July 24, 1862, in Huntsville, Alabama by Captain Bankhead for three years at the age of 28. He was on daily duty as a blacksmith. The Regimental Descriptive book states he was 28 years old, 5'-11¾" tall, light complexion, gray eyes, auburn hair, born in Morgan County, Alabama and a farmer by occupation. In December 1862, he was absent, sick in Nashville, Tennessee. In January and February 1863, he was absent on courier duty. In February 1863 he was shown as being absent because he was sick in the hospital. His Muster Roll for July and August 1864 stated he died August 17, 1864, of typhoid and congestive fever in hospital in Rome, Georgia. He served as Sergeant until January 1, 1863, when he was reduced to Private by order of Col. Stokes of the 1st Middle Tennessee Cavalry which later became the 5th Tennessee Cavalry and are the regiments in which the 1st Alabama Cavalry, USV merged when they arrived in Nashville, Tennessee.

A letter from Hospital 39, Iowa Volunteer Infantry, Rome, Georgia to Lt. J.H. Hornback stated: "Sir, Your note requesting a statement of the death of John Bell, a Blacksmith in Company K, 1st Alabama Cavalry, is before me. By reference of our books, I find that he died with Congestive Fever on the 17th of August inst.. His effects were turned over in compliance with an order from M.K. Flint, Captain Commanding.

I have to say in this connection that no requests for statements has ever been received of this office prior to this one and if you would condescend to listen to a word of friendly advice, I would respectively suggest that you be less hasty in your remarks at another time. Very respectively your obedient servant, William S. Leonard, Surgeon, 7th Illinois Infantry, Senior Surgeon, 3rd Brigade, 2nd Division, 16th A.C.

John Bell is buried in the Marietta National Cemetery in Marietta, Georgia.

Bell, Robert - Pvt. Robert Bell enlisted and mustered into Company A of the 1st Alabama Cavalry, USV as a Private on January 20, 1863, at Glendale, Mississippi for one year at the age of 30. He was under the command of Capt. Frank Cortez Burdick. When he joined, the company in January and February 1863, it was on active duty as scouts and guides and on an expedition in Alabama from February 5th – 13th and also from February 15th - 28th. They were on active duty as scouts with the expedition through Alabama from April 15, 1863 – May 2, 1863. Robert Bell was caught up in the Battle of Vincent's Crossroads, Mississippi, now Alabama, on October 26, 1863, and was captured and held prisoner of war by the Confederates who later sent him to Andersonville Prison in Georgia. William P. Lowrimore, a private in Co. K, was a cousin to Robert and he witnessed his capture. A Muster-Out Roll dated December 22, 1863, from Memphis, Tennessee stated he was missing in action. Under that it stated he died "August 3, 1864, whilst a prisoner of war". A Memorandum of Prisoner of War Records stated he was captured at Bay Springs, Mississippi on October 25, 1863. He was paroled at Mobile, Alabama November 2, 1863. Robert died of scurry and dysentery on August 3, 1864, while still being held POW. He was buried in Grave #4622 in camp. He is buried in Andersonville National Historic Cemetery in Andersonville, Georgia. His tombstone states he was in Co. E, 1st Middle Tenn. Cav. Information submitted by Tommy Martin and the author.

Bellamy, Nathan P. - Nathan P. Bellamy enlisted in Company C of the 1st Alabama Cavalry, USV on February 20, 1864, in Memphis, Tennessee for a period of 3 years. He was mustered in March 10, 1864, in Memphis. He was appointed Sergeant March 1, 1864, but was reported to have deserted November 9, 1864, from Rome, Georgia with two Colt revolvers, one Smith Carbine, horse and accoutrements. The Muster and Descriptive Roll showed Nathan to have been 24 years of age, 5'-4" tall, having a fair complexion, blue eyes, light hair, born in Franklin County, Georgia and a farmer by occupation. The July and August 1864 Muster Roll stated he was absent, on detached service as a scout for General Vandiver. He was shown as being mustered out on October 20, 1865, in Huntsville, Alabama, owing the U.S. Government $52.80 for the lost equipment. He was still shown as having deserted on his Muster-Out Roll. Nathan was listed as being single.

Bennett, William - William Bennett enlisted in Company C of the 1st Alabama Cavalry, USV on December 24, 1862, in Corinth, Mississippi for a period of one year. He was mustered in on December 28, 1862, at Corinth. The September and October 1863 Muster Roll listed him as being absent, on detached service with Brigadier General G.M. Dodge. The Regimental Descriptive Book showed William Bennett to have been 27 years of age, 6'-2" tall, having a fair complexion, blue eyes, dark hair, born in White County, Tennessee, and a farmer by occupation. He was mustered out December 27, 1863, at Camp Davies, Mississippi due to expiration of term of service. William's name appeared on the returns for December 1863, stating he was on extra or daily duty as a scout since September 7, 1863.

Benson, George W. - George W. Benson enlisted in Company B of the 1st Alabama Cavalry, USV on January 12, 1864, at Camp Davies, Mississippi for a period of 3 years. He was mustered in February 5, 1864, in Memphis, Tennessee. The Muster and Descriptive Roll listed him as being 22 years of age, 5'-8" tall, having a light complexion, gray eyes, dark hair, born in Franklin County, Alabama, and a Professor by occupation. On October 1, 1864, George was appointed Sergeant from Private on February 5, 1864, and promoted from 1st Sergeant to 2nd Lieutenant of Company A. The January through August 1865 Muster Rolls listed him as being absent, assigned to special duty with Company A, Special Order Number 8, Headquarters, 1st Alabama Cavalry, USV on January 23, 1865. Benson was shown as being discharged October 1, 1864, by reason of promotion to 2nd Lieutenant of Company B in Rome, Georgia. A letter dated June 21, 1865, from Huntsville, Alabama stated: Sir, I have the honor to make application for a leave of absence for twenty (20) days to go to Louisville, Kentucky to attend to some very important business. I have been in service about 18 months and have never been absent from the regiment neither with or without leave. Captain West and Lieutenant Smith are present with the company. Signed G.W. Benson, 2nd Lieutenant, Company B, 1st Alabama Cavalry. A note dated June 21, 1865, stated: George W. Benson makes leave of absence to visit Louisville, Kentucky to attend to important business. Been in service 18 months and has not been absent with or without leave. Leaves 2 officers present for duty. Signature was not legible. Another note from headquarters dated the same day stated: Approved and respectfully forwarded with the earnest recommendation that the leave be granted. This officer has been constantly on duty with the regiment since joining the service, and in the campaigns of the last year, has at his post and in every instance did his duty nobly. He can not be spared from the regiment for 20 days without detriment to the service. Signed Jerome Hinds, Commanding. George W. Benson was mustered out on October 20, 1865 in Huntsville, Alabama.

Bergin, James A. - James A. Bergin enlisted and mustered into Company M of the 1st Alabama Cavalry, USV on November 11, 1863, at Camp Davies, Mississippi for a period of one year. He was enrolled by Captain Lomax. The March and April 1864 Muster Roll stated he was absent with leave, on recruiting service. He was still recruiting in Alabama in May and June. The July and August 1864 Muster Roll stated he was absent, sick in hospital at Decatur, Alabama. The September and October 1864 Muster Roll states Bergin was absent, reported to have deserted with arms, while on recruiting service in Alabama October 29, 1864. His name appeared on the Returns dated June 1865 stating Bergin deserted June 1, 1865, from Mooresville, Alabama. A note at the bottom stated he appeared also as James A. Burgar. The Company Descriptive Book listed Burgin to have been 37 years of age, 5'-10" tall, having a fair complexion, gray eyes, dark complexion, born in Tuscaloosa County, Alabama, and a farmer by occupation.

Berry, Doctor Morgan - Doctor Morgan Berry enlisted in Company A of the 1st Alabama Cavalry, USV as a private on January 10, 1864, in Camp Davies, Mississippi and was later assigned to Company D. He was enrolled by Captain Shurtliff for a period of 3 years. He was mustered in February 5, 1864, at Memphis, Tennessee, and mustered out October 20, 1865, in Huntsville, Alabama with the rest of the regiment. The Company Muster-In and Descriptive Roll listed him as being 25 years of age, 5'-9" tall, having a fair complexion, gray eyes, dark hair, born in Marshall County, Alabama, and a farmer by occupation. The January and February 1864 Muster Roll stated he had been assigned to duty with Company A by Regimental orders. On February 29, 1864, he was reported to have been absent, on detached service with Company D by Regimental Order Number 47 or 49. The July and August 1864 Muster Roll stated Doctor Morgan Berry was a Corporal and was absent, on recruiting service by order of Colonel Spencer, and his pay was stopped for losing one Remington Revolver at a cost of $20.00. He was mustered out October 25, 1865, in Huntsville. The Muster-Out Roll stated he was transferred August 1, 1864 in Rome, Georgia per Regimental Order Number 69 to Company D for promotion. At the time he mustered out, he owed the U.S. Government $15.80 for losing one shelter tent, one saddle blanket, one curry comb and one surcingle. He was paid $180 for bounty and was still owed $120 to equal the $300. Berry was appointed Corporal July 1, 1864, by Regimental Order #70, but was reduced to ranks September 1, 1864 by Colonel Spencer. (Transcribed by the author)

Berry was born March 1839 in Alabama and died in 1900 in Tennessee. He was the son of George Washington Berry and Elizabeth South. He married first: Nancy Derrick, born about 1840 in Morgan County, Alabama (daughter of William Derrick & Margaret Waggoner.) Children from this marriage were: Baby Berry, born September 1867 and died at birth. The child's mother, Nancy Derrick Berry, also died at this time. Doctor Morgan Berry married second to Elizabeth Pierson Hubbert, on February 27, 1868, in Fayette County, Alabama. Elizabeth Pierson was married first to John Green Hubbert, who was born 1836 in Fayette County, Alabama and died 1863 as a prisoner of war at Rock Island Civil War Prison, Arsenal Island, Illinois. From this marriage there were two children: Josephine (Josey) Hubbert born about 1860; Tolbert A. Hubbert born about 1862.

Children of Elizabeth Pierson Hubbert and Doctor Morgan Berry were: Martha Jane "Mattie" Berry, born July 1869 in Alabama, and married John Press Prince; Mary Elizabeth Berry born March 13, 1871 in Florence, Lauderdale Co., Alabama and married John Richard Kelly October 25, 1887; Lucy Berry, born about 1873 and died shortly thereafter. She was mentioned in Doctor Morgan Berry's Civil War Papers. Doctor Berry is buried at Holly Creek Cemetery in Wayne County, Tennessee. (Submitted by Donna Cuillard)

Doctor Morgan Berry married third to Sarah Caroline Beasley. Children were: Jasey, born 1860; Tolbert A., born 1862; Mattie, born July 1869, married John P. Prince; Mary Elizabeth, born March 13, 1871, in Florence, Alabama, married October 25, 1887, in Wayne County, Tennessee to John Richard Kelly, and died in 1959 in Compton, California. After the death of Elizabeth Pierson, he married Sarah Caroline Beasley January 19, 1876, and had the following children: William M., born February 1880, married July 20, 1897, to Leona Briuce; Roxie, born August 1882, married November 7, 1903, to James Coburn; John Thomas, born November 11, 1884, married Georgia Allison "Allie" Seinea, and died August 17, 1963; Cynthia Morgan, born November 23, 1887, married May 6, 1905, to William Thomas Broadfoot, died February 27, 1973; Ida Miranda, born January 23, 1892, married December 30, 1909 to William Andrew Camper and died August 10, 1972; and Nancy, married a Coleman. Submitted by Anthony & Margo Harper.

Berry, Elijah - Elijah Berry enlisted and mustered into Company E of the 1st Alabama Cavalry, USV on March 5, 1863, at Glendale, Mississippi for a period of 1 year. He was next shown as being absent, sick in the hospital in Corinth, Mississippi, however, the May and June 1863 Muster Roll listed him as being present. The January and February 1864 Muster Roll listed him as being absent, on detached service as teamster in Quartermaster Department since January 25, 1864, in Vicksburg, Mississippi. On March 18, 1864, he was discharged, mustered out of service at Memphis, Tennessee due to expiration of term of service.

Berry, James M. - James M. Berry enlisted in Company D of the 1st Alabama Cavalry, USV on April 19, 1864, at Decatur, Alabama for a period of 3 years. He was enrolled by Lieutenant Pease, and was mustered in June 16, 1864, at Decatur. The Muster and Descriptive Roll listed him as being 19 years of age, 5'-10" tall, having a light complexion, blue eyes, brown hair, born in Blount County, Alabama, and a farmer by occupation. His Volunteer Enlistment Form stated he was born in Tennessee and joined the 1st Alabama in Larkinsville, Alabama. According to James Berry's Prisoner of War Record, he was captured September 19, 1863, at Chickamauga, Georgia and confined at Richmond, Virginia September 29, 1863. He was admitted to Hospital Number 21 at Richmond, Virginia on November 14, 1863, of Scorbutus and returned to prison December 12, 1863, sent to Danville, Virginia December 12, 1863. He was admitted to the hospital at Andersonville, Georgia May 3, 1864, where he died June 17, 1864, of diarrhea. He was buried in Grave Number 2111 at Andersonville Cemetery in Andersonville, Sumpter County, Georgia.

Berry, Samuel - There was only one muster roll found for Samuel Berry, and it showed he enlisted in September, no year given, in Fayette County, Alabama by Captain Tramel.*

Berry, Sylvester - Sylvester Berry enlisted as a private in Company L of the 1st Alabama Cavalry, USV as a private on September 25, 1863, at Fayette County, Alabama for a period of one year. The Muster Roll for November and December 1863, ordered his pay to be stopped for owing the U.S. Government fifty-three cents for lost ordnance. The Company Muster Roll for December 31, 1863, to April 30, 1864, stated he was absent, on detached duty as an orderly by order of General Veach April 18, 1864. He was reported to have deserted from Camp Davies, Mississippi January 10, 1864, but returned to Camp Davies January 22, 1864. In April 1864, he was on extra or daily duty as acting orderly sergeant. Sylvester was discharged September 28, 1864, at Rome, Georgia at age 30, by reason of expiration of term of service, and paid in full by Major Holt in Nashville, Tennessee.

Story of Sylvester Berry (sic)

Sylvester Berry was born about 1829 in Limestone County, Alabama to William and Sarah Nelson Berry. Other children were: John Nelson, born September 26, 1823, in Georgia, married Elizabeth Moore, and died March 13, 1883, in Fayette County, Alabama; Nancy, born May 15, 1825, in Georgia, married George Washington Brazil and died November 26, 1906; Elizabeth Ann, born about 1833 in Alabama, married John Rainey; Henry B., born about 1837 in Alabama; Robert, born about 1839 in Alabama; Cinthia, born March 8, 1844, in Fayette County, Alabama, married Albert Dobbs and died April 23, 1899, in Fayette County, Alabama; William, born June 6, 1842, married Mariah G. Culpepper September 20, 1868, and died June 12, 1913, in Fayette County, Alabama; Joshua, born December 6, 1844, and died January 31, 1862; Sarah M., married John Collier February 13, 1845; and Tarpling, born March 16, 1850, married Emma Collier February 12, 1874, in Texas and died June 23, 1926, in Pushmataha County, Oklahoma.

Sylvester married Sarah Redman Johnson July 7, 1852, in Fayetteville, Fayette County, Alabama, and had the following children: Sherman, Jasper A.; Mathilde Jane, born June 15, 1854, married John Canterbury 1873 in Hardin County, Tennessee; William Sanford, born January 21, 1856, died February 20, 1922, in Johnston County, Oklahoma; Henry B., born August 10, 1858, died September 24, 1942, in Colorado City, Texas, married Martha Estelle Heard; George W., born August 19, 1860, died June 20, 1940, in Pontotoc County, Oklahoma; Emma, born 1864; John F., born 1871; Ulysses L., born October 12, 1873; Lee, born January 25, 1877. Sylvester's son, Ulysses, married Annie Mae Watson and this union produced thirteen children: Sally Leo, Audy Edmond, Claudy, Sherman Edwin, Fredrick Earl, Roscoe Shelby, Neva Agnes, Carl Darwin, Arzelle, Eula Faye, Maymie, Hazel Argene, and Sherley Berry.

In 1950, Kenneth Foree wrote an article about Ulysses L. Berry entitled *NO RAILROADS RAN TO DALLAS HE SAW.* Due to the faded ink, some of the words are illegible. The article goes something like this: "It's strange how the whirligig of life handles a man at times. It turns him about. It really does.

There's U.L. Berry, for instance. Berry, whose initials stand for Ulysses because his father was a soldier under Ulysses S. Grant, has the distinction few living men have. He saw Dallas before the railroads came.

A small man is Berry, who once was five feet ten but who has shrunk a bit by seventy-eight years. He's also slightly stooped but so would you be if you'd followed as many mules as many miles along a cotton row. And a paradoxical sun has burned into him a rich complexion that city life has not removed and bleached his hair, at the same time thinning it down to almost silver wisps on the top of his head. However he is much more active than when he first saw Dallas. Then he was 2 years old. A couple of years back he laid his own concrete sidewalks and built on a front porch.

Berry naturally recalls that glimpse of Dallas through the stories of his parents who were a part of the great westward movement that settled up Texas. Early 1872 it was when his father, Sylvester Berry, his wife, their ten children including Ulysses and possessions and set out from Alabama with one ox wagon. The larger boys walked with the dogs or rode a horse that Sylvester Berry probably owned for he has fought with the Yankees although his brother, Tarp Berry, was a Confederate. (sic) Westward they picked up company, nine ox wagons eventually in all, leaving a war-wrecked land for raw, free Texas. The Berrys were headed for Delta County and a soil blacker'n any slave, deeper'n the ocean, rich as all git out, or so John Collier, a brother-in-law, had written. They had no intention of staying in Dallas in the first place. But when they saw it they thought less of it.

As they came down the long slope through the post oaks where skyscrapers are now, they saw a shirttail full of houses, mostly log cabins. Down near the end of them they stopped in front of a log saloon and a log store. In a hog wallow in front of the saloon was a big dead dog.

"Howdy," said Sylvester Berry to a knot of men in front of the saloon. "Whar's a good place to camp?"

"Right ahead less'n a quarter." (This is where the ink begins to fade.) "Whar ye frum?"

Shortly, the wagon train moved on .... to the river where they found a wel .... camp ground. They also found some ....else: That big dead dog tied to their .... axle. "I swan," said Sylvester Berry.... "No, leave him thar."

Next day they started out for .... County. No use in fiddling in this on .... town. The oxen slowly climbed in the rise .... Berry stopped them in front of the s.... where stood the same gang of men. .... got down, went back, untied the dead .... and said, "You Texas fellers can't git n.... on an Alabamian."

The Texans grinned. "Come in an' .... set 'um up." They did.

Up by the store and cabins .... Greenville, John Cantebury, brother-in .... gave a pony for forth acres which G....ville n.... month later offered two ponies for the .... acres Cantebury snapped him up. Texa.... lots of acres but not too many ponies.

Up in Delta County they found .... Collier hadn't told the half of it. They f.... 20 acres with brush, planted it to c.... and that fall they had picked 27 bales .... cattle got in one night and ate up .... three more.

But you've got to sell cotton. So Sy....ter Berry and other farmers loaded up ....wagons and started for old Jefferson .... mean sort of young fellow who wouldn't .... his name or where he was from ta.... along. They tried to get shut of him .... and couldn't. One night after they campe.... Indian came in with a load of hides .... and made motions he wanted to sell. The .... young fellow said they oughta kill him ... take his hides. The others said no not a.... But the young fellow grabbed up a gun .... shot the Indian who whooped before he ....

Purty soon there were 100 In.... whooping around the camp. A wrinkled .... one made motions which they said they w.... kill only the killer if someone would .... him out; otherwise all. Finally Mi.... Jackson pointed him out. The Indians p.... him down with forked sticks, then ski.... him alive. Ultimately they cut his head.... put it on a lance and rode away. Sylv.... Berry and the rest yoked up and lit out ....

Father Berry made many trip.... Jefferson, but later he moved his family .... the Nations. He died at Roff in the Ch.... saw Nation in the 90's after son U.L. B.... had married and gone. U.L. farmed .... ranched all over the Nations before .... finally went back to their first love, ... County and its black waxy.

He made twenty-five cotton crops up in that deep soil around Mount Joy until the early 1920's. Then he moved to near New Hope, Dallas County. Why did he leave that black waxy paradise? "Got

109

tired wadin' black mud. When it rained I'd hitch four mules to the front wheels, put a box on it and stop every quarter to punch mud out. At New Hope they had fine roads." That whirligig of time was turning.

It turned further. Berry's family of ten children was already breaking up. George D. Cummings, son-in-law and his wife Leo moved here. Then Sherman came to Dallas to work for Dr. Pepper and Roscoe for the R.B. George Machinery Company, both of them finally forming Berry Brothers Machine and Repair Works.

U.L. Berry moved in to the Big World Store area, quit farming and did some carpentering. By 1945 all of his children but one had been attracted by the magnet of Dallas. Then that whirligig spun again and Berry came back .... to the town he came through seventy-six years ago. But this time didn't find any dead dog in a mudhole in front of a saloon. Gosh! But it was bigger'n all git out." Submitted by Shonie Frederick Hill.

Berry, William - The only muster roll found for William Berry stated he was a Corporal in Company D and was on detached service recruiting in Decatur, Alabama in October 1864.*

Berryhill, William R.A. - William R.A. Berryhill enlisted in Company E of the 1st Alabama Cavalry, USV on March 1, 1863, in Glendale, Mississippi, and was mustered in the same day at Corinth, Mississippi. He was mustered out March 1, 1864, in Memphis, Tennessee by reason of expiration of term of service. He was 28 years of age when he mustered out.

Besow, George W. - See George W. Benson.

Bess, William Jasper - William Jasper Bess enlisted and mustered into Company A of the 1st Alabama Cavalry, USV as a private on June 25, 1863, in Glendale, Mississippi for a period of one year. The January and February 1863 Muster Roll listed him as being absent, sick in hospital in Corinth, Mississippi. The July and August 1863 Muster Roll showed him to be a 5th Corporal, stating he was promoted July 1, 1863. He was promoted to Quartermaster Sergeant on September 16, 1863. He was mustered out December 22, 1863, at Memphis, Tennessee at age 20.

William Jasper Bess was born November 11, 1842, in Jasper, Walker County, Alabama. He had come from South Carolina and became a Baptist minister and farmer. He lived in Howell County, Missouri for most of his life after the war where he founded the White Baptist Church, which was disbanded about after about 20 years. He died in February 18, 1919, in Mountain View, Howell County, Missouri, and is buried in the Mountain View Cemetery. (Mike Bess)

Bice, John C. - John C. Bice enlisted in Company L of the 1st Alabama Cavalry, USV on September 25, 1863, in Fayette County, Alabama for a period of one year, and was mustered in the same day at Glendale, Mississippi. John's father, Nathaniel, was a Corporal in Company M of the 1st Alabama Cavalry. On October 26, 1863, John was reported as missing in action from the Battle of Vincent's Crossroads, Alabama. He was still reported as missing in action through October 1864, when he was listed as a prisoner of war at Andersonville Prison in Andersonville, Wilkes County, Georgia. John C. Bice died in Andersonville Prison on September 11, 1864, of Scorbutus. The Prisoner of War Record stated John C. Bice was captured at Bay Springs, Mississippi on October 25, 1863, and confined at Andersonville, Georgia, where he was admitted to the hospital on September 10, 1864, and died the same day. John was only 17 years old when he enlisted and died. He was buried in Grave Number 8425 at Andersonville.

Bice, Nathaniel - Nathaniel Bice enlisted in Company M of the 1st Alabama Cavalry, USV as a private on October 30, 1863, at Glendale, Mississippi for a period of 3 years. He was enrolled by Captain Lomax, and was mustered in December 29, 1863, at Corinth, Mississippi. On the January and February 1864 Muster Roll he was shown as a Corporal, and it stated he was entitled to $300 bounty. The November and December 1864 Muster Roll listed him as being absent, on detached service recruiting in Alabama since November 3, 1864, by order of Colonel Spencer. The March and April 1864 Muster Roll listed Nathaniel Bice as absent, prisoner of war since March 10, 1865, which was the date of the Battle of Monroe's Crossroads near Fayetteville, North Carolina. The Company Descriptive Book listed Nathaniel Bice as having been 45 years of age, 5'-11" tall, having a dark complexion, dark eyes, dark hair, born in Winston County, Alabama, and a farmer by occupation. He was mustered out October 20, 1865, in Huntsville, Alabama owing the U.S. Government $16.66 for losing one Carbine swing and swivel, a carbine cartridge box, 2 saddle blankets, and one bridle. His Muster-Out Roll stated he was paid $180 for bounty and was still owed $120 to make the $300. Nathaniel was a private from October 30, 1863, to January 1, 1864, when he was appointed Corporal. His name appeared on the Muster Roll of a Detachment of Paroled Prisoners at Camp Chase, Ohio for January and February 1865, stating he was present, captured March 10, 1865, from Solomon Grove, North Carolina. The Prisoner of War Record stated he was captured at Bentonville, North Carolina on March 10, 1865, and brought from Raleigh, North Carolina and confined at Richmond, Virginia March 28, 1865. He was paroled at Boulware and Cox's Wharf in Virginia March 30, 1865, reported at Camp Parole, Maryland March 27-31, 1865, sent to Camp Chase, Ohio where he arrived April 5, 1865. Nathaniel Bice was the father of John C. Bice, above, who died while being held prisoner of war at Andersonville Prison in Georgia. John was only 17 years of age.

Bickerstaff, John W. - John W. Bickerstaff, also spelled Bakerstaff enlisted in Company E of the 1st Alabama Cavalry, USV on March 27, 1863, at Glendale, Mississippi for a period of one year. Another muster roll stated he enlisted April 1, 1863, and stated he was absent with leave. His name was shown on a Descriptive List of Deserters as having deserted July 25, 1863. His name appeared on the Returns as having returned from desertion January 8, 1864, at Camp Davies, Mississippi. John was discharged and mustered out of service on March 3, 1863, due to expiration of term of service at Memphis, Tennessee. A Notation in John's military records from War Department of the Record and Pension Office in Washington, DC, dated May 14, 1894, stated: see also William J. Bickerstaff, Company E, 12th Tennessee Cavalry, and Company D, 2nd Tennessee Mounted Infantry. William J. Bickerstaff was shown as thirty-six years of age when he mustered out on March 1, 1864, at Memphis, Tennessee.

On May 24, 1873, John's wife, Mahuldah "Huldy" Lovel Bickerstaff filed a Widow's Claim For Pension stating she was 40 years of age and was the widow of John Wilkerson Bickerstaff, who was shot and killed by the Rebels three miles below Eastport, Mississippi on August 22, 1864. She stated they married August 7, 1856, at Bay Springs in Tishomingo County, Mississippi by John Martin. She stated she knew of no record of their marriage except in Henry Bickerstaff's Bible. Mahulda gave the names of their children under sixteen years of age at the time of her husband's death were: Isadora C., born January 7, 1863, (there was a mark over the 3 so it may be different). John W. Bickerstaff, born March 27, 1865. She gave her Post Office Address as Iuka, Mississippi. Mahuldah signed her name and the affidavit was witnessed by Henry Bickerstaff and William A. McRae.

A letter from the War Department, Adjutant General's Office, 209.820, dated April 6, 1883, stated: "Respectfully returned to the Commissioner of Pensions. William J. Bickerstaff, a Private of Company E, 12th Regiment Tennessee Cavalry, Volunteers, was enrolled on the 1st Day of April, 1865 at Eastport, Mississippi 2 years and is reported on muster roll of Co. April 30th 1865, absent – sick at Ft. Leavenworth, Kansas since June 18th 1865. Mustered out on Detach ____ _ at Fort Leavenworth, Kansas July 1, 1865 in accordance with General Orders No. 77 War Department dated April 28, 1865.

Enlistment paper on file for it___ man reports prior service in 1st Alabama Cavalry from which discharged March 1, 1865. Name John W. Bickerstaff is not borne on rolls of Co. E 12th Tennessee Cavalry or on any rolls of Tennessee Mounted Infantry on file in this office. No enlistment paper of any similar name on file among Tennessee Volunteers. Nature of sickness may & June 1865 not stated. Regimental Hospital Records not on file of either organization

In another affidavit (typed sic) dated December 14, 1891, in Tishomingo County, Mississippi, Mahuldah stated she was a resident of Highland in Tishomingo County, Mississippi, and the widow of John W. Bickerstaff who was killed on his return to the U.S. Army on August 22, 1864, near Eastport, Mississippi and that she was without any means of support other than her daily labor.

J.J. Lovell, aged 46 and Mary C. Bickerstaff, aged 54, signed a General Affidavit stating they were present at and witnessed the marriage of John W. Bickerstaff and Mahuldah H. Lovell at Bay

Springs, Tishomingo County, Mississippi and that they were married on August 7, 1856, by Esquire Jack Martin.

An undated General Affidavit signed by William J. Bickerstaff, aged 58, a resident of Highland in Tishomingo County, Mississippi, stated "I do solemnly swear or affirm that I was with John W. Bickerstaff on our return to the Army when we were captured by the Rebel Soldiers near Eastport, Mississippi and marched out ____ August 22, 1864, where they fired and killed John W. Bickerstaff and I saved myself by jumping down a steep bluff into the river."

A Form on United States of America, Bureau of Pensions, Letterhead stated: "Increased to $12.00 per month from April 19, 1908, by act of that date. It is hereby certified that Mahuldah Bickerstaff, widow of John W. Bickerstaff, who was a Private in Co. E 1st Regiment Alabama Vol. Cavalry, and she is entitled to a pension under the provisions of the Act of June 27, 1890, at the rate of Eight dollars per month to commence on the Nineteenth day of December 1891, and to continue during her widowhood.

Deposition A for Mahuldah Bickerstaff, No. 209.820, dated April 2, 1895, near Mingo, Tishomingo County, Mississippi signed by William Ragsdale states the following:

"I live with my daughter and son-in-law – P.O Highland, Tishomingo Co., Miss. I am the claimant in this case as widow of John W. Bickerstaff who enlisted in Co. E, 1st Alabama Cavalry Volunteers in March 1863 and was discharged after serving about 9 months as near as I can recollect. He did not get his discharge papers, he was out on duty he said when the time came to pay off and he did not get his discharge or pay. He was killed by the Confederate soldiers near Eastport, Mississippi in August 1864 or 1865 on his way from his home in Highland, Mississippi to join the Union Army then at Savannah, Tennessee. All I know about his death is what William J. Bickerstaff, his brother has told me. My husband, William J. Bickerstaff, John W. Bickerstaff and Madison Neal started off together and were captured and my husband and William Neal were killed and William J. Bickerstaff made his escape. My husband was never in any other service than the 1st Alabama Cavalry.

I was married to John W. Bickerstaff under the name of Mahuldah Lovell , on the 7th day of August 1856 at Bay Springs, Mississippi by Squire Jackie Martin. Neither of us had ever been previously married. I have not remarried since his death, nor lived with any man as his wife. I have no property of any kind and am entirely dependant on my relatives and children for support. I am unable to work, and have no one legally bound for my support. I first made an application for pension along while ago I don't know just how long – 20 years I reckon- with a Mr. Avery, but it never went through, and I heard the law was fixed so as I could draw and I put in again about 3 years ago. No sir, I never signed my name to any of the papers but held the pen while someone else wrote it for me. Mr. Avery wrote my name himself to the first paper and I was not sworn to it. But Mr. Gurley wrote my name and swore me to the last claim I put in, but Mt. Stewart? Wrote it for me the other times, three I think and Jack Bickerstaff wrote it for me once I think, and Mr. Stewart? swore me to the papers he wrote my name on. Sometimes I held to the pen and sometimes not touch it at all. Yes, they always read the papers over to me. No sir, I don't know what law my claim is under. Mr. Frank Blount and Jack Bickerstaff have been tending to it for me and Mr. Le___ at Washington DC has charge of the case there." Signed Mahuldah X Bickerstaff and witnessed by G.M. Cornelison and ? Cornelison.

Deposition B, dated April 2, 1895, for Mahuldah Bickerstaff and signed by William J. Bickerstaff, John W. Bickerstaff's brother, stated the following:

"My age is 63, occupation farming, P.O. Highland, Miss. I am a brother of John W. Bickerstaff, and have lived in this county ever since I was 4 years old. I was present when my brother John was married to this claimant, Mahuldah Lovell, she was there at Bay Springs, Miss. this county, by Jack Martin. John had never been previously married. We were raised up together. Claimant has not remarried since John died. She has no property of any kind and is old and unable to work and depends upon her relatives for support, sometimes she lives with me. Sometimes with her brothers and sometimes with some of her children. There is no one legally bound to support her. She has always lived in this neighborhood ever since she married my brother John August 7, 1856. My brother was killed in the following manner. He and I and Madison Neal were on our way from our house in Highland Miss. to join the Union Army there at Savannah, Tenn. I was at the time a Private of Co. D 2nd Tennessee Mounted Infantry. And had been home on furlough and Neal and brother John having served a term in the 1st Ala. Cav. and been discharged were going to reenlist in the 12th Tennessee Cavalry to who I expected soon to be transferred. We started out in August 1864, the exact day I cannot give but we crossed the Tennessee River at Eastport, Mississippi. Savannah was about 20 miles further down the river and we had gotten 10 or 12 miles further on our way when we were captured by a squad of Confederate Cavalry, under a Captain who said his name was Danner (?) and who brought us back to almost opposite Eastport. They took our money and all our papers from us and said something about our being spies. They had us then surrounded – or nearly so. We were on the bank of the river and I saw they meant to kill us and one of them raised his gun to fire at me and the cap snapped and I made a jump down the bluff and made good my escape. They fired several shots, the balls hitting the water and earth around me but I got to the cane break where they couldn't pursue me further. They of course killed John and Neal. About two weeks after this I saw Tynes Terry, a young man who said he had deserted that very squad and who had cau___(?) to us at Clifton, Tennessee to join the Union Army. He told me that he and old man Knolan had helped to bury them, that old man Knolan knew my brother and identified his body. Old man Knowlen is ___? And I have never seen Terry since that day. He did not join my regiment and I do not know what regiment he joined." Signed Wm. J. Bickerstaff

Deposition C signed by Mary C. Bickerstaff on April 2, 1895, states the following: My age is 57. I am the wife of William M. Bickerstaff and a sister of this claimant. I was present and one of her 'waiters' when she married John W. Bickerstaff at Bay Springs, this county on August 7, 1856. Squire Jack Martin performed the ceremony. She had never been married before. She has not remarried since her husband, John W. Bickerstaff's death. We have lived in each others immediate neighborhood ever since. She is poor, has no property of any kind and is unable to work and is entirely dependant upon her relatives for a living. She sometimes lives with us and sometimes with her other relations. There is no doubt what ever of her husband's death just as stated to you in my husband's deposition. I heard even before I saw my husband, after John and Madison Neal went off together that time that they all three had been captured and killed and it was nearly a year after this before I saw my husband and learned the straight of it. I can't say now just how the news first reached me but I think it was that some of the soldiers – Confederate soldiers – brought the news to some of the citizens and thus it got scattered about and I heard it. I have heard my husband relate the circumstances of John's and Mr. Neal's death and his own except many a time. Yes sir, I made an affidavit in this case and swore to it before Mr. Storment (?). No sir, that is not my own signature, my son Jack wrote my name for me while I touched the pen. Yes sir, I can sign my name but I have a fil___ on my right fore finger now so I cannot do it at this time." Signed Mary C. X Bickerstaff and witnessed by Alice Bickerstaff and William J. Bickerstaff

Deposition D was signed by Thomas Lovell and dated April 3, 1895. He stated his age was 47, occupation was a farmer, his address was P.O. Highland, Mississippi, and he was the brother of the claimant, Mahuldah Lovell Bickerstaff. He went on to swear to the fact of their marriage and John W. Bickerstaff's death.

Deposition E, dated April 3, 1895, and signed by J.J. Lovell. He also testified to the same information as the people in the other depositions. It was witnessed by F.M. Blount and T.E. Lovell.

Deposition F was by T.J. Storment and was dated April 3, 1895 and, and stated the following: My age is 36, occupation farmer, also member of the Board of Supervisors of this Company. I have "qualified" the claimant and a good many of her witnesses to papers in her claim. I identify my signatures to BJ 6 to 14 inclusive, and the parties were all well known to me and were sworn as certified. No sir, they did not always sign their own names. It was sometimes done by F.M. Blount and sometimes by Jack Bickerstaff. They, the affiants, authorizing their names to be signed for them usually in my presence." The rest of this deposition is about how the affiants signed their names or gave permission for someone else to sign their names, and about them being sworn in before testimony. It was signed: T.J. Storment, M.B.S.

Deposition G was by J. R. Bickerstaff and was dated April 8, 1895. It stated he was 27 years old and a son of W.J. Bickerstaff and nephew of claimant. He had been assisting her in the preparations of affiants and getting the proof for her claim. He stated he had also signed her name for her to several of the papers, she holding the pen as he wrote her name. He stated he also did that for several other witnesses that were unable to write. He went on to give the names of some of the people he helped sign their names.

Biddel, Simeon - Simeon Biddle enlisted and was mustered into the 1st Alabama Cavalry, USV on March 14, 1864, in Decatur, Alabama for a period of 3 years. The Muster and Descriptive Roll listed him as being 38 years of age, 6' tall, having a fair complexion, gray eyes, black hair, born in Walker County, Alabama, and a farmer by occupation. The Remarks at the bottom of this muster roll stated the roll was torn, and the name was not taken up on the muster rolls of the regiment. This was the only muster roll in his records.

Biford, Perry - See Perry Byford.

Biford, Quiller J. - See Quiller J. Byford.

Billinger, John - See John Dillinger.

Billings, Thomas - Thomas Billings enlisted in Company F of the 1st Alabama Cavalry, USV on June 30, 1863, at Corinth, Mississippi and was mustered in August 13, 1863, at Corinth. He was enrolled by Captain L.S. Pierce. He was reported to have deserted on July 11, 1863, from Glendale, Mississippi. The Company Descriptive Book showed Thomas to have been 30 years of age, 6' tall, having a dark complexion, brown eyes, brown hair, born in McNairy County, Tennessee and a farmer by occupation. Thomas Billings and his family lived at Ripley, Tippah County, Mississippi, and his wife was pregnant with their son, William Thomas. It is thought that Thomas was so concerned about his wife since the war was all around the area, and he went back to see about them. He might have been better off remaining with his company because he was killed August 11, 1863, at Tuscumbia, in Colbert County, Alabama in a battle between the Confederates and Union soldiers.

Thomas Billings was born about 1833 in McNairy County, Tennessee, and in June 1857, he married Mary Jane Pate, daughter of Jackson and Mariah Pate. Their children were: Rosalie Victoria, born October 17, 1859, died March 5, 1933; John Booker, born August 14, 1862, died March 8, 1900, and William Thomas Billings, born November 21, 1863, and died December 24, 1940. After Thomas died August 11, 1863, he was first buried in Barton, Alabama and later removed to the Corinth National Cemetery where his tombstone gives his name as John Billings. (Family information submitted by Judy Mount)

Bird, John A. - John A. Bird enlisted in Company D of the 1st Alabama Cavalry, USV as a private on June 1, 1863 at Glendale, Mississippi for a period of 3 years. The March and April 1864 Muster Roll stated he was on detached service as an orderly at Headquarters, 16th Army Corps. He was discharged June 16, 1864, due to expiration of term of service. The Regimental Descriptive Book showed John A. Bird to be 20 years of age, 5'-9" tall, having a dark complexion, blue eyes, dark hair, born in Denton, (Cocke County) Tennessee, and a laborer by occupation.

Birdsong, Milton M. - Milton M. Birdsong enlisted in Company G of the 1st Alabama Cavalry, USV as a private on December 14, 1862, at Pocahontas, Tennessee for a period of 1 year. He was mustered out November 26, 1863, at Memphis, Tennessee at 17 years of age.

Birt, Henry - Henry Birt, could be Henry Bird, enlisted in Company D, and was shown as being in DeCamp USA General Hospital at David's Island, New York. He was mustered out June 8, 1865. No further information relative to this soldier was found.*

Bishop, Calvin - Calvin Bishop enlisted in Company M of the 1st Alabama Cavalry, USV as a private on December 2, 1863, at Camp Davies, Mississippi, and mustered in December 29, 1863, at Corinth, Mississippi. He was reported as having deserted January 19, 1964, from Camp Davies, Mississippi. A Descriptive List of Deserters stated he deserted January 19, 1864, lives in Marion County, Alabama and was supposed to have gone home. The Company Book showed Calvin Bishop to have been 26 years old, 5'-10" tall, having a fair complexion, blue eyes, dark hair, born in St. Clair County, Alabama, and a farmer by occupation. He was enrolled by Captain Lomax for a period of one year. (He had served more than one year when he deserted.) He is buried in the Sand Springs Cemetery, Wood County, Texas

Bishop, Columbus - Columbus Bishop enlisted in Company M of the 1st Alabama Cavalry, USV on December 2, 1862, at Camp Davies, Mississippi, and mustered in December 29, 1863, at Corinth, Mississippi. He was enrolled by Captain Lomax. He enlisted as a private for a period of one year. On the September and October 1863 Muster Roll he was listed as being absent, on detached service as orderly for General Vandiver since September. He was discharged December 17, 1864, at Savannah, Georgia by reason of expiration of term of service. Subsistence furnished to and including January 15, 1865. Transportation furnished by Quartermaster to Decatur, Alabama. A Notation from the Adjutant General's Office of the War Department dated October 31, 1864, stated: A.W. Edwards, Captain and A.A.A.G. Headquarters, District of Marietta, Georgia reports him on detached service at these headquarters by authority of S.F.O. Number 134, Headquarters of the Army of Tennessee near Kennesaw Mountain October 10, 1864. Columbus Bishop's name appeared on a Hospital Muster Roll at Adams U.S.A. General Hospital in Memphis, Tennessee dated March and April 1864, stating he was returned to duty on April 29, 1864. The Company Descriptive Book shows Columbus Bishop to have been 18 years of age, 5'-8" tall, having a fair complexion, blue eyes, dark hair, born Spartanburg District, South Carolina, and a farmer by occupation.

Bishop, David H. - David H. Bishop enlisted and mustered into Company M of the 1st Alabama Cavalry, USV on December 16, 1863, at Camp Davies, Mississippi. He died January 11, 1864, in the Regimental Hospital at Camp Davies, in Corinth, Adams County, Mississippi, of typhoid pneumonia. The Company Descriptive Book showed David to have been 18 years of age, 5'-6" tall, having a fair complexion, hazel eyes, light hair, born in Marion County, Alabama and a farmer by occupation. Another muster roll stated he was 16 years of age.

Bishop, Francis M. - Francis M. Bishop enlisted in Company C of the 1st Alabama Cavalry, USV on November 11, 1863, at Camp Davies, Mississippi, for a period of one year. He was enrolled by Captain Alexander T. Cameron, and was mustered in the same day at Marion County, Alabama. On September 1, 1864, he was shown as being absent, on detached service in Decatur, Alabama. The November and December 1864 Muster Roll listed him as being absent, on detached service since November 11th with Major Shurtliff in Nashville, Tennessee. He was mustered out January 12, 1865, due to expiration of term of service. From November 1864 to April 1865, Bishop was on detached service recruiting in North Alabama. The Regimental Descriptive Book listed Francis M. Bishop as being 18 years of age, 5'-6" tall, having a fair complexion, hazel eyes, light hair, born in Marion County, Alabama, and a farmer by occupation.

Bishop, James M. - James M. Bishop enlisted in Company M of the 1st Alabama Cavalry, USV on December 6, 1863, at Camp Davies, Mississippi for a period of one year. He was enrolled by Captain Lomax and was mustered in December 29, 1863, at Corinth, Mississippi. He was reported to have deserted from Camp Davies on January 13, 1864, with his revolver. The Descriptive List of Deserters stated he had gone to his home in Marion County, Alabama. A Notation from the Record and Pension Division of the War Department dated October 24, 1889, stated: Application for removal of the charge of desertion and for an honorable discharge has been denied. The Company Descriptive Book shows James M. Bishop to have been 44 years of age, 5'-8" tall, having a fair complexion, blue eyes, auburn hair, born in Bibb County, Alabama, and a farmer by occupation.

Bishop, Robert Wesley - Robert Wesley Bishop enlisted in Company B of the 1st Alabama Cavalry, USV on January 5, 1863, in Glendale, Mississippi for a period of one year. He was enrolled by P.A. Sternberg and was mustered in January 22, 1863, at Corinth, Mississippi. The March and April 1863, Muster Roll listed him as being absent, sick in the hospital at Jackson, Tennessee. On August 3, 1863, he died in the regimental hospital at Glendale, Mississippi. The Regimental Descriptive Book listed Bishop as being 37 years of age, 5'-8" tall, brown complexion, black eyes, dark hair, born in Bibb County, Alabama, and a farmer by occupation. Robert W. Bishop's name appeared on the Returns

115

March and April 1863 stating he was absent with leave since March 28th to take his family to Jackson, Tennessee.

Black, J. - J. Black enlisted in Company F and was recorded as being sick in a USA General Hospital from June 1865 to September 1865. No further information relative to this soldier was found.*

Black, William A. - William A. Black enlisted in Company D of the 1st Alabama Cavalry, USV on May 20, 1864, at Decatur, Alabama for a period of 3 years. He was enrolled by Lieutenant Pease. He was appointed Sergeant on July 1, 1864, by Regimental Order Number 70, but was reduced to ranks on September 1, 1864, by order of Colonel Spencer. The Company Descriptive Book showed William to have been 28 years of age, 6' tall, having a dark complexion, blue eyes, dark hair, born in Marshal County, Alabama, and a farmer by occupation. He was mustered out October 20, 1865, in Huntsville, Alabama, owing the U.S. Government $2.25 for losing one halter, two cartridge boxes, one curry comb and hand brush, and one saddle blanket.

Blackburn, Andrew J. - Andrew J. Blackburn enlisted in Company M of the 1st Alabama Cavalry, USV as a private on October 31, 1863, at Glendale, Mississippi for a period of 3 years, and was mustered in December 29, 1863, at Corinth, Mississippi. He was enlisted by Captain Lomax. In January 1864, he was on extra or daily duty as company cook. In March 1864, he was also on extra or daily duty as company cook. In October 1864, he was on detailed service as scout at department headquarters, since October 12, 1864. In April 1865, he was listed as absent without leave since April 20, 1865, in Orange County, North Carolina with arms. The September and October 1864 Muster Roll stated he was absent, on detail as scout and guide at department headquarters since October 12, 1864, by order of General Corse. The March and April Muster Roll listed Andrew. Blackburn as being absent without leave since April 20, 1865. The May and June 1865 Muster Roll stated he deserted from absent without leave May 20, 1865, in North Carolina with a Spencer Carbine, horse saddle, bridle and spurs. In May 1865, Andrew was dropped from the rolls April 20 at Durham's Station by reason of desertion. A Descriptive List of Deserters stated Andrew J. Blackburn deserted May 1, 1865 from Durham's Station, North Carolina. It also stated he deserted with Spencer Carbine and accoutrements, horse, saddle, bridle and equipment. He was shown on the Company Muster-Out Roll as being 26 years of age, and owing the U.S. Government $132.78 for lost equipment. A Notation from the Record and Pension Office of the War Department dated June 27, 1894, stated: Amendment of Record to show death in the service has been denied. The Company Descriptive Book showed Andrew J. Blackburn to have been 36 years of age, 5'-8" tall, having a fair complexion, blue eyes, light hair, born in Wilkes County, Georgia, and a farmer by occupation.

Blackstock, Thomas H. - Thomas H. Blackstock enrolled in Company L of the 1st Alabama Cavalry, USV as a Corporal on September 25, 1863, in Fayette County, Alabama for a period of 1 year. He was mustered in and promoted to Sergeant the same day in the camp at Glendale, Mississippi, which was about ten miles out of Corinth. He was shown as being 32 years of age. He was captured October 26, 1863, at the Battle of Vincent's Crossroads and held prisoner of war at Cahaba Prison in Alabama, where he died of disease on February 1, 1864. Cahaba was an atrocious prison, as were most of them.

Thomas was the brother of Hanna Blackstock, who married Jonathan Barton. Jonathan and four of his brothers, and two brothers-in-law all served in the 1st Alabama Cavalry, USV.

Another affidavit dated June 18, 1866, in Winston County, Alabama, stated the following: I Peyton Baughn Judge of the Probate Court in and for said County certify that letters of guardianship were on the 18th day of June 1866, granted to Oziah N. Holt for Martha Jane Blackstock, minor heir of Thomas H. Blackstock, deceased now the said Oziah N. Holt guardian will take in his possession the ward of his guardianship and property moneys, books, papers, rites and credits belonging in anywise to said minor and will take good care of the same that may come into said guardians possession belonging to said minor and the said Oziah N. Holt has complied with the requisitions of the law and is authorized to exercise authorities as such guardian according to law. Dated June the 18th day 1866. Signed Peyton Baughn, J.P.

Guardianship papers filed by Oziah N. Holt, second husband of Martha, and also a member of the 1st AL Cav., USV: "State of Alabama, Winston County. On this 24th day of July A.D. 1866 personally appeared Jonathan Barton and James G. Curtis, persons well known to be of Respectability and truth both residing in the County of Winston and State of Alabama and after first being duly sworn by me according to Law do on their oath say that they were present and saw Thomas H. Blackstock and Frances M. Baughn joined in the Holy Bonds of wedlock on the 12th day of December 1861 by Clinton Tittle a Justice of the Peace of the County and State aforesaid. Sworn to and subscribed before me this 24th day of July A.D. 1866 and is not relatives to either party. Peyton Baughn" Judge of Probate. Courtesy of Joyce Farris.

On July 24, 1866, Jonathan Barton and James G. Curtis signed an affidavit stating they resided in Winston County, Alabama and stated they were present and saw Thomas H. Blackstock and Miss Frances M. Baughn joined in the Holy Bands of wedlock on the 12th day of December 1861, by Clinton Tittle, a Justice of the Peace of the county and State aforesaid. Sworn to by Jonathan Barton and James G. Curtis and signed by Peyton Baughn, Justice of the Peace.

On August 7, 1866, Jonathan Barton signed an affidavit stating he was a resident of Winston County, Alabama and was personally acquainted with Thomas H. Blackstock and Oziah N. Holt and knew Oziah married Frances Blackstock. It was signed by Peyton Baughn, Judge of Probate.

On February 12, 1867, Hanna (X, her mark) Barton, Susan (X, her mark) stated they were present at the birth of Frances and Thomas H. Blackstock's daughter, Martha J. on October 30, 1862, and it was witnessed by W.H. Hyde and George W. Holt.

Names and dates of birth of minor: Martha J. Blackstock, born October 30, 1862, shown by witnesses to be the only child. Oziah N. Holt married Frances M. Blackstock November 12, 1865. Francis M. Blackstock Holt drew a pension of $8 per month. Francis married 2nd Oziah N. Holt on December 12, 1861, by Clinton Tittle. Holt was the legal guardian of Martha J. Blackstock.

On December 15, 1868, James Chastain signed an affidavit stating to John D. Terrell stating he was personally acquainted with Thomas Blackstock in his life time, that he was in the Federal Army with the said Thomas Blackstock and was with him at the time he was imprisoned at Cahaba, Alabama and there while in prison in the custody of the Confederate Army and was taken prisoner of war at the same time as Blackstock and was with him at the time of his death on or about the last of January or first of February 1864. It was signed by James Chastain and witnessed by John D. Terrell, Judge of Probate.

On July 24, 1866, Jonathan Barton and James G. Curtis signed an affidavit stating they resided in Winston County, Alabama and stated they were present and saw Thomas H. Blackstock and Miss Frances M. Baughn joined in the Holy Bands of wedlock on the 12th day of December 1861, by Clinton Tittle, a Justice of the Peace of the county and State aforesaid. Sworn to by Jonathan Barton and James G. Curtis and signed by Peyton Baughn, Justice of the Peace. Pension records submitted by Jeanette Maddox and transcribed by the author.

Blackstock, William H. - William H. Blackstock did not have any muster rolls in the records of the 1st Alabama Cavalry, USV, but had one record misfiled in the National Archives that stated he was a private in Company L, and was recorded as being absent, a prisoner of war on October 26, 1863, which was the day of the Battle of Vincent's Crossroads near Bay Springs, Mississippi. No further information relative to this soldier was found.*

Blackwell, John G. - John G. Blackwell, some descendants state his middle name was Glen while others say it was Gilbert, enlisted in Company M of the 1st Alabama Cavalry, USV on October 31, 1863, in Glendale, Mississippi for a period of 3 years. He was enrolled by Captain Lomax, and mustered in the same day in Corinth, Mississippi. The Company Descriptive Book recorded him as being 25 years of age, 6'-2" tall, having a fair complexion, blue eyes, light hair, born in Floyd County, Georgia, and a farmer by occupation. The November and December 1863 Muster Roll recorded him as a 6th Sergeant. The July and August 1864 Muster Roll recorded him as a 2nd Master Sergeant. The March and April 1865 Muster Roll recorded him as being absent, a prisoner of war in the hands of the enemy since March 10, 1865, from Solomon Grove, North Carolina, which is when the Battle of Monroe's Crossroads was fought. A Prisoner of War Record stated Blackwell was captured in

Fayetteville, North Carolina March 10, 1865, brought from Raleigh, North Carolina to Richmond, Virginia where he was confined March 28, 1865, paroled at Boulware and Cox's Wharf in Virginia on March 30, 1865, transferred to Camp Chase, Ohio on April 2, 1865, and reported at Camp Chase, Ohio April 5, 1865. He was sergeant from October 31, 1863, until August 1, 1864, when he was appointed to 2nd Master Sergeant. Blackwell was mustered out October 20, 1865, in Huntsville, Alabama owing the U.S. Government $17.10 for losing 1 saber, 1 belt plate, 1 watering bridle, saddle blankets and a halter and strap. He was due a bounty of $300 and was paid $180 and shown as being due another $120 to make up the rest of the bounty.

John G. Blackwell was born July 21, 1838, and died November 24, 1924. He was married March 10, 1856, to Nancy Bolt, who died in 1864 and he then married Martha Copeland April 30, 1867. Martha died August 18, 1889, and John married Arabelle Lututia Pearson on July 22, 1901. Arabelle was born April 14, 1857, and died February 17, 1925. John's children were: Twin girls born Circa 1864; Lawson G., born March 10, 1868, died before 1915; Marcus G., born December 1869, died Circa 1882; Lewis Grant, born April 17, 1872, died July 30, 1930, married Kitty Blakemore who died two years after marriage and he then married Dolly Williams; Walter Gilbert, born March 11, 1874, died October 25, 1954, married Emma Christine Gord who was born February 8, 1875, and died August 1, 1930; and Rutherford Gailor Blackwell, born February 25, 1877, and died before 1915.

Blakeney, Alfred - Alfred Blakeney enlisted in Company A of the 1st Alabama Cavalry, USV as a private on January 23, 1864, at Camp Davies, Mississippi for a period of 3 years. He was enrolled by Lieutenant Hinds. He was mustered in February 5, 1864, at Memphis, Tennessee. The Company Muster-In and Descriptive Roll recorded the soldier as being 35 years of age, 5'-10" tall, having a fair complexion, blue eyes, light hair, born Chesterfield District, South Carolina, and a farmer by occupation. A Company Muster Roll dated February 29, 1864, stated Alfred Blakeney deserted at Memphis, Tennessee on February 23, 1864. When Alfred Blakeney deserted, he owed the U.S. Government $17.15 for deserting with one pistol, one saber belt, and accoutrements, complete. Alfred Blakeney was able to sign his name to his enlistment forms.

Alfred Blakeney was born about 1829 in Chesterfield County, South Carolina and married Nancy Moore. In the 1910 Lamar County, Alabama Census, he was shown with a wife, Mary, who was 53 years of age. They lived in the Fayette County, Alabama area for several years. Alfred was shown as 90 years of age on the 1920 Lamar County, Alabama Census and probably died between 1920 and 1930. Nancy apparently died between 1880 and 1910 as Alfred was living with a Mary at that time. There was an Alfred M. Blakeney, Born October 25, 1796, in Chesterfield County, South Carolina, and died 1836 in Wilcox County, Alabama. There were two groups of Blakeneys in nearby Lamar/Fayette County Alabama. Alfred Blakeney lived near Millport and it is thought he was a doctor. The family of Thomas Blakeney lived not far away in Newtonville. Thomas came from Chesterfield County South Carolina about 1830 and lived near Newtonville until his death about.......1890? All of these Blakeneys descended from John Blakeney though his sons. Family information submitted by Gary Stevens, 3rd Great Grandson of Thomas Blakeney.

Blalock, James Madison - James Madison Blaylock enrolled in Company H of the 1st Alabama Cavalry, USV on September 18, 1863, at Glendale, Mississippi at the age of 38 for a period of one year. He was shown as 1st Sergeant on the September and October 1863 Muster Roll. He apparently reenlisted July 1, 1864, at Rome, Georgia as a Lieutenant, for a period of 3 years. He was promoted from 1st Sergeant, Company H by authority of Secretary of War, by Major General Dodge. Orders in the field January 1864. James was assigned to duty with Company G, November 1, 1864, at Rome, Georgia, by Regimental Order #102. The January and February 1865 Muster Roll showed him to be absent, sick in hospital in Savannah, Georgia since January 20, 1865. In February and March 1865, he was absent, sick in the hospital at Savannah, Georgia January 20, 1865. He returned from hospital April 25, 1865. The July and August 1865 Muster Roll showed James Blaylock to be absent with leave since July 29, 1865. His name appeared on the Returns dated September 1863, on extra or daily duty as Company Farrier. A letter from U.S. Forces, Goldsboro, North Carolina, dated April 23, 1865, stated: Special Order No. 12, Lieutenant J. Blaylock, 1st Alabama Cavalry, with one enlisted man and private servant will proceed to join his command at Raleigh, North Carolina without delay. The

Quartermaster's Department will furnish transportation. By Command of Brevet Major General Birge. A Letter from James M. Blaylock, dated June 16, 1865, from Huntsville, Alabama stated the following: Captain, I have the honor to respectfully request a leave of absence for 30 days for the following reasons. Viz, I have been in the service of the United States since September 1, 1863. I have never had a leave of absence or been absent without leave. I have not seen my family for nearly two years, and have it from positive authority that they have been stripped of all they had to live on, and this by our own army, too, General Wilson's Cavalry. It is absolutely necessary that I go to their relief. Hoping this request may be granted, I have the honor to be your obedient servant. James M. Blaylock, 2nd Lt., Company G, 1st Alabama Cavalry Volunteers. He was mustered out October 20, 1865, at Huntsville, Alabama. The Muster-Out Roll stated he was appointed to 2nd Lieutenant by the authority of the Secretary of War.

According to descendant Taylor F. Crowe, James Madison Blalock served as a scout for the Union Armies----supposedly led them across Lookout Mountain from Valley Head, Alabama to Alpine--They didn't trust him and turned back to Valley Head. Next he took them to a gap up the mountain where they went on to LaFayette or Chickamauga. William Blaylock never changed his name back to Blalock.

James Madison Blalock was born about 1829 in Monroe or Roane County, Tennessee to Squire Blalock and Katherine Aldridge who were married January 15, 1818, in Person County, North Carolina. James married Emmaline Rutledge on August 19, 1848, in Marshal County, Alabama. Emmaline was the daughter of Robert and Malinda Rutledge. Children of James and Emmaline were: Mary; Robert; William; Margaret; Eliza; Edward and Walter Blalock. James Madison Blalock died March 19, 1874, in Whitesboro, Grayson County, Texas and is buried in the Oak Wood Cemetery in Whitesboro.

Blalock, William C. - See William C. Blaylock.

Blanset, C. - Only one card was found for a soldier with the surname of Blancit, which was filed at the end of the last roll of microfilm of the 1st Alabama Cavalry, USV records. It recorded him as a 1st Lieutenant in Company C and stated he died November 11, 1863. No further information relative to this soldier was found.*

There was a Clement C. Blansit born December 20, 1828, in DeKalb County, Alabama to William Blancett or Blancit, and his wife, Elizabeth R. Hamman. Clement Blancitt married Eliza Jane Lee on January 12, 1849, in Valleyhead, DeKalb County, Alabama, and had the following children: William Allen; James Newton; Clement Clay; John Chambers; America Leanah Jane; Georgia; and Eliza Jane Blansit. Eliza Jane Lee Blancit was born August 25, 1832, in Camp Duncan, Clarksville, Montgomery County, Tennessee, and died October 11, 1916, in Walnut Shade,Taney County, Missouri. Clement C. Blancit died November 11, 1863, in Valley Head, DeKalb County, Alabama. There is a picture of James Newton Blancit in the back of the book.

Blankenship, Robert S. - It is thought Robert, William and Zephaniah Blankenship were brothers and sons of Miles G. Blankenship and Penelope Vest.

Robert S. Blankenship enlisted as a private in Company B of the 1st Alabama Cavalry, USV on March 17, 1864, at Athens, Alabama, and was mustered in March 27, 1864, at Decatur, Alabama. He was enrolled by Lt. Judy. The Company Muster and Descriptive Roll stated Robert as being 29 years of age, 5'-10" tall, having a dark complexion, gray eyes, brown hair, born in Shelby County, Alabama, and a farmer by occupation. The Company Muster Roll dated April 30, 1864, stated Blankenship was absent, on furlough from April 17, 1864, to May 1, 1864, to settle his family in Pulaski, Giles County, Tennessee. The November and December 1864 Muster Roll listed him absent, sent on recruiting service to Decatur, Alabama November 9, 1864. November 1864 to January 1865, Robert was on detached service as a scout since November 9, 1864. The January and February 1865 Muster Roll also listed him as being absent, on recruiting service in Decatur, Alabama since November 9, 1864. February and March 1865, he was on detached service in north Alabama. April 1865, he was absent, sick in U.S. General Hospital. In May 1865, he was on detached service in north Alabama with Major Shurtleff. He recruited until May 1865. Robert S. Blankenship died August 15, 1865 at Pulaski, Tennessee, killed in a

Railroad accident. Another note stated he died August 25, 1865. A Notation from the Adjutant General's Office of the War Department dated June 30, 1874, stated: Was detailed to go to Nashville, Tennessee to look after deserters and while returning to his command and under military orders was killed during a Railroad accident on August 25, 1865, by the falling in of the train of cars through the bridge at Richland Creek, Giles County, Tennessee. The Inventory of Effects had a note that stated "See outside of jacket", but there was nothing on the outside of the jacket.

Blankenship, William W. - It is thought Robert, William and Zephaniah Blankenship were brothers and sons of Miles G. Blankenship and Penelope Vest.

William W. Blankenship enlisted and was mustered into Captain Jones Company of the 1st Alabama Cavalry, USV as a private on July 21, 1862, at Huntsville, Alabama at age 22 for the duration of the war. He was with the group that was immediately shipped to Nashville, Tennessee and merged with Company D, 1st Middle Tennessee Cavalry, USV. The November and December 1862 Muster Roll stated he was absent, with wagon train at Nashville since December 27, 1862. In July and August 1863, William was back with Company I, 1st Alabama Cavalry, USV. In February 1864, he was on extra or daily duty as Company Cook. The March and April 1864 Muster Roll showed him to have been absent, sick in hospital in Nashville from April 1864. His name appeared on the Returns as being absent April 1864, sick in hospital at Decatur, Alabama He died of disease on April 29, 1864, at Nashville, Tennessee. The Company Muster-Out Roll dated July 19, 1865, stated he died in Decatur, Alabama. The Company Descriptive Book showed William W. Blankenship to have been 22 years of age, 5'-10½" tall, having a dark complexion, black eyes, black hair, born in Winston County, Alabama, and a farmer by occupation. The Casualty Sheet wasn't signed until November 20, 1883, and signed by Hugh R. Hedrick, and only stated: William W. Blankenship died of disease November 29, 1864, per roll May and June 1864. The Records of Discontinued Commands stated he died of disease at Nashville, Tennessee April 29, 1864. No evidence of disability or death. It also stated name of disease not shown.

Blankenship, Zephania H. - It is thought Robert, William and Zephaniah Blankenship were brothers and sons of Miles G. Blankenship and Penelope Vest.

Zephaniah Blankenship enlisted and mustered into Captain Jones Company of the 1st Alabama Cavalry, USV as a private on July 21, 1862, at Huntsville, Alabama at age 24 for the duration of the war. He was enlisted by Captain H.C. Bankhead. He was with the group that was immediately shipped to Nashville, Tennessee and merged with Company D, 1st Middle Tennessee Cavalry, USV. The November and December 1862 Muster Roll stated he was absent with leave with wagon train in Nashville, Tennessee since December 27, 1862. The Company Muster Roll dated December 31, 1862, to June 30, 1863, stated Zephaniah was absent, sick in hospital in Murfreesboro, Tennessee from March 26, 1863. The July and August 1863 Muster Roll stated he died in the hospital at Murfreesboro, Rutherford County, Tennessee. The July and August 1863 Muster Roll from Station-Nashville, stated he died in April 1863. The Company Muster-Out Roll dated July 19, 1865, stated he died of disease in April 1863. The Company Descriptive Book described Zephaniah Blankenship as being 24 years of age, 5'-9" tall, having a dark complexion, black eyes, black hair, born in Shelby County, Alabama, and a farmer by occupation. Zephaniah appeared on the Returns for December 1862, stating he was absent, on detailed service with wagon train since December 26, 1862. No full date was given for his death.

Blankenship, Jessie - Jessee Tobe Blankenship, sometimes spelled Jessie, enlisted in Company G of the 1st Alabama Cavalry, USV as a private on March 10, 1864, in Decatur, Alabama for a period of three years. He was enrolled by Lt. D.A. Pease. He was mustered in April 13, 1864, at Decatur. The Muster and Descriptive Roll showed him to have been 18 years of age, 5'-5" tall, having a light complexion, hazel eyes, brown hair, born in Lawrence County, Alabama, and a farmer by occupation. Jessee was mustered out October 20, 1865, at Huntsville, Alabama, with a note on his muster out card that he owed the U.S. Government $9.50 for losing one comb, bridle, one Carbine Cartridge Box, one cap pouch, one saber belt and plate, and one mess pan. Jessee died July 1, 1928, and is buried in the Landersville Church of Christ Cemetery in Lawrence County, Alabama.

Jessee Blankenship was born August 29, 1848, in Lawrence County, Alabama. It is believed by descendants that his parents were Hudson Hardin Blankenship and Martha "Patsy" Wallis, who married January 23, 1832, in Lawrence County, Alabama. Other children of Hudson and Martha were: Joshua L.; William; Sampson M.; Doctor B.; Martha; Elizabeth; Jonathan; and James B. Blankenship.

Blaylock, William Curtis - William Curtis Blaylock enlisted and mustered into Company L of the 1st Alabama Cavalry, USV as a Corporal on September 25, 1863, at Fayette County, Alabama for a period of one year. He was enrolled by Captain Sanford Trammel. The Company Descriptive Book showed William to have been 18 years of age, 5'-5" tall, having a fair complexion, blue eyes, light hair, born in Pickens County, Alabama, and was a farmer by occupation. He was discharged on the surgeon's certification of a disability on December 31, 1863, by orders of General Hurlburt. However, his name was listed on the Returns dated September 1864 which stated: W. C. Blaylock was discharged by reason of expiration of term of service September 29, 1864, in Rome, Georgia. His name appeared on another Return dated January 1864, which stated he was discharged by order January 1, 1864, at Camp Davies, Mississippi. The Certificate of Disability for Discharge stated: I certify that I have examined the said William C. Blaylock, Corporal of Captain S. Trammel's Company and find him incapable of performing the duties of a soldier because of General Debility, the result of chronic rheumatism existing before entering the service and a recent ____ of Rheumatic Fever. He is and will be unfit for duty in any department of the service. Is not a probable case for a pension. Is not able for duty in Invalid Corps. Signed A.B. Stuart, 1st Alabama Cavalry Surgeon. Also signed by Ozro Dodds as Commander.

William Curtis Blaylock was born June 25, 1845, in Pickens County, Alabama to Jeremiah Blaylock and Celia B. Hicks, who were married March 8, 1843, in Itawamba County, Mississippi. William married Amanda "Mandy" Catherine Weatherford on March 8, 1863, in Itawamba County, Mississippi and had the following children: Celia Dora, born September 1865, died 1931; Sarah E., born February 18, 1868, died January 14, 1933; John Basil, born February 6, 1869, died November 30, 1940; William Henry, born September 4, 1876, died February 28, 1907; Anna L., born April 3, 1877, died March 25, 1904; Vertie Lee, born December 29, 1883; Myrtle, born November 10, 1890, died May 20, 1911; and Estle Porter Blaylock, born September 3, 1893, died May 1, 1962. William died December 20, 1902, in Hartford, Sebastian County, Arkansas and is buried across the state line in the Monroe Cemetery in Le Flore County, Oklahoma. His wife and some of his children are also buried there.

Blevins' Brothers : Armistead, Dillard and John H. Blevins

Armistead Elzie Blevins, Sr. was born March 4, 1812, in Sullivan County, Tennessee to Josiah and Rebecca Blevins. Josiah was born 1780 in the Shenandoah Valley of Virginia, Augusta County and died July 15, 1859, in Morgan County, Alabama. Rebecca, last name unknown, was born about 1790 in Tennessee and died April 11, 1851, in Morgan County, Alabama. Armistead, Sr., married Celia Cranford March 29, 1829, and died March 23, 1882, in Winston County, Alabama.

The Civil War must have been devastating for the Blevins family as they had at least three sons who went off to fight for the 1st Regiment Alabama Cavalry Union Army but only one of them lived to return home. John H. Blevins was born February 18, 1837, in Walker County, Alabama, enlisted and mustered in Company K of the 1st Alabama in Huntsville, Alabama on July 24, 1862, as a Private when he was 25 years old. His service would only last a few months before he died February 4, 1863, of typhoid fever in Hospital #8 in Nashville, Davidson County, Tennessee. He is buried in the Nashville National Cemetery.

There were other Blevins who served in this regiment; Jacob Jonathan, Nathanial and William Blevins, who were distant cousins to the above Blevins. Armistead, Sr. had a son, William, and it is possible he was the one in the 1st Alabama but there is not enough available information to know for sure. Nathaniel and Jacob Jonathan were brothers and sons of John and Elizabeth Badgett Blevins

Blevins, Armistead E. - Armistead E. Blevins enlisted in Company L of the 1st Alabama Cavalry, USV as a private on March 1, 1865, in Stevenson, Alabama for a period of 3 years. He was enrolled by Lieutenant Bolton and was mustered in April 18, 1865, in Nashville, Tennessee. From the date and place he enlisted, it would appear he may have previously enlisted in this regiment about the same time his brothers did and then reenlisted in 1865. The Muster and Descriptive Roll recorded him as being 19 years of age, 5'-10" tall, having a fair complexion, gray eyes, dark hair, born in Walker County, Alabama, and a farmer by occupation. The March and April 1865 Muster Roll listed him as being absent, sick in hospital in Nashville, Tennessee since April 20, 1865, however, the May and June 1865 Muster Roll listed him as being present. Armistead was mustered out October 20, 1865, in Huntsville, Alabama, and was paid a bounty of $100. He was able to sign his name on the Volunteer Enlistment Form.

Armistead E. Blevins, Jr. was born February 17, 1844, in Walker County, Alabama. Armistead Blevins was married to Julia A. Campbell on October 28, 1868, in Walker County, Alabama. Julia was born in Forsythe County, Georgia to Adam Campbell, born November 12, 1802, in SC, died at Smith Lake, Walker County, Alabama and his wife, Lucinda Green, born 1806 in NC, died September 2, 1862 in Walker County, Alabama. Children of Armistead and Julia were: General Jackson, born April 9, 1870; Peggy, January 15, 1872; Mary, March 25, 1874; Benjamin F., October 3, 1875; Byrd B., February 12, 1879; Joe E., 22 July 22, 1881; Dillard E. Blevins, February 15, 1884; and Armistead A. Blevins, August 11, 1888. One of his descendants stated there was another unknown infant born June 12, 1886. Armistead died December 15, 1924, in Cullman County, Alabama and is buried in the Blevins Family Cemetery. Julia died January 14, 1921, in Cullman County and is buried beside Armistead. They share a tombstone.

Obituary of Armistead E. Blevins - *The Cullman Democrat December 18, 1924,* Pioneer Minister Buried. Rev. Arm Blevins, one of the oldest and most respected ministers in the county, died at his home on Bremen Route 1, on Monday. He was 83 years of age at the time of his death. He was preceded in death by his wife, who passed away two years ago. Mr. Blevins spent his long life mostly in this county. The funeral was conducted by the Masons and he was buried Wednesday in the Blevins cemetery in Bremen. From History of Methodism in Alabama and West Florida, by Marion Eliza Lazenby, 1960, North Alabama Conference and Alabama-West Florida Conference of the Methodist Church. (Submitted by Robin Sterling) A.E. Blevins enlisted March 1, 1865, in the Union Army and was mustered out in October 1865. In 1867 he was born of the spirit and united with the M.E. Church. He was licensed to preach in 1890. He served from 1897 until 1913, when he retired. He loved the church and went cheerfully to every charge to which appointed.

Blevins, Dillard - Dillard "Dillon" Blevins was born November 18, 1835, in Tennessee or Alabama. On July 21, 1862, he enlisted and mustered into Company K of the 1st Regiment Alabama Cavalry, Union Army as a Private at age 26 for a period of 3 years. He was enlisted by Captain Bankhead. The Regimental Descriptive Book listed Dillard as being 5'-2" tall, having a light complexion, gray eyes, light hair, born in Walker County, Alabama and a farmer by occupation. He was in one of the early groups that enlisted and were immediately shipped to Nashville, Tennessee where they were merged with the 1st Middle Tennessee and 5th Tennessee Cavalry. Dillard was with the 5th Tennessee, however, his Casualty Sheet stated he was in Company E of the 1st Tennessee Cavalry. The Casualty Sheet stated the information was taken from the Roll of Honor Number 22, Page 242. One Casualty Sheet was signed by R. Henry Wevill, Surgeon, U.S.V. in charge. There was a notation that stated "See case of Joseph R. Wood, same regiment. Dillard Blevins' service came to an abrupt end within less than three months when he died of measles on October 17, 1862, in General Hospital #14 in Nashville, Davidson County, Tennessee. He is buried in the Nashville National Cemetery. Dillard had married Mary E. Morris on April 19, 1860, in Morgan County, Alabama. It is not known to the writer if he had any children, in the less than two years they were married before he went off to war.

Blevins, Jacob Jonathan - Jacob J. Blevins was born in Morgan County, Alabama February 12, 1825, to John and Elizabeth Ryan Blevins. On May 8, 1849, he married Mary Ann Davis, daughter of Colonel Samuel Davis, Sr., in Morgan County, Alabama. Jacob and Mary Ann had five children: Rosa Anne Elizabeth, born February 26, 1850; Martha Catharine Adiller, born May 22, 1851; Mary Louisa Jane, born 3 May 1853; William Carroll, born January 10, 1855; and Sarah Caroline, born September 27, 1859. Martha Catharine Adiller died at the age of three on January 21, 1855. Mary Louisa Jane died before 1860 but the exact date is unknown. By 1860, Jacob had moved to Winston County, Alabama. He is listed in the 1860 census with children Rosanna, William, and Sarah. His occupation in the census was listed as "hatter." Although most records list Jacob's address as Houston, the 1860 census says he was living near what is now the Trimble community in what is now western Cullman County. Cullman County was carved out of parts of Winston and Blount Counties in 1877. Jacob had an older brother, Abraham Blevins, who moved to Texas before the war and enlisted in the Confederacy.

On June 27, 1862, Jacob Jonathan Blevins traveled from Winston County, Alabama by horseback to Huntsville, Alabama and enlisted as a Sergeant in Company K of the First Alabama Cavalry, USV on July 24, 1862, in Huntsville, Alabama and was mustered in the same day. He was enrolled by Captain Bankhead. The Regimental Descriptive Book listed Jacob as being 37 years of age, 5'-11" tall, having a light complexion, gray eyes, auburn hair, born in Morgan County, Alabama, and was a farmer by occupation. These early enlistees were immediately shipped to Nashville, Tennessee where they were merged with the 1st Middle Tennessee Cavalry, which went on to be the 5th Tennessee Cavalry. Jacob served with both of these regiments. Almost immediately, he contracted typhoid fever. The associated symptoms plagued him constantly and ultimately caused his medical discharge from military service on November 22, 1862, in Nashville, Tennessee. He had been in the Union Army four months. A Company Descriptive Book stated he was put back into the ranks September 1, 1862, at his own request on account of sickness. The Company Muster Roll dated October 31, 1862, recorded Jacob as being absent, sent to hospital in Nashville, Tennessee September 8, 1862. He was discharged from General Hospital No. 8 in Nashville. The Company Surgeon of the 5th Tennessee Cavalry stated Jacob was incapable of performing the duties of a soldier because of chronic diarrhea, four months standing, supervening upon Typhoid Fever. Jacob's post office was listed as Houston, Winston County, Alabama.

After his discharge, he went back to Winston County and shortly thereafter packed up his belongings and moved to Effingham County, Illinois. Jacob's son William Carroll died October 10, 1863. It is not known if William Carol is buried in Winston County, or Effingham County, Illinois. Not long after he moved to Illinois, Jacob moved to Benton County in the northwest corner of Arkansas and then down south to Scott County. By then, the household consisted of Jacob and his wife Mary Ann and two daughters, Rosa Anne, and Sarah Caroline. Rosa Anne married Isaac James Lucas, marriage date unknown. The Lucas home in Scott County, Arkansas was located near the settlement of Lucas, named for the family of the man who married Rosa Anne.

Jacob's wife Mary Ann died October 9, 1878. She is buried in the Cedar Grove Cemetery in Scott County, Arkansas. A year to the day afterward, daughter Sarah Caroline Blevins married James Berry Hurt in Scott County on October 9, 1879. On November 14, 1886, 61-year-old Jacob remarried Rhody Amena Rice Ramsey in Scott County. Less than a year later, Sarah Caroline Hurt died at the age of 28 on October 27, 1887. Sarah is buried near her mother in the Cedar Grove Cemetery in Scott County.

Jacob first applied for a Federal pension on his brief service as a Union soldier about 1890. Ten years later, after many applications and affidavits from some of his neighbors who had known him for many years, Jacob was recognized for his short length of service to the Union Army and received his military pension for a little while before he died February 3, 1901. He was buried next to his first wife in the Cedar Grove Cemetery.

His only remaining daughter, Rosa Ann, lived until December 14, 1933. She is also buried in the Cedar Grove Cemetery in Scott County, Arkansas. Submitted by Robin Sterling – Some military information transcribed by the author, Robin Sterling, wanted to give special credit to Artela Tyler for supplying some additional information about Jacob Jonathan Blevins to this story.

Blevins, John - John Blevins #1 enlisted and mustered into Company K of the 1st Alabama Cavalry, USV as a private on July 24, 1862, in Huntsville, Alabama for a period of 3 years. He was enrolled by Captain Bankhead. He was also sent to Nashville, Tennessee and merged with Company E of the 1st Middle Tennessee Cavalry. The Company Muster Roll for January 1, to June 30, 1863, listed him as being absent, wounded by the accidental shot from the pistol of William H. Hefner on January 6, 1863.

This is supposedly the John Blevins who was the son of John Blevins and Elizabeth Badgett, who married July 4, 1822, in Morgan County, Alabama. Apparently Elizabeth Badgett was Elizabeth Ryan when she and John married. According to Robin Sterling, John Blevins #1, was one of the earliest settlers of the Tennessee Valley area in the late 1810's and early 1820's following Andrew Jackson's defeat of the Creek Indians at the Battle of Horseshoe Bend in 1813. Jacob's mother was Elizabeth. Elizabeth was first married to Phillip Ryan. When Phillip died in 1822, she married John Blevins. Elizabeth's maiden name is unknown. Jacob had one older brother, Abraham, and two younger siblings, Elisha and Sarah. (One of the descendants of John and Elizabeth stated Elizabeth's maiden name was Badgett.)

Blevins, John H., called John Blevins #2 – John Blevins enlisted in Company K of the 1st Alabama Cavalry, USV as a private on July 24, 1862. in Huntsville, Alabama for a period of 3 years and was mustered in the same day. He was enrolled by Captain Bankhead. John was one of the early enlistees sent to Nashville and he was merged with the Company E of the 1st Regiment Middle Tennessee Cavalry. The Company Descriptive Book listed him as being 25 years of age, 5'-7½" tall, having a light complexion, gray eyes, light hair, born in Walker County, Alabama, and a farmer by occupation. A Company Muster Roll dated October 31, 1862, stated he was absent, sent to hospital in Nashville on September 30, 1862. The November and December Muster Roll listed him as being absent, in hospital at Nashville, Tennessee since December 26, 1862. John Blevins #2 died February 14, 1863, in General Hospital #8 in Nashville, Davidson County, Tennessee of typhoid fever. John was first buried in the Nashville City Cemetery but later removed to the Nashville National Cemetery. He was listed as being single, the son of Armistead Blevins, and lived in Jasper, Alabama before enlistment. John was still attached to Company E of the 1st Middle Tennessee Cavalry when he died, and because of this, his tombstone indicates he fought for Tennessee rather than Alabama and had J.H. Blevins on it. He had three blanks in his possession at his death. After the war, John's mother, Celia, filed for a Civil War Pension for John's military service.

Blevins, Nathaniel - Nathaniel Blevins enlisted and mustered into Company K of the 1st Alabama Cavalry, USV as a private on July 24, 1862, in Huntsville, Alabama for a period of 3 years. He was enrolled by Captain Bankhead. The Company Descriptive Book stated he was 39 years of age, 5'-11" tall, had light complexion, gray eyes, light hair, born in Morgan County, Alabama and a farmer by occupation. In January and February 1863, Nathaniel was absent on courier post. On April 23, 1863, he was sent to the hospital in Tuscumbia, Alabama. The January 1 through June 30, 1863, Muster Roll recorded him as absent, left in hospital in Tuscumbia, Alabama April 26, 1863. As the 1st Alabama soldiers arrived in Nashville, Tennessee, they were merged with Company E of the 1st Middle Tennessee Cavalry, US. On June 30, 1863, he was still hospitalized in Tuscumbia. The January and February 1864 Muster Roll recorded him as being absent, sick in hospital in Memphis, Tennessee since February 21, 1864. He died March 1, 1864, of smallpox in the hospital in Memphis and is buried in Grave #1-46 in the Memphis National Cemetery.

Nathaniel, Jacob Jonathan, and John Blevins (the 2nd John, there were two John Blevins in this regiment) were sons of John and Elizabeth Blevins. It is not clear exactly who their mother was, some researchers say it was Elizabeth Badgett while others say it was Elizabeth Ryan. John, the father, was born about 1802 in Kentucky and died about 1870, probably in Morgan County, Alabama. John and Elizabeth had the following children: Sarah; Josiah, born about 1823; Nathaniel, about 1823; Abraham, June 10, 1823, died March 9, 1900, in Cason, Titus County, Texas; Jacob Jonathan, see below; Elisha, December 24, 1826, died January 27, 1862, in Morgan County, Alabama, and John Blevins, see below.

Jacob Jonathan was born February 12, 1825, in Morgan County, Alabama and died February 3, 1901, in Scott County, Arkansas. On May 8, 1849, he married Mary Ann Davis in Morgan County, Alabama and they had the following children: Rosa Ann Elizabeth, born February 26, 1850, died December 14, 1933; Martha Catherine, May 22, 1851, died January 21, 1855; Mary Louisa Jane, born May 3, 1853; William Carroll, January 10, 1855; Sarah Caroline, September 27, 1859, died October 27, 1887; and Josiah Blevins. On July 24, 1862, Jacob Jonathan enlisted and mustered in the 1st Alabama Cavalry US as Sergeant in Company K, in Huntsville, Alabama at age 37, along with his brothers, Nathaniel and John Blevins. He was discharged with a disability on November 22, 1862.

Nathaniel Blevins was born about 1823 in Morgan County, Alabama and died of smallpox March 1, 1864, in Memphis, Shelby County, Tennessee. He is buried in the Memphis National

Cemetery. He had enlisted and mustered in the 1st Alabama Cavalry, USV in Huntsville, Alabama on July 24, 1862, with his brothers Jacob Jonathan and John. Nathaniel had married Sabrina G. Hart on August 27, 1845, in Morgan County, Alabama. It is not known to the writer if they had any children but none were listed with them on the 1860 Winston County, Alabama Census. Sabrina Blevins was not found on the 1870 census and they could have had some children between the time the 1860 census was enumerated and his death in 1864. It is possible Sabrina had remarried by 1870 and was enumerated under a different surname.

John Blevins was born about 1827 in Morgan County, Alabama and enlisted and mustered in the 1st Alabama Cavalry, USV with his brothers, Nathaniel and Jacob Jonathan. On January 6, 1863, he was wounded by an accidental gun shot from the pistol of William H. Hefner. He was again wounded at the Battle of Monroe's Crossroads in Solomon Grove, North Carolina on March 10, 1865. There was a John Blevins listed on the 1870 Winston County, Alabama Census with wife, Elizabeth, age 46, and children: Mary R., 19; Aggie S., 16; Sarah J., 14; and Elizabeth Blevins, age 12. It is not known if this is the same John Blevins, but it is not the other John who enlisted in this regiment. John was mustered out of service July 19, 1865, in Nashville, Tennessee.

The following is a letter found in Nathaniel's military files:

Thunderbolt, Georgia, Jan 14th, 1865,

In compliance with your order dated Sept 1st, 1864, I herewith transmit Final Statements of the Cases of Privates Blevins, Bell, and Huey, Company K, 1st Alabama Volunteer Cavalry.

It has been impossible to attend to it sooner having been on a active campaign the whole time since the receipt of your letter.

I had furnished Blevins Descriptive Roll when he was sent to the hospital at Memphis, Tennessee and the Surgeon in charge had all the necessary documents to render Final Statements. Huey and Bell were left sick at Decatur, Ala without descriptive Rolls. I being a prisoner to the rebels in Arkansas at the time and the Co. being commanded by Lieut. Tupper 1st Ala. Cav.

There are some facts in the case of Blevins to which I would most earnestly invite attention, Viz, he had $211.50 dollars in his pocket when he was sent to the hospital but a few days before his death (March 1st 1864). Our camp was not a half mile from the small pox hospital and we knew of Blevins death next day. But I received no official notice till the 9th. I had to make a written request for it. John Blevins, private Co. K, 1st Ala. Vol. Cav. had called at the hospital before I had received a Statement and ascertained from the clerks that the money of his brother Nathaniel was there but Surgeon Geo. F. Huntingdon was not willing to admit but $101.00 dollars but the clerks had told John Blevins of $201.00. He finally admitted it and the figures on the Inventory he sent me shows a 1 altered to a 2. John Blevins offered to identify himself as brother to the deceased and his legal representative but Surgeon Huntingdon refused to hear the testimony offered on the case and preferred to pay the money over to the paymaster if he has done so his receipts were sent up with the papers he should have sent. I reported the facts of the case to the proper authorities at Memphis immediately but was captured by the rebels in Arkansas on the 21st of March and detained there till 24th April by which time the Regt had moved to Decatur, Ala. and it was impossible for me to attend to it. I intended to prefer charges against Surgeon Huntingdon and have the matter investigated but have had other duties of more importance of the service to attend to. There are the main facts in the case which I can fully prove and if Surgeon Huntingdon has not sent receipts from some Paymaster, I would respectfully ask to be informed of it so that I can prefer charges against Asst. Surgeon Geo. F. Huntingdon and get justice done to a faithful and good soldier.

Yours respectfully, your obedient servant, J.H. Hornback, 1st Lieut. 1st Ala. Vol. Cav., Commanding Co. K. Most Blevins family information was submitted by Robin Sterling.

<u>Blevins, William Carl</u> - William Carl Blevins was born November 11, 1839, in Winston County, Alabama to Armistead Elzie Blevins, Sr., born March 4, 1812, in Sullivan County, Tennessee and Celia Selah Cranford, born about 1812 in Chester County, South Carolina. Armistead and Celia married March 29, 1829, in Morgan County, Alabama. Armistead and Celia watched four of their sons go off to fight for the Union Army. Besides William C. Blevins, his brothers, Dillard "Dillon", John H., and Armistead E. Blevins, Jr., all joined. William joined Captain Trammel's Company L of the 1st Alabama Cavalry, USV on September 25, 1863, in Fayette County, Alabama, as a private for a period of 1 year

at age 25. He was mustered in the same day at Glendale, Mississippi, a camp about ten miles from Corinth. From September 25th to October 31st, he was reported as being absent with leave. In November and December 1863, he was reported to have been missing in action at Vincent's Crossroads since October 26, 1863. In November 1863, he appeared on the Returns as absent, sick left in Alabama by order of Colonel Spencer. On the same Return dated December 1863, it stated he was absent in Alabama since the raid October 26, 1863. (This would have been the Battle at Vincent's Crossroads, Alabama. In January and February 1864, he was reported as absent, sick in Overton U.S.A. General Hospital in Memphis, Tennessee since February 16, 1863. He was still sick in May through October. On June 29, 1865, he was reported sick in the hospital in Nashville, Tennessee. He returned from absent, sick on April 3, 1865. On June 30, 1865, he was discharged by reason of expiration of term of service. He was due a $21 Clothing Allowance and $100 for Bounty. A Company Muster-Out Roll dated September 28, 1864, from Rome, Georgia stated he had been advanced a Clothing Allowance of $59. 36. There was one Prisoner of War Record in his Military Records.

William C. Blevins married Editha Jane Sullivan July 10, 1878, in Oakville, Lawrence County, Alabama. William and Editha had the following children: Melinda, born about 1878; Robert Lee, born Margaret, born June 1881; Lawson, born May 1883; James A., born February 1887; Cora, born April 1889; Daniel, born April 1893; William W., born October 1898, died August 12, 1905; and Killis Blevins, born March 18, 1900, died September 11, 1900. William had previously been married to Elizabeth Daniels sometime before 1866, and had the following children: Celia, Martha E., Thomas, Sarah E., Ann, Mack Farland, Lewis, and Malinda Blevins.

Bodkins, Charles W. - Charles W. Bodkins, also spelled Botkins, enlisted in Company H of the 1st Alabama Cavalry, USV on March 1, 1865, at Stevenson, Alabama, and was mustered in April 18, 1865, at Nashville, Tennessee. He was enrolled by J.W. DeVaney. He was appointed Sergeant April 1, 1865. The Muster and Descriptive Roll shows Charles to have been 20 years of age, 5'-9" tall, having a fair complexion, black hair, black eyes, born in Marion County, Alabama, and a farmer by occupation. On July 15, 1865, he was reduced to ranks from Sergeant for disobedience of orders, theft and general worthlessness. He was mustered out October 20, 1865, in Huntsville, Alabama, and paid $100 bounty. His name appeared on the Returns for July 1865 stating he was absent, sick in Huntsville, Alabama since July 25, 1865. There was a Notation in his file from the Record and Pension Office of the War Department dated January 10, 1898, and stated: The man under the name of Charles W. Bodkins deserted from Company H of the 6th Regiment of Missouri Infantry on January 7, 1863, and enlisted in this organization in violation of the 22nd, now 50th Article of War. The Notation of April 26, 1886, is cancelled.

Boen, Archie - See Archie Bowen.

Bolding, Augustus Madison – Augustus Madison Bolding was a brother to Thomas J. Bolding and Wyley V. Bolding, below. He enlisted in Company C of the 1st Alabama Cavalry, USV on August 24, 1863, at Glendale, Mississippi for a period of 1 year, and was mustered in September 27, 1863, at Corinth, Mississippi due to expiration of term of service. A Company Muster Roll stated he lost one Remington revolver. He was reduced from sergeant to private on August 18, 1864. His term of service expired April 24, 1864. Bolding was mustered out on September 28, 1864, in Rome, Georgia. It said subsistence had been furnished to September 30, 1864, and transportation was to be furnished to Nashville, Tennessee by the G.M. Department. The Company Descriptive Book showed Bolding to have been 21 years of age, 6'-1" tall, having a fair complexion, dark eyes and dark hair, born in Hamilton County, Tennessee, and a farmer by occupation. He was shown as being single.

Augustus Madison Bolding was born in March 1842. His first wife (stated in his pension paperwork) was Nancy "Nannie" A. Wade, widow of fellow soldier, William Henry "Buck" Baker, whom he married in the summer of 1864 in Rome, Georgia. Nannie died a couple of months later. On March 11, 1866, in Jackson County, Illinois, he was married to Julia Davis, daughter of Singleton Davis and Sarah Collier. (There is some controversy about Sarah's last name.) Julia's mother, Sarah (maiden name unknown), died with the last name of her "4th" husband, Collier...she married Samuel Daniel Collier as her 3rd or 4th husband. Her first child was a Qualls but no marriage record has been found for her marrying a Qualls as her first husband. Her "2nd" husband was William Bennett with whom she had two surviving children, "3rd" husband, Singleton Davis, and "4th" husband was Collier. Julia was born in about 1847, and died before September 6, 1883. Children of Augustus and Julia Bolding were: Marie Modine, born December 19, 1868, died June 20, 1951; Robert Jefferson, born February 27, 1872, died July 31, 1936; James Arthur, born August 26, 1875, died after September 12, 1918; an infant daughter, born January 1883, died the same day. paperwork did not identify sex of infant nor when the infant died...assumption is the infant died Feb 28, 1883 Julia Davis Bolding died between Feb 6, 1882 - Feb 28, 1883, and Augustus M. Bolding then married Mary Texana Easley, daughter of James D. and Elizabeth Warren Easley August 15, 1884 in Shelby County, Tennessee. Children from this union were: Samuel Wesley, born October 6, 1888, died October 1897; and Corina Senobia Bolding, born June 6, 1894. Augustus M. Bolding died September 4, 1908 in Oceola, Mississippi County, Arkansas, and his widow, Mary Texana, died October 22, 1915 in Tipton County, Tennessee. Family information submitted by Betty Ridgeway.

Bolding, Thomas Jefferson - Thomas J. Bolding enlisted in Company C August 24, 1863, at Glendale, Mississippi, and was mustered in September 27, 1863, in Corinth, Mississippi. He enlisted for a period of one year. He was mustered out September 28, 1864, at Rome, Georgia at age 18. He was overpaid $28.60 by error of Major Brewer, U.S. Paymaster. Subsistence was furnished to September 30, 1864. Transportation to be furnished by the G.M. Department to Nashville, Tennessee. Mustered out by reason of expiration of term of service. The Company Descriptive Book showed Bolding to have been 19 years of age, 5'-10" tall, having a fair complexion, gray eyes, dark hair, born in Franklin County, Alabama, and a farmer by occupation. He was shown as being single.

Thomas Jefferson Bolding was a brother to Augustus Madison Bolding, above, and Wyley V. Bolding, below. He was born May 15, 1845, in Franklin County, Alabama and was married April 16, 1871, in Osceola, Mississippi County, Arkansas to Matilda Josephine Stephenson, who was born about 1848 in Kentucky and died April 4, 1882, in Sans Souci, Mississippi County, Arkansas. Known children of this couple were: Robert M., born December 01, 1874, died before 1899; William Alexander, born September 5, 1877, died after March 9, 1922, and Lucy Ann Bolding, born August 27, 1879, died after 1910. Thomas J. Bolding died December 21, 1925, in Osceola, Mississippi County, Arkansas, and was buried in the Violet Cemetery in Osceola. See Augustus Bolding, above, for information on parents. Thomas Jefferson's 2nd wife was Texanna Hilton (she was divorced from James Wilson), born August 8, 1861, in Pikeville, Alabama. They married May 19, 1889, Mississippi County, Arkansas. She died April 11, 1939 in Mississippi County, Arkansas. They had one known daughter, Jean? Lorine? Bolding, born February, 1891, died before 1899.

Thomas Jefferson Bolding's Pension (sic)

Thomas Jefferson Bolding filed for a Civil War Pension and stated the following. "Was wounded in my home by a gun shot at Butler, AR. In 1897 I was shot in right arm accidentally by my step-son.

Lost the sight of my right eye during the Civil War. "he is suffering by the loss of his right eye caused from being struck in the eye by another soldier with a stick" "While acting as teamster at or near Memphis, Tenn, on or about Jan 1863, I became involved in a quarrel with one of my comrades on account of him unhooking my team. He struck me from which I incurred loss of sight of right eye, from which I have suffered continuously since, and on which I now claim pension"

"In the month of November 1863 he was a private in Co C 1st Regiment U.S. Alabama Cavalry and that while in Memphis Tenn at the time above named and while in the discharge of his duty when or with a wagon train he was struck over the head by a drunken soldier named James Jarratt of the same Regiment and without the slightest provocation on the part of claimant. that said soldier with a heavy stick struck him the claimant on the head and broke the cord of his eye as he was informed by surgeon--- Smith that his eye was thrown??? out. That he does not know the address of any of his officers or comrades tho he has endeavored to ascertain them."

"In the year 1863 during the month of November at Memphis Tenn a drunken soldier came into the wagon train where claimant was at work and with a heavy stick struck claimant over the head and broke the cord of the eye. That claimant was at the time in the discharge of his duty. I know of the occurrence by reson of being in the same company and coming upon the scene a few moments later and being informed by claimant and commander of the occurrence.   signed Aug M. Bolding"

"this applicant states that while acting as a teamster hauling supplies from the landing at Memphis to the Camp in the vicinity a dispute arose between him and another teamster about the right to a certain pair of mules he says belonged to his team and while unhitching at Camp after dark, the other part treacherously came behind him and struck him a violent blow on the right temple with a stretcher? stunning him for a short time, but he went on and attended to his team, but on returning to the Camp the he discovered that with the right eye he could not see the campfire. was treated by the regimental surgeon, has received no treatment since discharge"

"...that while in the service and line of duty, at Memphis, Tenn, about Nov. 15, 1863, he had his right eye put out by a blow from a stick in the hands of a comrade."

Thos J Bolding is the claimant in the above-mention cause, and that "he received a gun shot wound on the 13th day of March 1897 caused by being shot by Emmett Wilson a boy age 15 years without any cause, he being angry with me not due to any vicious habits on my part as it was at the supper table eating my supper with my family" (sic...lost the use of his right arm...infection caused a very bad wound). One of the witnesses to the shooting was T.J's future son-in-law, Sidney Harris.

"#5. Where had you lived before you enlisted? Answer: 22 miles south of Iuka, Miss."
Submitted by Betty Ridgeway.

Bolding, Wyley V. – Wyley V. Bolding enlisted and was mustered into Company C of the 1st Alabama Cavalry, USV on January 10, 1863, at Corinth, Mississippi. His name appeared on the Returns for March to December 1863, stating he was detailed as regimental teamster since March 10, 1863. The Regimental Descriptive Book showed Bolding to have been 22 years of age, 6' tall, having a fair complexion, gray eyes, dark hair, born in Ducktown, Tennessee, and a farmer by occupation. He was mustered out January 31, 1864, at Memphis, Tennessee, owing the U.S. Government $18.41.

Wyley V. Bolding was a brother to Augustus M. Bolding and Thomas Jefferson Bolding, above. He was born about 1841 in Ducktown, Polk County, Tennessee, and died sometime after September 22, 1891. Family information submitted by Betty Ridgeway. See Augustus Bolding, above, for information on parents.

Boling, Ozias D. - Ozias D. Boling enlisted in Company H of the 1st Alabama Cavalry, USV on January 1, 1865, in Stevenson, Alabama as a private for a period of 3 years. He was mustered in April 5, 1865, in Nashville, Tennessee. Boling was enrolled by Sergeant James W. DeVaney. The Muster and Descriptive Roll showed him to have been 18 years of age, 6' tall, having a fair complexion, blue eyes, dark hair, born in Grundy County, Tennessee, and a farmer by occupation. He was mustered out October 20, 1865, in Huntsville, Alabama and paid a bounty of $100.

Boling, William C. - William C. Boling enlisted and was mustered into Company K of the 1st Alabama Cavalry, USV on June 26, 1862, in Limestone County, Alabama for a period of 3 years. He was one of the first enlistees who were immediately shipped to Nashville, Tennessee and merged with the 1st Middle Tennessee Cavalry, which went on to become the 5th Tennessee Cavalry. William was shown to have been with the 5th Tennessee Cavalry. The Muster and Descriptive Roll showed William to have been 21 years of age, 5'-10" tall, having a dark complexion, dark eyes, dark hair, born in Warren County, Tennessee, and a farmer by occupation. A record in Boling's file stated he had been transferred from Company K of the 21st Ohio Volunteers by Special Order, Headquarters, Army of the Ohio, and appointed Sergeant on September 1, 1862, of Company E of the 1st Middle Tennessee Cavalry. The November and December 1862 Muster Roll listed him as being absent, dick in hospital in Nashville, Tennessee since December 26, 1862. The Muster Roll from January 1st to June 30th 1863, stated Boling had been sick and sent to the hospital in Nashville on September 30, 1862. The March and April 1864 Muster Roll listed him as being on daily duty as acting 1st Sergeant. His name appeared on the Returns as William C. Boling, No. 1, Sergeant, Company E, 1st Middle Tennessee Cavalry, and stated the following: December 1862, Absent, sick at Nashville since December 26, 1862; January, February and June 1863, absent, sick in hospital; July 1863, absent, sick. The December 31 to April 30,

1865, stated William C. Boling was killed in action at the Battle of Monroe's Crossroads near Fayetteville, North Carolina on March 10, 1865. This was considered one of the worst, if not the worst, battles during their North and South Carolina Campaign.

Bolley, George - See George Boxley.

Bolton, Hugh L. - Hugh L. Bolton enrolled in Company L of the 1st Alabama Cavalry, USV on September 29, 1863, in Fayette County, Alabama for a period of 1 year, and was mustered in the same day at Glendale, Mississippi. He was shown as being 22 years of age. The Company Muster Roll from December 31, 1863, through April 30, 1864, stated Bolton was absent, recruiting in Alabama by order of Colonel Spencer since April 15, 1864. The July and August 1864 Muster Roll stated he had been promoted to 2nd Lieutenant of Company L on July 1, 1864. He was mustered out June 30, 1864, at Rome, Georgia and reenlisted and was mustered in July 27, 1864, in Rome, Georgia for a period of 3 years and was promoted to 2nd Lieutenant by authority of the Secretary of War, by General Dodge. It showed his residence as Fayette County, Alabama. On January and February 1865, he was shown as absent, on duty with dismounted men by Special Order Number 7. March and April 1865 showed Bolton to be a prisoner of war since March 10, 1865. On March 31, 1865, Bolton was granted a 30 day leave of absence by Special Order Number 153, by the War Department. The May and June 1865 Muster Roll stated Bolton, 2nd Lieutenant of Company F had been transferred from Company F by special orders by Regimental Headquarters May 1, 1865. The July and August Muster Roll stated he was due pay as company commander since May 1, 1865. He was mustered out May 20, 1865, in Huntsville, Alabama. The Muster-Out Roll stated he was transferred to Company L, 1st Alabama Cavalry on April 7, 1865, by Special Order Number 16. The officer made an affidavit that he had rendered all requisite returns relating to public property for which he had been accountable as required by Army regulations. The Company Descriptive Book listed Hugh L. Bolton to have been 22 years of age, 6' tall, having a fair complexion, blue eyes, dark hair, born in Pickens County, Alabama, and a farmer by occupation. The Prisoner of War Record showed Bolton to have been captured at Monroe Plantation March 10, 1865, brought to Fayetteville, North Carolina, confined at Richmond, Virginia on March 21, 1865, paroled at Boulware and Cox's Wharf in Virginia on March 26, 1865, and reported to Camp Parole, Maryland March 27, 1865. He was sent back to his regiment on May 1, 1865. He was paid $217.95 from January 1, 1865 through February 28, 1865, by Thomas J. Wilson, Paymaster, U.S.A. On May 1, 1865 in Annapolis, Maryland, he was paid $178.78 which was from April 1, 1865 through April 30, 1865, by the same paymaster.

Bolton, John – John Bolton enlisted in Company H of the 1st Alabama Cavalry, USV on October 23, 1863, at Glendale, Mississippi for a period of one year, and was mustered in the same day at Camp Davies, Mississippi. In February 1864, he was on detached service in the Refugee Camp in Memphis, Tennessee. The March and April 1864 Muster Roll listed Bolton as being absent, sick in the hospital in Memphis, Tennessee. He was still listed as sick in hospital in May and June, 1864. The July and August 1864 Muster Roll stated John Bolton had died August 7, 1864, at Rome, Georgia. The Inventory of Effects listed John as having been 27 years of age, 5'5" tall, having a light complexion, blue eyes, dark hair, and a farmer by occupation. He died in the post hospital at Rome, Georgia of Typhoid Fever. The following are his effects when he died: one hat, one great coat, one uniform jacket, one pair of boots and one blanket, and they were in the possession of Captain Joseph Ford. John Bolton was buried in Grave #1630 in the Marietta National Cemetery in Marietta, Georgia.

Bone, James - James Bone, also spelled Boin, enlisted in Company H of the 1st Alabama Cavalry, USV on March 1, 1865, in Stevenson, Alabama for a period of 3 years. He was enrolled by Captain James W. DeVaney, and mustered in April 5, 1865, in Nashville, Tennessee. William L. Bone signed a Consent to Enlist as the father of James Bone, who was a minor at the time he enlisted. The Muster and Descriptive Roll listed James as having been 17 years of age, 5'-4" tall, having a light complexion, blue eyes, light hair, born in Paulding County, Georgia and a farmer by occupation. He had been paid a bounty of $100. He was listed on the October 20, 1865, Muster-Out Roll stating he had deserted from Blountsville, Alabama on September 6, 1865, owing the U.S. Government $57.19 for taking 1 Remington revolver, 1 Colt pistol, 1 belt and plate, 1 pistol cartridge box, 2 pistol holsters, 1 saber, 1 curry comb, 2 spurs and straps, and 1 shelter tent. No discharge was issued at muster out of organization.

James Bone was born about 1848 in Paulding County, Georgia to William L. Bone and Lucinda Box, who were married July 12, 1840, in Paulding County, Georgia.

Booker, William W. - William W. Booker enlisted in Company E of the 1st Alabama Cavalry, USV as a private on August 27, 1863, at Glendale, Mississippi for a period of 1 year. He was mustered in the same day at Corinth, Mississippi. The September and October 1863 Muster Roll listed him as being absent, missing in late action, which was probably the Battle of Vincent's Crossroads on October 26, 1863, at Bay Springs, Mississippi. The November and December 1863 Muster Roll showed him as being absent, prisoner of war since October 26, 1863. He was still listed as prisoner of war through the September and October 1864 Muster Roll and it stated he died August 13, 1864, at Andersonville Prison in Andersonville, Georgia. The March and April 1865 Muster Roll still listed William as absent, prisoner of war since October 26, 1863, at Vincent's Crossroads, even though they previously stated he died in August 1864. The July and August 1865 Muster Roll stated William W. Booker died of chronic diarrhea on August 13, 1864, at Andersonville Prison while a prisoner of war in the hands of the enemy. The Muster-Out Roll dated October 20, 1864, in Huntsville, Alabama stated he transferred from one year organization of the 1st Alabama Cavalry on October 1, 1864 by order of Colonel Spencer. William was listed as being 30 years of age, 5'-10" tall, having a light complexion, blue eyes, dark hair, born in McNairy County, Tennessee, and a farmer by occupation. He was buried in Grave #5505 in the Andersonville National Cemetery in Andersonville, Sumter County, Georgia.

Bookout, Abel - Abel Bookout enlisted in Company H of the 1st Alabama Cavalry, USV on September 18, 1863, at Glendale, Mississippi. The September and October 1863 Muster Roll listed him as being absent, in hospital wounded. He was probably wounded October 26, 1863, during the Battle of Vincent's Crossroads in Bay Springs, Mississippi. He died December 18, 1863, in Memphis, Tennessee from pneumonia and wounds received in battle on October 26, 1863. Abel Bookout was 28 years of age, 5'-10" tall, had a dark complexion, blue eyes, dark hair, born in Cleveland County, North Carolina, and a farmer by occupation. He was buried in the Memphis National Cemetery in Memphis, Shelby County, Tennessee.

Boon, John W. - John W. Boon, also spelled Boone, enlisted in Company C of the 1st Alabama Cavalry, USV on February 15, 1864, in Memphis, Tennessee for a period of 3 years. He was enrolled by John Latty and was mustered in on March 10, 1864, in Memphis. The Muster and Descriptive Roll showed him to have been 18 years of age, 5'-8" tall, having a dark complexion, blue eyes, dark hair, born in Yancy County, North Carolina, and a farmer by occupation. The Company Muster Roll dated to April 30, 1864, stated John was absent, on detached service as orderly at General Veach's Headquarters. He was still there through August 1864, but was listed as present on all of the other muster rolls with the exception of March 10, 1865, when he was captured and taken prisoner of war, which was the date of the Battle of Monroe's Crossroads near Fayetteville, North Carolina. The Muster-Out Roll dated October 20, 1865, in Huntsville, Alabama stated he was paid $180 in bounty was still owed $120 to make up for the $300 bounty. He was mustered out owing the U.S. Government $5.15, for losing one carbine sling, one swivel, one cap pouch, one saber belt, one thong and wiper, one screw driver, and one pair of spurs. There was a Notation in his file from the Adjutant General's office of the War Department dated September 4, 1884, stating his application for a lost Certificate for a lost Discharge was furnished. John W. Boon's name appeared on the Muster Roll of General Staff and Enlisted Men on Detached Service at Headquarters, 4th Division, 16th Army Corps.

Booth, George William Pinkney - George William Pinkney Booth enlisted and mustered into the 1st Alabama Cavalry, USV as a Veterinary Surgeon on April 13, 1863, at Glendale, Mississippi for a period of 1 year. He was appointed by order of General G.M. Dodge. In September 1863, he was recorded as being absent, on furlough. He was appointed veterinary surgeon April 13, 1863, by authority of the Secretary of War and approved by General Dodge. He was promoted from private in the 64th Illinois Infantry Volunteers, where he enlisted August 13, 1862, in Springfield, Illinois. He was mustered out April 12, 1864, in Decatur, Alabama. According to descendant, Connie, George W.P. Booth also served in Company A of Blythe's Cavalry, CSA.

Borden, Francis M. - Francis M. Bordon enlisted in Company A of the 1st Alabama Cavalry, USV as a private on June 12, 1863, at Glendale, Mississippi for a period of 1 year. He was mustered in the same day in Memphis, Tennessee. He was mustered out December 22, 1863, in Memphis, Tennessee.

Borolin – Only one card was found for a soldier with the surname of Borolin, which was filed at the end of the last roll of microfilm of the 1st Alabama Cavalry, USV records. It recorded him as a private in Company L of the 1st Alabama Cavalry on December 16, 1863. No further information relative to this soldier was found.*

Bostic, William F. - William F. Bostic, also spelled Bostick, enrolled in Company K of the 1st Alabama Cavalry, USA as a private on December 1, 1863, at Camp Davies, Mississippi. He was enrolled by Lieutenant Hornback for a period of 3 years. Bostic traveled 90 miles by horseback from his home in Marion County, Alabama to join the Union Army. The January and February 1864 Muster Roll listed him as being absent, on detached service as teamster in General Sherman's expedition in Vicksburg, Mississippi since January 24, 1864, by order of General Grierson. In July and August 1864, and October 1864, Bostic was on detached service as orderly for Quartermaster Kingsbury, since July 19, 1864, at Rome, Georgia. The Company Descriptive Book listed William F. Bostic as having been 21 years of age, 5'-10" tall, having a light complexion, gray eyes, auburn hair, born in Cass County, Georgia, and a farmer by occupation. He was mustered out July 19, 1865, at age 19, in Nashville, Tennessee.

Boswell, Andrew G. - See Andrew G. Basnell.

Botkins, Charles W. - See Charles W. Bodkins.

Bourland, Gabriel L. - Gabriel Lee Bourland enlisted in Company B of the 1st Alabama Cavalry, USV as a private on December 19, 1862, in Glendale, Mississippi. He was enrolled by Captain Frank C. Burdick for a period of 1 year, and was mustered in December 31, 1862, at Corinth, Mississippi. The Regimental Descriptive Book showed him to have been 35 years of age, 5'-8" tall, having a light complexion, gray eyes, auburn hair, born in Franklin County, Alabama, and a farmer by occupation. In March 1863, Gabriel was shown as being absent, on leave to take his family to Jackson, Tennessee. On June 19, 1863, he was absent with leave to take his family north. They were shipped up there in boxcars. He was gone from June 19, 1863, until January 1864, taking them up there and getting them settled. (In June 1863, the U.S. Army escorted about 300 Union wives, children and disabled Union men to Illinois for their safety. The Confederate Home Guard had been molesting and abusing the Union families, burning their houses, barns, crops, etc. and stealing their meat, corn, meal and anything of use to them. After the war, many of them remained in the Marion County, Illinois and surrounding areas and were buried there.)

Gabriel Lee Bourland was born March 12, 1827, in Franklin County, Alabama to Ebenezer Jackson Bourland and Mary "Polly" Hester, who married February 25, 1830, in Franklin County, Alabama. Gabriel married Milda "Milly" Oliver about 1849 and had the following children: John Henderson, born March 8, 1849, died December 22, 1921, in Green County, Missouri; Susan C., born 1851; Talitha Altha, born 1852; Modenia J., born 1855; Joseph McDonald, born 1856 and Walter B. Bourland, born 1859. There may have been other children. One descendant stated Gabriel's wife, Milly, died between 1862 and 1863. She was the daughter of John C. Oliver and his wife, Susanna Blackledge. Gabriel died February 12, 1913, in Wilzetta, near Prague, Lincoln County, Oklahoma Some family information submitted by Greg Bourland.

Bowlin - William Bowlin, also spelled Bolen and Bowling, enlisted in Company M of the 1st

Alabama Cavalry, USV as a private on December 16, 1863, at Camp Davies, Mississippi for a period of 3 years. He was enrolled by Captain John Lomax and mustered in the same day at Corinth, Mississippi. The Company Descriptive Book listed William as having been 18 years of age, 5'-11" tall, having a fair complexion, blue eyes, brown hair, born in Marion County, Alabama, and a farmer by occupation. The January and February 1864 Muster Roll listed him as being absent, sick in the hospital in Memphis, Tennessee since January 25, 1864. His name was listed as William Bowling on the Hospital Muster Roll of the Small Pox U.S.A. Hospital in Memphis, Tennessee stating he was admitted February 8, 1864, but was returned to his regiment on March 15, 1864. The March and April 1864 Muster Roll stated William Bolen died April 6, 1864, in the hospital in Nashville, Tennessee of inflammation of the lungs. He died in the Cumberland U.S.A. General Hospital Number 778 and was first interred in Grave Number 7128 in the Nashville City Cemetery. He was listed as being single. The Inventory of Effects of Private William Bowlin were listed as: one coat, one overcoat, one jacket, one pair of trousers, 2 shirts, one pair of drawers, one pair of shoes, and 4 blankets. Another Inventory of Effects listed him as having: one cap, one great coat, one uniform jacket, one pair of trousers, one pair of cotton drawers, 2 flannel shirts, one pair of shoes and 4 blankets.

In 2009, during her research, the author found that the names of at least eleven of the 1st Alabama Cavalry, USV soldiers had been recorded as belonging to the CSA and as being buried in Confederate Circle at Mt. Olivet Cemetery in Nashville, Tennessee. This error was due to the government undertaker not showing if they were Union or Confederate and apparently since they were from Alabama, he, like many others, assumed they were Confederates. These names and their dates of death were published in the *Nashville Union Newspaper*. Then in 1977, a member of UDC (United Daughters of the Confederacy), wanting to help with the cemetery, added these names from the newspaper to the Mt. Olivet Cemetery Records. This was confirmed by the Roll of Honor. This was brought to the attention of the cemetery staff and these names are supposed to be stricken from their records soon, due to the diligent work of a member of Friends of Metro Archives who has been researching this for almost two years. The names of the other soldiers recorded as being Confederates and buried in Confederate Circle were: James H. Downum, Calvin Guthrie, Thomas Huey, Isaac R. Perrett, John B. Pitts, Jeremiah Russell, Daniel Sharpton, Henry C. Sinyard, John W. Stokes, and John B. West. These men are actually buried in the Nashville National Cemetery, some in unmarked graves.

Bowman, Isaac V. - Isaac V. Bowman and his father, Lorenzo, first enlisted in Company A of the 1st Tennessee and Alabama Independent Vidette Cavalry, US which was only in service about one year. After it disbanded, they enlisted in Company H of the 1st Alabama Cavalry, USV, as did many of the other soldiers in the Vidette Regiment. Isaac enlisted in the 1st Alabama Cavalry, USV as a private on April 1, 1865, in Stevenson, Alabama with his father, Lorenzo Dow Bowman and his brother, Robert B. Bowman. He was enrolled for a period of 3 years by Captain James W. DeVaney and was mustered in April 18, 1865, at Nashville, Tennessee. The Muster and Descriptive Roll listed Isaac as having been 18 years of age, 5'-6" tall, having a fair complexion, blue eyes, light hair, born in Cass County, Georgia, and a farmer by occupation. He was mustered out October 20, 1865, at Huntsville, Alabama, and was paid $100 bounty. Isaac listed his home as Larkinsville, Alabama.

According to descendants, Isaac V. Bowman was born January 29, 1846, in Cass County, Georgia to Lorenzo Dow Bowman and Nancy Ann Baker, who were married October 29, 1840, in Bartow, Georgia. Isaac first married Carrie Ward, who died August 23, 1886, in Dayton, Rhea County, Tennessee. He then married Mollie W. Cullifer on August 24, 1893, and had the following children, James V., born September 11, 1895, and Artie A. Bowman, born September 4, 1897. Isaac V. Bowman died February 2, 1905, in Little Rock, White County, Arkansas.

Bowman, Lorenzo D. - Lorenzo D. Bowman and his son, Isaac, first enlisted in Company A of the 1st Tennessee and Alabama Independent Vidette Cavalry, US. This regiment was only in service for about one year and after it was disbanded, they enlisted in Company H of the 1st Alabama Cavalry, USV, along with two of his sons, Isaac V. Bowman and Robert Bowman, on April 1, 1865, in Stevenson, Alabama. He was enrolled for a period of 3 years by Captain James W. DeVaney and was mustered in April 18, 1865, in Nashville, Tennessee. The Muster and Descriptive Roll listed him as being 44 years of age, 5'-10" tall, having a fair complexion, blue eyes, light hair, born in Gwinnett County, Georgia and a blacksmith by occupation. He was mustered out October 20, 1865, in Huntsville, Alabama and paid $100 bounty.

Lorenzo Dow Bowman was born about 1821 in Gwinnett County, Georgia to Sherrod or Sherwood Bowman and Elizabeth Muir. According to the Georgia Marriage Records to 1850, Lorenzo married Nancy Ann Baker November 1, 1840, in Bartow County, Georgia. Nancy Ann Baker was born in March 1824 in Georgia and died in 1869 in Bedford County, Tennessee. Lorenzo and Nancy had at least 7 children: Isaac V. Bowman; Robert B. Bowman; Martha Ann Bowman; S.P. Bowman (Female); F.M. Bowman (Male); James M. Bowman, and M.E. Bowman (Female). One descendant stated that after Nancy died, Lorenzo married Malvina M. Stephenson on August 23, 1869 in Bedford County, Tennessee, and then married Mary Ann Huff on January 2, 1887, in White County, Arkansas. Lorenzo died July 21, 1904, in White County, Arkansas and is buried in the Carter Cemetery in Russell, White County, Arkansas.

Bowman, Robert B. - Robert B. Bowman enlisted in Company H of the 1st Alabama Cavalry, USV on April 1, 1865, in Stevenson, Alabama, with his father, Lorenzo Dow Bowman and his brother, Isaac V. Bowman, above. He was enrolled for a period of 3 years by Captain James W. DeVaney and mustered in April 18, 1865, in Nashville, Tennessee. The Muster and Descriptive Roll listed him as being 18 years of age, 5'-5" tall, having a fair complexion, blue eyes, light hair, born in Cass County, Georgia, and a farmer by occupation. He was mustered out October 20, 1865, in Huntsville, Alabama, being paid $100 bounty. He was charged 60 cents for losing a pistol cartridge box.

Robert was born about 1848 in Cass County, Georgia to Lorenzo Dow Bowman and his wife, Elizabeth Muir, and died in 1897 in White County, Arkansas.

Bowen, Archie - Archie Bowen enlisted in Company D of the 1st Alabama Cavalry, USV as a private on October 14, 1864, in Decatur, Alabama for a period of 3 years. He was enrolled by Lieutenant Emrick and mustered in November 10, 1864, in Rome, Georgia. The Muster and Descriptive Roll shows Archie to have been 46 years of age, 5'-6" tall, having a fair complexion, gray eyes, dark complexion, born in Kershaw County, South Carolina, and a farmer by occupation. Archie Bowen was killed by the enemy in action on March 10, 1865, which was during the Battle of Monroe's Crossroads near Fayetteville, North Carolina.

Bowland, William - This William Bowlin, cards filed with William Bowland, enlisted in Company E of the 1st Alabama Cavalry, USV on March 1, 1863, at Glendale, Mississippi, and mustered in the same day at Corinth, Mississippi. There was a letter in William's file from Headquarters, Company E, 1st Alabama Cavalry, Camp Davies, Mississippi, dated November 24, 1863, with the subject William Bowlin, Company E, 1st Alabama Volunteer Cavalry, Charge - 1st Murder, Specification, In this that the said William Bowlin, private Company E, 1st Alabama Volunteer Cavalry, did on or about the 14th day of November 1863, shoot one Neal Morrison, a citizen of Tishomingo County, Mississippi, with a revolver which resulted in the death of said Neal Morrison. All this near Camp Davies, Mississippi. Charge 2nd, Dissention, In this that the said William Bowlin, private Company E, 1st Alabama Volunteer Cavalry, did absent himself from his company and regiment without permission on or about the 14th day of November, 1863 and remained away from his command until the 18th day of November when he was captured by a scouting party near Glendale, Mississippi, and returned to his command, all this near Camp Davies, Mississippi. Signed Albert E. Murdock, 1st Lieutenant Commanding Company E. Witnessed by the following: Miss Sarah Morrison, Mrs. D.E. Harmon, Miss N.P. Morrison, Mrs. Neal Morrison, 1st Lieutenant A.E. Murdock, Company E, 1st Alabama Volunteer Cavalry, and 2nd Lieutenant Q.A. Gardner, Company E, 1st Alabama Volunteer Cavalry. William Bowland was alleged to have also been in Company G of the 44th Illinois Infantry as William Bowlin.

William Bowland and John Brooks were charged with the murder of Neal Morrison, a citizen of Tishomingo County, Mississippi, on or about November 14, 1863, near Camp Davies, Mississippi. He deserted and was captured by a scouting party near Glendale, Mississippi and returned on or about November 18, 1863. He was alleged to also be in Company G, 44th Illinois Infantry as William Bowlin.

William Bowlin, along with several other 1st Alabama Cavalry, USV deceased soldiers, were recorded as belonging to the CSA and buried in Confederate Circle at Mt. Olivet Cemetery in Nashville, Tennessee in 1977. This error was due to the government undertaker not showing if they were Union or Confederate and apparently since they were from Alabama, he, like many others, thought they were Confederates. This was confirmed by the Roll of Honor, which recorded his date of death as April 6, 1864. This was brought to the attention of the cemetery and these names will probably be stricken from their records.

Bowyer - Cards filed under Boyer.

Box, Francis E. - Francis E. Box enlisted in Company H of the 1st Alabama Cavalry, USV on October 16, 1863, in Glendale, Mississippi, and was mustered in the same day at Camp Davies, Mississippi. His name appeared on the Returns and stated in November and December 1863 Francis E. Box was on extra or daily as a teamster, probably in Vicksburg, Mississippi. In January 1864, he was on extra or daily duty as a barber. In February 1864, he was sick in Alabama since February 18, 1864. The January and February 1864 Muster Roll listed him as being absent, sick in the Adams U.S.A. General Hospital at Memphis, Tennessee. He was still shown as being sick, in the hospital at Memphis on the March and April Muster roll but on the next roll, he was shown as being sick in the hospital at Jefferson Barracks, Missouri in April 1864. However, another March and April 1864 Muster Roll listed him as being in the Adams U.S.A. General Hospital in Memphis, Tennessee. He was reported to have deserted April 30, 1864. The May and June 1864 Muster Roll stated he was sick in the hospital in Memphis, Tennessee with a note that it had been corrected. The July and August 1864 Muster Roll again listed him as being absent, sick in the General Hospital in Jefferson Barracks, Missouri. The Company Descriptive Roll recorded him as 23 years of age, 5'-11" tall, had a light complexion, blue eyes, dark hair, born in Blount County, Alabama, and was a farmer by occupation. Frances E. Box died of chronic diarrhea on May 17, 1864, in Jefferson Barracks, Missouri. The Inventory of his Effects listed the following items: 1 hat, 1 uniform jacket, 1 pair of pants, 1 pair of shorts, 1 pair of socks, 1 pair of drawers, 1 flannel shirt, and 1 blanket.

Boxley, George - Boxley, George - George Boxley enlisted as a private in Company M of the 1st Alabama Cavalry, USV on August 5, 1863, in Chewalla, Tennessee for a period of 3 years. He was enrolled by Captain Lomax and was mustered in December 29, 1863, in Corinth, Mississippi as a teamster. The March and April 1864 Muster Roll showed him to have been a wagoner but was absent, sick in the hospital in Decatur, Alabama. It stated he had never been paid any bounty and was due $300. He was shown as being present on the other muster rolls until the one for January and February 1865, which showed him as being absent, on duty as nurse in the Small Pox Hospital in Savannah, Georgia since January 10, 1865, by order of Colonel Spencer. He was still on detached duty as a nurse in Savannah the next two months. The Company Descriptive Book listed Boxley as having been 31 years of age, 5'-6" tall, having a fair complexion, gray eyes, dark hair, born in Meigs County, Tennessee, and a farmer by occupation. George Boxley was mustered out October 20, 1865 in Huntsville, Alabama, owing the U.S. Government $14.31 for losing 1 carbine sling and swivel, a carbine cartridge box, 1 cap pouch and pick, 1 saber belt and plate, bridle and saddle. He was paid $180 for bounty and still owed $120 for the bounty.

Boxley, W. - W. Boxley had one card misfiled in the military records of the 1st Alabama Cavalry, USV which showed he enlisted in Company F, and recorded him as being absent, sick in U.S.A. General Hospital. However, it does not give the name or place of the hospital. No further information relative to this soldier was found.*

Boyd, Doctor T. - Doctor Tandy Boyd enlisted in Company K of the 1st Alabama Cavalry, USV as a private on December 21, 1863, at Camp Davies, Mississippi for a period of 3 years. He was enrolled by Captain Hornback. He traveled over 150 miles from his home in Walker County, Alabama to Camp Davies, Mississippi to enlist in the Union Army. The Company Descriptive Roll listed Doctor Tandy Boyd as being 34 years of age, 6'-1" tall, having a light complexion, black eyes, auburn hair, born in

Morgan County, Alabama, and a farmer by occupation. The May and June 1864 Muster Roll showed him to have been absent, on recruiting service in Winston County, Alabama by order of Major Cramer. The March and April 1864 Muster Roll listed him as being captured and taken prisoner of war on March 21, 1864, in Arkansas near Memphis. In August 1864, he was on recruiting service in Walker County, Alabama. The September and October 1864 Muster Roll listed him as being absent, on recruiting service in Alabama May 25, 1864, by order of Major Fairfield. He was still on recruiting service in July and August 1864. In January through March 1865, he was on recruiting service in Decatur, Alabama, since November 10, 1864. He mustered out July 19, 1865 in Nashville, Tennessee.

Story of Doctor Tandy Boyd

Doctor Tandy Boyd was the son of Hannah James and James Lee Boyd, Sr. and brother of Tillman Boyd, below. He was born May 6, 1829, in Morgan County, Alabama and on October 19, 1852, he married Sarah Reid in Walker County, Alabama on October 19, 1852. Sarah was born October 25, 1834, and died November 9, 1904. Children of Tandy and Sarah were: John Daniel, born January 12, 1854, died April 4, 1936, married Mary Bell Godfrey; James Wesley, born May 21, 1858, died 1938, married Willie Burrel; Martha Jane, born August 8, 1860, died April 23, 1943, married Thomas Clemons; Sarah Ann, born April 29, 1866, died October 4, 1937, married John W. Wood and Green Williams; Joseph Monroe, born January 2, 1877, died April 18, 1947, married Ida Childers; and Gereda Elizabeth Boyd, born September 30, 1870, and died about 1880.

In 1862 Doctor Tandy Boyd and several other men including his three brothers, were locked in the Walker County Courthouse until they either joined the Confederacy or were conscripted into the Confederate Army. After refusing twice, Doctor T. finally agreed to go and shoe horses for Captain E.J. Rice of the Confederate Army where he remained for five or six days and then escaped. In December 1863 Doctor T. and his brother, Tillman, walked 150 miles from Walker County, Alabama to Camp Davies Mississippi where they enlisted in Company K of the 1st Alabama Cavalry Volunteers. While on his way to Camp Davies, Doctor T. was repairing his gun lock when the main spring flew out and penetrated his left eye causing him to loose site in that eye. On March 21, 1864, in Arkansas near Memphis, Tennessee, Doctor T. was held prisoner by the Rebels where he was exposed to very cold and rainy weather, without shelter or sufficient food causing him to have liver, kidney, rheumatism and heart disease. Due to these medical conditions, he was able to draw a pension of twenty dollars per month after the war. During the war he recruited in Walker, Winston and Morgan Counties in Alabama. Doctor T. died January 11, 1908, and he and his wife, Sarah, are buried in Antioch Cemetery at Bug Tussle near Bremen, Alabama. Sarah Narcissa Boyd, sister of Doctor T. and Tillman Boyd, married William P. Ramey who was also in Co. K, First Alabama Cavalry, U.S.V. Doctor Tandy Boyd is buried in the Antioch Cemetery at Bug Tussle near Bremen, Alabama. Family information submitted by Vicki Corrick.

Boyd, Elisha F. - Elisha F. Boyd enlisted in Company B of the 1st Alabama Cavalry, USV as a private on August 1, 1864, at Wedowee, Alabama for a period of 3 years, and mustered in August 1, 1864, at Rome, Georgia. He was enlisted by Captain West. The Muster and Descriptive Roll listed him as being 21 years of age, 5'-9" tall, having a fair complexion, hazel eyes, dark hair, born in Meriwether County, Georgia and was a farmer by occupation. It stated he was due a bounty of $300. Sometime before the January and February 1865 Muster Roll, Elisha was appointed to Sergeant. On the March and April 1865 Muster Roll, it stated he was killed by the enemy at Richland, North Carolina on April 1, 1865. The Company Muster-Out Roll dated October 20, 1865, in Huntsville, Alabama stated Elisha F. Boyd died April 1, 1865, of wounds received in action at Richland, North Carolina. Elisha's name appeared on a return stated he was killed April 3, 1865, while on scout. However, the Casualty Sheet for Sergeant Elisha F. Boyd stated he was killed April 1, 1865. (See Robert A. Boyd, below, for family information as he and Elisha were brothers.)

Boyd, Joseph A. - Joseph A. Boyd had one card which was misfiled with the military records of the 1st Alabama Cavalry, USV. It recorded him as a private in Company I, and stated he died of fever August 25, 1863, in the hospital in Corinth, Mississippi. However, it did not say which hospital. His effects were delivered to his brother, who was not named but could have been Robert Alexander or Elisha F. Boyd. No further military records relative to this soldier were found.

Joseph A. Boyd was the son of Alexander P. Boyd and his wife, Sarah Ann Hinton. Other children of Alexander and Sarah Boyd were: William James; John D.; Robert Alexander; Elisha F.; Elizabeth C.; Sarah A. "Sallie"; Rufus J.; and Martha B. Boyd.

<u>Boyd, Robert Alexander</u> - Robert Alexander Boyd enlisted in Company A of the 1st Alabama Cavalry, USV on September 15, 1864, in Rome, Georgia at age 29. He was on the March from Rome, Georgia to Savannah, Georgia and back through North Carolina to Huntsville, Alabama. He was treated in Savannah where the army physician removed a tumor from his neck and as soon as he was able he was given transportation to Salisbury, North Carolina where he went back to his company. He went from there back to Huntsville, Alabama. Boyd received a gunshot wound on March 10, 1865, at Monroe's Crossroads in North Carolina.

Robert Alexander Boyd was not on the original microfilm of soldiers who served in the 1st Alabama Cavalry, US Volunteers, however, his military and pension files indicate he did indeed serve in this regiment and was on Sherman's march to the sea. One statement in the pension file states he was never mustered in, he just joined in with the soldiers in Rome, Georgia on the way to Savannah, Georgia from Rome, Georgia. However, a muster roll in his military records stated he was enlisted September 15, 1864, and was discharged October 20, 1865. He was treated in Savannah, Georgia by the army physician and was left in the hospital, while a tumor was removed from his neck; until able to travel at which time he acquired regular transportation to Salisbury, North Carolina where he was reunited with his company. He then received a gunshot wound while participating in the Battle of Monroe's Crossroads. In his Declaration for Invalid Pension dated September 4, 1890, he stated he was 53 years of age, lived in Rockdale, Randolph County, Alabama His disability was listed as disease of the heart, like heart dropsy and he also had chronic rheumatism which disabled him from plowing at times. One report stated Boyd had pain in muscles of left arm and leg, pain in hip and shoulder and had fluttering of his heart and especially when he exerted himself or got too warm. The pain from his sciatic nerve in left hip ran all the way down his leg, and he had a heart murmur. The records state Boyd drew $4.00 per month pension for the gunshot wound he received in North Carolina. Robert was able to sign his name on affidavits and signed it R.A. Boyd. An affidavit from the Department of the Interior, Bureau of Pensions, dated June 22, 1891, No. 973.449, R.A. Boyd, A. 1st Alabama Cavalry. It is desired in this case that the examination be made with special reference to rheumatism and disease of Heart. Please make a thorough and careful examination of this soldier and describe the pathological conditions existing from any and all causes. Describe definably condition of all joints, ligaments, tendons, and muscles. Is there a lot of cintra__ion of muscles? Is there lameness and if so, to what degree. What is the condition of the heart as shown by auscultation and percussion. State pulse rate sitting, standing and after moderate exercise. Make your report full and definite. Upon examination we find the following objective conditions: Pulse rate, 89; respiration 20; temperature 99; height 5'- 10"; weight 160 pounds; age 56 years. I find the Sciatic nerve of left leg very tender all the way down the leg….Doctor's report illegible.

Robert Alexander Boyd was born July 24, 1838, in Meriwether County, Georgia to Alexander and Sarah Ann Hinton Boyd. Robert married Elizabeth Caroline Green, daughter of Rev. John Cephus Green and his wife, Nancy Huckaby, who were married April 28, 1836, in Coweta County, Georgia. Children of Robert and Elizabeth were: Sarah Jane, born December 7, 1859; John Carter, born April 17, 1860, died December 19, 1935; Thomas F., born March 11, 1864, died January 16, 1912; James Washington, born September 19, 1866, died December 15, 1955; Robert Lincoln, born February 20, 1869, died February 1, 1954; David Nathanial, born May 31, 1871, died July 12, 1954; Charles Henry, born February 20, 1873, died November 5, 1958; Martha Lula, born 14 July 14, 1876, died December 16, 1940; William Augustus, born April 3, 1879, died April 16, 1957; Andrew Jackson, born September 15, 1881, died September 19, 1954; Dallas Blain, born August 9, 1884, died November 25, 1965; and Hattie Boyd, born November 1887. Robert A. Boyd died May 6, 1930 and was Buried in McDonald Chapel Cemetery in Jefferson County, Alabama. Robert was the brother of Elisha and Joseph Boyd, also of this regiment. Descendant Ron Boyd recorded a story passed down from other family members which stated Robert Alexander Boyd swam across the Tennessee River near Guntersville, Alabama to return home to Randolph County, Alabama. He was home when the unit mustered out October 20, 1865.

Story of Robert Alexander Boyd

"Robert Alexander Boyd and his brother John went through the Confederate lines to the Yankees at Rome, Georgia. Their brother Bill stayed at home and the Confederates forced him to join their ranks. Bill ran away and returned to his kinfolk in Georgia. Of course, he had to hide out for the rest of the war."

"Before Grandfather Boyd (R.A. Boyd) could join the First Alabama Regiment to serve as a cook he had to have a large tumor removed from his neck. The Federals took him to Savannah, Georgia, and removed it at a very great risk to his life. The operation was performed free of charge. Two of Grandma Boyd's superior officers were General Gorman and Captain Hines. Once he prepared a special dinner for several high ranking officers of the Union Army. He said he baked and stuffed a turkey and four ducks. He made a tubful of coffee and plenty of cornbread. He said the Yankees relished the cornbread "as they would a juicy fresh cocoanut cake!"

"When the war was over Grandpa Boyd walked home from Chattanooga. He swam the river at Guntersville, Alabama. At that time there was no ferry at the Guntersville Crossing of the Tennessee River. Today there is a beautiful modern bridge at Guntersville."

"After the Civil War Grandpa moved his family to a farm north of Wedowee, Alabama. He and his sons farmed, ginned cotton, made syrup, and operated a big store until the store burned in 1890. The family attended New Home Methodist Church. He sent three of his sons to school at the old Mt. Zion Methodist Institute, Mt. Zion, Georgia."

"Grandfather was a loyal Mason, joining the Masonic Order in Wedowee, Alabama in 1856. He was a member of the Sawyer's Lodge at Wedowee. He lived to be 93 years of age. He was married to Elizabeth Caroline Green, September 27, 1858. Her father was an old pioneer circuit rider preacher. He built a log cabin on his farm east of Wedowee. He established a country church in Randolph county which bears his name today." Submitted by descendant Ron Boyd, written by his aunt, Estelle Boyd Braswell.

Boyd, Tillmon S. - Tillman S. Boyd, sometimes spelled Tillmon, enrolled and was mustered into Company K of the 1st Alabama Cavalry, USV as a private on December 21, 1863, at Camp Davies, Mississippi for a period of 3 years. He was enlisted by Lt. Joseph Hornback, and rode 150 miles on horseback from his home to Camp Davies, Mississippi to enlist in the Union Army. The May and June 1864 Muster Roll stated he left sick at Ackworth, Georgia on June 20, 1864, was present for pay. Tillman's name appeared on the July and August 1864 Hospital Muster Roll, U.S.A. Field Hospital in Rome, Georgia stated Tillmon was a patient. The name William S. Boyd was written at the bottom of the muster roll. The Company Muster and Descriptive Book listed Tillmon as being 21 years of age, 5'-6" tall, having a light complexion, blue eyes, light hair, born in Walker County, Alabama, and a farmer by occupation. A Company Muster Roll dated December 31, 1864, to April 30, 1865, stated Tillmon Boyd was absent, he was a paroled prisoner of war at Annapolis, Maryland. A Notation from the Record and Pension Office of the War Department dated January 11, 1897, stated: Discharge Certificate was on file. However, written across that was a note that stated: Cancelled, see Notation of February 20, 1897. The Notation from the Record and Pension Office dated February 20, 1897, stated: Discharge Certificate withdrawn and transmitted to the owner this date. The Notation of January 11, 1897, is cancelled. Tillman S. Boyd, Private Company K, 1st Regiment Alabama Cavalry, was listed on a Muster Roll of Detachment of Paroled Prisoners at Camp Chase, Ohio, dated April 10, 1865, stated he was present and was captured March 10, 1865, at Solomon Grove, North Carolina. That was the day of the Battle of Monroe's Crossroads. He was discharged June 12, 1865 from Camp Chase, Ohio by General Orders of the War Department 77, April 28, 1865. His name was listed on a Detachment Muster-Out Roll dated June 13, 1865, at Camp Chase, Ohio, stating he was due a bounty of $100, and that he owed the U.S. Government $6.26 for transportation, and says three months extra pay due the above enlisted man by order of the Secretary of War, dated Washington, D.C. dated May 31, 1865. A note in Tillmon S. Boyd's file stated: Hospital Department U.S.A., Rome, Ga., Sept. 22, 1864,

Paymaster of the 1st Alabama Cavalry, I have this day paid Tillmon S. Boyd Private, Company K, $32.00 in full from July 1, 1864. It was signed by T. Price, Paymaster U.S.A. Tillmon's Prisoner of War Record stated he was captured March 10, 1865, from Solemn (Solomon's) Grove in Fayetteville, North Carolina, brought from Raleigh, North Carolina, paroled at Boulware and Cone's Wharf, Virginia March 30, 1865, reported at Camp G. B. Maryland March 31, 1865, sent to Camp Chase April 2, 1865, reported there April 5, 1865, furloughed April 9, 1865, for 30 days, returned April 18, 1865, mustered out of service June 13, 1865, at Camp Chase, Ohio. Boyd's pension records state after he was captured, he was forced to walk barefoot in the snow for 200 miles from Monroe's Crossroads to Richmond, Virginia

Tillman S. Boyd was born 18 Feb 1842, in Walker County, Alabama. He died 16 May 1915, in Arkadelphia, Alabama and was buried in the Sulpher Springs Cemetery, Blount County, Alabama. He never married. Tillman served on both sides during the Civil War. He enlisted on September 6, 1862, in Walker County, in Company B, 13th Battalion Partisan Rangers, (later consolidated as 15th Battalion Alabama Partisan Rangers on June 5, 1863). At some time between this enlistment and December 21, 1863, Tillman deserted the Confederate service and enlisted in Company K, of the First Alabama Cavalry, U.S. The first Alabama Cavalry was actively recruiting, near Tillman's home, in Walker County. He was mustered in at Camp Davis, Mississippi on 21 Dec 1863. During June-August 1864 he was listed as absent, sick at Rome, Georgia, with typhoid fever and chronic diarrhea. On 10 Mar 1865, Tillman was captured by Confederate forces at Solomon Grove, North Carolina. In his pension application, he states that he was forced to march barefoot, in the snow, approximately 200 miles from Monroe Cross Roads to Richmond, Virginia. Frostbite from this experience, caused his feet to swell and burst. Many a captured Yank lost his shoes to his captors. At Camp Chase, Ohio, on March 30, 1865, he was paroled, released and later discharged from the Union Army at the end of the war. He returned to his home in Walker County on July 4, 1865. He later moved to Blount County. Tillman applied for a pension, based on his disability from suffering of the forced march in the snow and typhoid fever. His parents wrote the U.S. Government to plead his case. In the letter, they describe their home remedies: "His feet had an offensive smell - we bathed them in warm water and bound them up in roasted turnips, which relieved them from bad smell. We then applied an ointment of spirits of turpentine and sheep tallow which gave some relief. But he still complains of his feet especially during the winter time. We gave him Simmonds liver regulating pills, Jaynes pills, McLanes pills, Walter Scott S. Lythia for the kidneys, cod liver oil and vinegar bitters. All seem to give no permanent relief. We have continued these medicines ever since he came home, until six weeks ago we took him to Blount Springs to use the water. We can see, but little or no change for the better. He has not been able to perform any kind of labor, since he came home." By the treatment described it is a wonder that Tillman did not die at the hands of his well meaning parents. Such was the treatment of the day in the "Good Ole Days." Submitted by: Edward Corrick, Cullman, Alabama and written by Richard Jesse, Cullman, Alabama. Source: The Cullman Tribune October 23, 1997.

Tillman S. Boyd's Pension Testimony: The State of Alabama Cullman County, Personally appeared before me John A. Johnson, Clerk of the Circuit Court of Cullman County Alabama. Tillmon S. Boyd who after being by me duly sworn deposeth and saith that I am the identical Tillman S. Boyd who was a private in Company K' 1st Regt. Of Alabama Cavy Volunteers, enlisted at Camp Davis, Miss on the 23rd of December 1863 and honorably discharged at Camp Chase, Ohio on the 13th day of June 1865. That while in the military service of the United States and in the line of duty I contracted chronic diarrhea and typhoid fever the same being contracted at Rome, Ga. on June 1st 1864

Caused by exposure, and that I was treated for said disability at Military Hospital at Rome, Ga. entering in July 1864 and leaving there Sept 1st 1864, after being discharged from said hospital I rejoined my regiment and was captured on the 10th day of March 1865 then with General Sherman command in North Carolina, and by reason of exposure caused by having to march a forced march barefooted from Monroe Cross Roads to Richmond Va. The chronic diarrhea again came on me and I remained at Camp Chase. I having been treated by a regimental surgeon stationed at that place, and since said discharge I have been suffering from said disease every since being unable to do any work. Tillmon S. Boyd, Sworn and subscribed before me this 5th day of August 1880, John A. Johnson, Clerk Circuit Court, Cullman County, Ala.

The State of Alabama Cullman County, Before me A. B. Hays, Judge of the Probate Court in and for said County, personally appeared Tillmon S. Boyd, the applicant whose name is signed to the foregoing affidavit, and who being duly sworn in relation to the interlineations in the said foregoing affidavit, states the words "June 1st 1865, as first interlined, an error made by the person writing the same, and that the interlineations about June 1st 1864" is to the best of his knowledge and recollection correct as now inserted. Tillmon S. Boyd, Sworn to and subscribed Before me this June 27th 1881, A.B. Hays, Judge of Probate, Cullman Co., Ala.

Researched and documented and by: Edward (Ed) Oliver Corrick, & Charlotte Victoria (Vicki) Sams Corrick, Cullman, Alabama.

<u>Boyd, Thomas J.</u> - See Thomas J. Byrd.

<u>Boyer, Thomas Henry</u> - Thomas Henry Boyer enlisted in Company F of the 1st Alabama Cavalry, USV as a private on May 23, 1863, in Corinth, Mississippi. He was enrolled by Captain Pierce for a period of one year. The September and October 1863 Muster Roll listed Thomas as being absent, in confinement at Corinth, Mississippi. He died of disease in November 13, 1863, in the hospital at Corinth. The Company Descriptive Book shows Thomas to have been 18 years of age, 5'-8" tall, having a fair complexion, blue eyes, dark hair, born in Oktibbeha County, Mississippi, and was a farmer by occupation. Bowyer was buried in Grave #B-3357 in the Corinth National Cemetery.

<u>Bradley, Samuel</u> - Samuel Bradley only had one card misfiled in the military records of the 1st Alabama Cavalry, USV showing he enlisted in Company A. He was recorded as being a patient in Overton U.S.A. Hospital in Memphis, Tennessee in January and February 1864. No further information relative to this soldier was found.*

<u>Bramman, William M.</u> - See William M. Branen.

<u>Bramley, Barton</u> - Barton Bramley, also spelled Bromley and Brumley, enlisted in Company B of the 1st Alabama Cavalry, USV as a private on January 20, 1863, in Glendale, Mississippi for a period of 1 year. He was enrolled by Phillip A. Sternberg, and was mustered in January 22, 1863, in Corinth, Mississippi. The Regimental Descriptive Book recorded him as 33 years of age, 5'-9" tall, having a dark complexion, dark eyes, dark hair, born in Fayette County, Alabama, and a farmer by occupation. The September and October 1863 Muster Roll recorded him as being absent, a prisoner of war in the hands of the enemy since October 26, 1863, which was the Battle of Vincent's Crossroads, near Bay Springs, Mississippi. The November and December 1863 Muster Roll recorded him a Corporal, and stated he was present. He mustered out January 22, 1864, in Memphis, Tennessee.

<u>Branen, William M.</u> - See William M. Brannan. His name was also spelled Branan, Branen and Brannon.

<u>Branhan, Andrew</u> - Andrew Branhan had one misfiled card in the military records of the 1st Alabama Cavalry, USV. It stated he enlisted as a private in Company F, and was in the U.S.A. Field Hospital in Bridgeport, Alabama. He returned to duty May 7, 1864. No further information was found on this soldier.*

<u>Brannan, William</u> - William Brannan enlisted in Company B of the 1st Alabama Cavalry, USV on January 16, 1863, at Glendale, Mississippi for a period of 1 year. He was enrolled by Captain Sternberg and was mustered in January 22, 1863, in Corinth, Mississippi. William's name appeared on the Returns dated March 1863 stating: absent, sick in hospital in Corinth, Mississippi since March 26th. November 1863, he was on detached service recruiting in Alabama since November 27, 1863, by order of Colonel Spencer. From October 1863 through January 1864, he was on extra or daily duty as Regimental Bugler. The Regimental Descriptive Book shows William to have been 17 years of age, 5'-7" tall, having a light complexion, blue eyes, light hair, born in Coosa County, Alabama, and a farmer by occupation. The November and December 1863 Muster Roll listed him as being absent, on

recruiting service in Alabama since November 27, 1863. There was a Notation in his file from the Record and Pension Division of the War Department dated October 20, 1890, stating: It has this day been determined by this department that its records that this soldier was mustered out with company January 22, 1864. Discharge Certificate furnished by October 18, 1890. This is apparently the same soldier as the William M. Brannan listed below.

Brannan, William M. - William M. Brannan, also spelled Branan, Branen and Brannon enlisted in Company A of the 1st Alabama Cavalry, USV as a Bugler on August 1, 1864, in Rome, Georgia for a period of 3 years. He was enrolled by Captain Jerome Hinds, and appointed Bugler August 1, 1864. The Company Descriptive Book showed William to have been 18 years of age, 5'-8" tall, having a fair complexion, blue eyes, light hair, born in Coosa County, Alabama, and a farmer by occupation. The November and December 1864 Muster Roll stated he was absent, sick in the hospital in Nashville, Tennessee November 8, 1864. The January and February 1865 Muster Roll stated he was absent, on detached service in Decatur, Alabama, probably recruiting. He was on detached service in Decatur through April 1865. He was captured and taken prisoner of war by the enemy on March 10, 1865, which was the date of the Battle of Monroe's Crossroads near Fayetteville, North Carolina. The May and June 1865 Muster Roll listed him as being absent, missing in action, however, he was present in July and August. He was shown as having deserted October 6, 1865, from Decatur, Alabama with 1 horse, saddle, bridle, halter, saber belt, shelter tent, and 1 Spencer Carbine. There was a Notation in William's military records from the Record and Pension Office of the War Department, dated June 10, 1893, that stated: The charge of desertion of October 6, 1865, against this man is removed and he is discharged to date October 6, 1865, under the provision of the Act of Congress, approved March 2, 1889. Discharge Certificate prepared by the War Department on January 10, 1893, and filed. See Company B, 1st Alabama Cavalry. There was a letter in William M. Brannon's file from the Assistant Quartermaster's Office in Cairo, Illinois dated August 2, 1864, which states: In compliance of General Order Number 49, Department of Tennessee, I have this day furnished transportation from Cairo, Illinois to New Albany, Indiana for W.M. Brannan in the amount of $6.50. Very Respectfully, Your Obedient Servant, A.C. Woolfolk, Captain and A.Q.M., Commanding Officer of Company B of 1st Regiment Alabama Cavalry. William was mustered out October 20, 1865, in Huntsville, Alabama.

Brantley, James M. - James M. Brantley enlisted in Company H of the 1st Alabama Cavalry, USV as a private on January 15, 1865, in Stevenson, Alabama for a period of 3 years. He was enrolled by Sergeant Major James W. DeVaney, and was mustered in April 18, 1865, in Nashville, Tennessee. His Muster and Descriptive Roll showed him to have been 20 years of age, 5'-6" tall, having a dark complexion, blue eyes, black hair, born in Walton County, Georgia and a farmer by occupation. The January and February 1865 Muster Roll stated James was a patient in the Granger U.S.A. General Hospital in Huntsville, Alabama, with name shown as James Bentley. He was mustered out October 20, 1865, in Huntsville, Alabama and was paid $100 bounty.

James M. Brantley was born December 29, 1844, in Walton County, Georgia to Reubin Wesley Brantley and Almeda Elmira Coker. James married Martha J. Oliver on December 25, 1870, in Bedford County, Tennessee, and had the following children: Mary E., born 1872; James Madison, born 1876; and Jenetta Brantley, born 1878. James M. Brantley died April 26, 1902 in Bedford County, Tennessee and was buried in the Willow Mount Cemetery in Bedford County, Tennessee. He died the same day as his brother, William.

Braswell, J.B. - Only one card was found for J.B. Braswell which was filed at the end of the last roll of microfilm of the 1st Alabama Cavalry, USV records. It only stated he enlisted in Company L on April 1, 1864, in Mooresville, Alabama as a Private. No further information relative to this soldier was found.*

Brasswell, James - Only one card was found for James Brasswell which was filed at the end of the last roll of microfilm of the 1st Alabama Cavalry, USV records. It recorded him as a Private in Company L stating he enlisted on June 4, 1864, in Ackworth, Georgia. No further information relative to this soldier was found.*

Bray, Stephen S. - Stephen S. Bray enlisted in Company L of the 1st Alabama Cavalry, USV as a private on September 25, 1863, at Fayette County, Alabama for a period of 1 year. He was enrolled by Captain Trammel and was mustered in the same day in Glendale, Mississippi. The Company Descriptive Book showed Bray to have been 18 years of age, 5'-6" tall, having a fair complexion, blue eyes, light hair, born in Winston County, Alabama, and a farmer by occupation. From September 25 through October 31, 1863, he was shown to have been absent with leave. The November and December 1863 Muster Roll stated he had returned from missing in action on December 25, 1863. The Muster Roll dated from December 31, 1863, to April 30, 1864, showed Bray as absent, sick in Nashville, Tennessee since April 2, 1864. He was discharged September 28, 1864, in Rome, Georgia by reason of expiration of term of service, and paid in full by Major Holt in Nashville. Stephen S. Bray's name was listed on the Returns stating: November 1863, absent, sick, left in Alabama by order of Colonel Spencer, and March and April 1864, absent, sick in hospital in Memphis, Tennessee.

Bray, William H. - William H. Bray enlisted in Company L of the 1st Alabama Cavalry, USV on September 25, 1863, in Fayette County, Alabama for a period of 1 year. He was enrolled by Captain Trammel and was mustered in the same day in Glendale, Mississippi. The Company Descriptive Book recorded Bray as being 42 years of age, 5'-10" tall, having a fair complexion, blue eyes, light hair, born in Winston County, Alabama, and a farmer by occupation. He was reported to have deserted from Camp Davies, Mississippi on January 2, 1864, with a revolver for which he owed the US Government $40. His name appeared on the returns as follows: October 1863, missing in action October 26, 1863, from the Battle of Vincent's Crossroads; November 1863, gained from missing in action November 1, 1863; March 1864; on detailed duty by order of Colonel Spencer. September 1864, discharged September 29, 1864 in Rome, Georgia due to expiration of term of service.

Brewer, Sanders - Sanders Brewer enlisted in Company C of the 1st Alabama Cavalry, USV as a private on December 1, 1862, in Corinth, Mississippi for a period of 1 year. He was enrolled by D.R. Adams and was mustered in December 22, 1862, at Corinth. The Regimental Descriptive Book recorded him as 45 years of age, 6'-½" tall, having a fair complexion, blue eyes, sandy hair, born in Anson County, North Carolina, and a farmer by occupation. The July and August 1863 Muster Roll recorded him as being absent, prisoner in the hands of the enemy. The September 1863 through December 1863 Muster Roll showed him as being absent, a prisoner of war in the hands of the enemy since October 26, 1863, which was the Battle of Vincent's Crossroads, near Bay Springs, Mississippi.

Sanders Brewer was killed on August 8, 1863, by a Bank of Rebels, while on his way to his command at Glendale, Mississippi, he having been home on sick leave in Tishomingo County, Mississippi, with chronic "dierra" (diarrhea). He was shot and taken to a hospital in Glendale, Mississippi, where he died, his body covered with dirt in a ravine. This information is taken from Jane Austin Brewer's request for Pension Pay #149895. She was living in Henderson County, Tennessee. Several documents stating that she and Sanders were married in Anson, North Carolina were given, along with a list of 5 children under the age of 16. Her pension was $8.00 per month with an additional $2.00 for each child, commencing on July 25, 1866. The above information taken from documentation from National Archives. Submitted by Becky Steward.

William H. Brewer - William H. Brewer enlisted as a Private in Company D of the 1st Alabama Cavalry, USV on February 1, 1863, in Glendale, Mississippi. He was mustered in February 4, 1863, in Corinth, Mississippi by W. Williams for a term of 1 year. The Regimental Descriptive Book recorded him as being 23 years of age, 6'-7" tall, having a dark complexion, blue eyes, dark hair, born in Marion County, Alabama, and a farmer by occupation. He was mustered in on February 4, 1863m at Corinth, Mississippi and was discharged July 10, 1863, by order of Major General Hurlburt due to a disability. His records state he had measles when he enlisted. He was born January 29, 1841, in Bear Creek, Marion County, Alabama. A Certificate of Disability was issued to William H. Brewer by Captain Jude H. Shurtliff stating the following: During the last two months this soldier has been unfit for duty 60 days. I know nothing personally of the time or place that the disease was contracted, not being with the company at the time, but have learned from reliable information that the said William H. Brewer was of debilitate constitution prior to enlistment and was taken to taken with measles the 12th of February 1863, and has not been fit for duty since. Surgeon A.B. Stuart signed the Certificate of Disability stating William H. Brewer was incapable of performing the duties of a soldier due to general debility significant of measles since entering the service, but I learn from himself and others that he has never been a healthy man. He has been in the service four months and only had four days on duty. He is 6'-7½" tall, and very slim. He is not a probably case for pension. Signed by A.B. Stuart, Surgeon, July 10, 1863, at Corinth, Mississippi by order of Brigadier General G.M. Dodge.

William H. Brewer was born January 29, 1841, in Bear Creek, Marion County, Alabama. He is buried in a family plot with 2 wives and 4 children, all apparently born to his first wife. His stone says born 1841, died 1933. The Marion County recorder did not have a death certificate for him so he did not die in that county. 1st wife, Nancy S, died July 28, 1881, at age 38 years and 5 months. His 2nd wife, Damaris, died December 14, 1899, at age 61 years and 4 months. His 1st child, Arthur O., died July 3, 1867, at age 2 years; 2nd child, Elmina E., died July 5, 1881, at age 9 years and 20 days; 3rd child, Nancy, died July 3, 1881, at age 2 years and 4 months; 4th child, Archie L., died August 8, 1890, at age 23 years, 9 months, and 29 days. William H. Brewer married Nancy S., last name unknown, in August 1861, and died December 9, 1933. He is buried in a large above ground concrete tomb in the far SW corner of Eastland Cemetery, 7600 Baylis Road, Kinmundy Township, Marion County, Illinois. This is just off of the Kinmundy-Alma Exit on I-57. Family information submitted by Bob Herr.

From The *Kinmundy Express* December 14, 1933: This community was saddened by the death of Mr. W.H. Brewer, which occurred Saturday evening in Biloxi, Mississippi. He had been in poor health for the past 2 years, but died rather suddenly from an ulcer of the stomach with internal hemorrhage. He had spent several past winters in Biloxi, and the summers here. He was always present at the Decoration Day Exercises, but unable to attend the last one on account of health. He was quite an interesting character. In height, he measured 6 feet and 7 inches, and he often remarked, "Everybody has to look up to me." And then again in relating his experiences during the Civil War, he said that he rode a mule but you couldn't tell it as his feet dragged the ground. He was one of our early settlers, coming here soon after the close of the war and settling on a farm southeast of this city. Here he remained until moving to town. He could relate much of the early history of our city and he took great pride in doing so. The body, accompanied by his son, Noah, of Urbana, Illinois. arrived here Tuesday and was taken to Nelms Undertaking Parlors. Services were held at the M.E. Church with interment in Eastland Cemetery in the concrete vault which was constructed by the deceased several years ago. William H. Brewer was born January 29, 1841, at Bear Creek, Marion County, Tennessee, and died in Biloxi, Miss. On December 9, 1933. He married Miss Nancy S. May in March 1861, and they had 8 children, all of whom are deceased except the youngest son, Noah, of Urbana. This companion was laid to rest in Eastland Cemetery, July 8, 1881. In April 1883 he married Mrs. Damaris Upton of Springerton, Illinois, who died March 6, 1899. In the fall of 1900, he married Mrs. Downs of Kinmundy, who died December 10, 1917. Mr. Brewer served his country during the Civil War with Company D, 1st Alabama Cavalry. He was a member of the Grand Army of the Republic, of the B.P.O.E. of Champaign, and an ex-minister of the Gospel of the Latter Day Saints. Besides his son, he is survived by 9 grandchildren, 16 great-grandchildren, and 3 great-great-grandchildren. Brewer is buried at Eastland Cemetery in Marion County, Illinois. Submitted by Becky Stewart.

Brice, John C. - See John C. Bice.

Brigman, James N. - James N. Brigman, also shown as James R. Brigman, enlisted in Company G of the 1st Alabama Cavalry, USV as a private on June 26, 1863, at Chewalla, Tennessee at age 27, for a period of 1 year. He was mustered in the same day at Corinth, Mississippi. He was reported to have deserted July 3, 1863. Another muster roll stated he deserted July 30, 1863.

Brigman, Moses - Moses Brigman was originally with the 11th Illinois Cavalry and was temporarily attached to Company G of the 1st Alabama Cavalry, USV as a private.

Britnell, William S. - William S. Britnell enlisted in Company A of the 1st Alabama Cavalry,

USV as a private on October 29, 1862, at Corinth, Mississippi and was mustered in December 31, 1862, in Corinth. He was enrolled by Captain Jerome J. Hinds. The May and June 1863 Muster Roll listed him as having deserted June 3, 1863, however, the July and August 1863 Muster Roll stated he returned from desertion on August 16, 1863. The September and October 1863 Muster Roll listed him as absent, missing in action from Vincent's Crossroads October 26, 1863. Returned from missing from action December 6, 1863. The Muster and Descriptive Roll listed William as being 26 years of age, 5'-6" tall, having a fair complexion, blue eyes, light hair, born in Franklin County, Alabama, and a farmer by occupation. He re-enlisted February 23, 1864 at Memphis, Tennessee for a period of 3 years, and was mustered in February 26, 1864 in Memphis. He was enrolled by Lieutenant Files. A Notation from the Adjutant General's Office of the War Department dated November 3, 1870 stated: This man was discharged October 20, 1870 , to date, October 20, 1865, date of muster out of his company. Another Notation from the Adjutant General's Office of the War Department dated April 29, 1884, stating William S. Britnell was a veteran volunteer by reason of prior service in Company A of the 1st Alabama Cavalry, (Old Organization.) A Notation from the Adjutant General's Office of the War Department dated August 19, 1887, stated: He deserted June 3, 1863, returned August 16, 1863, was tried before a GCM (General Court Martial), found guilty of desertion, and sentenced to forfeiture of pay for 3 months and 17 days, as he was convicted of desertion by a GCM, the sentence of which appears to have been carried into execution, the charge of desertion no longer stands against him. The record of the fact that he was absent in desertion from June 3, to August 16, 1863, cannot...... William Britnell's name appeared on a Hospital Muster Roll from the U.S.A. General Hospital in Savannah, Georgia, Ward 3, dated February 28, 1865, stated Britnell was a patient in the hospital February 5, 1865. Britnell's name appeared on the Returns stating the following: May 1863, deserted May 1, 1863 from Glendale, Mississippi; June 1863, deserted June 3, 1863 from Glendale, Mississippi; August 1863, joined from desertion at Glendale August 16, 1863; October 1863, missing in action from Vincent's Crossroads October 26, 1863; February 1865, absent, sick in USA General Hospital; April 1865, absent, left sick in Savannah, Georgia January 23, 1865. The Company Descriptive Book shows William Britnell to have been 26 years of age, 5'-6" tall, having a fair complexion, blue eyes, light hair, born in Franklin County, Alabama, and a farmer by occupation. Britnell was mustered out October 20, 1865, in Huntsville, Alabama. His Muster-Out Roll stated he was paid $180 for bounty and was still owed $120 for bounty, and he owed the U.S. Government $2.15 for losing one saber belt, complete. Sick at Burleson, Alabama since September 4, 1865. No discharge furnished on muster out of organization. William was able to sign his name to his Enlistment Forms.

Britton, John - John Britton enlisted in Company K of the 1st Alabama Cavalry, USV as a private on October 13, 1862, in Corinth, Mississippi for a period of 1 year. He was mustered in October 14, 1862, in Corinth. The January and February 1863 Muster Roll stated he was discharged and final statement was given on February 24, 1863. A Certificate of Disability for Discharge: In the case of John Britton, a private in Company K of the 1st Alabama Cavalry, USV, Headquarters 16th Army Corps, Memphis, Tennessee, March 4, 1863, To be discharged, Pay Order of Major General Hurlburt, Adjutant General's Office, March 30, 1863, Duplicate sent to the Pension Office, Assistant Adjutant General; Entered on Casualty Rolls. Another Certificate of Disability for Discharge was issued to John Britton, a private of Captain Frank C. Burdick, Company K of the 1st Alabama Cavalry, USV, was enlisted by F.C. Burdick of the 1st Alabama Cavalry at Corinth, Mississippi, on October 13, 1862, to serve one year. He was recorded as being 45 years of age, 5'-7" tall, having a light complexion, gray eyes, dark hair, born in Edgefield, South Carolina, and was a farmer by occupation. It went on to state that during the last 2 months, the said soldier had been unfit for duty for 40 days, and his disability was listed as old age, loss of eyesight, broken constitution, and general debility. It was signed Frank C. Burdick, Glendale, Mississippi, and dated January 28, 1863. The assistant surgeon, Noble Holton, stated that John Britton was incapable of performing his duties as a soldier due to old age, a broken constitution, debility from diarrhea and fever, and deficiency of sight in left eye. Degree of disability is one-half. Discharged March 16, 1863, by order of Brigadier General G.M. Dodge, Commanding the Post District.

Britton, N.H. - Only one card was found for N.H. Britton which was filed at the end of the last roll of microfilm of the 1st Alabama Cavalry, USV records. It recorded him as a Private in Company E, stating he was discharged July 27, 1864, in Rome, Georgia due to expiration of term of service. No further information relative to this soldier was found.*

Brodigan, Peter - Peter Brodigan enlisted in Company F of the 1st Alabama Cavalry, USV as a private on June 29, 1863, in Corinth, Mississippi for a period of 1 year. He was enrolled by Captain Pierce and was mustered in August 13, 1863, in Corinth. The Company Descriptive Book shows him to have been 27 years of age, 5'-6" tall, having a fair complexion, blue eyes, dark hair, born in New York City, New York, and a printer by occupation. The September and October 1863 Muster Roll listed him as being absent, supposed to have been taken prisoner of war at the Battle of Vincent's Crossroads on October 26, 1863. He was returned from missing in action on November 24, 1863. In April 1864, he was on extra or daily duty as a stable guard. He was discharged July 27, 1864, in Rome, Georgia due to expiration of term of service.

Brogden, Charles J. - Charles J. Brogden enlisted in Captain Frank C. Burdick's Company of the 1st Alabama Cavalry, USV as a Bugler on September 8, 1862, in Iuka, Mississippi, and was mustered in on October 1, 1862, at Corinth, Mississippi. The Company Descriptive Book recorded him being 30 years of age, 5'-8" tall, having a sandy complexion, blue eyes, sandy hair, born in Warren County, Tennessee, and a farmer by occupation.

Brogdon, Claborne - Claborne Brogdon enlisted in Company G of the 1st Alabama Cavalry, USV on March 2, 1864, in Decatur, Alabama for a period of 3 years. He was enrolled by Lieutenant Pease, or Pierce, and was mustered in March 15, 1865, in Decatur. The Muster and Descriptive Roll shows him to have been 40 years of age, 5'-5" tall, having a dark complexion, gray eyes, dark hair, born in Morgan County, Alabama, and a farmer by occupation. In April 1864, Brogdon was listed as being absent, on detached service recruiting. The July and August 1864 Muster Roll stated he was absent with leave. The September and October 1864 Muster Roll listed him as being absent, having deserted in October 1864, while on furlough at Rome, Georgia. He returned from desertion July 14, 1865, at Decatur, Alabama. His name appears on a Hospital Muster Roll in the U.S.A. General Hospital in Hilton Head, South Carolina as being a patient from February 6, 1865. His name was also on the same hospital muster roll stating he was transferred north March 15, 1865. The March and April 1865 Hospital Muster Roll from the McDougall U.S.A. General Hospital in Fort Schuyler, New York Harbor, stated he was transferred to Nashville, Tennessee April 26, 1865. The next Hospital Muster Roll (Detached Soldiers) was from the U.S.A. Hospital #14 , in Nashville, Tennessee for March and April 1865, listed him as present. The May and June 1865 Hospital Muster Roll listed Brogdon as being a patient in the Cumberland U.S.A. General Hospital in Nashville, Tennessee. He was mustered out October 20, 1865, in Huntsville, Alabama.

Bromley, Barton - See Barton Bramley.

Bromley, Riley Y. - Riley Y. Bromley enlisted in Company K of the 1st Alabama Cavalry, USV as a private on November 5, 1862, in Corinth, Mississippi for a period of one year. He was enrolled by Captain Phillip A. Sternberg, and was mustered in December 31, 1862, at Corinth, Mississippi. He was reported to have deserted December 31, 1862, however, the March and April 1863 Muster Roll stated he was present. The September and October 1863 Muster Roll listed him as being absent, prisoner of war in the hands of the enemy since October 26, 1863, which was when the Battle of Vincent's Crossroads was fought near Bay Springs, Mississippi. The May and June 1863 Muster Roll listed him as being absent with leave. Riley Y. Brumley's name appeared on the Returns as being in Company B, and stated: May 1863 to July 1863, absent with leave since May 10, 1863, in Alabama. October and November 1863, absent, prisoner of war in the hands of the enemy since the engagement at Vincent's Crossroads October 26, 1863. The Regimental Descriptive Book listed him as being 35 years of age, 5'-6" tall, having a gray complexion, dark eyes, dark hair, and a farmer by occupation. He was mustered out January 22, 1864, at Memphis, Tennessee.

<u>Bronson, David A.</u> - See David A. Brunson.

<u>Bronson, William H.</u> - See William H. Brunson.

<u>Brooks, George W.</u> - George W. Brooks enlisted and was mustered into Company A of the 1st Alabama Cavalry, USV on August 27, 1864, in Rome, Georgia as a private, for a period of 3 years. He was enrolled by Captain Hinds. The Muster and Descriptive Roll showed Brooks to have been 40 years of age, 5'-9" tall, having a fair complexion, blue eyes, light hair, born in Henry County, Georgia, and a farmer by occupation. It stated he was due a $300 bounty. George W. Brooks died of disease of the heart, in the hospital June 17, 1865, in Huntsville, Alabama.

<u>Brooks, Henry F.</u> - Henry F. Brooks enlisted and was mustered into Company K of the 1st Alabama Cavalry, USV on July 22, 1862, in Huntsville, Alabama for a period of 3 years. He was enrolled by Lieutenant Millard. He was one of the first enlistees who were shipped to Nashville, Tennessee where they were merged with the 1st Middle Tennessee Cavalry, and the 5th Tennessee Cavalry, and Henry was assigned to Company E of the 1st Middle Tennessee Cavalry, and also served in the 5th Tennessee. The Regimental Descriptive Book shows him to have been 24 years of age, 5'-7¼ " tall, having sandy complexion, blue eyes, sandy hair, born in Lauderdale County, Alabama, and a farmer by occupation. Brooks was sent to the hospital at Camp Chase, Ohio on May 22, 1863. The January 1, to June 30, 1863, Muster Roll stated he was left sick in the hospital in Camp Chase, Ohio where he remained through April 1865. The May and June 1865 Muster Roll stated Henry F. Brooks had not been heard from since May 22, 1863, and was supposed to dead, not heard from since May 23, 1863. His name appeared on the Returns as follows: January and February 1863, on Courier Post, probably in Reedyville, Tennessee. June 1863, absent, sick in the hospital. Henry's name appeared on the Dennison U.S.A. General Hospital, 3rd Division, Camp Dennison, Ohio for September and October 1864 as being sick. The May and June 1863 Muster Roll from the Dennison U.S.A. General Hospital at Camp Dennison, Ohio, showed Henry F. Brooks to have been in Company C of the 63rd Regiment O.V.I. (Ohio Volunteer Infantry). There was a Notation in Henry's records from the Adjutant General's Office of the War Department, dated February 1, 1868, stating he had been transferred to Company G of the 15th V.R.C. (Veterans Reserve Corps). There was a Notation in his records that stated: Number of Bed: H.F. Brooks, Company E, 1st Middle Tennessee Cavalry, Date of Admission, May 22, 1863, Date of Discharge: General Hospital, Camp Chase, Ohio, Where Sent And By What Authority: Rogersville, Alabama. His effects included 1 blanket. The Prisoner of War Records stated Henry F. Brooks was captured at Rome, Georgia on May 3, 1863, confined at Richmond, Virginia on May 9, 1863, paroled at City Point, Virginia on May 15, 1863, reported to Camp Parole, Maryland on May 18, 1863, sent to Camp Chase, Ohio on May 19, 1863, where he reported on May 22, 1863. Enrolled as Henry F. Brooks, Company E, 1st Middle Tennessee Cavalry, subsequently Company K, 1st Alabama Cavalry. The name H.T. Brooks. N.N.F. or Henry Brooks not born February 21, 1883, Pen Case returned March 2, 1883. A Note dated February 23, 1883, stated the records would be corrected accordingly.

<u>Brooks, James L.</u> - James L. Brooks enlisted in Company D of the 1st Alabama Cavalry, USV as a private on May 20, 1864, in Decatur, Alabama for a period of 3 years. He was enrolled by Lieutenant Pease and was mustered in June 16, 1864, in Decatur. The Muster and Descriptive Roll showed him to have been 30 years of age, 6' tall, having a light complexion, blue eyes, dark hair, born in Carroll County, Georgia, and a farmer by occupation. The July through December 1864 Muster Rolls listed him as being absent, recruiting in Decatur, Alabama by order of Colonel Spencer. The January through April 1865 Muster Rolls listed him as being absent, on detached service in Decatur, Alabama. The May and June 1865 Muster Roll showed Brooks as being absent without leave, however, he was present in July and August 1865. James L. Brooks was mustered out October 20, 1865 in Huntsville, Alabama, owing the U.S. Government $25.45 for losing a revolver, 2 cartridge boxes, 1 halter and saddle, and blankets. His Muster-Out Roll stated the U.S. Government owed him $100 in bounty.

James L. Brooks was born in June 1834 in Carroll County, Georgia to William and Isabelle,

"Icy" Mullins Brooks. On February 20, 1859, James married Susan Penelope Fields in Jefferson County, Alabama. Susan was the daughter of William Hampton Fields and Mary Ann "Polly" Harden who married March 14, 1835. James died December 28, 1902, in Mount Olive, Jefferson County, Alabama.

James L. Brooks was reputed to be one-half Choctaw Indian, but was probably Cherokee Indian, his mother Isabell "Icy" Mullins Brooks being full-blooded Indian. This information submitted by Connie Gilbreath Belcher who stated she had not found any verification of Isabelle Mullins being full-blooded Indian.

Brooks, John A. - John A. Brooks enlisted and mustered into Company K of the 1st Alabama Cavalry, USV as a private on August 22, 1862, in Huntsville, Alabama. He was enrolled by Lieutenant Millard for a period of 3 years. The Company Descriptive Roll recorded him as being 28 years of age, 5'-8" tall, having a light complexion, blue eyes, sandy hair, born in Lauderdale County, Alabama and a farmer by occupation. On October 13, 1863, he was shown as being absent, sick in Hospital #14 in Nashville, Tennessee where he died of measles November 7, 1864, in Nashville, Davidson County, Tennessee. He is buried in Grave A-5186 in the Nashville National Cemetery.

Brooks, John C. - John C. Brooks was a Sergeant and 2nd Lieutenant and was temporarily attached from the 66th Illinois Volunteers.

Brooks, John W. - John W. Brooks enlisted in Company E of the 1st Alabama Cavalry, USV as a private on March 1, 1863, in Glendale, Mississippi for a period of 1 year, and was mustered in the same day in Corinth, Mississippi. The November and December 1863 Muster Roll listed him as being absent, in confinement at Corinth, Mississippi since November 22, 1863. His name appeared on the Returns as follows: March 1863, absent, sick; April 1863, absent with leave at Corinth, Mississippi; December 1863, absent, in close confinement under charge in Corinth, Mississippi since November 22, 1863; March 1864, term of service expired. John W. Brooks was charged with the murder of Neal Morrison, a citizen of Tishomingo County, Mississippi, on or about November 14, 1863, also charged with desertion but captured by scouting party near Glendale, Mississippi and returned. A letter in his file from Headquarters, Company E, 1st Alabama Cavalry, Camp Davies, Mississippi, dated November 24, 1863, stated: Private John W. Brooks, Company E, 1st Alabama Cavalry, Charge 1st, Murder, Specification – In this that the said John W. Brooks, Private, Company E, 1st Alabama Cavalry, did on or about the 14th Day of November 1863, shoot one Neal Morrison, a citizen of Tishomingo County, Mississippi with a revolver which resulted in the death of Neal Morrison, all this near Camp Davies, Mississippi. Charge 2nd, Desertion, Specification, in this that the said John W. Brooks, Private Company E, 1st Alabama Cavalry, did absent himself from his company and regiment without permission on or about the 14th Day of November 1863, and remained away from his command until the 18th Day of November 1863 when he was captured by a scouting party, and returned to his command, said Brooks was captured near Glendale, Mississippi. Signed Albert E. Murdock, 1st Lieutenant Commanding Company. Witnesses: Mrs. Sarah Morrison; Mrs. D.E. Harmon; Miss N.P. Morrison; Mrs. Neal Morrison; 1st Lieutenant A.E. Murdock, 1st Lieutenant Commanding; and 2nd Lieutenant John Q.A. Gardner, Company E, 1st Alabama Cavalry. The March and April 1864 Muster Roll stated he was discharged March 3, 1864 due to expiration of term of service at Memphis, Tennessee. (John W. Brooks was not the only man charged in the murder of Neal Morrison.)

Bross, J.A. - Only one card was found for J.A. Bross which was filed at the end of the last roll of microfilm of the 1st Alabama Cavalry, USV records. It recorded him as being in Company E, stating he was in arrest in Corinth, Mississippi since November 22, 1863. This name is apparently misspelled and the soldier could have been part of the group who were arrested for the murder of Neal Morrison. No further information relative to this soldier was found.*

Brown, Elijah - Elijah Brown enlisted in Company K of the 1st Alabama Cavalry, USV as a private on July 24, 1863, in Huntsville, Alabama for a period of 3 years. He was enrolled by Captain Bankhead, and was one of the early enlistees who were immediately shipped to Nashville, Tennessee where they were merged with the 1st Middle Tennessee, which later became the 5th Tennessee Cavalry. Elijah was also recorded as being in the 5th Tennessee Cavalry. The October 31, 1862, Muster Roll stated Elijah was also with the 1st Middle Tennessee Cavalry. The Regimental Descriptive Book listed him as having been 44 years of age, 5'-11" tall, having a light complexion, blue eyes, light hair, born in Lawrence County, Alabama, and a farmer by occupation. He died from a relapse of measles on October 30, 1862, at Camp Campbell in Nashville, Davidson County, Tennessee and was buried in Grave B-6968 in the Nashville National Cemetery.

Elijah Brown was born about 1818 in Lawrence County, Alabama to William Brown and Jane Stover, who were married June 29, 1820. Jane was the daughter of Obediah and Catherine Stover. Elijah and his brother, Merrill Brown enlisted the same day in the 1st Alabama Cavalry, USV. Elijah Brown died October 30, 1862, in Nashville, Davidson County, Tennessee and is buried in the Nashville National Cemetery.

Brown, George L. - George L. Brown enlisted in Company I and was on detached service as courier at Reedyville, Tennessee January 27, 1863. No further information relative to this soldier was found.*

Brown, George S. - Only one card was found for George S. Brown, however, the other George S. Brown, below, may be the same soldier. It stated he enlisted in Company I on August 1, 1863, in Shelbyville, Tennessee and was enrolled by Lieutenant Snelling. No further information relative to this soldier was found.*

Brown, George S. - One card was found for a George S. Brown stating he enlisted in Company D of the 1st Alabama Cavalry, USV. He was recorded as being on Courier Post in January and February 1863. No further information relative to this soldier was found.*

Brown, George W. - George W. Brown enlisted in Company K of the 1st Alabama Cavalry, USV in Corinth, Mississippi on December 13, 1862, for a term of 1 year, and was mustered in December 31, 1862, at Corinth. In January and February 1863, he was recorded as being absent, sick in the hospital in Corinth. The September and October 1863 Muster Roll recorded him as a wagoner or teamster. In November 1863, he was on extra or daily duty as a teamster. The Returns for November 1863 stated he was on extra or daily duty as a teamster. He was reassigned to Company A, and was mustered out December 22, 1863, in Memphis, Tennessee at 37 years of age, due to expiration of term of service.

Brown, John - John Brown, also shown as John Brown, Jr., enlisted in Company G of the 1st Alabama Cavalry, USV as a private on March 10, 1864, in Decatur, Alabama for a period of 3 years. He was enrolled by Lieutenant Pease and mustered in April 13, 1864, in Decatur. The Company Descriptive Book showed John to have been 36 years of age, 5'-7" tall, having a fair complexion, blue eyes, dark hair, born in Pike County, Georgia, and a farmer by occupation. The September and October 1864 Muster Roll stated he was on extra or daily duty as company cook. He was reported to have deserted from the camp at Atlanta, Georgia on November 17, 1864, with a Colt Revolver and accoutrements, but returned to Decatur, Alabama July 5, 1865. He was mustered out October 20, 1865, in Huntsville, Alabama owing the U.S. Government $80.95 for losing his side arms and equipment. There was a letter in his file from the Adjutant General's Office of the War Department in Washington, DC dated November 20, 1883, stating: The Application for removal of the charge of desertion has been denied.

John Brown was born April 2, 1828, in Pike County, Georgia, and was married to Martha C. Self. John died August 22, 1890, in Walker County, Alabama and was buried in the Williams Chapel Methodist Church Cemetery, Walker County. Martha was born August 15, 1836, in Blount County, Alabama. Some of the children of John and Martha Self Brown included: Martha Elizabeth; John C.; Amanda Josephine; Daniel, Frances P.; and Wilburn Milton Brown.

Brown, John - Only one card was found for John Brow which was filed at the end of the last roll of microfilm of the 1st Alabama Cavalry, USV records. It recorded him as enlisted in Company F, stating he was absent, sick in USA General Hospital in May 1865.   No further information relative to this soldier was found.* No further information relative to this soldier was found.*

Brown, M.V. - Only one card was found for M.V. Brown which was filed at the end of the last roll of microfilm of the 1st Alabama Cavalry, USV records. It recorded him as having enlisted in Company D on June 1, 1863, in Glendale, Mississippi. No further information relative to this soldier was found.*

Brown, Merrill - Merrill Brown enlisted and mustered into Company K of the 1st Alabama Cavalry, USV as a private on July 24, 1864, in Huntsville, Alabama for a period of 3 years. He was enrolled by Captain Bankhead and was one of the first enlistees to be shipped to Nashville and merged with the 1st Middle Tennessee Cavalry, which went on to become the 5th Tennessee Cavalry. The Regimental Descriptive Book recorded him as having been 30 years of age, 5'-8½" tall, having a light complexion, gray eyes, black hair, born in Lawrence County, Alabama, and a farmer by occupation. His name appeared on the Returns for Company K of the 1st Alabama Cavalry, as follows: November 1862, reported to have deserted from picket post, took horse, arms and accoutrements November 2, 1862 in Nashville, Tennessee. He was not apprehended.

Merrill Brown was born about 1833 in Lawrence County, Alabama to William and Jane Brown, and was a brother to Elijah Brown, above. He married Margaret Taylor on April 15, 1852, in Summerville, Morgan County, Alabama. One descendant stated he died or was killed in 1863, in Athens, Limestone County, Alabama, however, he was still being listed on the census records, at least through 1880, where he and Margaret had the following children: Arlinda and John Brown. In the 1870 Limestone County, Alabama Census listed the following children for Merrill and Margaret Brown: Samuel, 15; Ann, 14; Josiah, 12; Jennie and Babe, 8, twins; Nancy, 6; and William Brown, 18 years of age. In addition to these names, there was a William Lovell, 23; Betsy Lovell, 21; and Amanda Lovell, 3 years of age. The 1860 Morgan County, Alabama listed the following children for Merrill and Margaret: William L., 9; Samuel, 7; Jack S., 5; Letha, 4; Letha, 4; Josiah, 3; Orlanda J., 1; and Daniel M. Brown, 6 months old.

Brown, Robert K. - Robert K. Brown enlisted in Company B of the 1st Alabama Cavalry, USV as a private on January 13, 1863, in Glendale, Mississippi for a period of 1 year. He was enrolled by Captain Phillip A. Sternberg, and was mustered in January 22, 1863, in Corinth, Mississippi. The March and April 1863 Muster Roll listed him as having deserted on March 9, 1863, from Glendale, Mississippi. On September 15, 1863, he returned from desertion to Glendale, Mississippi, where he was taken up on the rolls as a private. His name appeared on the Returns as follows: October 1863, absent, prisoner of war in the hands of the enemy since engagement with the enemy at Vincent's Crossroads on October 26, 1863, near Bay Springs, Mississippi. The Regimental Descriptive Book listed him as having been 18 years of age, 6' tall, having a dark complexion, hazel eyes, dark hair, born in Marion County, Alabama, and a farmer by occupation.

Brown, Robert M. - Robert M. Brown enlisted in Company F on May 27, 1863, in Corinth, Mississippi as a private, for a period of 1 year. He was enrolled by Captain Pierce, and was mustered in August 13, 1863, in Corinth. The Company Descriptive Book showed Robert to have been 27 years of age, 5'-8" tall, having a fair complexion, blue eyes, light hair, born in Sumner County, Tennessee, and a farmer by occupation. He died of disease September 17, 1863, in the Regimental Hospital at Glendale, Mississippi. Many of the soldiers who died at Glendale were reinterred in the Corinth National Cemetery if their family didn't claim their bodies and bury them in a family plot.

Brown, Spencer R. - Spencer R. Brown enlisted in Company A of the 1st Alabama Cavalry, USV as a private on May 12, 1863, and was mustered in the same day in Corinth, Mississippi. He was shown as being mustered out on December 22, 1863, however, there is a Spencer R. Brown who died in April 1864, who is buried in Grave #B234 of the Corinth National Cemetery in Corinth, Mississippi. The tombstone has "ALA" (Alabama) engraved on his tombstone. Apparently the Spencer R. Brown who was mustered out of the 1st Alabama Cavalry did indeed die in April 1864 and is the Spencer R.

Brown who was buried in the Corinth National Cemetery. He was listed on the 1850 Marion County, Alabama Census with his parents, John and Frances Brown, and on the 1860 Marion County Alabama Census with wife, Phebe and children Carroll and Marshall Brown. He was not found on any records after the 1860 Census other than his burial.

Brown, William - William Brown enlisted in Company F of the 1st Alabama Cavalry, USV as a private on June 25, 1863, in Memphis, Tennessee for a period of 1 year. He was enrolled by Lieutenant Hinds and was mustered in August 13, 1863, in Corinth, Mississippi. The Company Descriptive Book showed him to have been 20 years of age, 5'-8" tall, having a dark complexion, blue eyes, brown hair, born in Chickasaw County, Mississippi, and a farmer by occupation. In August 1863, he was on extra or daily duty as company cook. The September and October 1863 Muster Roll listed Brown as absent and in the hospital in Memphis, Tennessee, having been wounded in battle October 26, 1863, which was the Battle of Vincent's Crossroads near Bay Springs, Mississippi. He was also listed as a Corporal on this muster roll. He was still in the hospital in Memphis in April 1864. The December 31, 1863, through June 30, 1864, Muster Roll listed him as being absent, sick in Louisville, Kentucky. The September and October 1864 Muster Roll showed him to have been absent, wounded in Louisville, Kentucky since March 28, 1864. He was still in the hospital in Louisville in December 1864. He returned from being wounded and in the hospital on June 27, 1865, having been there since March 20, 1864. William Brown's name appeared as a Corporal on a Hospital Muster Roll for Overton U.S.A. General Hospital in Memphis Tennessee as a patient on November15, 1863. He was also listed on a Hospital Muster Roll for the Small Pox U.S.A. General Hospital in Memphis, Tennessee, dated January and February 1864, stating he sick and attached to the hospital on February 18, 1864. In May and June 1864, William Brown's name appeared on a Hospital Muster Roll for the Number 1, U.S.A. General Hospital in Nashville, Tennessee, as a patient. He was then listed on a Hospital Muster Roll for the Clay U.S.A. General Hospital in Louisville, Kentucky, stating he was attached to the hospital August 26, 1864. There was a Notation in his file from the Military Secretary's Office of the War Department dated March 28, 1901, Washington, D.C., stating the following: This man under the name David W. Hess, (or David N. Hess) deserted from Company B of the 57th Regiment of the Ohio Infantry, on January 15, 1863, and enlisted in this organization in violation of the 22nd (now 50th) Article of War. It has been determined that the action of the Adjutant General of the Army purporting to discharge this man October 27, 1879, to date from June 30, 1865, by reason of desertion was taken under a misapprehension of the powers of the War Department, and is void and without effect. Signed E.R. Rochester. The charge of desertion against this man arising from absence of any records, evidence of him after June 30, 1865, is removed and he is discharged to date July 1, 1865, under the provisions of the Act of Congress, approved March 2, 1889. Discharge Certificate furnished by the War Department March 29, 1911. The Notations of August 30, 1876, July 27, 1877, October, 1879, May 5, 1890, and September 22, 1893, are cancelled. There was a letter in William Brown's File, dated August 8, 1865, from Headquarters, 1st Alabama Cavalry, Huntsville, Alabama, July 14, 1865, Special Orders Number 24, Corporal William Brown, 1st Alabama Cavalry, is hereby ordered to report to Lieutenant D.A. Snelling for the purpose of mustering out, his term of service having expired, Signed Major F.S. Cramer.

Brown, William - William Brown enlisted and mustered into Company K of the 1st Alabama Cavalry, USV on July 24, 1862, in Huntsville, Alabama for a period of 3 years. He was enrolled by Captain Bankhead and was one of the early enlistees who were immediately shipped to Nashville and merged with the 1st Middle Tennessee and 5th Tennessee Cavalry. William was merged with the 5th Tennessee Cavalry. The Regimental Descriptive Book shows him to have been 28 years of age, 5'-10¾" tall, having a light complexion, blue eyes, light hair, born in Lawrence County, Alabama, and a farmer by occupation. The Company Muster Roll dated October 31, 1862, listed William as being absent, sent to hospital in Nashville, Tennessee October 25, 1862. The November and December 1862 Muster Roll showed William Brown as being in Company E of the 1st Middle Tennessee Cavalry. It also stated he died December 13, 1862, in Hospital # 14, in Nashville, Davidson County, Tennessee, which was formerly the Nashville Female Academy until the Union Army took it over to use as a hospital. William Brown is buried in the Nashville National Cemetery.

149

Brown, William E. - William E. Brown enlisted in Company C of the 1st Alabama Cavalry, USV as a private on February 15, 1864, in Memphis, Tennessee for a period of 3 years. He was enrolled by Captain Latty and was mustered in March 10, 1864, in Memphis. The Muster and Descriptive Roll listed him as being 18 years of age, 5'-7" tall, having a fair complexion, blue eyes, light hair, born in Marshall County, Mississippi, and a farmer by occupation. The Company Descriptive Book showed him to have been single. An undated muster roll stated he was absent, on detached service as orderly in General Veach's Headquarters. The March and April 1865 Muster Roll stated William E. Brown was killed by the enemy while on scout, on April 7, 1865, at Faison's Station in North Carolina.

Brown, William G. - William G. Brown enlisted in Company H of the 1st Alabama Cavalry, USV on January 15, 1865 in Huntsville, Alabama as a private for a period of three years by J.W. DeVaney. He was mustered in the same day in Nashville, Tennessee. The Muster and Descriptive Roll shows him to be 18 years old, having a dark complexion, black eyes, black hair, 5'-5" tall, and a farmer by occupation. He was paid a $100 bounty and was credited to Chautauqua County, New York. He was mustered out October 20, 1865, in Huntsville, Alabama with $26.76 due him for Clothing Allowance. He owed the government $2.50 for losing one belt and plate (saber) and one pistol cartridge box. Buried: Glover Hill Cemetery, Marion County, Tennessee.

William G. Brown was born June 16, 1847, and married a lady by the name of Byancy Byers around 1877, in Jackson County, Tennessee. According to descendants William took his own life in July 1907, and was buried in the Glover Hill Cemetery in Marion County, Tennessee.

Brown, William M. - William Marion Brown enlisted in Company D of the 1st Alabama Cavalry, USV as a private on June 1, 1863, in Glendale, Mississippi for a period of one year. Another muster roll stated he enlisted in Company B. He was reported to have deserted June 22, 1863, from Glendale, Mississippi while on scout, however, some soldiers reported that he had been killed by the Confederate Home Guard and since his death date is shown as 1864, he probably was. According to Olva Jones, William M. Brown was born December 16, 1835, in Georgia and died March 12, 1864, in Marion County, Alabama. He was buried in the Brown Ballard Cemetery in Marion County, Alabama and has a broken tombstone.

(There are two William Browns buried in the Nashville National Cemetery: William F. Brown, died December 12, 1862, and is buried in Grave B-6102; and William M. Brown, who died December 20, 1862, and is buried in Grave N-10742.)

Brumley, Barton - See Barton Bramley.

Brumly, J.L. - Only one card was found for J.L. Brumly which was filed at the end of the last roll of microfilm of the 1st Alabama Cavalry, USV records. It recorded him as a Private in Company G, and stated he was transferred August 24, 1863, by order of Colonel Mercy. No further information relative to this soldier was found.*

Brumley, Riley Y. - See Reley Y. Bromley.

Brumly, Larkin J. - Only one card was found for Larkin J. Brumly which was filed at the end of the last roll of microfilm of the 1st Alabama Cavalry, USV records. It recorded him as a private in Company G, stating the following: This man was temporarily attached to the organization named above. His cards are filed with the 11th Illinois Cavalry to which organization he belonged. No further information relative to this soldier was found.*

Brunson, David A. - David A. Brunson, also spelled Bronson, enlisted in Company L of the 1st Alabama Cavalry, USV as a sergeant on September 25, 1863, in Fayette County, Alabama for a term of 1 year. He was enrolled by Captain Trammel and was mustered in the same day in Glendale, Mississippi. The Company Descriptive Roll recorded him as being 31 years of age, 5'-8" tall, having a fair complexion, blue eyes, light hair, born in Wilkes County, Georgia, and was a farmer by occupation.

He died of jaundice on December 28, 1863, in the Regimental Hospital in Camp Davies, Mississippi. He is buried in the Corinth National Cemetery and classified with the unknown dead.

Brunson, William H. - William H. Brunson enlisted as a Corporal in Company L of the 1st Alabama Cavalry, USV as a Corporal on September 25, 1863, in Fayette County, Alabama for a period of one year. He was enrolled by Captain Trammel, and was mustered in the same day in Glendale, Mississippi. The Company Descriptive Book listed him as being 23 years of age, 5'-7" tall, having a dark complexion, black eyes, dark hair, born in Wilkes County, Georgia, and a farmer by occupation. He died December 9, 1863, of remittent fever, in Camp Davies, Mississippi. He was buried in the Corinth National Cemetery and classified with the Unknown Dead.

Bryant, Henry - Henry Bryant enlisted in Company F of the 1st Alabama Cavalry, USV as a private on March 27, 1863, in Corinth, Mississippi. He was enrolled by Captain Pierce and was mustered in April 18, 1863, in Florence, Alabama. The Company Descriptive Book listed him as being 36 years of age, 5'-6" tall, having a dark complexion, yellow eyes, black hair, born in Florence County, Alabama, and a factory man by occupation. A Company Muster Roll that was just dated "to June 30, 1863, listed him as being absent without leave since April 27, 1863. He was reported to have deserted April 17, 1863 from Glendale, Mississippi.

Bryant, John A. - John A. Bryant enlisted and mustered into Company M of the 1st Alabama Cavalry, USV as a private on December 7, 1863, in Camp Davies, Mississippi for a period of 3 years. Another muster roll stated he was enrolled by Captain Lomax for a term of 1 year. The Company Descriptive Book recorded him as being 24 years of age, 6' tall, having a fair complexion, blue eyes, dark hair, born in Tippah County, Mississippi, and a farmer by occupation. The March and April 1864 Muster Roll recorded him as being absent, sick in the Gayoso USA General Hospital in Memphis, Tennessee. The May and June 1864 Muster Roll recorded him as being absent, sick in the 2nd Division USA Field Hospital in Rome, Georgia. The November and December 1864 Muster Roll recorded him as being absent, sick in hospital in hospital in Rome, Georgia since September 15, 1864. However, another muster roll dated November and December 1864, stated he was in the Jefferson USA General Hospital in Jeffersonville, Indiana, where he was admitted December 3, 1864. The January and February 1865 Muster Roll recorded him as being absent, sick in Mound City, Illinois since September 15, 1864. A Jefferson USA General Hospital Muster Roll recorded him as being in Ward #3 in that hospital in January and February 1865. A note in his file stated the following: Post of Cairo, Cairo, Illinois, May 31, 1865, In compliance with telegram of A.G.O. May 6, 1865, John A. Bryant, Company M, 1st Alabama Cavalry Volunteers, a patient in Mound City General Hospital and without descriptive roll was this day discharged. He was received at said hospital March 31, 1865. He brought with him nothing, has since drawn no clothing, and has been paid nothing. A Notation in Bryant's file from the Record and Pension Office of the War Department dated September 24, 1898: it has this day been determined by this department by records on file and information furnished by the auditor for the War Department that this man was mustered out of service May 31, 1865, in accordance with General Order #77. One record stated no discharge was given at muster out of organization, while another one stated he was mustered out May 31, 1865. A Stop was put on his pay for $16.71 due to him losing 1 carbine sling and swivel, 2 saddle blankets, bridle, and 2 spurs and straps. A Hospital Card filed in Bryant's records stated he was in Hospital # 70321, Ward #3, age 25, married, wife Margaret Bryant, PO Address Rienca, Mississippi, admitted December 3, 1862, to Jefferson General Hospital in Jeffersonville, Indiana, and received from Hospital #9, in Nashville, Tennessee. Diagnosis was chronic rheumatism. He was transferred to Cairo March 28, 1863.

Bryant, J.H. - Only one card was found for J.H. Bryant which was filed at the end of the last roll of microfilm of the 1st Alabama Cavalry, USV records. It only stated he enlisted in Company L on December 7, 1863. No further information relative to this soldier was found.*

Buchanan, Thomas S. -Thomas S. Buchanan enlisted in Company L of the 1st Alabama Cavalry, USV as a private on October 15, 1864, in Rome, Georgia for a period of 3 years. He was mustered in October 17, 1864, in Rome, Georgia. The Muster and Descriptive Roll listed him as being 27 years of age, 5'-5" tall, having a fair complexion, gray eyes, light hair, born in Anderson District, South Carolina, and a farmer by occupation. He was credited to Cherokee County, Alabama. He was reported to have deserted November 10, 1864 from Rome, Georgia.

Buford, Jerry - Jerry Buford enlisted in Company A as a private, and was recorded as being sick in the hospital in Memphis, Tennessee from February 14, 1864, to October 1864. This was a misfiled card and no further information relative to this soldier was found.*

Buford, John H. - John H. Buford enlisted in Company H of the 1st Alabama Cavalry, USV as a private on November 26, 1864, in Huntsville, Alabama for a period of 3 years. He was enrolled by Sergeant Major James W. DeVaney, who had been with the 50th Illinois Infantry, and was mustered in April 5, 1865, in Nashville, Tennessee. The Muster and Descriptive Roll listed him as being 18 years of age, 5'-4" tall, having a fair complexion, blue eyes, black hair, born in Madison County, Alabama, and a farmer by occupation. He was mustered out October 20, 1865, and paid $100 bounty.

Buford, Stanfield - Stanfield Buford enlisted in Company H of the 1st Alabama Cavalry, USV as a private on November 26, 1864, in Huntsville, Alabama for a period of 3 years. He was enrolled by Sergeant Major James W. DeVaney of the 50th Illinois Cavalry. The Company Descriptive Book shows him to have been 18 years of age, 5'-3" tall, having a fair complexion, blue eyes, dark hair, born in Madison County, Alabama, and a farmer by occupation. He reenlisted on November 25, 1864, in Huntsville, Alabama, and was mustered in October 16, 1865. A Note at the bottom of this muster roll stated he was absent, sick at time of company organization. Another Muster Roll stated Stanfield Buford enrolled and joined on November 26, 1865, in Huntsville, Alabama, and stated he was absent, sick and had not been mustered. The May and June 1865 Muster Roll stated he was absent, sick since January 15, 1865, and had not been mustered. The July and August 1865 Muster Roll stated he was absent, sick at his home in Alabama by permission of Post Surgeon, Huntsville, Alabama, since January 1865. His name appeared on the Returns stating: July and August 1865, sick in his home in Alabama since January 1865. September 1865, absent, sick in hospital in Huntsville, Alabama since January 15, 1865. He was shown as being mustered out with the company on October 20, 1865, with his pay stopped for losing one saber belt and plate.

Bullen, Robert - Robert Bullen enlisted in Company B of the 1st Alabama Cavalry, USV as a private on December 17, 1862, in Glendale, Mississippi for a period of 1 year. He was enrolled by Captain Frank C. Burdick and was mustered in December 31, 1863, at Corinth, Mississippi. The Regimental Descriptive Book recorded him as being 45 years of age, 6' tall, having a dark complexion, black eyes, dark hair, born in Bay Chilton, Mississippi, and a farmer by occupation. He was appointed Saddler on March 1, 1863. His name appeared on the Returns as follows: March, 1863, absent with leave to take his family to Jackson, Tennessee since March 28, 1863. August to November 1863, on extra or daily duty as a saddler. He was mustered out December 7, 1863, in Camp Davies, Mississippi by reason of expiration of term of service.

Robert Bullen, spelled Bullion by family, was born June 18, 1818, in Franklin County, Georgia to William Bullion and his wife, Naomi Amelia "Amy" Bolling. Robert married Sarah Ann Hawkins July 20, 1841, in Itawamba County, Mississippi, and died June 17, 1888, in Liberty Hill, Williamson County, Texas. He was buried in the Williams-Buck Cemetery in Liberty Hill, Williamson County, Texas.

Bullen, Robert (2nd) - Robert Bullen was listed as being 19 years of age and was possibly the son of the Robert, above and brother to William C. Bullen, below. He enlisted in Company B of the 1st Alabama Cavalry, USV as a private on March 2, 1863, as a private for a period of 1 year at Glendale, Mississippi. The September and October 1863 Muster Roll listed him as being absent, prisoner of war in the hands of the enemy since October 26, 1863, which would have been during the Battle of Vincent's Crossroads near Bay Springs, Mississippi. However, his name appeared on the Returns as having returned from prison of war in December 1863. He was mustered out January 22, 1864, in Memphis,

Tennessee.

Robert was born September 12, 1844, in Bay Chilton, Mississippi and on October 11, 1865, he married Serena C. Tiffin, who was born January 24, 1845, in Red Bay, Franklin County, Alabama and died April 15, 1922. Children of Robert and Serena Bullen were: William Asbury, Thomas, Marcus B.F., Edward, Lafayette, and Eva Bullen. Robert Bullen died May 4, 1939 in Franklin County, Alabama.

Bullen, William C. - William C. Bullen enlisted in Company B of the 1st Alabama Cavalry, USV as a private on March 2, 1863, for a period of 1 year and was mustered in the same day in Corinth, Mississippi. The September and October 1863 Muster roll listed him as being absent, a prisoner of war in the hands of the enemy since October 26, 1863, which would have been during the Battle of Vincent's Crossroads near Bay Springs, Alabama. He was mustered out January 22, 1864, in Memphis, Shelby County, Tennessee. His name appeared on the Returns as follows: May, 1863, absent without leave May 24, 1863. August and September 1863, on extra or daily duty as company cook. William C. Bullen was shown as being 22 years of age.

Bumper, David A. - Only one card was found for David A. Bumper which was filed at the end of the last roll of microfilm of the 1st Alabama Cavalry, USV records. It stated he enlisted in Company L of the 1st Alabama Cavalry, USV and died of bilious fever on December 18, 1863, in the regimental Hospital, but did not say where. No further information relative to this soldier was found.*

Bumper, William H. - Only one card was found for William H. Bumper which was filed at the end of the last roll of microfilm of the 1st Alabama Cavalry, USV records. It recorded him as a Corporal in Company L, stating he died December 9, 1863, of lung fever in the regimental hospital. No further information relative to this soldier was found.*

Bunders, J.B. - Only one card was found for J.B. Bunders which was filed at the end of the last roll of microfilm of the 1st Alabama Cavalry, USV records. It recorded him as a Private in Company H, and recorded him as absent, a prisoner of war November 1863. No further information relative to this soldier was found.*

Burden, John H. - John H. Burden enlisted in Company G of the 1st Alabama Cavalry, USV as a private on March 10, 1864, in Decatur, Alabama, for a period of 3 years. He was enrolled by Lieutenant Pease and was mustered in March 13, 1864, in Decatur. The Muster and Descriptive Roll listed him as being 19 years of age, 5'-9" tall, having a fair complexion, blue eyes, light hair, born in Lincoln County, Tennessee, and a farmer by occupation. The May 1864 through August 1865 Muster Rolls listed him as being absent, sick in the hospital in Decatur, Alabama since May 1, 1864. In April 1864, he was listed as being on extra or daily duty as a company cook. He was not given a discharge at the muster out of the organization. There was a notation in his file from the Adjutant General's Office of the War Department dated June 30, 1927, which stated: John H. Berden, Private, Company G, 1st Alabama Cavalry, A.G. 201. It has this day been determined by this department by the records and from information furnished by the General Accounting Office that the above named soldier was HONORABLY discharged October 20, 1865, by reason of the muster out of his company, on that day, he being at the time, absent sick. By authority of the Secretary of War. John signed his Enlistment Forms.

Burdick, Fernando "Frank" Cortez - A Company Muster Roll dated September and October 1862, stated Frank C. Burdick enlisted in Company K of the 1st Regiment Alabama Cavalry on June 11, 1861, in Belleville, Illinois for a period of 3 years, and was mustered in June 25, 1861, in Caseyville, Illinois. He was promoted from 1st Sergeant, Company C of the 22nd Illinois Infantry on September 8, 1862. The November and December 1862 Muster Roll stated he had been promoted from 1st Lieutenant to Captain December 18, 1862, and furnished his own horse and equipment. The January and February 1863 Muster Roll recorded him as being in Company A of the 1st Alabama Cavalry, USV. It stated: "Lieutenant, Co. A Ala. Cav. Vols. from Sept. 8, 1862, as it appears from the muster roll for Jany & Feb. 1863; the only evidence obtainable on the subject, that he was mustered in as of said grade, Co. & Regt. from that date and the same is accepted under its provisions of letter from this office of June 5, 1863." His name appeared on the Returns dated November 1863, stating he was present but sick in quarters. He was mustered out June 16, 1864, in Decatur, Alabama due to expiration of term of service. A Special Order 288 from the Adjutant General's Office in Washington, DC dated September 1, 1864, stated: The honorable muster out and discharge of Captain Frank C. Burdick , 1st Alabama Cavalry, dated December 23, 1863, is hereby revoked and he is dishonorably discharged the service as of that date, and will be paid no final pay and allowances for fraudulent conduct in attempting to bear his name on the rolls for pay after that date. By order of Secretary of War, E.D. Townsend, Assistant Adjutant General. Another form stated Frank C. Burdick was dishonorably discharged by Special Order # 288, September 1, 1864. This officers accounts not settled. A note in Burdick's military records states the following: Par (Paragraph) 28, September 1, 1864, from this office as dishonorable discharged him from service as of dates of his honorable muster out and discharge December 23, 1863, is hereby amended to read December 22, 1863, (Par 4) (Par 5) so much of S.O. 288-Par 28. September 1, 1864, from this amended by Special Order #74-Par 4, February 12, 1867, from this office as dishonorably discharged Capt. Burdick to date December 22, 1863, is hereby revoked and his honorable muster out upon expiration of term of service, dated December 22, 1863, is permitted to stand satisfactory - evidence having been furnished this office that his _____ in service after that date, although unauthorized, was not attributable to any fraud or connivance on his part. Vide 8074, Par 4 & 5, A.G.O., February 12, 1867. He was mustered out at age 26, on June 16, 1864, in Decatur, Alabama due to expiration of term of service, to date from June 16, 1864. This officer's accounts not settled.

Fernando "Frank" Cortez Burdick

By the time Frank arrived in Winston County, the Burdick family had been in America for over 200 years. Frank's great-great-great-grandfather, Robert Burdick, arrived in Newport, Rhode Island, from England in 1651; nearly all Burdicks in North America can trace their ancestry to him.

The Burdicks were instrumental in settling America's first "westward" expansion, becoming one of the founding families of Westerly, Rhode Island, situated on the border of what would become Connecticut (the Burdick's had a hand in the formation of that colony, also.)

Frank's family has been involved in all of America's expansions, as well as all of the country's wars. The first expansion was from New England into New York and Pennsylvania. From there the Burdicks helped settle the wild territories of Ohio, Michigan, Illinois, Wisconsin and other future states. So it was only natural that Frank, born in 1838, would be involved in those treks, becoming a Lieutenant in the 11th Ill. Infantry in 1861.

Early life must have been difficult for Frank. His mother, Queen Esther (Whiting) Burdick, died when Frank was only 3 years old. His father, Russell Burdick, who was a veteran of the War of 1812, died when Frank was 12. While there is no record of his life in the 11 years before he enlisted in the Union Army, it is known he went to New York City shortly after the death of his father.

Frank was somewhat unique among his Burdick relatives in that he was the only recorded family member who moved south before or during the Civil War. The Burdick family history mirrors America's westward expansion. Leading up to the Revolutionary Ward, they became farmers in places like upstate New York and central Pennsylvania. During America's early growth years, the Burdicks moved into Indiana, Iowa, Nebraska and other plains states. In the final expansion years, Burdicks moved into California, Oregon and Washington. As some of the original Mormons, Burdicks are prevalent throughout Utah and Colorado.

But none moved south. Except for Frank. While it was duty that initially brought him to Alabama, what kept him there was something else. He found his place in life and his family amongst the strong people of Winston County. Thanks to today's mobile society, the Burdick family is spread throughout the United States, but 150 years ago Frank was one of a few intrepid Northerners who helped make our country whole. (Written and submitted by Howard Burdick)

Frank Burdick was born August 26, 1838, and was the son of Russell Burdick, born January 5, 1797, and died December 29, 1850. He was married to Nancy Margaret Feltman. He first enrolled

June 25, 1861, as a private in Company C, 22nd Regiment of Illinois Volunteers, commanded by Colonel Daugherty, and was discharged September 8, 1862. He re-enlisted on that same date in Company A, 1st Alabama Volunteer Cavalry near Bridgeport, Alabama with a commission as 1st Lieutenant near Bridgeport, Alabama, (near Chattanooga, Tennessee) and served until his final discharge as Captain on December 22, 1863. He was a clerk, teacher, county clerk and probate judge of Winston County, Alabama. He died April 10, 1884, in Houston, Winston County, Alabama.

After Frank Burdick's father, Russell Burdick, died he went to New York City and worked as a clerk in a store. He remained there until he enlisted in the Union Army for service in the Civil War.

He applied for a pension (#463519) on October 30, 1862, based on a disability. According to his pension papers "he was greatly disabled and was compelled to resign his position as Captain." His widow, Nancy Margaret Feltman Burdick, and the older children were away from home when he died. She applied for a widow's pension (#292479) on September 26, 1888, which was denied on the grounds that the soldier's death was not the result of military service. The claim was referred for special examination, and several depositions were taken and affidavits obtained.

In April of 1927, Probate Judge John B. Weaver wrote to the U.S. Pension Department on behalf of his "door neighbor" Nancy M. Burdick to inquire if she was not entitled to more than $30.00 per month in pension benefits. A June 13, 1927 response from Winfield Scott indicated she would be entitled to no such increase as she was not the wife of soldier during his period of service.

Fernando "Frank" Cortez Burdick was left behind in the surgeon's tent after having contracted the disabling condition. He was treated by the post surgeon in his tent for 27 (or 37) days, being unable to leave it. Between his illness and apparent paperwork confusion of mustering out of the Illinois regiment to accept a promotion into the First Alabama Cavalry, he somehow wound up being reported "deserted" August 27, 1862, though another roll reports him left sick in Tuscumbia, Alabama on August 27, 1862. A War Department communication dated May 11, 1888, reports "The charges of desertion of August 27, 1862, on a Regimental return for December, 1862, against this man are removed as erroneous."

He received his discharge December 23, 1865, and remained in Alabama which began the Burdick family there. He was a clerk, teacher, county clerk, and probate judge of Winston County; and he assisted in re-establishing postal service in northwest Alabama. See also, petition to Brigadier General William Smith on behalf of Fernando "Frank" Cortez Burdick to be appointed Register of Votes, by loyal and true Union Men formerly of the 1st Alabama Cavalry.

Among his friends were the Feltman brothers from Walker County in Alabama. When he obtained his army discharge in 1865 he remained with his Feltman friends and married Nancy Margaret Feltman and they made their home in Winston County, Alabama. Both are buried at the Burdick Family Cemetery near Houston, Alabama which was named for his family and is maintained by the Houston Community. Directions to the Burdick Cemetery: From Arley Town Hall go north on County Road 41, .9 miles, turn left on Houston Road and go 4.9 miles. Turn left in front of the old jailhouse then immediately left on the dirt road. Cemetery is .4 mile on the left. Family information submitted by Sally Cox. Directions to cemetery submitted by Ryan Dupree.

<u>Burlison, James M.</u> - James M. Burleson, also spelled Burleston, enlisted in Company C of the 1st Alabama Cavalry, USV as a private on March 15, 1864, in Memphis, Tennessee for a period of 3 years. He was enrolled by Captain John Latty and was mustered in March 19, 1864, in Memphis. He was shown as being single. The Muster and Descriptive Roll listed him as being 18 years of age, 5'-7" tall, having a light complexion, dark eyes, auburn hair, born in Calhoun County, Mississippi, and a farmer by occupation. He was listed on the March and April 1864 Hospital Muster Roll for the Cumberland U.S.A. Hospital in Nashville, Tennessee. The November 1864 through April 1865 Muster Rolls listed him as being absent, a prisoner of war since December 3, 1864, when captured at Station 6½ on the Savannah and Macon Railroad at Millen, Georgia. He was paroled at Wilmington, North Carolina on February 27, 1865, reported to Camp Parole, Maryland on April 4, 1865, sent to Camp Chase, Ohio on April 6, 1865, where he arrived April 10 or 13, 1865. He was mustered out October 20, 1865 in Huntsville, Alabama, owing the U.S. Government $56.48 1 carbine sling, 1 swivel, 1 cartridge box, 1 cap pouch, 1 saber belt, 1 thong and wiper, 1 screwdriver, 1 pair of spurs and straps, and 1 curry comb. He was paid $180 for bounty with $120 still due him for bounty.

Burleston – A Burleston, or Burlison, enlisted in Company C and was recorded as being absent, sick in hospital in Memphis, Tennessee in March 1864, and was also absent, sick in the hospital in Nashville, Tennessee in April 1864. This was a card found by itself and is apparently the James M. Burlison, above.*

Burnett, Peyton - Peyton Burnett enlisted in Company K of the 1st Alabama Cavalry, USV on December 1, 1863, in Camp Davies, Mississippi for a period of 3 years. He was enrolled by Captain Hornback. He traveled 90 miles from his home in Marion County, Alabama to Camp Davies, Mississippi to enlist. A note in his file stated that he furnished his own horse which failed on June 15, 1865, for want of forage and was abandoned. The March and April 1864 Muster Roll listed him as being absent, a prisoner of war in the hands of the enemy in Arkansas near Memphis, Tennessee since March 21, 1864, however, he was shown as being present on the May and June 1864 Muster Roll. His name appeared on the Returns stating from January to April 1865, he was on extra or daily duty as orderly at Brig. Headquarters. The Company Descriptive Book listed Peyton Burnett as having been 27 years of age, 5'-5" tall, having a light complexion, gray eyes, auburn hair, born in Spartanburg District, South Carolina, and a farmer by occupation. He was mustered out July 19, 1865 in Nashville, Tennessee and his muster-out roll stated the following: Entitled for pay for his own horse he brought into service at his enlistment. Kept himself mounted until June 15, 1865, when his horse failed for forage and was abandoned. See information about Peyton and Lemuel Burnett under Jasper Newton Green. Jasper married Peyton Burnett's sister and the Burnett and Green family information is together. See information about Peyton and Lemuel Burnett under Jasper Newton Green. Jasper married Peyton's sister and the Burnett and Green information is together.

Burney, Francis A. - Francis A. Burney enlisted in Company B of the 1st Alabama Cavalry, USV as a private on February 10, 1864, for a period of 3 years in Pulaski, Tennessee. He was enrolled by Lieutenant Judy and was mustered in March 17, 1864, in Decatur, Alabama. The Muster and Descriptive Roll showed him to have been 20 years of age, 5'-2" tall, having a fair complexion, dark eyes, black hair, born in Lauderdale County, Tennessee and a farmer by occupation. He was credited to Athens, Limestone County, Alabama. The Company Muster Roll for April 30, 1864, listed him as being a Corporal. He was reported to have deserted from Rome, Georgia on March 10, 1864, owing the U.S. Government $109.57 for deserting with horse, equipment, arms, and accoutrements. There was a letter in his file from Headquarters of the Provost Marshall in Nashville, Tennessee, dated May 19, 1865, to a Captain Hunter Brooks, Post Provost Marshall, Post of Nashville, Tennessee, which stated: I have the honor to forward under guard one F.A. Burney, Company B, 1st Alabama Cavalry with charges and specifications to be held until further orders. Signed Captain J.W. Plummer, Provost Marshall, District of Middle Tennessee. Another letter was in his file from Headquarters District of Northern Alabama, Office Provost Marshall, Huntsville, Alabama, May 18, 1865, to Captain J.W. Plummer, Provost Marshall, District of Middle Tennessee which stated: I have the honor to forward to you F.A. Burney, Private Company B, 1st Alabama Cavalry with charges and specifications in his case. Very Respectfully, Your Obedient Servant, A.H. Babcock, Captain 18th Michigan Infantry. No further information was found but apparently the charges were for desertion.

Burns, James L. - James L. Burns enlisted in Company F of the 1st Alabama Cavalry, USV as a Sergeant for a period of 1 year on April 3, 1863, in Corinth, Mississippi. He was enrolled by Captain L.W. Pierce, and was mustered in August 13, 1863, in Corinth. The Company Descriptive Book shows him to have been 21 years of age, 6'-1" tall, having a light complexion, gray eyes, brown hair, born in Chattooga County, Georgia, and a farmer by occupation. He was reported to have deserted from Glendale, Mississippi on September 11, 1863.

Burns, Perry - Perry Burns, also shown as Berry Burns, was enlisted in Company L of the 1st Alabama Cavalry, USV on September 25, 1863, in Fayette County, Alabama for a period of 1 year. He was enrolled by Captain Trammel and was mustered in the same day in Glendale, Mississippi. The Company Descriptive Book listed him as having been 18 years of age, 5'-8" tall, having a fair complexion, blue eyes, light hair, born in Itawamba County, Mississippi, and a farmer by occupation.

Final Statements given December 12. Discharged on Surgeon's Certificate of Disability on February 10, 1864, by order of Major General Hurlburt, 16th Army Corps. He was shown on a Hospital Muster Roll for the Gayoso U.S.A. General Hospital in Memphis, Tennessee, as a patient, dated January and February 1864. He was discharged due to phthisis pulmonalis (consumption of the lungs, or better known as T.B.), and partial paralysis of left side existing before entering the service. He is not able for duty in the Invalid Corps, and is not entitled to pension. Signed A.B. Stewart, Surgeon. Also signed by Ozro J. Dodds, Lieutenant Colonel. There was a letter in Perry Burns' file that stated: Office Gayoso Hospital Memphis, Tennessee, November 16, 1864, Sir, In compliance with your requests of September 10th and October 30th 1864, I have the honor to forward herewith the Final Statements of the following named deceased soldiers as complete as I am able to give them, their descriptive lists never having been furnished this office:

Sergeant James Moore, Company L, 1st Alabama Cavalry, USV
Private Perry Burns, Company L, 1st Alabama Cavalry, USV
Private William H. Ward, Company L, 1st Alabama Cavalry, USV
Private Levi Guin, Company L, 1st Alabama Cavalry, USV

In explanation of the delay in furnishing the required papers, I have to state that it has been occasioned by the failure of the company commanders with whom the deceased were serving to comply with my requests that their descriptive lists be forwarded to this office in order that I might make out their final papers in accordance with instruction recently received from Washington. Thinking longer delay useless, I forward the papers incomplete. You will undoubtedly meet with many like cases from the hospital as it is but recently that descriptive lists have been furnished promptly to men absent from their commands. Very Respectfully, your obedient servant, _____ V. Jessup, Assistant Surgeon.

Burrell, John - John Burrell enlisted in Company D of the 1st Alabama Cavalry, USV as a private on April 19, 1864, in Decatur, Alabama for a period of 3 years. He was enrolled by Lieutenant Pease, was mustered in June 16, 1864, in Decatur. The Muster and Descriptive Roll recorded him as being 26 years of age, 6' tall, having a dark complexion, black eyes, black hair, born in Walker County, Alabama, and a farmer by occupation. He was appointed sergeant on July 1, 1864, by Regimental Order #70. A stop was put on his pay for $20.00 for losing 1 Remington revolver. He was later charged $2.70 for losing 1 halter and 1 curry comb. He was mustered out October 20, 1865, in Huntsville, Alabama.

Burroughs, William Harrison - William Harrison Burroughs enlisted in Company H of the 1st Alabama Cavalry, USV on March 20, 1865, in Stevenson, Alabama, and mustered in April 5, 1865, at Nashville, Tennessee for a period of 3 years. He was enrolled by Captain James W. DeVaney. His Muster and Descriptive Roll recorded him as 18 years of age, 5'-4" tall, having a fair complexion, gray eyes, dark hair, born in Marion County, Tennessee, and a farmer by occupation. William was mustered out October 20, 1865, at Huntsville, Alabama. Later in life, William H. Burroughs signed a Declaration For Invalid Pension dated January 16, 1903, stating he was aged 55 years, a residence of Bridgeport in Jackson County, Alabama. He stated he enlisted in Company H of the 1st Alabama Cavalry, USV as a private on March 20, 1865, (in Stevenson, Alabama, was mustered in April 5, 1865, in Nashville, Tennessee), and was discharged November 20, 1865, in Huntsville, Alabama. He stated he was unable to earn a support by manual labor by reason of rheumatism and general debility. It was signed: William H (X) Burroughs, and witnessed by L.M. Merriman and Jackson J. Woody.

William H. Burroughs stated in his request for pension that he was born April 19, 1844, however, his father stated in his pension records that William was born April 19, 1848. William married Caroline Daly October 2, 1873, in Jasper, Tennessee, and they were married by Squire William Bennett. Caroline was the daughter of Patrick and Martha Henson Daly. Patrick was born January 1, 1817, in Limerick, Ireland and died October 22, 1892, in Bridgeport, Jackson County, Alabama. Martha Henson Daly was born February 5, 1824 in Tunnel Hill, Georgia, and died March 16, 1899, in Bridgeport, Jackson County, Alabama. He stated he and Caroline had 3 children: Anna, born August 10, 1873; Patrick, born November 2, 1874; and Garret, born June 8, 1878. Caroline Daly Burroughs died October 22, 1929, in Memphis, Shelby County, Tennessee. William Harrison Burroughs died June 5, 1916.

In another Declaration For Invalid Pension, William H. Burroughs stated he was aged 44 years old and stated he was unable to earn a support by manual labor by reason of neuralgia, disease of kidney's, dyspepsia, rheumatism, and nervous debility,

According to grandson, James T. Burroughs of Houston, Texas, Union soldiers were trying to steal the Daly cow and the Daly girl fought them off. William H. Burroughs was among these soldiers and he so admired Carolina for her courage, that he later married her.

An affidavit signed by William H. Burroughs and dated February 27, 1895, stated he was aged 48, a resident of Bridgeport in Jackson County, Alabama. He stated: Owing to circumstances over which I had no control I was prohibited from reporting to the board of surgeons within the time required in order for examination such as sickness of myself and also my family and I am very anxious and willing to obey all orders from the commissioner of pensions that he may make relative to my claim for pension. The above is my oral statement dictated by myself and written by T.J. Scruggs in my presence at the residence of said T.J. Scruggs in the County of Jackson and State of Alabama and it is my earnest desire to have another order for examinations. I shall report promptly. Signed Wm. H. x Burroughs, his mark.

On October 15, 1898, William H. Burroughs stated he married Caroline Daly on October 2, 1873, at Jasper in Marion County, Tennessee, and they were married by Squire William Bennett. He stated he had three children and their names were: Anna Burroughs, born August 10, 1873; Patrick Burroughs, born November 2, 1874; and Garret Burroughs, born June 8, 1878. He signed his name Wm. H. x Burroughs, his mark.

An affidavit dated June 7, 1901, to the Department of the Interior, from William H. Burroughs of Bridgeport, Jackson County, Alabama stated the following in answer to the questions: He was born April 19, 1844, (contradicts previous date) in Marion County, Tennessee. He enlisted March 20, 1865 in Marion County, Tennessee where his Post Office address was Jasper, Tennessee. He was a Farmer, and was discharged October 20, 1865, at Huntsville, Alabama.

He stated he had only lived in Jackson County, Alabama since his discharge. He stated he was 5'7" tall, weight 140 pounds, had gray eyes, dark hair and sandy complexion. He stated he had a mark on his left jaw and a scar on his back. He signed his name William H. x Burroughs, his mark

In a General Affidavit stamped April 29, 1908, by Burrell Lasater, aged 58, and T.J. Lewis, aged 64, of Marion County, Alabama, state: That they were well acquainted with William H. Burroughs, the claimant before and during the late war of the rebellion, and that they know that he never at any time served in the Confederate Army, or gave any aid, comfort, or assistance to the cause for which they fought. On the contrary, he has always been known to us as a strong Union man, fought in the Federal Army and was always loyal to the United States. Signed B.B. Lasater and T. J. Lewis

In a Declaration For Pension signed by William H. Burroughs and dated May 23, 1912, he stated he was 65 years of age, and a resident of Bridgeport in Jackson County, Alabama. He stated he enrolled in the 1st Alabama Cavalry in Stevenson, Alabama under the name of William H. Burroughs on March 17, 1865, as a Private in Company H, in the Civil War. He was honorably discharged at Huntsville, Alabama on October 17, 1865. His description was listed as 5'-7¼" tall, fair complexion, gray eyes, brown hair, and his occupation was a farmer. He stated he was born near Jasper in Marion County, Tennessee in 1847. His pension certificate number was 107099. This Declaration was witnessed by C. Wall and W.C. Choat.

The State of Alabama, Jackson County, I.C.F. Hartung, age 37 years, do hereby certify that I was the attending physician during the last illness and death of William H. Burroughs of Bridgeport, Alabama, who died on the 5th day of June A.D. 1916 at his home at Bridgeport, Alabama. I do further certify that I am regular qualified practicing physician located at Bridgeport, Alabama, and that I have no interest whatever in the prosecution of this claim, and am not interested in the result thereof.

In witness whereon I hereunto set my hand this the 14th day of July A.D. 1916. C.T.J. Hartung.

A note dated November 7, 1916, stated, Doctor Keenan, Chief, Civil War Division: You may accept April 19, 1847, as the date of soldier's birth.

A General Affidavit stamped July 22, 1916, stated: I.R.A. McFarlane, a resident of Bridgeport, in the county of Jackson, and State of Alabama, aged 60 years, on oath depose and say in relation to the claim of Caroline Burroughs as follows: Affiant says that he has known the said Caroline Burroughs for 60 years, affiant and the applicant being raised up in the same community together, near

Bridgeport, Alabama, and have still continued to live in the same neighborhood till this time. Affiant says further that on or about the 2nd day of October 1872, it was reported that the said Caroline Burroughs, whose maiden name was Caroline Daly, had gone to Jasper, Tennessee, a distance of some fifteen ,miles, and married, and from that time on, till the death of William H. Burroughs she and said William H. Burroughs were recognized as man and wife in the neighborhood where they loved. Affiant says he meant to say that said Caroline Burroughs married William H. Burroughs at Jasper, Tennessee at above date. Affiant says further he has lived in the same community with the said William H. and Caroline Burroughs since the above date of their marriage, and has never heard of any divorce proceedings of any kind, and in his judgment and honest belief there never has been any divorce proceedings, and from his close association and knowledge of the parties continuously from the above date of their marriage to the date of the death of the said William H. Burroughs, he believes if there had been any divorce proceedings he believes he would have heard of it, which he never did but that the said Caroline Burroughs, this applicant, is the true and lawful widow of the said William H. Burroughs, deceased. I further state that I have no pecuniary interest in this claim, and that my post office address is Bridgeport, Alabama. Signed R.A. McFarland

A General Affidavit stamped July 22, 1916, signed by Caroline Burroughs states: Caroline Burroughs, a resident of Bridgeport, in the County of Johnson and state of Alabama, aged 70 years on oath depose and say in relation to the claim of myself, I and William H. Burroughs, deceased, was married at Jasper, Tennessee on the 2nd day of October 1872, and lived together as husband and wife till the 5th day of June 1916, when the said William H. Burroughs died at our home near Bridgeport, Alabama. Affiant says she and said William H. Burroughs were never divorced and that she is the true and lawful widow of said William H. Burroughs, who was a pensioner of the U.S. Affiant says there are no minor children of herself and said William H. Burroughs though they are adult children. Signed Caroline Burroughs

An undated Claimant's Affidavit states: State of Alabama, County of Jackson, In the pension claim of Caroline Burroughs personally appeared before me, a Notary Public in and for the County and State aforesaid, Caroline Burroughs, aged 70 years, whose Post Office address is Bridgeport, Alabama, well known to me to be reputable and entitled to credit, and who, being duly sworn, declares in relation to the aforesaid case as follows: That she is the applicant in above claim; that she was married at Jasper, Tennessee October 2, 1872, to William H. Burroughs, that her true and correct maiden name was Caroline Daly; that the "C" in her marriage Certificate is for Caroline; and all the explanation that she is able to give of the "S" being in such certificate is that when she was a girl she was sometimes called "Tesela" and that Mr. Burroughs in getting the marriage license may have intended the "S" to stand for "Seta". Again she says that when a young woman, she was sometimes was called a nick name, "Sallie the Wog", and that Mr. Burroughs in getting marriage license may have thought "Sallie" formed part of applicant's given name, but it did not. Affiant says further that the correct way to spell her maiden name was Caroline Daly, and not "Daily", though lots of the neighbors now spell it "Daily". Signed Caroline Burroughs

A General Affidavit stamped August 11, 1916, and signed by Jesse Thatch, a resident of Jasper, Marion County, Alabama stated: I was personally acquainted with William H. Burroughs before he married Caroline Daly on the 2nd day October, 1872, and had been personally acquainted with him from his boy hood days till his marriage as upon stated. I never heard of said William H. Burroughs marrying anyone till above marriage, and I believe I would have heard of it had he married anyone before he married Caroline Daly at above date. I was present when above parties married. In fact they were married at my house by Esquire Burnette, October 2, 1872. Signed Jesse x Thatch, his mark.

A letter written on November 9, 1929, to the Department of the Interior, Bureau of Pensions, from 974 Oakland Avenue in Memphis, Tennessee from J.A. Thomas stated: "Sir, Caroline Burroughs died on October the 22nd at my home 974 Oakland Avenue. I am returning check if any part of this check can be applied to her expenses it will be appreciated by the family. Your Rep. J.A. Thomas

William H. Burroughs was paid at $13.50 to May 4, 1916, and was dropped from the roll because of death, June 5, 1916.

Caroline Burroughs of Memphis, Tennessee was last paid at the rate of $40 per month to October 4, 1929, and was dropped from the roll because of death, October 22, 1929.

William Harrison Burroughs Obituary - William Harrison Burroughs, 69, orchardist north of South Pittsburg, Tennessee for many years, died at 9:30 P.M. Sunday in a Bridgeport, Alabama hospital. Mr. Burroughs represented Start Brothers Nursery in the area for many years and before that time was foreman at Aycock Hosiery Mill. He was an active member of First Baptist Church. South Pittsburg. Surviving are his wife. Mrs. Bessie Young Burroughs, South Pittsburg; a son, James Harrison Burroughs, Jasper, Tennessee; numerous nieces and nephews. Funeral services will be held at 2 p.m. CST Tuesday at First Baptist Church, South Pittsburg with the Rev. Norman O. Baker officiating. Interment in Cumberland View Cemetery. Active pallbearers will be Chester Vaughn, James O. Young, Dallas Young, Donald Young, Eugene Young, and Willard Elledge. Honorary pallbearers will be the Men's Class of First Baptist Church and Drs. James B. Hayron and W.M. Headrick. The body is at Rogers Funeral Home here, but will be moved to the church to lie in state for one hour before the service.

Burton, H. - Only one card was found for H. Burton which was filed at the end of the last roll of microfilm of the 1st Alabama Cavalry, USV records. It recorded him as being in Company L, stating he served as a nurse in a hospital in November 1863. No further information relative to this soldier was found.*

Butler, H.H. - Only one card was found for H.H. Butler which was filed at the end of the last roll of microfilm of the 1st Alabama Cavalry, USV records. It recorded him as being in Company D, stating he was absent, supposed deserted in August 1863. No further information relative to this soldier was found.*

Butler, John C. - John C. Butler enlisted in Company G of the 1st Alabama Cavalry, USV as a private on June 15, 1863, in Chewalla, Tennessee for a period of 1 year. He mustered in the same day in Corinth, Mississippi and was shown as 26 years of age.. He was reported to have deserted from Glendale, Mississippi on July 2, 1863.

Butler, Nathan B. - Nathan B. Butler, also spelled Napoleon Butler, listed as 22 years of age enlisted in Company E on June 24, 1863, in Glendale, Mississippi for a period of one year. He was reported to have deserted July 9, 1863, but returned January 23, 1864, and was returned to duty with loss of pay while absent by Special Order No. 50, Brigadier General G.H. Grierson. He was discharged July 27, 1864, at Rome, Georgia due to expiration of term of service. He is the son of the Napoleon H. Butler, below.

Butler, Nathan H. - Nathan B. Butler, shown as age 45, enlisted in Company E of the 1st Alabama Cavalry, USV as a private on June 24, 1863, at Glendale, Mississippi for a period of one year. He was reported to have deserted July 9, 1863. The Descriptive List of Deserters stated he deserted from Glendale, Mississippi. He returned January 23, 1864, at Camp Davies, Mississippi and was restored to duty with loss of pay while absent by Special Order Number 50, by Brigadier General Grierson. He was detailed as teamster in Quartermaster Department at Vicksburg, Mississippi on January 25, 1864. The January and February 1864 Company Muster Roll stated he was absent, on detached service as teamster since January 25, 1864. Nathan was discharged at expiration of term of service on July 27, 1864. A Notation from the Adjutant General's Office of the War Department dated August 21, 1887, stated: This man deserted on or about July 9, 1863, and returned on or about January 23, 1864. As he was subsequently restored to duty with loss of pay while absent by Special Order Number 50, Brigadier General B. H. Grierson March 10, 1864, without trial, but upon conditions which appear to have been complied with (so far as not waived by the Government), the charge of desertion no longer stands against him. The record of the fact that he was absent in desertion from on or about July 9, 1863, to on or about January 23, 1864, cannot however be expunged. He was discharged July 27, 1864, in Rome, Georgia due to expiration of term of service. He is the father of the Nathan Butler, above.

Butler, William Jasper - In 1863, at age 32, William Jasper Butler was living in Lee County,

Mississippi. He was a loyal Union man, and true to his convictions, on January 20, 1864, he enlisted in Company A of the 1st Alabama Cavalry, USV as a Private, at Camp Davies, Mississippi. He then traveled to Memphis, Tennessee where on February 5, 1864, he was mustered in. Between June 26, 1864 and November 6, 1864, Butler was on duty at Rome, Georgia with the rest of the regiment, scouting and foraging in all directions from the city, acting as the eyes and ears for the army, while operating in the rear of General Sherman's forces during the Atlanta Campaign. On several occasions they crossed the paths with the scouts of General Joseph Wheeler's Confederate Cavalry, but no serious confrontations took place during that period. However, on one such occasion Private Butler, for his own safety, felt compelled to conceal his whereabouts for a brief time to prevent his being captured. He took cover in the crawl space under a house which is long since destroyed, that was located in the southern part of Walker County, Georgia, until his enemies left the area and it became safe for him to rejoin his company. He was undercover long enough to carve his name and regiment on one of the foundation stones of the house. He recorded in stone: W.J. BUTLER 1st ALA CAVALRY US (See pictures of stone in back of book). Through the generosity of the late Dr. D.R. Mahan, this stone is now one of the items in the Hamilton House in Dalton, Georgia and is on public display in their Civil War Collection. Information and pictures submitted by Marvin Sowder.

According to descendants of William Jasper Butler, he was born about August 1834 in Shelby County, Alabama to Sanders Walker and Elizabeth Butler. Sanders Walker Butler was born about 1809 in Elbert County, Georgia and died April 9, 1867, in Guntown, Mississippi. Elizabeth died about 1880 in Lee County, Mississippi. Other children of Sanders and Elizabeth were: James N., born about 1856; Melissa C., born October 5, 1835; Harriett Ann, born May 26, 1837, died February 20, 1909; Mary Jane, born about 1838; Thomas Nathan, born 1842, died 1900; Sarah, born February 23, 1845, died January 17, 1891; and Susan Amanda, born, about November 1850, died 1923. This was one of the many families torn apart during the Civil War, with William J. serving in the 1st Alabama Cavalry Union Army while his brother, Thomas Nathan, served in the Confederacy. William Jasper Butler was apparently married three times, Sarah Elizabeth Mayhall, on November 12, 1857; Bodicia Clevia, on September 1, 1859, and Olivia Bailey, about 1868. Since there is a contradiction between descendants as to which child belongs to which mother, I will just list them as children of William Jasper Butler. According to the 1900 Newton County, Mississippi Census, William was born in August 1834 and E. Ellen was born September 1848. Children listed were: Camilla, born August 1874; Emma, born February 1881; Henry, born January 1882; Leona, born January 1884; Venie, born August 1887; Clarence, born January 1890; Clara, born January 1890; and May Butler, born January 1896. Sallie Yarber was living with them and was shown as a daughter, born January 1870, and she had a daughter, Clara R., who was born September 1899. William and Olivia supposedly had at least three children: Theodicea Eveline, born February 24, 1862 and died June 16, 1908;Laura, born 1864 and died April 9, 1867; and Sanders Walker Butler, born November 10, 1869 and died 16 Feb 1955. William Jasper Butler died about March 1880 in Guntown, Lee County, Mississippi, and is buried in the Guntown Cemetery.

Byars, John H. - John H. Byers, also spelled Byars, enlisted on Company G of the 1st Alabama Cavalry, USV as a private on March 10, 1864, for a term of 1 year, in Decatur, Alabama. He was enrolled by Captain Trammel, and was mustered in April 13, 1864, in Decatur. The Company Descriptive Book recorded him as being 19 years of age, 5'-8" tall, having a dark complexion, blue eyes, dark hair, born in Pickens County, Georgia, and a farmer by occupation. The November and December 1863 Muster Roll recorded him as returning from absent, sick December 3, 1863. The January and February 1864 Muster Roll recorded him as being absent, sick in hospital in Memphis, Tennessee since February 8, 1864. The Company Muster Roll dated December 31, 1863, to April 30, 1864, recorded him as being absent, sick in Nashville, Tennessee since April 2, 1864. The May and June 1864 Muster Roll records him as being absent, sick. The July and August 1864 Muster Roll recorded him as being present, and having pay due as Corporal from December 31, 1863, through August 28, 1864, at which time he was reduced to ranks per Special Order #89, Regimental Headquarters. In January and February 1864, he was recorded as a patient on the Gayoso U.S.A. General Hospital in Memphis, Tennessee. The March and April 1864 Muster Roll stated he was returned to duty. In May and June 1864, he was recorded in the Brown U.S.A. General Hospital in Louisville, Kentucky in the 7th

Ward. His name appeared on the Returns as follows: October 1863, missing in action from Vincent's Crossroads since October 26, 1863; January and February 1864, absent, sick in hospital in Memphis, Tennessee; March and April 1864, absent, sick in hospital in Nashville, Tennessee. He was discharged September 28, 1864, in Rome, Georgia by expiration of term of service.

Byers, Joseph Pinson - Joseph Pinson Byers, also spelled Byars, was the brother of Robert Jarrett Byers and Samuel Phillip Byars, below. He enlisted in Company G of the 1st Alabama Cavalry, USV on March 10, 1864, in Decatur, Alabama for a period of 3 years. He was enrolled by Lieutenant Pease, and was mustered in April 13, 1864, in Decatur. The Muster and Descriptive Roll recorded him as being 23 years of age, 6' tall, having fair complexion, blue eyes, dark hair, born in Habersham County, Georgia, and a farmer by occupation. He was appointed Sergeant on May 1, 1864. He was mustered out October 20, 1865, in Huntsville, Alabama owing the U.S. Government $1.30 for losing 1 curry comb and 1 horse brush.

Joseph Pinson Byers was born December 19, 1839, in Habersham County, Georgia to James Kuykendall Byers and Ary Ann Burch, who were married October 1, 1829, in Rabun, Georgia. James Kuykendall Byers and his wife are buried in the Old Sterrett Cemetery in Shelby County, Alabama. Joseph married Clarissa "Carrie" Turner in October 1869 in Little Rock, Pulaski County, Arkansas. Carie was born January 1, 1852, in Jefferson County, Alabama and died October 4, 1933, in Mansfield, Sebastian County, Arkansas. Joseph died August 13, 1913, in Mansfield, Sebastian County, Arkansas and he and Carrie are buried in the Buggy Hill Cemetery in Sebastian County, Arkansas. Children of Joseph and Carrie were: Frances J., born November 12, 1870, died January 1871; John Henry, born September 27, 1872, died February 25, 1953; James Washington, born December 1, 1874, died December 17, 1952; Ara Elizabeth, born April 4, 1876, died September 7, 1944; Prentice Pinson, born January 16, 1879, died May 9, 1963; Robert Forrest, born July 9, 1882, died 1964; Mary Elzie Mamie, born March 17, 1864; died March 18, 1930; Amos Marshman, born February 22, 1886, died January 8, 1964; Ora Maude, born July 1, 1888, died 1969; and Justin Nirum Byers, born February 16, 1893.

Byers, Robert Jarrett – Robert Jarrett Byers, also spelled Byars, was a brother to Joseph Pinson Byers, above and Samuel Phillip Byers, below. He enlisted in Company G of the 1st Alabama Cavalry, USV as a private on March 10, 1864, in Decatur, Alabama and was mustered in April 13, 1864, in Decatur. He was appointed Sergeant on May 1, 1864. The Muster and Descriptive Roll listed him as being 26 years of age, 6'-1" tall, having a fair complexion, blue eyes, dark hair, born in Habersham County, Georgia and was a farmer by occupation. He was promoted to Sergeant on May 1, 1864. The July and August 1864 Muster Roll showed him to have been absent, on leave. The September and October 1864 Muster Roll stated he was absent, supposed to be prisoner of war since August 9, 1864, however, his name appeared on the Returns for September and October 1864 stating he was on daily or extra duty recruiting in north Alabama since August 24, 1864. He was mustered out October 20, 1865, in Huntsville, Alabama owing the U.S. Government $4.70 for losing 2 spurs and straps, 1 screw driver and 1 curry comb.

Robert Jarrett Byers was born August 6, 1837, in Habersham County, Georgia and is a brother to Joseph Pinson Byers, above. See Joseph's information for parents of Robert. Robert married Ann Elizabeth Dyke on May 19, 1861, in Shelby County, Alabama, and they had the following children: Robert Pinson, born March 1, 1862, died June 10, 1890; Almedia J., born August 16, 1866, died December 12, 1917; John Marion, born August 2, 1870, died June 15, 1916; Elsie Clemanthy, born October 12, 1873; died January 31, 1945; Madison Hendrix "Matt", born December 1, 1877, died April 27, 1958; Maude Lavada, born September 19, 1880, died November 1965; Earnest Earl, born July 10, 1886, died November 15, 1907; and Curtis Embrey Byers, born December 24, 1890. Robert J. Byers died February 28, 1918, in Jefferson County, Alabama and is buried in the Buried in the Old Sterrett Cemetery in Shelby County, Alabama.

Byers, Samuel Phillip - Samuel Phillip Byers, also spelled Byars, was a brother to Robert Jarrett Byers and Joseph Pinson Byers, above. He enlisted in Company G of the 1st Alabama Cavalry, USV as a private on April 10, 1864, in Decatur, Alabama for a period of 3 years. He was enrolled by Lieutenant Pease and was mustered in the same day in Rome, Georgia. The Muster and Descriptive

Roll showed him to have been 33 years of age, 6½" tall, having a sandy complexion, blue eyes, dark hair, born in Habersham County, Georgia, and a farmer by occupation. He was promoted to Sergeant on May 1, 1864. He was promoted from 2nd master sergeant to 1st sergeant on January 1, 1865. Byers had received a furlough from August 14, 1865, to August 24. 1965. He was mustered out October 20, 1865 in Huntsville, Alabama owing the U.S. Government $6.70 for losing 1 screwdriver and one pair of spurs and straps. He was furnished transportation from Nashville to Clarksville and return.

Byers, William A. - William A. Byers, also spelled Byars, enlisted in Company L of the 1st Alabama Cavalry, USV as a Corporal on September 25, 1863, in Fayette County, Alabama for a period of one year. He was enrolled by Captain Sanford Trammel and was mustered in the same day in Glendale, Mississippi. The Company Descriptive Book listed him as being 19 years of age, 5"-8" tall, having a dark complexion, blue eyes, dark hair, born in Pickens County, Georgia and was a farmer by occupation. His name appeared on the Returns dated October 1863, stated he was missing in action on October 26, 1863, which would have been in the Battle of Vincent's Crossroads near Bay Springs, Mississippi. The November and December 1863 Muster Roll stated he had returned from being absent on December 2, 1863. The Company Muster Roll dated from December 31, 1864, to April 30, 1864, listed him as being absent, stating he was sick in Nashville, Tennessee since April 2, 1864. The January and February 1864 Muster Roll listed him as being absent, sick in the Gayoso U.S.A. General Hospital in Memphis, Tennessee since February 8, 1864. The May and June Hospital Muster Roll for Brown U.S.A. General Hospital in Louisville, Kentucky, listed him as being a patient in May and June 1864. The July and August 1864 Muster Roll listed him as being present. Byars was discharged September 28, 1864, in Rome, Georgia due to expiration of term of service, at which time he was reduced to ranks from Corporal.

Byford, Perry - Perry Byford enlisted in Company A of the 1st Alabama Cavalry, USV as a private on December 22, 1863, at Camp Davies, Mississippi for a period of 3 years. He was enrolled by Lieutenant Hinds, and was mustered in February 5, 1864, in Memphis, Tennessee. The Company Muster and Descriptive Roll listed him as being 20 years of age, 6'-1" tall, having a fair complexion, blue eyes, dark hair, born in Winston County, Alabama, and a farmer by occupation. His name appeared on the Hospital Muster Roll for the Small Pox U.S.A. General Hospital in Memphis, Tennessee on the January and February 1864 Muster Roll stating he was admitted to the hospital on February 18, 1864. His name was also shown on the same Hospital Muster Roll dated March and April 1864, stating he was returned to his regiment on April 25, 1864. He was mustered out October 20, 1865 in Huntsville, Alabama owing the U.S. Government $3.22 for losing 1 carbine swing, swivel, curry comb and brush. He was paid $180 for bounty and was still owed $1.20 to make up the $300 bounty he was due.

Byford, Quiller J. - Quiller J. Byford, together with his brother, Perry, above, enlisted in Company A of the 1st Alabama Cavalry, USV as a private on December 22, 1863, at Camp Davies, Mississippi for a period of 3 years. He was enrolled by Lieutenant Hinds, and was mustered in February 5, 1864, in Memphis, Tennessee. The Company Muster and Descriptive Roll listed him as being 18 years of age, 5'-8" tall, having a fair complexion, blue eyes, dark hair, born in Winston County, Alabama, and a farmer by occupation. The Company Muster Roll dated through February 29, 1864, stated he was absent, sick in the U.S. General Hospital in Memphis, Tennessee. Quiller J. Byford's name appeared on the Hospital Muster Roll for the Overton U.S.A. General Hospital in Memphis, Tennessee, dated January and February 1864. The March and April 1864 Muster roll stated he died of measles and inflammation of the lungs in the Overton U.S. Military Hospital in Memphis Tennessee on March 1, 1864. The Inventory of Effects of Byford included the following: 1 great coat, and 1 blanket. The Final Statement listed him as having died March 2, 1864. Quiller J. Byford is buried in the Memphis National Cemetery in Memphis, Tennessee.

Byram, William T.G. - William T.G. Byram, sometimes listed William T.C. Byram, enlisted in Company C of the 1st Alabama Cavalry, USV on February 20, 1863, under the name of William T.C. Byram. He enlisted at Corinth, Mississippi for a period of 1 year and was mustered in February 25,

1863, at Corinth. The Regimental Descriptive Roll showed William to have been 23 years of age, 5'-11½" inches tall, having fair complexion, dark eyes, light hair, born Tishomingo County, Mississippi, and a farmer by occupation. Capt. A.C. Cameron signed a Casualty Sheet confirming Byram died August 21, 1863, in the hospital at Glendale, Mississippi, while another Casualty Card stated he died August 6, 1863, at Glendale. However, information in Byram's pension records signed by Surgeon A.B. Stuart, stated he died August 21st, 1863, at the Regimental Hospital of Typhoid Pneumonia.

William Byram was married to Mary E. Shook on January 31, 1860, in Highland, Mississippi, and they had one child, Nancy Ann, born January 24, 1861. William's wife, Mary, had applied for a pension but was remarried to J. Dawson on January 27, 1866, and her pension was rejected because she had remarried prior to the completion of her claim. John McRae became the guardian of Nancy Ann Byrum and he was allowed $8 per month pension beginning August 12, 1870, and retroactive to August 25, 1863. He gave his address as Jacinto, Tishomingo County, Mississippi. On July 29, 1865, Mrs. Mary Byram, aged 26 years , a resident of Ridge Precinct, County of Jackson, State of Illinois, and that she was the widow of William T. Byram, who was a private in Company C commanded by Captain A.T. Cameron, of the 1st Regiment of Alabama Cavalry, US Volunteers, Commanded by Colonel George E. Spencer, and that her said husband enlisted at Corinth, Mississippi on or about February 14, 1863, for the term of one year and continued in actual service until he died at Glendale, Mississippi on or about the twenty-first day of August 1863 of measles received while in service. Mary Shook stated she was married to William T.G. Byram on December 25, 1859, in Tishomingo County, Mississippi by Harden Patterson, M.G., however, their marriage certificate states they were married on January 31, 1860. Henry Shook and William L. Armor signed an affidavit stating they were acquainted with William and Mary Byram and knew of their wedding and their child, Nancy Ann Byram.

Byrd, H.H. - H.H. Byrd was taken prisoner of war on October 26, 1863. This was a card by itself in the military records and actually should be in Marshall H. Byrd's records, below.*

Byrd, Josephus - Josephus "Jo" Byrd enlisted and was mustered into Company E of the 1st Alabama Cavalry, USV on August 27, 1863, in Glendale, Mississippi, at age 23. Another muster roll stated he enlisted August 27, 1863, in Corinth, Mississippi for a period of 3 years. His name appears on the Returns for July 1864 as J.S. Byrd and stated he was on extra or daily duty as a farrier. He was mustered out September 28, 1864, in Rome, Georgia. He was advanced a Clothing Allowance of $25.53. Subsistence was furnished to September 30, 1864.

Josephus Byrd was the son of Thomas W. Byrd. He was born February 01, 1839, in Hardin County, Tennessee and died September 27, 1873, in Hardin County, Tennessee. Thomas W. Byrd was born March 10, 1812, in Martin County, North Carolina and died November 18, 1885, in Hardin County, Tennessee. His first wife was Minerva J. Miller, born December 08, 1834. Second wife of Thomas W. Byrd was Mariah Smith. Minerva Miller Byrd died December 08, 1834, so apparently the children all belonged to Mariah Smith. Other siblings of Josephus Byrd were: William Rufus Byrd, born 1836, married 1st to Mary F. (?) and 2nd to Irene Robertson (this William Byrd was probably the William R. Byrd who served in the 1st Alabama Cavalry, USV with Josephus and Marshall Henderson Byrd); Martha J. Byrd, born 1841, married James Thomas; Eveline Byrd, born 1842 in Hardin County, Tennessee married Unknown Bryson; James M. Byrd, born 1844 in Hardin County, Tennessee; Thomas J. "Jeff" Byrd, born December 3, 1845, in Hardin County, Tennessee, died March 22, 1912, in Hardin County, Tennessee, married Vicky Eaves, 2nd wife of Jeff was Almeda George, born June 2, 1841, married October 23, 1873; Henry C. Byrd, born 1848 in Hardin County, Tennessee; Susan Byrd, married a Counts/Counce; Calvin C. Byrd; and Elizabeth Byrd. Thomas W. Byrd was the son of William Edward Byrd and Lovey Cherry of Martin County, North Carolina. William was the son of Edward Byrd, who was married to Elizabeth Razor, but it is not clear if she was the mother of his children.

Byrd, M.C. - M.C. Byrd enlisted in Company E, and was recorded as missing in action October 26, 1863, from the Battle of Vincent's Crossroads near Red Bay, Alabama. No further information relative to this soldier was found.* (This may be the Marshal Henderson Byrd, below.)

Byrd, Marshal Henderson - Marshall Henderson Byrd enrolled in Company E of the 1st Alabama Cavalry, USV on September 1, 1863, at Glendale, Mississippi at age 35 for a period of 1 year. His life as a Union soldier was short-lived as he was killed in action during the Battle of Vincent's Crossroads near Red Bay, Alabama on October 26, 1863. Thomas J. Byrd also enlisted with Marshall on the same day and place as Marshall.

Marshall Byrd was born August 28, 1828, in Hardin County, Tennessee to John Richard Byrd and Susan Rebecca Nichols. He married Nancy Eleanor Robertson, daughter of Major Robertson and Sarah Young, on January 20, 1848, in Hardin County, Tennessee and had the following children: Sarah E., born January 31, 1848, died June 12, 1876; James Jackson born June 23, 1850, died March 18, 1925; William A. born July 11, 1852, died August 21, 1866; Susan E. born April 8, 1854, died June 12, 1876; Major Henderson, born April 18, 1856, and died March 12, 1903; and David H or K Byrd, born 1859 and died July 17, 1862. Marshall's wife, Nancy Eleanor Robertson Byrd, was born January 20, 1827 in Hardin County, Tennessee and died January 31, 1862 in Hardin County. Noel C. Byrd (brother of Marshall) was appt. guardian of minor heirs and affidavit was signed by T.J. Byrd, who was also a member of the 1st Alabama Cavalry, USV regiment. Noel C. Byrd was appointed guardian of minor heirs and affidavit was signed by T.J. Byrd, who was also a member of this regiment. Some siblings of Marshall Henderson Byrd were: James N., William Carroll, Noel Cherry, and Lovey Nancy Byrd. Family information submitted by Bettie Byrd Hickman.

Byrd, Thomas Jefferson "Jeff"- Thomas Jefferson "Jeff" Byrd, also spelled Boyd, enlisted and mustered into Company E of the 1st Alabama Cavalry, USV on October 1, 1863, in Glendale, Mississippi for a period of 1 year. Thomas J. was 18 years old at enlistment. He was mustered out September 28, 1864 at Rome, Georgia. He was discharged by reason of expiration of term of service.

Thomas Jefferson "Jeff" Byrd was born December 3, 1845, in Hardin County, Tennessee to Thomas W. and Mariah Smith Byrd. He was a brother to William Rufus Byrd, below. His father, Thomas W. Byrd was born March 10, 1812, in Martin County, North Carolina, and died November 18, 1885, in Hardin County, Tennessee. His wife, Mariah, was born in 1814 in Hardin County, Tennessee and died 1864, in Hardin County. "Jeff" Byrd married 2nd to Minerva Jane Miller, born December 8, 1834, in Tennessee.

Byrd, William Rufus - William Rufus Byrd enlisted in Company B of the 1st Alabama Cavalry, USV on August 27, 1863, at Glendale, Mississippi for a period of 1 year at Corinth, Mississippi. He was mustered out at age 26 on September 28, 1864, at Rome, Georgia by reason of expiration of term of service.

William R. Byrd was born March 13, 1836, in Hardin County, Tennessee to Thomas W. Byrd and Mariah Smith. He was a brother to Thomas Jefferson Byrd, above. He married Arena "Irene" Robertson in 1855, in Hardin County, Tennessee.

Byres, John J. – See John H. Byers.

Byres, Joseph P. – See Joseph P. Byers.

Byres, Robert J. – See Robert J. Byers.

Byrum, B. - B. Byrum enlisted in Company D as a private, and was recorded as being sick in the hospital in Nashville, Tennessee in July and August 1864. No further information relative to this soldiers was found.*

Byram, Cavalier H. - Cavalier H. Byram, also spelled Byrum enlisted in Company D of the 1st Alabama Cavalry, USV on March 15, 1863, at Glendale, Mississippi for a period of 1 year. He was mustered in on February 4, 1863, at Corinth, Mississippi. In May 1863, he was shown as being on daily duty as company cook. The May and June 1863 Muster Roll listed him as absent, sick in Corinth, Mississippi, but he was present for the next muster roll. On the March and April 1864 Muster Roll, Cavalier was shown as being absent, sick in hospital in Memphis, Tennessee. The May and June 1864 muster roll stated he enrolled on November 15, 1863, at Glendale, Mississippi, and mustered in November 24, 1863, at Corinth, Mississippi, but was still sick in the hospital at Memphis, Tennessee since March 18, 1864. In November and December 1863, he was shown as being sick in Refugee Camp at Corinth since November 20, 1863. The July and August 1864 Muster Roll still listed him as sick in hospital in Memphis. Cavalier Byrum was still in the USA General Hospital in Memphis, Tennessee when the company was mustered out on October 20, 1865. He was 45 years old and had been in the hospital since March 18, 1864. He was not furnished with a discharge. The Company Descriptive Book shows Cavalier H. Byrum to have been 49 years of age, 5'-6" tall, having light complexion, blue eyes, dark hair, born Madison County, Alabama, and a farmer by occupation. His Certificate of Discharge, which allows soldiers to receive their pay, stated: Death by pneumonia in Adams U.S.A. General Hospital in Memphis, Tennessee on the 21st Day of April 1864, and is buried in the Memphis National Cemetery, possibly in an unmarked grave.

Cavalier H. Byram was born October 5, 1814, in Madison County, Alabama to Alden Byram and Elizabeth Horner. Other children of Alden and Elizabeth Byram were: Miriam A., Silas Condict, Lydia, Alden, Elizabeth, Ebenezer B., Rebecca and Lewis Byram. Alden was born November 12, 1764, in Mendham, Morris County, New Jersey, and Elizabeth was born January 17, 1771, in Tennessee. They married September 16, 1788. Cavalier Byram married Sarah Lair or Laear on November 2, 1839, in Tishomingo County, Mississippi, and they had two children, William and James M. Byram, before Cavalier succumbed to pneumonia April 21, 1864, in Adams U.S.A. General Hospital in Memphis, Shelby County, Tennessee while serving with the 1st Alabama Cavalry, USV during the Civil War.

Byram, William T.C. - William T.C. Bryam was the alias of William O.G. Byram. He enlisted under the name of William T. C. Byram in Company C of the 1st Alabama Cavalry, USV as a Private on February 20, 1863, in Corinth, Mississippi for a period of 1 year. He was enrolled by D.R. Adams. The Company Descriptive Book showed him to have been 23 years of age, 5'-11½" inches tall, having a fair complexion, dark eyes, light hair, born Tishomingo County, Mississippi, and a farmer by occupation. He died of disease in the hospital at Glendale, Mississippi on August 21, 1863.

Byrum, Noah D. - Noah D. Byrum enlisted in Company D as a private and was recorded as being a prisoner of war in the hands of the enemy on January 8, 1864. No further information relative to this soldiers was found.*

Byrum, W. - W. Byrum, also spelled Byram, enlisted in Company D as a private, and was recorded as being on daily duty as a hospital nurse. No further information relative to this soldier was found.*

Byrum, William A. - William A. Byrum, also spelled Byram, enlisted in Company L on November 14, 1863, and was a Bugler. No further information relative to this soldier was found.*

- C -

Cabaniss, Madison Lewis "Mack" - Madison Lewis "Mack" Cabaniss enlisted and mustered into Company K of the 1st Alabama Cavalry, USV as a private on December 1, 1863, in Camp Davies, Mississippi for a period of 3 years. He was enrolled by Lieutenant Hornback, and traveled over 90 miles on horseback from his home in Marion County, Alabama to Camp Davies, in Corinth, Mississippi, to join the regiment. The Company Descriptive Book recorded him as being 36 years of age, 5'-10" tall, having a light complexion, black eyes, black hair, born in Tuscaloosa County, Alabama, and a farmer by occupation. The January and February 1864 Muster Roll recorded him as being absent, in Marion County, Alabama since January 6, 1864. Absent without leave since January 26, 1864. The March and April 1864 Muster Roll stated the following: This man was sent on recruiting service, when one time was reported as absent without leave and is now dropped and recorded as deserted. His name appeared on the Company Muster-Out Roll dated July 19, 1865, from Nashville, Tennessee, and stated he had leave of absence dated January 6, 1864, for 20 days, was not apprehended and listed as a deserter. He was originally on detached service in January and February 1864, recruiting in Marion County, Alabama

Madison Lewis "Mack" Cabaniss was born in 1827 in South Carolina or Tuscaloosa County, Alabama, to Peter Randolph Cabaniss, born February 7, 1800, in Nottoway County, Virginia, died April 12, 1834, in Tuscaloosa County, Alabama, and his wife Catherine Mayfield, born 1808 in South Carolina and died November 23, 1854, in Tuscaloosa County, Alabama. Madison was a brother to Obediah Cabaniss, below.

Cabiness, Obediah - Obediah Cabiness, also spelled Cabaniss, enlisted into Company M of the 1st Alabama Cavalry, USV as a private on December 16, 1863, in Camp Davies, Mississippi and was mustered in December 29, 1863, in Corinth, Mississippi. He was enrolled by Captain Lomax for a period of 3 years. The Company Descriptive Book recorded him as being 30 years of age, 5'-8" tall, having a dark complexion, black eyes, black hair, born in Holmes County, Mississippi, and a farmer by occupation. In February 1864 he was recorded as being on daily duty as company cook. The March and April 1864 Muster Roll recorded him as having deserted from Memphis, Tennessee on March 18, 1864, with 1 Remington revolver and 1 belt plate and box. The May and June 1864 Muster Roll stated he deserted with 1 Smith carbine and 1 Remington revolver.

Obediah Cabiness was born in 1832 in Mississippi and first enlisted in Company C, 41st Alabama Infantry, CSA on May 15, 1862, at Tuscaloosa, Alabama. Muster Roll of June 30, 1862, states he was absent in hospital at Knoxville, TN, Muster Roll of March & April state he was furloughed from hospital to Marion Co., AL and never returned to his unit. He then enlisted in the Union army. He was charged with desertion by the CSA and found guilty. He was sentenced to be shot to death with musketry. (Some of the men charged had their sentences remitted.) See Madison Cabaniss note about parents.

The Confederate charge and trial for the desertion of Obediah Cabaniss stated the following: Continuation of the proceedings of a General Court Martial, convened at the Camp of Johnson's Division, by virtue of Special Orders Number 239, Head Quarters Department of Northern Virginia (current series), before which were arraigned and tried the following named Prisoners - Private Obadiah Cabaniss, Co. A, 41st Ala. Regiment. Charge – Desertion - Specification - In this, that he Private Obadiah Cabaniss of Company A, of the forty-first Alabama Regiment, a duly enlisted soldier in the service of the Confederate States, and having drawn pay as such, did, on or about the first day of December in the year of our Lord one thousand eight hundred and sixty-two, in Marion County, in the state of Alabama, desert the said service, and did remain absent there from until the thirteenth day of September in the year of our Lord one thousand eight hundred and sixty-four, when he was brought back to his company under guard, near Petersburg, Virginia.

Finding: Of Specification - Guilty; Of Charge – Guilty; Sentence: And the Court (two-thirds concurring) do therefore sentence the said Private Obadiah Cabaniss of Company A, of the forty-first Alabama Regiment, to be shot to death with musketry, at such time and place as the General commanding may direct. The proceedings, findings, and sentences in the foregoing cases are approved. The sentences are confirmed, and with the exceptions herein after indicated, will be duly executed. The sentences respectively in the cases of...and of Private Obadiah Cabaniss of their respective brigades, seven days after the publication of their sentences to the same, under the direction of their division commander. Some of the men had their sentences remitted.

Cabit, Headley - See Headley Coburn.

Cadle, Kinard A. - Kinard A. Cadle enlisted in Company H of the 1st Alabama Cavalry, USV as a private December 25, 1864, in Rome, Georgia and was mustered in the same day in Nashville, Tennessee. Another muster roll stated he mustered in February 13, 1865, in Nashville. The Muster and Descriptive Roll recorded him as being 23 years of age, 5'-7" tall, having a fair complexion, blue eyes, light hair, born in Randolph County, Alabama, and a farmer by occupation. He was paid a bounty of $100, and his enlistment was credited to Ripley, Chautauqua County, New York. He was appointed sergeant April 1, 1865. He was mustered out October 20, 1865, in Huntsville, Alabama.

Cagh, Charles B. - Charles B. Cagh enlisted in Company A of the 1st Alabama Cavalry, USV as a private on December 5, 1862, in Glendale, Mississippi for a period of 1 year, and mustered in December 31, 186,2 in Corinth, Mississippi. He was 45 years of age when he enlisted. He was reported to have deserted on January 24, 1863.

Cagh, John H. - John H. Cagh enlisted in Company A of the 1st Alabama Cavalry, USV as a private on December 5, 1862, in Glendale, Mississippi, and was mustered in on December 31, 1862, in Corinth, Mississippi. He was reported to have deserted January 24, 1863. He was 16 years of age at the time he enlisted and was probably the son of Charles B. Cagh, above. They enlisted together and most probably deserted together.

Cagle, Albert S. - Albert S. Cagle enlisted in Company A of the 1st Alabama Cavalry, USV as a private on January 7, 1864, in Camp Davies, Mississippi for a period of 3 years. He was enrolled by Captain James W. DeVaney and was mustered in February 5, 1864, in Memphis, Tennessee. Another Muster Roll stated he was enrolled by Lieutenant Hinds. The Company Muster and Descriptive Roll shows him to have been 29 years of age, 6' tall, having a fair complexion, blue eyes, light hair, born in Winston County, Alabama, and a farmer by occupation. The May and June 1865 Muster Roll showed him to have been absent, on furlough since June 24, 1864. The July and August 1865 Muster Roll listed him as being present. He was mustered out October 20, 1865, in Huntsville, Alabama owing the U.S. Government $2.15 for losing 1 saber belt complete. His name appeared on the Returns as being on duty as a blacksmith in the regimental shop in July 1864. Albert S. Cagle is buried in Rock Creek Baptist Church Cemetery in Winston County, Alabama.

Cagle, David C. - David Crockett Cagle enlisted in Company L of the 1st Alabama Cavalry, USV as a private on September 25, 1863, in Fayette County, Alabama for a period of 1 year. He was enrolled by Captain Trammel and was mustered in the same day at Glendale, Mississippi. The Company Muster Roll dated from September 25 to October 31, 1863, stated he was absent with leave. The November and December 1863, Muster Roll stated he was present and had returned from missing in action on December 25, 1863. He was possibly captured during the Battle of Vincent's Crossroads on October 26, 1863, near Bay Springs, Mississippi. The Company Muster Roll dated from December 31, 1863, to April 30, 1864, stated he was absent, on daily duty in the Quartermaster Department since December 20, 1863. David C. Cagle re-enlisted December 24, 1864, in Stevenson, Alabama for a period of 3 years, and was mustered in the same day in Nashville, Tennessee, being paid $100 bounty. His enlistment was credited to Ripley, Chautauga County, New York. The Muster and Descriptive Roll listed David as having been 28 years of age, 6'-1" tall, having a fair complexion, blue eyes, dark hair, born in Hall County, Georgia, and a farmer by occupation. David C. Cagle's name appeared on the Returns as follows: November 1863, absent, sick, left in Alabama by order of Colonel Spencer; January 1864 to April 1864, on duty as regimental teamster; September 1864, discharged by reason of expiration of term of service September 29, 1864, in Rome, Georgia; and June 1865, enlisted in regiment December 21, 1864, in Stevenson, Alabama. He was mustered out October 20, 1865 in Huntsville, Alabama.

David Crockett Cagle was born May 11, 1834, in Gainesville, Georgia. He married Mary Ann Herdon on August 21, 1861, in Alabama. He died May 6, 1923, and is buried in Fanshawe Cemetery in LeFlore Co., Oklahoma. His parents were William C. Cagle, born 1797 in North Carolina and Mary (last name unknown) born in 1798 in North Carolina. Children of David and Mary were: James William, born 1863; Sarah T., born 1866; Thomas A., born 1868; Joseph Newton, born 1870; Phillip C., born 1872; Jacob M., born 1874; Otto A., born 1876; Virgil W., born 1879; Mary "Janie" E., born 1881 and Flora C. Cagle, born 1888. William C. Cagle was the son of Jacob Cagle, born 1766 and died 1850. Jacob was the son of John Cagle, born 1710 and died 1799. John was the son of Leonard Leonhart Kagle who was the original immigrant of this family. He was born in 1684 in Germany, arrived in Philadelphia in 1732, and died in 1754.

He was listed in the Civil War Pension Index filed in Connecticut and in Oklahoma with Mary A. Cagle listed as his widow. Fair complexion, blue eyes, dark brown/black hair.

David grew to adulthood in Hall County, Georgia, and appeared in the household of William and Mary Cagle in the Federal Census of 1850 in Hall County, at the age of 14. David has not been located for the Federal Census of 1860, but it is known that he had migrated to Winston County, Alabama by the early 1860's for on August 21, 1861, he was married to Mary A. Herndon at Larissa, Winston County, Alabama. The names, dates of births, place of birth, dates of marriage and death were taken from the family bible of David and Mary and provided by Helen O'Dell who is the daughter of John McKinley Cagle, 1898-1956. Three Cagle cousins, from the states of Georgia, Arkansas and Tennessee, but whose ancestors were among the Cagle pioneers of Old Cumberland County, North Carolina, served as soldiers in the Civil War as young men, and then, in later years, all made their way, by separate routes, to the old Choctaw Nation, and settled permanently in what eventually became LeFlore County, Oklahoma with the coming of Oklahoma Statehood in 1907. These were David, Charles T. Cagle 1839-1887, a native of Jackson County, Arkansas, is buried in the Hall Cemetery in Rural LeFlore County; Enoch Cagle, 1847-1934, a native of East Tennessee, is buried in the City Cemetery in Howe, Oklahoma. In the July 1862 term of the Inferior Court in Hall County, Georgia, David was summoned as a prospective juror, but did not appear in court, having already left some time previously. While a resident of Winston County, Alabama, David served as a soldier in the Civil War, and was one of several Cagle men across the South who served in both the Confederate and Union armies. He enlisted first in the CSA on September 6, 1862, at Jasper, Walker County, Alabama, in Company A, 13th Battalion, Alabama Partisan Rangers, but his service lasted less than a month, and by the end of September he was noted as being absent without leave. The reason for David's change of heart during the course of the War is not known, but it might be noted that Winston County was a Union stronghold during the Civil War and attracted many volunteers to the Union Army, most of whom enlisted in the 1st Alabama Cavalry (USA). David enlisted in Company L, 1st Alabama Cavalry on September 25, 1863, for a one-year period, and re-enlisted on December 21, 1864, and served until his discharge after the close of the War. After the Civil War, David remained in Winston County, Alabama for a few years, but by 1872 had moved to Howell County, Missouri and by 1880 to Independence County, Arkansas. During the 1880's, he migrated to the Choctaw Nation, and , after living for a period of time in St. Clair County, Missouri near the time of the 1900 Federal Census, returned permanently to the Choctaw Nation in the early 1900's, where he eventually established his home near Fanshawe, in what would soon become LeFlore County, Oklahoma. Family information submitted by Louis Cagle.

Cagle, Enoch - Enoch Cagle, son of David C. Cagle, above, enlisted in Company A of the 1st Alabama Cavalry, USV as a private on January 7, 1864, in Camp Davies, Mississippi for a period of 3 years. He was enrolled by Lieutenant Hinds, and was mustered in February 5, 1864, in Memphis, Tennessee. The Company Muster and Descriptive Roll records him as being 23 years of age, 5'-9" tall, having a fair complexion, blue eyes, light hair, born in Winston County, Alabama, and a farmer by occupation. On February 29, 1864, he was listed as being absent, sick in the Adams U.S.A. General Hospital in Memphis, Tennessee but was returned to duty on April 6, 1864. He was next listed on the Hospital Muster Roll for the U.S.A. General Hospital #6 in New Albany, Indiana as being a patient from December 31, 1863 through April 30, 1864, and then died there of measles and phthisis pulmonalis (consumption of the lungs) on May 3, 1864, in the General Hospital in New Albany, Indiana. He was buried in the New Albany National Cemetery, New Albany, Indiana.

Cagle, James - James Cagle enlisted in Company A of the 1st Alabama Cavalry, USV as a private on October 14, 1864, in Decatur, Alabama for a period of 3 years. He was enrolled by Lieutenant Emrick and was mustered in November 10, 1864, in Rome, Georgia. The Muster and Descriptive Roll shows him to have been 19 years of age, 5'-9" tall, having a fair complexion, blue eyes, auburn hair, born in Walker County, Alabama, and a farmer by occupation. He was mustered out October 20, 1865, owing the U.S. Government $2.02 for losing one carbine sling and swivel. He was paid a bounty of $100.

Cagle, James Riley - James R. Cagle enlisted in Company A of the 1st Alabama Cavalry, USV as a private on January 7, 1864, in Camp Davies, Mississippi for a period of 3 years. He was enrolled by Lieutenant Hinds and was mustered in on February 5, 1864, in Memphis, Tennessee. The Company Muster and Descriptive Roll showed him to have been 39 years of age, 5'-11" tall, having a fair complexion, blue eyes, light hair, born in North Carolina, and a blacksmith by occupation. In March and April 1864, he was on daily duty as a blacksmith, and from August 1864 to September 1865, he was on duty as a regimental blacksmith. He was mustered out October 20, 1865 in Huntsville, Alabama owing the U.S. Government $2.15 for losing 1 saber belt complete.

James Riley Cagle was born in December 1824 in Winston County, Alabama to Charles Cagle and Martha Johnson. He first married a cousin, Malinda Cagle, daughter of John Adam Cagle and Sarah Ann Lovett. Malinda was born December 18, 1824, in Warren County, Tennessee, and died September 9, 1863, in Haleyville, Marion County, Alabama. They had the following children: Sherard W.; Tamsey W.; Samantha; and Delilah Emaline Cagle. After Melinda's death, James married Emaline Cagle, sister to his first wife, Malinda on October 23, 1882, in Winston County, Alabama. Emaline was born September 15, 1830, and died January 1, 1912, in Winston County, Alabama. James Riley Cagle died January 9, 1904, in Winston County, Alabama and was buried in the Sardis #1 Baptist Church Cemetery in Winston County.

Cain, James - James Cain enlisted in Company C of the 1st Alabama Cavalry, USV as a private on July 27, 1863, in Glendale, Mississippi for a period of 1 year. He was enrolled by Captain Alexander T. Cameron and was mustered in on August 15, 1863, in Corinth, Mississippi. The Company Descriptive Book showed him to have been 18 years of age, 5'-8" tall, having a fair complexion, blue eyes, light hair, born in Tishomingo County, Mississippi, and was a farmer by occupation. He was shown as being single. James Cain died March 26, 1864, of small pox in Memphis, Tennessee. He is buried in the Memphis National Cemetery.

Cain, William - William Cain enlisted in Company A of the 1st Alabama Cavalry, USV as a private on December 22, 1863, in Camp Davies, Mississippi for a period of 3 years. He was enrolled by Lieutenant Hinds and was mustered in February 5, 1864, in Memphis, Tennessee. The Company Muster and Descriptive Roll showed him as being 46 years of age, 5'-8" tall, having a dark complexion, blue eyes, dark hair, born in Buncombe County, North Carolina, and a farmer by occupation. On February 29, 1864, he was shown as being absent, sick in the Overton U.S.A. General Hospital in Memphis, Tennessee. His name appeared on the Returns dated August 1864 stating he was absent, sick in the hospital in Nashville, Tennessee. He was still shown as being in the Overton U.S.A. General Hospital in Memphis through February 1865. The March and April 1865 Muster Roll listed him as absent, sick in the U.S.A. General Hospital in Jefferson Barracks, Missouri. The July and August 1865 Muster Roll stated William was still sick in Jefferson Barracks the last time they heard from him. William Cain was mustered out May 31, 1865, in St. Louis, Missouri. There was a note in his files from the Surgeon General's Office dated May 4, 1865, stating muster out to take effect May 31, 1865.

Caldwell, Stephen N. - See Stephen N. Colwell

Calvert, Jonathan - Jonathan Calvert, brother to Ralphord Calvert, below, was 27 years of age when he enlisted in Company I of the 1st Alabama Cavalry, USV as a private on December 21, 1863, in Camp Davies, Mississippi, for a period of 3 years. He was mustered out July 19, 1865 in Nashville, Tennessee. See Ralphord Calvert, below, for family information.

Calvert, Ralphord Randolph - Ralphord Randolph Calvert, brother to Jonathan Calvert, above, enlisted and mustered into Company I of the 1st Alabama Cavalry, USV as a private on August 18, 1862, in Huntsville, Alabama. He was enlisted by Captain Bankhead, and was with the early group of enlistees who were immediately shipped to Nashville, Tennessee and merged with the 1st Middle Tennessee and 5th Tennessee Cavalry. Ralphord was assigned to Company D of the 1st Middle Tennessee Cavalry, US. The Company Muster Roll dated November 30, 1862, listed him as being absent, sick in Hospital #12 in Nashville, Tennessee. He died of disease on November 7, 1862, in Nashville at age 30. His name appeared on the Company Muster-Out Roll stating he died October 21, 1862. The Company Descriptive Book showed him to have been 30 years of age, 5'-11" tall, having a dark complexion, hazel eyes, black hair, born in Winston County, Alabama, and a farmer by occupation.

Ralphord Calvert, some say his name was Ralphord Randolph Calvert, was born May 17, 1832, in Winston County, Alabama to Thomas and Elizabeth Calvert, who married February 18, 1830, in Walker County, Alabama. He was the brother of Jonathan Calvert, above. Ralphord's father, Thomas, was born March 29, 1804, in Tennessee, and died July 7, 1875, in Cullman County, Alabama. Elizabeth, last name unknown, was born December 19, 1813, in Tennessee and died October 13, 1867, in Cullman County, Alabama. Other children of Thomas and Elizabeth besides Jonathan and Ralphord were: Thomas Bird, Abner, Sarah, Jane, William R., Mary E., John H., and Simeon Calvert. Thomas Bird Calvert, brother of Jonathan and Ralphord, served in Company H of the 32nd Alabama Infantry, CSA.

Cameron, Alexander T. - Alexander T. Cameron was enrolled in the 1st Alabama Cavalry, USV on March 30, 1863, at Glendale, Mississippi at age 23, by order of Brigadier General G. M. Dodge to date from March 30, 1863. He was detailed to take command of Company C by order of Brigadier General Dodge and was listed as 1st Lieutenant on April 1, 1863. In May 1863, he was shown as being absent with leave since May 19, 1863, and in June 1863, he was listed as absent, on court martial in Corinth, Mississippi. In February 1864, the Returns stated: Present (numerically) AGO, is anointed out of service of US from this date, March 29, 1864, the reports from and records of regiment being irregular and conflicting, not to receive final payment under this order until he shall have fully satisfied the Pay Department that he is not indebted to the Government and that he has not previously occupied or presented any discharge papers upon which final dues were paid. A note in Alexander T. Cameron's records stated: S.O. 290, Par? 20, AGO September 2, 1864, the following officers of the 1st Alabama Cav. are announced as out of the service as of the date set opposite of their respective names. Captain Alex T. Cameron, March 29, 1864. Signed J.N. Kirkley. An officer's casualty sheet shows Captain Alexander T. Cameron to have resigned or mustered out March 29, 1864.

A letter to the Disbursing Clerk, Bureau of Pensions in Washington, D.C. dated April 7, 1922, from Margaret Cameron Lewis (Mrs. Harrison C. Lewis) stated: My mother, Nancy A. Cameron, Hotel Carlton, Berkeley, California, died March 26th, 1922. She left no estate and I am her only child. I shall make no claim for the amount of pension due at her death, if any. Her pension certificate has been sent to me here, No. 181,182. If anything more than this notice of her death is necessary, please let me know. I do not know whether the certificate should now be returned to the Pension Bureau or not. If so, I will send it upon hearing from you. Mrs. Lewis' address at the time was 238 West 11th Street, New York City.

Alexander and his brother, James both enlisted in Company A of the 64th Illinois Infantry, Yates Sharpshooters. On April 15, 1863, James was detailed by order of General Dodge to command the 1st Regiment of Alabama Cavalry Volunteers. However, James was killed in action on April 17, 1863, at Bear Creek, Alabama and his brother, Captain Alexander Cameron, requested permission to be absent from his command for 30 days to take the remains of his brother to the family burial ground at Ottawa, Illinois.

Alexander T. Cameron was born April 5, 1840, in Argyllshire, Scotland to James and Ann Cameron. Ann was the daughter of Alexander Cameron and Jessie Campbell. She was born in July 1809 in Ardnamurchan, Scotland and died April 26, 1888, in Austin Cottages, South Geelong, Victoria, Australia. James, Alexander's father, was born December 15, 1801, and died in January 1841. After emigrating from Scotland, Alexander settled in Ottawa, Illinois. He married Nancy A. Nelson on October 19, 1865, in La Salle County, Illinois. They were married by E.N. Lewis, Minister of the Gospel. After the war, he moved to Santa Barbara, California in 1875 where he worked as an attorney. He died December 17, 1877, in Santa Barbara and was buried in the Santa Barbara Cemetery and his grave is marked with a military headstone which is engraved "Co. C, 1st Alabama Cav." However, it is covered with lichen and almost impossible to read. He is in the Summit Section, Lot 353, Grave 08. His wife, Nancy, is also buried there. In the same lot Nancy Nelson Cameron ashes were buried on April 22, 1922. His obituary described him as "Lieutenant Colonel." A memo in the cemetery register states: "According to the deed book this lot was sold to Mrs. A.F. Cameron and she gave rights of interment to Margaret Cronise and her heirs 'full use of lot.' See minutes of directors' dates October 25, 1901. There are several Cronise burials in this lot.

Captain Alexander Cameron requested permission to be absent from his command for 30 days to take the remains of his brother, James C. Cameron, who was killed in the engagement at Barton Station, Alabama April 17, 1863, to the family burial ground at Ottawa, Illinois. Leave was approved.

Cameron, James C. - James C. Cameron was from Ottawa, Illinois and was 22 years old when he enlisted with the Union Army on December 3, 1861. He became a First Lieutenant in Yates' Sharpshooters, Company A of the 64th Illinois Volunteer Infantry Regiment; the regiment was sent south in 1862 and he was listed as wounded in the battle of Corinth, Mississippi 3-4 October 1862. Recovered, he was assigned to General Grenville Dodge's staff in Corinth and detailed to Iuka to become Provost Marshall of the District of Corinth. Dodge's command was part of the Army of the Tennessee under General Grant. He was released from this command to join the 1st Alabama Cavalry in April 1863, and assigned to march with Dodge's screening force to protect Colonel Abel D. Streight's raiders headed for Alabama. Dodge's force encountered Confederate Colonel Philip Roddey's cavalry while Dodge was enroute to meet Streight. Several minor battles were fought, and in the battle near Bear Creek, Alabama on April 17, 1863, he was killed while leading a charge against Roddy's men.

There was a James C. Cameron living in the Hoag Household in Marquette, Michigan in the 1860 Census. He was shown as a Bricklayer and born in Scotland. His brother, Alexander, was living in the Tharp Household in Ottawa, LaSalle County, Illinois, born in Scotland. I'm not sure this is the same James C. Cameron, but by him being born in Scotland I would imagine it was. Their parents may have not come over from Scotland or were already deceased by this time.

James C. Cameron, brother to Alexander, above, first enlisted in 64th Regiment Illinois Infantry, Company A., Yates Sharpshooters. He was promoted to captain September 12, 1862. On April 15, 1863, he was detailed by order of General Dodge to command 1st Regiment Alabama Cavalry Volunteers. He was killed in action April 17, 1863 at Bear Creek. After his death, his brother, Captain Alexander Cameron requested permission to be absent from his command for 30 days to take his remains to the family burial ground at Ottawa, Illinois. There is a memorial dedicated to James Cameron and four other Civil War Soldiers located in the Ottawa Avenue Cemetery in Ottawa, LaSalle County, Illinois, where Cameron was buried. Submitted by Robert Willett.

Camp, Alfred B. - Alfred B. Camp enlisted into Company E of the 1st Alabama Cavalry, USV as a private on August 1, 1864, in Wedowee, Alabama and was mustered in the same day in Rome, Georgia. The Muster and Descriptive Roll shows him to have been 18 years of age, 5'-8" tall, having a fair complexion, blue eyes, dark hair, born in Chambers County, Alabama, and a farmer by occupation. He reenlisted August 4, 1864, in Company B in Rome, Georgia or Wedowee, Alabama and was enrolled by Captain West. He was transferred to Company E on October 9, 1864. The November and December 1864 Muster Roll listed him as being absent, sick and sent to the hospital in Decatur, Alabama on November 5, 1864, from Rome, Georgia, where he remained sick through April 1865. He re-enlisted January 1, 1865, in Stevenson, Alabama, and was mustered in the same day in Nashville, Tennessee. His enlistment was credited to Sherman, Chautauga County, New York, and he was paid $100 bounty. He was mustered out October 20, 1865, in Huntsville, Alabama, and paid $100 bounty. Alfred B. Camp's name appeared on the Returns as follows: November 1864, absent, sick in General Hospital; December 1864, absent, sick in Rome, Georgia; January 1865 to April 1865, sick in U.S. General Hospital. He was able to sign his name on his Enlistment Forms.

Camp, William Anderson - William Anderson Camp enlisted in Company B of the 1st Alabama Cavalry, USV as a private on August 1, 1864. in Wedowee, Alabama for a period of 3 years, and was mustered in the same day in Rome, Georgia. The Muster and Descriptive Roll showed him to have been 19 years of age, 5'-8" tall, having a fair complexion, blue eyes, light hair, born in Randolph County, Alabama, and a farmer by occupation. He was promoted to Corporal on June 13, 1865. He was mustered out October 20, 1865, in Huntsville, Alabama.

Corporal William A. Camp was born November 29, 1845, in Randolph County, Alabama to John Jackson and Irene Camp. He died December 1, 1929, and is buried in the Forrest Chapel Cemetery in Wedowee, Randolph County, Alabama. William's father, John Jackson Camp was born July 28, 1818, in Georgia, and died August 21, 1880. in Heflin, Cleburne Alabama. John's wife, Irene, was born February 16, 1810, and died October 20, 1858. William A. Camp is buried in the Forrest Chapel Cemetery in Wedowee, Randolph County, Alabama.

<u>Camp, William M.</u> - William M. Camp enlisted in Company B of the 1st Alabama Cavalry, USV as a private on August 1, 1864, in Wedowee, Alabama, and was mustered in the same day in Rome, Georgia. He was enrolled by Captain West for a period of 3 years. The Muster and Descriptive Roll listed him as being 27 years of age, 5'-9" tall, having a fair complexion, blue eyes, dark hair, born in Chambers County, Alabama, and a blacksmith by occupation. He was transferred to Company E in October 1864. From December 1864 through February 1865, he was on duty as regimental ambulance driver. The March and April 1865 Muster Roll listed him as being absent, prisoner of war in the hands of the enemy since March 10, 1865, through May, in North Carolina. That would have been during the Battle of Monroe's Crossroads near Fayetteville, North Carolina. William M. Camp was discharged June 12, 1865, according to General Order Number 77, by the War Department, dated April 28, 1865. William M. Camp was listed on a Hospital Muster Roll stating he was a patient in the Dennison U.S.A. General Hospital, 3rd Division, Camp Dennison, Ohio, in March and April 1865. He was discharged June 12, 1865 at Camp Chase, Ohio. William M. Camp was able to sign his name to his Enlistment Forms. His POW Record states he was captured March 10, 1865, near Fayetteville, North Carolina, confined at Richmond, Virginia on March 28, 1865, paroled at Boulware and Cox's Wharf March 30, 1865, reported at CGB, Maryland on March 31, 1865, sent to Camp Chase, Ohio April 2, 1865, no Surgeon's Certificate on file, no further record.

William M. Camp was born in 1836, in Chambers County, Alabama and died in September 1867, in Wedowee, Chambers County, Alabama. He married Mary Ann, last name unknown, born July 15, 1840, and died August 25, 1899, in Wedowee, Chambers County, Alabama. William was buried in the Wedowee Masonic City Cemetery in Randolph County, Alabama.

<u>Campbell, Adam</u> - Adam Campbell enlisted in Company K of the 1st Alabama Cavalry, USV as t private on July 24, 1862, in Huntsville, Alabama, for a period of 3 years. He was enrolled by Captain Bankhead. The Regimental Descriptive Book showed Adam to have been 24 years of age, 5'-5" tall, having a light complexion, gray eyes, light hair, born in Pendleton County, South Carolina, and was a farmer by occupation. Adam was with the group of early enlistees who were immediately shipped to Nashville, Tennessee, where they were merged with the 1st Middle Tennessee and 5th Tennessee Cavalry. He was with Company E of the 1st Middle Tennessee Cavalry, US. He died October 23, 1862, in Hospital #14 in Nashville, Tennessee of measles. However, his Casualty Sheet states he died October 24, 1862. There was a Notation in his file from the Adjutant General's Office of the War Department, dated March 7, 1874, which stated: This man was admitted to #14 General Hospital, Nashville, Tennessee, October 6, 1862, and died October 24, 1862, of chronic diarrhea. The Muster -Out Roll stated he died October 23, 1862, of measles. His name was listed on the Roll of Honor No. 22, Page 244. He is buried in Grave A-5062 in the Nashville National Cemetery with the death date shown as December 24, 1862.

<u>Campbell, Alexander</u> - Alexander Campbell enlisted and mustered into Company K of the 1st Alabama Cavalry, USV as a private on July 24, 1862, in Huntsville, Alabama for a period of 3 years. He was enrolled by Captain Bankhead. The Regimental Descriptive Book recorded him as being 30 years of age, 5'9" tall, having a dark complexion, gray eyes, auburn hair, born in Pendleton County, South Carolina, and a farmer by occupation. He died of chronic diarrhea December 5, 1862, in Hospital #12, in Nashville, Tennessee. A Notation in his file from the Adjutant General's Office of the War Department dated June 25, 1883, stated the following: Admitted to Hospital #12 in Nashville, Tennessee on November 27, 1862, of bronchitis, and died of same disease December 5, 1862. Campbell was one of the early enlistees who were shipped to Nashville, Tennessee and merged with Company E of the 1st Middle Tennessee Cavalry, which is the company to which he was assigned when he died. He was buried in the Nashville National Cemetery. His effects at his death included 1 great coat, 1 blanket, 1 pair of boots, 1 shirt, 1 hat, 1 pocket knife, and 1 portmanteau.

Alexander Campbell was born 1828/1832, married Millie Noles/Knowles in Cass County, Georgia December 1, 1848, and they had the following children: Thomas Jefferson, born June 2, 1850; John Robert, born August 3, 1852; Samuel Henry, born November 1854; Sarah Ann, born June 3, 1857; Andrew Jackson, born July 1, 1859 and William Green Campbell, born July 1, 1861. Family information submitted by Rhett Campbell.

Campbell, Andrew J. - Andrew J. Campbell enrolled in Company G of the 1ˢᵗ Alabama Cavalry, USV as a private on May 29, 1863, in Chewalla, Tennessee for a period of 1 year. He was temporarily attached from the 11ᵗʰ Illinois Cavalry, US. He was mustered out November 26, 1863, in Memphis, Tennessee.

Campbell, Andrew J. - Only one card was found for Andrew J. Campbell which was filed at the end of the last roll of microfilm of the 1ˢᵗ Alabama Cavalry, USV records. It recorded him as a Private in Company G, and recorded him as having deserted July 7, 1863, from Glendale, Mississippi. However, his military records stated he mustered out November 26, 1863, in Memphis, Tennessee. No further information relative to this soldier was found.*

Campbell, George B. - George B. Campbell enlisted in Company H of the 1ˢᵗ Alabama Cavalry, USV as a private on December 16, 1864, in Stevenson, Alabama for a period of 3 years. He was enrolled by Captain James W. DeVaney. The Descriptive Book recorded him as being 43 years of age, 5'7 ½" tall, having a dark complexion, blue eyes, light hair, born in Halifax County, Virginia, and was a farmer by occupation. He died of smallpox and measles on February 5, 1865, in the U.S.A. Post Hospital in Huntsville, Alabama.

Campbell, John R. - John Robert Campbell enlisted and mustered into Company K of the 1st Alabama Cavalry, USV as a private for a period of 3 years on July 24, 1863, in Huntsville, Alabama. He was enrolled by Captain Bankhead with his brothers Adam and Alexander Campbell. John was with the group of early enlistees who were immediately shipped to Nashville, Tennessee, where they were merged with the 1st Middle Tennessee Cavalry which was later the 5th Tennessee Cavalry. He was with Company E of the 1st Middle Tennessee Cavalry. The Company Descriptive Book showed him to have been 23 years of age, 5'-8½" tall, having a light complexion, blue eyes, light hair, born in Pendleton District, South Carolina, and a farmer by occupation. On April 30, 1863, he was reported missing in action from the Battle of Day's Gap in Alabama. The January 1, to June 30, 1863, Muster Roll listed him as being absent, supposed to have been captured at Crooked Creek in Alabama near Day's Gap on April 30, 1863. He was also shown as missing in action on Streight's Raid through Alabama but returned December 1, 1863. The January and February 1864 Muster Roll listed him as being absent, on detached service as teamster in General Sherman's expedition in Vicksburg, Mississippi since January 24, 1864, by order of General Grierson. In June and July 1864, he was absent, on duty as an orderly for General Vandiver. The September and October 1864 Muster Roll shows him to have been absent, on recruiting service in Alabama by order of Colonel Spencer. However, the Returns stated he was on furlough from September 22, 1864, through December 1864. The Returns also recorded the following information; December 1863 – December 21, 1863, Returned to Camp Davies, Mississippi from missing in action on Streight's Raid; January 1864 – February 1864, on detached service in Vicksburg, Mississippi January 24, 1864: July 1864, absent, orderly for General Vandiver since June 1864; October 1864 – December 1864, on furlough since September 22, 1864; June 1, 1865 – May 1865, absent, recruiting in Winston County, Alabama since September 1864 by order of Colonel Spencer. The November and December 1864 Muster roll also showed him as being absent, on recruiting service in Alabama since September 1, 1864. He was still recruiting in Winston County, Alabama through April 20, 1865, by order of Colonel Spencer. He was mustered out July 19, 1865.

John R. Campbell was born about 1839, married first, Jane Catharine Blevins and had the following children: Flora Ann, born August 22, 1857; Sarah Tayor, born March 29, 1859: and John Nathaniel Campbell, born March 2, 1863. After Jane's death March 6, 1863, he married Rachel Blevins November 23, 1864, and had the following children: General Strate, born December 20, 1865; Bird Sherman, born January 26, 1868; Lucretia, born August 4, 1871; Susannah Elizabeth, born April 3, 1876; Alexander, born May 8, 1878; and Henry Jackson Campbell, born October 18, 1880. John died October 28, 1908 and is buried in the Wilson Cemetery in Winston County, Alabama. Family information submitted by Rhett Campbell.

Campbell, William - William Campbell enlisted in Company M of the 1st Alabama Cavalry,

USV as a private on August 2, 1863, in Corinth, Mississippi for a period of 3 years. He was enrolled by Captain Lomax, and was mustered in December 29, 1863, in Corinth. The Company Descriptive Book showed him to have been 30 years of age, 6' tall, having a dark complexion, gray eyes, dark hair, born in White County, Tennessee, and a farmer by occupation. The January and February 1864 Muster Roll stated William Campbell was reported to have deserted from Lagrange, Tennessee on January 28, 1864, with a Smith Carbine and Colt Revolver, for which he owed the U.S. Government $44.55. It stated that perhaps he went northwest to McNairy County, Tennessee. His name was listed on the Returns as follows: November 1863, absent, sick, left at post in Chewalla, Tennessee on October 13, 1863; December 1863, on duty as company cook; January 1864, Deserted January 28, 1864, at LaGrange, Tennessee with revolvers.

<u>Campbell, William H.</u> - William H. Campbell enlisted in Company D of the 1st Alabama Cavalry, USV as a private on May 20, 1864, in Decatur, Alabama for a period of 3 years. He was enrolled by Lieutenant Pease, and was mustered in June 16, in Decatur. The Muster and Descriptive Roll shows him to have been 19 years of age, 6'-1" tall, having a light complexion, blue eyes, dark hair, born in Jefferson County, Alabama, and a farmer by occupation. He was appointed Corporal September 1, 1864, by order of Colonel Spencer. He was mustered out October 20, 1865, in Huntsville, Alabama, owing the U.S. Government $1.80 for losing 1 surcingle and a curry comb.

<u>Canady, John H.</u> - John H. Canady, also shown as Canada, enlisted in Company L of the 1st Alabama Cavalry, USV as a private on September 25, 1863, in Fayette County, Alabama for a period of 1 year. Another Muster Roll stated he enrolled in Glendale, Mississippi. He was enrolled by Captain Trammel and mustered in September 25, 1863, in Glendale, Mississippi. The January and February 1864 Muster Roll shows him to have been absent, sick in hospital in Memphis, Tennessee, February 16, 1864. He was discharged September 28, 1864, in Rome, Georgia due to expiration of term of service. John H. Canady re-enlisted in Company L on September 29, 1864, and was mustered in October 17, 1864, in Rome, Georgia for a period of 3 years. His re-enlistment was credited to Winston County, Alabama. The Muster and Descriptive Roll listed him as having been 19 years of age, 5'-7" tall, having a fair complexion, blue eyes, dark hair, born in Heard County, Georgia, and a farmer by occupation. Canada was transferred to Company F at some time during his enlistment but was transferred back to Company L in May 1865. A Stop was put on his pay for $20, due to losing a Colt revolver. He was mustered out October 20, 1865, in Huntsville, Alabama, and his Muster-Out Roll stated he was 32 years of age. Another Muster-Out Roll stated he mustered out October 20, 1865, and was age 19. He was paid $100 bounty. John H. Canada's name appeared on a Hospital Muster Roll for Adams U.S.A. General Hospital in Memphis, Tennessee, stating he was attached to the hospital as a patient on February 5, 1864. There were apparently two men by the name of John H. Canady who served in the 1st Alabama Cavalry, USV, as there were two Muster and Descriptive Rolls, one giving his age as 19 and the other giving his age as 32. This is possibly a father and son, John H. Canada, Sr., and John H. Canada, Jr. The Company Descriptive Book that gave the age as 32 stated he enlisted September 29, 1864, in Rome, Georgia for a period of 3 years. He was enrolled by Lieutenant Bolton, and was transferred to Company L of the 1st Alabama Cavalry, USV on April 1, 1865, by Special Regimental Order Number 16. His name appeared on the Returns as follows: November 1864, enlisted in regiment November 11, 1864, in Rome, Georgia; June 1865, Transferred to Company L June 26, 1865, in Huntsville, Alabama.

<u>Canada, Russell</u> - See Russell L. Kenedy.

<u>Canady, Isaac A.</u> - Isaac A. Canady, also spelled Canada, enlisted and was mustered into Company I of the 1st Alabama Cavalry, USV as a private on July 21, 1862, in Huntsville, Alabama. He was enrolled by Captain Bankhead. He also served in Company D. The Company Descriptive Book showed him to have been 33 years of age, 5'-11½" tall, having a light complexion, hazel eyes, dark hair, born in Morgan County, Alabama, and a farmer by occupation. He died of disease November 22, 1862, in Nashville, Tennessee.

Canterbury, Andrew Sylvester - Andrew Sylvester Canterbury enlisted in Company M of the 1st Alabama Cavalry, USV as a private on December 19, 1863, in Camp Davies, Mississippi for a period of 3 years. He was enrolled by Captain Lomax, and was mustered in on December 29, 1863, in Corinth, Mississippi. The Company Descriptive Book showed him to have been 44 years of age, 5'-10" tall, having a light complexion, blue eyes, light hair, born in Bibb County, Alabama, and a farmer by occupation. He was entitled to a $300 bounty. The November and December 1864 Muster Roll listed him as being absent, sick in hospital since November 12, 1864, place not known. The January and February 1865 Muster Roll also listed him as absent, sick in hospital, place not known. He was still listed as being sick on the March and April 1865 Muster Roll but was listed as present on the July and August 1865, Muster Roll. He was mustered out October 20, 1865 in Huntsville, Alabama, owing the U.S. Government $13.16 due to losing 1 carbine sling and swivel, 1 carbine cartridge box, 1 cap, pouch and pick, 1 saber belt and plate, 1 curry comb, halter and strap, 2 spurs, straps, and a saddle blanket. He was paid a bounty of $180 but was still due $120 to make the $300 bounty some of the trooper received.

Andrew Sylvester Canterbury's brother, Nicholas J. Z. Canterberry, enlisted in Co. B. of the 44th Alabama Infantry Regiment at Selma, Alabama, on March 29, 1862. He and 44th arrived in Richmond on July 1, but the unit was decimated by illness and many, including Nicholas, were listed as not fit for duty on August 31, 1862, and missed the Second Battle of Bull Run. Nicholas was also reported ill on September 17, 1862, and missed the Battle of Sharpsburg. He was discharged from duty for health reasons on October 1, 1862, and he returned to Alabama. He later enlisted in the Bibb County Militia. Their parents were Zachariah Canterbury and Sarah Canterbury. About 1811, they moved to present day Bibb County, Alabama.

TESTIMONY BY ZACHARIAH C. CANTERBURY AT PENSION HEARING FOR STEP MOTHER NANCY JANE CANTERBURY ON MAY 10, 1890, Case No. 282,585 (sic)

Zachariah C. Canterbury identified himself as a 45-year-old farmer, the son of Andrew Sylvester Canterbury and his first wife, Olia Mary Ann Bolen. They were married in Marion County, Alabama near Jasper.

Zachariah testified that he was the 11th of 12 children born to Andrew and Mary, and that he was the sole survivor of those 12 children. He stated that he was born on April 12, 1845. He identified his 11 siblings as Oliver, James, William, Sarah T.E., Permelia, Elizabeth, Mary Jane, Sarah, John D., David L. Elmore, and Mollie. He said seven of the children - he did not identify which - were buried in Tuscaloosa. The 1850 Census of Marion County, Alabama, only lists only six children - Permelia, Elizabeth, Sarah, Rhoda, James and William. There is no mention of Zachariah. His age is contradicted by his step mother's testimony.

Zachariah testified that he was 15 years (1860?) old when his mother died of smallpox in Nashville, Tennessee. He said he, too, contracted smallpox, but survived. There were four brothers alive at the time of their mother's death, Zachariah, James, David L. and John D., but two of his brothers, David L. and John D. died "right after" their mother from smallpox. According to Zachariah's testimony, James died in 1889. Zachariah testified that two months after his mother died he joined his father at Huntsville and remained with him until Andrew mustered out. Zachariah was not in the Army but served as personal servant to "M" Company Commander, Capt. Lomax. (Zachariah testified the man's name was "Romax," but Andrew's mustering out documents and the 1st Alabama Cavalry USV roster list him as "Lomax.")

Zachariah testified that Andrew's health was good the first year he was with him but then Andrew came down with a cough (consumption?) And then erysipelas (a bacterial infection) in his right arm. Zachariah testified his father was treated by the regimental surgeon and never went to the hospital. Andrew stayed with his command and in his tent when he was too sick.

Zachariah testified he "tented" with his father, Corp. Bias (Nathaniel Bice?) and 1st Sgt. (John G.) Blackwell. Andrew's health was "right bad" when he mustered out. Zachariah testified Andrew coughed and had pain in his right breast and erysipelas in his right arm and shoulder. The arm would swell "mightily inflamed" and would break out raw frequently. The erysipelas would clear up and the arm would "look well."

Andrew married Nancy Jane Croft Canterberry (sic) at Rogersville, Lauderdale County, Alabama, on Dec. 5, 1865, two and a half months after mustering out of the Union Army. Nancy was the widow of Lewis F. Canterberry, a cousin of Andrew's, who died March 28, 1864, at the Union POW camp at Rock Island, Illinois (grave No. 941). Nancy Jane brought four children to the marriage (by Lewis F. Canterberry), Elizabeth Ann, Poke (Polk?)Walker, George Washington and Sarah F. Nancy Jane and Andrew S. Canterbury had one child together, Mary Jane, who, as an adult, married Yeeley Little. At the time of Zachariah's testimony the Littles lived about 4 miles south of Courtland in Lawrence County, Alabama.

Zachariah testified his father died of consumption and erysipelas in early spring of 1867 at Shoal Creek, Alabama, nine miles NE of Florence, Alabama. Pension records submitted by Jack Moore.

Cantrell, Daniel C. - Daniel C. Cantrell enlisted in Company A and was also on detached service in Company M since February 5, 1864. No further information relative to this soldier was found.*

Cantrell, Dennis Cody - Dennis Cody Cantrell enlisted in Company D of the 1st Alabama Cavalry, USV on February 1, 1863, in Glendale, Mississippi for a period of 1 year. He was enrolled by W. Williams and was mustered in February 4, 1863, in Corinth, Mississippi, about ten miles from Glendale. The Regimental Descriptive Book showed him to have been 45 years of age, 5'-11" tall, having a dark complexion, blue eyes, dark hair, born in Spartanburg, South Carolina, and a farmer by occupation. The May and June 1863 Muster Roll listed him as being a 2nd Sergeant. The January and February 1864 Muster Roll showed him as a Sergeant. On February 4, 1864, he was mustered out as Sergeant in Memphis, Tennessee due to expiration of term of service.

Story of Dennis Cody Cantrell

Dennis Cody Cantrell enlisted in Company D of the 1st Alabama Cavalry, USV on February 1, 1863, in Glendale, Mississippi, at age 45. He was mustered in February 4, 1863, in Corinth, Mississippi, about ten miles from Glendale. On February 4, 1864, he was mustered out as Sergeant in Memphis, Tennessee. Dennis was the son of Lanceford and Martha "Patsy" Cartwell Cantrell. Lanceford was born in 1787 in Rockingham County, North Carolina (his Company Descriptive Roll recorded him as being born in Spartanburg, South Carolina) and died in 1850 in Union County, Georgia. Martha "Patsy" was born November 17, 1800, in Spartanburg, South Carolina and died 1870 in Georgia. Dennis was born October 16, 1821, in Spartanburg, South Carolina, and died July 7, 1891, in Winston County, Alabama of typhoid fever, according to Dr. C.H. Johnson. In 1842, he married Sarah Jane Robbins, who was born in January 1822 in Spartanburg, South Carolina and died in 1900 in Winston County, Alabama. Some of the children of Dennis and Sarah were: James H., born January 11, 1842, died January 27, 1921; Tennessee A., born 1846; John D., born January 25, 1848, died April 6, 1924; Edie C., born 1850; Rebecca Jane, born February 1852, died February 1924; Martha J., born October 31, 1854, died March 9, 1932; William Dennis, April 1858; Temper R., born 1861; Thomas M., born July 1865, died 1920; and Sherman Hanford Cantrell, born August 1867, died February 5, 1933.

Dennis Cantrell's brother, John Sterling Cantrell, also served in Company D of the 1st Alabama Cavalry, USV, (see below).

Southern Claim for Dennis C. Cantrell - That the property was removed to camps near Mooresville and 2nd to camps near Paint Rock, Jackson County, Alabama and used for or by said officers and soldiers, all this on or about the 1st, the last of August or first of September and first of December in the year 1864.

That no voucher, receipt, or other writing was given for the property thus taken.

That your petitioner verily believes that the property described was taken under the following circumstances, or one or more of such circumstances, Viz: (sic)

177

1. For the actual use of the army, and not for the mere gratification of individual officers or soldiers already provided by the Government with such articles as were necessary or proper for them to have.

2. In consequence of the failure of the troops of the United States to receive from the Government in the customary manner, or to have in their possession at the time, the articles and supplies necessary for them, or which they were entitled to receive and have.

3. In consequence of some necessity for the articles taken, or similar articles; which necessity justified the officers or soldiers taking them.

4. For some purpose so necessary, useful, beneficial or justifiable as to warrant or require the Government to pay for it.

5. Under the order or authority of some officer, or other person connected with the army, whose rank, situation, duties, or other circumstances at the time authorized, empowered, or justified him in taking or receiving it, or ordering it to be taken or received.

That your petitioner remained loyally adherent to the cause and the Government of the United States during the war, and so loyal before and at the time of the taking of the property for which this claim is made, and he solemnly declares that, from the beginning of hostilities against the United States to the end thereof, his sympathies were constantly with the cause of the United States; that he never, of his own free will and accord, did anything, or offered, or sought, or attempted to do anything, by word or deed to injure said cause or retard its success, and that he were at all times ready and willing, when called upon, or if called upon, to aid and assist the cause of the Union, or its supporters, so far as his means and power, and the circumstances of the case, permitted.

That said claim has not been presented to any branch of the government or department thereof. That Thomas C. Fullerton, of Washington D.C., is hereby authorized and empowered to act as Attorneys for the prosecution of this claim.

Wherefore your petitioner prays for such action of your Honorable Commission in the premises as may be deemed just and proper. [signed] Dennis C. Cantrell, Witnesses: [signed] William Dodd, Jr. and Carroll Dodd.

State of Alabama, County of Winston: I, Dennis C. Cantrell, being duly sworn, deposes and says that he is the petitioner named in the foregoing petition, and who signed the same; that the matters therein stated are true, of the deponent's own knowledge except as to those matters which are stated on information and belief, and as to those matters he believes them to be true; and deponent further says that he did not voluntarily serve in the Confederate army or navy, either as an officer, soldier, or sailor, or in any other capacity, at any time during the late rebellion; that he never voluntarily furnished any stores, supplies, or other material aid to said Confederate army or navy, or to the Confederate government, or to any officer, department or adherent of the same in support thereof, and that he never voluntarily accepted or exercised the functions of any office whatsoever under, or yielded voluntary support to, the said Confederate government. [signed] Dennis C. Cantrell, Witnesses: [signed] William Dodd, Jr., and Carroll Dodd.

Sworn to and subscribed in my presence, the 25th day of November 1872. A.B. Hays, J.P.

Names and residences of witnesses who will be relied upon to prove loyalty:

Buckner Walker, of Houston, Winston County, Alabama, Captain J.J. Hinds, of Decatur, Morgan County, Alabama

Names and residences of witnesses who will be relied upon to prove the other facts alleged in the foregoing petition: Tennessee A. Williams, of Houston, Winston County, Alabama, Richard Penn, of Basham's Gap, Morgan County, Alabama, Mary S. Carter, of Basham's Gap, Morgan County, Alabama, John D. Cantrell, of Houston, Winston County, Alabama, James Penn, of Houston, Winston County, Alabama, Post office address of claimant: Houston, Winston County, Alabama. Post office address of attorney: Washington, D.C.

State of Alabama, County of Winston: I, Dennis C. Cantrell, being duly sworn, deposes and says that he is the petitioner named in the foregoing petition, and who signed the same; that the matters therein stated are true, of the deponent's own knowledge except as to those matters which are stated on information and belief, and as to those matters he believes them to be true; and deponent further says that he did not voluntarily serve in the Confederate army or navy, either as an officer, soldier, or sailor, or in any other capacity, at any time during the late rebellion; that he never voluntarily furnished any stores, supplies, or other material aid to said Confederate army or navy, or to the Confederate government, or to any officer, department or adherent of the same in support thereof, and that he never voluntarily accepted or exercised the functions of any office whatsoever under, or yielded voluntary support to, the said Confederate government. [signed] Dennis C. Cantrell, Witnesses: [signed] William Dodd, Jr., and Carroll Dodd.

Names of witnesses called upon to prove loyalty: Buckner Walker, Captain J.J. Hinds, Tennessee A. Williams, Richard Penn, Mary S. Carter, John D. Cantrell, and James Penn.

My name is Dennis C. Cantrell and I am 52 years of age. I reside in the County of Winston and State of Alabama and have so resided most of the time for 16 years. My occupation is that of a farmer. I resided in said County of Winston from the year 1859 until March 1864. At this time, I moved through the lines in to Limestone County, Alabama where I made a crop in the year 1864. In the winter of 1864, I moved to Stevenson, Alabama. In the spring of 1865, I moved back to Limestone County, Alabama and there I remained until after the surrender. When I first moved from said County of Winston in the year 1864, I moved because a man of my principles could not live here in safety. I never followed any business during the rebellion except farming excepting the time I was in U.S. service.

I served as a U.S. soldier for 12 months. I also in the years 1862 and 1863 fed scores of Union men and U.S. solders. I fed Dock Spain and William Looney, who was a U.S. scout and many Union layouts, whose names I can't now recollect. I also fed W.W. Young who belonged to the 1st Alabama Cavalry.

I had one brother, John S. Cantrell in the 1st Alabama Regiment Cavalry. He entered service at Camp Davis (Davies), Mississippi in the year 1863 in Company D. He was captured by Stokely Robert's Rebel forces and turned over to Moreland's Battalion and was by them murdered. I also had a son, James H. Cantrell, in the 1st Regiment Alabama Cavalry Volunteers in Company D. My son entered said service the 4th day of February 1863 at Glendale, State of Mississippi and was honorably discharged 11th day of February 1864 at Memphis, Tennessee. I carried him with me into service. We both entered service and were both discharged at the same time.

Dennis C. Cantrell was buried in the Cantrell Cemetery near Addison in Winston County, Alabama. No dates were recorded on his monument. The Winston County Register of Deaths recorded Cody Cantrell died of typhoid fever on July 7, 1891, at the age of 69 years. He was born October 16, 1821.

Cantrell, George D. - George D. Cantrell enlisted in Company C of the 1st Alabama Cavalry, USV as a private on February 20, 1863, in Corinth, Mississippi for a period of 1 year. He was enrolled by D.R. Adams, and was mustered in February 25, 1863, in Corinth. The Company Descriptive Book shows him to have been 25 years of age, 5'-11" tall, having a fair complexion, blue eyes, light hair, born in McMinn County, Tennessee, and a farmer by occupation. He was discharged March 26, 1864, in Memphis, Tennessee due to expiration of term of service. His name appeared on the Returns as follows: August 1863, he was on daily duty as a cook; March 1864, he was transferred to Company C in Memphis, Tennessee on March 3, 1864. He was shown as being single.

George D. Cantrell was born May 10, 1838, in McMinn County, Tennessee and died March 22, 1910, in Boone County, Arkansas. He was buried in the Crawford Cemetery in Everton, Boone County, Arkansas.

Cantrell, James H. - James H. Cantrell enlisted in Company D of the 1st Alabama Cavalry, USV as a private on February 1, 1863, in Glendale, Mississippi for a period of 1 year, and was mustered in February 4, 1863, in Glendale, Mississippi. The Regimental Descriptive Book showed Cantrell as having been 20 years of age, 5'-8½" tall, having a dark complexion, blue eyes, dark hair, born in Spartanburg, South Carolina, and a farmer by occupation. He was mustered out February 4, 1864, in Memphis, Tennessee due to expiration of term of service. See James' father under Dennis C. Cantrell, above.

James' father stated the following: "John S. Cantrell was in the 1st Alabama Regiment Cavalry. He entered service at Camp Davis (Davies), Mississippi in the year 1863 in Company D. He was captured by Stokely Robert's Rebel forces and turned over to Moreland's Battalion and was by them murdered. I also had a son, James H. Cantrell, in the 1st Regiment Alabama Cavalry Volunteers in Company D. My son entered said service the 4th day of February 1863 at Glendale, State of Mississippi and was honorably discharged 11th day of February 1864 at Memphis, Tennessee. I carried him with me into service. We both entered service and were both discharged at the same time." See note under James' father, Dennis C. Cantrell's file above.

Cantrell, John Starling - John Starling Cantrell, also listed as John Sterling Cantrell, enlisted in Company D of the 1st Alabama Cavalry, USV as a Private in Glendale, Mississippi on October 26, 1863, at age 35. His brother, Dennis, had already enlisted in the 1st Alabama in February. John was mustered in at Camp Davies, Mississippi on the same date. On January 18, 1864, he was captured and taken prisoner of war in Jacinto, near Corinth, Mississippi. He was killed by the Rebels on June 18, 1864, in Franklin County, Alabama while still a prisoner of war. See note in John Cantrell's brother's file above about his brother, Dennis C. Cantrell.

John Starling Cantrell was born about 1828 in Lumpkin County, Georgia to Lanceford and Martha "Patsy" Cantrell. He was a brother to Dennis C. Cantrell, above. About 1846, he married Nancy Manerva Chastain, daughter of Edward and Sarah Shelton Chastain. Nancy was born June 11, 1810. in Haywood County, North Carolina and died May 3, 1913. in Licking, Texas County, Missouri.

John S. Cantrell's wife, Nancy, had two brothers, James Knox Polk Chastain, and David D. Chastain, who also served in the 1st Alabama Cavalry, USV. See information on them later.

On April 27, 1869, Nancy M. Cantrell stated in her Request for Pension in Winston County, Alabama that she was the widow of John S. Cantrell, who was killed by gun shot near Frankfort, Franklin County, Alabama, on or about January 14, 1864. while a prisoner of war. She stated she had enclosed an affidavit of A.T. Bonds and the said affidavit was the best evidence of the death of her husband that was known to exist or could be obtained, to her knowledge or the knowledge of any other person. The affidavit was signed by Andrew D. Mitchell and E.P. Hughes, and witnessed by W.C. Hyde and J.W. Wilhite.

On April 30, 1869, Nancy M. Cantrell stated she was a resident of Littlesville in Winston County, Alabama, and she lists her children who are under 16 years of age as: Sarah E. Cantrell, John C. Cantrell and Thomas L. Cantrell. The affidavit was witnessed by James Osborn and Samuel Spain of Houston, Winston County, Alabama.

Lydia A. Coward and Teresa E. Osborn stated on January 25, 1871, that they were present and witnessed the marriage of John S. Cantrell and Nancy M. Chastain on January 22, 1850, in Shady Grove, in Union County, Georgia. They also stated they were witnesses to the births of the following children of John S. and Nancy M. Cantrell: Martha Ann, born March 2, 1852; Sarah E., born March 26, 1854; John C., born August 25, 1856; and Thomas Cantrell, born February 20, 1859, all born in Thorn Hill, Marion County, Alabama. This affidavit was signed by Lydia A. Coward and Teresa E. Osborn on January 23, 1871.

On June 5, 1913, John C. Cantrell, son of John and Nancy Chastain Cantrell, completed an Application For Reimbursement due to his mother's death on May 3, 1913. He stated her Certificate No. was 154392. He stated the cause of her death was old age, and her doctor was Dr. S.L. Mitchell of Licking, Missouri. Nancy had been living with her son, J.C. Cantrell at his home. He listed the following items for which payment was due: Dr. S.L. Mitchell, $7.25; Medicine, $1.00; nursing care from March 15, 1913, to May 3, 1913, $16.30, Casket, $19.00, for a total of $43.55. It was signed by J.C. Cantrell of Licking, Texas County, Missouri. Dr. Mitchell added a note saying "Pensioner required a great deal of care and attention because of her extreme feebleness." Nancy M. Cantrell's pension of $12 per month was stopped February 4, 1913, due to her death on May 3, 1913, in Licking, Texas County, Missouri.

Cantrell, Moses B. - Moses B. Cantrell enlisted in Company D of the 1st Alabama Cavalry, USV as a private on April 19, 1864, in Decatur, Alabama for a period of 3 years. He was enrolled by Lieutenant Pease, and was mustered in June 16, 1864, in Decatur, Alabama. The Muster and Descriptive Roll showed him to have been 25 years of age, 5'-11" tall, having a light complexion, blue eyes, brown hair, born in Lumpkin County, Georgia, and a farmer by occupation. A Stop was put on his pay for $20 due to him having lost 1 Remington revolver. The November and December 1864 Muster Roll listed him as being absent in Alabama with leave. However, the Company Descriptive

Book stated he was missing in action December 15, 1864. The January and February 1865 Muster Roll stated he was absent, on detached service in Decatur, Alabama. The May and June 1865 Muster Roll listed him as being absent and stated: Dropped from prisoner of war and reported missing in action. The Muster- Out Roll stated he had been a prisoner of war since December 18, 1864, not mustered out. A Notation from the Records and Pension Office of the War Department dated May 6, 1892, stated Investigation fails to elicit any further information relative to this soldier. Cantrell's name appeared on the Returns as follows: December 1864 to April 1865, absent, sick in U.S. General Hospital; May 1865, supposed to be dead in the field May 1, 1865.

Cantrell, Reuben - Reuben Cantrell enlisted in Company D of the 1st Alabama Cavalry, USV as a private on February 1, 1863, in Glendale, Mississippi, for a period of 1 year. He was mustered in February 4, 1863, in Corinth, Mississippi. The Regimental Descriptive Book listed Cantrell as having been 29 years of age, 5'-7½" tall, having a dark complexion, black eyes dark hair, born in Gwinnett County, Georgia, and a farmer by occupation. His Muster-In Roll stated he was absent with leave to move family to Jackson, Tennessee on April 3, 1863. The September and October 1863 Muster Roll listed him as being absent, sick in hospital in Corinth, Mississippi. The November and December 1863 Muster Roll listed him as being absent, sick in the hospital in Memphis, Tennessee. He was discharged February 4, 1864, by reason of expiration of term of service.

Reuben Cantrell was born November 12, 1834, in Gwinnett County, Georgia to Elijah and Rebecca Ann Cantrell, who were married October 31, 1817, in Spartanburg, South Carolina. Rebecca was the daughter of Charles Cantrell and Milliage M. Lillard. Reuben first married Sarah, last name unknown, about 1854 and had the following children: William J.; Martha C.; Aaron J.; and Isaac J. Cantrell. He was married next to Mary Frances Sullivan on November 19, 1865, in Jackson County, Illinois, and they had the following children: Sarah Rebecca; Brada; Elijah S.; Reuben J.S.; Margaret I.; Stephen A.; Laura F.; Texanna Louisa; and Pearl D. Cantrell. The 1880 Marion County, Arkansas Census showed Reuben Cantrell as being a Minister. Reuben died December 13, 1913, in Sugarloaf Township, Boone County, Arkansas and was buried in the Cedar Grove Cemetery in Lead Hill, Boone County, Arkansas. [The Marriage Record of Reuben Cantrell and Mary Frances Sullivan can be found in the "Illinois Marriages, 1851-1900". It can also be found in the Jackson County, Illinois Court Records, Film #0968927 – 0968929.]

Cantrell, William - William Cantrell enlisted in Company D of the 1st Alabama Cavalry, USV as a private on February 1, 1863, for a period of 1 year, in Glendale, Mississippi. He was mustered in February 4, 1863 in Corinth, Mississippi. He died of disease on February 20, 1863, in Glendale, Mississippi.

Cape, Thomas K. - Thomas K. Cape enlisted in Company L of the 1st Alabama Cavalry, USV as a private on September 25, 1863, in Fayette County, Alabama for a period of 1 year. He was enrolled by Captain Trammel, and was mustered in the same day in Glendale, Mississippi. The Company Descriptive Book showed him to have been 33 years of age, 6'-3" tall, having a fair complexion, blue eyes, light hair, born in Hall County, Georgia, and a farmer by occupation. He was promoted to Sergeant on December 2, 1863. He was mustered out September 28, 1864, in Rome, Georgia due to expiration of term of service.

Thomas K. Cape was the son of King Hiram Cape and his wife, Nancy L. Cagle, who married January 15, 1824, in Hall County, Georgia. Nancy L. Cagle was the daughter of Jacob Cagle and Elizabeth Gilmore.

Carnelius, William R. – See William R. Cornelius.

Carpenter, Frazier E. - Frazier E. Carpenter enlisted in Company C of the 1st Alabama Cavalry, USV as a private on December 18, 1862, in Corinth, Mississippi for a period of 1 year. He was enrolled by D.R. Adams, and was mustered in on December 22, 1862, in Corinth. The Regimental Descriptive Book showed Carpenter to have been 35 years of age, 5'-7½" tall, having a fair complexion, blue eyes, dark hair, born in Anson County, North Carolina, and a farmer by occupation. The March and April 1863 Muster Roll listed him as being absent, stating he was captured and taken prisoner of war on April 14, 1863, from Glendale, Mississippi, however, the May and June 1863 Muster Roll showed him to be present. When he was taken prisoner of war, he was sent to Camp Parole, Maryland and from there to B.B. Missouri, and back to his regiment on May 18, 1863. The July and August 1863 Muster Roll stated Frazier E. Carpenter died of disease on August 9, 1863, at Glendale, Mississippi. He was buried in the Corinth National Cemetery.

Carroll, Anderson B. - Anderson B. Carroll enlisted in Company B of the 1st Alabama Cavalry, USV on May 10, 1863, at Glendale, Mississippi at age 20, for a period of one year. He was mustered in the same day in Corinth, Mississippi. Another roll stated he enlisted for a period of 3 years. The September and October 1863 Muster Roll listed him as being absent, prisoner of war in the hands of the enemy since October 26, 1863, which would have been at the Battle of Vincent's Crossroads. However, the November and December 1863 Muster Roll listed him as being present. He was mustered out January 22, 1864, in Memphis, Tennessee and was last paid to August 31, 1863.

Anderson B. Carroll was born January 14, 1843, in Georgia, married Mary Elizabeth Clement on August 8, 1862, in Franklin, Alabama and died May 4, 1896, in Paducah, McCracken County, Kentucky. Mary Elizabeth Clement was the daughter of Eunice C. Sullivan and William Benjamin Clement and she had two brothers, William and Harvey, who also served in the 1st Alabama Cavalry, USV. Children of Anderson and Mary were: Joseph N., born November 25, 1863, in Alabama, died July 25, 1945; John B., born September 30, 1865, in Centralia, Illinois, died July 4, 1903; James R., born August 28, 1867, in Livingston, Kentucky, died January 23, 1876; William Jefferson, born August 23, 1869, in Livingston, Kentucky, married Maggie Blackwell July 12, 1888, and died July 3, 1957; Mattie Belle, born August 24, 1871, died February 13, 1888; Lydia R., born June 7, 1873, died May 7, 1927; Anderson Bailey, born April 23, 1875 in Livingston, Kentucky, died 1958; Mary Elizabeth, born April 23, 1875, died February 20, 1903; Hugh Harvey, born September 28, 1880, died October 15, 1890; Georgia, born August 25, 1883, died March 16, 1884; and Annice Beatrice Carroll, born October 31, 1885 in Paducah, Livingston County, Kentucky, married John Benton Carroll on April 18, 1903, and died March 31, 1981 in Paducah, Kentucky. Family information submitted by Vicki Ruth Ebbert.

Carroll, James K.P. - James K.P. Carroll enlisted in Company B of the 1st Alabama Cavalry, USV on December 23, 1862, at Glendale, Mississippi by Frank Burdick, and was mustered in December 31, 1862, at Corinth, Mississippi. He was appointed Corporal January 22, 1863. The September and October 1863 Muster Roll listed James as absent, prisoner of war since October 26, 1863, which was probably during the Battle of Vincent's Crossroads. He was shown as being discharged December 27, 1863, by reason of expiration of term of service. The Regimental Descriptive Book shows James to have been 17 years of age at time of discharge, 5'-8" tall, having a light complexion, blue eyes, auburn hair, born Floyd County, Georgia and a farmer by occupation. James K.P. Carroll's name appeared on the returns as absent in the hands of the enemy since the engagement of Vincent's Crossroads October 26, 1863.

James Knox Polk Carroll was born April 12, 1840, in Floyd County, Georgia to John G. Carroll and Sarah McElroy. He married Melissa Jane Guinn on October 15, 1876, in Red Rover County, Texas. Melissa was born March 13, 1858, to William Guinn and Louisa Marion Wolverton. Children of James Knox Polk and Melissa Jane Guinn Carroll were: Mary Isabelle, born January 23, 1878, died May 10, 1979; Maggie Mae, born March 12, 1879, died August 9, 1960; Lula, born May 1880; Ollie Florence, born May 31, 1880, died March 5, 1900; Daisy Carroll, born October 1881; Lily Day, born October 27, 1881, died April 4, 1964; Nettie James, born May 7, 1883, died April 25, 1918; Susie Jane, born April 16, 1886, died March 27, 1980; Alice Lucinda "Lucy", born February 1, 1888, died February 21, 1971; Callie Vera, born September 10, 1889; Charles Jesse, born March 27, 1892, died August 4, 1892; Ross, born December 8, 1895, died September 3, 1972; and Alma F. Carroll, born August 20, 1901, and died June 11, 1996.

Carter, Andrew Johnson - Andrew Johnson Carter enlisted and mustered into Company D of the 1st Alabama Cavalry, USV on June 1, 1863, at Glendale, Mississippi, for a period of one 1 year, and was discharged June 16, 1864, for reason of expiration of term of service. The Regimental Descriptive

Book showed Andrew to have been 18 years of age, 5'-3" tall, having light complexion, gray eyes, light hair, born Lewis, Tennessee, and listed his occupation as a Factory Hand.

Andrew J. "Andy" Carter was born April 1846 in Lewis County, Tennessee to Gideon G. and Comfort Carter. Andrew married Susan Emaline, last name unknown, about 1866, and they had the following children: Martha E. born 1868; W.M., born 1871; John H., born 1873; Annie L., born May 1875; Edward, born August 1876; Robert Frank, born September 1878; and Lucy M. Carter, born September 1881. The 1870 Giles County, Tennessee Census listed Andrew as a Cloth Bailer, and the 1880 Giles County Census stated he worked in a Cotton Factory. Andrew is buried in the Florence City Cemetery in Florence, Alabama, Section N1-07 with a Union tombstone. Submitted by James H. Carter, Jr.

<u>Carter, James T.</u> - James T. Carter was enrolled in Company D of the 1st Alabama Cavalry, USV by Lieutenant Lukins on November 25, 1864, in Gordon, Georgia for a period of 3 years or the end of the war. He was mustered in on July 13, 1865, in Huntsville, Alabama. However, Remarks at the bottom of a muster roll stated he was mustered into service from date of enlistment. His Muster and Descriptive Roll showed him to be 18 years of age, 5'-8" tall, having a dark complexion, hazel eyes, dark hair, born in Paulding County, Georgia and a farmer by occupation. It showed he was due $300 for bounty. The January and February 1865 Muster Roll listed him as being absent, sick in U.S. General Hospital since January 28, 1865. He was shown as present on the March and April Roll. James T. Carter was mustered out October 20, 1865, at Huntsville, Alabama owing the U.S. Government $3.90 for losing one halter and one Surcingle (A girth that binds a saddle, pack, or blanket to the body of a horse.) His Muster-Out Roll stated he was due $100 for bounty. A Hospital Muster Roll from U.S.A. General Hospital in Savannah, Georgia, Ward #3, stated Carter was admitted February 1, 1865, as a patient. Another Hospital Muster Roll from the same hospital dated March and April 1865, stated he had been a patient there since February 1, 1865. He was returned to duty March 6, 1865. James Carter's name appears on the Returns and states he was enlisted at Louisville, Georgia. In January and February 1865, he was on detached service in North Alabama with Major Shurtleff. James T. Carter was able to sign his name and signed it J.T. Carter on some forms and James T. Carter on others.

<u>Carter, John</u> - John Carter enlisted in Company A of the 1st Alabama Cavalry, USV as a private on January 14, 1864, in Camp Davies, Mississippi for a period of 3 years. He was enrolled by Captain Jude Shurtliff and was mustered in February 5, 1864, in Memphis, Tennessee. The Company Descriptive Roll listed him as being 18 years of age, 5'-10" tall, having a fair complexion, gray eyes, dark hair, born in Spartanburg, South Carolina, and a farmer by occupation. Another form stated he was born in Anderson District, South Carolina. The Company Muster Roll dated February 29, 1864, listed him as being absent, on detached service with Company D by Regimental Order Number 47. Another Muster Roll stated he was sick and sent to the hospital in Memphis, Tennessee on February 28, 1864. He was present for the March and April 1864 Muster Roll. The July and August 1864 Muster Roll stated he had been transferred to Company D by Regimental Order Number 69, and he was absent, on recruiting service by order of Colonel Spencer. John Carter was listed as a Sergeant on the July and August 1864 Muster Roll. He was still on detached service recruiting through December 1864. The January and February 1865 Muster Roll stated John Carter was killed in action October 1, 1864. His name appeared on a Company Muster-Out Roll stated he was killed in action on August 10, 1864. It also stated he was appointed Sergeant on July 1, 1864. The Company Descriptive Book stated John Carter was killed in action on October 1, 1864, near Decatur, Morgan County, Alabama. His name was listed on a Hospital Muster Roll for Overton U.S.A. General Hospital in Memphis, Tennessee for January and February 1864. A Final Statement listed John Carter as having died August 10, 1864. According to the Quarter Master General's Report of burial sites of 1st AL soldiers, John Carter is buried in Grave N-4516 in the Marietta National Cemetery in Marietta, Georgia.

<u>Carter, Samuel L.</u> - Samuel L. Carter enlisted in Company F of the 1st Alabama Cavalry, USV as a private on April 5, 1863, in Corinth, Mississippi, and was mustered in August 13, 1863, in Corinth. He was enrolled by Captain Pierce for a term of 1 year. The Company Descriptive Book recorded him as being 30 years of age, 6'-3" tall, having a dark complexion, dark eyes, dark hair, born in Hamilton

County, Tennessee, and a machinist by occupation. The July and August 1863 Muster Roll recorded him as being absent, on furlough for 30 days. He was recorded as being a farrier for Company F. His name was listed on the Returns as follows: August 1863, absent on furlough; September 1863, on detached duty as farrier; December 1863, on detached duty as farrier; January 1864, on detached duty as farrier; April 1864, mustered out April 5, 1864, at Mooresville, Alabama due to expiration of term of service.

Cartwright, Asbury - Asbury Cartwright enlisted in Company G of the 1st Alabama Cavalry, USV as a private on June 8, 1864, in Chewalla, Tennessee for a period of 1 year at age 24. He was mustered in June 8, 1863, in Corinth, Mississippi, and was reported to have deserted from Chewalla, Tennessee on June 19, 1863.

Caruthers, John - John Caruthers enlisted in Company E of the 1st Alabama Cavalry, USV as a private for a period of 1 year at Chewalla, Tennessee, and was mustered in the same day in Corinth, Mississippi. He was listed as having been taken prisoner of war on January 20, 1863, near Chewalla, Tennessee. A Descriptive List of Deserters listed him as having deserted on March 3, 1863, from Glendale, Mississippi. No further military records relative to this soldier were found.

Case, Thomas L. - Thomas L. Case enlisted in Company C of the 1st Alabama Cavalry, USV on December 10, 1862, in Corinth, Mississippi, for a period of 1 year. He was enrolled by D.R. Adams, and was mustered in December 22, 1862, in Corinth. He was appointed Sergeant on January 1, 1863. The Regimental Descriptive Book showed him to have been 29 years of age, 5'-7" tall, having a dark complexion, dark eyes, dark hair, and was born in Jefferson County, Alabama. On September 1, 1863, he was on daily duty as a horse farrier. He was mustered out December 17, 1863 in Memphis, Tennessee due to expiration of term of service.

Cash, Francis M. - Francis M. Cash enlisted in Company M of the 1st Alabama Cavalry, USV as a private on November 11, 1863, in Camp Davies, Mississippi, for a period of 3 years. He was enrolled by Captain Lomax and was mustered in the same day in Corinth, Mississippi. The Company and Descriptive Book showed Cash to have been 30 years of age, 5'-10" tall, having a fair complexion, hazel eyes, brown hair, born in Abbeville District, South Carolina, and was a farmer by occupation. The November and December 1863 Muster Roll showed him to have been a 2nd Sergeant. The January and February 1864 Muster Roll showed him to be a 3rd Sergeant. The March and April 1864 Muster Roll stated he was a Commissary Sergeant on November 11, 1863. The May 1864 through August 1864 Muster Rolls listed him as being absent, sick in the hospital in Madisonville, Indiana since May 14, 1864, however the September and October 1864 Muster Roll stated he was present. There was a card in his military records that stated he was in Hospital Number 4849, Ward 10, Bed 6, giving his residence as Big Pond in Fayette County, Alabama, and showed his wife as Martha J. Cash, who was a resident of Fayette County, Alabama. He had been admitted July 9, 1864, from Hospital Number 8 in Nashville, Tennessee. His diagnosis was chronic diarrhea, and he was in the Jefferson General Hospital in Jeffersonville, Indiana. He was mustered out October 20, 1865, in Huntsville, Alabama owing the U.S. Government $17.10 for losing 1 saber, 1 saddle blanket, halter and strap, watering bridle, belt and plate. When he was mustered out, he was paid a bounty of $180 and the U.S. Government still owed him another $120 to make up the $300 bounty he was due.

Casteel, James H. - James H. Casteel, also spelled Castile, enlisted and mustered into Company K of the 1st Alabama Cavalry, USV as a private on August 22, 1862, in Huntsville, Alabama. He was enrolled by Lieutenant Millard for a period of 3 years. James was one of the early enlistees who were immediately shipped to Nashville, Tennessee where they were merged with the 1st Middle Tennessee Cavalry, and the 5th Tennessee Cavalry. James was merged in Company E of the 1st Middle Tennessee Cavalry. In January and February 1863, he was shown as being absent, on courier post. The June 30, 1863, to October 31, 1863, Muster Roll stated he was absent, sent to hospital in Corinth, Mississippi on October 12, 1863, where he was back with Company K of the 1st Alabama Cavalry, USV. The Regimental Descriptive Book listed him as having been 20 years of age, 6'-4" tall, having a dark complexion, gray eyes, brown hair, born in Limestone County, Alabama, and was a blacksmith by occupation. On October 10, 1863, James H. Casteel was sent to the hospital at Corinth, Mississippi from an accidental pistol shot on September 15, 1863, in Nashville, Tennessee. In March 1864, he was shown as being on detached duty guarding ordnance in Memphis, Tennessee. The July and August 1864 Muster Roll stated he was appointed Corporal on August 1, 1864. On January 1, 1865, he was promoted to Sergeant. On March 10, 1865, he was wounded in action during the Battle of Monroe's Crossroads near Fayetteville, North Carolina. He was mustered out July 19, 1865, in Nashville, Tennessee. There was a Notation in Casteel's records from the Adjutant General's Office of the War Department in Washington, DC, dated December 9, 1878, which stated: Company Descriptive Book reports him sent to hospital in Corinth, Mississippi on October 12, 1863, from an accidental pistol shot September 15, 1863, at Nashville. Nature and location of wound and circumstances under which wounded was not stated. There was a Prisoner of War Record in his file that stated he was captured at Blountsville, Alabama on April 30, 1863, (the date of May 1, 1863 was written above the other date.) He was confined at Richmond, Virginia on May 9, 1863, paroled at Richmond, Virginia on May 14, 1863, reported to Camp Chase on May 22, 1863, and sent back to his regiment June 9, 1863.

James H. Casteel was born March 31, 1842, and died November 14, 1892. His parents were Henry Casteel and Elizabeth Jane Hicks. He married Teresa Lentz and had at least two children, Mary, born 1866 and Albert, born 1869. He and his father were both Blacksmiths. His father died November 18, 186, at the age of 48. James is buried in the Athens Cemetery in Athens, Limestone County, Alabama. Family information was submitted by Lisa Casteel McLaurin.

Castleberry, David - David Castleberry enlisted and mustered into Company E of the 1st Alabama Cavalry, USV as a private on May 1, 1863, in Glendale, Mississippi for a period of 1 year at the age of 20. His name appears on the Returns which stated: September 1863, on detached duty as nurse in hospital; January and February 1864, on detached service detailed as teamster in Quartermaster Department in Vicksburg, Mississippi since January 25, 1864; March and April 1864, on detached duty as company cook. He was mustered out June 13, 1864, at Decatur, Alabama due to expiration of term of service.

David A. Castleberry was born June 8, 1843, to David and Nancy Castleberry, and died April 4, 1928, in Thaxton, Pontotoc County, Mississippi. He is buried in the Thaxton Cemetery in Thaxton, Pontotoc County, Mississippi. He was married to Matilda Allred, born in 1847, and died October 27, 1917, in Pontotoc County.

Castleberry, Robert B. - Robert B. Castleberry, also shown as Castlebury, enlisted in Company G of the 1st Alabama Cavalry, USV as a private on April 10, 1864, in Decatur, Alabama. He was enrolled by Lieutenant Pease for a period of 3 years. The Company Descriptive Book showed him to have been 32 years of age, 6' tall, having a dark complexion, gray eyes, dark hair, and a farmer by occupation. Robert B. Castleberry died of chronic diarrhea on June 28, 1864, in the Field Hospital in Chattanooga, Hamilton County, Tennessee. The Inventory of Effects showed Robert to have had: 1 hat, 1 uniform jacket, 1 flannel shirt, and 1 pair of boots. Robert B. Castleberry is buried in Grave #E-11506 in the Chattanooga National Cemetery.

Castleberry, Solomon - Solomon C. Castleberry, and his brother, David A., enlisted and mustered into Company E of the 1st Alabama Cavalry, USV as a private on April 1, 1863, in Glendale, Mississippi for a period of 1 year. The January and February 1864 Muster Roll listed him as being absent, on detached service as teamster in Quartermaster Department in Vicksburg, Mississippi since January 25, 1864. He was mustered out March 18, 1864, in Memphis, Tennessee due to expiration of term of service. The Muster-Out Roll stated he was mustered out March 1, 1864.

Solomon Castleberry was born September 24, 1831, in Southern Mississippi, married Nancy Emaline Treadway, who was born May 8, 1824, and died October 1, 1892, in Fayette County, Alabama. Solomon died December 16, 1899, in Fayette County, Alabama and was buried in the Studdard's Crossroads Cemetery in Fayette County, Alabama. See David A. Castleberry, above, for parents of Solomon.

Cathey, John - John Cathey enlisted in Company C of the 1st Alabama Cavalry, USV as a private on January 1, 1864, in Corinth, Mississippi for a period of 3 years. He was enrolled by Captain John Latty, and was mustered in March 10, 1864, in Memphis, Tennessee. The Muster and Descriptive Roll shows him to have been 18 years of age, 5'-8" tall, having a fair complexion, blue eyes, light hair, born in Tishomingo County, Mississippi, and a farmer by occupation. He was appointed Corporal on March 1, 1864. He was mustered out October 20, 1865 in Huntsville, Alabama, owing the U.S. Government $5.26 for losing one Carbine sling, 1 swivel, 1 cap pouch, 1 saber belt, 1 thong and brush wiper, 1 screwdriver, and 1 pair of spurs. He was due a bounty of $300 and was paid $180 and still owed $120 at the time of his discharge. He was shown as being single.

Cothran, Daniel R. - Daniel R. Cothran, also listed as Caughorn and Caughren, enlisted in Company E of the 1st Alabama Cavalry, USV as a private on January 1, 1863, in Chewalla, Tennessee, and was mustered in the same day in Corinth, Mississippi. The Muster and Descriptive Roll recorded him as being 18 years of age, 5'-5" tall, having a fair complexion, blue eyes, light hair, born in Pontotoc County, Mississippi, and a farmer by occupation. The Company Descriptive Book recorded him as being 17 years of age, 5'-5" tall, having fair complexion, blue eyes, light hair, born in Lauderdale County, Alabama, and a farmer by occupation. He served as a Bugler. He was discharged February 5, 1864, due to expiration of term of service. He reenlisted January 1, 1864, in Camp Davies, Mississippi. He was enrolled by Captain Lomax and mustered in February 5, 1864, in Memphis, Tennessee as a Bugler. On February 29, 1864, he was recorded as being absent, on detached service in Company M by Regimental Order #47, reenlisted and never received any bounty. In December 1864, he was on duty in Company M as a Regimental Bugler. He was mustered out October 20, 1865, in Huntsville, Alabama. The Company Muster-Out Roll showed him to have been 17 years of age. He mustered out owing the U.S. Government $11.50 for losing 1 Saddle Blanket, cap pouch and pick, saber belt and plate, 1 curry comb, 1 brush, 2 spurs and straps, 1 halter and strap, 1 thong, and brush wiper, 1 pistol and 1 screwdriver. He was paid a bounty of $180, and shown as being due a bounty of $120, to make up for the $30 bounty due him.

Daniel R. Cothran was born December 7, 1847, married Margaret M., last name unknown, and died January 28, 1927. He is buried in the Moore School House Cemetery west of Selmer, Tennessee.

Cayne, Thomas C. - Thomas C. Cayne enlisted in Company F and was recorded as being sick in the hospital in Memphis, Tennessee and was wounded October 26, 1863, which would have been during the Battle of Vincent's Crossroads in Bay Springs, Mississippi. No further information relative to this soldier was found.*

Chafin, John H. - John H. Chafin, brother of William M. Chafin, below, enlisted in Company B of the 1st Alabama Cavalry, USV on January 6, 1863, at Glendale, Mississippi for a period of one year, and was mustered in January 22, 1863. He was appointed Sergeant the day he was mustered in. The July and August 1863, Muster Roll stated he was a Duty Sergeant. John H. Chafin's name, sometimes spelled Chaffin, appeared on the Returns stated he was absent without leave since April 18, 1863. He was mustered out January 22, 1864, at Memphis, Tennessee at age 28. John H. and William M. Chaffin had a sister, Martha Rachael, whose husband, William J. Baker, also enlisted in the 1st Alabama Cavalry, USV in Glendale, Mississippi.

John H. Chafin married Sarah J. Baker on November 6, 1856, in Cobb County, Georgia and they had the following children: Mary R., born January 14, 1857; James William, born January 21, 1859, died July 24, 1923; and Nancy E. Chafin, born December 10, 1862. John and his family moved to Centralia County, Illinois where he died January 27, 1864, of pneumonia.

Chafin, William Marion - William Marion Chafin, brother of John H. Chafin, above, enlisted in Company B of the 1st Alabama Cavalry, USV on January 6, 1863, at Glendale, Mississippi for a period of one year. They were sons of William Chafin and Sarah Jones, who were married August 4, 1834, in Newton County, Georgia. William was enrolled by P.A. Sternberg. He died June 28, 1863, in the Regimental Hospital. The Regimental Descriptive Book showed William to have been 22 years of age, 5'-5" tall, having a dark complexion, blue eyes, light hair, born in Pickens County, Alabama, and stated he died of dysentery on June 23, 1863. His name appeared on the Returns for June 1863, stating William died in the Regimental Hospital in Glendale, Mississippi on June 28, 1863. The Company Muster-Out Roll stated William died May 26, 1863, in Glendale, Mississippi. The Records of Discontinued Commands stated William H. Chafin died of dysentery June 28, 1863, company stationed at Glendale, Mississippi on that date. The Casualty Sheet also shows William as having died June 28, 1863. (Many of these soldiers who died at Glendale, Mississippi were buried in the Corinth, National Cemetery in Corinth, Mississippi. It is possible that William Marion Chafin was also buried there.)

Chalmers, Andrew J. - Andrew J. Chalmers was a Veterinary Surgeon and was temporarily attached from 9th Illinois Cavalry, which is where his cards are filed.

Chambers, Bailey G. - Bailey G. Chambers, also listed as Baley Y. Chambers, enlisted and mustered into Company B of the 1st Alabama Cavalry, USV on September 1, 1864, in Rome, Georgia for a period of 3 years. He was enrolled by Captain West. The Muster and Descriptive Roll recorded him as being 18 years of age, 5'-5" tall, having a dark complexion, gray eyes, dark hair, born in Edgefield District, South Carolina, and a farmer by occupation. He was mustered out October 20, 1865, in Huntsville, Alabama. His Muster-Out Roll stated he was due a bounty of $100. It also stated he owed the US Government $9.90 for losing some equipment.

Elisha Chambers – See Elisha Chambles.

Chambless, Elisha - Elisha Chambless, also spelled Chambles, enlisted in Company A of the 1st Alabama Cavalry, USV as a private on September 8, 1862, in Iuka, Mississippi for a period of 1 year, and was mustered in October 1, 1862, in Corinth, Mississippi. He was shown as having deserted from Glendale, Mississippi on March 31, 1863, but returned from desertion on August 16, 1863, in Glendale. He was discharged September 16, 1863, due to expiration of term of service. He re-enlisted February 1, 1864, in Memphis, Tennessee for a period of 3 years, and was mustered in February 26, 1864, in Memphis. The Muster and Descriptive Roll listed him as having been 18 years of age, 5'-5" tall, having a fair complexion, blue eyes, light hair, born in Franklin County, Alabama, and a farmer by occupation. In February, June and July 1864, he was on daily duty as company cook. He was mustered out October 20, 1865, in Huntsville, Alabama, owing the U.S. Government $2.15, for losing one saber belt complete. He was due a bounty of $300 and was paid $180 and the Muster-Out Roll stated he was due $120.

Elisha Chambless was born March 11, 1845, in Franklin County, Alabama to James Madison Chambless and his wife, Cynthia M. Peterson. He married Martha Frances McClelland on September 6, 1865, in Winston County, Alabama. He then married Sarah Ann Linton on October 7, 1869. Elisha died March 21, 1906, in Wagoner, Wagner County, Oklahoma. In 1900, Elisha and wife Ellen E. were living in the Creek Nation, Indian Territory, with children Albert J.; Pearl A. Chambless, and a daughter, Ada E. Haley, and her 3 month old daughter, Ruth Haley.

Chambless, Isaac J. - Isaac J. Chambless and his brother, Elisha, above, enlisted in Company A of the 1st Alabama Cavalry, USV as a private. Isaac enlisted on October 29, 1862, in Corinth, Mississippi for a period of 1 year, and was mustered in December 31, 1862, in Corinth. He was reported to have deserted March 31, 1863, and then reported as having been arrested, tried, and returned to duty on August 16, 1863, in Glendale, Mississippi, with loss of pay for 3 months. He was discharged November 28, 1863, in Memphis, Tennessee.

Isaac was born April 16, 1811, in Powderly Texas and married Sarah Ann Fredericks who was born August 24, 1845, and died July 11, 1911. Isaac died November 3, 1913. They are buried in Riverside Cemetery, McLoud, Oklahoma. Family information submitted my Linda Worley.

Chambless, James Madison - James Madison Chambless, also listed as Chambles, enlisted in Company A of the 1st Alabama Cavalry, USV on October 29, 1862, in Corinth, Mississippi at age 46. He was reported to have deserted March 31, 1863. His name appears on the returns as follows: March and April 1863, absent without leave since March 25, 1863; May 1863, deserted May 1, 1863, from

Glendale, Mississippi. There was one Prisoner of War Record in his files which only stated there was no record subsequent to March 30, 1863.

According to Lindy Worley, this James M. Chambless was the father of Isaac and Elisha Chambless. He was married to Cynthia M. Peterson, and died in 1863, in Tuscumbia, Colbert County, Alabama. There were only records for one James M. Chambless.

Chambless, James M. - James M. Chambless enlisted in Company H of the 1st Alabama Cavalry, USV on December 20, 1864, in Stevenson, Alabama, and was mustered in the same day in Nashville, Tennessee. His enlistment was credited to Ripley, Chautauqua County, New York The Muster and Descriptive Roll listed him as having been 18 years of age, 5'-8" tall, having a dark complexion, gray eyes, black hair, born in Calhoun County, Alabama, and a farmer by occupation. He was appointed corporal on April 1, 1865, and was mustered out October 20, 1865, in Huntsville, Alabama. James was able to sign his name on his enlistment forms.

Chandler, Erasmus D. - Erasmus D. Chandler enlisted in Company B of the 7th Illinois Cavalry, US on September 5, 1861, in Lightsville, Illinois, and was mustered in October 5, 1861, in Springfield, Illinois. He was promoted to Captain when he was detached to the 1st Alabama Cavalry, USV on January 28, 1863, in Corinth, Mississippi, for a period of 1 year and had to use his own horse. He was appointed by order of General Dodge. He was killed in action on October 26, 1863, which would have been during the Battle of Vincent's Crossroads near Bay Springs, Mississippi. Erasmus D. Chandler was buried in Grave #C-9 in the Corinth National Cemetery.

Chaney, Alexander - Alexander Chaney enlisted on Company D of the 1st Alabama Cavalry, USV as a private on February 15, 1863, in Glendale, Mississippi for a period of 1 year, and was mustered in March 13, 1863, in Corinth, Mississippi. He was transferred to Captain in Company E of the 1st Alabama Cavalry, USV. The Company Muster Roll dated July and August 1863, stated his pay had been stopped for $46.63 because of losing a saddle, 1 Austrian rifle and accoutrements, however, a line was drawn through it stating it was settled September 1, 1863. Chaney was reported to have deserted September 6, 1863, from Glendale, Mississippi. His name appeared on the Returns and stated the following: March 1863, supposed to have joined another company March 12; May 1863, absent without leave, to be dropped as deserter after date; June 1863, deserted May 8, 1863, from Glendale, Mississippi; "Gain" from desertion, May 4, 1863 in Glendale.

Chaney, Artemus - Artemus Chaney enlisted in Company D of the 1st Alabama Cavalry, USV as a private on February 15, 1863, in Glendale, Mississippi for a period of 1 year, and was mustered in March 13, 1863, in Corinth, Mississippi, and was transferred to Company E. His name appeared on the Returns and stated the following: March 1863, supposed to have joined another company March 18; May 1863, absent without leave to be dropped as a deserter after date; June 1863, deserted May 8, 1863, at Glendale, gained from desertion at Glendale; December 1863, on detached service at Refugee Camp in Corinth, Mississippi December 15, 1863; January and February 1864, on detached service at Refugee Camp in Memphis, Tennessee December 15, 1863; March 1864, term of service expired March 1, 1864, and mustered out at age 36. The May and June 1863 Muster Roll stated he was absent with leave. He was reported to have deserted May 8, 1863, from Glendale, Mississippi, but returned in July and was on duty at the Refugee Camp in Corinth, Mississippi on December 28, 1863. the November and December 1863 Muster Roll stated he was absent, on duty in Refugee Camp at Corinth, Mississippi since December 28, 1863. In January and February 1864, he was still detailed at the Refugee Camp in Corinth. He was mustered out March 3, 1864, in Memphis, Tennessee due to expiration of term of service.

Chaney, John - John Chaney enlisted in Company M of the 1st Alabama Cavalry, USV as a private on November 20, 1863, in Camp Davies, Mississippi for a period of 1 year. He was enrolled by Captain Lomax and mustered in November 29, 1863, in Corinth, Mississippi. Another muster roll stated he enlisted for a term of 3 years. The March and April 1864 Muster Roll recorded him as being absent, sick in USA General Hospital #1 in Nashville, Tennessee. The May through August 1864 Muster

Rolls recorded him as being absent, sick in the hospital in Decatur, Alabama. However, the July and August 1864 USA General Hospital #1 Muster Roll stated he had been transferred to Totten USA General Hospital in Louisville, Kentucky August 2, 1864. The July and August 1864 Muster Roll for Totten USA Hospital recorded him to be present and sent to Barracks #1. His name was listed on the Returns which recorded the following: December 1863 to April 1864, on detached duty as a hospital nurse; August 1864, on detail in hospital in Decatur, Alabama; October 1864, on duty as company cook. A Totten General Hospital #2193 record, recorded him as 42 years of age, single, nativity was Alabama, living in Illinois, diagnosis was rheumatism, and no nearest relative that they knew of. He was admitted to the hospital August 3, 1864, from Nashville and returned to duty September 6, 1864. He was mustered out October 20, 1865, in Huntsville, Alabama owing the U.S. Government $14.56 for losing 1 carbine swing and swivel, 1 carbine cartridge box, 1 cap pouch and pick, 1 saber belt and plate, 1 halter and strap, 2 spurs and straps, 1 carbine screwdriver, and 1 thong and brush wiper. He was paid a bounty of $180 and shown as being owed $120 to make up the $300 bounty he was due.

Chapman, Joseph A. - Joseph A. Chapman enrolled in Company E of the 1st Alabama Cavalry, USV on March 1, 1863, at Glendale, Mississippi for one year as a Private at age 36. On the Company Muster Roll for May and June 1863, he was shown as absent with leave. The July and August 1863 Muster Roll stated he was present, but had been absent for two months and pay allowance was stopped for that time. Joseph was mustered out March 3, 1864, due to expiration of term of service at Memphis, Tennessee. He appears on Returns as follows: April -1863, enlisted at Glendale April 1; June 1863, absent, gone with refugees. (In June 1863, the Confederate Home Guard was murdering Unionists in northwest Alabama, burning their homes, barns, crops, etc. and making it too dangerous for them to remain at home unprotected. The U.S. On June 20, 1863, the Union Army escorted approximately 300 Unionists to Illinois for their safety, and this is possibly where Joseph A. Chapman had gone to escort the refugees; December – 1863, Absent, sick in regimental hospital; January – 1864, Absent, nurse in General Hospital in Memphis, Tennessee; March – 1864, Term of Service expired, Memphis, Tennessee, March 1.

After the war, Joseph A. Chapman bought a 40 acre farm in Centralia, Illinois. He was born January 18, 1833, in Georgia and died July 14, 1887, in Dix, Jefferson County, Illinois. He is buried in the Ebenezer Cemetery, eight miles north of Mt. Vernon, Illinois. He married first, Malinda Bennett December 1850, and had the following children: Frances Elizabeth, born October 10, 1853; Levinia Ann Adaline, born April 19, 1856, died January 23, 1859; Martha, born August 8, 1859, died November 12, 1865; William Allen, born March 3, 1862, died August 16, 1863; and Wanda Ann Chapman, born September 15, 1863, died October 20, 1863. After the death of Malinda, on January 5, 1864, Joseph married Celia Ann Gossett on November 5, 1864 in Centralia, Marion County, Illinois. Celia had been Malinda's nurse during her illness for several years. Children of Joseph and Celia were: James Lafayette, born February 16, 1861, died December 30, 1938; John Allen, born September 23, 1865; Henry Franklin, born March 9, 1868, died April 5, 1943; Nancy Ann, born December 12, 1871, died January 19, 1956; Emma L., born April 14, 1876, died 1953; Cora L., born April 11, 1880, died 1948; and Charles W. Chapman, born August 5, 1885, and died April 19, 1950. (Family information submitted by Michael Sloat)

Michael R. Sloat states the Methodist Church in Dix, Jefferson County, Illinois has a foundation that Joseph built as a mason, and he did a lot of other brick work for the town of Dix.

The James Edward Chastain Family And the Civil War

During the Civil War, many families were split, with members fighting on both sides. Chastains were no exception. Including alternate spellings and misspellings (Chastain, Chastaine, Chasteen, Chasteene, Chastian, Chastine, Chesteen, and Chestine), military rosters from the war list 128 Chastains in the Union Army and 355 in the Confederate Army. Most, if not all, were descendants of French Huguenot immigrant Pierre Chastain, who arrived in 1700.

Edward Chastain was born in Haywood County, North Carolina on May 10, 1805. Edward's descent from immigrant Dr. Pierre Chastain is: 1. Pierre 2. Peter, Jr., 3. Rev. John 4. Elijah, 5. James

Edward Chastain. Edward married Sarah Shelton in Haywood County, North Carolina on October 7, 1825. Sarah was born in Haywood County on June 10, 1810. Soon after, they moved to north Georgia and had all their children there. In 1859 Edward moved his family to Thorn Hill, Marion County, Alabama, leaving some of his adult children in Georgia. Certainly Edward's younger, unmarried children went to Alabama with him (James, David, Sarah, and "Cobb"), but it appears some of his married children accompanied him as well, or moved into the area later.

Why did Edward move to Alabama? Don Umphrey wrote a book about his ancestor, John R. Phillips, who lived near Edward Chastain in Alabama (Umphrey, Don, *Southerners in Blue*, Quarry Press, 2002). He states on page 20: "One day in the spring of 1858, he was handed a tattered notice that told of land for sale at 12-1/2 cents per acre in Winston county (sic), Alabama. It was available through the Graduation Land Act, a federal program designed to encourage pioneers to move to undeveloped parts of the country. Prices of these lands kept decreasing until someone finally purchased them.

Phillips arrived in the fall of 1858. The same opportunity may have drawn Edward the next year. However, he may not have been the first in the family to respond to the offer of cheap land. His daughter, Theresa Emmaline Chastain, gave birth to Sarah Ann Osborne in Marion County Alabama on January 22, 1858. This was before John Phillips even heard about the program."

When the Civil War began, Edward supported the Union instead of the Confederacy. This was a dangerous position anywhere in the South, and even though Northwest Alabama was a stronghold of Union sympathy some of Edward's neighbors paid dearly for supporting the Union. It is well known that there were many Union sympathizers in the South. Every state except South Carolina had at least one regiment in the Union forces. It is also known that there were pockets of strong Union support such as Northwest Alabama, East Tennessee, and Western Virginia. Because of its proximity to Union states, Western Virginia was able to "secede" from Virginia and become the new state of West Virginia, but Northwest Alabama and East Tennessee were surrounded by the Confederacy. There was talk of creating a Union state by combining these two districts, but it never happened.

Chastains have known, at least as far back as 1981 when Mary Avilla Farnsworth-Milligan released her work, *Chastain Kith and Kin*, that Edward's family in Alabama was pro-Union, but Don Umphrey's 2002 work, *Southerners in Blue* paints a picture of Edward that is more than just sympathetic to the Union. It presents Edward as pro-active in supporting those who hid out to avoid being drafted into the Confederate Army. He also cooperated in recruitment efforts for the Union Army. His home was a regular stop on the "underground railroad" that facilitated the hiding and movement of Alabama men on their way to join Union forces. At least once he paid a scout to lead a group of recruits safely to the Union camp, and he helped feed and support the families of local men who joined Union forces. When Edward had the opportunity, he traveled 100 miles to a Union facility in Glendale, Mississippi, where he took an oath of loyalty to the United States.

On May 17, 1867, two years after the war ended, Edward was killed by a horse. He is buried at the Phillips family cemetery about a mile from the Thornhill Church of Christ in Thornhill, Marion County, Alabama. His wife, Sarah died July 17, 1891, and is buried in the same cemetery.

The Naming of Sons - A clue to Edward's predilection toward the Union may be found in the names he chose for his sons. His youngest, William Howell, was nicknamed Cobb. Evidently, his namesake was the Georgia politician, William Howell Cobb. William Howell Cobb was Speaker of the House in the United States Congress, Governor of Georgia, and Secretary of the Treasury under President Buchanan. He was a leading Unionist in the South. William Howell Chastain's birth in 1850 was before William Howell Cobb's Governorship and Cabinet position, so Cobb must have been a popular congressman (1843-1851) even before his rise in office. He became Speaker of the House on December 22, 1849, just five months before William Howell Chastain was born. However, though he was a Unionist, once South Carolina seceded after the 1860 election Secretary Cobb resigned his cabinet post and went home to Georgia to urge secession. But parents don't name their children based on what the namesakes will do in the future!

A second son was James K. Polk Chastain. This is a more familiar name. James K. Polk was President of the United States from 1845-1849. He was a Jacksonian throughout his political career, so much so that he was called "Young Hickory", a reflection of Andrew Jackson being "Old Hickory." Jacksonians were Unionist through and through. President Jackson stated, "The Federal Union--it must be preserved," and he threatened South Carolina with military force when they hinted at independence. However, James K. Polk Chastain was born in 1839 before Polk was president. At that time he had just completed five years as Speaker of the House (1835-1839).

A third son was Martin Shelton. Shelton was the maiden name of Martin's mother, so the two names appear not to belong to a single namesake. Martin was a fairly common name, but not in the Chastain family. A search of known Chastains shows that there were 5 Martin Chastains before 1840, and they were all of family lines distant from Edward's. In fact one of those was a Martin Van Buren Chastain, born in 1836, named for Martin Van Buren, President from 1837 to 1841. Martin Shelton Chastain was likely named for the same person, however, he was born in 1827 ten years before Van Buren was President. From 1821-1829 Van Buren was a U.S. Senator from New York. A Jacksonian, he emerged as the principal northern leader for Andrew Jackson. Jackson made him Secretary of State and later chose him as Vice-President. Van Buren succeeded Jackson as President.

The naming of his sons in such a way reinforces the likelihood that Edward was a Jacksonian, and pro-Union, prior to his moving to Alabama. Edward had four sons, at least three of whom were in the fight. Edward's youngest son, William Howell "Cobb" Chastain, was just over 10 1/2 years old when Alabama seceded from the Union, so he was too young to fight in the army. However, by the time of Lee's surrender on April 9, 1865, Cobb was almost 15. There is no tradition or documentation in the Chastain family that Cobb was in the military, but a W. H. Chastine is listed in the Confederate 22nd Regiment, Alabama Infantry. It is possible that Cobb was drafted in the last years or months of the war.

Chastain, David D. - James K. Polk's younger brother, David D. Chastain, was born August 11, 1841, in Union County, Georgia and was enlisted in Company A of the 1st Alabama (Union) on January 12, 1864, at Camp Davies, Mississippi by Lieutenant Hinds for a period of 3 years. He mustered in February 5, 1864, in Memphis, Tennessee. By this time, his brother James K. Polk Chastain had been a prisoner of war for almost three months. David is listed in the 1st Alabama records as David D. Chestaine. It is interesting that the person filling out the volunteer enrollment form spelled the name *Chesteine*, but later on the form the name is spelled *Chestain*. David's Company Muster-In and Descriptive Roll listed him as being 18 years of age, 5'-6" tall, having a fair complexion, black eyes, black hair, born in Union County, Georgia, and a farmer by occupation. The 1st Alabama was an important component of Sherman's march through Atlanta, Savannah, and the Carolinas, serving as scouts in the march to Atlanta and as Sherman's personal escort in the march to Savannah.

At his website regarding the 1st Alabama Cavalry, Richard Nelson Current says: From April to September 1864 the First Alabama then took part in William T. Sherman's campaign for Atlanta, acting as scouts (whose value Sherman himself acknowledged) and as rear guards for the supply line. And from September to December the Alabamians joined in the march from Atlanta to the sea... During January - March 1865 Spencer led the Third Cavalry Brigade as Sherman's army moved from Savannah up though the Carolinas...After advancing into North Carolina, Spencer's brigade fought off another Confederate attack in what developed into the battle of Monroe's Cross Roads. One morning at reveille his men awoke to find the enemy charging their camp from opposite directions - under the lead of two of the most famous rebel cavalry commanders, Wade Hampton and Joseph Wheeler. The rebels overran almost the entire camp before Spencer's men, "By desperate fighting behind trees," succeeded in driving them off. For two and a half hours the Federals stood up against repeated charges, until finally "the enemy retreated in confusion," leaving behind more than a hundred of their men killed, a larger number wounded, and a few dozen captured. "Our loss... was 18 killed, 70 wounded, and 105 missing."

Among the missing at the battle of Monroe's Crossroads, North Carolina on March 10, 1865, was David Chastain who became a prisoner of war in that battle. From that point, his records have conflicts. The March and April 1865 Muster roll showed him to be absent, a prisoner of war since March 10, 1865. However, he was shown as present in May and June 1865. His Individual Muster-Out Roll dated June 12, 1865, from Camp Chase, Ohio, stated he was paid a bounty of $100 and he was due three months extra pay by order of the Secretary of War, dated Washington, May 31, 1865. He was shown as absent, again, in July and August 1865, captured March 10, 1865, paroled and sent to Camp Chase, Ohio, and not heard from since. The Company Muster-Out Roll dated October 20, 1865, stated that David was a prisoner of war since March 10, 1865, captured near Fayetteville, North Carolina and not mustered out. It stated he was owed $300.00 for bounty. A Notation from the Adjutant General's Office of the War Department in Washington, D.C. dated June 19, 1883, stated David D. Chastain mustered out at Camp Chase, Ohio June 12, 1865, in accordance with G.O. #77 of 1865 A.G.O. A Muster Roll of a Detachment of Paroled prisoners at Camp Chase, Ohio stated David was captured March 10, 1865, at Solomon's Grove, North Carolina. On coming back to his Regiment, David was no longer fit for duty. Captured March 10, 1865, he was mustered out on June 12, 1865 and returned to his home in Marion County, Alabama, where he died February 22, 1866, of complications from military service. In 1883, Jerome J. Hinds, former Captain of Company A, 1st Regiment Cavalry, in a sworn deposition said that he was well acquainted with David D. Chasteen (sic) who was in active service from his enlistment to the date of his capture. He indicated that up to the date of his capture David was a healthy able bodied man and ever ready soldier and the severe treatment received by him while in the hands of the enemy completely destroyed his health rendering him totally unfit for military duty. This was corroborated by David's mother in a sworn statement on May 12th, 1886: My son David D. was a strong healthy boy when he enlisted January 12, 1864. When David came home from the Army in June 1865 he had the chills and diarrhea and he had them both all the time. He was a skeleton, he never did any work, was not able, would be able to be about the day he had no chill and then was unable he died. We thought from Congestive chills, he had one in the morning and one at night the day he died. We never had no physician to treat him. There was no doctor to be had...Everything was torn up so and we just doctored him at home the best we could. His symptoms were continuously from discharge to death varying some chills, high fever following, running off at bowels, and cold sweats at times. The fever would make him almost deranged. He had no appetite when the fever was off, he would be able to be up move around, he did not have the color of blood in his lips...He said when they captured him in North Carolina they stripped his boots and clothes off to his shirt tail and marched him and put him in prison somewhere and the exposure caused his sickness. I know he never was sick until he went to the army and he came home sick.

David D. Chastain was born August 11, 1841, in Union County, Georgia, and died February 22, 1866, in Marion County, Alabama, and is buried in the Phillips Family Cemetery near Thorn Hill in Marion County, Alabama. Jan Curtis, a John R. Phillips descendent-in-law, shared with us additional information on the Phillips Cemetery. There are four Chastains buried in the Phillips family cemetery about a mile away from the Thornhill Church of Christ Cemetery: Edward Chastain, born May 10, 1806, died May 17, 1867; David D. Chastain Company A, 1st Alabama Cavalry (no dates given); Sarah Chastain, wife of Edward, born June 11, 1810, died July 17, 1891; and Chastain Infant, William Thomas, son of William & M.H., born September 7, 1899, died December 9, 1899.

Chastain, James Knox Polk was born June 3, 1839, in Union County, Georgia. On May 10, 1860, he married Martha Emeline Dykes. Their address was Haleyville, Marion County, Alabama. Researcher Glenda McWhirter Todd states that Thomas L. Dykes, the brother of Martha Emaline, was also in the 1st Alabama Cavalry and lost his life on October 7, 1864, in Charleston, South Carolina. *Pierre Chastain and His Descendants*, contains an error; Volume 2, page 139, states that James K. Polk Chastain "was a Confederate soldier in Company K. 1st Alabama Cavalry." The information is correct except that the 1st Alabama Cavalry was Union, not Confederate.

James enlisted and was mustered into the 1st Alabama (Union) July 24, 1862, in Huntsville, Alabama. He was enrolled by Captain Bankhead for a period of 3 years. He was promoted to sergeant less than three months later. A naming exercise with James K. Polk Chastain produces similar results to that of his father, demonstrating that his pro-Union activity arose from personal conviction rather than his simply following his father and friends. In the years just after the war, he gave his sons distinctive names. John Sheridan Chastain was likely named for General Philip Henry Sheridan, a high ranking General of the Union army during the war. For whom might Ulysses G. Chastain have been named? Ulysses Grant was President (Republican) when Ulysses Chastain was born. Edward Colfax Chastain was likely named for Schuyler Colfax, who was Republican Vice-President under Ulysses Grant when Edward Colfax Chastain was born. He had been Speaker of the House from 1863-1869. Sheridan, Ulysses, and Colfax are not usual names in the Chastain family.

Glenda Todd has done a great service in compiling information on James K. Polk Chastain from military records (as she has done for many other soldiers of the 1st Alabama). The following information relies heavily on her research.

James K. Polk Chastain was one of the early volunteers enlisted July 24, 1862. in Huntsville, Alabama by Captain Bankhead for a period of three years. They were shipped immediately to Nashville, Tennessee and merged with the 1st Middle Tennessee Cavalry which later became the 5th Tennessee Cavalry. James was first with of the 5th Tennessee Cavalry. The Company Descriptive Book showed him to be 21 years of age, 5'-6½" tall, having light complexion, dark gray eyes and dark brown hair, born in Union County, Georgia, and a farmer by occupation. James was not only in the in the battle of Neely's Bend on the Cumberland River in Tennessee on November 5, 1862, and Stone's River in Murfreesboro, Tennessee from December 31, 1862, through January 2, 1863, but he was part of the unsuccessful Streight's Raid through Alabama and North Georgia where he fought in the battle of Rome, Georgia May 3, 1863, and was part of Streight's surrender. And he fought in the Battle of Vincent's Crossroads near Red Bay, Alabama on October 26, 1863. The Muster Roll dated October 31, 1862, states that James was a Sergeant in Company E of the 1st Regiment of the Tennessee Cavalry. He had been appointed Sergeant October 1, 1862. In November 1862, he was listed as being absent, prisoner of war November 5, 1862, at Nashville, Tennessee. This would have been during the Skirmish of Neely's Bend. The November and December 1862 Muster Roll states he was a 1st Sergeant in the 1st Regiment Tennessee Cavalry and was a paroled prisoner of war. James appeared on the returns as having been captured in action near Nashville, and his arms and accoutrements were lost but returned on the 15th under parole. He was captured at Rome, Georgia May 3, 1863, confined at Richmond, Virginia May 9, 1863, paroled at City Point, Virginia May 15, 1863, and reported at Camp Parole, Maryland on May 18, 1863.

The June 30, 1863, to October 31, 1863, Muster Roll stated James was absent, missing in action at the Battle of Vincent's Crossroads (the town is now called Red Bay) October 26, 1863. A POW record shows he was paroled more than a year later in Savannah on November 20, 1864. as Sherman's army approached the city. He did not rejoin the 1st Alabama at this time. He is next found on a Hospital Muster Roll of Division No. 1 U.S.A. General Hospital at Annapolis, Maryland on December 4, 1864, by which time Sherman had not yet taken Savannah. The name James P. Chastain appear on the Annapolis, Maryland hospital records in November and December 1864, and his name appears again on the same hospital roll for January and February 1865, stating also that he was transferred to Wilmington, Delaware on February 26, 1865.

The Detachment Muster Roll for paroled prisoners dated December 24, 1864. at Annapolis, Maryland, states that he had been paid for September and October 1864. He was charged $2.50 for transportation by the Provost Marshall. He was returned to duty February 4, 1865. The May and June 1865 Muster Roll stated that he was present with Company K of the 1st Alabama Cavalry, USV and had been paid in Annapolis, Maryland by Major Mixon. James K. P. Chastain was mustered out July 19, 1865, at Nashville, Tennessee and was due $35.23 by the government, along with $100 for bounty. His Muster-Out Roll states he was Corporal until October 1, 1862, when he was appointed Sergeant by Colonel Stokes.

A few years after the war, James K. Polk Chastain and his wife Emeline moved from Marion County, Alabama to Missouri. He married a second wife, Mary Bets "Mollie" Skeets. Apparently he was married to both wives at the same time. James K. Polk Chastain died May 15, 1901, in Ponce deLeon, Stone County, Missouri. He was 61 years old. He is buried in the Ponce de Leon Cemetery in Christian County, Missouri.

Chastain, Martin Sheldon in the Confederacy - Meanwhile, Edward's older son, Martin Shelton Chastain, who had remained in Georgia, served in Georgia's 52nd Regiment Volunteer Infantry, Company E of the Confederate Army. The Georgia 52nd served in the west, defending Vicksburg, Mississippi for example, but the 52nd was moved east to confront Sherman's army in the Atlanta campaign, along with many other units. The 52nd was in North Georgia from May to September, 1864 and participated in a number of battles: Rocky Face Ridge, Resaca, New Hope Church, Dallas, Kennesaw Mountain, Peach Tree Creek, Atlanta, Ezra Church, the Atlanta Siege (July-Sept 1864), and Jonesboro. It is possible that David and Martin unknowingly fired on each other, but we really do not know whether the Georgia 52nd ever engaged the 1st Alabama.

Martin contracted measles, apparently during the Atlanta campaign and traveled home while he was still recovering. Shortly after he arrived, he died at his uncle's home in Acworth, Cobb County, Georgia on August 4, 1864 (*Pierre Chastain and His Descendants*, volume 2, page 136). Disease was often rampant in military camps on both sides and resulted in a high number of deaths. Since the Georgia 52nd was in North Georgia, perhaps Martin's journey home was a short one.

(See Hiram Lambert and John Sterling Cantrell for information on Edward's sons-in-law.) Hiram Lambert, husband of Sarah Chastain, served in the 1st Alabama. He and David Chastain joined at the same time. However, he was not Edward's son-in-law at that time. Hiram and Sarah were married October 7, 1867, after the war was over and after the death of both David and Edward. Six months after he joined the military, Hiram was in the hospital with typhoid fever. He was discharged June 28, 1865.

Nancy Ann married John Sterling Cantrell, and they had a son born in Georgia in 1860, but they must have moved to Alabama within the next couple years, and Nancy is buried in Marion County. *Pierre Chastain and His Descendants*, volume 2, page 137, shows that Cantrell died in the Civil war, but does not state how, nor whether he served in either army. The records of the 1st Alabama list a John S. Cantrell. He became a prisoner of war on January 18, 1864, and was killed by Confederates while a prisoner of war June 18, 1864, in Franklin County, Alabama, not far from his home. Researcher Glenda Todd identifies John S. Cantrell as our John Sterling Cantrell and says further that John Sterling's brother, Dennis Cody Cantrell, also served in the 1st Alabama, Union. In a sworn document, this Dennis Cody Cantrell says about his brother, "I had one brother, John S. Cantrell in the 1st Alabama Regiment Cavalry. He entered service at Camp Davis (Davies), Mississippi in the year 1863 in Company D. He was captured by Stokely Robert's Rebel forces and turned over to Moreland's Battalion and was by them murdered."

Cousins and Other Relatives

Many families in the South had members in both the Union and the Confederate Armies. Edward Chastain had two sons in the Union Army and one in the Confederate. Edward's own brother, Renny Marion Chastain, served in the Confederate Army, and his first cousin, Elijah Webb Chastain, a former US Congressman, was a Confederate Colonel. Edward's sons had at least six first cousins in the war, and there were probably many more as they had 20 sets of aunts and uncles on the Chastain side alone. We know of only one first cousin who served in the Union Army--Nathan P. Chastain (Missouri Cavalry). Family information submitted by Tim Chastain.

Cheak, George M. - George M. Cheak enlisted in Company C of the 1st Alabama Cavalry, USV as a private on January 1, 1864, in Corinth, Mississippi for a period of 3 years. He was enrolled by Captain John Latty and was mustered in March 10, 1864, in Memphis, Tennessee. The Muster and Descriptive Roll recorded him as being 18 years of age, 5'-9" tall, having a fair complexion, gray eyes, light hair, born in Tishomingo County, Mississippi, a farmer by occupation and he was single. He was appointed sergeant on March 1, 1864. He was on duty from September 1864 through June 1865 as Regimental Forage Master in the Quartermaster Department, and was mustered out October 20, 1865, in Huntsville, Alabama owing the U.S. Government $5.41 for losing one carbine sling, 1 cap pouch, 1 saber belt, 1 thong and wiper, 1 screwdriver, 1 pair of spurs and 1 swivel. He had previously lost a Remington revolver but it did not say if it was recovered.

Cheek, Edmund/Elijah S. - The records for Edmund Cheek and Elijah S. Cheek were mixed in together, but there was a note on a muster roll which stated: Elijah Cheek filed with Edmund S. Cheek, name Elijah not born on any other roll. Elijah S. Cheek, enlisted in Company E of the 1st Alabama Cavalry, USV as a private on March 1, 1863, in Corinth, Mississippi. Edmund S. Cheek's description stated he was 23 years of age, 5'10" tall, having a light complexion, blue eyes, brown hair, born in Green County, Missouri, and a farmer by occupation. The July and August 1863 Muster Roll listed Cheek as being absent, sick in hospital. September and October 1863 also showed him to be absent, sick in the hospital in Corinth. The November and December 1863 Muster Roll listed Edmund S. Cheek as being absent, a nurse in the Post Hospital in Corinth since November 22, 1863. Edmund S. Cheek's name was listed on the Returns as follows: March and April 1863, absent with leave; July 1863, on daily duty as teamster; August to October 1863, absent, sick in hospital; February 1864, died of disease in Memphis February 6, 1864. The January and February 1864 Muster Roll stated Edmund A. Cheek died of smallpox on February 6, 1864 at Smallpox Hospital in Memphis, Tennessee. He is buried in the Memphis National Cemetery.

Cheek, Elisha - Elisha Cheek enlisted in Company A of the 1st Alabama Cavalry, USV on January 5, 1865, in Savannah, Georgia for a period of 3 years. He was enrolled by Captain Jerome Hinds, and was mustered in July 13, 1865, in Huntsville, Alabama. The Muster and Descriptive Roll recorded him as being 18 years of age, 5'-8" tall, having a dark complexion, dark eyes and dark hair, born in Franklin County, Georgia, and a farmer by occupation. He was mustered out October 20, 1865, in Huntsville, Alabama owing the U.S. Government $31.73 for losing a saber belt, complete, and pistol cartridge box. He retained one pistol under Special Order Number 101. The Company Descriptive Book showed him to have been born in Cobb County, Georgia. His Civil War Discharge was included in his military records.

Elisha Cheek was enumerated November 27, 1850, on the Franklin County, Georgia Census residing with James F. Cheek and Nesse, at age 3 and born in Georgia. He is supposed to have lived for a time in Toccoa, Georgia. Elisha married Sarah Moss, born 1836, daughter of John and Nancy Boatright Moss. Sarah had first married Sanford N. Swilling on April 10, 1854, and he died in the CSA Army at Knoxville, Tennessee, August 11, 1862. Sarah and Elisha, along with her two children, Mary Jane and Samuel Swilling, moved to Van Buren and White County, Tennessee where she had three children by Elisha Cheek, James R., Sallie Elisabeth "Lizzie", and William M. Cheek. Elisha disappears between 1874 and 1880 when the White County, Tennessee Census shows Sarah to be a widow. Sarah remarried when James R. Cheek was about 17 years old, (1886). Elisha appears in the 1880 Federal Census of Clay County, North Carolina Census with a wife Lavina Holmes and children. No divorce from Sarah or marriage certificate to Lavina has been found. Elisha was a Blacksmith. He was disabled from falling off of a horse. He was discharged in conformance of surrender. Deeds: Squire Johnson conveyed to Elisha Cheek two acres in District 5, Van Buren County, Tennessee on December 25, 1871, for $30.00, Deed Book E, Pages 222-223, recorded April 15, 1872. Family information submitted by Norm Ricker.

Cheek, Samuel M. - Samuel M. Cheek enlisted in Company A of the 1st Alabama Cavalry, USV as a private on October 18, 1864, in Rome Georgia for a period of 3 years. He was mustered in the same day in Rome, Georgia. The Muster and Descriptive Roll shows him to have been 18 years of age, 5'10" tall, having a light complexion, blue eyes, light hair, born in Hart County, Georgia, and a farmer by occupation. Another Descriptive Roll stated he was born in Cobb County, Georgia. The March and April 1865 Muster Roll listed him as being absent, in arrest at Raleigh, North Carolina since April 20, 1865, however, he was present for the May and June 1865 Muster Roll. He was mustered out October 20, 1865, in Huntsville, Alabama, owing the U.S. Government $2.75 for losing 1 saber belt complete and pistol cartridge box. Samuel Cheek's name appeared on a Roll of Federal prisoners in charge of the Provost Marshall, Army of the Ohio, dated April 23, 1865, charge plundering and stealing, by order of General Schofield. Turned over to Colonel Zent (?), Provost Marshall, Raleigh, North Carolina.

Cheney, N. - N. Cheney enlisted in Company E and was reported to have deserted September 12, 1863, from Glendale, Mississippi. No further information related to this soldier was found.*

Cheney, William H. - William H. Chaney enlisted and mustered into Company F of the 1st Alabama Cavalry, USV in Corinth, Mississippi on March 23, 1863, for a period of 1 year. He was appointed 1st Lieutenant by order of Brigadier General G.M. Dodge on March 23, 1863. He was promoted from private of Company F of the 2nd Iowa Cavalry. The Company Muster Roll for December 31, 1863, to June 30, 1864, showed Cheney as being absent; pay due for commanding company October 18, 1863, to April 30, 1864. Dropped from rolls for expiration of term of service from May 23, 1864. There was an Officer's Casualty Sheet in Cheney's military records that stated he had resigned September 2, 1864.

<u>Chastain, David D.</u> - See information on David D. Chastain with the other Chastain family information, above.

<u>Childers, Samuel</u> - Samuel Childers enrolled in Company C of the 1st Alabama Cavalry, USV as a private on December 1, 1862, in Corinth, Mississippi. He was enrolled by Captain John Latty for a term of 1 year. The Regimental Descriptive Book shows him to have been 27 years of age, 6'-2" tall, having a fair complexion, dark eyes, dark hair, born in Greenville, South Carolina, and a farmer by occupation. The September and October 1863 Muster Roll listed him as being absent, on detached service with the surgeon. A Notation found in his records from the Adjutant General's Office of the War Department in Washington, DC, dated August 9, 1870, stated the following: Investigation fails to elicit any further information relative to this soldier. Samuel Childers' name appeared on the Returns as follows: May 1863 – October 1863, detailed as nurse in hospital since May 18, 1863; November 1863 through December 1863, prisoner of war in the hands of the enemy since October 26, 1863, which would have been during the Battle of Vincent's Crossroads, near Bay Springs, Mississippi. After Samuel Childers was captured, he was held prisoner at Cahaba Prison in Alabama then Andersonville Prison in Georgia, then Charleston, South Carolina. He died October 13, 1864, of Chronic Diarrhea at Charleston, South Carolina. His grave is marked as W. Childness. Samuel was buried in Charleston Race Course - "Potter's Field" Cemetery in South Carolina and then later reinterred in the Beaufort National Cemetery

<u>Childress, M. (or W.)</u> - M. Childress enlisted in Company C as a private, and died October 13, 1864, at Charleston, South Carolina. No further information relative to this soldier was found.*

<u>Chowley, Pvt.</u> - Chowley, first name unknown, enlisted in Company F and was recorded as being on Detached service as an orderly in the 2nd Quartermaster and A.A.G. Departments. No further information relative to this soldier was found.*

<u>Clannahan, W.D.</u> - W.D. Clannahan enlisted in Company H as a private and was discharged October 25, 1864, in Rome, Georgia due to expiration of term of service. No further information relative to this soldier was found.*

<u>Clark, Daniel C.</u> - Daniel C. Clark enlisted in Company B of the 1st Alabama Cavalry, USV on January 20, 1863, in Glendale, Mississippi, and was appointed Corporal on January 22, 1863. The Descriptive Roll listed Daniel as having been 18 years of age, 5'-8" tall, having a dark complexion, dark eyes, dark hair, born in Marion County, Alabama, and a farmer by occupation. The September and October 1863 Muster Roll listed Clark as a sergeant and stated he was absent, a prisoner of war since October 26, 1863, which would have been during the Battle of Vincent's Crossroads near Bay Springs, Mississippi. He was shown as present on the next muster roll. There was a Notation in his file from the from the Record and Pension Division of the War Department, dated March 10, 1890, stating: See Company A, 1st Alabama Cavalry for subsequent service. Daniel C. Clark re-enlisted on December 23, 1863, in Camp Davies, Mississippi for a period of 3 years, and was mustered in February 5, 1864, in Memphis, Tennessee and appointed sergeant on that date. He was promoted to 1st sergeant on October 1, 1864. Clark was enrolled by Captain Phillip A. Sternberg. The Regimental Descriptive Book at his re-enlistment listed him as having been 17 years of age, 5'-3" tall, having a light complexion, blue eyes, light hair, born in Marion County, Alabama, and a farmer by occupation. The November and December 1864 Muster Roll listed him as being absent and stated: Sergeant Clark is in the hospital in Hilton Head, South Carolina due to wounds received November 27, 1864, at Balls Ferry, Georgia. He remained in the hospital until sometime in April 1865. He was shown on the U.S.A. General Hospital in Hilton Head, South Carolina Muster Roll until he returned to duty on April 22, 1865. Clark was mustered out on October 20, 1865, in Huntsville, Alabama. He was due a bounty of $300 and was paid $180 and stated he was still due $120 to make up the $300.

Daniel C. Clark was born about 1846 in Marion County, Alabama and died July 22, 1890, in Huntsville, Madison County, Alabama. He married Lavina Ada Street on January 18, 1866, in

Huntsville, Alabama and had the following children: Nella Marcella, born November 18, 1865; Stella Elizabeth, born August 5, 1873; Daniel Charles, born October 18, 1875; John William, May 14, 1878; Henrietta Celest, born September 12, 1881; and Edward Irby Clark, born December 30, 1883. Daniel is buried in the Maple Hill Cemetery in Huntsville, Madison County, Alabama.

Clark, George W. - George W. Clark enlisted in Company A of the 1st Alabama Cavalry, USV as a private on December 25, 1863, in Camp Davies, Mississippi. He was enrolled by Lieutenant Jerome Hinds for a period of 3 years, and was mustered in February 5, 1864, in Memphis, Tennessee. The Muster and Descriptive Roll showed him to have been 19 years of age, 5'-8" tall, having a fair complexion, gray eyes, light hair, born in Tipton County, Tennessee and was a saddler by occupation. He was able to sign his Enlistment Forms. A Company Muster Roll dated February 29, 1864, listed George W. Clark as having deserted from Memphis, Tennessee on February 17, 1864 with arms and accoutrements. He was shown as owing the U.S. Government $42.65 for arms and equipment, and $50.19 for his clothing account. Some of the equipment he took with him included 1 Smith carbine, pistol saber belt and accoutrements complete.

Clark, Jonathan W. - Jonathan W. Clark enlisted in Company G of the 1st Alabama Cavalry, USV as a private on March 21, 1864, in Decatur, Alabama for a period of 3 years. He was enrolled by Lieutenant Pease and was mustered in April 13, 1864, in Decatur. The Company Descriptive Book listed him as having been 36 years of age, 5'-8" tall, having a dark complexion, gray eyes, dark hair, born in Madison County, Alabama, and a farmer by occupation. Jonathan W. Clark's name appeared on the Returns as follows: April 1864, on daily duty as company cook; September and October 1864, on daily duty as company cook; March and April 1865, absent, sick in Wilmington, North Carolina March 10, 1865, and in hospital. This was the date of the Battle of Monroe's Crossroads. Clark was mustered out October 20, 1865, in Huntsville, Alabama owing the U.S. Government $11.30 for losing 1 saber belt and plate, 1 bridle, 1 halter, 1 carbine cartridge box and 1 mess kit (?). Jonathan was able to sign his name on his Enlistment Forms. Jonathan W. Clark is buried in the Upshaw Friendship Baptist Church Cemetery in Winston County, Alabama.

Clark, Martin - Martin Clark enlisted in Company B of the 1st Alabama Cavalry, USV as a private on March 6, 1864, in Decatur, Alabama and was mustered in April 13, 1864, in Decatur. He was enrolled by Lieutenant Judy for a period of 3 years. The Muster and Descriptive Roll showed him to have been 18 years of age, 5'-6" tall, having a fair complexion, blue eyes, light hair, born in Lawrence County, Tennessee, and a farmer by occupation. Another Descriptive Roll stated he was born in Turner, Tennessee. Martin Clark was reported to have deserted May 11, 1864, near Chattanooga, Tennessee with a horse and equipment, Smith Carbine, sling and swivel, cartridge box, cap pouch and pick, waist belt and plate, for which he owed the U.S. Government $24.96.

Clayton, John M. - John M. Clayton enlisted in Company B of the 1st Alabama Cavalry, USV on April 10, 1863, at Glendale, Mississippi for a period of one year. He enrolled as a 21-year old private. The May through October 1863 Muster Rolls stated he was absent with leave, had a pass from Brigadier General G.M. Dodge to go North. In June 1863, the U.S. Army escorted about 300 Union wives, widows, children, and disabled men to Illinois for their protection from the roaming Confederate guerilla gangs who were burning the homes, barns, crops, etc. of Union families and taking the meat from their smoke houses, corn, meal, and anything of value or use to their army. There was a Notation in his file from the War Department dated October 13, 1888, stating: Investigation fails to elicit any further information relative to this soldier. John M. Clayton's name appeared on the Returns as follows: June 1863 to January 1864, Absent with leave, gone North with family June 19, 1863.

Affidavit of Samuel Reid dated March 3, 1890, stated: In a letter dated June 18, 1863, from the hospital of 1st Alabama Cavalry, 16th Army Corps (USA) in Glendale, Mississippi. A request was made by the Company surgeon A. B. Stuart, that Private John M. Clayton, "being in the advance stages of Consumption", be sent North with his family and his discharge paper forwarded to him when ready. The request was forwarded to Headquarters in Corinth, Mississippi and granted by order of Brigadier General G. M. Dodge. John Clayton was later discharged from the Army on February 6, 1864, in

Memphis, Tennessee; he was not present when discharged.

John M. Clayton was born 1839 in Georgia, according to the 1860 Marion County, Alabama Census. He married Serena Ann Stidham on October 22, 1858, in Itawamba County, Mississippi. Serena was the daughter of Winston Dilmus Stidham and Mary M. Markham, who are buried in the Shottsville Cemetery in Marion County, Alabama with a large monument dedicated to Winston. Winston was a strong Unionists who helped the Union wives and widows whose husbands were away. It is thought he helped to escort the group of Union wives, widows, children and disabled Union men to Illinois in June 1863, for their protection. Children of John and Serena Stidham Clayton were: Merrill Winston "Bud", born September 7, 1859, died August 30, 1949; Safrona Jane, born March 10, 1861, died May 5, 1885; Sarah Ann Josephine, born February 4, 1865, died February 14, 1931; and Nancy Lucinda Clayton, born February 1868. John M. Clayton died March 16, 1869 in Centralia, Marion County, Illinois and descendants say he is supposedly buried in a military cemetery close to Centralia. They also state he was either a doctor or interested in medicine.

Clearman, William D. - William D. Clearman enlisted and mustered into Company H of the 1st Alabama Cavalry, USV as a private on October 17, 1863, for a period of 1 year. His name appeared on the Returns and stated the following: January 1864 to April 1864, on daily duty as company cook; August 1864, and on daily duty as company cook. He was listed as being present on all of the Company Muster Rolls and was mustered out October 24, 1864, at Rome, Georgia due to expiration of term of service. He was shown as being 44 years of age when he mustered out, and his pay had been stopped because he had lost 1 thong and brush wiper, 1 haversack, and 1 painted blanket, for which he owed the U.S. Government $2.93.

Clemen, Lewis - Lewis Clemen enlisted in Company F as a private on December 6, 1863. No further information relative to this soldier was found.*

Clement, Curtis Beason - Curtis Beason Clement was born about 1837 in St. Clair County, Alabama to William Washington Clement and Martha Jane Lord. (There is a controversy as to the middle name of Curtis.) See William Riley Clement, brother to Curtis, for information on their parents. Curtis married Mary Ann Cole on November 15, 1856, in Franklin County, Alabama. Mary Ann Cole was born December 25, 1839, and died July 10, 1905, in Elmore, Chickasaw Nation, Indian Territory. She was the daughter of Harbird Cole and Susan Helton. Curtis had died June 25, 1863, in Corinth, Adams County, Mississippi. The only known children of Curtis and Mary were: Mary Elizabeth "Molly", born December 21, 1857, died October 10, 1932; and James D. "Jimmy" Clement, born March 9, 1860, and died sometime after 1930, possibly in Oklahoma.

Curtis B. Clement enlisted in Company A of the 1st Alabama Cavalry, USV as a Private on October 5, 1862, at age 25. He was mustered in December 31, 1862, at Corinth, Mississippi for one year. In November and December 1862, he was listed as absent, in hospital at Corinth from an accidental wound to knee. In January and February 1863, he was listed as absent from being sick in Purdy, Tennessee. In March and April 1863, he was absent, sick in Jackson, Tennessee. March to May 1863, sick in Corinth, Mississippi. Died June 25, 1863, at Glendale, Mississippi. Another muster roll stated he died at Corinth, Mississippi of measles.

Inventory of the effects of Curtis Clement, late, a Private of Captain Frank C. Burdick of Company A of the 1st Regiment of Alabama Cavalry Volunteers who was enrolled as a Recruit in Corinth, Mississippi on the 25th Day of October 1862, at Corinth, in Company A, 1st Regiment Alabama Cavalry Volunteers to serve one year or until the end of the war. He was born in St. Clair County, Alabama; he was 25 years of age, 5'-9" high, Light Complexion, hazel eyes, dark hair, and by occupation a farmer. He died in the General Hospital in Corinth, Mississippi on the 25th Day of June 1863, by reason of measles. The Record of Death and Interment stated Curtis Clement died of Pneumonia and was buried on June 23, 1863.

Curtis B. Clement married Mary Ann Cole November 15, 1856. in Franklin County, Alabama.

Curtis B. Clement Pension Records

On June 18, 1864, John R. Coal [Cole] and William Clement [probably William Riley Clement], residents of Marion County, Illinois appeared to verify Mary's identity in her application for pension. John R. Coal was present at their wedding on November 15, 1856 and William stated he knew them to have lived as husband and wife.

Mary filed for a pension on June 25, 1864. On December 8, 1864, information was requested from Assistant Adjutant-General, Pensions Bureau by Commissioner, Board of Pensions, Department of Interior.

On December 10, 1864, Information of Curtis' service and death was supplied from Assistant Adjutant-General's office.

On January 4, 1865, and July 18, 1865, verifications were requested by the Commissioner.

On July 17, 1865, Receipt of pension application was acknowledged – information from Nov-Dec muster roll regarding Curtis' hospitalization for being "accidentally wounded" and death from measles reported.

Mary was residing in Carbondale, Jackson County, Illinois on October 21, 1865, when she stated she was age 25, and that her husband, Curtis Clement, died June 23, 1863, of measles.

Abram R. Cole and Julia Ann Hawthorne witnessed her declaration that both were present at her wedding.

On January 13, 1866, Captain Edgar M. Lowe, aged 39 of Carbondale, Jackson County, Illinois stated while he served in Regiment G of the 9th Illinois Infantry and was stationed in the Spring of 1864 at Corinth, Mississippi, he became acquainted with Curtis B. Clement and saw him to be "very much reduced by disease" typhoid and dysentery; Curtis occupied a house near to the parade ground but was removed to a hospital in Corinth sometime about the last of April. He stated he believed that Curtis died on June 23, 1863. (One death date in Curtis Clement's records stated he died on June 23, 1863, while another one stated he died on June 25, 1863. Julia A. Hawthorne, age 22 years stated she was a resident of Carbondale and she waited on Curtis in the hospital and knew that he died there about June 23 1863. On January 15, 1866, a verification of enlistment October 25, 1862, muster in December 31, 1862 died June 25, 1863, was requested. On September 4, 1866, Curtis' service and death (June 25, Corinth, measles) was verified October 16, 1869, Mary signed an affidavit giving the death date of her husband, Curtis Clement as June 23, 1863, Beda Davis stated she was the mid-wife at the birth of Mary's daughter, Mary Elizabeth, and that Charity Shook was the mid-wife at the birth of James.

Mary stated they were "compelled by the Rebels to leave the neighborhood in which she lived at the time when the rebellion broke out". Julia A. Webley, aged 27, a resident of Jackson County, Illinois verified Mary's information , that she lived in Franklin County, Alabama at the time of the birth of the Clement children. Bradford Scott, aged 52, and a resident of Jackson County, Illinois verified that he lived in Franklin County, Alabama. On October 23, 1869, John G. Bentley, JP of Franklin County, Alabama verified marriage date as November 15, 1856. Mary's Pension was approved on February 10, 1870, for the amount of $8 per month, beginning June 25, 1863, and beginning July 25, 1866, an additional $2 per month was added for each child. The Administration of Mary's Pension was transferred from Chicago, Illinois to Topeka, Kansas on May 7, 1877. September 4, 1878, Pension of $8/month commenced – paid until December 4, 1878. September 8, 1878, Mrs. Mary Ann Clemons married to Hiram Heiple in Marion, Williamson County, Illinois by JP. April 1, 1880, Heiple's first wife, Vinette A. Welman, reappeared and claimed to be his wife, Mary and Hiram immediately separated. March 4, 1882, Mary dropped from pension roll (Chicago) because of "limitation" April 21, 1882, Appeared to file for restoration – resided in Williamson County, Illinois since 1878 commencement of her pension. April 25, 1882, Filed for restoration of pension. August 24, 1885, Hiram Heiple, age 55, filed his statement with notary public agreeing with Mary's characterization of what had transpired "that justice may be done."

Ronald Mayhall obtained the pension file of Curtis B. Clement, in hopes that a connection could be made showing Curtis and Peter Richard were brothers since they enlisted the same day on October 25, 1862. However, nothing in the pension file establishes their relationship.

Curtis married Mary Ann Cole in Franklin County, Alabama on November 15, 1856. Officiating was John G. Bently, Justice of the Peace. They had two children: Mary Elizabeth "Molly" born December 21, 1857, in Alabama and James D. L. born March 9, 1860, in Mississippi. Mid-wife for Molly's birth was Beda Davis, who later married William Riley Clement, consistent with my belief that William was brother to both Curtis and Peter Richard.

Mary testified October 16, 1869, that she, "as well as most of her acquaintances and friends were compelled by the rebels to leave the neighborhood where [we] lived at the time when the rebellion broke out."

Curtis' muster-in date is given as December 31, 1862, but he was in Corinth from the time of his enlistment on October 25. The November and December muster roll reported him "absent in hospital, at Corinth, accidentally wounded."

Captain Edgar M. Lowe, Company G, 9th Illinois Regiment testified January 13, 1866, that he was on duty with his company at Corinth in the Spring of 1863, that "while there he became acquainted with Curtis B. Clement...that he knows that he was...very much reduced by disease" which he "supposed to be a low grade of typhoid fever or dysentery," that he was "at the time he knew him occupying a house near to the parade ground of said Regiment and was removed to the Hospital at Corinth sometime about the last of April." The last time he saw Clement, he was "so low with the disease from which he suffered that he believed that he died in the hospital on or about the 23 day of June 1863." Other records give cause of death as measles and Mary adds diarrhea as a cause [it was probably a combination of all these factors].

When Mary filed for pension on June 25, 1864, she was living in DeSoto, Jackson County, Illinois. William [Riley?] Clement appeared to certify her identity (he was residing in Marion County, Illinois at that time). She received pension of $8 per month with additional $2 per month for each of her children. This continued until she became ineligible by marrying Hiram Heiple on September 8, 1878, at Marion, Williamson County, Illinois. On April 1, 1880, a previous wife of Heiple's (his third wife) appeared at their doorstep with her claim to be his wife. Heiple testified that she had left him three years previous to his marriage to Mary Clement and that he had been told that his previous wife was deceased. Mary requested that the court declare this marriage void and restore her surname as Clement (which it did); she then applied for resumption of Curtis' pension (which was granted).

Mary died on July 10, 1905. Following up on her children I learned that Molly married John Heiple (a son of Hiram -- she had better luck with her Heiple experience -- they had two children and lived together until his death in 1914). James D. L. married a woman named Jennie, had a brood of children with her, including a son named for his grandfather, Curtis Beardford Clement (I haven't found any other documentation that Curtis B. Clement had the middle name of Beardford, but maybe so if the grandson was named literally for him). Submitted by Ronald Bruce Mayhall.

Clement, John Harvey - John Harvey Clement in Company B of the 1st Alabama Cavalry, USV as a Private on June 10, 1863, in Glendale, Mississippi for a term of 1 year. He was mustered in at Corinth, Mississippi, and mustered out January 22, 1864, in Memphis, Tennessee with the US Government owing him $59.09 for Clothing Allowance. The Company Descriptive Book recorded him as being 19 years of age, 5'-6" tall, having a light complexion, gray eyes, light hair, born in St. Clair County, Alabama, and a farmer by occupation. Harvey, as he was listed, was shown in September 1863 as Company Cook and from December 1863 until January 1864, he was an Orderly at Regimental Headquarters.

John Harvey Clement was the son of Eunice C. Sullivan and William Benjamin Clement and brother to William Clement, below. He was born in October 1844 in St. Clair County, Alabama and married Martha J. Carroll on April 25, 1869. Family information on Harvey and William Clement submitted by Vickie Ruth Ebbert.

Clement, Peter Richard - Peter Richard Clement enlisted in Company A of the 1st Alabama Cavalry, USV as private on October 25, 1862, and mustered in December 31, 1862, in Corinth, Mississippi. He was promoted to sergeant December 18, 1862. The January and February 1863 Muster Roll recorded him as being absent, with sick leave, however he was shown as present on the March and April Muster Roll. He was discharged November 28, 1863, in Memphis, Tennessee due to expiration of term of service. His name appeared on the Returns stating he was discharged November 7, 1863, in Glendale, Mississippi.

Peter Richard Clement was born January 8, 1840, in Pickens County, Alabama. He moved to Franklin County (Hodges) with his parents William Washington and Martha Jane Lord near the end of 1854. At the time of the 1860 census, the family was living in the Chalk Bluff area of Marion County. Their farm was near that of Thomas and Jane Rayburn. Peter married Elizabeth "Molly" Rayburn on January 6, 1861. He joined the First Alabama Cavalry, USV in October, 1862 and mustered out on November 28, 1863. in Memphis. Peter was present for duty in part of January and February, 1863 but was absent in part of February and March on sick leave. A statement signed in 1898 when filing for disability pension says that he contracted measles on March 1 "while at home." He suffered complications from this illness: his attending doctors in his final illness -- chronic asthma -- stated on his death certificate that this condition started "45 or 50 years ago," probably a result of this bout of measles. Actually, Peter's wife, Molly, died from smallpox in a military hospital in Memphis in April 1864. Peter also had small pox at this time. After Molly's death, Peter went to Smithland, Kentucky where he joined Captain Keesee's Company B North Cumberland Battalion, Kentucky Home Guards (Union). After the war, he returned to Smithland, Kentucky where he married Sarah Isabelle Reed. Her parents moved to Mound City, Illinois. Peter and Sarah lived in Mound City for a brief time, but also lived in Paducah Kentucky, Iuka, Mississippi, Ballard County, Kentucky, and Joppa, Illinois before returning to Alabama in 1879. By April 14 Peter was fighting again. He mustered out in Memphis on November 28, 1863.

Peter Richard did not go back to Alabama immediately after his wife's death and his service with the First Alabama. He moved to Mound City, Illinois and married Sarah Isabelle Reed on September 6, 1865. Eight children were born before they moved back to Marion County, Alabama about 1880. Peter and Sarah had three more children after returning to Alabama.

Sarah died on April 23, 1891. Seven months later Peter married twenty-year old Julia Ann McAnally. They lived for a time at Bartonville, Walker County, then for a short time in Cullman County, then back to Walker County. By 1906 they were back in Marion County. Peter and Julia had seven children before his death at Hackleburg, Marion County on December 20, 1914. He was buried at Lower Hackleburg Cemetery near the grave of Sarah Isabelle Reed. The month after his death, his widow Julia applied for Civil War Pension based on her husband's service. After her death in 1953 she was buried next to Peter Richard. Family information submitted by Bruce Mayhall.

Clement, William C. - William C. Clement enlisted in Company B of the 1st Alabama Cavalry, USV as a private on January 6, 1863, in Glendale, Mississippi. He was enrolled my Phillip A. Sternberg and was mustered in January 22, 1863, in Corinth, Mississippi. The Company Descriptive Book recorded him as being 23 years of age, 5'-6" tall, having a fair complexion, blue eyes, light hair, born in Pickens County, Alabama, and a farmer by occupation. The September and October 1863 Muster roll recorded him as being absent, prisoner of war in the hands of the enemy October 26, 1863, from the Battle of Vincent's Crossroads. He was mustered out January 22, 1864, in Memphis, Tennessee.

William C. Clement was the son of Eunice C. Sullivan and William Benjamin Clement who were married January 4, 1844, in St. Clair County, Alabama. He was born in September 1849 in Pickens County, Alabama and married Martha E. "Mattie" Doublin on December 15, 1872. Other children of William Benjamin and Eunice Clement were: Jasper, John "Harvey", Mary Elizabeth, James Richard, and Benjamin Clement.

Clement, William Riley - William Riley Clement enlisted in Company B of the 1st Alabama Cavalry, USV on January 6, 1863, at Glendale, Mississippi for one year, and was Mustered In on January 22, 1863, in Corinth, Mississippi. He was captured by the enemy and taken Prisoner of War on October 26, 1863 at the Battle of Vincent's Crossroads near Red Bay, Alabama, then Mississippi. His Muster Roll for October and November 1863, say he was absent, in the hands of the enemy since the engagement of Vincen's (Vincent's) Crossroads October 26, 1863. He was mustered out on January 22, 1864, at Memphis, Tennessee. Clothing Allowance due William from the U.S. was $41.04. His Muster Rolls state he was transferred from Company A to Company B in March 1863. The Regimental Descriptive Book shows William Riley Clement as being 23 years of age, 5'6" high, having a fair complexion, blue eyes, light hair, born in Pickens County, Alabama, and a farmer by Occupation.

William Riley Clement was born November 23, 1835, in Pickens County, Alabama to William Washington Clement, Jr. and Martha Jane Lord. William Washington was born March 9, 1806, in Clark County, Georgia and died January 30, 1889, in Marion County, Alabama. He married Martha Jane Lord on October 16, 1825, in St. Clair County, Alabama. Martha Jane was born May 12, 1809, in North Carolina and died June 11, 1887, in Marion County, Alabama. Other children of William Washington and Martha Jane Clement were: Martha Jane, born 1830, died March 1929; Andrew Jackson, born 1833, KIA February 4, 1863; William Riley; Mary, born 1835, died in the 1850's; Curtis Beason, born 1837, died June 23, 1863; Sarah M., born 1837, died February 12, 1899; Peter Richard, born February 5, 1840, died December 20, 1914; and Green G., born 1849. William Riley Clement married Beady Davis about 1853 and had the following children: William M., born November 1860; James Lafayette, born April 18, 1861; Mary E., born January 6, 1865; Thomas Isom, born September 20, 1869; Laura, born about 1872; Robert F., born June 9, 1874; and Arthur Clement, born in February 1881.

Civil War Pension File - February 4, 1892, Declaration for Invalid Pension: Resident at Pegram, Colbert County, Alabama, filed Tishomingo County, Mississippi; 54 years old. Enrollment January 6, 1863; discharged Memphis February 6, 1864. "Now unable to earn a support by reason of the loss of one eye and the other injured, so as to make it quite difficult to see. Also rheumatism and palpitation of the heart. Attested by J.J. Cornan, Joel W. Williams. May 29, 1893. It stated proof of Disability and Incapacity to Labor filed at Tishomingo County, Mississippi by William Riley Clement. Henry Wadkins, age 52 of near Iuka, Mississippi and J.W. Carter, age 33 of near Iuka, Mississippi testified that they knew William Riley and that he had been, since December AD 1891, afflicted with the following disabilities: Rheumatism, Palpitation of the Heart and the loss of the sight of one eye and the other eye injured. That the said William Riley "is disabled from manual labor to the extent of one half, and they know of the facts from personal observation, having seen him suffering from said afflictions and that the disability of the claimant is not caused by his vicious habits."

November 15, 1894, P.D. Hall appeared before Justice of the Peace in Hardin County, Tennessee. He was 49 years old and resident of Victory, Wayne County, Tennessee. He swore: "I was Corporal of Co. B 1st Alabama Volunteer Cavalry and personally knew William R. Clements of said Company and Regiment during the latter part of the Spring or early part of Summer (I Believe in June) 1863. Said claimant was taken sick (I do not remember the nature of his disease). The reason I know of his taking sick is I remember the doctor could not prevail with him to go to the hospital and had to treat him at the house of his brother inside our lines and he was unable for duty for same length of time, I do not remember how long, but he would visit the camp from day to day and just barely able to walk about. He finally returned to duty but complained some until discharge and I last saw him in April 1864 on his way to Illinois until I met him a few days ago. His appearance shows him to be suffering from same disabilities. I further state this to be in my own handwriting from the best of my memory." Filed December 7, 1894.

November 22, 1893, Information returned to Commissioner of Pensions: enrolled January 6, 1863, and was mustered out February 4, 1864. On October 31, 1864, he was shown as being absent, a prisoner of war since October 26, 1863, which is when he was captured at the Battle of Vincent's Crossroads. Medical records show him treated as W. Clements, Private Company B, 1st Alabama Cavalry April 8-10 1863 for storvatis (possibly Scorbutus), and returned to duty. Nothing additional found.

February 26, 1907, Declaration for Pension: Resident at Savannah, Hardin County, Tennessee; enlisted Glendale, Mississippi January 6, 1863; honorably discharged February 6, 1865, at Memphis, Tennessee (previous records gave the year as 1864). His description listed him as 5'-8" high, fair complexion, blue eyes, light hair; and occupation, a farmer. He was born 1836 at Pickens County, Alabama. Since service lived 2 years in Illinois, then Mississippi, Alabama and Tennessee. Witnesses A.A. Watson and J.H. Harrison, witnesses, swore that they had known him 15 years.

November 29, 1907, William R. Clement appeared before L.L. Hurbert, Clerk of County Court, Hardin County, TN swearing that "the family record was destroyed during the Rebellion 1861-5 and he has no record either public or private of his birth, and his parents always told him he was born November 23, 1835."

March 31, 1911, Application for Reimbursement for last expenses of William R. Clement was filed by T.I. Clement (age 40, Administrator of the will of his father). Pension last paid November 4, 1910. States he was married once to Beedie Davis; she died November 18, 1907. At his death William left plow tools ($10), corn ($20), hay ($5), hogs ($18), all sold at public sale by Administrator. He owned no real estate. William died of "heart trouble." Last sickness began "about December 15, 1910;" requiring constant attendance from "January 1, 1911." In this sickness he was treated by Dr. G. C. Morrison and Dr. O.C. Doty of Savannah, Tennessee and was nursed by "J.L. Clement, Vester Clement, and Lester Clement." During last sickness he lived with "John Scott, Nixon, Tennessee." He died at home of J.L. Clement near Savannah and was buried at Mt. Hermon Cemetery near Savannah. Outstanding debt included $68 to Drs. Morris and Doty (unpaid) and $34.50 to J.L. Clement for shrouding and casket.

Statement of Attending Physicians: Pensioner's death was February 2, 1911;

Commencement of illness "about December 15, 1910; attended him from January 1, 1911, to January 31, 1911, for "organic disease of the heart;" he died from "stacis due to organic disease of the heart." Dr. W.P. King made one visit about the last of December 1910. Other facts: "In my judgment the Clements Family the father deceased and all the Family are reliable and would do nothing wrong in this mater." Signed G. C. Morris. Filed April 3, 1911.

March 31, 1911, L.L. Hurbert, Clerk of County Court, Hardin County, Tennessee received record from J.L. Clement of money furnished to buy shrouding and casket for William R. Clement, deceased:

William Riley Clement, the sixth child of William Washington Clement, moved from Franklin County, Alabama to Tishomingo County, Mississippi, near Iuka, sometime between 1863 and 1865. His move was probably prompted by the fact that he had served with the Yankee Army and was not welcome in Franklin County any more. The Iuka, Mississippi area was in Yankee hands when he made his move.

On October 20, 1863, the 1st Alabama Cavalry, USV, consisting of about 650 men, rode out of Corinth, Mississippi, directly southeastward, toward Columbiana, Alabama. It was supposed to destroy the railroad from Line Station to Eleyton. However, 40 miles out of Glendale, Mississippi at a place called Jones Cross Roads, they were attacked by Confederate troops commanded by Brig. Gen. Samuel W. Ferguson who, according to official reports, "....scattered the Alabama Tories over the country, killing 20, including two captains, the adjutant of the regiment and a lieutenant." It was said the battle of Vincent's Crossroads was fought over such a long, densely wooded area that some of the bodies were not found for several days. For several days following the battle, stragglers were still being caught throughout the countryside. It was during this time that William Riley Clement was captured as he made his way back to Corinth. Family information submitted by Janie Hayes.

Clements, Edward - Edward Clements, also spelled Clemens, enlisted in Company L of the 1st Alabama Cavalry, USV as a private on September 25, 1863, in Fayette County, Alabama for a period of 1 year, and was mustered in the same day in Glendale, Mississippi. Clements was shown as having been 22 years of age, 6' tall, having a fair complexion, blue eyes, light hair, born in Georgia, and a farmer by occupation. He was missing in action October 26, 1863, from the Battle of Vincent's Crossroads near Red Bay, Alabama. He continued to be missing in action and a prisoner of war through October 1864. The Memorandum From Prisoner of War Records stated he was captured November 25, 1863, from Walker County, Tennessee, probably should have been Walker County, Alabama. He was admitted to Hospital 21 at Richmond, Virginia on January 2, 1864 where he died January 12, 1864, of pneumonia at a Confederate Military Prison. Edward Clements was buried in the Richmond National Cemetery in Virginia.

Clements, Phillip O. - Phillip O. Clements enlisted in Company B of the 1st Alabama Cavalry, USV as a private on April 12, 1864, in Decatur, Alabama for a period of 3 years. He was mustered in April 13, 1864, in Decatur, and on April 17, 1864, he was sick in the Hospital at Decatur, Alabama. The Muster and Descriptive Roll, recorded him as being 18 years of age, 6' tall, having a dark complexion, gray eyes, light hair, born in Calhoun County, Alabama and a farmer by occupation. The next several Muster Rolls through July and August 1865, state he was left sick in the hospital at Decatur, Alabama on April 17, 1864. On October 20, 1865, he was Mustered Out with pay due since enlistment of $60.00 and Bounty due, $100.00. At the bottom of the Muster-Out Roll it states: Left sick in U.S. General Hospital in Decatur, Alabama since April 17, 1864, no discharge furnished on Muster Out of Organization. Phillip O. Clements also appears in the records as P.A. Clements, Phillip J. Clements, and P.W. Clements.

<u>Clements, Smith Leroy</u> - Corporal Smith Leroy Clements, or Leroy Smith Clements, enlisted in Company B of the 1st Alabama Cavalry, USV on April 2, 1864, at Decatur, Alabama for a period of 3 years. He was enrolled by Lieutenant Judy and was mustered in April 13, 1864, in Decatur. The Muster and Descriptive Roll recorded as being 23 years of age, 5'-10" tall, having a fair complexion, blue eyes, dark hair, born Walker County, Alabama, and a farmer by occupation. He was also listed as Smith Z. Clements on one muster roll, and was shown to be a Corporal. He was reported to have deserted July 16, 1864, from Rome, Georgia with a Smith Carbine Sling, several box caps, Pouch Waist Belt and Plate. A Descriptive List of Deserters showed Smith to have deserted July 16, 1864, from Rome, Georgia with arms and accoutrements. However, his name was listed on the Company Muster-Out Roll dated October 20, 1865, in Huntsville, Alabama with pay due from enlistment, but he owed the U.S. Government $16.40 for losing the arms and accoutrements.

Smith was born August 9, 1841, in Walker County, Alabama to Jacob Clements and Louisa Ann Busby, who married December 5, 1832, in Tuscumbia, Alabama. Smith married Mary Elizabeth Tubb, who was born April 7, 1844, and died January 2, 1918, in Itawamba County, Mississippi. Children of Smith and Louisa were: Dave, Emaline, Annie Lou Frances, Malinda "Mindie", Jacob, Gertrude, Colonel David, and Dock Walker Clements. Smith Clements died May 5, 1908, in Itawamba County, Mississippi, and is buried in the Salem Cemetery. He and his wife, Mary, have one tombstone with their names engraved side-by-side.

<u>Cline, Jacob Hobert</u> - Jacob Hobert Cline enlisted in Company A of the 1st Alabama Cavalry, USV as a Private on January 23, 1864, in Camp Davies, Mississippi, leaving his wife, Mary Guin Cline, at home with eleven of their young children. Jacob was mustered in on February 5, 1864, in Memphis, Tennessee. The Muster and Descriptive Roll recorded him as being 41 years of age, 6'-1" tall, having a dark complexion, gray eyes, dark hair, born in Wayne County, Tennessee, and a farmer by occupation. He was and mustered out on October 20, 1865, owing the US Government $3.45 for losing 1 saber belt complete and 1 carbine cartridge box. He later served as Tax Collector in Sanford County, Alabama (changed to Fayette County, Alabama later) in 1869. He was buried at the Old Liberty Church of Christ Cemetery in Lamar County Alabama, later Fayette County.

Jacob H. Cline was born October 1, 1822, in Wayne County, Tennessee to Michael and Sophia Lentz Cline. About 1841, Jacob married Mary Guin, daughter of Levi Guin, Sr. and his wife, Nancy, last name unknown. Children of Jacob and Mary were: Cordelia Clementine, born May 14, 1844, died January 18, 1838; Frances Adeline, born October 7, 1846, died August 15, 1930; Thomas William, born May11, 1848, died June 21, 1930; Martha Jane, born January 3, 1849, died June 1, 1915; Lewis Andrew, born 1851, died 1930; Susan E. February 1, 1863, died November 27, 1909; Parthenia "Thenia", born 1855, died 1938; Lavanda L., born July 27, 1857, died June 13, 1873; Savannah, born 1857; Benjamin Franklin, born October 4, 1860, died October 21, 1937; Jacob Ephraim, born May 24, 1863, died January 18, 1888; and James E. Cline, born August 3, 1866, and died February 17, 1884. Jacob H. Cline's father, Michael, was born August 7, 1799, in Cabarrus County, North Carolina and died August 5, 1887, in Tuscaloosa, Tuscaloosa County, Alabama. He married Sophia Lentz, daughter of Peter and Susannah Brown Lentz, about 1820 in Rowan County, North Carolina. Sophia was born March 7, 1800, in Rowan County, North Carolina, and died May 3, 1883, in Tuscaloosa, Tuscaloosa County, Alabama. Children of Michael and Sophia Cline, and Jacob's siblings were: Catherine, born 1820, died 1921; Mahaley, born 1824, died 1911; Andrew, born July 29, 1826, died July 1, 1903; Sarah R., born 1827, died 1851; Jane, born 1831, died 1864; John, born 1832, died 1921; Elizabeth, "Betty", born 1833, died 1926; Delilah "Dilly" Cline, born 1834, died 1928; Susan "Kitty" Cline, born 1836, died 1852; Jackson, born 1838, died 1928; and Samuel T. Cline, born about 1840, and died 1936. Jacob's father, Michael Cline was the son of George and Maria Meisenheimer Cline.

Cloer, Andrew J. - Andrew J. Cloer, also listed as Cloar and Clear, enlisted and was mustered into Company H of the 1st Alabama Cavalry, USV on September 13, 1863, at Glendale, Mississippi as a private for a period of 1 year. The November and December 1863 Muster Roll showed him to be absent, on sick leave. His name appeared on the Returns as follows: January 1864, absent, sick in Memphis, Tennessee since November 10, 1863; February 1864, sick in Alabama since December 6, 1863; August 1864, absent, sick at Memphis; October 1864, absent, sick in General Hospital.

Andrew Jackson Cloer was born in July 1839 in Fayette County, Alabama to Elijah J. Cloer and his wife, Elizabeth A. "Betsy" Weathers, who were married March 6, 1829 in Lauderdale County, Alabama. Elijah was born December 21, 1803, in Burke County, North Carolina and died sometime after 1881 in Lamar County, Alabama. Elizabeth was born in January 1804 in Williamson County, Tennessee, and died sometime after 1900 in Lamar County, Alabama. Other children of Elijah and Betsy were: Sarah, Charlotte, Michael, Martha Elizabeth, John H., Susan Ann, James R.P., and Mary Caroline Cloer. Another unnamed infant died in birth or shortly after in 1836.

Andrew J. Cloer married Nancy Francis "Fannie" Tackett on January 30, 1861, in Fayette County, Alabama. Nancy was born April 19, 1846, in Fayette County, Alabama to Michael and Catherine Tackett. Children of Andrew Jackson and Nancy Tackett Cloer were: Frances Jane, born October 19, 1863, died December 27, 1941; Thomas Jefferson, born May 16, 1864, died October 30, 1945; Mary Elizabeth, born February 20, 1868, died July 2, 1952; James Andrew, born August 5, 1870, died October 2, 1954; Germinia, "Jamie" Lee, born June 15, 1872, died May 14, 1958; Raymon Monroe, born 1874, died sometime before 1885; William "Doc" Jonas, born July 22, 1876, died October 17, 1961; George Washington, born February 5, 1878, died July 8, 1949; Helen Vanetta, born February 14, 1879, died July 2, 1941; Edward Hansford "Ed", born January 27, 1882; died April 3, 1932; and Jaline, "Jalie" Irene, born June 25, 1883, died May 26, 1963. They had two unnamed children who died in infancy in 1866 and 1885. Andrew Jackson Cloer died October 10, 1922, in Terrill, Kaufman County, Texas.

Clutter, William H. - William Harrison Clutter was the Assistant Surgeon in Companies F&G of the 1st Alabama Cavalry, USV. His appointment, enrollment or muster was not given. His name was only listed on two Field and Staff Muster Rolls as being present. He could have been from one of the Illinois Regiments.

The following family information was sent by a descendant of William H. Clutter stating she wasn't sure this information was on his ancestor but was 98% sure. According to her, he was born September 5, 1830, in Washington County, Pennsylvania (could have been in one of the Pennsylvania Regiments) to Jacob Clutter and Mary Ann Lindley. He married Sarah Ann Friedline on October 7, 1854, in Athens, Ohio. Sarah was born December 31, 1830, in Somerset, Pennsylvania, and died January 20, 1894, in Farnhamville, Calhoun County, Iowa. William Harrison Clutter died August 6, 1892, in Farnhamville, Calhoun County, Iowa. Children of William and Sarah Clutter were: Margaret J., born August 6, 1855, died April 11, 1918; Mary H., born October 25, 1856, died October 18, 1900; Francis Marion, born June 27, 1858, died February 5, 1861; Armeda P., born July 29, 1860, died May 6, 1943; Abraham Arza, born May 22, 1862, died November 11, 1921; William Sherman, born May 25, 1865, died May 13, 1934; Alva Lindley, born June 12, 1867, died June 16, 1931; John Eben, born July 26, 1871, died March 1874; and Archie Clayton, born February 17, 1876, died July 27, 1853.

Cobb, Alexander - Alexander Cobb was enrolled in Company E of the 1st Alabama Cavalry, USV on February 10, 1863, in Corinth, Mississippi, for a period of 1 year. He was shown as absent without leave on the March and April 1863 Muster Roll and it stated his name was not borne on any subsequent muster rolls of the company. He was listed on the Descriptive List of Deserters of Company E stating he deserted May 20, 1863, from Glendale, Mississippi. The name Alex Cobb appears on the Returns as having deserted April 1, 1863.

Alexander Cobb was born March 16, 1849, in Bibb County, Alabama to Levi Banks Cobb, born February 17, 1819, died May 10, 1883, and his wife, Amanda Davenport, born November 7, 1823, and died November 5, 1892. Lee and Amanda were married October 6, 1841. Alexander A. Cobb married Sarah M. Brasher December 15, 1870 in Union County, Arkansas and had the following children: John N., born about 1872; James M., born March 26, 1874, died April 27, 1895; Alexander, born about 1874;

William Willis, born July 20, 1876, died October 31, 1906; Bennie F., born January 24, 1879, died July 28, 1885; Julia Etta, born January 1879; Avah Dottie, born May 1884; and Sabina Cobb, born February 1887.

Cobb, I.M. - I.M. Cobb enlisted in Company F and was recorded as being absent without leave on April 29, 1863. No further information relative to this soldier was found. *

Cobit, Headley - See Headley Coburn.

Cobleigh, Edward J. - Lieutenant Edward J. Cobleigh was promoted by Special Order 200, Headquarters, District of Corinth, Mississippi, Private, Company L, 15th Illinois Cavalry, May 25, 1863. Cobleigh's Individual Muster-In Roll dated December 28, 1863, stated he enlisted November 1, 1863, at Glendale, Mississippi for a period of 3 years. He was promoted to Lieutenant by Brigadier General Granville M. Dodge, November 1, 1863. He was listed as age 21. He was mustered in December 28, 1863, at Camp Davies, Mississippi. In March and April 1864, he was on detached service with Company G, 1st Alabama Cavalry, US. In May and June 1864, he was still on detached duty as above. He was detailed from Company M to take care of Company G April 15, 1864. July and August 1865, Cobleigh was still on detached service commanding Company G of the 1st Alabama Cavalry, USV. Edward J. Cobleigh's Muster-Out Roll stated he was age 26, mustered out in Huntsville, Alabama on October 20, 1865. The Remarks stated he was appointed by authority of Secretary of War. This officer makes affidavit that he has rendered all required of all public property for which he has been accountable.

A letter written by Cobleigh from Memphis, Tennessee on March 10, 1864, stated: I have the honor to request that I be granted a leave of absence for four days for the following reasons. I was formerly a member of the 15th Illinois Cavalry and when I detached to the 1st Alabama Cavalry, I retained my horse, arms, and equipments. I now desire to go to Helena, Arkansas and return the above property to my original commander, and also to secure my final statements. I would most respectfully call your attention to my having received permission to apply for leave of absence and also to the fact of Lt. Tupper of this Regiment having a leave of absence granted for the same purpose except he had no property to turn over. It is indispensable that I should have my final statements that I may receive my pay. I have the honor to be your obedient servant, E.J. Cobleigh, 1st Lt. Co. M, 1st Alabama Cavalry.

Another letter from Savannah, Georgia dated February 11, 1865, from Cobleigh stated: I would respectfully request leave of absence for 30 days to visit my home in Northfield, Vermont for the following reasons. 1st, I have been in the U. S. Service since April 18, 1861, and have never been home and never been absent without leave. Also, I will state that I have been in the field in active service over three years of the time. 2nd, I have just been discharged from hospital where I have been for the first time since entering service, and I cannot get to my command for twenty or thirty days in all probability. 3rd, the constant service I have been doing has so reduced my health that I am quite unfit for field duty. 4th, my family needs my immediate presence and will suffer if I don't go to their relief. Hopefully this request may be granted. I have the honor to be, Colonel, your obedient servant. E.J. Cobleigh, 1st Lieut., 1st Alabama Cavalry Volunteers, Company G. The leave was granted.

On March 21, 1865, Cobleigh wrote a letter from Northfield, Washington County, Vermont stating the following: I would respectfully request a second extension of twenty days to a leave of absence given at Savannah, Georgia February 14, 1865, by order of Maj. Gen. W. T. Sherman, and assign reasons as shown by the Surgeon's Certificate. Hoping this request may be granted, I have the honor to be your obedient servant, E.J. Cobleigh, 1st Lt., 1st Alabama Cavalry Vols., Company G.

On the 21st Day of March 1865, a statement by Dr. Samuel Keith of Northfield, Washington County, Vermont, stated that 1st Lt. E.J. Cobleigh having applied for a certificate on which to ground a leave of absence, I do hereby certify that I have carefully examined this officer and find that he is suffering from bilious difficulties which are probably the sequila of Bilious fever he had before leaving South Carolina, and that in consequence thereof, he is in my opinion unfit for duty. I further declare my belief that he will not be able to resume his duties in a less period than twenty days and I further state that he is unable to travel without incurring the risk of permanent disability. It was signed by Sam'l Keith, M.D.

Cobleigh was born March 22, 1837, in Northfield, Vermont to George H. Cobleigh, born about 1792 in Vermont, and his wife, Electra "Electy" Frizzel. Edward was enumerated on the 1850 Northfield, Washington County, Vermont Census with his parents and siblings, George, Caroline, Martin, Dennison and Charles. He was next enumerated as a Boarder on the 1860 Chicago Ward 2, Cook County, Illinois Census in the household of Nancy Bishop of Vermont who owned a Boarding House, as age 23 and shown as a Peddler. In 1870, he was enumerated on the Harrison County, Iowa, St. John Township, as age 32, a Railroad Baggage Master, after having married Georgianna A. Woodward on March 28, 1865, in Lowell, Massachusetts, and having one daughter, Lillian Gertrude Cobleigh, born 19 Dec 1867.

Georgianna A. Woodward was born December 16, 1842, in New Hampshire to Jacob Andrews Woodward, born April 10, 1811, in Lyndeborough, Hillsboro City, New Hamphshire, and his wife, Julia Bowen of Holderness, born April 2, 1809, and died November 27, 1878. Jacob died July 20, 1846, in Lyndeborough, Hillsboro City, New Hampshire. He was the son of Daniel Woodward and Lucy Burnham.

In 1880 Edward was living in Missouri Valley, Harrison County, Iowa with his age shown as 42 and occupation as American Express Agent. Georgianna was shown as 39 years old and Lillian 12. They had two boarders in the household, David Richardson, 50, born in New York and Ethan Daget, 39, born in New York.

By 1900 Edward and his family were back in Evanston Ward 2, Cook County, Illinois, shown as age 63 and married 35 years. Georgianna was and Lillian, 32. There was a Dress Maker, Louisa C. Heldt, living in the household with them, age 33, born in Illinois.

By 1910, the family was still in Cook County, Illinois, Ridgeville Township and Edward was shown as age 73 and occupation was Sewing Machine Agent. Georgianna was 67 and their daughter, Lillian was still home at age 42. Internment records show his date of death as June 13, 1912, and he was buried in the Rose Hill Cemetery in Cook County, Illinois.

<u>Coburn, James Headley</u> - James "Headley" Coburn enlisted in Company I of the 1st Alabama Cavalry, USV as a private on April 20, 1863, (another muster roll stated he enrolled April 22, 1863) in Murfreesboro, Rutherford County, Tennessee for a term of 3 years, and was mustered in the same day. He was enrolled by Lieutenant Shipp. The Company Descriptive Book listed Coburn as being 18 years of age, 5' tall, having a light complexion, blue eyes, light hair, born Winston County, Alabama, and a Tanner by occupation. His name on some the muster rolls was shown as "Headley Cobit" but there was a note stating his cards were filed with "Headley Coburn". Another muster roll stated he mustered in on September 27, 1863, at Glendale, Mississippi. He was mustered out September 28, 1864, due to expiration of term of service at Rome, Georgia. However, his discharged showed he was discharged in October 1864, in Rome, Georgia. During the Civil War, James served as a private in Company I of the 1st Alabama Cavalry. James was enlisted, into the unit in Murfreesboro, Tennessee where he wound up after having run away from his older, abusive brother, Elijah. During the war a Rebel musket ball shot off his left ear lobe.

James Headley Coburn was born January 4, 1848, in Lauderdale County, Alabama. The 1st Alabama Company Descriptive Book recorded him as being born in Winston County, Alabama to Charles and Elizabeth Coburn. His Military Muster Roll stated he was born in Winston County, Alabama and died October 18, 1934, in Lonoke County, Arkansas when a team of mules he was driving bolted, throwing him from the wagon which then ran over him and fractured his skull. He is buried in Tomberlin Cemetery in Lonoke County. In 1863 he emigrated from Colbert County, Alabama to Murfreesboro, Rutherford County, Tennessee. After the war he returned to Colbert County, Alabama where he remained until 1881 when he emigrated to Lonoke County, Arkansas, and in 1902 he moved to Durant, Oklahoma, Indian Territory. By 1910 he was living in Tomberlin, Arkansas farming about 400 acres. He married first, Martha June Mayes, August 6, 1865, and had the following children: Mary Lou, born May 26, 1866; Robert E., born October 15, 1869, died October 15, 1870; Elizabeth Permelia, born July 8, 1872; Agnes Elizabeth, born April 25, 1876, died January 14, 1957; and Lydia A., born October 9, 1878, died August 5, 1888. His wife, Martha, died February 18, 1879 in Colbert County, Alabama and James married Julia Fureigh on December 21, 1879. and they had the following children: Mattie Bell, born October 23, 1881; James Franklin, born February 3, 1884; John Thomas, born November 18, 1885; Minnie L., born July 10, 1889; Sallie S., Jan. 22, 1892, died August 15, 1895; Edna E., born December 11, 1893, died July 1, 1894; Margrette I., born February 7, 1895, died September 16, 1896; Charles Sidney, born April 6, 1897; Jerry and Joel, (twins), September 13, 1899, died October 20, 1899; and Julia H. Coburn, born July 21, 1902. James had three other sons who died at birth and were not named. After the death of Julia, his second wife, August 20, 1910, James married Etha Elizabeth Poteet September 2, 1914.

James' family was not happy about him marrying Julia. They thought that 10 months was too soon after his first wife's death. Julia was supposedly Eastern bred, a Catholic school girl with wealthy parents and a rather sophisticated background. Her parents were also unhappy with the marriage, feeling that James, a farmer, was not good enough for their daughter. Julia had her hands full, but she took his small children and raised them after they lost their mother and even after she had fifteen children of her own with James. Four of the fifteen children died at birth, a set of twins died in infancy, two others didn't make it to their second birthday, and one child died before the age of four. Family information submitted by John Kopp.

The following was written by another descendant: James Headly Coburn was born January 1848 in Lauderdale County, Alabama, to Charles and Elizabeth Coburn.

During the Civil War, James served as a private in Company I of the 1st Alabama Cavalry. James was Enlisted, into the unit in Murfreesboro, Tennessee in 1863 where he wound up after having run away from his older, abusive brother, Elijah. During the war a Rebel musket ball shot off his left ear lobe. He was discharged at Rome, Georgia in October of 1864.

After the war he returned to Colbert County, Alabama where he remained until 1881 when he moved to Lonoke County, Arkansas. In 1902 he moved to Durant (Oklahoma), Indian Territory. By 1910, he was living in Tomberlins, Arkansas, farming about 400 acres.

James married Martha June Mayes, 6 August 1865 in Alabama. They had five children. Martha died 18 February 1879 in Colbert County, Alabama, and James married Julia Fureigh on 21 December 1879.

James' family was not happy about him marrying Julia. They thought that it was too soon after his first wife's death (10 months). Julia was supposedly Eastern bred, a Catholic school girl with wealthy parents and a rather sophisticated background. Her parents were also unhappy with the marriage, feeling that James, a farmer, was not good enough for their daughter.

Julia had her hands full, but she took his small children and raised them after they lost their mother and even after she had fifteen children of her own with James. Four of the fifteen children died at birth, a set of twins died in infancy, two others didn't make it to their second birthday, and one child died before the age of four. Julia died 20 August 1910, and James married for a third time. Her name was Etha Elizabeth Poteet and they had no children.

James Headly died 19 October 1934 in Lonoke County, Arkansas when a team of mules he was driving bolted, throwing him from the wagon which then ran over him and fractured his skull. He is buried in Tomberlin Cemetery in Lonoke County.

Cochran, Levi - Levi Cochran enlisted and mustered into Company K of the 1st Alabama Cavalry, USV as a private on August 5, 1862, in Huntsville, Alabama. He was enrolled by Captain Bankhead for a term of 3 years. He was one of the early enlistees shipped to Nashville, Tennessee where they were merged with the 1st Middle Tennessee Cavalry which was later the 5th Tennessee Cavalry, US. The Regimental Descriptive Book recorded him as being 21 years of age, 5'-10" tall, having a dark complexion, black eyes, auburn hair, born in Marion County, Alabama, and a farmer by occupation. He was reported to have deserted October 22, 1862, from Camp Campbell in Nashville, Tennessee. He was not apprehended.

Cock, Charles C. - Charles C. Cock [could be Cook] enlisted and mustered into Company K of the 1st Alabama Cavalry, USV as a private on July 24, 1862, in Huntsville, Alabama. He was enrolled by Captain Bankhead for a term of 3 years. He was with the early enlistees who were immediately shipped to Nashville, Tennessee where they were merged with Company E of the 1st Middle Tennessee Cavalry, which was later the 5th Tennessee Cavalry, US. In January and February 1863 he was absent on courier post. He was shown as being missing in action on October 26, 1863, from the Battle of

Vincent's Crossroads near Red Bay, Alabama, but returned January 14, 1864. On April 30, 1863, he was captured and taken prisoner of war by the Rebels at the Battle of Day's Gap, Alabama, having been cut off from Colonel Streight's expedition. The Regimental Descriptive Book recorded him as being been 18 years of age, 5'-8½" tall, having a light complexion, blue eyes, light hair, born in Lafayette, Chambers County, Alabama, and a farmer by occupation. He was still shown as being absent on October 31, 1863, but was listed as being present on the March and April 1864 Muster Roll. Cock's name appeared on the Returns as follows: January and February 1863, absent January 27, 1863, on courier post; September 1863, gained September 21, 1863, Glendale, Mississippi, having been cut off from Colonel Streight's Expedition April 1863; October 1863, missing in action, Bay Springs, Mississippi, Vincent's Crossroads October 26, 1863; January 1864, returned from missing in action at Vincent's Crossroads on January 4, 1864, to Camp Davies, Mississippi; January to February 1864, on detached service January 24, 1864, in Vicksburg, Mississippi; March 10, 1865, absent, prisoner of war. A Prisoner of War Record stated Charles C. Cock/Cook was captured at Fayetteville, North Carolina on March 10, 1865, brought from Raleigh, North Carolina, and confined at Richmond, Virginia on March 28, 1865; paroled at Boulware and Cox's Wharf in Virginia March 30, 1865; reported at Camp Parole, Maryland on March 31, 1865; Furloughed April 9, 1865, for 30 days, returned May 3, 1865. His name appeared on the January and February 1865 Muster Roll of a detachment of Paroled Prisoners at Camp Chase, Ohio, dated April 10, 1865, stated Charles C. Cock was captured April 10, 1865, at Solomon Grove, North Carolina. The Muster Roll for December 31, 1864, to April 30, 1865, showed him as being absent, a paroled prisoner of war at Annapolis, Maryland. He was discharged April 28, 1865, at Camp Chase, Ohio by General Order #77 of the War Department. Another muster roll stated he was mustered out June 12, 1865, at Camp Chase, Ohio. He was paid a bounty of $25 and shown as being due another $75 for the rest of the bounty. He owed the US Government $2.46 for transportation

Charles C. Cock was born in August 1844 and died in 1927. He was buried in the Oakwood Cemetery in Fort Worth, Tarrant County Texas. He married Mary Purdy Adams who was born in February 1840 and died in 1903 in Forth Worth, Tarrant County, Texas. Charles and Mary share the same tombstone in the Oakwood Cemetery in Fort Worth, Texas

Cock, Charles J. - Charles J. Cock enlisted in Company L of the 1st Alabama Cavalry, USV as a private on September 25, 1863, in Fayette County, Alabama for a period of 1 year. He was enrolled by Captain Trammel, and was mustered in the same day at Glendale, Mississippi. The Company Descriptive Book showed Cock to have been 42 years of age, 5'-9" tall, having a fair complexion, blue eyes, light hair, born in Union County, North Carolina, and a farmer by occupation. The November and December 1863 Muster Roll stated he had been absent with leave since October 20, 1863, by order of Colonel Spencer. The January and February 1864 Muster Roll listed him as being absent, missing in action October 26, 1863, from Vincent's Crossroads, which was near Red Bay, Alabama. The September and October 1864 Muster Roll showed him as being a prisoner of war in the hands of the enemy since October 26, 1863. His name appeared on the Returns as follows: October 1863, Absent with leave; November 1863, absent, left sick in Alabama by order of Colonel Spencer; December 1863, Absent in Alabama since the raid October 26, 1863; March through August 1864: Absent, prisoner of war since October 26, 1863; September and October 1864: Absent, sick; June 1865: Missing in action October 26, 1863, from Vincent's Crossroads, Mississippi, before reported as prisoner of war. Charles J. Cock died of disease on February 23, 1864, in Richmond, Virginia while still a prisoner of war. He is buried in the Richmond National Cemetery, in Richmond, Virginia.

Charles J. Cock was born about 1820 in Union County, North Carolina and was married to Nancy Ann Whitley on September 27, 1848, in Fayetteville, North Carolina. Nancy Ann was the daughter of Henry Clay Whitley and Nancy Bridges. Children of Charles and Nancy Ann Whitley Cock were: Martha J., born February 17, 1850, died July 2, 1894; James A., born July 29, 1852, died December 13, 1911; Jesse E., born February 7, 1853, died September 25, 1931; Mary Ann, born March 12, 1855; Henry Thomas, born October 2, 1859; and John A. Cook, born October 1, 1862.

Cock, I. - Only one card was found for I. Cock [could be Cook] which was filed at the end of the last roll of microfilm of the 1st Alabama Cavalry, USV records. It recorded him as being in Company H, and reported him as having deserted in October 1864, while on detached service. No further information relative to this soldier was found.*

Cock, Jeremiah D. - Jeremiah D. Cock [could be Cook] enlisted in Company B of the 1st Alabama Cavalry, USV on January 20, 1863, in Glendale, Mississippi for a term of 1 year. He was enrolled by Captain Phillip A. Sternberg and was mustered in January 22, 1863, in Corinth, Mississippi. The Regimental Descriptive Book recorded Jeremiah as being 17 years of age, 5'-8" tall, having a dark complexion, blue eyes, dark hair, born in Fayette County, Alabama, and a farmer by occupation. The September and October 1863 Muster Roll recorded him as being absent, prisoner of war since October 26, 1863, which would have been during the Battle of Vincent's Crossroads. He was mustered out January 22, 1864, in Memphis, Tennessee. His name appeared on the Returns as follows: October and November 1863, absent in the hands of the enemy since the engagement of Vincent's Crossroads October 26, 1863.

Coe, Edward D. - Edward D. Coe enlisted in Company B of the 1st Alabama Cavalry, USV on November 1, 1863, in Glendale, Mississippi for a term of 1 year, and was mustered in the same day in Corinth, Mississippi. He was appointed 2nd Lieutenant in the 1st Alabama Cavalry, USV from a private in Company I of the 11th Illinois Cavalry Volunteers by Brigadier General G.M. Dodge, by authority of the Secretary of War, on November 1, 1863. There was a Notation in his records from the Record and Pension Office of the War Department dated June 16, 1894, which stated: It has this day been determined by this Department from records on file, that the charges of desertion of July 1, 1864, on medical records against this officer is erroneous. Another Notation from the Adjutant General's Office of the War Department dated March 29, 1884, stated: This officer was mustered out and honorably discharged as of date of muster out of his company on February 6, 1864. His name appeared on the Returns as follows: November 1863, Assigned to duty by order of Colonel George E. Spencer November 13, 1863; December 1863 and January 1864, absent on detached service as superintendent of Refugee Camp in Corinth, Mississippi, by order of Brigadier General J.D. Stevenson, Commanding District of Corinth. Absent since December 14, 1863; March 1864, relieved from duty by expiration of term of service. A letter in his file stated the families in the Refugee Camp totaled to about 1000, and called them "very unfortunate people." A form in his file from Head-Quarters District of Memphis, Tennessee, dated January 30, 1864, Special Orders #5, stated: Lieutenant E.D. Coe of the 1st Alabama Cavalry is hereby detailed to take charge of refugees in District of Memphis and will report at once to these headquarters for instructions. By order of Brigadier General Buckland. Another form from Head-Quarters 16th Army Corps, Memphis, Tennessee, March 18, 1864, Special Orders #63, stated: Lieutenant E.D. Coe, 1st Alabama Cavalry, Volunteers, has permission to proceed beyond the limits of the Department of the Tennessee and await the settlement of his accounts with the Department at Washington, D.C. previous to his being mustered out of service; his company having been mustered out of the United States Service and he being not liable to duty, nor entitled to pay. By order of Major General S.A. Hurlburt.

Coffman, Robert R. - Only two cards were found for Robert R. Coffman which were filed at the end of the last roll of microfilm of the 1st Alabama Cavalry, USV Muster Rolls. They recorded him as a private in Company M. His name appeared on a Hospital Muster Roll for No. 3 USA General Hospital in Nashville, Tennessee as a patient since June 28, 1864. No further information relative to this soldier was found.*

Cohorn, David R. - Only one card was found for David R. Cohorn which was filed at the end of the last roll of microfilm of the 1st Alabama Cavalry, USV records. It recorded him as a private in Company M. He was recorded as being on extra or daily duty as the Regimental Bugler January through June 1865 On June 30, 1865, he was returned from absent, on daily duty. No further information relative to this soldier was found.*

Cole, John R. - John R. Cole enlisted in Company B of the 1st Alabama Cavalry, USV as a private on January 20, 1863, in Glendale, Mississippi for a term of 1 year. He was enrolled by Captain Phillip A. Sternberg and was mustered in January 22, 1863, in Corinth, Mississippi. The Regimental

Descriptive Book recorded him as being 27 years of age, 6'-1" tall, having a fair complexion, blue eyes, light hair, born in Franklin County, Alabama, and a farmer by occupation. The September and October 1863 Muster Roll recorded him as being absent, prisoner of war since October 26, 1863. His name appeared on the Returns as follows: August and September 1863, on daily duty as company cook; October and November 1863, absent in the hands of the enemy since the engagement of Vincent's Crossroads on October 26, 1863. He was mustered out January 22, 1864, in Memphis, Tennessee due to expiration of term of service.

John R Cole, Private, Company B, First Alabama Cavalry, Pension File, July 15, 1890, Declaration for Invalid Pension: John R Cole (age 53 years), a resident of Joppa, Massac County, Illinois was enrolled on January 14, 1863; honorably discharged at Memphis, Tennessee on the 22nd day of January 1864. He is wholly unable to earn a support by reason of eyresephilas and granulation of eyes, and blood poisoning resulting there from. Signed John R Cole by his mark; Attested by John H. Wood and Martha A Wood.

January 15, 1898. Circular with questions forwarded to pensioner with quarterly payment:

Married: Mrs. Sarah M. maiden name Clement; married at Franklin County, Alabama, Lem Nelson, J. P. June 22, 1855; records burned during War. Living children: Martha A., born November 29, 1856, Isabel, born February 14, 1859, Mary E., born February 11, 1865, Florence E., born July 14, 1877, Susan, born September 13, 1861. Replied July 5, 1898; Signed: John R. Cole by his mark.

May 7, 1907: Marriage Certificate for John R. Cole to Mrs. Elizabeth Benton by O. J. Taylor, Justice of the Peace. Filed by Clerk of the County George C. Schneeman, January 2, 1908, at Metropolis, Massac County, Illinois.

January 24, 1908: Affidavit by Sadie Maxfield, age 27, Joppa, Massac County, Illinois in the matter of the Claim for Accrued Pension of Elizabeth Cole, widow of John R. Cole: "That she was well acquainted with John R. Coles former wife, having lived near them for a number of years and that she was frequently present during the last illness of Mrs. Cole and helped to take care of and sit up with her. And that she saw Mrs. Cole after she was dead. And was at the church during the funeral service when she was buried. Affiant states that the funeral occurred on or about the 14th of February, 1901, as she remembered being at the Post Office on the day of the funeral and getting in her mail a comic Valentine that made her angry. Affiant further states that she cannot remember the year but that it has been seven or eight years. Filed January 29, 1908.

January 24, 1908: Affidavit by J. M. Elliott, a resident of Metropolis, Massac, County Illinois: "That he is an undertaker and as such sold the funeral outfit for the above named soldier, who died at Joppa, Massac County, Illinois on the 18 day of Nov. 1907. Filed January 20, 1908.

January 27, 1908: Report of Finance Division of Bureau of Pensions of removal of John R. Cole from roll: died November 18, 1907; last paid at $15 per month to October 4 1907, has this day been dropped from the roll. Signed Charles Bent, Agent. January 27, 1908.

February 26, 1908: Affidavit by Elizabeth Cole, age 57 of Metropolis, Massac County, Illinois: "That she was previously married to William S. Benton who died on the 16th of April 1901 at Wyatt Missouri. That he was never in any military or naval service. That she never was married to anyone except William Benton. And. John R. Cole. That after her marriage to said John R Cole; she lived with him as husband and wife that they were never parted until his death November 18, 1907. Said John R. Cole was previously married and his first wife who died on the 12th day of February 1901. That there is no record evidence of deaths. That the affidavits of William and Rosa Wyatt have been forwarded to the department in regard to the death William S. Benton. And evidence of death of Sarah Cole first wife of soldier, who died February 12, 1901, and John R. Cole who died November 18, 1907. Witnessed by Leona M. Kidd and Thomas Liggett.

February 28, 1908: Declaration for Widow's Pension: Elizabeth Cole, age 57, a resident of the city of Metropolis, Massac County, Illinois appeared before George C. Schneeman, returned the pension certificate 662,630 of John R Cole and filed for pension. She was married under the name of Elizabeth Benton to John R Cole on the 7 day of May 1907 by O. J. Taylor, J. P. at Joppa, Illinois. She appointed Thomas Liggett of Metropolis her attorney. Signed Elizabeth Cole. Attested by Palestine Rew (Kew?), Cora Meyer. Filed March 2, 1908. Transcription of Pension Records for John R. Cole, submitted by Ronald Mayhall.

Coleman, Edward - Only one card was found for Edward Coleman which was filed at the end of the last roll of microfilm of the 1st Alabama Cavalry, USV records. It recorded him as a private in Company B. stating he enlisted on February 11, 1864, in Pulaski, Tennessee. The Company Descriptive Book recorded him as 21 years of age, 5'-6" tall, having fair complexion, gray eyes, light hair, born in Shelby County, Tennessee, and a printer by occupation. His enlistment was credited to Pulaski, Giles County, Tennessee. He was enrolled by Lieutenant Judy for a period of 3 years. No further information relative to this soldier was found.*

Coleman, Thomas M. - Thomas M. Coleman, also listed as Thomas C. Coleman, enlisted in Company B of the 1st Alabama Cavalry, USV on February 20, 1864, in Pulaski, Tennessee for a term of 3 years. He was enrolled by Lieutenant Judy and was mustered in March 27, 1864, in Decatur, Alabama. His enlistment was credited to Pulaski, Giles County, Tennessee. The Muster and Descriptive Roll recorded him as being 21 years of age, 5'-10" tall, having a light complexion, gray eyes, light hair, born in Giles County, Tennessee, and a farmer by occupation. He was appointed to Corporal on August 1, 1864. The September and October 1864 Muster Roll recorded him as being absent, sent to the hospital in Rome, Georgia October 14, 1864. The November and December 1864 Muster Roll recorded him as being wounded in action and sent to the hospital in Rome, Georgia October 14, 1864. He was mustered out on October 20, 1864, in Huntsville, Alabama.

Collier, Allen - Allen Collier enlisted in Company C of the 1st Alabama Cavalry, USV as a private on February 10, 1863, in Corinth, Mississippi for a period of 1 year, and was enrolled by Captain John Latty. The Regimental and Descriptive Book showed Collier to have been 21 years of age, 5-5" tall, having a dark complexion, black eyes, black hair, born in Tishomingo County, Mississippi, and a farmer by occupation. He was shown as being absent without leave on February 21, 1863, and was reported to have deserted from Glendale, Mississippi on June 28, 1863.

Collier, George W. - George W. Collier enlisted in Company C of the 1st Alabama Cavalry, USV as a private on February 10, 1863, in Corinth, Mississippi. He was enrolled by D.R. Adams The Regimental Descriptive Book recorded him as being 30 years of age, 5'-5" tall, having a fair complexion, blue eyes, dark hair, born in Perry County, Tennessee, and a farmer by occupation. A Notation in his records from the Record and Pension Division of the War Department dated May 5, 1892, stated: "Investigation fails to elicit any further information relative to this soldier."

Collier, Squire - Squire Collier and his brothers, Allen and George W. Squire, enlisted in Company C of the 1st Alabama Cavalry, USV as a private, in Corinth, Mississippi. He was enrolled by Captain John Latty for a term of 1 year. The Regimental Descriptive Book recorded Squire as being 23 years of age, 5'-6" tall, having a fair complexion, blue eyes, dark hair, born in Perry County, Tennessee, and a farmer by occupation. He was absent without leave on February 21, 1863, and was reported to have deserted from Glendale, Mississippi on June 28, 1863. It appears that Squire and his two brothers, Allen and George W. Collier, all deserted. He was a brother to Allen and Squire Collier and they all deserted

Collins, Christopher C. - Christopher C. Collins enlisted in Company M of the 1st Alabama Cavalry, USV as a private on December 16, 1863, in Camp Davies, Mississippi. He was enrolled by Captain Lomax and was mustered in the same day in Corinth, Mississippi for a term of 1 year. Another muster roll stated he enlisted for a term of 3 years. The Company Descriptive Roll listed him as being 18 years of age, 5'-8" tall, having a dark complexion, black eyes, brown hair, born in Marshall County, Mississippi, and a farmer by occupation. He was promoted to Corporal for meritorious conduct in the field on December 1, 1864. He was mustered out October 20, 1865, in Huntsville, Alabama as a Sergeant, owing the U.S. Government $15.90 for losing 2 saddle blankets, 1 bridle, halter and strap. It had originally stated he had lost 1 Remington revolver. He was due a bounty of $300 and was paid $180 and shown to be due the other $120 for the total of the $300.

C.C. Collins was born March 17, 1846, in Mississippi and died December 8, 1937, in Polk County, Texas. He married Letha Keeton on January 16, 1868, in Walker County, Alabama. Letha died February 20, 1926, in Polk County, Texas. Christopher was a minister and farmer. Children: Silvester Chumway, born November 19, 1868; William Theophilus, born July 17, 1870; L. (Lovella?), born April 10, 187?; Arletta, born May 26, 1876; Volney Adolphus, born June 20, 1878; Asalea/Azalea, born December 16, 188?; Josephine, born June 1, 188?; and Thula Collins, born July 4, 1883. Christopher is buried in Camp Ruby Cemetery just outside of Livingston, Polk County, Texas. Family information submitted in part by Lisa Collins and David Collins

    Collins, John A. - This John A. Collins had a Pension Index Card on file, stating he served in Company C of the 1st Alabama Infantry, which was the original name of the regiment, but he was not listed on the microfilm of soldiers in the 1st Alabama Cavalry, USV that was purchased from the National Archives and transcribed. His pension records were then ordered from the Veterans Administration who stated the records had been shipped to Kansas for storage and they were unable to locate them. The records were again ordered from the Veterans Administration, who stated the following: "The service records you requested are not located at our station. We unfortunately were unable to locate a known record on Veteran John A. Collins. We worked with two National Archive Storage Facilities, and a thorough search was conducted at both sites. We apologize for the delay in processing your request, and for not being able to provide a more favorable response." They do, however, have a Pension Index Card for John A. Collins showing he did indeed serve in Company C of the regiment and he filed for a pension June 21, 1924, from Alabama. He may have already been drawing a pension and this was a request for an increase in his pension, but apparently we will never know. One Prisoner of War Record was found for John Collins which was filed at the end of the last roll of microfilm of the 1st Alabama Cavalry, USV Muster Rolls. It recorded him as being in Company D and stated he was captured at Lebanon, Alabama November 24, 1864, paroled at Vicksburg, Mississippi April 22, 1865, reported to Benton Barracks April 27, 1865, and sent to Camp Chase, Ohio May 14, 1865.

    There was a John A. Collins listed on the 1860 Tuscaloosa County, Alabama Census as age 20, born in Alabama, and son of David A. and Martha L. Collins. Other children in household were: Andrew J., Jane E., William S., Thomas D., and Wash M. Collins. There was also a John A. Collins listed on the 1860 Lowndes County, Alabama Census as age 33, with the following people in the household: Martha, James B., John, Eliza C., Caroline Collins, age 75, Sarah Grimes, B.F. Grimes, and H.A. Grimes. It is uncertain which or if either of these was the John A. Collins who served in the 1st Alabama Cavalry, USV.

    Collins, Volney B. - Volney B. Collins enlisted in Company M of the 1st Alabama Cavalry, USV as a private on December 16, 1863, in Camp Davies, Mississippi for a period of 3 years. He was enrolled by Captain Trammel, and was mustered in December 29, 1863, in Corinth, Mississippi. The Company Descriptive Book recorded him as being 24 years of age, 6' tall, having a dark complexion, gray eyes, dark hair, born in Spartanburg District, South Carolina, and was a farmer by occupation. He was promoted to Corporal December 16, 1863. He died of typhoid pneumonia on January 15, 1864, in the Regimental Hospital in Camp Davies, Mississippi.

    Coltman, J.R. - Only one card was found for J.R. Coltman which was filed at the end of the last roll of microfilm of the 1st Alabama Cavalry, USV records. It recorded him as a private in Company H, stating he enlisted October 18, 1863, in Glendale, Mississippi. No further information relative to this soldier was found.*

    Colwell/Caldwell, Stephen N. - Stephen N. Colwell, also spelled Caldwell, enlisted and mustered into Company F of the 1st Alabama Cavalry, USV as a private on August 5, 1864, in Rome, Georgia for a period of 3 years. He was enrolled by Lieutenant Fishback. The Company Descriptive Roll showed Colwell to have been 18 years of age, 5'-8" tall, having a fair complexion, gray eyes, light hair, born in Buncombe County, North Carolina, and a farmer by occupation. The November and December 1864 Muster Roll listed him as being absent, sick in Nashville, Tennessee since November 6, 1864, and did not return from being sick in the hospital until June 27, 1865. He was reported to have deserted October 1, 1865, from Moulton, Alabama with 1 horse, saddle and equipment, Spencer

Carbine and accoutrements, saber belt, spurs and straps.

Con, John W. - See John W. Crow, his records were filed under John W. Con.

Conaway, Andrew J. - Andrew Jackson Conaway, also known as William Andrew Jackson Conaway, enlisted in Company C of the 1st Alabama Cavalry, USV on March 22, 1863, in Glendale, Mississippi for a period of 1 year. He was enrolled by Captain John Latty, and was mustered in November 17, 1863, in Corinth, Mississippi. The Company Descriptive Book recorded him as being 19 years of age, 5'-7" tall, having a dark complexion, dark eyes, dark hair, born in Lumpkin County, Georgia, and a farmer by occupation. The July and August 1863 Muster Roll listed him as being absent, sick in the hospital in Corinth. The September and October 1863 Muster Roll listed him as being absent, a prisoner of war in the hands of the enemy on October 26, 1863, which would have been from the Battle of Vincent's Crossroads near Red Bay, Alabama. On November 17, 1863, he returned to Camp Davies, Mississippi from being a POW. He was discharged March 26, 1864, due to expiration of term of service. However, the Muster-Out Roll stated he was mustered out on March 22, 1864. He was shown as being single.

William Andrew Jackson Conaway was born about 1843 in Lumpkin County, Georgia, according to his military records. One descendant stated he was born in Newton County, Georgia. He was the son of William J. Conaway, and his wife, Mary Tyler, who married March 23, 1825, in Newton County, Georgia. William was born 1798 in Georgia and died June 8, 1864, in Coosa County, Alabama. Mary Tyler Conaway was born June 4, 1808, in Newton County, Georgia, and died June 4, 1883 in Weatherford, Parker County, Texas. Other children of William J. and Mary Tyler Conaway were: Martha M., born 1825, died 1899; John Monroe, born May 30, 1829, died July 28, 1878; James H., born 1831, died April 27, 1855; Thomas Jefferson, born 1833, died July 15, 1862; Sarah E., born 1836, died April 11, 1857; and Francis Marion Conaway, born 1838, died December 1862. William Andrew Jackson Conaway married Amanda Kilgore July 18, 1865, in Coosa County, Alabama and they had the following children: William H.; James M.; Roser (?); John; Virginia "Jennie"; Norah; and Augustus Conaway. In the 1900 Sevier County, Arkansas Census, Amanda Conaway was enumerated as the head of household and it stated she had 10 children with only 3 alive. William Andrew Jackson Conaway may have also served in the 13th Alabama Infantry, CSA,

Conaway, John E. - John E. Conaway, probably brother to the Andrew Jackson Conaway, above, enlisted in Company C of the 1st Alabama Cavalry, USV as a private on March 22, 1863, in Glendale, Mississippi by John Latty, and was mustered in April 10, 1863. The Company Descriptive Book stated he was 21 years of age, 5'-10" tall. Having a dark complexion, dark eyes, dark hair, born in Lumpkin County, Georgia, and a farmer by occupation. His name appeared on the Returns stating he was on detached service in July 1863, as a company cook. A Notation in his file from the Adjutant General's Office of the War Department in Washington, DC, dated May 10, 1887, stated the following: A Notation in his records from the Adjutant General's Office of the War Department dated May 10, 1887, stated the following: This man died in Regimental Hospital January 15, 1864, of inflammation of the tonsils, but did not state which hospital or where.

John E. Conaway married Margaret Lay on January 3, 1861, in Walker County, Alabama. They were married by William Neasmith, a Justice of the Peace. John was the son of Norris Connaway and Cynthia Abbott, who were married May 20, 1841, in Lumpkin County, Georgia. John E. Conaway died January 15, 1864, in the regimental hospital of inflammation of the tonsils.

Connelin, L. - Only one card was found for L. Connelin which stated he was in Company H and was discharged October 25, 1864, by reason of expiration of term of service. No further information relative to this soldier was found.*

Conner, Lewis E. - Lewis E. Conner enlisted in Company F of the 1st Alabama Cavalry, USV as a private on December 6, 1863, in Camp Davies, Mississippi, for a period of 1 year. He was enrolled by Lieutenant W.H. Cheney, and was mustered in February 24, 1864, in Memphis, Tennessee. The Muster and Descriptive Roll recorded him as being 36 years of age, 6'-6" tall, (another Descriptive Roll stated he was 6'-½" tall) having a dark complexion, dark eyes, dark hair, born in Lincoln County, North Carolina, and a farmer by occupation. A Stop was put on his pay for $12.00 losing 1 Remington revolver. He was killed in action near Rome, Georgia on September 6, 1864. His name appeared on the Returns as follows: August 1864, Detailed as Scout at General Vandiver's Headquarters in Rome, Georgia; September 1864, Killed in action September 6, 1864, near Rome, Georgia.

Connor, Marion - Marion Conner enlisted in Company D of the 1st Alabama Cavalry, USV as a private on April 19, 1864, in Decatur, Alabama. He was enrolled by Lieutenant Pease for a period of 3 years. The Company Descriptive Book recorded Conner as being 24 years of age, 6' tall, having a light complexion, blue eyes, dark hair, born in DeKalb County, Alabama, and a farmer by occupation. He was on detached service from the time he enlisted through August 1864, recruiting in Alabama by order of Colonel Spencer. The September and October 1864 Muster Roll listed him as being absent in Alabama with leave. After he returned from leave, he was absent in Alabama recruiting to April 1865. January through March 1865, he was on detached service with Major Shurtleff in north Alabama. In April 1865 he was on detached service in north Alabama with Captain Lomax. The May and June 1865 Muster Roll listed him as being absent without leave. The July and August 1865 Muster Roll showed him to have deserted July 10, 1865, from Moulton, Alabama, and ordered his pay stopped for 1 saddle, Pat. 59. $28.10. There was a Notation in his file from the Adjutant General's Office of the War Department in Washington, DC, dated May 4, 1888, which stated: "All charges of Absent Without Leave, and desertion on or subsequent to June 30, 1865, against this man are removed and he is discharged to date June 30, 1865, under the provisions of the Act of Congress, approved July 5, 1884. Discharge Certificate furnished by Adjutant General's Office May 10, 1888.

Cook, Charles J. – Charles J. Cook enlisted in Company L of the 1st Alabama Cavalry, USV as a Private on September 25, 1863, in Fayette County, Alabama for a period of 1 year. He was enrolled by Captain Trammel, and was mustered in the same day at Glendale, Mississippi. The Company Descriptive Book showed Cook to have been 42 years of age, 5'-9" tall, having a fair complexion, blue eyes, light hair, born in Union County, North Carolina, and a farmer by occupation. The November and December 1863 Muster Roll stated he had been absent with leave since October 20, 1863, by order of Colonel Spencer. The January and February 1864 Muster Roll listed him as being absent, missing in action October 26, 1863, from Vincent's Crossroads, which was near Red Bay, Alabama. The September and October 1864 Muster Roll showed him as being a prisoner of war in the hands of the enemy since October 26, 1863. His name appeared on the Returns as follows: October 1863, Absent with leave; November 1863, Absent, left sick in Alabama by order of Colonel Spencer; December 1863, Absent in Alabama since the raid October 26, 1863; March through August 1864: Absent, prisoner of war since October 26, 1863; September and October 1864: Absent, sick; June 1865; Missing in action October 26, 1863 from Vincent's Crossroads, Mississippi, before reported as prisoner of war. Charles J. Cook also served in the U.S. - Mexican War which began on April 25, 1846. It ended when the Treaty of Guadalupe Hidalgo was signed on February 2, 1848. However, fighting between Mexican guerrillas and U.S. troops continued for several months afterward. The last American troops left Mexico on August 2, 1848. He died of disease on February 23, 1864, in Richmond, Virginia while still a prisoner of war. He is buried in the Richmond National Cemetery, in Richmond, Henrico County, Virginia.

Charles J. Cook was born about 1821 in Union County, North Carolina, and on September 27, 1848, he married Nancy Ann Whitley, daughter of Henry Clay Whitley and Nancy Bridges, in Fayetteville, North Carolina. Children of Charles and Nancy Ann were: Martha J., born February 17, 1850, died July 2, 1894; James A., born July 29, 1852, died December 13, 1911; Jesse E., born February 7, 1853, died September 25, 1931; Mary Ann, born March 12, 1855; Henry Thomas, born October 2, 1859; and John A. Cook, born October 1, 1862. Charles J. Cook died February 23, 1864, in Richmond, Wise County, Virginia. Nancy Ann died January 26, 1896, in Fayette County, Alabama.

Cook, Daniel, L. - Daniel L. Cook, enlisted in Company A of the 1st Alabama Cavalry, USV as a private on January 23, 1864, at Camp Davies, Mississippi for a period of 3 years. He was enrolled by Lieutenant Hinds and was mustered in February 5, 1864, in Memphis, Tennessee. The Muster and Descriptive Roll showed him to have been 35 years of age, 5'-11" tall, having a fair complexion, gray eyes, light hair, born in Tennessee, and a farmer by occupation. His name appeared on the Returns as follows: April 1864, on detached duty as a teamster; July to October 1864, on duty as regimental teamster. A letter in his file stated the following: Charges and specifications preferred against Private Daniel L. Cook, Company A, 1st Alabama Cavalry Volunteers. Charge: Assault with intent to commit murder. Specification: In this that he the said Daniel L. Cook, Private Company A 1st Alabama Cavalry did whilst engaged in a difficulty with one John Abernathy, Company A, 1st Alabama Cavalry, draw his revolver and with the intent to kill said John Abernathy, did fire at him and seriously wound him. This near the came of the 1st Alabama Cavalry on the march between Hillsboro and Greensbury, North Carolina on or about the 5th day of May 1865. Signed George W. Benson, 2nd Lieutenant Commanding Company A, 1st Alabama Cavalry. Witnesses: Elisha Chambless, Perry Byford, and Aaron B. Pollard, all privates in the 1st Alabama Cavalry, USV. It does not reveal the outcome of the charges. Cook was mustered out October 20, 1865, in Huntsville, Alabama owing the U.S. Government $2.02 for losing 1 carbine sling and swivel. He was due a bounty of $300, but was only paid $180 and stated he was due $120 to make up the $300 bounty.

Cook. George L. - George L. Cook enlisted and mustered into Company H of the 1st Alabama Cavalry, USV as a private on December 13, 1863, in Camp Davies, Mississippi for a term of 1 year. He was 36 years of age when he enlisted. The May 1864 through August 1864 Muster Rolls listed him as being absent, sick in General Hospital in Nashville, Tennessee since March 26th. The September and October 1864 Muster Roll listed him as having deserted, and his pay was stopped for taking one Remington revolver with him that belonged to the U.S. Government.

Southern Claim No: 21671: Date of Hearing: May 28, 1877

Place of Residence: Walker County, Alabama (lived near Dublin, Fayette County, when petition filed in 1873)

Length of Residence in Fayette County: Since at least "six months prior to the rebellion and during the whole of the late war" (moved to Walker County about 1875)

Age: 69 years; Place of Birth: Georgia; Place of Residence at Time of Incident/s: At or near Dublin, Alabama.

Remarks: He was known, recognized and treated as a friend to the Union by both Confederates and Unionists. He was threatened with death by the rebels and hid in the woods for 6 months to avoid them. He eventually was arrested and put in jail for his loyalty and was released by a Union scout named John Stout (General Dodge's"favorite spy"). He persuaded his son to join the Union army and also had a brother who served.

Brief Description of Incident/s: On or about March 25, 1865, Colonel Tompkins of General Wilson's army took from claimant's residence livestock, feed and foodstuffs valued at about $700.

Witnesses, Testifiers and Others:

Francis M. Black, age 73; resident of Fayette County for about 30 years

Charles Cook, brother, enlisted 1863 in 1st Alabama Cavalry, Company L, at Glendale, Mississippi; captured by the rebels October 26, 1863, near Vinsons (Vincent's) Cross Roads, Mississippi, "and was brutally murdered by them at Andersonville Prison in the state of Georgia"

James Cook, son, enlisted 1864 in 1st Alabama Cavalry, Company D, at Decatur, Alabama; living in Mississippi in 1877

Mary A. Cook, daughter, age 34; resident of Walker County, Alabama, for two years

James C. Cooner, age 41, resident of Walker County, Alabama, "all my life"; acquainted with claimant for 17 years; lived 2½ miles from him during war; Union soldier

Elijah A. Jeffreys, age 43, resident of Fayette County for 30 years; acquainted with claimant for 20 years; lived three miles from him during war; conscripted by the rebels, escaped and hid out with claimant's assistance

Capt. Stoke Roberts, CSA; arrested claimant in Marion County, Alabama in 1864.

James F. Stovall, age 46, resident of Fayette County and acquainted with claimant for 20 years; lived two miles from him during war; Union soldier

Capt. D.H. Whatley, CSA; threatened to hang claimant

Joseph Adkins, Isham Cock, A.J. Files, G.W. Jeffreys, Richard Panter, Jacob Phelpman (Feltman), John A.W. Shaw, David Studdard & Samuel Studdard (prominent Unionists in Dublin area)

<u>Cook, James</u> - James Cook enlisted in Company D of the 1st Alabama Cavalry, USV as a private for a period of 3 years on May 1, 1864, in Decatur, Alabama. He was enrolled by Lieutenant Pease and was mustered in June 16, 1864, in Decatur. The Muster and Descriptive Roll showed him to have been 18 years of age, 5'-7" tall, having a light complexion, blue eyes, light hair, born in Marion County, Alabama, and a farmer by occupation. He was mustered out October 20, 1865, in Huntsville, Alabama, owing the U.S. Government $6.50 for losing 1 saddle blanket, 1 curry comb, and 1 surcingle. His Muster-Out Roll stated he was due a bounty of $100. There was an unusual form in James Cook's file that stated: Camp of Distribution, Middle Department, Eighth Army Corps, Baltimore, June 5, 1865: Sir: Please take notice of the following clothing to be charged upon your company rolls as per receipt the following article of clothing: 1 flannel sack coat or blouse, 1 pair trowsers; 1 flannel shirt, and 1 pair of drawers. Total Money Value, $14.54.

<u>Cook, Riley P.</u> - Riley Parker Cook enlisted in Company C of the 1st Alabama Cavalry, USV as a Private on January 12, 1863, in Corinth, Mississippi for a period of 1 year. He was enrolled by Captain John Latty and was mustered in January 20, 1863, in Corinth. On August 1, 1863, he was detailed as Bugler. The Regimental Descriptive Book recorded him as being 33 years of age, 5'-8½" tall, having a fair complexion, blue eyes, light hair, born in Haywood County, North Carolina, and a farmer by occupation. He mustered out January 31, 1864, in Memphis, Tennessee.

Riley Parker Cook was born March 11, 1828, in Haywood County, North Carolina, and married Mary Ann Pratchard February 3, 1849, in Hamilton County, Tennessee. Children of Riley and Mary Ann were: Patience Elizabeth, born November 3, 1850; Amanda Jane, born January 17, 1852; George Thomas, born January 17, 1852; Jasper, born January 13, 1854; Catherine Julia, born July 22, 1855; Louisa, born February 14, 1857; Martha Emmaline, born January 3, 1859; Riley, born April 24, 1861; and Mary Ann Cook, born March 15, 1863. Riley's wife, Mary Ann, had died on April 22, 1869, in Crawford County, Missouri, and he married Mary Susan White on February 2, 1870, in Crawford County, Missouri. She was born July 11, 1842, and died April 13, 1910. Mary Susan White was the daughter of Alfred William White and his wife Nancy Dawson, who were married August 20, 1839, in Cole County, Missouri. Riley Parker Cook died April 24, 1902, in Crawford County, Missouri, and was buried in the old Farrar Cemetery on Dry Creek, on the Franklin Ware farm, near Westover, Crawford County, Missouri.

<u>Cook, Thomas Kinzie</u> - Thomas Kinzie Cook enlisted in Company H of the 1st Alabama Cavalry, USV on December 30, 1864, as a private in Stevenson, Alabama for a period of 3 years. He was enrolled by Captain James W. DeVaney and mustered in February 13, 1865, in Nashville, Tennessee. The Muster and Descriptive Roll recorded him as being 36 years of age, 6' tall, having a dark complexion, blue eyes, black hair, born in Wall County, Georgia, and a farmer by occupation. His enlistment was credited to Ripley, Chautauqua County, New York. He was mustered out October 20, 1865, in Huntsville, Alabama owing the US Government $1.20 for transportation from Huntsville to Stevenson, Alabama on September 11, 1865. He was paid a bounty of $100 when he mustered out.

Thomas was born 1828 in Hall County, Georgia, and married Jane Grizzell, daughter of James and Mary Ray Grizzell, on July 22, 1852, in Lumpkin County, Georgia. Thomas and Jane had seven children, all but one born in Georgia. Children of Thomas and Jane were: Amanda Jane, born July 2,1853, died December 28, 1901; Asbury Thomas, born Jun 28, 1856, died December 4, 1940; William J., born December 14, 1858, died May 25, 1935; Sarah Jane, born September 8, 1862, died June 29, 1924; Alfred Sherman, born January 25, 1868, died May 22, 1947; Elijah Isaac, born July 1880, died January 17, 1913; Andrew Cook, born 1872;

He first enlisted in Atlanta, Georgia in Company C, 35th Georgia Infantry, CSA and was involved in the battles of Seven Pines (Fir Oaks), Chickahominy (Mechanicsville), Cedar Mountain, Second bull Run, Fredericksburg, Chancellorsville, Gettysburg, The Wilderness, and Spotsylvania. He is reported as having deserted at Petersburg on August 26, 1864, signed the oath of allegiance to the USA on October 21, 1864, and sent to prison at Chattanooga, Tennessee. He then enlisted in the First Alabama Cavalry USV in December. In 1872 he took his wife and five children and moved to northern Arkansas in a covered wagon. They settled on a farm in Marion County near Yellville. He died August

5, 1877, in Marion County, Arkansas and is buried in Fairview Cemetery near Flippin, Arkansas. Family information submitted by Gary Long,

Another descendant stated that in 1872, Thomas took his wife and five children and moved to northern Arkansas in a covered wagon. They settled on a farm in Marion County in Yellville.

<u>Cook, William W.</u> - William W. Cook enlisted and mustered into Company I of the 1st Alabama Cavalry, USV as a private in Huntsville, Alabama for a period of 3 years. He was enrolled by Captain Bankhead, and was mustered in August 18, 1862, in Huntsville. Cook was one of the early enlistees who were immediately shipped to Nashville, Tennessee and merged with the 1st Middle Tennessee Cavalry, and 5th Tennessee Cavalry, US, and Cook was merged with Company D of the 1st Middle Tennessee Cavalry. The Company Descriptive Roll listed him as having been 46 years of age, 5'-6" tall, having a light complexion, hazel eyes, light hair, born in Wayne County, North Carolina, and was a blacksmith by occupation. His name appeared on a Muster and Descriptive Roll dated July 2, 1863, and stated: Muster and Descriptive Roll of a detachment forwarded from Columbus, Ohio to Cincinnati, Ohio pursuant to orders. Paroled prisoner of war, and exchanged. The November and December 1862 Muster Roll listed him as being absent, sick in hospital in Nashville, Tennessee since October 24, 1862. His name appeared on a Hospital Muster Roll for Dennison U.S.A. General Hospital in Camp Dennison Ohio, stating he was attached to the hospital on December 27, 1862, as a patient. The Company Muster Roll from December 31, 1862, through June 30, 1863, stated Cook was missing in action from the Battle at Day's Gap, Alabama, since April 28, 1863. Rejoined regiment August 2, 1863. The July and August 1863 Muster Roll stated: Missing in action after Battle of Cedar Bluff, Alabama May 9, 1863, injured August 1, 1863. A note at the bottom of this muster roll stated "Corrected March 30, 1899. He was shown as being present on the June 30th to August 31, 1863 Muster Roll. In November 1863, he was on daily duty as a blacksmith. The Prisoner of War Record for William W. Cook stated he was captured at Cedar Bluff, Alabama on May 23, 1863, reported at Camp Parole, Maryland, May 25, 1863, sent to Camp Chase, Ohio, June 23, 1863, reported there July 2, 1863, and was sent to regiment the same day. He died of disease (ruptured aorta) December 1, 1863, at Camp Davies, Mississippi.

<u>Cooksey, Enoch C.</u> - Enoch C. Cooksey enlisted in Company B of the 1st Alabama Cavalry, USV on December 23, 1862, in Glendale, Mississippi. He was enrolled by Captain Frank C. Burdick and was mustered in January 22, 1863, in Corinth, Mississippi for a period of 1 year. The Regimental Descriptive Book recorded him as being 28 years of age, 5'-10" tall, having a light complexion, blue eyes, auburn hair, born in Warren County, Tennessee, and a farmer by occupation. He died of measles February 22, 1863, in the Seminary Hospital at Corinth, Mississippi. Another muster roll stated he died February 25, 1863. He was buried in Grave #B-230 in the Corinth National Cemetery.

<u>Cooksey, Martin L.</u> - Martin L. Cooksey enlisted in Company C of the 1st Alabama Cavalry, USV as a private on December 1, 1862, in Corinth, Mississippi for a term of 1 year. He was enrolled by D.R. Adams, and was mustered in December 22, 1862, in Corinth. The Regimental Descriptive Book showed him to have been 37 years of age, 5'-6" tall, having a fair complexion, gray eyes, dark hair, born in Buncombe County, North Carolina, and a farmer by occupation. He was detailed as hospital nurse on May 18, 1863. On November 9, 1863, he was shown as being sick in Corinth. He mustered out December 17, 1863 at Memphis, Tennessee due to expiration of term of service.

<u>Cooley, John H.</u> - John H. Cooley, also listed as Cooly, enlisted in Company A of the 1st Alabama Cavalry, USV as a private on September 5, 1864, in Rome, Georgia for a period of 3 years. He was enrolled by Captain Jerome Hinds. The Company Descriptive Book recorded him as being 21 years of age, 5'-9" tall, having a fair complexion, blue eyes, light hair, born in Coweta County, Georgia, and a farmer by occupation. The September through December 1864 Muster Rolls listed him as being absent, prisoner of war since October 3, 1864. The January and February 1865 Muster Roll listed him as being absent, captured near Rome, Georgia on October 2, 1864. His Muster Rolls through December 1865, state he was absent, prisoner of war since October 26, 1864, never heard from since. The Muster Roll stated: Prisoner of war since October 3, 1864, captured near Rome, Georgia. No discharge

furnished on muster out of organization. Not mustered out. His name appeared on the Returns and stated the following: October 1864, on detached service as a guide; January to September 1865, absent, prisoner of war since October 3, 1864, captured at Cave Springs, Georgia.

Cooner, James Carroll - James Carroll Cooner enlisted in Company A of the 1st Alabama Cavalry, USV as a private on March 18, 1864, in Decatur, Alabama for a period of 3 years. Another record stated he enlisted March 28, 1864. He was enrolled by Captain John H. Hogan, and was mustered in April 13, 1864, in Decatur. The Muster and Descriptive Roll listed him as having been 28 years of age, 5'-7" tall, having a sandy complexion, blue eyes, sandy hair, born in Walker County, Alabama, and a farmer by occupation. The March and April 1864 Muster Roll stated he had been transferred to Company G by Regimental Order #62. His name appeared on the Returns and stated he was transferred to Company D on April 18, 1864, in Mooresville, Alabama. He was promoted to Corporal on May 1, 1864. On November 17, 1864, he was reported as having deserted from Atlanta, Georgia and left with side arms. However, these charges were removed April 21, 1886 as he returned June 17, 1865. The Returns also stated Cooner returned to Walker County, Alabama from desertion on March 15, 1865, and had reported to his company on June 8, 1865. He had been acting as a guide for General Wilson from March 15, 1865, to March 27, 1865. He had been captured by the CSA and forced to join the 13th Alabama Cavalry, CSA under Captain Shepherd. It wasn't long until he was able to escape and make his way back to the Union lines where he returned to his regiment June 17, 1865. He was mustered out October 20, 1865, in Huntsville, Alabama. There was a Notation in his records from the Adjutant General's Office of the War Department in Washington, DC, dated April 21, 1886, which stated: The Charge of desertion of November 17 and 20, 1864, against this man are removed under the provisions of the act of Congress, approved July 5, 1884. He was absent without proper authority from November 20, 1864, to March 15, 1865.

James was able to read and write and he signed all of his pension records. He is buried in the Files Cemetery in Walker County, Alabama with the following inscription on his tombstone: Cooner, James C., CORPL CO G, 1st ALA CAV USA

James C. Cooner was the son of James Patman Cooner and Martha Lollar. He was born December 25, 1835, near Pleasant Grove on Lost Creek in Walker County, Alabama. The Company Descriptive Book shows him to have been 5'-10" inches tall, weighing 155 pounds, having sandy hair, a fair complexion, blue eyes and no permanent marks or scars. He was able to read and write, and he signed all documents in his pension file. James Carroll Cooner married Mahalia Martha Lawson March 16, 1854, in Walker County, Alabama. Martha was the sister of Patmon Lawson, who also served in the 1st Alabama Cavalry. She and Patmon were the children of John Lawson and Sarah H. Ball. Martha was born April 24, 1833 in Walker County, Alabama and died December 23, 1927, in Walker County. Children of James and Martha Lollar Cooner were: Irene Elizabeth, born September 1855, died 1914; John W., born November 28, 1857, died April 2, 1904; Mary, born October 26, 1860, died September 11, 1935; Samuel S. December 1865, died May 12, 1947; Spencer Monroe, born 26 Nov 1868; Daniel J., born February 27, 1871; and Martha M. Cooner born October 25, 1873.

James Patman Cooner was born April 10, 1787, in Abbeville, South Carolina, and died about 1855 in Walker County, Alabama. His wife, Martha, was born December 13, 1794, in Abbeville District, South Carolina, and died in 1856 in Walker County, Alabama.

James Carroll Cooner stated that in August 1865, during a battle at Rome, Georgia he was overcome by sun-stroke, which left him highly susceptible to overheating the rest of his life; he claimed this as a "nervous disability." He said that he had been treated for this problem by Dr. J.F. Martin, Assistant Surgeon of the 1st Alabama Cavalry, at Rome in Sept 1864, and during the summer and fall of 1865 at Decatur; that he was treated later by L.C. Miller; and that he "used patent medications mostly all the time." In a later claim, he also said that he suffered from piles, heart trouble, rheumatism and Kidney Diseases."

James attested to the following: (sic)"I was forsed out in the confederate Armey by the Conscript ofiser but i left and went to the Federal Armey as soon as i cold git acros The lines." He enrolled 8 or 28 Mar 1864 at Decatur, AL as private in Co. G of the 1st AL Cavalry under Captain John H. Hogan and was honorably discharged at Huntsville on 20 or 25 Oct 1865. In Aug 1865 during a battle at Rome, GA, he was overcome by sun-stroke, which left him highly susceptible to overheating the rest of his life; he claimed this as a "nervous disability." He said that he had been treated for this problem by Dr. J.F. Martan, Assistant Surgeon of the 1st AL Cavalry, at Rome in Sept 1864, and during the summer and fall of 1865 at Decatur; that he was treated later by L.C. Miller; and that he "used pattent medisans mostly all the time." In a later claim, he also said that he suffered from "Piles, Heart Truble, Rhumitism and Kidney Deases."

George Allison Myers was a soldier in the Confederate Army, but when the Federal Army got to Huntsville, he, his brother Howell, his brother-in-law Jim Tindall, Carol Cooner and Dave Wolf (with Dave acting as a guide) went through the woods from Walker Co. to Huntsville and joined the Union Army. Some of them at least, were imprisoned. (Howell Myers, Jim Tindall and Carol Cooner appear in the roster of the 1st AL Cavalry; the others don't.) Carol Cooner's wife, Mahaley Lawson, was the aunt of George Allison Myers' wife, Sarah Ann Lawson. Also, a number of the Lawsons served in the same company in the 1st AL Cavalry.

He was designated as a corporal only on his gravestone and in one of two claims by his widow. James Carroll Cooner was buried in the Files Cemetery in Walker County, Alabama. Family information submitted by John Bush.

George Allison Myers was a soldier in the Confederate Army, but when the Federal Army got to Huntsville, he, his brother Howell, his brother-in-law Jim Tindall, Carol Cooner and Dave Wolf (with Dave acting as a guide) went through the woods from Walker Co. to Huntsville and joined the Union Army. Some of them at least, were imprisoned. (Howell Myers, Jim Tindall and Carol Cooner appear in the roster of the 1st AL Cavalry; the others don't.) Carol Cooner's wife, Mahaley Lawson, was the aunt of George Allison Myers' wife, Sarah Ann Lawson. Also, a number of the Lawsons served in the same company in the 1st AL Cavalry.

Carol and Mahala lived at Wolf Creek. They always lived in Walker Co., with their residence/post office listed variously as Holly Grove (1864, 1915), Beech Grove (1889), Chickasaw (1896, 1902), and Townley (1911, 1914-1916).

He is buried in Files Cemetery, Walker Co., AL. Gravestone inscription:
COONER, JAMES
CORPL CO G
1st ALA CAV USA

Cooper, James Mack - James M. Cooper enlisted in Company E of the 1st Alabama Cavalry, USV as a private on April 1, 1863, in Glendale, Mississippi for a term of 1 year. He was mustered in the same day in Corinth, Mississippi. The January and February 1864 Muster Roll recorded him as being absent, on detached duty as a teamster in Quartermaster Department in Vicksburg, Mississippi since January 25, 1864. He was discharged March 18, 1864, in Memphis, Tennessee due to expiration of term of service.

James Mack Cooper was born about 1822 in Alabama to Isaac Zack Cooper and Mahala Jane Blevins, who married January 21, 1823, in Marion County, Alabama. James Mack Cooper married Sophia Ann Glenn on December 4, 1853.

The previous James M. Cooper and the below Mack Cooper could possibly have been a father and son. In the 1850 Itawamba County, Mississippi Census, there was a family listed in this census with the head of household as James Cooper with wife, Mary Ann Cooper. They had a son, James M. Cooper, who was 9 years old and would have been old enough to have served during the Civil War. Other children in this family were: Leroy, John, Elizabeth, F.M., Eliza, William J., Emily S., George W., and Martha S. Cooper. However, it is not proven that this is the same family.

Cooper, Mack - Mack Cooper enlisted in Company E of the 1st Alabama Cavalry, USV on April 1, 1863, in Glendale, Mississippi for a term of 1 year, and mustered in the same day in Corinth, Mississippi. The May through August 1863 Muster Rolls recorded him as being absent, taken prisoner of war between Glendale and Burnsville, Mississippi June 11, 1863. The September and October 1863, Muster Roll recorded him as being missing in late action. A Muster Roll of 19 Company 1, Battalion, Paroled Men in Benton Barracks, Missouri listed the name of Mack Cooper and stated he was sick in the hospital, never settled clothing allowance. A Prisoner of War Record stated Cooper was captured June 11, 1863, at Corinth, Mississippi, confined at Richmond, Virginia June 26, 1863, paroled at

220

Richmond July 2, 1863, reported at Camp Parole, Maryland July 3, 1863, and reported at Benton Barracks July 19, 1863. A Casualty Sheet stated Mack Cooper was killed in action at Vincent's Crossroads December 15, 1863. The November and December 1863, Muster Roll stated he was killed in action December 15, 1863.

Corgan, William W. - William W. Corgan enlisted in Company F of the 1st Alabama Cavalry, USV for a period of 1 year on November 25, 1863, in Corinth, Mississippi. He was enrolled by Lieutenant W.H. Cheney, and was mustered in February 24, 1864, in Memphis, Tennessee. The Muster and Descriptive Roll shows him to have been 27 years of age, 5'-9" tall, having a fair complexion, blue eyes, dark hair, born in Union County, Illinois, and a carpenter by occupation. He was appointed sergeant on December 10, 1863. His name appeared on the Returns for November 1863 and stated he was gained from missing in action November 27, 1863. Corgan was promoted to 1st Sergeant March 1, 1864. He was appointed Sergeant Major on October 10, 1864, and mustered out December 17, 1864, in Savannah, Georgia due to expiration of term of service. There was a note in Corgan's file that stated the following: Mustered out by reason of being on the March from Atlanta to Savannah, Georgia. Mustered out by reason of expiration of term of service. Post Office, Jonesboro, Union County, Illinois

Corghanny, J.H. - Only one card was found for J.H. or I.H. Corghanny which was filed at the end of the last roll of microfilm of the 1st Alabama Cavalry, USV records. It recorded him as being discharged October 25, 1864, in Rome, Georgia due to expiration of term of service. No further information relative to this soldier was found.*

Corley, Holis M. - There was one card for Holis M. Corley, Card # 31833913, which stated he was in Company I of the 1st Alabama, but no further information relative to this soldier was found.*

Cornick, W. - Only one card was found for W. Cornick, which was filed at the end of the last roll of microfilm of the 1st Alabama Cavalry, USV records. It recorded him as a being in Company E, stating he was absent without leave July 1, 1863. No further information relative to this soldier was found.*

Cornelin, L. - Only one card was found for L. Cornelin which was filed at the end of the last roll of microfilm of the 1st Alabama Cavalry, USV records. It recorded him as a private in Company H, stating he was discharged October 25, 1864, at Rome, Georgia by reason of expiration of term of service. No further information relative to this soldier was found.*

Cornelius, Cargell - Cargill Cornelius, also spelled Cargell, was enlisted and was mustered into Company H of the 1st Alabama Cavalry, USV as a private on October 10, 1863, in Glendale, Mississippi for a period of 1 year. He was shown as being 34 years of age. On the September and October 1863 Muster Roll, he was shown as a 4th Sergeant; on the November and December 1863 Muster Roll, he was shown as a 4th Corporal; on the March and April 1864 Muster Roll, he was shown as a 2nd Corporal; on the July and August 1864 Muster Roll he was shown as a corporal. When Cornelius mustered out, he was charged $2.45 for losing 1 thong and brush wiper and 1 painted blanket. Cargill Cornelius died in 1885 in Blount County, Alabama and was buried in the Dailey's Chapel Cemetery in Blount County. He was the father of Zion Cornelius, below.

Cornelius, Zion - Zion B. Cornelius enlisted in Company H of the 1st Alabama Cavalry, USV on October 19, 1863, in Glendale, Mississippi and mustered in the same day in Camp Davies, Mississippi. He was listed on the Muster Rolls as a patient in Gayoso U.S.A. General Hospital in Memphis, Tennessee from February 23, 1864, until July 19, 1864, when he was returned to his company. He mustered out October 24, 1864, in Rome, Georgia.

       Zion B. Cornelius served in the Union Army in the Civil War. Zion was born in March 12, 1847, to Cargile Cornelius and Nancy C. Blackwood. Zion served in the place of an older brother. Zion was ill during most of his enlistment. He met Lucinda Jane (Jennie) Keen Grigsby. Lucinda Jane was a widow of John H Grigsby, who also served in the Civil War and died at Gettysburg. He was a descendant of Aaron Grisgby the privateer in the American Revolutionary War. Lucinda and John's eldest daughter was Elizabeth who married Louis. Aaron Grigsby, the privateer, married Phebe Harrison a daughter of Benjamin Harrison V, Signer of the Declaration of Independence of Virginia. The Grigsby's and Harrison's lived in Stafford County, Virginia. Zion and Lucinda married after a short courtship and lived in Blount County, Alabama until Zion's death in 1916. Following Zion's death, Lucinda continued to live in Jefferson County Alabama with her daughter Elizabeth and husband Louis Turnbow.

Zion Cornelius - The Southern Democrat, November 2, 1916

Zion Cornelius Dead. Zion B. Cornelius died very suddenly at his home near Blountsville on October 25th. While Mr. Cornelius had been in ill health for quite a while he was able to be up and had been to Blountsville on the day of his death. The deceased was about 72 years of age and he had made his home for many years in the community where he died. He had many friends in the county who will regret to learn of his death. The deceased is survived by his widow, two sons and two daughters.

Mr. Cornelius had been a member of the Primitive Baptist church for 36 years. The remains were laid to rest in Graves cemetery, near Royal, the funeral services being conducted by Rev. J.J. Herring. [Zion B. Cornelius, March 12, 1847 – October 25, 1916.

The Southern Democrat, November 9, 1916

Royal News. Many friends of Zion Cornelius were surprised and grieved to hear of his death Wednesday. He went to Blountville Wednesday, bought a lot of merchandise and was planning to have a working on Friday. He carried his goods into the house and sat down by the fire and was dead in a few minutes. He seemed to be all right and in his usual health when he came in.

He was a good old man and had a lot of friends. He always attended to his own affairs and bothered no one. He was a member of the Primitive Baptist church. He was buried at the Graves Cemetery. Rev. Jimmie Herring conducted the funeral services. He will be greatly missed in his community. He leaves an aged wife, 5 children and a host of friends and relatives to mourn his death. The bereaved ones have the sympathy of this community. Both obituaries submitted by Robin Sterling.

Cornelius, William R. - William R. Cornelius, also spelled Carnelius enlisted on Company H of the 1st Alabama Cavalry, USV on February 20, 1865, in Huntsville, Alabama for a period of 3 years. He was enrolled by J.W. DeVaney, and was mustered in May 20, 1865, in Nashville, Tennessee. The Muster and Descriptive Roll listed him as being 19 years of age, 5'-9" tall, having a fair complexion, blue eyes, light hair, born in Blount County, Alabama, and a farmer by occupation. It showed him to be due $100 for bounty. The May and June 1865 Muster Roll showed him to have been absent without leave since June 27, 1865. He was mustered out October 20, 1865, in Huntsville, Alabama owing the U.S. Government $9.05 for losing a shelter tent.

William R. Cornelius was born about 1846 in Blount County, Alabama to William and Martha Chambers Cornelius, who were married November 28, 1839, in Blount County, Alabama. Other known children of William and Martha Cornelius were: Ellender L. "Nelly", and Andrew Cornelius. William, the father was listed as a Miller in the 1850 Blount County, Alabama Census.

Cossett, Henry - Henry Cossett first enlisted in Company F of the 6th Iowa on June 14, 1862, and was mustered in June 14, 1862. He was reported to have deserted July 6, 1862. He also enlisted in Company G of the 11th Illinois Cavalry, US on September 1, 1862, in Bolivar, Tennessee, and was temporarily attached from that regiment to Company G of the 1st Alabama Cavalry, USV. No further information relative to this soldier was found.*

Cothern, George W. - George W Cothern enlisted in Company K of the 1st Alabama Cavalry, USV as a private on November 1, 1863, in Glendale, Mississippi for a period of 3 years. He was enrolled by Lieutenant J.H. Hornback, and mustered in the same day in Camp Davies, Mississippi. The Company Descriptive Book recorded him as being 28 years of age, 5'-3" tall, having a light complexion, blue eyes, brown hair, born in Henry County, Georgia, and a farmer by occupation. The January and February 1864 Muster Roll listed him as being absent, on detached service as a teamster in General Sherman's Expedition since January 24, 1864, by order of General Grierson. The July and August 1864 Muster Roll shows his name on a Hospital Muster Roll for 2 Division U.S.A. Field Hospital in Rome,

Georgia. The Company Muster Roll from December 31, 1864, through April 30, 1865, show Cothern as being absent at Annapolis, Maryland, wounded in battle March 10, 1865, which was when the Battle of Monroe's Crossroads was fought. He was discharged May 16, 1865, by a Surgeon's Certificate of Disability by order of General Dix, by being wounded March 10, 1865, during the Battle of Monroe's Crossroads, near Fayetteville, North Carolina. In March and April 1865, he was listed on a Hospital Muster Roll for Grant U.S.A. General Hospital at Willett's Point, New York Harbor, admitted March 30, 1865. The Surgeon's Certificate of Disability stated the following: I certify that I have examined the said George W. Cothern and find him incapable of performing the duties of a soldier because of paralysis of left forearm and hand and may alter contractions of left hip. This a result of a gunshot wound.

George Cothern was born in 1835 in Henry County, Georgia and a brother to William R. Cothern. He had a brother, Collins Cothern, who served in the 25th Alabama Infantry, CSA throughout the war. George was wounded twice during the war. After the war he lived in Madison County, Alabama, before moving to Cross County, Arkansas, approximately 1890. He was married three times and had six children. He died in St. Francis County, Arkansas. Family information submitted by John W. Cothern.

Cothern, Joel Alexander - Joel Alexander Cothern enlisted and mustered into Company K of the 1st Alabama Cavalry, USV on December 1, 1863, in Camp Davies, Mississippi for a period of 3 years. He was enrolled by Lieutenant Hornback, and traveled 90 miles on horseback from his home in Marion County, Alabama to Camp Davies, Mississippi, to enlist in the Union Army. The Company Descriptive Book recorded him as being 18 years of age, 5'-8" tall, having a light complexion, blue eyes, auburn hair, born in Spartanburg District, South Carolina, and a farmer by occupation. The January and February 1864 Muster Roll recorded him as being absent, on detached service as teamster in General Sherman's Expedition since January 24, 1864, by order of General Grierson. On January 28, 1865, he was left sick in Savannah, Georgia. His name appeared on a DeCamp General Hospital Muster Roll in David's Island, New York Harbor stating he was a patient March 3, 1865, with remarks that patient was on temporary duty in Section B. He was mustered out under Telegraphic Order from the War Department May 4, 1865. To receive pay from February 28, 1865. Transportation and pay allowances suspended for future settlement. Has drawn clothing allowance in hospital of $16.11. Date of discharge from Roll Number 51, DeCamp Hospital Records.

Joel A. Cothern was born about 1845 in Spartanburg, South Carolina and married Isabella Clementine Wylie on December 23, 1869, in Marion County, Alabama. Isabella was born November 29, 1849 in Ireland Hill, Marion County, Alabama and died April 12, 1922. After the war, they moved to Hope, Hempstead County, Arkansas. They had the following children: Mary; Rosie; Henry J.; John Kelsey, born July 24, 1877; died November 14, 1943; James Edward, born March 2, 1881; Zanna Belle, born April 22, 1883, died 1984; and Joseph Wylie Cothern, born February 15, 1889, and died February 4, 1969. Joseph Wylie Cothern was enumerated with the USS Albany Submarine in San Francisco, California Military and Naval Forces 1910 Census. Joel A. Cothern died January 7, 1889, in Hempstead County, Arkansas.

Cothern, William R. - William R. Cothern enlisted in Company K of the 1st Alabama Cavalry, USV as a private on November 1, 1863, in Glendale, Mississippi for a term of 3 years, and was mustered in the same day in Camp Davies, Mississippi. He was enrolled by Lieutenant Hornback. The Company Descriptive Book showed him to have been 25 years of age, 5'-4" tall, having a light complexion, gray eyes, black hair, born in Carroll County, Georgia, and a farmer by occupation.

William Cothern was born in 1838 in Carroll County, Georgia. After the war he lived in Madison County, Alabama. He was a brother to George Cothern, above, and their brother Collins Cothern served in the 25th Alabama Infantry, CSA, throughout the war. Family information submitted by Joel W. Cothern.

Cotton, James H. - James H. Cotton enlisted in Company M of the 1st Alabama Cavalry, USV as a private on December 16, 1863, in Camp Davies, Mississippi for a period of 3 years. He was enrolled by Captain Lomax and mustered in the same day in Corinth, Mississippi. The Company Descriptive

Book showed him to have been 31 years of age, 5'-10" tall, having a fair complexion, blue eyes, light hair, born in Fayette County, Alabama, and a farmer by occupation. Cotton died of measles in the hospital in Memphis, Tennessee on January 27, 1864. James H. Cotton is buried in the Memphis National Cemetery in Memphis, Shelby County, Tennessee.

Couch, Benjamin - Only one card was found for Benjamin Couch which was filed at the end of the last roll of microfilm of the 1st Alabama Cavalry, USV records. It recorded him as a private in Company L. His name was recorded on a Hospital Muster Roll for the USA General Field Hospital in Bridgeport, Alabama in May and June 1864. No further information relative to this soldier was found.*

Coughman, Jesse R. - Jesse R. Coughman enlisted and mustered into Company H of the 1st Alabama Cavalry, USV as a private on October 17, 1863, in Glendale, Mississippi for a period of one year at the age of 19. The March and July 1864 Muster Rolls listed him as being absent, sick in Hospital #2 in Nashville, Tennessee. His name appeared on the Returns as follows: March and April 1864, sick in hospital in Memphis, Tennessee. (Different cities recorded in Returns from Muster Rolls); July and August 1864, absent, sick in Nashville, Tennessee since March 26, 1864. His name appeared on another Hospital Muster Roll stating he was in No. 3 U.S.A. General Hospital in Nashville, Tennessee. He was mustered out October 24, 1864, in Rome, Georgia due to expiration of term of service, and his pay was stopped because of losing 1 thong and brush wiper, and 1 haversack. However, it stated he was overpaid $32.00, paid by Major Brown in General Hospital without Descriptive Roll for May and June.

Counce, John A. - John Anderson Counce stated he enlisted and mustered into Company E of the 1st Alabama Cavalry, USV as a private on August 27, 1863, in Glendale, Mississippi for a period of 1 year. A Notation from the Record and Pension Office of the War Department in Washington, DC, dated May 12, 1894, stated the following: It has this day been determined by this department by evidence on file that this man (enrolled August 27, 1863) was discharged the service on or about November 30, 1863, Robert M. Reed having been accepted to serve in his place instead. Discharge Certificate prepared by the War Department May 12, 1894, and filed. Apparently John Anderson Counce did not serve in the 1st Alabama Cavalry, USV since he had Robert M. Reed serve for him. (Cards filed with Robert M. Reed, true name of soldier.)

John Anderson Counce was born about 1820 in Lauderdale County, Alabama, married Paralee Malissa Chesney on March 5, 1846, in Hardin County, Tennessee, and died September 4, 1864 in Jackson County, Illinois. Paralee was born October 25, 1827, in Alabama and died September 2, 1886 in Hardin County, Tennessee. Children of John and Paralee Counce were: James R.: William T.; Mary F.; Caladona "Dona"; Judy, and Martha J. Counce.

Notation in file states he took the place of John A Counce and assumed his name.

Cowen/Cowan, George W. - George W. Cowan, also spelled Cowen, enlisted in Company B of the 1st Alabama Cavalry, USV as a private on April 1, 1865, in Faison, North Carolina for a period of 3 years. He was enrolled by Captain West. The Company Descriptive Book showed him to have been 18 years of age, 5'-5" tall, having a fair complexion, gray eyes, light hair, born in Onslow County, North Carolina, and a farmer by occupation. He was reported to have deserted about June 20, 1865, from Huntsville, Alabama

Cox, Jefferson, M. - Jefferson M. Cox enrolled in Company H of the 1st Alabama Cavalry, USV on December 25, 1864, in Huntsville, Alabama, and was mustered in the same day in Nashville, Tennessee. The Muster and Descriptive Roll recorded him as being 18 years of age, 5'-6½" tall, having a light complexion, black eyes, light hair, born in Greenville, District, South Carolina, and a farmer by occupation. He was paid a bounty of $100 and was credited to Ripley, Chautauqua County, New York. He was mustered out October 20, 1865, in Huntsville, Alabama.

Cox, Mordecai Michael - Mordecai Michael Cox enlisted and mustered into Company A of the 1st Alabama Cavalry, USV as a 2nd Master Sergeant on December 22, 1863, for a period of 3 years. He was enrolled by Lieutenant Jerome Hinds and was mustered in February 6, 1864, in Memphis,

Tennessee. The Muster and Descriptive Roll recorded him as being 26 years of age, 5'-11" tall, having a fair complexion, gray eyes, light hair, was born in Habersham County, Georgia, and was a farmer by occupation. He was appointed 2nd Master Sergeant on February 5, 1864. The March and April 1864 Muster Roll listed him as a Quartermaster Sergeant, and showed him to have been absent, on recruiting service in Alabama since April 17, 1864. He was still on recruiting service with Major Shurtleff through February 1865. The March and April 1865 Muster Roll showed him to be absent, on detached service with Major Shurtleff at Decatur, Alabama. The July and August 1865 Muster Roll showed him to be present. He was mustered out October 20, 1865, in Huntsville, Alabama, owing the U.S. Government $17.65 for losing 1 pistol and belt. He paid a bounty of $180 and due $120 to make up the $300 bounty he was due. Mordecai M. Cox was able to sign his name on his Enlistment Forms.

Sergeant Mordecai Michael Cox, Sr. was born January 12, 1837, in Habersham County, Georgia, and married Nancy Emmaline Dodd, daughter of Michael and Mary Wright Dodd, on December 2, 1858. Mary was born June 11, 1841, in Winston County, Alabama, and died March 11, 1926, in Marion County, Alabama. Mordecai M. Cox died May 2, 1923, in Marion County, Alabama, and is buried in the Thorn Hill Church of Christ Cemetery in Marion County, Alabama. Children of Mordecai and Mary were: Emily Lucille; Rufus Napoleon; Nancy Mariah; Mordecai Michael, Jr.; Theodore S.; Petronelie Annah; and Julias Benton Cox. They may have had other children.

Crabb, William P. - William P. Crabb enlisted in Company C of the 1st Alabama Cavalry, USV as a private on December 1, 1862, in Corinth, Mississippi, for a period of 1 year. He was enrolled by D.R. Adams, and was mustered in December 22, 1862, in Corinth. The Company Descriptive Book listed William as having been 35 years of age, 5'-10" tall, having a fair complexion, blue eyes, dark hair, born in Giles County, Tennessee, and a farmer by occupation. He was appointed corporal June 18, 1863, and was mustered out at age 35, December 17, 1863, in Memphis, Tennessee.

William P. Crabb was born in 1829 in Giles County, Tennessee to Joseph Crabb, born May 19, 1805, in White County, Tennessee, and died after 1880, and his wife, Catherine Rogers, daughter of William Perry Rogers and Rosannah Herd. Catherine Rogers was born March 8, 1804, in Tennessee and died February 20, 1873, in Prentiss County, Mississippi. Other children of Joseph and Catherine Crabb were: Fountain Rogers; James Hurd; Malinda Jane; Elizabeth Ann; Thomas Wesley; Catherine Rebecca; Joseph; Rhoda E.; C.A.; and Rosa Narcissa Crabb. William P. Crabb first married Elizabeth Horn, daughter of John Horne and Nancy Hall, on December 12, 1850, in Lawrence County, Texas. He married his second wife, Lucinda Livingston, on December 30, 1879, in Prentiss County, Mississippi. Lucinda was born about 1846 in Tennessee and died in 1894 in Danville, Vermilion County, Illinois. Three of William's brothers served in the Confederacy. William P. Crabb died in 1893 in Yell County, Arkansas. William's brother, Joseph, died November 7, 1863, in Point Lookout, Maryland, which was a Union prison, so he was likely a prisoner of war in the hands of the Union when he died, while his brother, William, was fighting for the Union.

William P. Crabb was born 1829 in Giles County, Tennessee and had three brothers who served in the C.S.A. His first wife was Elizabeth Horn, born 1828 in Tennessee and died 1878 in Prentiss County, Mississippi. His father was Joseph Crabb, born 1805. William died in 1893 in Yell County, Arkansas. Family information submitted by Mary Ellen Ledford.

Craddock, Pleasant G. - Pleasant G. Craddock had three cards which was filed at the end of the last roll of microfilm of the 1st Alabama Cavalry, USV Records. It recorded him as a private in Company I, of the 1st Middle Tennessee Cavalry. The early enlistees in the 1st Alabama Cavalry, USV were shipped to Nashville, Tennessee and merged with the 1st Middle Tennessee Cavalry, US, which later became the 5th Tennessee Cavalry. The card stated there was 1 Burial Record in his files. There was a Record of Death and Interment in his file stating he died January 20, 1863, in the University Hospital #2 of typhoid pneumonia, and was buried in the Nashville Cemetery No. 2832. That was probably the Nashville City Cemetery. The record stated he was 23 years of age, born in Cannon County, Tennessee, and was single. (This soldier may have just served with the 1st Middle Tennessee Cavalry, US, but his records were filed with the 1st Alabama Cavalry, USV.)

Cramer, Francis L. - Francis Lytle Cramer enlisted in the 1st Alabama Cavalry, USV as a

Major on October 22, 1863, in Memphis, Tennessee for a term of 3 years. He received and accepted the appointment and entered on duty October 24, 1863. He was appointed Major by General Dodge. The Field and Staff Muster Roll for March and April 1864 stated he was granted a 6-day leave of absence from April 1-6, 1864, by Special Order Headquarters, 16th Army Corps. The Field and Staff Muster Roll for March and April 1865, stated he was absent, on leave of absence for 30 days due to wounds March 14, 1865, (he was actually wounded March 10, 1865, during the Battle of Monroe's Crossroads.) He had a gunshot wound to the left hip, was captured by the enemy and held for 7 days without extracting the ball. A General Order #67, in his military records dated July 16, 1867, from the Adjutant General's Office of the War Department, stated he was appointed Colonel by Brevet in the volunteer force, Army of the United States, for gallant and meritorious services during the war, to date from March 30, 1865. Another General Order stated he was appointed Brigadier General. He was mustered out October 20, 1865, in Huntsville, Alabama. He had been appointed from 1st Lieutenant and Adjutant, 1st Nebraska Infantry by authority. A letter written by Cramer from Page County, Iowa dated April 20, 1865, requested an extension of his leave of absence for the following reasons: "I was wounded in the fight of March 10, 1865, at Monroe's Plantation between Major General Kilpatrick and Major General Wade Hampton. Granted a leave of absence for 30 days by General Sherman from the nature of my wound, I was unable to reach home until lately. Enclosed is the certificate of examining surgeon."

A Surgeon's Certificate in Cramer's file stated the following: I hereby certify that I have carefully examined F.L. Cramer, Major of the 1st Alabama Cavalry, and find him laboring under the effects of a recent gunshot wound of the hip. The ball was not extracted by the enemy in whose hands he was for seven days. From the condition of the wound and soreness in the region of the ball, together with the neuralgic pains in the region, I am of the opinion that he is unfit to perform the duties of a soldier, and will not be in a less time than thirty days. Signed: N.L. VanLauen (?), Surgeon appointed to examine applicant. Subscribed and sworn to before me Jacob Butler, Clerk of the District Court, Page County, Iowa, this the 20th Day of April A.D. 1865. Jacob Butler, Clerk.

Charge and Specification preferred against Major Kramer, 1st Alabama Cavalry

Charge: Conduct of _____ of good order and military discipline.

Specification: In this, that he Major F.L. Kramer, 1st Alabama Cavalry, did on or about November 16, 1864, during the March of the Army of the Tennessee from Atlanta, Georgia release against the protest of the Provost, and by assumed and illegal authority, from the custody of said Guard, two prisoners named F. Burdick and S. Peak, or Peck, of 1st Alabama Cavalry. Signed Hempstrost, Captain and Provost Marshall, 1st Division, 17th Army Corps. Witnesses: Captain Wm. Hempstrost; J.W. Clemens, Company G, 18th Missouri Volunteers; F. Burdick, Company A, 1st Alabama Cavalry; S. Peak, Company I, 1st Alabama Cavalry.

A letter from Cramer in his military records dated December 4, 1863, from Corinth, Mississippi states: Dear Blackes, Allow me this beautiful morning to address unto you a few lines for I do want to hear from you and I know you won't write to me unless I commence. Since joining my new regiment, I have been on 3 Scouts, one lasting for 5 days and extending into Colona, Mississippi, or near there. The first one I took I had a nice little brush with the enemy in which I lost 2 wounded and one prisoner. The enemy lost 5 killed and 2 wounded. Yesterday I went 15 miles South towards Ripley and while feeding and men eating, the enemy scouts attacked my advance. Maybe we did not get into line and mounted quick, and when I found out what the matter was the thing was all over they had got away. My men being dismounted could not follow them so they escaped. It would amuse you to have heard my Alabamian's asking what they must do. I suppose they are so used to used to being ordered to do this and ordered to do that that they cannot help asking whether to fight or run but there is one advantage, they will do just what you tell them to do and fight as well as any men I ever seen if you do as they think you should they will call you a powerful pert chap, if you do anything that does not suit them they will say, you ain't much account. In a word, Blakes, they talk and act very much like Mrs. Brakebone of Helena. While sojourning in Memphis I almost failed to find any of our old friends. All had either left or been driven to the wall and living in shanties or Negro quarters. Old Colonel Sanderson of the 23rd Indiana is president of a Court Martial and is in Memphis. Colonel Anthony is commanding a brigade with Dodge. General Stevenson of the 7th Missouri Volunteer Infantry is commanding District of Corinth, and playing poker all of his time. Colonel Spencer is commanding Camp Davies, which is 7 miles from Corinth, where our regiment are not stationed. I suppose by this time your regiment is all on horseback and joining in on the cavalry where he was recruiting all the time from 10 to 20 a day, the regiment was originally mustered in for 12 months, but nearly all are reenlisting for 5 years. They cannot help themselves; it is our army or the Southerners. If the regiment is ordered to Florence or Huntsville I think another regiment can easily be raised for Greenback or patriotism, have a great influence with most of the Southerners that I have seen and woman suffrages from Alabama, Mississippi and Tennessee, more than can be taken care of – all are on it or at least most all. This would be a fine field for the 1st Nebraska to display their talents in that line. Blackes, remember me to friends Ribble, Bob, Howard & c. and be sure enough to write me a long letter. Your Friend, F.L. Cramer, District of Corinth, 1st Alabama Cavalry.

During Sherman's March to the Sea, Major Cramer's 1st Alabama regiment was a member of the 3rd Cavalry Division, commanded by Brevetted Major General Hugh J. Kilpatrick, 3rd Brigade commanded by Colonel George E. Spencer.

On March 10, 1865, Lieutenant General Wade Hampton and his Confederate forces attacked the Union forces at dawn in their camp at Monroe's Crossroads. The battle would eventually be regarded as one of the largest all-cavalry engagements of the Civil War. The Union casualties at Monroe's Crossroads were 18 killed, 70 wounded, and 105 missing. Among the killed and wounded were some of the best officers of the command. The 1st Alabama Cavalry lost eight officers, including both of its field officers, Major Cramer being both wounded and a prisoner. Major Cramer would later return to service and eventually achieved the rank of Brevetted Brigadier General, U.S. Volunteers.

Francis Lytle Cramer was born February 8, 1835, probably in Page County, Iowa, and died February 20, 1890, in Oklahoma City, Oklahoma County, Oklahoma. He is buried at Fairlawn Cemetery in Oklahoma City, Plot: Block 7, Lot 166.

Crandell, Levi - Only one card was found for Levi Crandell which was filed at the end of the last roll of microfilm of the 1st Alabama Cavalry, USV records. It recorded him as a private in Company M, stating he was enlisted February 3, 1864, in Memphis, Tennessee by Captain Lomax. The Company Descriptive Book recorded him as 17 years of age, 5'-4" tall, having a dark complexion, hazel eyes, dark hair, born in Dark County, Ohio, and a farmer by occupation. He may have been temporarily assigned to the 1st Alabama Cavalry from an Ohio regiment. No further information relative to this soldier was found.*

Cranford, W.H. - Only one card was found for W.H. Cranford which was filed at the end of the last roll of microfilm of the 1st Alabama Cavalry, USV records. His name appeared on a Return stating he was a sergeant in Company E of the 1st Alabama Cavalry, USV. The Return was dated March 1864; however, it stated Cranford mustered out in January 1864 in Memphis, Tennessee due to expiration of term of service.

Crawfords in the 1st Alabama Cavalry, USV
Samuel A., John T., James D. Sr. & Jr., William H., & William L. Crawford

Contrary to what some researchers think about the Crawfords who served in the 1st Alabama Cavalry, USV, the following information shows who the parents were of each Crawford soldier. It has been very confusing with the different parents giving their sons the same names, but this is the breakdown.

Samuel A. Crawford, John T. (which was listed as John F. on the muster roll), and James D. Crawford, Sr. were the sons of William Andrew and Susannah Emaline Dobbins Crawford. More on them later.

James D. Crawford, Jr. and William H. Crawford were the sons of Alfred and Mary A. Crawford. More on this later.

William L. Crawford of the 1st Alabama Cavalry was not the son of Samuel and Emaline as some have suggested but rather the son of James and Eliza Ataline Dobbins Crawford. Susannah Emaline Dobbins and Eliza Ataline Dobbins were sisters and may have married brothers but I haven't proven that. I will give the proof for the above statements later in the family information of each soldier.

James Dobbins Crawford, Sr. (I believe the reason these James D. Crawfords were listed as Jr. and Sr. was to be able to tell them apart and keep up with them.) James married Harriett A. Johnson February 27, 1868, in Sanford, later Lamar County, Alabama and had the following children: Jeanettie Ann America "Merrikey", born December 26, 1868, died December 6, 1956; Mary Etta, born December 15, 1870, died June 21, 1936; John Rufus, born 1872, died 1872; William Andrew, born March 24, 1874, died February 26, 1956; Valulu Lavina, born December 26, 1876, died March 1958; Sarah Emaline, born March 4, 1879; Nancy Mortimer, born March 4, 1879; and Margaret Elizabeth, born January 22, 1886.

On October 17, 1863, James, Sr. enlisted and mustered in the 1st Alabama Cavalry, US as Private in Company H in Glendale, Mississippi at age 22. He was mustered out November 24, 1864 in Rome, Georgia. His pension index card states his widow, Harriett A., applied for his pension March 30, 1891. It stated he also served in the 11th Illinois Cavalry, US.

Corporal John Thomas Crawford (listed on the muster roll as John F.) enlisted and mustered in the 1st Alabama Cavalry US on September 14, 1863, as a Private in Co. H in Glendale, Mississippi at age 19. He was mustered out September 29, 1864, in Rome, Georgia. On January 25, 1866, he married Selena Ellen Ponder in Fayette County, Alabama. and after her death, he married Clarrisa E. Pruitt about 1896. John T. Crawford was listed on the 1890 Dunklin County, Missouri Veterans' Census.

Samuel A. Crawford was born in Abbeville District, SC and died in Campbell, Dunklin County, Missouri. He was married to Martha E. Ponder on March 4, 1858, in Fayette County, Alabama and had the following children: William M., born 1862; John J., 1866; Mary C., 1867; James or Joseph M., 1870; Frances P., 1871; and Ida H. Crawford, 1879. All of these birth dates are approximate as they were taken from the census records. Samuel may have had other children but these were the only ones found on the census.

Samuel A. Crawford enlisted and mustered in the 1st Alabama Cavalry, US October 17, 1863, as Private in Company H in Glendale, Mississippi at age 25 and mustered out October 24, 1864, in Rome, Georgia. His pension index card stated his widow, Martha A. filed for a pension on September 19, 1891, from Mississippi. Martha Crawford, widow of Samuel A. Crawford, was listed on the 1890 Dunklin County, Missouri Veterans' Census.

William Andrew Crawford was born about 1816 in Abbeville District, South Carolina and died some time before 1900. He was married to Susannah Emaline Dobbins, daughter of James Dobbins, Jr. and Elizabeth A. Porter. William and Susannah had the following children: Samuel A., born about 1838, died June 23, 1886, in Dunklin County, Missouri; William Lindsey, born September 17, 1840, died 1864; James Dobbins Crawford, Sr., born April 5, 1841, died February 17, 1923; Margaret E., born about 1843; John Thomas, born November 3, 1844, died March 29, 1916; Joseph W., born about 1847, died about 1877; Nancy M., born March 16, 1849, died September 30, 1870; Thompson A., born March 1851, died 1926; Ebenezer Pressley "Ebbey", born July 5, 1853, died February 12, 1917; and Mary Jane Crawford, born March 9, 1856, died February 9, 1933.

Sgt. William H. Crawford was born about 1837 in Alabama to Alfred and Mary A. Bunch Crawford. His father, Alfred, was born about 1800 in Edgefield District, South Carolina and died in 1861 in Lowndes County, Alabama. His mother, Mary A. was born about 1812 in Edgefield District, South Carolina and died in 1860 in Lowndes County, Alabama. She was the daughter of David Bunch. Other siblings of William H. Crawford were: James D.; Jr.; Mary Ann Matilda; Charles A.; Lucretia Winford "Sallie"; Frances E. "Fannie"; Adrianna E.; Florence A.; Laura L.; Lewis; and Wiley Crawford. William H. enlisted in Company E, of the 1st Alabama Cavalry but no date or place was given. He mustered out March 1, 1864, in Memphis, Shelby County, Tennessee by reason of expiration of term of service. He was born about 1837 in Alabama and married Mary F. Miles on September 15, 1861, in Lowndes County, Alabama. William's wife, Mary, must have died before 1880 when he was enumerated in Navarro County, Texas as age 43 and wife, Mary F., age 36. At that time, they had the following children: Mary E., age 17; Leila M., 14; Aseanath, age 7 and Willie, a daughter, born August 1879. In 1900 there was a William H. Crawford, born December 1836 enumerated in Childress County, Texas with one son, Charles F., age 13, born in Texas and both of his parents were born in South Carolina. They were the only two living in the household.

William L. Crawford was born about 1841 in South Carolina to James and Eliza Ataline/Adaline Dobbins Crawford. There has been some confusion over this William L. and some descendants think he was the William Lindsay Crawford, son of William Andrew and Susannah Emmaline Dobbins but his pension index card clearly shows this is not true.

Eliza Ataline Dobbins was the daughter of James and Elizabeth A. Porter Crawford and sister of Susannah Emaline Dobbins, wife of William A. Crawford. James and William A. Crawford were quite possibly brothers but I have found no proof of that. On October 17, 1863, William L. Crawford enlisted and mustered in as Private in Company H of the 1st Alabama Cavalry USV in Glendale, Mississippi at age 22. Just a few days later on the 26th of October 1863, he was captured and taken prisoner of war from Vincent's Cross Roads near Red Bay, Alabama. So far nothing has been found on him after he was captured. His pension index card states his parents, James and "Adaline" Crawford filed for his pension in July 1873. He must have died or been killed while in the hands of the enemy.

Crawford, James Dobbins, Jr. - James D. Crawford, Jr., also shown as Cranford, enlisted and mustered into Company H of the 1st Alabama Cavalry, USV as a Private on October 17, 1863, in Glendale, Mississippi, for a period of 1 year. All of the Company Muster Rolls recorded him as present. He was mustered out of service on October 24, 1864, in Rome, Georgia at 22 years of age, on account of expiration of term of service, and shown as owing the US Government thirty-five cents for losing 1 thong and brush wiper. See Crawfords in the 1st Alabama Cavalry, USV, above.

Crawford, James D., Sr. - James D. Crawford, Sr., also shown as Cranford, enlisted and mustered into Company H of the 1st Alabama Cavalry, USV as a Private for a period of 1 year. The Company Muster Rolls recorded him as present during his enlistment. His name was found on a Return stating the following: January 1864, absent, orderly for Brigadier General Stevenson. He was mustered out of service on October 24, 1864, at Rome, Georgia due to expiration of term of service, and shown as owing the US Government forty-eight cents for losing 1 haversack. Crawford also served in Company F of the 38th Alabama, CSA, but deserted and joined the Union. See Crawfords in the 1st Alabama Cavalry, USV, above.

Crawford, John Thomas - At age 19, John Thomas Crawford, also shown as John F. Crawford, enlisted and mustered into Company H of the 1st Alabama Cavalry, USV as a Private on September 14, 1863, in Glendale, Mississippi for a period of 1 year. The September and October 1863 Muster Roll recorded him as a Corporal. He mustered out September 29, 1864, in Rome, Georgia due to expiration of term of service. He mustered out owing the US Government forty-one cents for losing 1 canteen. John T. Crawford was listed on the 1890 Dunklin County, Missouri Veterans' Census.

John Thomas Crawford was born November 3, 1844, in Abbeville, District, South Carolina, He first married Selina Ellen Ponder on January 25, 1866, in Fayette County, Alabama, and after her death, he married Clarissa Pruett about 1896 in Dunklin County, Missouri. Children of John and Selena were: James W., born 1870; Martha J., 1872; Andrew, 1874; and John, 1877. All children were born in Dunklin County, Missouri. James and Clarrisa had a son, Charlie G. Crawford born January 1897 in Missouri. Two of Clarissa's children by a previous marriage were living with them when the 1900 Dunklin County, Missouri Census was enumerated and they were: William E. Prewitt, born October 1882 and Shelby Prewitt, July 1886, both born in Missouri. John's pension index card stated Clarissa E. Crawford filed for his pension on January 10, 1905, or 1915 from Missouri.

Crawford, Samuel A. - At age 25, Samuel A. Crawford enlisted and mustered into Company H of the 1st Alabama Cavalry, USV as a Private on October 17, 1863, in Glendale, Mississippi for a period of 1 year. The November and December 1863 Muster Roll recorded him as absent, sick in US General Hospital in Corinth, Mississippi. He mustered out of service on October 24, 1864, due to expiration of term of service. When he mustered out, he was charged eighty-three cents for losing 1 thong and brush wiper, and 1 haversack. In November and December 1863, he was recorded as a patient in the USA Post Hospital in Corinth, Mississippi. His name appeared on a Return stating the following: January 1864, absent, sick in Alabama since October 26, 1863; August and September 1864, on duty as company cook. See Crawfords in the 1st Alabama Cavalry, USV, above.

Crawford, W.H. - Only one card was found for W.H. Crawford which was filed at the end of the last roll of microfilm of the 1st Alabama Cavalry, USV records. It recorded him as a Sergeant in Company E stating he mustered out March 1, 1864, due to expiration of term of service. No further information relative to this soldier was found.*

Crawford, William L. - William L. Crawford enlisted in Company E of the 1st Alabama Cavalry, USV as a Private on October 17, 1863, in Glendale, Mississippi, for a period of 1 year. He was recorded as 22 years of age. The September and October 1863 Muster Roll recorded him as absent, supposed prisoner of war in the hands of the enemy. The November 1863 through October 1864 Muster Rolls recorded him as absent, prisoner of war since October 26, 1863, which was the date of the Battle of Vincent's Crossroads near Bay Springs, Mississippi. A Notation from the Adjutant General's Office of the War Department dated September 21, 1869, stated: Investigation fails to elicit any further information relative to this soldier. Crawford's name appeared on a Return and recorded him as sick in the General Hospital. His term of service expired March 1, 1864, in Memphis, Tennessee. See Crawfords in the 1st Alabama Cavalry, USV, above.

Creekmore, Brison C. - Bison C. Creekmore, also spelled Brison, enlisted in Company A of the 1st Alabama Cavalry, USV as a private on September 8, 1862, in Iuka, Mississippi for a period of 1 year, and was mustered in October 1, 1862, in Corinth, Mississippi. He died of disease on February 27, 1863, in the General Hospital in Corinth, Mississippi. The Company Descriptive Book recorded Bison Creekmore as being 27 years of age, 6' tall, having a light complexion, blue eyes, light hair, born in Wilkes County, North Carolina, and a farmer by occupation.

Creel, John T. - John T. Creel, also listed as John F. Creel and Creal, enlisted and mustered into Company D of the 1st Alabama Cavalry, USV as a private on June 10, 1863, in Glendale, Mississippi, for a term of 1 year. He was enrolled by J.H. Shurtliff. The Regimental Descriptive Book recorded him as being 19 years of age, 5'-9" tall, having a dark complexion, dark eyes, dark hair, born in Bibb County, Alabama, and a farmer by occupation. He was mustered out June 16, 1864, in Decatur, Alabama due to expiration of term of service.

Creel, Joshua D. - Joshua D. Creel enlisted and mustered into Company D of the 1st Alabama Cavalry, USV as a private on June 10, 1863, in Glendale, Mississippi for a term of 1 year. He was enrolled by J.H. Shurtliff. The Regimental Descriptive Book recorded him as being 26 years of age, 5'-8½" tall, having a dark complexion, dark eyes, dark hair, born in Bibb County, Alabama, and a farmer by occupation. His Muster-In Roll stated he was 20 years of age. He was mustered out on June 16, 1864, in Decatur, Alabama due to expiration of term of service. Joshua D. Creel and John T. Creel, above are probably brothers.

On November 13, 1897, Joshua D. Creel signed a Deposition in Salem, Fulton County, Arkansas for Morgan C. Barnes concerning Barnes' request for pension. The Deposition stated the following: I was a private in Company D. 1 Alabama Cavalry, I remember Cleve Barnes well - Don't remember of any sickness, injury or wound he may have incurred while in the service. As I recollect him he was nearly always on duty.

Yes, I was with that scouting party that cold New Year - January 1, 1864. We were out some four or five days through Collierville, Tennessee a day or so later and returned to camp at Camp Davis (Davies), near Corinth, Mississippi. I don't remember of any thing happening to Barnes on that said frostbitten feet: Well if he says so I don't doubt it but I don't remember it myself and hearing his statement does not refresh my memory - either as to the frost bitten feet, varicose veins or some wound. Barnes was a good and honorable man and if he claims he contracted said ailments I don't doubt it in the least. I have read this and it is correct. Signed Joshua D. Creel (Creel had a very nice penmanship.)

Crigar, Charles alias William Johnson - Charles Crigar, also shown as Creger, Criger and Crigor, enlisted under the name of William Johnson. See William Johnson in Company F for additional information.

<u>Crittenden, William</u> - William F. Crittenden enlisted in Company A of the 1st Alabama Cavalry, USV December 13, 1862, in Glendale, Mississippi and on December 18, 1862, he was promoted from Private to 2nd Corporal. He mustered in December 31, 1862, at Corinth, Mississippi, and mustered out December 22, 1863. From June to September 1863, he was on duty as a saddler. He was sick and in the hospital quite a bit during his term in the Union Army. His widow, America M. Parrish Crittendon, filed for a pension July 22, 1873, but was apparently unable to furnish the documents needed for proof of his service. On May 25, 1888, a claim was filed for the minor, William R. Crittenden, which was rejected January 5, 1895, on the ground that the minor had no title as he became 16 years of age prior to filing the claim.

<u>Crocker, James D</u>. - James D. Crocker enlisted in Company D of the 1st Alabama Cavalry, USV as a private on May 20, 1864, in Decatur, Alabama for a period of 3 years. He was enrolled by Lieutenant Pease and was mustered in June 16, 1864, in Decatur. In July 1864, he was transferred from Company D to Company A on July 28, 1864. The Muster and Descriptive Roll recorded him as being 22 years of age, 6' tall, having a dark complexion, blue eyes, black hair, born on Jefferson County, Alabama, and a farmer by occupation. He was reported to have deserted from Rome, Georgia on July 7, 1864, with 1 Smith Carbine, 1 Remington revolver and accoutrements complete.

<u>Crocker, John Y.</u> - John Y. Crocker enlisted in Company G of the 1st Alabama Cavalry, USV on November 27, 1862, in Grand Junction, Tennessee for a period of 3 years, and was mustered in the same day in Corinth, Mississippi. He was appointed Corporal April 1, 1863, and was mustered out November 26, 1863, in Memphis, Tennessee.

<u>Crocker, William Roundtree, alias Henry Curtis</u> - William Roundtree Crocker was born about 1838 in Washington County, North Carolina to Alfred Bradbury Crocker and Pearcey Wilson. He and also served in the 30th Illinois Infantry. He enlisted in the 1st Alabama Cavalry, USV on May 15, 1863, as 1st Sergeant in Company F in Memphis, Tennessee at age 23, under the name of Henry Curtis. He mustered in at Corinth, Mississippi on August 13, 1863. On February 5, 1864, he was promoted to 2nd Lieutenant from 1st Sergeant, and he was discharged on September 14, 1864. He is buried in Greenwood Cemetery on Church Street in Decatur, Illinois.

William married Martha Ann Caroline Perkins on January 5, 1867, in Hutsonville, Crawford County, Illinois. Martha was born January 10, 1845, Laurens County, Georgia and died January 15, 1927, in Oakland, Alameda County, California. They had the following children: Julia Curtis, born 1865; Mary, born February, 1870; Charles Matthew, 1872; William Franklin, July 22, 1875; Isaac "Fred", July 22, 1883; Arthur Roland, June 24, 1887; and Sarah "Sadie" Curtis, February 9, 1922. Martha was the daughter of Isaac and Indiana Perkins.

Notation from Record and Pension Office dated January 24, 1896, states, "This man under the name William R Crocker deserted from 30th Reg't Illinois Volunteers. On or about April 30, 1863, and enlisted in this organization in violation of the 22d (now 50th) Article of War. The notation of December 17, 1886, is cancelled." According to Martha A.C. Crocker, William R. Crocker apparently deserted from the 30th Illinois Infantry and joined the 1st Alabama Cavalry. US under the alias of Henry Curtis.

Pension Records for William R. and Martha Ann Caroline Perkins Crocker: On March 21, 1895, Martha A.C. Crocker signed a Declaration For Widow's Pension in Macon County, Illinois stating she was 49 years of age, a resident of the City of Decatur, County of Macon, State of Illinois, who being duly sworn according to law, declares that she is the widow of William R. Crocker, who enlisted under the name of Henry Curtis on the 5th day of February 1864 in Company F, 1st Alabama Cavalry Volunteers. He resigned September 15, 1864, and died March 18, 1895. She was married under the name of Martha A.C. Perkins to said William R. Crocker on the 6th day of January 1868 by Rev. John Cox, M.G. at Crawford County, Illinois, there being no legal barrier to said marriage. Neither of them was previously married. She stated since the death of the said William R. Crocker Alias Henry Curtis, she was without other means of support. She listed her living children under age 16 as Isaac F., born July 22, 1883, and Arthur Roland, born June 24, 1887. She stated she had previously applied for pension and her husband drew pension under Certificate No 797619. It was signed Martha A.C. Crocker.

On July 8, 1895, John T. Perkins signed a General Affidavit in Jasper County, Illinois stating Martha A.C. Crocker was not married to any other person until she married W.R. Crocker. I have known her for the last 30 years. This is in my own hand writing and in the preparation of the same I was not aided or prompted by any written or printed statement, dictated or prepared by any one else.

In August 1895, Martha A.C. Crocker was living in Crawford County, Illinois. E. Barlow, M.D., stated Martha Crocker gave birth to a son June 24th 1887, and he was the attending physician. The facts were taken from his birth records written in his own hand, the 30th day of April 1895. He stated Mr. Crocker appeared in his records as William C. but he was pretty sure it should be William R. and that he made a mistake in making up the record.

In August 1895, a W.A. Perkins of Cooke County, Texas signed a General Affidavit stating he was 48 years old and a citizen of Gainesville, Cooke County, Texas. He states: "I have known Martha A.C. Crocker from childhood and I know that she was not previously married prior to the time that she was married to William R. Crocker, and I also state that was the only time she was ever married. This affidavit is in my own hand writing, and in the preparation of the same I was not aided or prompted by any written or printed statements prepared or dictated by any one else. This is the second day of August 1895, at Gainesville, Texas.

There is a document signed by Charles O. Harper, County Clerk stating William R. Crocker and Miss Martha A.C. Perkins were married on the 5th of January 1868 in Crawford County, Illinois by J. T. Box, Minister of the Gospel. Another document "Any Ward, Widows, ETC." Martha's remains were buried in Lot 56, Grave 174, Mountain View Cemetery in Oakland, California It was signed by William F. Crocker, guardian. 1603 Ashby Avenue, Berkeley, California. That would probably be her son, William Franklin Crocker. She lived in Georgia, Alabama, Illinois, Missouri, Texas, and California maybe a few more states in between.

Mary L. Cheek, City of Washington, Daviess County, Indiana signed a General Affidavit stating the following: "I was a near neighbor of claimant and her late husband at Carthage, Missouri, in 1883, living next door to her. I was present at her house when she gave birth to a child one Sabbath evening, when the weather was very warm, and the date of said birth was July 22, 1883. I fix this date from memory and my memory has been refreshed by letter written me by claimant. I state these facts to Ezra Mattingly who wrote them in my presence and at my dictation, and in preparing these. I was not aided by any printed or written memoranda not dictated hereto, save claimants said letter." The child mentioned was Isaac F. Crocker which was written at the bottom of the affidavit.

Sarah Rhoades of Jasper County, Missouri signed an affidavit stating: "I was a near neighbor to the claimant at this time she was confined which occurred about July 22, 1883. she gave birth to a boy. I fix this date by reference to the age of my child who was eight weeks old at the time. Miss Adams another woman who was there is dead! My first impression is that she acted as the midwife but of this I am not quite positive."

In Martha's Declaration For Widow's Pension, she states that William R. Crocker enrolled in the 30th Illinois Infantry under the name of Henry Curtis. Martha was living in Sonoma, California when she signed this affidavit for pension. On September 18, 1916, Martha signed an affidavit saying she was 72 years old, was born January 10, 1845. in Lawrence County, Georgia. She was living in Santa Rosa, California at the time she filed this.

A document signed by Dr. Howard M. Wood, Decatur Arcade Office Building, stated William R. Crocker died age 68 years old on March 18, 1895, and cause of death was La Grippe. (This has been described as the "Spanish Flu", and there was a pandemic of it that spread through the world in 1918. Webster describes it as simply "Influenza") He stated he was buried March 20. 1895. by Undertaker Mr. Reeves in Decatur, Illinois.

Alameda County, California, March 25, 1911. "I Charles M. Crocker, being duly sworn say that I am a son of the said William R. Crocker and the said Martha A.C. Crocker and have known them for 35 years and know of my own knowledge that they lived together as husband and wife from date of marriage until date of his death. My address is 1528 Bonita or Burrito Avenue, Barkley, California. There is no interest in this case further than a son naturally feels in such matters."

September 18, 1916, Widow's Certificate Number 721101, Soldier William R. Crocker, alias Henry Curtis, Sergeant and second Lieutenant in Company F, 1st Regiment Alabama Volunteer Cavalry. Sir: I am pensioned under the above certificate number because of the service of the soldier named. I married January 5, 1868. I am 72 years old, having been born January 10, 1845, at Laurence County, Georgia." Signed Martha A.C. Crocker, Santa Rosa, California.

January 4, 1927, William F. Crocker, Guardian, makes oath that he is the rightful holder of pension certificate No. 721101, in his possession and now exhibited, as guardian of Martha A.C. Crocker, who remains buried in lot 56, grave 174, Mountain View Cemetery in Oakland, California and died January 15, 1927. Signed William F. Crocker, Guardian, 1603 Ashby Avenue, Berkeley, California

Obituaries for William Roundtree Crocker

Obituary for William R. Crocker: The funeral of the late William R. Crocker a veteran of the late war, took place this forenoon from the family residence, Rev. J.D. Jordan, of the Baptist church officiating. Members of Dunham Post, G. A. R. (Grand Army of the Republic) attended in a body, and the interment in Greenwood was with military honors. The pallbearers were S. L. Kern, James W. Reavis, S. A. Wilson, J. W. Kennedy, Joseph Baxter and George W. Stoy.

William Roundtree died at 3:00 AM at his home on Church Street in Decatur Illinois on March 18, 1895, of complications from his breast injury in the war. Apparently he had a bullet lodged from his time in the Illinois infantry. As for his desertion and joining up I think 13 days later in the 1st Alabama Cavalry, the Regiment he joined was a Union Regiment. They were known as "Tories" or "Men of the Hills" southerners who fought for the North so he didn't join the Confederacy but stayed true to the flag. In your muster rolls and so forth it states that charges were dropped on December 1886, a year after he died so I assume the G.A.R. helped Martha to receive a pension as he was a member of the Post# 141 in Decatur. Also, the post was in charge of his funeral and there were 6 pall bearers from the post at the funeral which was with honors.

Cross, John W. - John W. Cross enlisted in Company B of the 1st Alabama Cavalry, USV as a private on June 10, 1863, in Glendale, Mississippi, for a term of 3 years. He was enrolled by Captain Phillip. A. Sternberg, and was mustered in the same day in Corinth, Mississippi. The Regimental Descriptive Book recorded him as being 32 years of age, 5'-6" tall, having a light complexion, gray eyes, light hair, born in Perry County, Alabama, and a farmer by occupation. The September through December 1863 Muster Rolls listed him as being absent, a prisoner of war in the hands of the enemy since October 26, 1863, which would have been from the Battle of Vincent's Crossroads near Bay Springs, Mississippi. No further information relative to this soldier's capture was found. He was mustered out June 22, 1864, in Memphis, Tennessee

Crow, John D. - John D. Crow enlisted and mustered into Company K of the 1st Alabama Cavalry, USV as a private on December 25, 1863, for a period of 3 years. He was enrolled by Lieutenant Hornback. He traveled 100 miles or horseback from his home in Marion County, Alabama to Camp Davies, Mississippi to enlist in the Union. The Company Descriptive Roll recorded Crow as being 39 years of age, 5'-10" tall, having a light complexion, gray eyes, light hair, born in Morgan County, Alabama, and a farmer by occupation. The January and February Muster Roll recorded him as being absent, on detached service as teamster in General Sherman's expedition in Vicksburg, Mississippi since January 24, 1864, by order of General Greirson. The March and April 1864 Muster Roll recorded him as being on daily duty as a regimental hospital nurse. The November and December 1864 Muster Roll recorded him as being on recruiting service in Decatur, Alabama since November 10, 1864. A Company Muster Roll from December 31, 1864, through April 30, 1865, recorded him as being absent, on recruiting service in Tennessee since November 10, 1864. Crow was mustered out July 19, 1865, in Nashville, Tennessee. His Muster-Out Roll showed him to be due a bounty of $300.

John D. Crow was born September 27, 1829, in Morgan County, Alabama and died May 6, 1899, in Fayette County, Alabama. He married Elizabeth "Betsy Jane" Whitehead, daughter of Archibald Whitehead, Sr. and Nancy Smith. Betsy Jane was born February 10, 1828, in Lauderdale County, Alabama, and died December 11, 1909, in Fayette County, Alabama. They are both buried in

Crow, John W. - John W. Crow enlisted in Company C of the 1st Alabama Cavalry, USV as a Corporal on December 15, 1862, in Corinth, Mississippi for a period of 1 year. He was enrolled by Captain John Latty and mustered in December 22, 1862, in Corinth. The Regimental Descriptive Book recorded him as being 27 years of age, 5'-6½" tall, having a fair complexion, blue eyes, light hair, born in Pickens County, Alabama, and a farmer by occupation. He died February 27, 1863, in the hospital in Corinth, Mississippi.

John W. Crow was the son of Nathaniel Sanders Crow and Nancy Buford Johnson who were married December 5, 1815, in Lunenburg County, Virginia Nathaniel was born March 19, 1792, in Lunenburg County, Virginia and died March 27, 1875, in Booneville, Prentiss County, Mississippi. Children of Nathaniel Sanders Crow and Nancy Buford Johnson were: Julius J.; Eliza Ann, b. 1818; Mary L., b. 1825; Emily M., born September 21, 1827, and died April 25, 1904; Sarah Jane, born 1830; Martha Sanders, born April 12, 1832, died March 21, 1876; and John W. Crow, born July 4, 1837, Pickens County, Alabama and died February 27, 1863, in Corinth, Mississippi.

Crowley, William Riley - William Riley Crowley, also appeared as Craulay, enlisted in Company F of the 1st Alabama Cavalry, USV as a private on November 20, 1863, in Corinth, Mississippi, for a term of 1 year. He was enrolled by Lieutenant Cheney, and was mustered in February 24, 1864, in Memphis, Tennessee. The Company Descriptive Book recorded him as being 21 years of age, 5'5½" tall, having a dark complexion, dark eyes, dark hair, born in Marion County, Alabama, and a farmer by occupation. The January and February 1864 Muster Roll stated his pay had been stopped until he had paid the U.S. Government $12.00 for losing 1 Remington revolver. William R. Crowley's name appeared on the Returns as follows: November 1863, gained from missing in action November 28, 1863; February 1864 to April 1864, on extra or daily duty as a mail carrier; July 1864, absent, an orderly with General Veatch; August 1864, an orderly at General Vandiver's Headquarters in Rome, Georgia; September 1864, absent, on detached service; October 1864, absent on detached service as orderly in Quartermaster and Assistant Adjutant General's Department; November 1864, on detached service; and December 1864, mustered out December 17, 1864 in Savannah, Georgia due to expiration of term of service. Another muster roll stated he mustered out due to being on the march from Atlanta to Savannah, Georgia.

Crumbley, Thomas - Thomas Crumbley enlisted in Company H of the 1st Alabama Cavalry, USV as a private on January 1, 1865, in Huntsville, Alabama. He was enrolled by James W. DeVaney for a period of 3 years, but died before he was mustered in. The Company Descriptive Book recorded him as being 22 years of age, 5'-11" tall, having a dark complexion, blue eyes, black hair, born in Lawrence District, South Carolina, and was a farmer by occupation. He died of smallpox on February 12, 1865, in the barracks in Nashville, Tennessee. The Physician's Statement of Death stated Crumbley died in the hospital of variola, which is smallpox. He is buried in Grave H-09225 in the Nashville National Cemetery in Nashville, Davidson County, Tennessee.

Crumbly, William W. - William W. Crumbley enlisted in Company H of the 1st Alabama Cavalry, USV as a private on February 10, 1865, in Stevenson, Alabama for a period of 3 years, and was mustered in the same day in Nashville, Tennessee. The Muster and Descriptive Roll recorded him as being 24 years of age, 5'-10" tall, having a dark complexion, blue eyes, black hair, born in Lawrence District, South Carolina, and a farmer by occupation. He was paid a bounty of $100 when he enlisted, and his enlistment was credited to Ripley, Chautauqua County, New York. He was appointed sergeant on April 1, 1865, and was mustered out October 20, 1865, in Huntsville, Alabama.

William W. Crumbley was born December 14, 1837, in Lawrence District, South Carolina, and died September 20, 1915, in Cullman, Cullman County, Alabama. He is buried in the Holly Pond Cemetery in Cullman County, Alabama.

Cunningham, James P.W. - James P.W. Cunningham enlisted in Company F of the 1st Alabama Cavalry, USV as a private on December 8, 1863, in Camp Davies, Mississippi for a period of 1 year. He was enrolled by Lieutenant Davis, and was mustered in July 27, 1864, in Rome, Georgia. Another muster roll stated he was enrolled by Lieutenant W.H. Chaney. The Muster and Descriptive Roll recorded him as being 32 years of age, 5'-8" tall, having a fair complexion, blue eyes, dark hair, born in Shelby County, Alabama, and a farmer and blacksmith by occupation. The January and February 1864 Muster Roll showed him to have been absent, sick in the hospital in Memphis, Tennessee. He was discharged December 17, 1864, due to expiration of term of service. His name was listed on the Adams U.S.A. General Hospital Muster Roll in Memphis, Tennessee showing he was admitted February 5, 1864. He was returned to duty March 12, 1864. In August 1864, he was shown as being on extra duty as a scout in General Vandiver's Headquarters in Rome, Georgia. In September 1864, he was on detached duty as a blacksmith. In October and November 1864, he was an orderly in the Quartermaster and Assistant Adjutant General's Department. He was returned to duty March 12, 1864. He was mustered out December 17, 1864, in Savannah, Georgia due to expiration of enlistment on detached service as a blacksmith, since July 20, 1864, but not before mustered out by reason of being on the march from Atlanta to Savannah, Georgia.

James P.W. Cunningham was born in February 1830 in Shelby County, Alabama and died in July 1906 in Bakersville, Ozark County, Missouri, and is buried in the Bakersville Cemetery.

Cupples, Elijah - Elijah Cupples enlisted in Company M of the 1st Alabama Cavalry, USV as a private, for a term of 3 years on September 14, 1863, in Chewalla, Tennessee. He was enrolled by Captain Lomax, and was mustered in the same day in Corinth, Mississippi. The Company Descriptive Book recorded him as being 23 years of age, 5'-8" tall, having a light complexion, hazel eyes, brown hair, born in Hardeman County, Tennessee, and a farmer by occupation. He was appointed sergeant September 14, 1863, to August 15, 1864, when he was appointed 1st sergeant. Elijah's name appeared on a U.S.A. Post Hospital Muster Roll in Huntsville, Alabama for May and June 1865, but did not state if he was a patient or working in the hospital. He was mustered out October 20, 1865, in Huntsville, Alabama. A stop had been put on his pay for $17.10 because of losing 1 saber, 1 saddle blanket, halter and strap, 1 saber belt and plate, and one watering bridle. He was paid a bounty of $180 and shown as being due $120 to make up the $300 bounty he was due.

Curtis, Henry, alias William R. Crocker - See William R. Crocker.

Curtis, Isaac R. - Isaac R. Curtis enlisted in Company G of the 1st Alabama Cavalry, USV. He was temporarily attached from the 11th Illinois Cavalry.

- D -

Dagger, George W. - Only one card was found for George W. Dagger which was filed at the end of the last roll of microfilm of the 1st Alabama Cavalry, USV records. It recorded him as a private in Company A, stating he had been on detached service in Company D of the 11th Illinois Cavalry since February 5, 1864. No further information relative to this soldier was found.*

Daily, Green - Green Daily, also listed as Dailey, enlisted in Company E of the 1st Alabama Cavalry, USV as a private on April 1, 1863, in Glendale, Mississippi, and was mustered in the same day in Corinth, Mississippi. He was shown as present through August 1863, but was reported as having deserted September 6, 1863, from Glendale, Mississippi.

Daughtery, William - William Daughtery, also spelled Daughtry, enlisted in Company G of the 1st Alabama Cavalry, USV as a private on July 11, 1863, in Glendale, Mississippi for a term of 1 year, and was mustered in July 17, 1863, in Corinth, Mississippi. He was mustered out November 26, 1863.

Davis, Adam Aaron - Adam Aaron Davis, enlisted and mustered into Company A of the 1st Alabama Cavalry, USV as a private on September 6, 1864, in Rome, Georgia. He was enrolled by Captain Hinds for a period of 3 years. The Company Descriptive Book records him as being 36 years of age, 5'-5" tall, having a dark complexion, gray eyes, dark hair, born in DeKalb County, Georgia, and a shoemaker by occupation. Davis was sick in Whiteside, Tennessee beginning October 1, 1865, and was still sick when the company mustered out on October 20, 1865. His pay was stopped for $3.32, due to losing 1 carbine swing and swivel and 1 carbine cartridge box. He also owed the U.S. Government $4.98 for clothing. His discharge was furnished October 29, 1865, and he was paid a bounty of $100.

Davis, Archibald M. - Archibald M. Davis enlisted and mustered into Company I of the 1st Alabama Cavalry, USV as a private on August 18, 1862, in Huntsville, Alabama. He was enrolled by Captain H.C. Bankhead for a period of 3 years, and also served in Company D. The Company Descriptive Book recorded him as being 18 years of age, 5'-8½" tall, having a light complexion, dark eyes, light hair, born in Blount County, Alabama, and a farmer by occupation. In November 1862, he was listed as being absent, sick in Hospital #8 in Nashville, Tennessee, where he died November 12, 1862. He was shown as having originally been buried in Grave No. 1235 of the Nashville City Cemetery, was in Ward #117 of Hospital #8 in Nashville, Davidson County, Tennessee, residence before death was Arkadelphia, Walker County, Alabama, he was shown as single and his father was William Davis. His age was listed as 17 on his death record although he had been listed earlier as 18. He died from chronic diarrhea, and was later reinterred in the Nashville National Cemetery.

Davis, Arthur - Arthur Davis enlisted in Company E of the 1st Alabama Cavalry, USV on December 13, 1862, in McNairy County, Tennessee for a term of 1 year, and was mustered in the same day in Corinth, Mississippi. He was 21 years old when he enlisted. A note in his file stated he was taken prisoner of war near Chewalla, Tennessee on January 20, 1863. He was mustered out December 17, 1863, in Memphis, Tennessee due to expiration of term of service.

Davis, Bird - Bird Davis enlisted and was mustered into Company G of the 1st Alabama Cavalry, USV as an Under Cook on July 1, 1864. He enrolled at Decatur, Alabama but was mustered in at Rome, Georgia for a period of 3 years. He was shown as being of African Descent. The Muster and Descriptive Roll recorded him as being 18 years of age, 5'-9" tall, having a black complexion with black eyes, black hair, born in Jackson, Hinds County, Mississippi, and a farmer by occupation. Another muster roll showed him as "Colored". In November 1864 Bird Davis was shown to be on daily duty as a Teamster. In June 1865, he was on daily duty as a Wagoner, and in August 1865, he was on daily duty as a Teamster. He mustered out October 20, 1865, at Huntsville, Alabama with pay being due from enrollment.

Davis, Charles - Charles Davis enlisted and mustered into Company E of the 1st Alabama Cavalry, USV as a Private on August 27, 1863, in Corinth, Mississippi for a term of 1 year. The September and October 1863 Muster Roll showed him to be a blacksmith. He was mustered out September 28, 1864, in Rome, Georgia. His Muster-Out Roll showed him to have been 33 years of age. It stated his clothing account had never been settled including subsistence furnished. Transportation to be furnished by the Quartermaster Department to Nashville, Tennessee. Mustered out by reason of expiration of term of service to date from September 28, 1864. His name appeared on the Returns as follows: October 1863 to April 1864, on daily duty as a blacksmith, and July 1864 to August 1864, on daily duty as a Regimental Blacksmith.

Davis, Charles M. - Charles M. Davis enrolled in Company G of the 1st Alabama Cavalry, USV as a private on March 5, 1863, in Chewalla, Tennessee, and enlisted the same day in Corinth, Mississippi. He was reported to have deserted on August 3, 1863, from Glendale, Mississippi. The September and October 1863 Muster Roll stated he had rejoined from desertion and was awaiting trial. He was mustered out November 26, 1863, in Memphis, Tennessee.

Davis, Christopher C. - Christopher C. Davis enlisted and mustered into Company K of the 1st Alabama Cavalry, USV as a private on July 27, 1862, in Huntsville, Alabama for a term of 3 years. He was enrolled by Captain Bankhead. The Regimental Descriptive Book recorded him as being 23 years of age, 5'-11" tall, having a light complexion, gray eyes, light hair, born in Marshall County, Alabama, and a farmer by occupation. He was appointed Sergeant October 1, 1862. The November 1862 through

February 1863 Muster Rolls listed him as being absent, sick in the hospital in Nashville, Tennessee since December 26, 1862. Christopher C. Davis was among the early enlistees who were immediately shipped to Nashville, Tennessee and merged with the 1st Middle Tennessee Cavalry, which later became the 5th Tennessee Cavalry. Davis was merged with Company E of the 1st Middle Tennessee Cavalry. He was discharged February 18, 1863, by reason of Surgeon's Certificate of Disability. He was shown as being sick in the U.S.A. General Hospital in Mound City, Illinois on the hospital muster roll. A Hospital Muster Roll from the U.S.A. General Hospital in Mound City, Illinois, showed Christopher C. Davis as being a private in Company E of the 1st Middle Tennessee Cavalry, US, and reported him as having deserted April 15, 1864. His name appeared on another Muster-Out Roll stating he was discharged at Nashville, Tennessee on Surgeon's Certificate of Disability on February 18, 1865. There was a Notation in his file from the Adjutant General's Office of the War Department dated October 12, 1888, stating he was discharged at Nashville, Tennessee on January 21, 1863, by reason of Surgeon's Certificate of Disability: origin not stated and paid to include that date. It is not clear as to the muster rolls from the hospital in Mound City, Illinois after he had been discharged.

Davis, D. - A Prisoner of War Record was found in the records of a D. Davis, who served in Company I of the 1st Alabama Cavalry, USV. He was captured and taken prisoner of war near Fayetteville, North Carolina on March 10, 1865, brought from Raliegh, North Carolina and confined at Richmond, Virginia March 28, 1865, and paroled at Boulware & Cox's Wharf May 30, 1865. (The date Davis was captured was the date of the Battle of Monroe's Crossroads.)

Davis, George W. - George W. Davis enlisted in Company C of the 1st Alabama Cavalry, USV on December 15, 1863, in Camp Davies, Mississippi for a period of 3 years. He was enrolled by Captain John Latty and was mustered in March 10, 1864, in Memphis, Tennessee. The Muster and Descriptive Roll recorded him as being 24 years of age, 5'-10" tall, having a fair complexion, black eyes, light hair, born in Walker County, Alabama and a farmer by occupation. From the time of his enlistment to April 30, 1864, he was shown as being absent, on detached duty recruiting in Alabama. His name appeared on the Returns stating: March 1864, On daily duty as company cook; April 1864, on daily duty recruiting. He was shown as being married. He was reported to have deserted October 1, 1865, from Moulton, Alabama with 1 horse and equipment, 2 bridles, 2 saddles, carbine and accoutrements, and 1 shelter tent. A Notation in his file from the Adjutant General's Office of the War Department, dated July 20, 1886, stated the following: The charge of desertion of October 1, 1865, against this man is removed and he is discharged October 1, 1865, under the provisions of the Act of Congress approved July 5, 1864. Discharge Certificate furnished by the Adjutant General's Office July 31, 1886.

George Washington Davis was born February 7, 1840, in Walker County, Alabama to William and Mary Catherine Davis. He was the younger brother of William Wallace Davis. George died August 17, 1921, in Walker County, Alabama

Davis, Henry H. - Henry H. Davis, also shown as Harvy H. Davis, enlisted and mustered into Company D of the 1st Alabama Cavalry, USV as a private in Glendale, Mississippi for a period of 1 year. He was enrolled by Lieutenant John A. Snelling. The Regimental Descriptive Book recorded him as being 18 years of age, 5'-5" tall, having a light complexion, blue eyes, light hair, born in Tuscaloosa, Alabama, and a farmer by occupation. His name appeared on the Returns as follows: July 1863, he was on daily duty as company cook; January to April 1864, he was on daily duty as orderly at Headquarters. He was discharged June 16, 1864, in Decatur, Alabama due to expiration of term of service. His pay was stopped for $12.00 due to him losing 1 Remington revolver.

Davis, James, Pvt. - James Davis enlisted in Company E of the 1st Alabama Cavalry, USV as a private on December 9, 1862, in Nabor's Mill, and enlisted the same day in Corinth, Mississippi. He was shown as being absent, taken prisoner of war January 20, 1863, near Chewalla, Tennessee. He was listed as having deserted from Corinth, Mississippi on March 3, 1863. No further information relative to this soldier was found.

Davis, Jeremiah B. - Jeremiah B. Davis, also listed as Jesse B. Davis, enlisted and mustered into

Company D of the 1st Alabama Cavalry, USV as a private on May 3, 1863, in Glendale, Mississippi for a term of 1 year. He was enrolled by Captain Jude H. Shurtliff. The Regimental Descriptive Book recorded him as being 18 years of age, 5'-8¾" tall, having a dark complexion, blue eyes, dark hair, born in Walker County, Alabama, and a farmer by occupation. He was discharged June 16, 1864, in Decatur, Alabama due to expiration of term of service. His pay had been stopped for $12.00 due to him losing 1 Remington revolver.

Jeremiah B. Davis was the son of Dennis and Rephena Davis. Other children of Dennis and Rephena were: Henry H.; William C.; Sarah E.J.; Darlin M.; Mahaly M.V.; Theodocea E.; and Rochana R.B. Davis.

Davis, Jesse - Jesse Davis enlisted and mustered into Company I of the 1st Alabama Cavalry, USV as a private on July 21, 1862, in Huntsville, Alabama for a period of 3 years. He was enrolled by Captain Bankhead. The Company Descriptive Book listed him as having been 25 years of age, 5'-10" tall, having a dark complexion, blue eyes, dark hair, born in Surry County, North Carolina, and a farmer by occupation. Jesse Davis died of disease on October 19, 1862, in Hospital #2 in Nashville, Davidson County, Tennessee, and is buried in Grave A-5045 in the Nashville National Cemetery.

Jesse Davis was born August 18, 1836, in Surry County, North Carolina. His parents were Joshua Davis, born July 8, 1805, in Wilkes County, North Carolina and Kisiah Stanfield, born 1813, who were married September 8, 1832, in North Carolina. Joshua died March 30, 1882, in Brown County, Indiana and Kisiah died October 2, 1906. Jesse married Margaret Spiegle January 10, 1861, and had the following children: Lou Allen, born November 13, 1861, in Winston County, Alabama; Jesse David, born February 12, 1863, (five months after his father died); Sarah, born 1838; Robert, born May 7, 1841; Mason, born December 31, 1842; Lucinda Jane, born June 14, 1846; Roxannah, born June 5, 1847; Martha, born June 7, 1849; and Joseph, and Jasper Newton Davis, born May 12, 1852. Family information submitted by Caroline Wright.

Davis, Joseph H. - Joseph H. Davis enlisted in the Field and Staff of the 1st Alabama Cavalry, USV on August 19, 1864, in Rome, Georgia as 1st Assistant Surgeon, and was mustered in the same day in Savannah, Georgia for a period of 3 years. He was appointed 1st Assistant Surgeon from a citizen of Alabama by authority of the Secretary of War. The March and April 1865 Field and Staff Muster Roll listed him as being absent, on leave of absence in April 1865. The May and June 1865 Field and Staff Muster Roll listed him as being absent, on detached service in Decatur, Alabama. His name was listed on the Returns for June and July 1865, stating he was absent, sick in Roanoke, Alabama June 25, 1865. He was mustered out October 20, 1865, in Huntsville, Alabama. This officer has made affidavit that he has made all requisite returns relating to public property for which he has been accountable, as required by army regulations.

Davis, Mason - Mason Davis enlisted and mustered into Company I of the 1st Alabama Cavalry, USV on August 18, 1862, in Huntsville, Alabama. He was enrolled by Captain Bankhead. The Company Descriptive Book recorded him as being 20 years of age, 5'-11½" tall, having a dark complexion, dark eyes, sandy hair, born Surry County, North Carolina, and a farmer by occupation. On November 30, 1863, he was listed as being absent, sick in Hospital #12 in Nashville, Tennessee. Mason was one of the early enlistees who were immediately shipped to Nashville, Tennessee and merged with the 1st Middle Tennessee Cavalry which was later the 5th Tennessee Cavalry. He was assigned to Company D of the 1st Middle Tennessee Cavalry. His name appeared on the Returns as follows: December 1862, on detached service with train since December 26, 1862; January 1863, On detached service as courier in Reedyville, Tennessee January 27th; December 1863, on detached service as teamster, September and October 1864; on daily duty as Regimental Ambulance Driver. He was mustered out July 19, 1865, in Nashville, Tennessee.

Mason Davis was born December 31, 1842, (his tombstone states his date of birth was January 1, 1842) in Surry County, North Carolina (see Jesse Davis, above, for family information) He was the brother of Jesse and Robert Davis, also members of the 1st Alabama Cavalry, USV. He married 1st, Christen Ann Young November 20, 1870, in Blue Earth Lake, Minnesota and had the following children: Ida Lucinda and Gerome. After Christen's death, Mason married Emma Jane Anthony and they had the following children: Jasper Newton; Lemuel; Grant E.; Ettie; and Nettie Davis. Mason died December 23, 1917, in Janesville, Waseca County, Minnesota. Family information submitted by Caroline Wright.

Davis, Robert - Robert Davis, brother of Mason and Jesse Davis, enlisted and mustered into Company I of the 1st Alabama Cavalry, USV as a private on August 18, 1862, in Huntsville, Alabama for a period of 3 years. He was enrolled by Captain H.C. Bankhead. The Company Descriptive Book recorded him as being 18 years of age, 5'-10" tall, having a dark complexion, blue eyes, dark hair, born in Surry County, North Carolina, and a farmer by occupation. From September 8, 1862, until his death, he was shown as being absent, sick in Hospital #8, in Nashville, Tennessee. He died of typhoid fever January 27, 1863, in Hospital #8, in Nashville, Davidson County, Tennessee. He is buried in Grave B-6554 in the Nashville National Cemetery.

Robert was born May 7, 1841, to Joshua Davis and Kisiah Stanfield. He was the brother of Jesse Davis and Mason Davis, also members of the 1st Alabama Cavalry, USV.

Davis, Thomas P. - Thomas P. Davis enlisted in Company D of the 1st Alabama Cavalry, USV as a private on May 1, 1864, in Decatur, Alabama for a term of 3 years. He was enrolled by Lieutenant Pease. The Company Descriptive Book recorded him as being 20 years of age, 5'-8" tall, having a light complexion, blue eyes, light hair, born in Walker County, Alabama, and a farmer by occupation. He was on detached service recruiting in Alabama, sometimes with Major Shurtliff and others with Captain Lomax. From the time he enlisted until July 30, 1865, he was shown as being absent, on detached service recruiting in Decatur, Alabama. However, on July 30, 1865, he was shown as having deserted from Moulton, Alabama, and his pay was stopped for $28.10 for deserting with a saddle. Another muster roll stated he deserted from Huntsville, Alabama May 10, 1865. A Notation in his file from the Adjutant General's Office of the War Department in Washington, DC, dated November 7, 1884, stated the following: The charge of desertion of May 10, 1865, and of July 30, 1865, are removed and he is discharged to date May 10, 1865, under the provisions of the act of Congress, approved July 5, 1884. Discharge Certificate furnished by Adjutant General's Office November 29, 1884, as of May 10, 1865.

Thomas P. Davis was born in April 1844 in Walker County, Alabama to George Tom Davis and Sarah Thacker. He married Mahala J. Pennington on February 19, 1873. The following children were listed in their household in the 1880 Walker County, Alabama Census, but obviously some of the children were by a previous wife as they were born before Thomas and Manala were married: Irvin, Sarah, Elizabeth, Arcena, Rufus, Thomas, Jasper R., and Lloyd Davis. Thomas P. Davis died October 25, 1916, in Tuscaloosa County, Alabama.

Davis, William - William Davis enlisted in Company B of the 1st Alabama Cavalry, USV as a private on May 1, 1864, in Decatur, Alabama for a term of 3 years. He was enrolled by Major Cramer and was mustered in the same day in Rome, Georgia. The Muster and Descriptive Roll recorded him as being 17 years of age, 5'-5" tall, having a fair complexion, yellow eyes, light hair, born in Roane County, Tennessee, and a farmer by occupation. William Davis was killed in action November 23, 1864, in Oconee River, Balls Ferry, Georgia.

Davis, William - William Davis enlisted in Company E of the 1st Alabama Cavalry, USV at age 28 on February 1, 1863, in Corinth, Mississippi for a period of 1 year. He was enlisted as a sergeant; however, he was reduced to rank on September 22, 1863, by order of Captain Chandler. He had been listed as a 2nd Sergeant, Sergeant, and 2nd Master Sergeant. He was mustered out of service due to expiration of term of service on March 1, 1864, in Memphis, Tennessee.

Davis, William - William Davis, shown as "Colored", enrolled in Company M of the 1st Alabama Cavalry, USV on January 9, 1865, in Savannah, Georgia. He was enrolled by Captain Lomax for a period of 3 years, and was shown as a "Colored Cook". The July and August 1865 Muster Roll showed William to have been absent, sick in the hospital in Decatur, Alabama since July 15, 1865. From August to September 1865, he was still listed as being absent, sick in Decatur, Alabama since July

15, 1865. The Company Descriptive Book records him as being 23 years of age, 6'-1" tall, having a black complexion, black eyes, black hair, born in Burke County, Georgia, and a farmer by occupation. He was listed as having mustered out October 20, 1865, with the rest of the organization but was not given a discharge at that time, apparently because of him still being sick.

Davis, William C. - William C. Davis enlisted and mustered into Company D of the 1st Alabama Cavalry, USV as a private on May 3, 1863, in Glendale, Mississippi for a period of 1 year. He was enrolled by Lieutenant John A. Snelling. The Regimental Descriptive Book showed him as being 19 years of age, 5'-6½" tall, having a light complexion, dark eyes, dark hair, born in Walker County, Alabama, and a farmer by occupation. In August 1863, he was on daily duty as a company cook. He was mustered out June 16, 1864, in Decatur, Alabama due to expiration of term of service. A stop was put on his pay for $1.25 for transportation.

Davis, William J. - William J. Davis enlisted in Company C of the 1st Alabama Cavalry, USV, on January 1, 1864, in Camp Davies, Mississippi for a period of 3 years. He was enrolled by Captain John Latty, and was mustered in March 10, 1864, in Memphis, Tennessee. The Muster and Descriptive Roll recorded him as being 20 years of age, 5'-11" tall, having a fair complexion, black eyes, light hair, born in Bibb County, Alabama, and a farmer by occupation. He was shown as being single. He was recorded as a Farrier for Company C. He was also listed as being on daily duty as Regimental Blacksmith. He was mustered out October 20, 1865, in Huntsville, Alabama, with a stop put on his pay for $6.16 for losing 1 carbine sling, 1 swivel, 1 carbine cartridge box, 1 cap pouch, 1 screwdriver, and 1 pair of spurs and straps. He was paid $180 bounty and shown as being due $120 to make up the $300 bounty. There was a Notation in his military records from the Adjutant General's Office of the War Department, dated January 31, 1877, which stated the following: William J. Davis was appointed blacksmith, by Regimental Order #44, August 2, 1864, date of reduction to private not stated.

Davis, William T. - William T. Davis enlisted in the 1st Alabama Cavalry, USV September 25, 1863, in Stevenson, Alabama, USV. He was recorded as being 18 years of age, 5'-5" tall, having a light complexion, blue eyes, light hair, born in Cincinnati, Ohio. The card was signed by Lieutenant Irvine of the 28th Kentucky but was filed with the 1st Alabama Cavalry, US Records and stated he enlisted in the 1st Alabama Cavalry, USV. No further information relative to this soldier were found.*

Davis, William W. - William W. Davis' name was shown on a Hospital Muster Roll for the Adams USA General Hospital in Memphis, Tennessee. It stated he was a private in Company M of the 1st Alabama Cavalry, USV, and was admitted to Adams USA General Hospital as a patient on January 21, 1864. (This William W. Davis and the one below may be for the same person.)

Davis, William W. - William Wallace Davis enlisted in Company C of the 1st Alabama Cavalry, USV on December 15, 1863, in Corinth, Mississippi for a term of 3 years. He was enrolled by Captain John Latty, and was mustered in March 10, 1864, in Memphis, Tennessee. The Muster and Descriptive Roll recorded him as being 26 years of age, 6' tall, having a fair complexion, blue eyes, light hair, born in Walker County, Alabama, and a farmer by occupation. It also stated he was a married sergeant. From March 1, 1864, through June 30, 1865, he was absent, on detached service recruiting in Alabama. He was appointed Sergeant on March 1, 1864. His name appeared on the Returns for April 1864 stating he was on daily duty on recruiting service. He was reported to have deserted from Moulton, Alabama on October 1, 1865, with saddle, bridle, halter, blanket, curry comb, brush, Spencer Carbine, and accoutrements. Another muster roll stated he deserted with 1 saddle, 2 saddle blankets, 1 Spencer Carbine and accoutrements, 2 bridles and 1 shelter tent. There is a Notation in his military records from the Record and Pension Office of the War Department in Washington, DC, dated December 26, 1895, which stated: The charge of desertion of October 1, 1865, against this man is removed and he is discharged to date, October 1, 1865, under the provisions of the act of Congress, approved March 2, 1889. Discharge Certificate furnished by the War Department December 26, 1895.

William Wallace Davis was the son of Mary Catherine and William Davis. He married Elizabeth Jane Handley in the late 1850's. Their children were: George Washington; William Mack;

Andy M.; Levi Henry; Mary Elizabeth; Dovie Ann; John Irvin; and Manley Carol Davis. He became a preacher in 1866, served one term as a state representative from Winston County, Alabama in 1890, died December 23, 1901, and is buried in Union Grove Cemetery in Winston County, Alabama. Solomon Curtis and two of his sons are also buried in Union Grove Cemetery. Family information submitted by Bill Davis.

Davlin, George W. - George W. Davlin enlisted in Company C of the 1st Alabama Cavalry, USV as a private on February 5, 1864, in Memphis, Tennessee for a term of 3 years. He was enrolled by Captain John Latty and mustered in March 10, 1864, in Memphis, Tennessee. The Muster and Descriptive Roll shows him to have been 18 years of age, 5'-8" tall, having a fair complexion, blue eyes, light hair, born in Panola County, Texas, and a drover by occupation. He was shown as being single. He was appointed corporal on March 1, 1864. His name appeared on the Returns as follows: March 1864, absent, sick in hospital in Memphis, Tennessee; April 1864, absent, sick in hospital in Nashville, Tennessee. He was reported to have deserted from Rome, Georgia on November 9, 1864, with 2 Colt Revolvers, 1 Smith's Carbine, horse, saddle and accoutrements.

Dawson, Lewis N. - Lewis N. Dawson enlisted in Company G of the 1st Alabama Cavalry, USV on March 5, 1863, in Chewalla, Tennessee for a term of 1 year, and mustered in the same day in Corinth, Mississippi. He was appointed corporal September 1, 1863. He was mustered out November 26, 1863, in Memphis, Tennessee

Day, Enos - Enos Day enrolled in Company B of the 1st Alabama Cavalry, USV on February 16, 1864, in Pulaski, Tennessee for a period of 3 years by Lieutenant Judy. His enrollment was credited to Pulaski, Giles County, Tennessee. He was mustered in March 27, 1864, at Decatur, Alabama. The Company Descriptive Roll, recorded him as being 20 years of age, 5'-9" tall, having a fair complexion, gray eyes, brown hair, born in Jackson County, Alabama, and a farmer by occupation. Enos Day was mustered out on October 20, 1865, at Huntsville, Madison County, Alabama. For some reason he owed the U.S. Government $100.86 but they owed him $300 for bounty.

Enos Day was born August 12, 1840, in Jackson County, Alabama to Wyatt Day and Elizabeth Isbella Grider who married March 6, 1840. Enos married Sarah Jane "Janie" Anderson on July 2, 1868, in Winston County, Alabama and had the following children: Louisa Elizabeth, born April 26, 1869, died March 3, 1962; Martha, born 1870; Orpha Jane, born May 14, 1870, died December 28, 1955; Pheby Ann, born April 27, 1872, died December 25, 1899; James Sherman, born June 26, 1873, died 1941; Oliver Washington, born June 28, 1875, died May 28, 1958; Emaline, "Emma" R., born April 18, 1877; and Lillie Viola Day, born August 31, 1886, and died November 1977. Enos Day's wife, Sarah, was born October 13, 1840, in Jackson County, Alabama to Horatio Alexander "Horacie" Anderson and his wife Elizabeth, last name unknown. Enos Day died May 29, 1915, in Cullman County, Alabama, and was buried in the Bethlehem Methodist Church Cemetery near Good Hope in Cullman County, Alabama.

From *The Cullman Tribune*, June 10, 1915 (sic)
Enoch Day is Dead
On May 29th at 8:30 pm the death angel called Mr. Enoch Day to the great beyond. He was born August 12, 1840, led the life of an average settler until the civil war when he joined the first Alabama cavalry Kilpatrick's division U.S.A. and fought through the Atlanta campaign and was with Sherman until the surrender in North Carolina, where he received an honorable discharge. While on the field of battle he fought with conspicuous bravery, standing after others had fled. At the close of the war he returned home and became one of Cullman county's best citizens. His death was due to cancer from which he suffered untold agony but bore it all like a true soldier. He married Miss Janie Anderson and unto them were born five daughters and two sons, all of whom are living except one daughter. Mrs. Day died a few years ago. Mr. Day was a member of the Baptist church, the I.O.O.F. and the Masons. The remains were laid to rest on Sunday evening at Bethlehem cemetery by the Odd Fellows. Rev. Smith conducted the funeral services. A Friend.

Day, F. - Only one card was found for F. Day which was filed at the end of the last roll of microfilm of the 1st Alabama Cavalry, USV records. It recorded him as a private in Company B of the 1st Alabama Cavalry, USV having enlisted February 1, 1864, in Pulaski, Tennessee for a period of 3 years. He was enlisted by Lieutenant Judy. He was on daily duty as a nurse in the hospital in April 1864, however, it did not say which hospital or where. No further information relative to this soldier was found.*

Day, Gardner C. - Gardner C. Day enlisted in Company B of the 1st Alabama Cavalry, USV on February 1, 1864, in Pulaski, Tennessee for a period of 3 years. He was enrolled by Lt. Judy. The Company Descriptive Book records him as being 18 years of age, 5'-6" inches tall, having a fair complexion, gray eyes, light hair, born in Lawrence County, Tennessee, and a farmer by occupation. No further information relative to this soldier was found.

Day, George William - George William Day enlisted and mustered into Company I of the 1st Alabama Cavalry, USV as a private on August 22, 1864, in Louisville, Kentucky. He was enrolled by Captain Smith for a term of 3 years. The Muster and Descriptive Roll recorded him as being 18 years of age, 5'-9½" tall, having a fair complexion, gray eyes, light hair, born in Morgan County, Alabama, and a farmer by occupation. The Company Descriptive Book stated he was born in Lawrence County, Alabama. He was mustered out July 19, 1865, in Nashville, Tennessee

George William Day was the son of David M. Day and Cyrena Dutton, the grandson of Richard Day and the great grandson of both David Day, Jr. and Stephen Penn. He had two uncles in the 1st Alabama Cavalry, USV, James H. Day and Richard B. Day. In 1870 he was living in the Crowdabout Community with his wife, Laura and young son, Lucian.

Day, James H. - James H. Day enlisted and mustered into Company D of the 1st Alabama Cavalry, USV as a sergeant on July 21, 1862, in Huntsville, Alabama. He was enrolled by Captain Bankhead for a period of 3 years. The Company Descriptive Book records him as being 23 years of age, 6'-1" tall, having a light complexion, blue eyes, sandy hair, born in Morgan County, Alabama and a farmer by occupation. The November and December 1862 Muster Roll recorded him as a 4th Sergeant. He was one of the early enlistees immediately shipped to Nashville, Tennessee and merged with the 1st Middle Tennessee Cavalry, which went on to become the 5th Tennessee Cavalry, US. He reenlisted October 12, 1863, in Glendale, Mississippi. James H. Day was discharged to accept appointment as 2nd Lieutenant October 12, 1863, and received pay as Sergeant to October 31, 1863. He was mustered out July 19, 1865, in Nashville, Tennessee. His Muster-Out roll stated: This officer makes affidavit that he has rendered all returns of public property for which he has been accountable as required by army regulations and existing order to date. Most of his time was spent on special duty commanding Company.

James H. Day was the son of Richard Day and Elizabeth Penn, the grandson of David Day, Jr. and Stephen Penn. On March 10, 1865, he was given command of Company K after its leader was killed in action in North Carolina. After he mustered out of service, he returned to his home community, married Martha Simpson and fathered four children, his first born being named George Spencer Day after Colonel George Spencer, Commander of the First Alabama Cavalry. James H. Day died January 1, 1881 in Morgan County, Alabama at the age of 40. He is buried in the Friendship Cemetery in Morgan County, Alabama.

Day, Lionel W. - Lionel W. Day and his younger brother George, answered President Lincoln's call for volunteers, enlisting as privates in Company A of the 64th Illinois Infantry on August 16, 1862. They were with the regiment during the Battle of Corinth, Mississippi in October 1862, when the regiment lost 70 men killed, wounded and missing. On March 3, 1863, Lionel transferred to the 1st Alabama Cavalry, USV at Corinth and was promoted to 1st Lieutenant serving as Regimental Adjutant. The 1st Alabama Cavalry, USV was very active in north Alabama, scouting and engaging the guerrilla bands in the area. He was mustered out march 2, 1864, at Memphis, Tennessee, and returned to Illinois. His brother, George, remained with the 64th Illinois Cavalry, and died August 7, 1864, of wounds received during the Atlanta Campaign.

Lionel W. Day first enlisted in Company A of the 64th Regiment Illinois Volunteer Cavalry. He then enrolled in Company A of the first Alabama Cavalry, USV at age 24, on March 3, 1863, for a period of one year. He was appointed to 1st Lieutenant by order of Gen. Dodge at Corinth, Mississippi. On the Field and Staff Muster Roll dated June 30, 1863, it stated Lionel W. Day was Adjutant and was commissioned or appointed on March 2, 1863, in Springfield, Illinois. In June 1863, Day was shown as relieved from duty on account of being sick June 7th. Discharged from 64th Illinois Cavalry.

On the Field and Staff Muster Roll for January and February 1864, it listed him as 1st Lieutenant and Adjutant. On March 2, 1864, he was relieved from duty due to expiration of term of service. He was shown as being Mustered out on October 20, 1865, at Huntsville, Alabama. He was also listed as being Mustered Out March 2, 1864, in Memphis, Tennessee. Lionel W. Day is buried in the Maplewood Cemetery in Huntsville, Alabama.

Lionel W. Day was born on a farm in Maine in 1839, one of 5 sons of Eben and Clarissa Day. In the late 1850s the family moved to the fertile prairie land in north-central LaSalle County, Illinois, where they prospered. Continued life as a farmer had no appeal to Lionel; he chose to study law and became licensed to practice in Illinois. Lionel didn't stay long in Illinois. He returned to Alabama in the summer of 1865, first to Selma, where he sought a location to set up a law practice, then to Montgomery in August, where he was employed by the Post Office. While there he met many influential men, and was appointed, in January, 1866, as Clerk of the United States District Court in north Alabama, which held court in Huntsville. He held that office for 8 years and was subsequently appointed Assistant United States District Attorney. He retired from that office in 1884, and entered private practice, ranking as one of the successful lawyers of Northern Alabama.

Lionel W. Day died suddenly of a massive stroke on March 15, 1891, at the age of 52. Obituaries printed in the local newspapers attest to his standing in the community. He was buried in the Maple Hill Cemetery in Huntsville, Madison County, Alabama.

The Weekly Gazette wrote "...Huntsville loses one of its most esteemed and widely known public men, an estimable citizen, a brave soldier; in all a chivalrous character. The funeral services were largely attended from the Episcopal Church and the remains were laid to rest with the honors of the I.O.O.F, the G.A.R., [Grand Army of the Republic] the Huntsville Bar, and the City authorities. Appropriate resolutions of respect have been adopted and tributes paid to the memory of the deceased by each of these organizations. Peace to his calm and tranquil spirit."

The Weekly Mercury wrote "...the largest concourse of people we have seen in our city for years, assembled to pay the last sad tribute to the memory of our esteemed fellow citizen, Captain Lionel W. Day. It was indeed a touching sight to see the remains of one who had come among us as a stranger and a Federal soldier, who had neither family or relative living in our community, followed to the grave by the representative of every class of Southern society, and the circumstances spoke in strong and unmistakable terms of the high appreciation our community had of the magnificent character that Captain Day had attained in the estimation of all who knew him. The gray-haired citizen, the Confederate veteran, and the fair women commingled tears of sorrow over his grave, nor did the colored people forget his merits, for they too in sincere sorrow followed him to his last resting place..."

Perhaps W.L. Clay, an ardent supporter of Secession, said it best when he wrote "...when Memorial Day comes again, and when flowers are scattered over the graves of the Confederate dead, that Captain Day's grave will be as kindly and liberally remembered by loving friends as the grave of any here that fell for the cause that was loved but lost." Submitted by Brian Hogan

Day, Richard B. - Richard B. Day enlisted in Company I of the 1st Alabama Cavalry, USV as a private on August 26, 1862, in Huntsville, Alabama for a term of 3 years, and was mustered in the same day in Nashville, Tennessee. His horse and equipment were furnished by the U.S. The Company Descriptive Roll recorded him as being 25 years of age, 6' tall, having a light complexion, gray eyes, dark hair, and a carpenter by occupation. He was appointed 1st Sergeant on September 30, 1862, by order of Colonel Stokes. Richard was one of the early enlistees who were immediately shipped to Nashville, Tennessee where they were merged with the 1st Middle Tennessee Cavalry which later became the 5th Tennessee Cavalry. He was merged with Company D of the 1st Middle Tennessee Cavalry. On January 27, 1863, he was detached as courier at Reedyville, Tennessee. On April 30, 1863, he was reported as missing in action at Cedar Bluff, Alabama. He rejoined the company November 10,

1863, in Camp Davies, Mississippi. From December 1863, to April 1864, he was on daily duty in the Ordinance Department, and in July 1864, he was on daily duty in same department. He was reduced from 1st Sergeant and appointed corporal November 10, 1863. Richard B. Day's name was listed on a U.S.A. Post Hospital Muster Roll in Huntsville, Alabama dated May and June 2865. He was mustered out July 19, 1865, in Nashville, Tennessee.

Corporal Richard B. Day was the son of Richard Day and Elizabeth Penn, and the grandson of David Day, Jr. and Stephen Penn. After he mustered out of service he returned to Crowdabout and married Martha Ellen Gibson on October 10, 1866, and they had six children. He was Justice of the Peace in his community and died February 22, 1923, at the age of 86. He was buried in the Pisqua Cemetery in Morgan County, Alabama. Family information from *Some Union Soldiers From a Place Called Crowdabout*, by Henry G. Sellers, Jr.

<u>Dean, Dudley</u> - Dudley Dean enlisted in Company H of the 1st Alabama Cavalry, USV. A note in his file headed Camden Street, Baltimore, Maryland, stated he died June 6, 1863. The Record of Death and Interment stated his residence before enlistment was "Sinclair County, Alabama" but probably should have been St. Clair County, Alabama. It also recorded him as married, born in Alabama, and 66 years of age. He was admitted to the hospital from Fort McHenry on June 3, 1863, and died of chronic diarrhea on June 6, 1863.

<u>Dean, William J.</u> - William J. Dean enlisted in Company G of the 1st Alabama Cavalry, USV on November 27, 1862, in Grand Junction, Tennessee for a term of 1 year, and was mustered in November 27, 1862, in Corinth, Mississippi. He was appointed Commissary Sergeant November 27, 1862. He was mustered out November 26, 1863, in Memphis, Tennessee due to expiration of term of service.

<u>Deaton, James</u> - James Deaton enlisted in Company B of the 1st Alabama Cavalry, USV as a private on December 20, 1862, in Glendale, Mississippi. He was enrolled by Captain Frank C. Burdick, and was mustered in December 31, 1862, in Corinth, Mississippi. The Regimental Descriptive Book recorded him as being 31 years of age, 5'-9" tall, having a dark complexion, gray eyes, dark hair, born in Bledsoe County, Tennessee, and a farmer by occupation. The January through April 1863 Muster Rolls listed him as being absent, sick in the hospital in Corinth, Mississippi. From May through November 1863, he was cooking in the Regimental Hospital. He was discharged December 27, 1863, in Camp Davies, Mississippi due to expiration of term of service.

<u>Delk, David M.</u> - David M. Delk enlisted in Company G, and was temporarily detached from the 11th Illinois Cavalry.

<u>DeVaney, James W.</u> - Captain James W. DeVaney enlisted and mustered into Company H (called the lost company) of the 1st Alabama Cavalry, USV on April 1, 1865, for 3 years, at age 24 in Huntsville, Alabama. He had previously enlisted in Company G of the 50th Infantry Illinois Cavalry, Colonel M.M. Bain Commanding. He was appointed Captain by Major General Dodge by authority of the Secretary of War, Left Wing, 16th Army Corps, Kennesaw, Georgia dated July 12, 1864, to fill an original vacancy. Later Sergeant Major of the 50th Illinois Volunteer Infantry. His pay was due from enrollment when he was mustered out October 20, 1865. His name appeared on the Returns as follows: June 1865 through July 1865, Present, assigned to duty April 1, 1865, not mustered. August 1865, Present; September 1865, present commanding company. He mustered out October 20, 1865, and his Muster-Out roll stated: Appointed by Major General Dodge by the authority of the Secretary of War. This officer makes affidavit that he has rendered all requisites returns waiting for public property for which he has been accountable as required by Army regulations.

Captain DeVaney was born October 29, 1840, in Ross County, Ohio. He married Phoebe C. Chicken November 24, 1860, near Bernadotte, Fulton County, Illinois. Phoebe was born November 27, 1841, in Bernodotte, Fulton County, Illinois and died January 28, 1929, in Owl Creek Township, Woodson County, Kansas. Children of James and Phoebe Chicken DeVaney were: Anna, born 1865; Nellie, born 1868; Samuel Sheridan, born November 1869; and J. William DeVaney, born 1870, and died 1954 in Sumner County, New Mexico. Phoebe was the daughter of Henry Farson Chicken and

Elizabeth Bogue, who married December 12, 1840, in Fulton County, Illinois. Henry was born September 16, 1816, in Freeport, Harrison County, Ohio and died April 4, 1894, in Vermont, Fulton County, Illinois. Elizabeth Bogue Chicken was born October 1, 1816, in Flushing, Belmont County, Ohio and died April 14, 1859, in Bernadotte, Fulton County, Illinois.

His widow filed for a pension after his death and the following was taken from the pension records. Her pension was denied because Devaney's death was not connected to his military service.

Affidavit from James DeVaney's widow states the following in her request for a pension after his death: "I will write a few lines to inform you of the services of James W. DeVaney. We were married near Bernadotte, Fulton County, Illinois on November 24th 1860. On the 12th day of September 1861 he enlisted at Bernadotte in Company G 50th Regiment Infantry Illinois Volunteers, Colonel M.M. Bain Commanding Regiment. James W. DeVaney was 4th Sergeant until the 4th day of March 1863 when he was made 1st Sergeant until the 19th day of May 1864 he was made Sergeant Major of the 50th Regiment of Illinois Volunteers.

On the 29th of December 1863 he was discharged at Springfield, Illinois by reason of re-enlistment as a veteran volunteer. He was sent home with Jacob Fleming to recruit for the Regiment and they got 9 recruits 8 new ones and a veteran. They reported to Captain G.S. Fairwell of the 28th Illinois Volunteers at Macomb, Illinois. Then about September 1864 he was discharged to raise a Company for the 1st Alabama Cavalry and was made Captain of Company H, 1st Alabama Cavalry, USV. He was left at Huntsville, Alabama until he was discharged from the service of the United States on the 20th day of October 1865 at Huntsville, Alabama. James W. DeVaney was born in Ross County, Ohio on the 29th day of October 1840. He was five feet nine inches tall, had dark complexion, hazel eyes, black hair, and by occupation was a farmer and school teacher. Him nor I ever applied for a pension except me, one time, when so many was getting one I thought since I had four small children maybe I could get one but when I said he was killed by accident that was all. James W. DeVaney was at Ft. Henry, Ft. Donalson and Shiloh where he had a wounded man shot off his shoulder that he was carrying off the battle field. Then he was on the advance on Corinth for 28 days and in the second battle of Corinth he was sun struck there so he never could work in the hot sun after he came home on November 2nd 1865, at Vermont Illinois. Then in the Spring of 1868, we came to Woodson County, Kansas where we settled on a homestead in 1870. Then on the 17th of November he went with a party of thirteen others on a buffalo hunt where he was shot accidentally. They never got him home and I never seen him again. On June 16, 1874, I married Charles Steffen of Company G, 5th Kansas Volunteer Cavalry and lived with him until his death July 24, 1910." Signed Phoebe C. Steffen and dated 16th Day of February A.D. 1911. His death date was shown as December 2, 1870. Pension records submitted by Johnny L.T.N. Potter.

Devine, J. - Only one card was found for J. Devine, also spelled Divine, which was filed at the end of the last roll of microfilm of the 1st Alabama Cavalry, USV records. It recorded him as a Sergeant in Company H and having deserted in October 1864. No further information relative to this soldier was found.*

Deweese, John P. - John P. Deweese, also listed as John P.J. Deweese, enlisted in Company A on March 28, 1864, in Decatur, Alabama for a term of 3 years. He also served in Company G. He was enrolled by Lieutenant Pease and was mustered in April 13, 1864, in Decatur. The Muster and Descriptive Roll recorded him as being 25 years of age, 5'-7" tall, having a fair complexion, blue eyes, dark hair, born in Dallas County, Alabama, and a farmer by occupation. He was reported to have deserted October 28, 1864, from Decatur, Alabama with arms and equipment, but was since found to be a prisoner of war in the hands of the enemy. He was transferred to Company G by Regimental Order 62, at Mooresville, Alabama. From April 13, 1864, through July 1864, he was on detached service recruiting in Decatur, Alabama. Supposedly deserted from Rome, Georgia while on detached service. He was also reported as having deserted from Decatur, Alabama October 28, 1864, with arms and equipment.

Dickinson, Rufus, B. - Rufus B. Dickenson, also spelled Dickenson, enlisted in Company G of the 1st Alabama Cavalry, USV as a private on March 10, 1864, in Decatur, Alabama for a term of 3 years. He was enrolled by Lieutenant Pease and was mustered in April 13, 1864, in Decatur. The Muster and Descriptive Roll recorded him as being 21 years of age, 5'-9" tall, having a fair complexion, blue eyes, light hair, born in Marion County, Alabama, and a farmer by occupation. On May 1, 1864, he was shown as being absent, sick in the hospital in Decatur, Alabama through August 1864. His name appears on the Returns as follows: June 1864, died of disease on May 1, 1864, in Decatur, Alabama; July 1864, absent, sick at Decatur since May 1, 1864. He was shown as being mustered out October 20, 1865, and a stop was put on his pay for $27.10, due to him losing 1 carbine, retained under General Order 101, War Department; 1 saber belt and plate; 1 carbine cartridge box; 1 cap pouch and 1 screwdriver. While the records state he died during the war, they also state he was mustered out October 20, 1865, which is when the organization was mustered out. It is unclear if this trooper Rufus B. Dickenson did indeed die during the war. Rufus is buried in the Old Ireland Cemetery in Marion County, Alabama.

Dickinson, James - James Dickinson, also spelled Dickenson, enlisted and mustered into Company F of the 1st Alabama Cavalry, USV as a private on November 25, 1863, in Camp Davies, Mississippi. He was enrolled by Captain Pierce. The Company Descriptive Book recorded him as being 26 years of age, 6' tall, having a fair complexion, dark eyes, dark hair, born in Hardin County, Tennessee, and a farmer and mechanic by occupation. From January 1, 1864, to February 1, 1864, he was on detached service detailed as a teamster in the Quartermaster Department in Vicksburg, Mississippi, since January 25, 1864. James Dickenson died February 15, 1864, while on detached service in Vicksburg, Mississippi. He was taken sick and never mustered in. A Notation in his files from the Adjutant General's Office of the War Department in Washington, DC, dated January 13, 1879, stated the following: Company Descriptive Book reports him died at Vicksburg, Mississippi, February 15, 1864, of diarrhea, died while on detached service. His Casualty Sheet spells his name Dickerson, and states he died February 15, 1864, of diarrhea. Another Casualty Sheet stated he died February 16, 1864.

James Dickinson was the son of George and Frances "Fannie" Ivie Dickinson and brother to George W. Dickinson, below.

Dickinson, George Washington - George Washington Dickinson, also shown as Dickerson and some descendants say his middle name was Wylie, was a brother to the John H. Dickinson, below. He enlisted in Company L of the 1st Alabama Cavalry, USV on March 1, 1865, in Stevenson, Alabama, and was mustered in April 18, 1865, in Nashville, Tennessee. The Muster and Descriptive Roll recorded him as 19 years of age, 5'-5" tall, having a fair complexion, dark eyes, light hair, born in Marion County, Alabama and a farmer by occupation. He was mustered out October 20, 1865, in Huntsville, Alabama and paid a bounty of $100.

George Washington Dickinson was born November 26, 1845, in Marion County, Alabama to John Irvin Hawkins Dickinson, and his wife, Leatha W. "Lithie" Harp. He met and married Leatha W. Harp about 1867. Leatha was born April 22, 1845, in Habersham County, Georgia, and died February 11, 1914, in Marion County, Alabama. A descendant stated George and his brother, Ben, both enlisted in the 1st Alabama Cavalry, USV. Another brother, James "Jim" and his wife, Hezzie, opened Dickinson Brothers General Store in Boston, Alabama in 1905, which was close to a coal mining camp close to Brilliant Coal Company. George W. Dickinson died sometime after the 1920 census and was buried in the Crooked Creek Cemetery in the Sunny Home Community, about ten miles from Natural Bridge. Family information submitted by Jim Dickinson.

Dickinson, Jonathan "John" H. - John H. Dickinson, brother to George Wylie Dickinson, above, enlisted in Company G of the 1st Alabama Cavalry, USV as a private on March 10, 1864, for a term of 3 years in Decatur, Alabama. He was enrolled by Lieutenant Pease and was mustered in April 13, 1864, in Decatur, Alabama. The Company Descriptive Book recorded him as 25 years of age, 5'-10" tall, having a fair complexion, gray eyes, dark hair, born in Marion County, Alabama, and a farmer by occupation. The April 1864 Muster Roll stated he was absent, sick. He died May 1, 1864, in the General Hospital in Decatur, Alabama. No further information relative to this soldier was found.

Digby, Benjamin F. - Benjamin F. Digby enlisted in Company B of the 1st Alabama Cavalry, USV as a private on December 23, 1862, in Glendale, Mississippi for a term of 1 year. He was enrolled by Captain Frank C. Burdick, and was mustered in December 31, 1862, in Corinth, Mississippi. The Company Descriptive recorded him as being 27 years of age, 6'-9" tall, having a dark complexion, dark eyes, dark hair, born in Bibb County, Alabama, and a farmer by occupation. The March and April 1863 Muster Roll listed him as being absent, a prisoner of war in St. Louis, Missouri in the hands of the enemy. However, he was present for the May and June 1863 Muster Roll. He was discharged on December 27, 1863, his term of enlistment having expired. The Prisoner of War Record for Benjamin F. Digby showed him to have been captured April 14, 1863, in Glendale, Mississippi; in custody of Confederate authorities April 23, 1863; confined at Richmond, Virginia on April 26, 1863; paroled at City Point, Virginia May 5, 1863; reported to College Green Barracks in Maryland on May 6, 1863; sent to Camp Parole, Maryland, where he reported May 8, 1863; sent to B.B. Missouri May 18, 1863, where he reported May 24, 1863; and was sent on to his regiment but date not given.

Dikes, Thomas L. - See Thomas L. Dykes.

Dill, James P. - James P. Dill enlisted in Company B of the 1st Alabama Cavalry, USV as a private on April 7, 1864, in Mooresville, Alabama for a period of 3 years. He was enrolled by Captain West and was mustered in October 17, 1864, in Huntsville, Alabama. The Muster and Descriptive Roll recorded him as being 23 years of age, 5'-10" tall, having a fair complexion, dark eyes, auburn hair, born in Walker County, Alabama, and a farmer by occupation. The July and August 1864 Muster Roll showed him to have been absent, on furlough to 26th of August. He was reported to have deserted on July 10, 1864, from Rome, Georgia while on furlough. He was mustered out October 20, 1865, in Huntsville, Alabama, with the remarks that he was erroneously reported as having deserted. The Company Descriptive Book was a little different from the Muster and Descriptive book. It stated James was 23 years of age, 5'-7" tall, having a sandy complexion, gray eyes, sandy hair, born in Winston County, Alabama, and farmer by occupation.

James P. Dill was born December 30, 1831, and died August 7, 1918. He married Surrenia Sullivan and had at least 3 children: Mary Jane, Phebe, and James L. Dill. James is buried in the Shady Grove Primitive Baptist Church Cemetery in Cullman County, Alabama near Bugtussel. Some family information submitted by James Quinn.

Dillard, James T. - Only one card was found for James T. Dillard which was filed at the end of the last roll of microfilm of the 1st Alabama Cavalry, USV military records. It recorded him as enlisting in Company M of the 1st Alabama Cavalry, USV on January 14, 1864, in Camp Davies, Mississippi for a period of 3 years. He was enrolled by Captain Lomax. The Company Descriptive Roll recorded him as 38 years of age, 5'-9" tall, having a dark complexion, blue eyes, black hair, born in Spartanburg District, South Carolina, and a farmer by occupation. No further information relative to this soldier was found.*

Dillard, Smith - Dillard Smith enlisted in Company B of the 1st Alabama Cavalry, USV as a private December 20, 1862, in Glendale, Mississippi for a period of 1 year. He was enrolled by Captain Frank C. Burdick, and was mustered in December 31, 1862, in Corinth, Mississippi. The Regimental Descriptive Book recorded him as 23 years of age, 5'-8" tall, had a dark complexion, hazel eyes, black hair, born in Spartanburg, South Carolina and a farmer by occupation. He died of disease March 14, 1863, at Glendale, Mississippi. One muster roll stated he died at Corinth, Mississippi but two others stated he died at Glendale.

Dillard, William - William Dillard enlisted in Company B of the 1st Alabama Cavalry, USV as a private on December 31, 1862, in Corinth, Mississippi for a period of 1 year. He was enrolled by Captain Frank C. Burdick. The Company Descriptive Book recorded him as 35 years of age, 5'-6" tall, having a dark complexion, gray eyes, dark hair, born in Spartanburg, South Carolina, and a farmer by occupation. The May and June Muster Roll stated he was detailed as an ambulance driver. He was discharged December 7, 1863, due to expiration of term of service. His name appeared on the Returns as follows: February 1863, on daily duty as ambulance driver; May 1863 to July 1863, on daily duty as ambulance driver; August 1863 to November 1863, on daily duty as teamster.

Dillinger, John - John Dillinger enlisted in Company M of the 1st Alabama Cavalry, USV as a private on November 19, 1863, in Camp Davies, Mississippi for a term of 3 years. He was enrolled by Captain Lomax and mustered in December 29, 1863, in Corinth, Mississippi. The Company Descriptive Book showed him to have been 19 years of age, 5'-8" tall, having a light complexion, blue eyes, brown hair, born in Lincoln County, North Carolina, and a farmer by occupation. The January and February 1864 Muster Roll listed him as being absent, sick in hospital in Memphis, Tennessee since January 31, 1864. His name was listed on the Overton U.S.A. General Hospital Muster Roll dated January and February 1864, stating he was present. He died of disease June 30, 1864, in the hospital in Rome, Georgia, and never received any bounty. Another muster roll stated he died July 18, 1864, in the Post Hospital in Rome, Georgia of debility. Another record stated he died of diarrhea. He is buried in Grave #1433 in Marietta National Cemetery in Marietta, Georgia.

Divine, J. - J. Divine was a Sergeant in Company H of the 1st Alabama Cavalry, USV, but was reported to have deserted October 1, 1864, while on detached duty. No further information relative to this soldier was found.*

Dixon, William - Two Prisoners of War records were found for William Dixon, shown as William Doxon which were filed at the end of the last roll of microfilm of the 1st Alabama Cavalry, USV Records. It recorded him as a private in Company I. They stated he was a muster roll for the Paroled Prisoners of War at College Green Barracks in Annapolis, Maryland. They stated he was admitted to the hospital on April 1, 1865, arrived April 25, 1865, and sent to regiment June 1, 1865. No further information relative to this soldier was found.*

Dobson, Benjamin P. - Benjamin Parks Dobson enlisted in Company B of the 1st Alabama Cavalry, USV as a private on August 1, 1864, in Wedowee, Alabama for a period of 3 years. He was enrolled by Captain West, and enlisted the same day in Rome, Georgia. The Muster and Descriptive Roll recorded him as 38 years of age, 5'-9" tall, having a fair complexion, blue eyes, dark hair, born in Macon County, North Carolina, and a farmer by occupation. He was promoted to sergeant from private on June 13, 1865. He was mustered out October 20, 1865, in Huntsville, Alabama owing the U.S. Government $23.97 for losing 1 saddle, holster, cap pouch, bridle and blanket.

His name first appeared on the roster for the Wedowee Volunteers, a pre-war Confederate Company of men formed in 1860 Randolph County. He enlisted 1863 [enlistment record states only Randolph County] as a private in Company A, 53rd Alabama Partisan Rangers CSA. His neighbor and brother-in-law, James M Bowen, had enlisted exactly six months prior and died Sept 12, 1863, of sickness at Roddey's encampment in Russellville, Alabama.

Benjamin had owned slaves as late as 1860, as did James Bowen's family. But Benjamin's Confederate service conflicted with his Whig-Republican family's convictions, being descended from hero Captain John Dobson, who died at the pivotal Battle of Ramsour's Mill during the Revolutionary War. Perhaps due to the death of James, the harassment of Yankee marauders back home, and the chronic hardships the 53rd was suffering, Benjamin had enough to desert the 53rd at near Tunnel Hill on March 6, 1864. Ironically, there were five Confederate deserters from Roddey's Battalion who showed up at one of the Union camps that same day and with valuable information -- can't help but wonder if Benjamin was one of them. Reportedly Benjamin joined the "Wedowee Volunteers" with his brother-in-law, James M. Bowen, on February 24th, 1860. He enlisted in the 53rd Alabama, Company A on June 1, 1863. He was AWOL in NW Georgia (probably around Tunnel Hill) on March 6, 1864. Ironically, the local Union camp was approached by a group of five deserters from Roddey's Battalion that day, with plenty of good information. I can't help but wonder if Uncle Ben was one of them, as the two Hughey and two Pollard brothers were also AWOL from Company A at the same time. The 53rd was suffering mass desertions so we may never know.

On March 6, 1864, Major-General John M. Palmer (Union) writes to Brigadier General W.D. Whipple, as follows:

General: Five deserters just brought in confirmation report that that Roddey passed through Rome on his way to Dalton. They say the brigades of Roddey and Patterson came together from Alabama, and that all the troops in that quarter are ordered to Dalton. I think the report now shows that there are four cavalry brigades in the neighborhood of Dalton- Davidson's, Hume's, Roddey's, and Patterson's. These deserters say horses are in bad condition. The brigades which came from Alabama are two regiments each.

By the time Ben deserted, the peace movement was well under way and his brother, Wallace Washington Dobson, was thoroughly involved. (Submitted by David Walker)

Benjamin Parks Dobson was born May 4, 1825, Macon County, Georgia. He was the son of John Williams Dobson, Jr. and Nancy "Anna" Parks who married November 19, 1803, in Randolph County, Alabama. Other children of John and Anna Parks Dobson, and siblings of Benjamin Parks Dobson were: Eliza, Nancy T., Wallace, Catherine Ann, Harriett, and John Dobson. Benjamin Parks Dobson married Mary J. Bowen, and they had the following children: Wallis B., John A., Catherine, James J., Nancy E., William Washington, Harriett C.A., Mary M.E., and Herman A. Dobson. Mary J. Bowen was born March 1, 1830, in Georgia, and died February 13, 1905. She was the daughter of Alanson and Jane Bowen. Benjamin Parks Dobson died June 27, 1901, in Randolph County, Alabama and was buried in the Mt. Pisgah Methodist Church Cemetery in Wedowee, Randolph County.

Dodd, Franklin - Franklin Dodd enlisted in Company L of the 1st Alabama Cavalry, USV as a private on September 25, 1863, in Fayette County, Alabama for a period of 1 year. He was enrolled by Captain Trammel and was mustered in the same day in Glendale, Mississippi. The September 25, 1863, to October 31, 1863, Company Muster Roll listed him as being absent with leave. The November and December 1863 Muster Roll stated he had returned from missing in action December 25, 1863, and was sick in the regimental hospital. His name appeared on the Returns dated November 1863, stating Dodd was absent, sick, left in Alabama by order of Colonel Spencer. The January and February 1864 Muster Roll listed him as being absent, sick in hospital in Memphis, Tennessee since January 15, 1864. The Company Muster-Out Roll stated Franklin Dodd died of disease in the hospital in Memphis, Tennessee April 14, 1864. The Company Descriptive Book records him as 21 years of age, 5'-11" tall, having a fair complexion, blue eyes, dark hair, born in Walker County, Alabama and a farmer by occupation. The Certificate of Death stated Dodd died April 15, 1864, of chronic diarrhea in Adams U.S.A. General Hospital in Memphis, Tennessee.

Franklin Dodd, also called George Franklin Dodd, was the brother to John Dodd, see below for family information. He September 24, 1857, he married Elizabeth Tucker in Winston County, Alabama. She was the daughter of Simeon Tucker who was also in this regiment. Children were: Mary Ann, born September 23, 1858, died March 10, 1930; George Franklin, Jr., born July 10, 1860, died March 29. 1940; William Simeon, born April 10, 1861, died August 7, 1949; and Mary or Maria Priscilla, born May 24, 1864 and died March 18, 1911. After Franklin's death, Elizabeth married George Washington Webb, Sr. Franklin Dodd is buried in the Memphis National Hospital in Memphis, Tennessee.

On January 7, 1873, William Dodd, brother of John and Franklin Dodd, filed a Southern Claim asking to be reimbursed for the following items which belonged to him and were taken by the army during the war: One sorrel mare, valued at $160; one saddle and bridle, valued at $15; 15 bushels of corn, valued at $30, for a total of $205. He stated they were taken from my premises in Winston County, Alabama on March 26, 1865, by Wilson's Cavalry, or at least the men who took the property, said they belonged to Wilson's Cavalry. The mare was taken out of the stable; the saddle was taken from the dwelling house, and the corn from the crib. During his deposition, he made some of the following statements: He stated he furnished provisions for recruits and recruiting officers of U.S. Army in the hills of Winston County, Alabama; that he was arrested and imprisoned and finally taken to Rome Georgia by the Rebels, whence he made his escape. He had two brothers in the Union Army, no relatives in the Rebel Army and was in no way complicated with the Rebellion. Since the war has served as Assessor of Internal Revenue and taken the Iron Clad Oath. Claimants testimony is confirmed by two witnesses, and we find him loyal. The supplies were taken by Gen Wilson's Command in March 1865, and we allow the sum of one hundred and thirty five dollars.

I was arrested by the so called Confederate officer Colonel McCaskill on the 17th day of April, 1864 and was put in the jail in the town of Jasper, Walker County, Alabama, and was kept there seven or eight days; from thence I was carried to Rome, Georgia where I made my escape and returned to my home in Winston County, Alabama. I never was arrested by the United States authorities. My corn and meal were taken regularly when they were about me for which I never received any pay. My house was robbed by one Captain Becknell of the Confederate Army. I was threatened by my wife's brother, Moses Holcombe, he drew a gun on me for my union principals, cocked it and threatened to shoot and was prevented by M.M. Cox. I carried provisions to recruiting officers of the United States' Army, Captain Jerome J. Hinds, John N. Bond, and Captain Sanford Trammel, who were in the hills of Winston County, Alabama, who dare to show themselves publicly.

At the beginning of the Rebellion I sympathized with the Union Cause. I felt just like our country was ruined, and I also said that our government would be ruined to be divided. I exerted my influence in behalf of the Union Cause. In 1860, I voted for Colonel C.C. Sheats, the Union candidate of Winston County, to the Secession Convention of Alabama. The Ordinance of Secession was not referred to the people of Alabama, and if it had been, I should have voted against it. And after the Ordinance of Secession was adopted, I still adhered to the Union Cause and did not go with the State.

John N. Baughn, a Bugler in Company L of the 1st Alabama Cavalry, signed an affidavit for William Dodd stating the following: While myself and others were scouting and recruiting, Claimant would inform us where the Confederate Cavalry was. Claimant expressed himself publicly and aloud as being opposed to the Rebellion. Claimant was publicly known to be a Union man from the beginning of the hostilities to the end thereof, as far as I know, and was so regarded by his neighbors and the United States Soldiers and that the United States Soldiers were not afraid to see Claimant during the whole war so far as carrying news to the Rebels.

Mordecai Michael Cox, a Sergeant in Company A of the 1st Alabama Cavalry, USV, filed an affidavit for Dodd stating the following: I was sent back to Winston County as a recruiting Officer, and my residence during of that time, was in the woods. The claimant very often gave me news of the whereabouts of the Rebels, and also gave me provisions to eat which took place in the year 1864 and 1865. Claimant often told me that he was opposed to the Confederacy and the cause in which it was engaged, and that he was in hopes that the United States authorities would suppress the Rebellion. Cox also stated that William Dodd fed him, and others, while they were engaged in such service and that he was in favor of the United States Government whipping the Confederacy back into the Union.

Dodd, John - John Dodd enlisted in Company L of the 1st Alabama Cavalry, USV on September 25, 1863, as a private at Fayette County, Alabama for a period of 1 year. He was mustered in the same day in Glendale, Mississippi. He was discharged December 27, 1863, by Major General Hurlburt, for a disability. The Company Descriptive Book recorded John as 18 years of age, 5"-10" tall, having a fair complexion, blue eyes, light hair, born in Walker County, Alabama, and a farmer by occupation. A Certificate of Disability for Discharge was issued John Dodd on December 3, 1863, stating: I certify that I have carefully examined John Dodd, private of S. Trammel's Company, and find him incapable of performing the duties of a soldier because of general debility, the result of a deformity in the chest, he said existing from infancy. He is wholly unfit for duty, even in the Invalid Corps, and is not entitled to a pension. Signed A.B. Stuart, Surgeon, and Ozro J. Dodds, Lt. Col.

John Dodd was born April 4, 1844, to Michael/Mikel and Mary "Polly" Knight Dodd. He married Nancy Elizabeth Ingle, daughter of Andrew Jackson Ingle, September 3, 1868, in Larissa, Winston County, Alabama and died March 15, 1928 at Haleyville, Winston County, Alabama. Their children were: Mary Elizabeth, born July 28, 1869, died January 12, 1896; Andrew M., born January 27, 1871, died November 28, 1877; Jessie, born September 15, 1872, died December 18, 1875; Jasper N., born August 28, 1874, died September 10, 1914; Nancy Jane, born 1876; Rufus Irving, born June 1, 1879, died December 26, 1909; Virgil Marion, born November 19, 1881, died June 18, 1938; Genia Adling, born October 12, 1884, died June 21, 1908; Emma and Anna (Twins) born October 28, 1886; Nancy Jane, born August 18, 1887, died September 12, 1894; Elzie "Otho", born October 2, 1889, died August 17, 1938, and Alta, born December 15, 1891, died June 21, 1924. John Dodd is buried in the Dodd Memorial Cemetery in Winston County, Alabama. Family information submitted by Patricia Dodd Greathouse.

Dodd, John - Although there were two different John Dodds listed in the microfilm of muster rolls, it is thought this is the same John Dodd as above. Apparently after he was discharged for a disability, he was determined to remain in the Union Army and fight for his country. The Muster and Descriptive Rolls for both of these men described them the same, with the exception he was a year older when he reenlisted.

John Dodd enlisted in Company L of the 1st Alabama Cavalry, USV as a private on December 23, 1864, at Stevenson, Alabama and mustered in the same day in Nashville, Tennessee. The Muster and Descriptive Roll showed him to have been 20 years of age, 5'-11" tall, having a fair complexion, blue eyes, light hair, born in Walker County, Alabama, and a farmer by occupation. He was given a $100 bounty, and was credited to Ripley, Chautauqua, 32nd Congressional District, New York. The January and February 1865 Muster Roll listed John as being absent, on duty with detached 1st Alabama Cavalry in Stevenson, Alabama since December 25, 1864. John Was mustered out October 20, 1865 in Huntsville, Alabama. His name appeared on the Returns dated September 1865, stating he was absent, sick since September 20, 1865.

The Advertiser Journal, Haleyville, Alabama, Thursday, December 16, 1926, Vol. XV, No. 49, Page 1

"Our readers will be glad to have this good picture of John Dodd, a leading member of one of Winston Counties eldest settlers. John Dodd lived at Lynn for many years but moved to our town about twelve years ago. He has been one of our county's most successful business men. He made large purchases in its mineral lands when few knew of the wealth that was underground. As founder of the Dodd Wholesale Grocery Company he helped start one of our most valued business concerns. Mr. Dodd is advanced in years but is still able to be in town at times."

John Dodd's Obituary: (The name of the newspaper along with the first line of the obituary are not legible)... spirit of Mr. John Dodd, one of Haleyville's oldest and most popular citizens and business men passed from this world into the life beyond. Mr. Dodd had been confined to his room since last August and had been under the constant care of members of the family since last September. Mr. Dodd was born April 4, 1844; married to Miss Nancy Ingle, September 3, 1868. To this union were born 6 boys and 6 girls, of which number there were living at the time of his death, only two of the boys, the six daughters having preceded him to the Great Beyond. He leaves besides these sons, 20 grandchildren and one great grandchild. He was 83 years, 11 months, 11 days of age and had been a member of the church for the past thirty years.

Mr. Dodd had been a citizen of Haleyville for 17 years and was well known and highly esteemed by a host of friends in Haleyville and Winston County.

Funeral services were held Saturday morning from the Church of Christ at Lynn and interment was made in the Bond grave yard about two miles south of Lynne. The funeral was conducted by Bro. C.A. Wheeler. A large crowd was present to pay their last tribute of respect to the remains of the deceased.

Dodd, Wyatt Newton - Wyatt Newton Dodd enlisted in Company L of the 1st Alabama Cavalry, USV on September 25, 1863, in Fayette County, Alabama for a period of 1 year. He was enrolled by Captain Trammel and was mustered in the same day in Glendale, Mississippi. He was discharged September 28, 1864, at Rome, Georgia by reason of expiration of term of service. He was paid in full by Major Holt at Nashville, Tennessee. There was a Hospital Muster Roll dated March and April 1864, from Cumberland U.S.A. General Hospital in Nashville, Tennessee, but does not state if Dodd was present or absent, however, his name appeared on the Returns for March 1864, stating W.N. Dodd was absent, sick in the hospital in Nashville, Tennessee. His name also appeared on the April 1864 Muster Roll stating he was still absent, sick in the hospital in Nashville. His name next appeared on the Returns from Rome, Georgia stating Dodd was discharged September 29, 1864, due to expiration of term of service. The Company Descriptive Book records Wyatt as 19 years of age, 6' tall, having a fair complexion, black eyes, dark hair, born in Walker County, Alabama, and a farmer by occupation. On October 9, 1864, there was a Requisition for Wyatt N. Dodd, Order No. 9311 stated: From Cairo, Illinois to St. Louis, Missouri, discharged, but transportation not furnished.

Wyatt Newton Dodd was born June 22, 1844, in Walker County, Alabama to William Royal

"Byler Bill" Dodd, and his wife, Elizabeth "Betsy" Tittle. Other children of William and Betsy were: Lydia, Silas, George Washington, Azalette, Martha A., Clarrisa, and Teddy Dodd. On October 23, 1867, Wyatt N. Dodd married Adalene Barnett in Harrison County, Iowa. Adalene was born October 6, 1855, in Marion County, Alabama, and died April 29, 1914, in Tensman, Iowa. Wyatt and Adelene had the following children: Wyatt Newton Dodd, Jr., born January 19, 1870, died March 7, 1932, in Marion County, Alabama, and Josephine Dodd, born 1868 in Iowa. In the 1870 Harrison County, Iowa Census, Adalene Barnett Dodd was living next door to a J.R. Barnett, age 57, and his wife, Sarah, but it is not known if that was her parents. Wyatt N. Dodd died July 10, 1869 in Harrison County, Iowa and is buried in the Magnolia Cemetery in Harrison County, Iowa.

Dodds, Ozro J. - Lieutenant Colonel, F&S, age 23, enlisted October 9, 1863, in Glendale, Mississippi. He was appointed from Captain of the 81st Ohio Infantry and resigned April 30, 1864, stating his father was in poor health; their manufacturing business was suffering and needed his immediate and personal attention.

Ozro John Dodds was born March 22, 1840, in Cincinnati, Hamilton County, Ohio. He died in Columbus, Ohio April 18, 1882, and was interred in Spring Grove Cemetery, Cincinnati, Ohio. (From the Biographical Directory of the United States Congress 1774 – 2005)

"Ozro John Dodds was a U.S. Representative from Ohio." A Biography of Ozro Jennison Dodds written by Betty Bettencourt Dodds, published in the 2010 Ohio Civil War Genealogy Journal, Vol. XIV, Issue 3, it states Lieutenant Ozro J. Dodd's middle name was "Jennison", while others have stated it was "John". She also stated the Honorable Ozro Jennison Dodds was the third generation of a Scotch-Irish immigrant family. In 1797 his grandfather, James Harvey Dodds, and wife, Martha Black, with brother-in-law, Rev John Black, left war-torn North Ireland and sailed for Philadelphia, settling in Western Pennsylvania. Ozro was the son of William Black Dodds, born 1808 and died 1885, who was the fourth child of James and Martha Dodds.

Ozro J. Dodds attended the common schools, and Miami University in Oxford, Ohio, for four years. At the outbreak of the Civil War, he organized Captain Dodd's Miami University Company and enlisted on April 18, 1861, as Captain of Company B, Twentieth Ohio Volunteer Regiment. He served as captain of Company F, Eighty-first Ohio Volunteer Infantry from September 1, 1861, to January 1, 1863. He became Lieutenant Colonel of the First Alabama Cavalry, USV on October 18, 1863. At the close of the war he was given his degree from Miami University. He studied law at Cincinnati Law School and was admitted to the bar in 1866. He began practice in Cincinnati and served as member of the Ohio House of Representatives in 1870 and 1871.

Dodds was elected as a Democrat to the Forty-second Congress to fill the vacancy caused by the resignation of Aaron F. Perry and served from October 8, 1872, to March 3, 1873. He was not a candidate for renomination in 1872. He resumed the practice of law at Cincinnati. He died in Columbus, Ohio, April 18, 1882. He was interred in Spring Grove Cemetery, Cincinnati, Ohio.

Dodds Hall, a residence hall on the Miami University Campus, was named in Ozro Dodds' memory.

Dodson, John W. - John W. Dodson, also shown as Dobson, enlisted in Company H of the 1st Alabama Cavalry, USV as a private on December 21, 1864, in Decatur, Alabama for a period of 3 years. He was enrolled by Captain James W. DeVaney and was mustered in the same day in Nashville, Tennessee. The Muster and Descriptive Roll recorded him as 31 years of age, 6' tall, having a dark complexion, hazel eyes, black hair, born in McMinn County, Tennessee, and a farmer by occupation. His enlistment was credited to Ripley, Chautauqua County, New York. He was paid a bounty of $100. He was appointed corporal April 1, 1865. He was reported to have deserted October 1, 1865, from Blountsville, Alabama, owing the U.S. Government $37 because he ran off with 1 Colt pistol, 1 belt and plate, 1 pistol cartridge box, 1 pistol holster, 1 shelter tent. No discharge furnished on muster out of organization. A note under this stated the entire entry was canceled. He was restored to duty per Special Order Number 38, Headquarters, District of Huntsville, Alabama, in the following letter: Company H, 1st Alabama Cavalry Volunteers, Huntsville, Alabama, October 20, 1865 – Major, I have the honor to respectfully request that Corporal John W. Dobson, Company H, 1st Alabama, be restored to duty with full pay and allowance. Corporal Dobson has always been a true and faithful soldier and I have never had any reason to doubt his word in any respect, he reports that he was sick and unable to join his company at the end of his furlough. I am Major, very respectfully your obedient servant, J.W. DeVaney, Captain, 1st Alabama Cavalry, Volunteers, Commanding Company H. The request was approved and he was mustered out October 20, 1865, in Huntsville, Alabama

Donner, Michael - Michael Donner enlisted in Company C of the 1st Alabama Cavalry, USV as a private on December 6, 1862, in Corinth, Mississippi for a period of 1 year. He was enrolled by John Latty, and was mustered in December 22, 1862, in Corinth. The Regimental Descriptive Book recorded him as 35 years of age, 5'-4½" tall, having a fair complexion, gray eyes, dark hair, born, possibly in Ireland, and a farmer by occupation. He was appointed Corporal on April 10, 1863. The September and October 1863 Muster Roll showed him as being absent, sick in the Union U.S.A. General Hospital in Memphis, Tennessee since October 16, 1863. He was released from the hospital and returned to Camp Davies, Mississippi on November 28, 1863, and was mustered out December 17, 1863, at Memphis, Tennessee due to expiration of term of service.

Dorris, N.J. - Only two cards were found for N.J. Dorris which were filed at the end of the last roll of microfilm of the 1st Alabama Cavalry, USV Muster Rolls. It recorded him as a being in Company B of the 1st Alabama Cavalry, USV. They stated he was killed at Cold Harbor, Virginia in June 1864. No further information relative to this soldier was found.*

Doss, Francis M. - Francis M. Doss enlisted in Company A of the 1st Alabama Cavalry, USV on January 1, 1864, in Camp Davies, Mississippi for a term of 3 years. He was mustered in February 5, 1864, in Memphis, Tennessee. He was enrolled by Lieutenant Hinds and appointed Corporal February 5, 1864. The Company Muster and Descriptive Roll recorded him as 26 years of age, 5'-10" tall, having a fair complexion, blue eyes, auburn hair, born in Chickasaw County, Mississippi, and a farmer by occupation. The March and April 1864 Muster Roll showed him to be absent, in confinement at Athens, Alabama. A letter in Doss' file stated the following: Charges and Specifications against Corporal Francis M. Doss, 1st Regiment, Alabama Cavalry Volunteers, Charge Desertion, In this that the said Corporal Francis M. Doss 1st Regiment Alabama Cavalry Volunteers, did on or about the 16th of April 1864, desert his company and regiment and attempted to pass the lines into the enemy's country taking with him arms and ammunition, the property of the Unites States, all this at or near Mooresville, Alabama. Signed J.J. Hinds, Captain 1st Alabama Volunteer Cavalry, Commanding Company A. Camp Mooresville, Alabama, April 20, 1864. Witnesses, Sergeant John H. Hogan, Sergeant George W. Benson, Sergeant Anderson Looney. He was shown as Corporal when he mustered in; however, the June and July 1864 Muster Roll stated he was reduced to ranks per Regimental Order #70. His name appeared on the returns dated April 1864, stating: Absent, in arrest in prison. Doss was reported to have deserted October 1, 1865, from Decatur, Alabama with 1 shelter tent, 1 horse, saddle, bridle, carbine saber belt, pistol, and accouterments complete, for which he owed the U.S. Government $188.80. He was paid a bounty of $180. A Notation in his file from the Adjutant General's Office of the War Department dated October 6, 1884, stated the following: The dishonorable discharge heretofore issued to this man is cancelled. Charge of desertion of October 1, 1865, is removed and he is discharged to date October 1, 1865, to complete his military record under the provisions of Congress approved July 5, 1884. Discharge Certificate furnished by Attorney General's Office October 11, 1884.

Douthit, William G. - William G. Douthit, also shown as William G. Douthet, enlisted in Company C of the 1st Alabama Cavalry, USV on December 3, 1862, in Corinth, Mississippi for a term of 1 year. He was enrolled by D.R. Adams and was mustered in December 22, 1862, in Corinth. The Regimental Descriptive Book recorded him as 51 years of age, 5'-6" tall, having a fair complexion, blue eyes, light hair, born in Rowan County, North Carolina, and a school teacher by occupation. A Notation in his file from the Adjutant General's Office of the War Department dated September 14, 1869, stated the following: Died of disease February 17, 1863, in hospital at Corinth, Mississippi. Another muster roll stated he died February 20, 1863. A note in his file dated September 20, 1869, stated he died of disease in the hospital in Corinth, Mississippi. February 17, 1863, is considered his actual date of death.

Downing, Thomas - Only one card was found for Thomas Downing which was filed at the end of the last roll of microfilm of the 1st Alabama Cavalry, USV records. It recorded him as a private in Company F, stating he was discharged December 17, 1864, in Savannah, Georgia by reason of expiration of term of service. No further information relative to this soldier was found.*

Downum, James Henry - James Henry Downum, also listed as Donnum and Donner, enlisted in Company F of the 1st Alabama Cavalry, USV as private on November 25, 1863, at Camp Davies, Mississippi and was never mustered. He was enrolled by Lieutenant W.H. Chaney for a term of 1 year. The Company Descriptive Book recorded him as 18 years of age, 5'-6½" tall, having a fair complexion, gray eyes, light hair, born in Marion County, Alabama, and a farmer by occupation. The January and February 1864 Muster Roll listed him as being absent, with Lieutenant Straight A.A.Q.M. 16th Army Corps. He was sent to the hospital in Nashville, Tennessee where he died April 13, 1864. His name appeared on the Returns as follows: January to February 1864, on detached service as teamster with the Quartermaster Department in Vicksburg, Mississippi, since January 25, 1864; April 1864, died of disease April 13, 1864, in Nashville, Tennessee. The Record of Death and Interment for James H. Downum stated he was in Hospital 356 Cumberland General in Nashville, Tennessee where he died of erysipelas (A type of skin infection. Symptoms: Blisters; Fever, shaking, and chills; Painful, very red, swollen, and warm skin underneath the sore), following measles. He was interred in Grave #7245 in the Old City Cemetery in Nashville, Tennessee where he was mistakenly left, as other Union soldiers buried there were removed to the Nashville National Cemetery. (The author is currently working with the Cemetery and Friends of Nashville Cemeteries to get this straightened out.) James was shown as being single and he lived with Hiram P. Downum in Pikeville, Marion County, Alabama. His effects were shown as: 1 hat – worthless, 1 great coat, 1 jacket, 1 pair of pants, 1 shirt - worthless, 1 pair of drawers, 1 pair of boots, 1 canteen, and 3 blankets. The total of his effects amounted to $1.69. James H. Downum was able to sign his name on all of his Enlistment Forms.

James Henry Downum was born about 1845 in Marion County, Alabama to Hiram P. and Nancy Miller Downum. Some of the other children of Hiram and Nancy were: Kissiah M.; William S.; Green C.; John W.; Margaret E.; and Martha A. Downum. James died April 13, 1864, in Nashville, Tennessee. James Henry Downum, along with several other 1st Alabama Cavalry, USV deceased soldiers, were recorded as belonging to the CSA and buried in Confederate Circle at Mt. Olivet Cemetery in Nashville, Tennessee. This error was due to the government undertaker not showing if they were Union or Confederate and apparently since they were from Alabama, he, like many others, thought they were Confederates. These names and dates of death were published in the *Nashville Union Newspaper*, and then in 1977, a member of UDC, wanting to help, added these names from the newspaper to the Mt. Olivet Cemetery Records. This was confirmed by the Roll of Honor, which recorded his date of death as April 13, 1864. This was brought to the attention of the cemetery and these names will probably soon be stricken from their records due to the diligent work of a member of Friends of Metro Archives who has been researching this for almost two years.

Downum, William T. - William T. Downum enlisted in Company F of the 1st Alabama Cavalry, USV as a private on November 25, 1863, in Camp Davies, Mississippi for a period of 1 year. He was enrolled by Lieutenant W.H. Chaney. The Company Descriptive Book recorded him to be 23 years of age, 5'-8" tall, having a fair complexion, gray eyes, light hair, born in Marion County, Alabama, and a farmer by occupation. The January and February 1864 Muster Roll showed him to be absent, on detached service with Lieutenant Streight in Vicksburg, Mississippi with the Quartermaster Department, 16th Army Corps since January 25, 1864. The Company Muster Roll dated April 30, 1864, showed him to be absent, sick in Nashville, Tennessee. His name was shown on a Hospital Muster Roll of Hospital #19 U.S.A. General Hospital in Nashville, Tennessee, dated March and April 1864. He was discharged December 17, 1864, due to expiration of term of service. He was mustered out December 17, 1864, in Rome, Georgia due to expiration of term of service. Another record stated he was discharged due to being on the march from Atlanta to Savannah, Georgia.

Doxon, William - William Doxon, or Dixon, was captured March 10, 1865, from the Battle of

Monroe's Crossroads near Fayetteville, North Carolina and was confined at Richmond, Virginia. He was paroled March 29, 1865, and admitted to the hospital April 1, 1865. His card was misfiled at the end of the last roll of microfilm of the 1st Alabama Cavalry records. No further information relative to this soldier was found.*

Doyle, Joseph C. - Joseph C. Doyle enlisted in Company A of the 1st Alabama Cavalry, USV as a private in September 6, 1864, in Rome, Georgia for a period of 3 years. He was enrolled by Captain Hinds. The Muster and Descriptive Roll recorded him as 43 years of age, 5'-10" tall, having a fair complexion, blue eyes, light hair, born in Jackson County, Alabama, and a farmer by occupation. He was mustered out October 20, 1865, in Huntsville, Alabama, owing the U.S. Government $2.15 for losing 1 saber belt complete. He was paid a bounty of $100.

Duckett, John T. - John T. Duckett enlisted in Company A of the 1st Alabama Cavalry, USV as a private on September 8, 1862, for a period of 1 year in Iuka, Mississippi, and was mustered in October 1, 1862, in Corinth, Mississippi. The Regimental Descriptive Roll recorded him as 24 years of age, 6' tall, having a light complexion, hazel eyes, auburn hair, born in McNairy County, Tennessee, and a farmer by occupation. He was promoted from private to Corporal December 18, 1862. He was mustered out September 16, 1863, due to expiration of term of service.

John T. Duckett was born September 14, 1838, in McNairy County, Tennessee to Mahala Massengill and Rignal Odell Duckett. After he mustered out of service he lived in Cairo, Illinois where he married his first wife, Nancy Wilhoit. His second wife was Mary Chasteen. From 1865-1890, he resided in Cullman, Morgan, Blount, and Cherokee Counties in Alabama. In 1900, he moved to Whitfield County, Georgia where he lived the rest of his life and had 11 children. John T. Duckett died April 5, 1913 in Whitfield County, Georgia and was buried in the Deep Springs Baptist Church Cemetery in Dalton, Whitfield County, Georgia. Some family information submitted by Wilma Duckett Morgan.

Dudley, Dean - See Dudley Dean.

Dugan, K.H. - Only one card was found for K.H. Dugan which was filed at the end of the last roll of microfilm of the 1st Alabama Cavalry, USV records. It recorded him as a captain or corporal in Company C, of the 1st Alabama Cavalry, USV. His name appeared on a Return stating the following: He was on detached service detailed to go North with the refugees June 20, 1863. This was when the US Army escorted about 300 Unionists to Illinois for their safety due to the Confederate Home Guard burning homes, barns and crops of the Union families, in some cases molesting the Union wives and widows and murdering their husbands. No further information relative to this soldier was found.*

Dugan, Richard Sanders - Richard Sanders Dugan enlisted in Company C of the 1st Alabama Cavalry, USV as a private on February 20, 1863, in Corinth, Mississippi, for a period of 1 year. He was enrolled by D.R. Adams and was mustered in February 25, 1863, in Corinth. The Regimental Descriptive Book recorded him as 27 years of age, 5'-9" tall, having a fair complexion, blue eyes, sandy hair, born in McMinn County, Tennessee, and a farmer by occupation. The May and June 1863 Muster Roll stated he was absent, on detached service, detailed to go North with Refugees. He was appointed Corporal June 10, 1863. The September and October 1863 Muster Roll stated he died of disease September 27, 1863, in the hospital at Glendale, Mississippi.

Richard Dugan was born July 3, 1836, in Monroe County, Tennessee and died September 27, 1863 in the hospital in Glendale, Mississippi. Most of the soldiers who died in Glendale were buried in the cemetery there and then removed to the Corinth National Cemetery, if their family didn't claim their body and take it home to be buried in a family cemetery. His sister, Minerva Jane Dugan, was born February 5, 1834, in Monroe County, Tennessee and married William L. Peoples, who was in Company E, 1st Alabama Cavalry USV. Minerva died October 26, 1876, in Marion County, Alabama. Richard and Minerva were the children of Absalom L. Dugan (1812-1862) and Susannah Sanders, who emigrated to Marion County, Alabama from East Tennessee in 1850. They were forced to leave in 1863 because of their Union sympathies and fled to Marion County, Illinois. Family information submitted by Richard Dugan.

Dumick, J. - Only one card was found for J. Dumick which was filed at the end of the last roll of microfilm of the 1st Alabama Cavalry, USV records. It recorded him as a sergeant in Company H, stating he was on detached service recruiting in Alabama in September 1864. No further information relative to this soldier was found.*

Duncan, John W. - John W. Duncan enlisted in Company C of the 1st Alabama Cavalry, USV as a private on February 20, 1863, in Corinth, Mississippi. The Regimental Descriptive Book showed him to have been 28 years of age, 5'-8" tall, having a fair complexion, blue eyes, dark hair, born in Perry County, Alabama, and a farmer by occupation. The March and April 1863 Muster Roll showed him to have been absent without leave April 18, 1863. He was reported to have deserted June 28, 1863, from Glendale, Mississippi. There was one muster roll in his files calling him Wesley Duncan, which might indicate his name to be John Wesley Duncan.

Dunn, Francis W - Francis "Wayland" Dunn enlisted and mustered into the F&S of the 1st Alabama Cavalry, USV on May 16, 1863, in Corinth, Mississippi. He was appointed Sergeant Major on May 16, 1863, by order of General Dodge. He was Sergeant Major from enrollment to December 4, 1863, when discharged to accept appointment to 2nd Lieutenant, assigned to duty by Brigadier General G.M. Dodge to date from November 1, 1863. On June 4, 1864, he was on special duty at Regimental Headquarters. He mustered out October 31, 1864, in Rome, Georgia due to expiration of term of service. He was first enlisted into the 64th Illinois Infantry with his brother, Newell Ransom Dunn on August 18, 1862, in Freedom, Illinois, and was mustered in August 28, 1862, in Springfield, Illinois. Francis W. Dunn was stationed in Glendale, Mississippi, while his brother Ransom, was in Corinth, still with the 64th Illinois Infantry, when he contracted typhoid fever. Wayland would travel to Corinth as often as he could to take his brother milk, eggs, or anything he thought might help him. He finally took pneumonia and died March 26, 1863, as Wayland looked on. Wayland asked for and received permission to take his brother back home to Illinois to be buried. After he returns to Glendale, he writes in his diary about how much he missed his brother and how worried he was about their father.

Francis Wayland Dunn was born January 29, 1843, in Wayne, Ashtabula County, Ohio. His father, Ransom Dunn, was a New England born preacher and missionary of the Free Will Baptist faith. In this capacity the family moved many times in the East and Midwest, starting or supporting new congregations. After the mid-1850's this travel also included the raising of money for Hillsdale College at Hillsdale, Michigan. The elder Dunn was instrumental in its founding and also taught there between trips.

Wayland and his older brother, Newell Ransom Dunn, both were graduated from Hillsdale College in June of 1862. In March of 1861, the family moved to a small undeveloped farm at Prairie Center, Illinois, twelve miles from Ottawa. They built a home there and it was from this place that both brothers enlisted in the 64th Illinois Infantry in September of 1862. On May 16, 1863, Wayland became Sergeant major of the 1st Alabama Cavalry, USV.

After his military service Wayland lived in Hillsdale. During the fall of 1865, he and his father took a year long tour of Europe. During 1867-1869 Wayland was an editor of "The Christian Freeman". This religious newspaper was published in Chicago. Poor health and the desire to travel caused work at the paper to be of short stints. During the spring of 1868 he made a trip to New Orleans and on the return to Chicago he visited former battlefields and Corinth, Mississippi where Newell, his brother, had died on March 26, 1863. That same year he went west with a college friend. This trip included a tour of Indian life, a buffalo hunt, and a study of the Mormons which included meeting Brigham Young. He purchased land in Richardson County, Nebraska and the family moved there in 1870, to farm. This move was also short lived. In 1872 his father became president of Hillsdale College and Ransom joined the facility as professor Dunn. They moved back into the old family house. He enjoyed teaching and was respected by his students. His traveling was over. At almost 32 years of age, Francis Wayland Dunn died in his sleep on December 13, 1874, and was buried in the Oak Grove Cemetery in Hillsdale, Hillsdale County, Michigan.

Francis Wayland Dunn Obituary - From the Free Will Baptist Cyclopedia

Dunn Francis Wayland, Son of Rev. R. Dunn, was born in Ashtabula County, Ohio January 29, 1843. Early and always he was very conscientious and decided. Nothing seemed to tempt him to violate his conscience or parental direction. Remarkable in the strictest regard for truth and purity of character from a child, he was soberly reverential, and when fifteen years of the age was baptized. With firm health and unbroken perseverance in study he graduated from the classical college course before he was nineteen years old. Soon after leaving college he enlisted as a private soldier, but was soon transferred to another regiment as sergeant major, then commissioned first lieutenant and commissary. The term for which his regiment enlisted expired in 1864, and as his only brother had died in the army and his father health was not good, he did not deem it his duty to re-enlist.

As a competent member of a successful business firm he spent a year in Chicago, and then spent nearly a year in eastern travel, visiting Egypt, Arabia, Syria, Turkey, and most of the European countries. Not long after his return from Europe he was elected editor of the Christian Freeman (q. v.). In 1869 a severe cough and other symptoms led his physician to advise the cessation of that mode of life. Remedies and changes of location and climates were but partially successful, and yet, having been elected a professor in Hillsdale College, he did valuable service in that institution during the last four years of his life. December 13, 1873, he peacefully closed a brief but useful life. In spite of a great heart, deeply emotional nature, and lively imagination, his conscious, firmness of purpose, and intellectual force secured evenness of temper, soundness of judgment and symmetrical piety, rendering him an able writer and good teacher.

Diaries (1862-1864) written while he was serving in Company A, 64th Illinois Infantry and in Company H, 1st Alabama Cavalry (Union) as sergeant major. The diaries give details of camp life, especially in Corinth, Glendale, and Rome, and make a point of his reaction to the profanity, drinking, quarreling and gambling. He accents foraging and scouting parties with descriptions of the country and its people; gives vivid pictures of skirmishes and battles; and expresses his loneliness, grief and faith after the death of his brother Ransom. Francis Wayland Dunn became editor of Christian Freeman and a professor at Hillsdale College. Letters of Dunn are found in the papers of his father, Ransom Dunn.

Francis Wayland Dunn and his brother, Newell Ransom Dunn, both enlisted in the 64th Illinois Infantry in September 1862. Wayland became Sergeant Major of the 1st Alabama Cavalry, US, May 16, 1863. He was born January 29, 1843, in Wayne, Ashtabula County, Ohio, to Ransom Dunn who was a minister and missionary of the Free Will Baptist faith. Newell Ransom Dunn died March 26, 1863, during the war, and Francis Wayland Dunn was given permission to take his brother home for burial. Wayland survived the war and taught at Hillsdale College where his father was president. Wayland died in his sleep December 13, 1874, just before he reached age 32. He is buried in Oak Grove Cemetery in Hillsdale, Michigan.

Dunn, Fred T. - Fred T. Dunn enlisted in Company G of the 1st Alabama Cavalry, USV. He was temporarily attached from the 11th Illinois Cavalry.

Dunn, John - Only one card was found for John Dunn which was filed at the end of the last roll of microfilm of the 1st Alabama Cavalry, USV records. It stated he enlisted in Company A, and was absent in the USA General Field Hospital at Bridgeport, Alabama in May 1864. He was returned to duty on May 15, 1864. No further information relative to this soldier was found.*

Dunn, Joseph F. - Joseph F. Dunn enlisted and mustered into Company H of the 1st Alabama Cavalry, USV as a private on September 18, 1863, in Glendale, Mississippi for a term of 1 year. The September and October 1863 Muster Roll recorded him as being a 5th Sergeant. The March and April 1864 Muster Roll stated a stop was put on his pay for 1 Remington Revolver. The May and June 1864 Muster Roll recorded him as being absent, on detached service recruiting in Decatur, Alabama since May 1, 1864. The September and October 1864 Muster Roll reported him as having deserted. There was no further information in his records.

Dunn, William - William Dunn enlisted in Company G of the 1st Alabama Cavalry, USV as a private on June 13, 1863, in Chewalla, Tennessee at age 25, and was mustered in the same day in

Corinth, Mississippi. The July and August 1863 Muster Roll recorded him as being discharged, was a member of the 1st West Tennessee Cavalry, sent back by order of Colonel Miller, 18th Missouri Volunteers. He was transferred to the 6th Regiment Tennessee Volunteers on June 25, 1863.

<u>Dunn, William D.</u> - William D. Dunn enlisted in Company G of the 1st Alabama Cavalry, USV as a private on November 27, 1862, at Grand Junction, Tennessee, at age 22, and was mustered in the same day in Corinth, Mississippi. In October 1863, he was on daily duty as company cook. He was mustered out November 26, 1863, in Memphis, Tennessee due to expiration of term of service.

<u>Durm, John</u> - Three cards were found for John Durm, could be Dunn, which were filed at the end of the last roll of microfilm of the 1st Alabama Cavalry, USV records. It recorded him as a private in Company D, stating he died August 15, 1863, in a hospital in Nashville, Davidson County, Tennessee. When the early enlistees of the 1st Alabama Cavalry, USV were shipped to Nashville, they were merged with the 1st Middle Tennessee Cavalry, which later became the 5th Tennessee Cavalry. Durm was recorded as being in both regiments.   No further information relative to this soldier was found.*

<u>Dwyer, William Lemuel</u> - William Lemuel Dwyer enlisted in Company K of the 1st Alabama Cavalry, USV as a private on December 13, 1862, in Nashville, Tennessee for a period of 3 years. He was enrolled by Lieutenant Joseph Hornback and was mustered in September 27, 1863, in Glendale, Mississippi. The Company Descriptive Book records him as being 24 years of age, 5'-11" tall, having light hair, blue eyes, auburn hair, born in Bibb County, Alabama, and a farmer by occupation. The January and February Muster Roll stated he was on Detached Service January 27, 1863, on courier post, probably in Reedyville, Tennessee. At this time, he was with Company E of the 1st Middle Tennessee Cavalry US. Dwyer was with the early enlistees who were immediately shipped to Nashville, Tennessee and merged with the 1st Middle Tennessee Cavalry, which went on to be the 5th Tennessee Cavalry. The Muster Roll from June 30, through October 31, 1863, he was recorded as being absent, missing in action from the Battle of Vincent's Crossroads October 26, 1863. His name appeared on the Muster-Out Roll for July 19, 1865, which stated he escaped from Cahaba Prison in Alabama and came to Winston County, Alabama December 1863. He was dropped from the rolls as a deserter in July 1864 but reported to his company June 6, 1865, in Huntsville, Alabama after escaping from prison again and walking back to Alabama. There was a Notation in his records from the Record and Pension Office of the War Department dated March 2, 1896, which stated: This man deserted November 30, 1863, and returned November 15, 1864. As he was subsequently restored to duty by competent authority without trial but upon conditions which appear to have been complied with (so far as not waived by the Government), the charge of desertion no longer stands against him. The record of the fact that he was absent in desertion from November 2, 1863, to November 15, 1864, cannot, however, be expunged. The notation of October 16, 1889, is cancelled. One Prisoner of War Record states William Dwyer was captured at Cedar Bluff, Alabama May 3, 1863, paroled at Rome, Georgia May 4, 1863, reported at Camp Chase, Ohio May 22, 1863, and sent to regiment June 9, 1863.

Affidavit from Thomas A McWhirter dated July 3, 1865, stated "William Dwyer was taken POW by the enemy with him at Vincent's Crossroads, MS in action October 26, 1863, and taken to Cahaba Prison, Alabama. After remaining there for two months, they both escaped from the prison and started together for the Union lines at Camp Davies, MS. After traveling six days, William Dwyer became exhausted and unable to travel any further when Thomas A McWhirter left him in a Union home about 150 miles from their lines. There are several documents on file that state how William tried to get back to his regiment. Due to weather conditions and his illness, he was not able to return until January 5, 1864, when he reported to Major Shurtleff who was the only officer left. The rest of the regiment had gone with Major General W.T. Sherman."

Affidavit from Thomas A McWhirter dated July 3, 1865, stated "William Dwyer was taken POW by the enemy with him at Vincent's Crossroads, MS in action October 26, 1863, and taken to Cahaba Prison, Alabama. After remaining there for two months, they both escaped from the prison and started together for the Union lines at Camp Davies, Mississippi. After traveling six days, William Dwyer became exhausted and unable to travel any further when Thomas A McWhirter left him in a Union home about 150 miles from their lines. There are several documents on file that state how

William tried to get back to his regiment. Due to weather conditions and his illness, he was not able to return until 5 January 1864 when he reported to Major Shurtleff who was the only officer left. The rest of the regiment had gone with Major General W.T. Sherman."

A letter in Dwyer's file from Camp 1st Alabama Cavalry Volunteers, dated July 3, 1865, stated: Before me the undersigned acting adjutant 1st Alabama Cavalry personally came Thomas A. McWhirter , Private Company K, 1st Alabama Cavalry Volunteers, says that Private William Dwyer was taken prisoner by the enemy with him at Vincent's Crossroads, Mississippi, on the 26th Day of October 1863, and was taken from there to Cahaba Prison Alabama. After remaining there near two months they both escaped from prison and started together for our lines at Camp Davies, Mississippi, where the regiment was stationed at that time. After traveling six days, William Dwyer became exhausted and unable to travel further, when McWhirter left him about 150 miles from our line. Signed Thomas A. McWhirter, Private Company K, 1st Alabama Cavalry. Subscribed and sworn to before me this 3rd Day of July 1865. Ira F. Pratt, 1st Lieutenant, Acting Adjutant 1st Alabama Cavalry.

Another letter from Headquarters District of Northern Alabama, Office Provost Marshall, Huntsville, Alabama, June 5, 1865. To Whom it may concern, William Dwyer, Private 1st Alabama Cavalry, a detailed scout for the District of Northern Alabama has been in my command for two months and has faithfully discharged his duty as a good soldier and trustworthy man. He has been always ready for duty, and has discharged his duties in a manner which entitles him to the confidence of all with whom he may have business connections. Signed, M.W. Reed, Captain, 18th Michigan Volunteer Infantry, and Chief of District Scouts.

Another letter in Dwyer's file from Headquarters District of Northern Alabama, Huntsville, Alabama, dated March 1st, 1865, Special Order # 36, William Dwyer, 1st Alabama Cavalry is hereby detailed as Scout and Guide for the District of Northern Alabama. He will report at these headquarters for duty immediately. Signed Colonel C.C. Doolittle.

One letter was from: Quarters Company K, 1st Alabama Cavalry Volunteers, Transfer Barracks, Nashville, Tennessee, July 18, 1865. Assistant Adjutant General, Military Division of Tennessee. Sir, I enlisted in Company K, 1st Alabama Cavalry, December 13, 1862, and on the 26th day of October 1862, I was captured by the enemy, at Vincent's Crossroads, Franklin County, Alabama during an action where we were badly defeated. I was taken to Cahaba Prison, 9 miles below Selma where I remained until January 1, 1863, when I succeeded in escaping, but owing to extremes of weather, and endeavors to elude pursuants, I did not reach our lines until November 15, 1864, at Decatur, Alabama when I reported to Major Julian H. Shurtleff, 1st Alabama Cavalry, who was the only officer of my regiment at that place. The regiment having gone with Major General Sherman. Major Shurtleff ordered me to stay with a detachment of my regiment and recruit for the same. I did so and on the return of my regiment I reported for duty to 1st Lieutenant Joseph Hornback, Commander of Company K, 1st Alabama Cavalry Volunteers. He informed me he had dropped me as "missing in action", and refuses to take my name up without orders from General Thomas. Hoping that justice may be done me and that my excuse for directly addressing you; the officer of my regiment having refused to render me any assistance, is sufficient. I am, Sir, very respectfully your most obedient servant, William Dwyer, Private, Company K, 1st Alabama Cavalry, USV. There were several letters in his files stating how he tried to get back to his regiment but due to the weather and his illness, he was not able to get there. Thomas A. McWhirter testified that he left Dwyer with a Union family who promised to care for him until he was well enough to travel.

William Lemuel Dwyer was born September 21, 1837, in Bibb County, Alabama to John and Jane Henry Dwyer. William married Hester Ann Tobitt on March 6, 1859, and they had the following children: Margaret; Sarah Elizabeth; Josephine "Josie"; William Samuel Ulysses Grant; Mary Roberta A.; Georgia Alice Virginia; John Edwin "Ed" Franklin; James Arthur; Florence Augusta Jane; Una, Hugh Nathanial; and Michael Dwyer. William's wife, Hester, was born August 19, 1844, in Tennessee and died in 1911. William Lemuel Dwyer died January 16, 1915, in Johnson City, Washington County, Tennessee, while living in the US National Home for Disabled Volunteer Soldiers where he was admitted September 9, 1901. He was buried in Site H-10– 8 of the Mountain Branch of the U. S. National Home for Disabled Volunteer Soldiers in Johnson City, Washington County, Tennessee.

<u>Dykes, Thomas L.</u> - Thomas L. Dykes, also listed as Dikes, enlisted in Company L of the 1st Alabama Cavalry, USV as a private on September 25, 1863, in Fayette County, Alabama for a period of 1 year. He was enrolled by Captain Tramel and was mustered in the September 25, 1863, in Glendale, Mississippi. The Company Descriptive Roll recorded him as being 18 years of age, 5'-4" tall, having a fair complexion, blue eyes, dark hair, born in Marion County, Alabama, and a farmer by occupation. The Company Muster Roll from September 25, through October 31, 1863, stated he was absent with leave. The November and December 1863 Muster Roll stated he was absent with leave since October 20, 1863, by order of Colonel Spencer. The January and February 1864 Muster Roll stated he was missing in action from the Battle of Vincent's Crossroads since October 26, 1863. In June 1865 he was listed as a prisoner of war since October 26, 1863. Thomas L. Dykes died October 2, 1864, in Charleston, South Carolina while a prisoner of war in the hands of the enemy. His Prisoner of War Record stated he died of chronic diarrhea, but did not say where he was when he died.

Thomas L. Dykes was born about 1846 in Fayette County, Alabama to Dr. Thomas G. Dykes and his wife, Zilpha Delilah Howell. Dr. Dykes was born about 1813 in Tennessee and died August 18, 1867, in Okalona, Chickasaw County, Mississippi. His wife, Zilpha, was born about 1813 in North Carolina, and died 1890 in Haleyville, Winston County, Alabama. Other children of Dr. Dykes and Zilpha, and siblings of Thomas L. Dykes were: Mary Elizabeth, Hester A., Harriet G., Rachel Matilda, Sarah Jane, Martha Emmaline "Emma", Stephen Franklin, John C., and Daniel C. Dykes.Thomas G. Dykes was born about 1813 in Tennessee and died August 18, 1867. His wife, Zilpha Delilah Howell, was born about 1813 in North Carolina and died in 1819 in Haleyville, Winston County, Alabama. Thomas L. Dykes died October 2, 1864, in Charleston, South Carolina while a prisoner of war in the hands of the enemy.

- E -

<u>Eakins, James B.</u> - See James B. Aikins

<u>Eakins, John</u> - See John Aikins.

<u>Eakins, Robert</u> - See Robert Aikins.

<u>Eakins, William T.</u> - See William T. Aikins.

<u>Earnest, David</u> - One card was found for David Earnest, also listed as Earnest David, which stated he enlisted in Company C of the 1st Alabama Cavalry, USV as a private. It recorded him as absent, sick in the hospital in Memphis, Tennessee since February 2, 1864. No further information relative to this soldier was found.*

<u>Earnest, Francis D.</u> - Francis D. Earnest, also shown as Francis D. Ernest, enlisted in Company C of the 1st Alabama Cavalry, USV on December 15, 1863, in Camp Davies, Mississippi for a period of 3 years. He was enrolled by Captain John Latty and was mustered in April 30, 1864, in Decatur, Alabama. The Company Descriptive Book recorded him as being 18 years of age, 5'-7" tall, having a dark complexion, dark eyes, light hair, born in Fayette County, Alabama, and a farmer by occupation. He was shown as being single and his residence was Fayette County, Alabama. A note in his file states: Mr. Cox, It has been ascertained from the V.A. that Francis D. Earnest died July 25, 1923, at Catalpa, Arkansas, and that his widow's name was Sarah. He served in Company C of the 1st Alabama Cavalry. March 4, 1939, Signed, GWS Headstone case disposed of March 4, 1939. Signed TEC. He was shown as being a patient on the January and February 1864 Hospital Muster Roll for the Gayoso U.S.S. Hospital in Memphis, Tennessee. He was mustered out October 20, 1865, in Huntsville, Alabama owing the U.S. Government $6.76 for losing 1 carbine sling, 1 swivel, 1 carbine cartridge box, 1 cap pouch, 1 saber belt, thong, wiper, and brush, 1 pair of spurs, and 1 curry comb.

Francis D. Earnest was born about 1845 in Fayette County, Alabama and died July 25, 1923, in Catalpa, Johnson County, Arkansas. He married Sarah C. Bruce, and is buried in the Bascom Cemetery (East) in Smith County, Texas with a Confederate tombstone.

<u>Earnest, William Calvin</u> - William Calvin Earnest enrolled in Company A of the 1st Alabama Cavalry, USV on January 5, 1864, at Camp Davies, Mississippi, for 3 years by Lt. Hinds. He was mustered in February 5, 1864, in Memphis, Tennessee. The Company Muster In and Descriptive Roll recorded him as 22 years of age, 5'-8" tall, having a dark complexion, gray eyes, dark hair, born in Tuscaloosa County, Alabama, and a farmer by occupation. A Company Muster Roll dated February 29, 1864, stated he had not received any bounty. William C. Earnest was captured by the enemy on March 10, 1865, and held prisoner of war. He was mustered out October 20, 1865, in Huntsville, Alabama with $178 due the U.S. Government for arms and equipment. He was paid $180 for bounty. William's Muster-Out Roll stated he deserted October 6, 1865, from Decatur, Alabama with one horse, saddle, bridle, halter, Carbine Pistol, saber belt, and one shelter tent. A Note from the Adjutant General's Office of the War Department dated September 30, 1887, stated he was captured at Fayetteville, North Carolina on March 10, 1865, brought from Raleigh, North Carolina, and confined at Richmond, Virginia March 28, 1865. He reported at College Green Barracks on March 31, 1865, sent to Camp Chase, Maryland in March 1865, where he arrived April 5, 1865, furloughed April 9, 1865 for 30 days, reported to regiment and retained by commanding officer on notification sent May 21, 1865. He was reported as having deserted October 10, 1865, from Decatur, Alabama. The charge of desertion against this man is removed and he is discharged to date, October 6, 1865, to complete his military record under the provisions of the act of congress approved July 5, 1884. Discharge certificate furnished by A.G.O. October 13, 1887. William C. Earnest was on a Muster Roll of a Detachment of Paroled Prisoners at Camp Chase, Ohio, dated April 10, 1865, shown as present, captured March 10, 1865, at Solomon Grove, North Carolina. William C. Earnest signed his name to his enlistment papers. His Prisoner of War Record stated Earnest was Paroled at Boulware's and Cox's Wharf. (This was located on the James River in Virginia.)

William Calvin Earnest was born April 27, 1841. in Tuscaloosa, Alabama. His parents were Moses and Mary Earnest. He had ten brothers and sisters including, Jane E. Earnest (b. 1833), Nancy Ann (b. 1835), Harriet S. (b.1837), John J. (b. 1839), Marion H. (b. 1845), Thomas P. (b. 1846), Barran D. (b. 1848), Sarah F. (b. 1854), Mary M. (b. 1857), and Jailor (b.1861). By 1860 the family had relocated to the Eastern Division of Fayette county, Alabama where they're enumerated on the census for that year. When the Civil War began, William was eighteen years old and living in a county that had strong Union sentiment. However, his older brother John J. Earnest, joined the Confederacy serving in the 51st Alabama and died in a Confederate hospital in April 1863. The following year, William joined with the Union. On January 5, 1864 he enlisted with the 1st Alabama Cavalry at Camp Davies for a period of 3 years and was placed in the "new" Company A.

While present most of 1864, it wasn't until the next year that William's record shows a lot of activity. On March 10, 1865, William participated in the action at Monroe's Cross Roads. That same day he was captured in Fayetteville, North Carolina and from Raleigh, he was sent to Richmond, Virginia. After being paroled at Bulvares and Coxes Wharf, Virginia, he reported at College Green Barracks, Maryland on March 30. Next, he was sent to Camp Chase in Ohio where he reported April 5, 1865. A few days later he was given a 30 day furlough after which he reported back and was present through the end of August. What happened after this is explained only through reading the various affidavits contained in William's pension records.

According to Elizabeth Mackey Earnest, widow of William Earnest, they married on September 17, 1865, at the home of Elizabeth's father in Tuscaloosa County, Alabama. It seems that the marriage took place during a furlough (one affidavit stated it was a sick furlough) and William was being treated by a Dr. Baker for a couple of months. William had been coughing violently and began coughing up blood and suffering from night sweats. Eventually, the doctor told him that he couldn't do anything else for him. He said he had contracted consumption from exposure while in the army and recommended that William go north- adding that this would either cure him, or kill him.

Elizabeth accompanied William and they made their way north. They got as far as Decatur, Alabama when he took a turn for the worse becoming very weak and could go no further. He died about two months later on December 21, 1865. In Elizabeth's affidavit she states that a Captain J.J. Hines (Hinds) was present at the time of her husband's death. He had been her husband's captain while in the army and was very kind. In fact, he even paid the $5.00 for her husband's burial. Another

261

affidavit given by Jere (Jeremiah) F. Files, Lt., says that he also saw William at the home of J.J. Hines (Hinds) while he was very sick with consumption just a few days before his death. Not only was J.J. Hinds apparently very good to both William and Elizabeth, but it's thanks to him that William was buried initially somewhere in Decatur with a marker bearing his name and the name of his regiment. This information was necessary when later he was moved to Corinth National Cemetery where he rests today. Family information submitted by Renee Kernan.

Earp, Daniel - Daniel Earp enlisted and mustered into Company M of the 1st Alabama Cavalry, USV as a private on September 5, 1864, in Rome, Georgia for a term of 2 years He was enrolled by Captain John Lomax. The Muster and Descriptive Roll showed him to have been 40 years of age, 5'-9" tall, having a fair complexion, blue eyes, dark hair, born in Anderson District, South Carolina, and a mechanic by occupation. The November 1864 through April 1865 Muster Rolls showed him to have been absent, sick in the hospital since November 3, 1864, place unknown. He was shown as being present on the May and June 1865 Muster Roll. His name appeared on the Returns as follows: October 1864, on daily duty in Regimental Carpenter Shop; November 1864, sent to hospital from the front November 3, 1864; December 1864 to May 1865, absent, sick since November 3, 1864, place not known; June 1865, on daily duty at Quartermaster Department by order of Captain Hinds; June 1865, returned from absent sick; July 1865, on daily duty as regimental carpenter. He was mustered out October 20, 1865, in Huntsville, Alabama. His pay was stopped due to owing the U.S. Government $10.31, for losing 1 carbine sling and swivel, 1 carbine cartridge box, 1 saber belt and plate, 2 spurs and straps, 1 saddle blanket, 1 thong and brush wipes and 1 carbine screwdriver. He was paid a bounty of $66.66 and showed him still due that same amount. Earp was able to sign his name on the Enlistment Forms.

East, James M. - James M. East enrolled in Company K of the 1st Alabama Cavalry, USV as a private on September 8, 1862, in Iuka, Mississippi, and was mustered in October 1, 1862, in Corinth, Mississippi for a period of 1 year. The Regimental Descriptive Book showed him to have been 19 years of age, 6'-1" tall, having a light complexion, gray eyes, light hair, born in Patrick County, Virginia, and a farmer by occupation. He was mustered out September 16, 1863 in Corinth, Mississippi due to expiration of term of service.

Eaton, Lewis Cass - Lewis Cass Eaton enlisted in Company F of the 1st Alabama Cavalry, USV as a Corporal on April 29, 1863, in Corinth, Mississippi, and was mustered in August 13, 1863, in Corinth for a period of 1 year. He was enrolled by Captain Pierce. The Company Descriptive Roll showed him to have been 32 years of age, 5'-6" tall, having a fair complexion, blue eyes, light hair, born in Whitley County, Kentucky, and a farmer by occupation. In July 1863, he was absent, on recruiting service. The September and October 1863 Muster Roll recorded him as absent, wounded in battle October 26, 1863, in Memphis, Tennessee. (This was probably during the Battle of Vincent's Crossroads which was fought on that date.) There was a Notation in his file from the Adjutant General's Office of the War Department dated February 7, 1870, stating he died November 19, 1863, at Church Military General Hospital in Memphis, Shelby County, Tennessee. He died of gangrene of the hip as a result of a gunshot wound. His only effects listed when he died were 1 uniform jacket or great coat and 1 flannel shirt. Lewis Cass Eaton is buried in the Memphis National Cemetery in Memphis, Shelby County, Tennessee.

Eaton, Monroe - Monroe Eaton enlisted in Company C of the 1st Alabama Cavalry, USV as a private in Corinth, Mississippi for a term of 1 year. He was mustered in December 22, 1862, in Corinth. He was enrolled by John Latty. The Company Descriptive Roll showed him to have been 18 years of age, 5'-4" tall, having a fair complexion, blue eyes, dark hair, born in Cass County, North Carolina, and a farmer by occupation. The March and April 1863 Muster Roll listed him as absent without leave since March 1, 1863. Another muster roll stated he had been absent without leave since February 21, 1863. The May and June 1863 Muster Roll recorded him as having deserted June 28, 1863, from Glendale, Mississippi.

Eaves, Dudley F. - Dudley F. Eaves enlisted in Company G of the 1st Alabama Cavalry, USV on December 8, 1862, in Oxford, Mississippi, and mustered in the same day in Corinth, Mississippi for a term of 1 year. Another muster roll stated he enrolled in Grand Junction, Tennessee. He was first appointed as 2nd Lieutenant of the Mississippi Rangers by Brigadier General C.S. Hamilton on December 8, 1862. He mustered out December 7, 1863, due to expiration of term of service. A note on his Muster Out Record stated he was not in debt to the government. His name appeared on the Returns as follows: June 1863 to August 1863, present; September 1863, absent, sick at home; October 1863, on duty with company.

Edgil, John - John Edgil enlisted in Company M on December 20, 1863, in Camp Davies, Mississippi. He was enrolled by Captain Lomax for a period of 3 years. The Company Descriptive Book was found in the back of the last roll of microfilm for records of the 1st Alabama Cavalry Soldiers. It stated he was 36 years of age, 5'-7" tall, having a fair complexion, blue eyes, dark hair, born in Morgan County, Alabama, and a farmer by occupation. He was rejected by the surgeon on December 20, 1863, due to imbecility. No further information relative to this soldier was found.*

Edmonds, Emanuel - Emanuel Edmonds enlisted in Company M of the 1st Alabama Cavalry, USV as a private on September 25, 1863, in Fayette County, Alabama and was mustered in the same day in Glendale, Mississippi, for a term of 1 year. He was enrolled by Captain Trammel. The Company Descriptive Book recorded him as 20 years of age, 6' tall, having a fair complexion, blue eyes, light hair, born in Georgia, and a farmer by occupation. The November and December 1863 Muster Roll listed him as being absent, sick in the Post Hospital in Corinth, Mississippi since December 5, 1863. The January and February 1864 Muster Roll recorded the following: Final Statements given February 24, 1864. He was discharged March 19, 1864, by the Surgeon's Certificate of Disability by order of Major General Hurlburt due to having smallpox. His name appeared on the November and December 1864 Hospital Muster Roll for the U.S.A. Post General Hospital in Corinth, Mississippi. The Surgeon's Certificate showed he had smallpox and chronic diarrhea and had been unfit for duty for 60 days.

Edwards, Alanson William - Captain Alanson William Edwards was in Company L of the 1st Alabama Cavalry, USV, being appointed on September 18, 1863, at Glendale, Mississippi, and promoted to Adjutant March 2, 1864. He was appointed Captain on July 1, 1864, in Savannah, Georgia. The January and February 1865 Muster Roll showed him to have been absent, on detached service on Brigadier General Corses' staff per S.P.O. 199 H.Q. A&D of the Tennessee dated near Savannah, Georgia December 19, 1864. His name appeared on an Individual Muster-in Roll dated November 20, 1863, in Corinth, Mississippi stating he enrolled September 18, 1863, at Glendale, Mississippi for a period of one year, and was promoted from a Private of Company I of the 122 Regiment of Illinois Infantry Volunteers by authority of the Secretary of the War, S.O. No. 2, Headquarters, L.W. 16 A.C. October 18, 1863. Another muster roll stated he enrolled for a period of 3 years. He was transferred from Company M to Company L by Regimental Order Number 24 on October 28, 1863. He began commanding Company L on November 1, 1864. The Field and Staff Muster Roll dated March and April 1864, stated Edwards had pay due as 1st Lieutenant Commanding Company L, from November 1, 1863 to March 2, 1864. The July and August 1864 Field and Staff Muster Roll stated: Resigned and promoted since last muster. Appointed Captain of Company L, 1st Alabama Cavalry July 1, 1864. He was mustered out from the company in June 1864, as 1st Lieutenant and Adjutant for promotion to Captain of the 1st Alabama Cavalry. The Company Muster Roll for September and October 1864 stated Edwards joined for duty and enrolled July 1, 1864, at Rome, Georgia and mustered in July 27, 1864, in Rome, Georgia. He was shown on this same muster roll as being absent, on detached service as A.A.A.G. for Brigadier General Vandiver in Marietta, Georgia per S.F.O. 131, Headquarters A & D of the Tennessee dated near Culpepper Farm in Georgia October 7, 1864. He was listed as 21 years of age. In January 1865, his name appeared on a Return of the 4th Division, 15th Army Corps, stating: In the field, Sister's Ferry, Georgia, January 31, 1865. The next Return dated February 1865, stated: In the field, Lynch Creek, South Carolina, February 28, 1865. The March 1865 Return stated: In the field near Goldsboro, North Carolina, March 31, 1865. The April 1865 Return stated they were near the Neuse River, absent per Special Order Number 39,

Headquarters 4th Division, 15th A.C. A.W. Edwards' name appeared on a General Order Number 65, dated War Department, Adjutant General's Office, June 22, 1867, appointed to be Major By Brevet in the Volunteer Force, Army of the United States for gallant and meritorious services in the field. Alonson W. Edwards was mustered out and honorably discharged per Special Order Number 362, War Department, A.G.O. July 11, 1865. The Field and Staff Muster-Out Roll was dated October 20, 1865, at Huntsville, Alabama.

Alanson W Edwards - From "The Fargo Forum" of Fargo, North Dakota, February 8, 1908.

Major Alanson W. Edwards passed quietly into rest at noon today, after an illness extending over quite a number of years, although he had only been confined to the house for a few months...when the end came it was as peaceful as could be imagined, and he was tenderly waited upon by his devoted wife and members of the family. The interment will be made in Fargo, the service being held Monday afternoon...and will be in charge of John F. Reynolds post of the G.A.R. (Grand Army of the Republic) The service will be at the residence of the deceased, on Seventh Street South.

Major Alanson William Edwards was born in Lorain County, Ohio, August 27, 1840, and his father removed his family to Macoupin County, Illinois in 1848. Major Edwards attended the county schools and was a student at McKendree College in Lebanon, Illinois, in 1856-7. After leaving school he was railroad and express agent and telegraph operator at Gillespie when the war broke out. On the first call for troops, April 15, 1861, he volunteered, but was rejected as he weighed some 300 pounds. He continued with the railroad company until 1862, when he enlisted and went into Camp Palmer at Carlinville, Illinois. He was mustered into Company I 122nd Illinois Infantry by Captain Charles Ewing. Two years afterwards he was adjutant general on General Vandeveer's staff, who commanded the district of Marietta.

Major Edwards served in the western army as a private, beginning at Columbus, Kentucky. He was a clerk in the office of the adjutant general of the district of Jackson and for General G. M. Dodge at Corinth, Mississippi. On the march through Georgia to the sea, Major Edwards commanded Company M of his regiment and for thirty-seven days did not draw a ration, but gained fifty pounds in weight. At Savannah he was detached from his company by order of General Sherman and assigned to duty A.A.G. 9th Division, 15th Corps and served with General Corse until after the general review in Washington, being finally mustered out by order of the war department July 11, 1865. He was brevetted major by order of Congress, March 18, 1865.

Major Edwards was present at the preliminary meeting of the officers of the army of Tennessee, to organize this society at Raleigh, North Carolina, April 25, 1865, and he became a member of the G.A.R. in Post No. 6 at Bunker Hill, there being only five earlier posts organized.

He returned to his old Illinois home after the war and resuscitated The Union Gazette at Bunker Hill, a paper he published before going to the war which suspended while he was away. In 1868, Major Edwards secured an interest in the Carlinville Free Democrat; a Republican paper started by Senator John M. Palmer, and was made warden of the Illinois State Penitentiary by the governor for the term of 1871-2.

After the big fire in Chicago he went into business in that city. He went to the Black Hills in 1876, going out via Fargo, and returned to this city in 1878 and started the Fargo Republican, being associated with Dr. J. B. Hall. He later sold the Republican and started The Daily Argus.

Territorial Governor Pierce appointed Major Edwards superintendent of the semi-decennial of Dakota territory in 1885 and in 1886 he was elected mayor of the city of Fargo. He was largely instrumental in organizing the original board of trade in the city of Fargo in 1879 and was its secretary for some time. He helped to organize the Fargo Southern Railway Company, which organization constructed 122 miles of road from Fargo to Ortonville, and was elected secretary and assistant manager. The road was built in 1883-4 and is now a part of the Milwaukee system. Major Edwards was a member of the first board of the North Dakota penitentiary, and directed the construction of the nucleus of the present building. He was elected a member of the state legislature in 1895 and received credit for maintaining the prohibition law.

Major Edwards left the Argus in 1891 and started the Daily Forum of that year in connection with Mr. Plumley, and in 1894 The Forum purchased The Republican, the first paper started by the major, and the two papers were consolidated. In March 1902, the major was made American consul general in Montreal which position he resigned in 1906 in consequence of poor health and returned to

Fargo where he has since resided.

The major married at Carlinville, Illinois in 1970 to Elizabeth Robertson and they have six sons and one daughter. The sons are Harry Goodell, stenographer for the district court at Fargo; William Robertson, advertising manager of The Forum; Alanson Charles, living in New York City; John Palmer, assistant manager of The Forum; George Washington, musical instructor at Danville, Kentucky, Female Seminary; Richard Roberts, collector in this city and the daughter is Marie Rosenfield Belknap, who also resides in Fargo.

Major Edwards has always taken much interest in politics and has been known as a hard fighter. During his residence of thirty years in Fargo, no one has done more to build up the territory, the state, and the city, than Major Edwards, and his death will be sincerely mourned. His work, however, lives after him. The Political Graveyard stated he died February 14, 1908.

Edwards, James - James Edwards enlisted and mustered into Company K of the 1st Alabama Cavalry, USV as a private on July 24, 1862, in Huntsville, Alabama. He was enrolled by Captain Bankhead for a period of 3 years, and was with the early enlistees who were immediately shipped to Nashville, Tennessee and merged with the 1st Middle Tennessee Cavalry which went on to be the 5th Tennessee Cavalry. The Company Descriptive Book recorded him as 32 years of age, 5'-10½" tall, having a light complexion, blue eyes, yellow hair, born in Morgan County, Alabama, and a farmer by occupation. There was one Return found at the end of the last roll of microfilm containing the roster and records of the 1st Alabama Cavalry, USV, which was for James Edwards of Company E, 1st Alabama Cavalry, and stated he was in the 3rd Regiment Tennessee Cavalry and enlisted June 28, 1863, in Nashville, Tennessee. That probably should have been the 1st or 5th Tennessee Cavalry. Edwards served with Company E of the 1st Middle Tennessee Cavalry. The November and December 1862 Muster Roll recorded him as absent, sick in hospital in Nashville, Tennessee since December 26, 1862. The July and August 1863 Muster Roll recorded him absent, died in hospital in Nashville, Tennessee January 28, 1863. Official Notice received August 13, 1863. Edwards died of phthisis pulmonalis, consumption of the lungs or tuberculosis. James Edwards is buried in Grave #G-5674 in the Nashville National Cemetery in Nashville, Davidson County, Tennessee.

Elkins, Francis C. - Francis C. Elkins enlisted in Company F of the 1st Alabama Cavalry, USV as a private on June 27, 1863, in Corinth, Mississippi for a period of 1 year. He was enrolled by Captain Pierce and mustered in August 13, 1863, in Corinth. The Company Descriptive Book recorded him as 22 years of age, 5'-0" tall, having a light complexion, gray eyes, brown hair, born Choctaw County, Mississippi, and a farmer by occupation. The January and February Muster Roll recorded him as being absent, sick in Gayoso USA General Hospital in Memphis, Shelby County, Tennessee. He was also listed on a Hospital Muster Roll as a patient in the Washington USA General Hospital in Memphis, Tennessee where he was admitted March 13, 1864. His name appeared on the Returns as follows: September 1863, deserted from Glendale, Mississippi on September 15, 1863; November 1863, Gain from missing in action November 11, 1863; November 1863, on daily duty as company cook; April 1864, absent; July 1864, discharged, term of service expired July 27, 1864, at Rome, Georgia.

Elkins, William J. - William J. Elkins enlisted in Company G of the 1st Alabama Cavalry, USV as a private on March 10, 1864, in Decatur, Alabama for a period of 3 years. He was enrolled by Lieutenant Pease and was mustered in April 13, 1864, in Decatur. The Muster and Descriptive Roll recorded him as 21 years of age, 5'-9" tall, having a dark complexion, blue eyes, black hair, born in Lawrence County, Alabama, and a farmer by occupation. The July and August 1864 Muster Roll showed him to have been absent with leave. The September and October 1864 Muster Roll showed him to have been absent, on detached service recruiting in Decatur, Alabama since August 7, 1864. He was promoted to Sergeant on November 20, 1864. Elkins' name appeared on the Returns for March and April 1865 stating he was sick in Wilmington, North Carolina since March 10, 1865. A note in his file stated the following: Regimental Returns March 1865 Historical Memorandum shows as follows: On the morning of the 10th (1865), our camp was surprised by an overwhelming force of the enemy, we fought desperately, regained our camp and held it with the loss of 11 killed, 257 wounded, and 41 prisoners (names of wounded not given) this return shows regiment was in action March 10, 1865, at

Monroe's Crossroads. William J. Elkins had a severe gunshot wound to the thigh. He was mustered out October 20, 1865, in Huntsville, Alabama. His Muster-Out Roll stated he owed the U.S. Government $13.83 for losing 1 carbine screwdriver, 1 cleaning rod, retained under General Order 101 of the War Department, 1 wiper and thong, $10.00.

<u>Elliott, Samuel</u> - Samuel Elliott enlisted in Company B of the 1st Alabama Cavalry, USV as a private on February 4, 1864, in Pulaski, Tennessee for a term of 3 years. He was enrolled by Lieutenant Judy and was mustered in March 27, 1864, in Decatur, Alabama. The Company Muster and Descriptive Roll recorded him as having been 36 years of age, 5'-11" tall, having a fair complexion, blue eyes, red hair, born in Hall County, Georgia (card stated Pall. County, Georgia so it could possibly have been Paulding County), and a farmer by occupation. His enlistment was credited to Pulaski, Giles County, Tennessee. He was appointed Sergeant from Corporal on August 1, 1864. He was mustered out October 20, 1865, in Huntsville, Alabama.

<u>Ellis, Charles</u> - Charles C. Ellis enlisted in Company D of the 1st Alabama Cavalry, USV as a private on April 19, 1864, in Decatur, Alabama for a period of 3 years. He was enrolled by Lieutenant Pease and was mustered in June 16, 1864, in Decatur. The Muster and Descriptive Roll records him as being 19 years of age, 6' tall, having a light complexion, blue eyes, light hair, born in Brandon, Calloway County, Kentucky, and a shoemaker by occupation. The March and April 1865 Muster Roll recorded him as being absent, captured and taken prisoner of war near Fayetteville, North Carolina since February 18, 1865. Another record stated he was captured March 10, 1865, which was when the Battle of Monroe's Crossroads was fought. A Notation from the Adjutant General's Office of the War Department dated June 20, 1870, stated he was captured March 10, 1865, near Fayetteville, North Carolina. Charles C. Elkins' name appeared on the Returns as follows: April 1864, enlisted in regiment April 19, 1864, in Decatur, Alabama; February to April 1865, absent, prisoner of war; May 1865, prisoner of war March 10, 1865; June 1865, Discharged June 13, 1865, at Camp Chase, Ohio, General Order #77, War Department 1865.

<u>Ellis, Isaac R.</u> - Isaac R. Ellis, name also appears as R. Ellis and J.B. Ellis, enlisted in Company F of the 1st Alabama Cavalry, USV as a private on March 27, 1863, in Corinth, Mississippi for a period of 1 year. He was enrolled by Captain Pierce, and was mustered in May 18, 1863, in Corinth. The Company Descriptive Roll shows him to have been 24 years of age, 5'-10" tall, having a dark complexion, gray eyes, light hair, born in Crawford County, Indiana, and shoe maker by occupation. He was shown as a saddler in all military records. The July 1863 through December 1863 Muster Rolls showed him to have been absent, sick at post hospital in Corinth, Mississippi. The January and February 1864 Muster Roll shows him to be absent, sick in hospital in Memphis, Tennessee since February 20, 1864. Strangely enough, the November 1864 through June 1865 Muster Rolls shows him to have been absent, a prisoner of war from Camp Davies, Mississippi since February 15, 1864. The July and August 1865 Muster Roll shows him to have been absent, prisoner of war since July 25, 1864. The Company Muster-Out Roll stated the following: Prisoner of war since February 1864, assigned to duty from 1 year organization 1st Alabama Cavalry July 25, 1864, by order of Colonel Spencer. Captured at Camp Davies, Mississippi. His name appeared on the Returns as follows: August 1863, on daily duty as farrier; September 1863, absent, in Corinth at home; October 18, 1863 to December 1863, sick at Corinth, Mississippi since July 21st; January to March 1864, absent, sick in hospital in Memphis, Tennessee; April 1864, absent; July to August 1864, absent, sick in Memphis, Tennessee since March 5, 1864; September 1864, absent, sick; October 1864 to March 1865, absent, sick in U.S. General Hospital; April 1865 to September 1865, prisoner of war since January 10, 1864.

<u>Ellis, Lorenzo D.</u> - Lorenzo D. Ellis enlisted in Company F of the 1st Alabama Cavalry, USV as a Corporal on June 25, 1863, in Memphis, Tennessee for a term of one year. He was enrolled by Captain Hinds, and was mustered in August 7, 1863, in Corinth, Mississippi. The November and December 1863 Muster Roll recorded him as a sergeant. A Stop was put on his pay for $12 for losing 1 Remington revolver. He was mustered out July 27, 1864, in Rome Georgia due to expiration of term of service. He also owed the Sutler $5.50 for clothing allowance. The Company Descriptive Roll recorded

him as 25 years of age, 6' tall, having a dark complexion, dark eyes, dark hair, born in Cocke County, Tennessee, and railroader by occupation.

Ellison, William J. - William J. Ellison enlisted in Company H of the 1st Alabama Cavalry, USV as a private on April 1, 1865, in Stevenson, Alabama for a period of 3 years. He was enrolled by James W. DeVaney and was mustered in April 5, 1865, in Nashville, Tennessee. The Muster and Descriptive Roll recorded him as 18 years of age, 5'-7" tall, having a light complexion, blue eyes, light hair, born in Cherokee County, Georgia, and a farmer by occupation. William J. Ellison died of rubella (measles) in the hospital in Huntsville, Alabama on May 22, 1865. The Record of Death and Interment stated he died in Hospital #333 in Huntsville, Alabama and was buried in Grave 212 in the Huntsville Cemetery. It also stated he was 17 years of age, his home address was Marshall County, Alabama, and he was single. His remains were later removed to Plot #L-9534 in the Chattanooga National Cemetery in Chattanooga, Hamilton County, Tennessee.

Emerick, George - George Emerick, also listed as Emerich, enlisted in Company A of the 1st Alabama Cavalry, USV as a 1st Lieutenant on February 4, 1864, in Camp Davies, Mississippi for a period of 3 years. He was appointed 1st Lieutenant by Brigadier General G.W. Dodge, by authority of the Secretary of War. Received and accepted appointment February 1, 1864. He had been duty sergeant in Company B, 2nd Illinois Light Artillery. George Emerick's name was found on a Return found at the end of the last roll of microfilm of the records for the 1st Alabama Cavalry, USV soldiers. It stated he was a sergeant in Company E of the 1st Alabama Cavalry, and that he transferred from the 2nd Illinois Artillery on August 13, 1863, in Glendale, Mississippi. It also recorded him as absent, on detached service, on recruiting duty since November 22, 1863. The March and April 1864 Muster Roll recorded him as being absent, on recruiting service. The July and August 1864 Muster roll records him as being absent, on detached service in Decatur, Alabama. The September and October 1864 Muster Roll records him as being absent, on recruiting service in Decatur, Alabama since August 7, 1864. In December 1864 through February 1865, he was on special duty commanding Company M. The March and April 1865 Muster Roll recorded him as being absent, wounded in action March 10, 1865, during the Battle of Monroe's Crossroads and sent to Berry House General Hospital in Wilmington, North Carolina. He was shown as present in the May and June 1865 Muster Roll. He was mustered out October 20, 1865, in Huntsville, Alabama. The Muster-Out Roll stated the following: This officer has made affidavit that he has rendered all requisite returns relating to public property for which he has been accountable as required by army regulations. The Company and Muster and Descriptive Roll listed him as being 25 years of age, born in Ross County, Ohio, and a farmer by occupation. Emerick wrote a letter requesting a 30-day leave of absence: Camp 1st Alabama Volunteer Cavalry, Faison's Depot, North Carolina, April 3, 1865. Major, I have the honor to respectfully apply for a leave of absence for thirty (30) days for the following reasons: I was severely wounded in the engagement with the enemy's cavalry at Monroe's Crossroads, North Carolina March 10, 1865. Surgeon's Certificate enclosed. Signed: I am, Major, very respectfully your obedient servant, George W. Emerick, 1st Lieutenant, 1st Alabama Volunteer Cavalry. The Surgeon's Certificate stated the following: Lieutenant George W. Emerick of the 1st Regiment Alabama Cavalry having applied for a certificate on which to ground an application for leave of absence I do hereby certify that I have carefully examined this officer, and find that he is suffering from the effects of a gunshot wound to the thigh and scrotum received in action at Monroe's Crossroads, North Carolina, 10th Day of March 1865; and that in consequence thereof, he is, in my opinion, unfit for duty. I further declare my belief that he will not be able to resume his duties in less period than thirty (30) days. Dated at Faison's Depot, North Carolina, this third day of April 1865. James H. Davis, Assistant Surgeon, 1st Alabama Cavalry. His name appeared on a Return for November 1863 stating the following: Transferred from 2nd Illinois Artillery August 13, 1863, at Glendale, Mississippi; and on November 22, 1863, he was absent, on detached service recruiting in Alabama since November 22, 1863.

There was another interesting letter in his military records but it is written extremely light and is almost illegible, but needs to be included: Headquarters 27th Missouri Volunteers, R_w__ Plantation, North Carolina, April 7, 1865, Doctor, On arriving at Wilmington, North Carolina on the 17th March, last, the sick and wounded of the 15th and 20th Corps were all crowded into the Railroad Depot (594 in number) and Assistant Surgeon Light of the 20th Corps left them next morning and during my stay in the city never came near the hospital. Nor did Doctor Audt of the 15th Corps. Having to hunt up cooking utensils for the hospital as well as attend to all these men in person I could not give them such particular as I would have wished. Relying on Assistant Surgeon Light's assertions that they were all (wounds) dressed. On the third day of going around the wards and selecting such cases as were badly wounded, for a transfer to a better house, I was very much surprised to find Lieutenant Emrick with fracture of the upper third of femur without any attention, his wound had never even been dressed. I removed all of the _____ of bone and found fracture extending from the Great _raca_ter to about the lower third of femur – this the great comminution _____ the course of the ball I was unable to trace but left the Lieutenant pretty comfortable as were all the rest of the sick and wounded of your Corps. As to Assistant Surgeon Light, I could hear him occasionally and saw him once or twice. I left him in Wilmington and urged him and Dr. Audt of the 4th Division, 15th Corps to return home with me but they would not. As to the doctors being drunk, I can say nothing as I never drink myself nor do I often associate with the class of men frequenting the house where the doctor stopped but I can say I think the doctor was criminally negligent of his patients. I will be glad to hear from you. Very Respectfully, Your obedient servant, B.N. Bond, Surgeon 27th Missouri, 1st Brigade, 1st Division, 15th Army Corps.

A letter written by Major Trammel in response to a 30-day leave of absence requested for Emerick and stated: Approved and respectfully forwarded, with the request that the leave be granted, as this officer is totally unfit for duty and has always been a faithful and efficient officer, always at his post. Another letter in his file states the following: Headquarters, 3rd Brigade, 3rd Cavalry Division, Faison's Depot, North Carolina, April 3, 1865, approved and respectfully forwarded. This officer was severely wounded at Monroe's Crossroads March 10, 1865. At first the wound was considered mortal, but he is now slowly recovering. He is lying in the hospital at Wilmington, North Carolina and it is thought by the surgeon that the trip north would be of incalculable benefit to him. Signed George E. Spencer, Commanding Company.

Emmerson, John - John Emmerson, also listed as John Emerson, enlisted in Company C of the 1st Alabama Cavalry, USV as a private on February 1, 1864, in Memphis, Tennessee for a period of 3 years. He was enrolled by John Latty, and was mustered in March 10, 1864, in Memphis. The Muster and Descriptive Roll showed him to have been 18 years of age, 4'-6" tall, having a fair complexion, blue eyes, light hair, born in McNairy County, Tennessee, and a farmer by occupation. He was shown as being single. The March and April 1865 Muster Roll recorded him as being absent, a prisoner of war since March 10, 1865, which would have been the Battle of Monroe's Crossroads near Fayetteville, North Carolina. He was mustered out of service June 12, 1865, in Camp Chase, Ohio according to General Order #77 of the War Department dated April 28, 1865. His name was listed on a Hospital Muster Roll for Tripler U.S.A. General Hospital in Columbus, Ohio for March and April 1865. Clothing draw in hospital $12.70. Discharged at Tripler U.S. Hospital March 29, 1865, by Lieutenant Rowley, 2nd U.S. Infantry. A Notation in his file from the Record and Pension office of the War Department dated April 7, 1896, stated: It has this day, April 7, 1896, been determined by this department from records on file and evidence furnished by the auditor of the War Department that this man was discharged the service at Tripler General Hospital, Columbus, Ohio, May 29, 1865, in compliance with telegrams. A record in his file stated he was in Hospital # 1273, Age 16; Nativity, Tennessee; Residence, Purdee, McNairy County, Tennessee; Nearest Relative, Father, Arch Emmerson; Admitted to hospital April 6, 1865; From what source, Parole Camp Annapolis, Maryland; Diagnosis, Pneumonia. A Prisoner of War Record stated John Emmerson was captured at Fayetteville, North Carolina March 10, 1865, brought from Raleigh, North Carolina to Richmond, Virginia March 28, 1865, paroled at Boulware's and Cox's Wharf March 30, 1865. His father was shown as Arch Emersin.

England, Francis Marion - Francis Marion England enlisted in Company K of the 1st Alabama Cavalry, USV at Glendale, Mississippi on November 1, 1863, for a period of 3 years. He was enrolled by Lieutenant Hornback, and was mustered in the same day at Corinth, Mississippi. The Company Descriptive Book recorded him as 17 years of age, 5'-7" tall, having a light complexion, gray eyes, red hair, born in Morgan County, Alabama, and a farmer by occupation. The March and April 1864

Muster Roll recorded him as being absent, sick in the General Hospital in Nashville, Tennessee since April 3, 1864. The May and June 1864 Muster Roll recorded him as being sick in the Jefferson USA General Hospital in Jeffersonville, Indiana where he was admitted May 14, 1864, and was sent there from the hospital in Nashville, Tennessee. The diagnosis appeared to be anemia. The Hospital Muster Roll stated he was in Ward 3 in tents. He was recorded as being single and the next of kin was Mrs. M.J. Williams of Morgan County, Alabama. He was mustered out July 19, 1865, in Nashville, Tennessee.

Francis Marion England was born about March 26, 1840, in Morgan County, Alabama to John and Mary Scott England. John was born about 1795 in Montgomery County, Virginia and was listed on the 1860 Morgan County, Alabama Census at age 65, with his third wife, Frances, who was 21 years old at the time. They lived in the Southwest Division of the Cedar Plains area. Other children listed were Martha J., 19; Newton, 17; Marion, 15 (this would be Francis Marion); Alfred, 13; Elizabeth, 11; John, 9; and Rebecca England, 3 years old. It is evident that some of these younger children belonged to Francis Marion's young step-mother, Francis. Records indicate this John England was the son of John England, born 1765 in Montgomery County, Virginia, died 1816 in Anderson County, Tennessee and married Vesta Zipporah Choate, born 1767 in Montgomery County, Virginia, died 1847 in Anderson County, Tennessee. She was the daughter of Christopher Choate and Prudence Staley. Francis Marion first married Delia Fox Jones from Walker County, Alabama, who was born about 1845 and died 1887. Francis Marion lost his wife and 12-year old son, John, the same day to the same illness. They are both buried in the Ebenezer Baptist Church Cemetery in West Point, Cullman County, Alabama. His second wife was Elsie Woodard from Cordova, Walker County, Alabama who is buried near Arley in Winston County, with a headstone that only shows her first name. It is a small cemetery, off the beaten path and is difficult to find. His third wife was Katherine/Catherine "Katie" Blevins who was born in 1860, and they married in Knox County, Tennessee. Francis Marion England died in 1943 and is buried in the Ebenezer Baptist Church Cemetery, near West Point in Cullman County, Alabama. Family information submitted by Stephen Caudle)

Entrican, John W. - John W. Entrican enlisted in Company G of the 1st Alabama Cavalry, USV as a private on March 5, 1863, for a period of 1 year in Chewalla, Tennessee, and was mustered in the same day at Corinth, Mississippi. In September and October 1863, he was on daily duty as company cook. He died December 20, 1863, at Camp Davies, Mississippi. Cause of death not known and no further information was found, other than he was buried in Grave B-3495 in the Corinth National Cemetery in Corinth, Alcorn County, Mississippi.

Epperson, Sanford Jackson - Sanford Jackson Epperson enlisted and mustered into Company K of the 1st Alabama Cavalry, USV as a private on December 1, 1863, in Camp Davies, Mississippi for a period of 3 years. He was enrolled by Lieutenant Hornback. He traveled 90 miles on horseback from his home in Marion County, Alabama to Camp Davies, Mississippi to enlist in the Union Army. From January through October 1864, he was on daily duty as a teamster in Regimental Headquarters Department. January and February 1865, he was Brigade Teamster. The Company Descriptive Book recorded him as 25 years of age, 5'-10" tall, having a light complexion, gray eyes, auburn hair, born in Cherokee County, Georgia, and a farmer by occupation.

Sanford Jackson Epperson was born May 10, 1842, in Cherokee County, Georgia to John and Emily Bell Epperson. John was born 1783 and died November 24, 1862. Emily was born September 7, 1791, and died February 17, 1883. Other children of John and Emily Bell Epperson were: Nancy P., Elizabeth, Green B., John Ira, Mary Ann, James B., and Jane Epperson. Sanford J. Epperson married Frances Nancy Holland, who was born March 26, 1838, and died 15 August 15, 1905 in Smith County, Texas. She was buried in the Bascom East Cemetery in Bascom, Smith County, Texas. Sanford was enumerated with a wife named Mandy F. on the 1910 Smith County, Texas Census. He died March 26, 1915, in Smith County, Texas and was buried in the Bascom East Cemetery in Bascom, Smith County, Texas.

Ernest, Francis D. - See Francis D. Earnest.

Ernest, William Calvin - See William Calvin Earnest.

Estell, William L. - William L. Estell, also spelled Estill, enlisted in Company M of the 1st Alabama Cavalry, USV as a private on December 12, 1863, in Camp Davies, Mississippi for a period of 3 years (another muster roll stated he enrolled for 1 year). He was enrolled by Captain Lomax and was mustered in December 29, 1863, in Corinth, Mississippi. The Company Descriptive Book listed him as being 25 years of age, 5'-10" tall, having a fair complexion, blue eyes, auburn hair, born in Marion County, Alabama, and a farmer by occupation. The January and February 1864 Muster Roll showed him to be absent with leave since January 9, 1864. The May 1864 through February 1865 Muster Rolls recorded him as being absent, sick in the hospital in Chattanooga, Tennessee since May 22, 1864. The March and April 1865 Muster Roll recorded him as being absent, on recruiting service (from absent sick since November 10, 1864, by order of Major General Shurtliff. The May and June 1865 Muster Roll recorded him as having deserted from absent, on recruiting service in Alabama since June 1, 1865, with Smith's carbine and accoutrements, colt revolver and spurs. Deserted from absent, sick in hospital in Chattanooga, Tennessee in June 1864. William L. Estell actually died of disease on June 1, 1865, in Decatur, Alabama.

Evans, Edmond R. - Edmond R. Evans enlisted in Company K of the 1st Alabama Cavalry, USV as a Sergeant on July 24, 1862, in Huntsville, Alabama by Captain Bankhead for 3 years. He mustered in as Sergeant and kept that title until he died. Edmond was one of the early enlistees who was immediately shipped to Nashville, Tennessee and were merged with the 1st Middle Tennessee Cavalry, and the 5th Tennessee Cavalry, USV. He was captured by the enemy in Rome, Georgia on May 3, 1863, and confined at Richmond, Virginia May 9, 1863. He was paroled at City Point, Maryland May 15, 1863, and reported to Camp Parole, Maryland May 18, 1863, The Regimental Descriptive Book shows him to have been 37 years of age, 5'-9½" tall, light complexion, hazel eyes, auburn hair, born in Morgan County, Alabama, and a farmer by occupation. In November and December 1864, Edmond R. Evans was listed as absent, on recruiting service in Tennessee November 10, 1864. On February 5, 1865, he was listed as having died in Post Hospital at Mooresville, Alabama of Smallpox. Edmond's Prisoner of War Record stated he was captured at Rome, Georgia May 3, 1863, confined at Richmond, Virginia May 9, 1863, paroled at City Point, Virginia on May 15, 1863, reported at Camp Parole, Maryland on May 18, 1863, and sent back to regiment May 9, 1863.

Edmond R. Evans was the son of Joseph and Mary Denson Evans. Joseph was born April 4, 1795, and died August 16, 1868. Mary Denson Evans was born about 1800 and died in Hartselle, Morgan County, Alabama Edmond's grandfather was Owen Evans, born May 14, 1754, and died March 13, 1827. He was a Revolutionary War Veteran of the South Carolina Militia who died in Huntsville, Alabama. Edmond R. Evans was born in 1825 in Morgan County, Alabama, brought up in Walker/Winston County near the Morgan County line. Edmond married Christina Parker, daughter of William and Mary Parker, December 14, 1844, in Morgan County, Alabama, and they had the following children: Mary Elizor, born December 23, 1845, died March 2, 1897 married Edward McAnear; Josiah, born 1847, died about 1911; William, born December 5, 1849, died after 1911; Emily, born September 6, 1852, died April 22, 1878; Martha Caroline, born April 15, 1853, died 1939, married George A. McAnear; Charles M., born November 6, 1857, died October 19, 1932; Zachariah P., born December 22, 1859, died August 27, 1930; and a twin Thomas Haywood Evans, born December 22, 1859, died May 26, 1911. Thomas H. Evans married Florence D. Sams on December 21, 1884 in Cullman, Alabama. They had two children Thomas H. Evans, Jr. and Fred Evans. My wife's grandmother was Ruby Evans, daughter of Thomas H. Evans Jr. Family information courtesy of descendant Benny Gordon.

Evans, John Wesley - John Wesley Evans enlisted in Company C of the 1st Alabama Cavalry, USV under the name William A. Andous, and various spellings. He enlisted as a private on February 15, 1864, in Memphis, Tennessee for a period of 3 years by John Latty, and was mustered in March 10, 1864, at Memphis. The Muster and Descriptive Roll listed him as being 18 years of age, having a fair complexion, gray eyes, dark hair, born in Green County, Georgia, and a farmer by occupation. He was shown as being single. His name appeared on a Company Muster Roll and the date was Enlistment to

June 30, 1864, absent, on detached service as orderly at General Veatch's Headquarters. The Returns listed him as: January 1865 to March 1865, Orderly at Regimental Headquarters; May 1865 to September 1865, Orderly at Regimental Headquarters. John W. Evans was mustered out on October 20, 1865, at Huntsville, Alabama. He was paid $180 bounty by the U.S. Government with $120 still due him. He owed the U.S. Government $5.36 for losing the following ordnance: One Carbine sling, one swivel, one cap pouch, one saber belt, one thong and brush, wiper, screw driver, one pair of spurs, and one curry comb.

Evans, William C. - William C. Evans, also listed as Evins, enlisted in Company D of the 1st Alabama Cavalry, USV as a private on May 20, 1864, at Larkinsville, Alabama for a period of 3 years, by Capt. J. H. Shurtliff. He was mustered in at Rome, Georgia on July 27, 1864. The Muster and Descriptive Roll listed him as being 18 years of age, 5'-3" tall, having a light complexion, blue eyes, brown hair, born in Marion County, Alabama, and a farmer by occupation. Another Muster Roll stated William enlisted in Decatur, Alabama. The November and December 1864 Muster Roll stated he was absent without leave since December 10, 1864, however, he was shown as present in January and February 1865. The March and April 1865 Muster Roll stated William was absent, a prisoner of war since March 10, 1865, which is when the Battle of Monroe's Crossroads in North Carolina took place. The May and June 1865 Muster Roll listed him as still absent, dropped from prisoner of war and listed as missing in action. The Company Muster-Out Roll dated October 20, 1865, at Huntsville, Alabama did not list William C. Evins except to say he was due a bounty of $100. It also stated he had been a prisoner of war since March 10, 1865, when he was captured near Fayetteville, North Carolina, and was not mustered out. The January and February 1865 Muster Roll stated he was a paroled prisoner of war at Camp Chase, Ohio, dated April 10, 1865, was present at Camp Chase, and captured March 10, 1865, at Solemn (Solomon's) Grove, North Carolina. William C. Evins name appeared on the Company Returns as follows: August 1864, he was on daily duty as company cook; December 1864, he was absent without leave; March 1865 to May 1865, he was absent, prisoner of war March 10, 1865; June 1865, he was Missing in Action from Huntsville, Alabama June 13, 1865, before being reported as prisoner of war. The Company Descriptive Book showed him to have been 19 years of age, 5'-7" tall, having a dark complexion, hazel eyes, black hair, born in Marion County, Alabama, and a farmer by occupation. He had been enrolled in the 1st Alabama by Lt. Pease. William was listed as being a paroled prisoner of war at Boulware and Cox's Wharf on March 30, 1865. William was furloughed for 30 days from April 9, 1865.

Ezell, James - James Ezell enlisted in Company M of the 1st Alabama Cavalry, USV on September 14, 1863, in Chewalla, Tennessee for a period of 3 years. He was enrolled by Captain Lomax but never mustered in. The Company Descriptive Book recorded him as being 18 years of age, 5'-10" tall, having a dark complexion, black eyes, dark hair, born in McNairy County, Tennessee, and a farmer by occupation. He was reported to have deserted October 26 1863, from Glendale, Mississippi. However, that was the day of the Battle of Vincent's Crossroads in Bay Springs, Mississippi, and he may have been captured or wounded, or both.

Ezell, Thomas L. - Thomas L. Ezell enlisted in Company M of the 1st Alabama Cavalry, USV as a private on August 9, 1863, in Chewalla, Tennessee for a period of 3 years, and was mustered in December 29, 1863, in Corinth, Mississippi. The Company Descriptive Book recorded him as 31 years of age, 5'-8" tall, having a dark complexion, hazel eyes, dark hair, born in Lauderdale County, Alabama, and a farmer by occupation. The January and February 1864 Muster Roll recorded him as being absent, sick in the hospital in Memphis, Tennessee since February 20, 1863. A receipt in his records stated his wife was Mrs. Nancy Ezell. His name appeared on the Hospital Muster Roll for Small Pox U.S.A. General Hospital in Memphis, Tennessee, stating he was admitted February 19, 1864. One of the Small Pox U.S.A. General Hospital Muster Rolls stated he died March 11, 1864. His name appeared on the Returns as follows: December 1863, on daily duty as company cook; December 1863 through January 1864, on daily duty as a wagon maker; February 1864, absent, sick in the hospital in Memphis, Tennessee; February 1864, on daily duty as wagon maker; March 1864 to March 10, 1864, in small pox hospital in Memphis, Tennessee. Thomas L. Ezell died March 10, 1864, of smallpox in the hospital at Memphis, and was buried in the Memphis National Cemetery in Memphis, Shelby County, Tennessee.

- F -

Fagan, William B. - William B. Fagan enlisted in Company G of the 1st Alabama Cavalry, USV on April 24, 1864, in Mooresville, Alabama, and mustered in the same day in Rome, Georgia. The Muster and Descriptive Book recorded him as 18 years of age, 5'-5½" tall, having a light complexion, blue eyes, light hair, born in Forsythe County, Georgia, and a farmer by occupation. He mustered out October 20, 1865, in Huntsville, Alabama owing the US Government $9.55 for losing 1 halter, 1 curb bridle, 1 carbine cartridge box, 1 mess pan and 1 camp kettle.

Fairfield, Micajah F. - Micajah F. Fairfield enlisted in the Field and Staff of the 1st Alabama Cavalry, USV as a major on April 22, 1863, in Corinth, Mississippi, for a period of 1 year at age 40. He was appointed Major from 1st Lieutenant of the 15th Illinois Cavalry by order of General Dodge, by authority of the secretary of war on April 23, 1863, when he was mustered in. He was relieved from duty April 22, 1864, due to expiration of term of service. His name appeared on the Returns as follows: April 1863, Present, detached from Ford's Independent Cavalry Company by Special Order District Headquarters and not aggregated; May 1863, Present, detached from Company L, 15th Illinois Cavalry; June 1863, Present, mustered as major since last return; July – September 1863, present, commanding regiment; October 1863, Absent, on leave by Special Order, Headquarters 16th Army Corps in Memphis, Tennessee; November 1863, Present, on duty with regiment; December 1863 – January 1864, Present; February, Present, numerically; March 1864, Numerically present. There was a letter in Fairfield's military records dated June 26, 1863, from Glendale, Mississippi to Brigadier General G.M. Dodge, Commanding District of Corinth, which stated: General, we the undersigned officers of the 1st Regiment Alabama Cavalry would respectfully request that you appoint Major M.F. Fairfield to be Lieutenant of our regiment. Signed: L.W. Day, Adjutant; William T. Gray; A.B. Stuart, Assistant Surgeon; Frank C. Burdick, Captain Company A; James M. Smith, 1st Lieutenant; G.W. Slaughter, 2nd Lieutenant; E.D. Chandler, Captain Company E; Sanford Trammel, 1st Lieutenant Company E; Albert E. Murdock, P.H. Reed, Captain Company G; Isaac A.J. Parker, 1st Lieutenant, Company G; Dudley F. Eaves, 2nd Lieutenant Company G; Phillip A. Sternberg, 1st Lieutenant Company B; James C. Swift, 2nd Lieutenant Company B; A.T. Cameron, Captain Company C; John Latta, Captain Company C; James D. Holly, 2nd Lieutenant, Company C; Jude H. Shurtliff, Captain Company D; and John A. Snelling, 2nd Lieutenant Company D. (These officers must have thought highly of Major Micajah F. Fairfield to have all requested him.) The following is a letter found in Fairfield's military records: Camp 1st Alabama Cavalry US Volunteers, Glendale, Mississippi September 13, 1863, W.F. Fairfield, Major 1st Alabama Cavalry USV has applied for a certificate on which to gain an application for leave of absence. I do certify that I have carefully examined this officer and find that he is laboring in general debility the result of an attack of remittent fever partaking of a typhoid character on or about the 1st of June 1863. The Major never having recovered from the attack has been gradually failing for the last six weeks. So that is my opinion that not only a change climate but a change of diet and a season of rest and quiet is necessary to prevent permanent disability and endangering of his life. I further declare that in my opinion he will not be able to resume his duties in a less period of 20 days. Signed A.B. Stuart, Surgeon, 1st Alabama Cavalry. On September 13, 1863, Major Fairfield requested a leave of absence to go to Ottawa, Illinois. His leave was granted.

The 15th Illinois Cavalry was based in Tennessee until March 1863 when they were transferred to Corinth, Mississippi where General Dodge detailed Fairfield to help recruit a regiment of patriotic white Southerners who would fight for restoration of the Union. He took command of the 1st Alabama Cavalry in April 1863.

It was during this duty that he contracted typhoid fever. In September of 1863, the regimental surgeon warned him that the two day scouting missions were doing him physical injustices and that he should no longer expose himself to the heat of the day or night air. He finally resigned and returned to Ottawa, but after his physician recommended a change of climate, he moved to Minnesota in 1866 and started a business. He died there in 1872 of tuberculosis. His wife died in 1899 of the same disease.

Major Fairfield was born in Pittsford, Vermont but was a resident of Ottawa, Illinois where he worked in the lumber industry. He was married and had three children. The 15th Illinois Cavalry was based in Tennessee until March 1863 when they were transferred to Corinth, Mississippi where General Dodge detailed Fairfield to help recruit a regiment of patriotic white Southerners who would fight for restoration of the Union. He took command of the 1st Alabama Cavalry US in April 1863. It was during this duty that he contracted typhoid fever. In September of 1863, the regimental surgeon warned him that the two day scouting missions were doing him physical injustice and that he should no longer expose himself to the heat of the day or night air. He finally resigned and returned to Ottawa, Illinois but after his physician recommended a change of climate, he moved to Minnesota in 1866 and started a business. He died there in 1872 of tuberculosis. His wife died in 1899 of the same disease. He is buried in Lakewood Cemetery in Minneapolis, Minnesota.

Farmer, Simon - Simon Farmer, name also appeared as Jack Farmer, was born in Spartanburg District, South Carolina. He enlisted in Company A of the 1st Alabama Cavalry, USV as an undercook on October 24, 1864, in Rome, Georgia for a period of 3 years. He was recorded as being "Colored". His Muster and Descriptive Roll recorded him as 39 years of age, 6'-1" tall, having a black complexion, black eyes, black hair, born in Spartanburg, South Carolina, and a farmer by occupation. His name appeared on the Returns for November 1864 as follows: November 1864 to September 1865, on daily duty as Regimental Teamster. He mustered out October 20, 1865, in Huntsville, Alabama and the Muster-Out roll recorded him as 30 years of age. The other records stated he was 39 years of age.

Faulkner, Frank - Frank Faulkner enlisted in Company E of the 1st Alabama Cavalry, USV, as a private on December 25, 1862, in Chewalla, Tennessee for a period of 1 year, and mustered in December 28, 1862, in Corinth, Mississippi where he operated as a scout. He died of fever on March 20, 1862, in the U.S. Military Hospital in Corinth, Mississippi. His age did not appear on the rolls.

Faulkner, William - Only one card was found for William Faulkner which was filed at the end of the last roll of microfilm of the 1st Alabama Cavalry, USV records. It recorded him as a private in Company H, stating he was on daily duty as company cook in March 1864. No further information relative to this soldier was found.*

Feamster, William J. - William J. Feamster enlisted in Company A of the 1st Alabama Cavalry, USV as a private on January 3, 1864, in Camp Davies, Mississippi for a period of 3 years. He was enrolled by Lieutenant Hinds, and was mustered in March 5, 1864, in Memphis, Tennessee. The Muster and Descriptive Roll listed him as being 18 years of age, 5'-8" tall, having a light complexion, gray eyes, dark hair, born in Lowndes County, Mississippi, and a farmer by occupation. In January and February 1864, he was listed on a Hospital Muster Roll for Overton U.S.A. General Hospital in Memphis, Tennessee as being present. The Company Muster Roll dated February 29, 1864, listed him as being absent, sick in the U.S.A. General Hospital in Memphis, Tennessee. He was also absent from October 3, 1864, through February 1865, sick in the hospital in Indianapolis, Indiana, and stated he had never received any bounty. The March and April 1865 Muster Roll showed him to have been absent, on detached service in Decatur, Alabama. William J. Feamster's name appeared on the Returns as follows: February 1864, absent, sick in General Hospital in Memphis, Tennessee since February 1, 1864; June 1864, absent, sick in Field Hospital near Ackworth, Georgia; December 1864, absent, sick in General Hospital; June 1865, discharged for disability at Jeffersonville, Indiana, time unknown. Another muster roll stated he was discharged in the hospital in Indianapolis, Indiana on November 21, 1864, on Surgeon's Certificate of Disability, have not received notice of this man's being paid since June 30, 1864, not any amount of clothing drawn since that date. The Surgeon's Certificate of Disability stated the following: "I certify that I have carefully examined the said William J. Feamster of Captain Hinds Company and find him incapable of performing the duties of a soldier because of chronic diarrhea and extreme emaciation contracted in the service and _____ on measles. Has done no duty in service for seven months. Not able for field duty and not physically able to enter or enlist in the Veteran Reserve Corps due to a total disability. Discharged this 23rd November 1864, at Indianapolis, Indiana. A note at the bottom of the Certificate of Disability stated Feamster desired to be addressed at Indianapolis, Marion County, Indiana. A letter from the Quartermaster's Office, U.S. Military, R.R. Transportation, Department of the Cumberland, Nashville, Tennessee, September 11, 1864, states: Captain: I have this day furnished transportation to Private William J. Feamster, of your command from Nashville, Tennessee to Louisville, Kentucky, on furlough distance 185 miles at cost to government ($3.80) Three Dollars and Eighty Cents. Same to be stopped against pay due him. I am, Captain, very respectfully, your obedient servant, S.B. Browal (?).

Feltman, Benjamin F. - Benjamin F. Feltman enlisted in Company L of the 1st Alabama Cavalry, USV on September 25, 1863, as a Private for 1 year in Fayette County, Alabama, and was stationed at Glendale, Mississippi. He was mustered out September 28, 1864, in Rome, Georgia by reason of expiration of term of service. His Muster-Out Roll stated his pay was due from enlistment. He reenlisted March 1, 1865, in Stevenson, Alabama for three years and mustered into service April 18, 1865, in Nashville, Tennessee. No bounty was paid and he served one year of this enlistment. His Muster and Descriptive Roll recorded him as 22 years of age, 5'-6" tall, having a fair complexion, blue eyes, light hair, born in Fayette County, Alabama, and a farmer by occupation. He was listed as being absent with leave in May and June 1865. Benjamin was mustered out October 20, 1865, in Huntsville, Alabama with the rest of the regiment with pay due from enlistment and a bounty of $100 due him.

Benjamin F. Feltman was born November 12, 1842, in Fayette County, Alabama and died February 13, 1918, probably in Fayette County, Alabama. He was buried in the Feltman Cemetery in Fayette County, Alabama. He was the son of Jacob Benjamin Feltman born August 27, 1799, and died February 5, 1879. On May 16, 1838, Benjamin F. Feltman married Elvira Traywick, born August 22, 1813, and died June 24, 1901. On October 5, 1867, Benjamin Franklin Feltman married Mary Jane Whitley at her home. Mary Jane Whitley was born February 18, 1847, in North Carolina and died May 27, 1929. According to one descendant, Benjamin and Mary Jane Feltman had the following children: George W., born September 10, 1868, died January 22, 1949; Nancy, born June 17, 1970, died August 15, 1874; Elvira, born May 7, 1872; Jerry Marcel, born June 15, 1874, died August 2, 1905; Hampton, born May 25, 1876, died December 25, 1954; Solomon Waco, born March 10, 1878, died December 20, 1972; Buck, born April 2, 1880; Lou, born July 3, 1884, died September 22, 1945; Pallie, born November 8, 1886; died December 20, 1972; Spencer, born April 1888, died April 24, 1962; Hester, born 1890 and Kyle Feltman, born November 15, 1892.

Feltman, Isham Botener - Isham Botener Feltman enlisted in Company L of the 1st Alabama Cavalry, USV as a private on September 25, 1863, in Fayette County, Alabama for a period of 1 year. He was enrolled by Captain Tramel. Apparently he and his brother, Benjamin, went together to join the Union Army. His enlistment was credited to Ripley, Chautauqua County, New York. He was mustered in the same day in Glendale, Mississippi, and mustered out on September 28, 1864, in Rome, Georgia, the same date as his brother. The Muster and Descriptive Roll recorded him as 24 years of age, 5'-5" tall, having a fair complexion, blue eyes, light hair, born in Fayette County, Alabama, and a farmer by occupation. The Company Muster Roll from December 31, 1863, through April 30, 1864, recorded Isham as absent, sent to Regimental Hospital April 28, 1864. However, he was recorded as present in May and June 1864. Isham also re-enlisted on January 1, 1865 in Stevenson, Alabama, mustered in the same day in Nashville, Tennessee and paid a bounty of $100. The January and February 1865 Muster Roll recorded him as absent, on duty with detached 1st Alabama Cavalry in Stevenson, Alabama since January 1, 1865. The May and June 1865 Muster Roll recorded him as absent with leave since June 5, 1865. Feltman and his brother, Benjamin, mustered out on October 20, 1865, discharged due to expiration of term of service.

Another twist in this family is, Nancy Margaret Feltman, daughter of Jacob Benjamin Feltman and Elvira Traywick, above, married Fernando "Frank" Cortez Burdick, who was a Captain in the 1st Alabama Cavalry, USV. (Read story about Burdick, earlier in book)

Isham B. Feltman was born November 10, 1840, in Fayette County, Alabama and died July 1, 1888, in Cross County, Arkansas of typhoid fever. On June 1, 1865, he married Sarah Elizabeth Rutledge, daughter of William Manley Rutledge and Nancy Ball Lawson. William was born in 1808 in Cumberland County, Kentucky and died 1866 in Walker County, Alabama. Sarah Elizabeth was born April 3, 1816, in St. Clair County, Alabama and died June 27, 1900, in Elmo, Kaufman County, Texas.

After the war, Isham filed a Southern Claim stating he had turned over a mule to the army in Rome, Georgia: To the Commissioners of Claims, Under Act of 3rd March, 1871, Washington, D.C.:

The petition of Isham Feltman, respectfully represents: That your petitioner is a resident of the county of Winston in the State of Alabama; that his post office address is Larissa, in said county and State; and that at the time his claim and each item thereof as above set forth accrued he was a resident of the County of Fayette, and State of Alabama; that he is the original owner of said claim; that he has never sold, assigned or transferred the same or any part thereof to any person; that no mortgage, bill of sale or other lien of like nature has at any time rested upon it, or any part thereof, nor has it been attached or taken in execution; that the same has not been paid by the United States or any of their officers or agents, nor have the United States any legal offset against the same or any part thereof; that he is the sole owner of the said claim, no other person being interested therein; that said claim does not contain any charge for property which was destroyed or stolen by the troops or other persons; that the rates or prices charged are reasonable and just, and do not exceed the market rate or price of like stores or property at the time and place stated; all of which your petitioner states of his own knowledge.

Your petitioner further states that he is now and was at the time the several items of his said claim accrued, as stated therein, a citizen of the United States; that he remained a loyal adherent to the cause and Government of the United States, during the war of 1861; and was so loyal before and at the time of the taking or furnishing of the property for which this claim is made. And your petitioner further represents, and of his own knowledge states, that on the 1st day of October, A.D. 1864, at Rome, Georgia, in the State of Georgia the following property or stores were furnished by your petitioner for the use of the army of the United States, and for which payment is claimed, viz:

1 mule ($125); 1 mare ($100).

Which said property or stores being of the kind, quantity, quality and value above stated was furnished to QM McWorkman belonging to the 1st Alabama Cavalry Volunteers, Department of the United states Army, in the service of the United states, whose rank was Lieutenant of the 1st Regiment of Alabama Cavalry Volunteers acting as quartermaster, who, as your petitioner has been informed and believes was stationed at Rome, Georgia under the command of Col. Godfrey, who at that time had command of the United States forces in the District in which said property was furnished.

And your petitioner further represents that he has been informed and believes that the said stores or property was furnished by your petitioner as above stated and removed to camp at Rome, Georgia for the use of Company L of the 1st Regiment of Alabama Cavalry Volunteers; that at the [taking] of said property, or stores, no vouchers, receipt or other writing was given therefor by the person taking the same as aforesaid or received at any time by your petitioner. Your petitioner further states that the claim, within and above mentioned has never been presented to Congress of any officer or agent of the U.S. Government or to any department thereof and that no action or decision has been had in regard to the same. Your petitioner hereby constitutes and appoints Thomas C. Fullerton, Attorney-at-Law, of Washington, D.C. true and lawful attorney, with full power of substation and association, to prosecute this claim, and to receive a draft payable to the order of your petitioner for such amount as may be allowed, and to do all acts necessary and property in the premises.

Your petitioner therefore prays that said claim may be examined and considered under the provisions of the Act of Congress approved 3rd March, 1871, dated this 4th day of February 1873 [signed] I.B. Feltman; Witnesses: [signed] John Randolph and David Hall

State of Alabama, County of Walker: I.B. Feltman, being duly sworn deposes and says, that he is the petitioner named in the foregoing petition, and who signed the same; that the matters therein stated are true, of the deponent's own knowledge except as to those matters which are stated on information and belief, and as to those matters he believes them to be true; and deponent further says that he did not voluntarily serve in the Confederate army or navy, either as an officer, soldier, or sailor, or in any other capacity, at any time during the late rebellion; that he never voluntarily furnished any stores, supplies, or other material aid to said Confederate army or navy, or to the Confederate government, or to any officer, department or adherent of the same in support thereof, and that he never voluntarily accepted or exercised the functions of any office whatsoever under, or yielded voluntary support to, the said Confederate government. [signed] I.B. Feltman. Sworn to, and subscribed before me this 4th day of February 1873 and I certify that the affiant is to me personally known, and that I read over to him this affidavit before made oath therein. [signed] John Brown, Judge of Probate.

The mule was large medium size, 6 years old, was sound and in good order. And a good riding mule, and at the time turned over to said Quartermaster Sergeant was worth $125 in U.S. money. Said mule was turned over for the use of the army of the U.S. and was used as such, by the troops of the 1st Regiment Alabama Cavalry Volunteers. [signed] I.B. Feltman, Attest: [signed] John C. Moore, Special Commissioner

To all whom it may concern: Know ye, that Isham B. Feltman, Private of Lieutenant Hugh L. Bolton's Company L, First Regiment of Alabama Cavalry Volunteers who was enrolled on the first day of January, one thousand eight hundred and sixty-five to serve three years of during the war, is hereby discharged from the service of the United States this twentieth day of October 1865, at Huntsville, Alabama. (No objection to his being re-enlisted is known to exist).

Remarks: The claimant was a soldier in the First Alabama Cavalry Regiment Federal service. He enlisted the 25th of September 1863, served one year, was discharged and re-enlisted in January 1865 and served until the October following. When the testimony was taken, the claim produced before the Special Commissioner was for a mule only. The petition was with the Commissioners at Washington. No mention was made of the mare and no testimony relating to the mare was given. If this claim was honest, something would have been said relating to the mare. The claimant testifies that he turned over the mule at Rome, Georgia to Ira Pratt, Quartermaster Sergeant on or about October 1, 1864. No voucher was given and none asked for. He is corroborated in this statement by his brother who is a witness. It is alleged that the Quartermaster promised to pay for the mule. No reason is given why payment was not made. No complaint was made and no efforts by the claimant to get pay. We believe there was some good reason why this mule was not paid for if it was really the property of the claimant and turned over as he alleges. Explanation upon this point is indispensable to a satisfactory establishment of the claim. It is disallowed. [signed] A.O. Aldis, J.B. Howell, O. Ferriss, Commissioners of Claims. (Transcribed and submitted by Robin A. Sterling. However, the author has condensed the claim.)

Felton, Abraham - Abraham Felton enlisted and mustered into Company I of the 1st Alabama Cavalry, USV on July 21, 1862, in Huntsville, Alabama. He was enrolled by Captain H.C. Bankhead for a period of 3 years. The Company Descriptive Book recorded him as 30 years of age, 5'-9½" tall, having a dark complexion, hazel eyes, dark hair, born in Paulding County, Georgia, and a teacher by occupation. Felton was one of the early enlistees shipped to Nashville immediately after they mustered in, and were merged with the 1st Middle Tennessee Cavalry which later became the 5th Tennessee Cavalry. He was merged with Company D of the 1st Middle Cavalry. A note in his records stated that Company D of the 1st Tennessee Cavalry became Company D of the 1st Middle Tennessee Cavalry, and then the 5th Tennessee Cavalry. When they left Nashville and went back to Alabama, they were in Company K of the 1st Alabama Cavalry, USV. The Company Muster Roll dated November 30, 1862, stated he was absent, sick in Hospital #12 in Nashville, Tennessee. Abraham Felton died of typhoid fever December 22, 1862, in Hospital #12 in Nashville, Davidson County, Tennessee. His effects at the time of his death were recorded as: 1 overcoat; 1 jacket; 1 pair of pants, worthless: 1 hat; 2 pair of breeches; 1 handkerchief; 1 comb; 1 purse containing .50 cents; 1 thin plaster, worthless; and 1 box of gun caps.

Ferguson, J.C. - Only one card was found for J.C. Ferguson which was filed at the end of the last roll of microfilm of the 1st Alabama Cavalry, USV records. It recorded him as a private in Company H, stating he enlisted on October 18, 1863, in Glendale, Mississippi. No further information relative to this soldier was found.*

Fielder, Enos T. - Enos T. Fielder enlisted in Company H of the 1st Alabama Cavalry, USV as a private on February 17, 1865, in Stevenson, Alabama for a term of 3 years. He was enrolled by Captain James W. DeVaney and was mustered in February 19, 1865, in Nashville, Tennessee. The Company Descriptive Book records him as being 19 years of age, 5'-6" tall, having a light complexion, black eyes, black hair, born in DeKalb County, Georgia, and a farmer by occupation. His enlistment was credited to Sherman, Chautauqua County, New York, and he was paid a bounty of $100. He mustered out

October 20, 1865, in Huntsville, Alabama owing the U.S. Government $10.50 for losing 1 Colt pistol, 1 saber belt and plate, and 1 pistol cartridge box. He was paid a bounty of $100.

Fielder, John N. - John N. Fielder and his brother, Enos, above, enlisted in Company H of the 1st Alabama Cavalry, USV as a private on February 17, 1865, in Stevenson, Alabama for a term of 3 years. He was enrolled by Captain James W. DeVaney and mustered in February 19, 1865. His enlistment was credited to Sherman, Chautauqua County, New York. The Company Descriptive Book recorded him as being 18 years of age, 5'-6" tall, having a light complexion, blue eyes, light hair, born in DeKalb County, Georgia, and a farmer by occupation. He was appointed Sergeant April 1, 1865. He was mustered out October 20, 1865, in Huntsville, Alabama owing the U.S. Government $11.40 for losing 1 Colt pistol, 1 saber belt and plate, 1 pistol cartridge box, and 1 pistol holster. He was paid a bounty of $100.

Fields, Isaac - Isaac Fields enlisted in Company D of the 1st Alabama Cavalry, USV as a private on May 20, 1862, at Decatur, Alabama for a period of 3 years. He was enrolled by Lieutenant Pease and was mustered in June 16, 1864, at Decatur. The Muster and Descriptive Roll recorded him as 45 years of age, 5'-10" tall, having a dark complexion, blue eyes, dark hair, born Jefferson County, Alabama and a farmer by occupation. He received no bounty. In September 1864, he was on daily duty as a company cook. The January and February 1865 Muster Roll listed him as being absent, sick in General Hospital since January 28, 1865. Isaac was mustered out October 20, 1865, in Huntsville, Alabama. He owed the U.S. Government $1.30 for losing one cartridge box. It stated he was due $100 for bounty. A Hospital Muster Roll from U.S.A. General Hospital in Savannah, Georgia dated February 28, 1865, stated Isaac had been attached to the hospital since February 1, 1865, as a patient. It also stated Isaac was last paid by August 31, 1864, by Major Hale, and was due a bounty of $300. Isaac was returned to duty March 6, 1865.

Isaac Fields, Jr. was born December 18, 1818, in Jefferson County, Alabama to Isaac Fields, Sr. and Anna LNU. Isaac, Jr. married Esther Wedgeworth August 24, 1841, in Greene County, Alabama and had the following children: Sarah Jane Fields and John Westley Fields. Esther died June 27, 1849, and Isaac married Elizabeth Linn on November 7, 1850, in Jefferson County, Alabama and had the following children: Andrew Jackson, James Elbert, William Joseph, Isaac Watson, Edward Gray H. "Babe", Maranda Elizabeth, Anna Elisa, and Mary Matilda Fields. Isaac died January 3, 1893, in Jefferson County, Alabama and is buried in the Fraternal Cemetery at Pratt City, Alabama.

Fields, William - William Fields enlisted in Company C of the 1st Alabama Cavalry, USV as a private on December 20, 1862, in Corinth, Mississippi for a period of 1 year and was mustered in December 22, 1862, in Corinth. The March and April 1863 Muster Roll recorded him as being absent, on detached service as scout from December 22, 1862, through December 1863, by order of Brigadier General G.M. Dodge. His name appeared on the Returns as follows: March 1863 through December 1863, on detached service as a scout from December 22, 1862, for General Dodge.

Files, James L. - One card was found for James L. Files which was filed at the end of the last roll of microfilm of the 1st Alabama Cavalry, USV records. It stated he was a private in Company L of the 1st Alabama Cavalry, USV, and was killed in action December 24, 1864, at Jack's Creek, Tennessee. Some of his records were mixed up with those of Jesse I. Files.

The Files Family of Alabama: A Family of Patriots

The blood of patriots flowed deeply in the veins of many members of the Files families of Blount, Fayette and Walker Counties, Alabama. Their patriarch, Captain John Files, was a soldier of the American Revolution and hero in the Battle of Cowpens (South Carolina.) Captain Files and his three sons served together with Colonel Andrew Pickens in the South Carolina Volunteers. One of those sons, Jeremiah Benton Files, moved south into what is now Blount County about 1800. His son, Jeremiah, Jr. married Peggy Dunn there in 1818 and they had three sons: Jesse (b. 1825), Jeremiah

Franklin (b. 1836) and Thomas Benton (b. 1839,) all of whom were patriots in the First Alabama Cavalry, U.S.V.

The oldest, Jesse, and his sons, John H. and Jesse Lee Files, mustered in at Glendale, Mississippi on September 25, 1863. All of them served in Company L with the rank of Private. The elder Jesse served primarily as a scout and recruiter and was on such an assignment on December 24, 1863 when his son Jesse Lee was wounded in the Battle of Jack's Creek, tended by his cousin John. The 18-year-old Jesse died three days later in the hospital at Corinth. Private John Files continues to serve until September 28, 1864, when he mustered out at Rome, Georgia. The elder Jesse Files mustered out at the same time. After the war he and his son John migrated to Stone County, Arkansas where Jesse died May 21, 1906.

The second son of Jeremiah Benton Files, Jeremiah Franklin, enrolled at Glendale at the same time as his uncle and cousins and served originally in Company L but later rose to the rank of 2nd Lieutenant and served with Company A. His service as a recruiter had begun before he enrolled in the Union army. Ill-equipped to serve as an officer, he resigned on May 13, 1864, at Snake Gap, Georgia.

On March 23. 1863, at Glendale, Mississippi. Thomas Benton enlisted as a Private in the First Alabama and was assigned to Company A. During the spring of that year the company served as guides and scouts for General Dodge's expedition in the area of Decatur in North Alabama. They took part in raids on Pikeville, Alabama, Fulton, Mississippi and on Tuscumbia and Barnesville, Mississippi. During the Barnesville, encounter on Yellow Creek, Thomas was wounded in the arm and was thrown from his horse. He landed on a tree stump, resulting in severe damage to his lungs, right shoulder and wrist. The muster rolls for September list him as First Sergeant.

On December 22nd, upon expiration of his term of enlistment, Thomas mustered out of the army at Camp Davis (Davies), Mississippi, but he remained at the camp until sometime in January 1864. Apparently fearing to return home, where he would have been subjected to forced service in the Confederate army or perhaps even to execution because of his service to the Union; he spent the rest of the war hanging out with various Union units. It is not known whether he participated in any of their skirmishes, but from February until September 10, 1864, he was in Pulaski, Illinois, near where the Ohio River joins the Mississippi. He then returned south, to Lavergne, Tennessee with Ohio troops under Captain Nash. There on December 4th, he was captured by Confederate troops under General Wood, and taken to a prison near Nashville where he was confined for about six weeks before being moved to Corinth. On January 17, 1865, he escaped and hid out in the mountains of Marion County, Alabama, where he encountered some Union troops from Indiana. With them, he went to Decatur but, having misplaced his discharge papers, he was arrested as a suspected Rebel and sent to a Union military prison in Nashville. In some way he was able to convince the Provost Marshall, Captain Goodwin, that he was not a Reb, and was released.

After General Lee's surrender at Appomattox on April 9, 1865, it was relatively safe for Thomas to return to his home on Wolf Creek in Walker County, where he arrived sometime in the late summer or early fall, about two years after mustering out of the army. One of his post-war children, Eva Lucinda, married James Patmon Cooner, Jr. who was the son of another veteran of the First Alabama, James Carroll Cooner. Written and submitted by John Bush.

<u>Files, Jeremiah Franklin</u> - Jeremiah Franklin Files enlisted in Company L of the 1st Alabama Cavalry, USV on September 25, 1863, in Fayette County, Alabama for a term of 1 year and was mustered into service as 2nd Lieutenant to date from October 8, 1863, at Glendale, Mississippi. The January and February 1864 Muster Roll recorded him as being absent, assigned to duty with Company A. Regimental Order 38, January 7, 1864. The Muster Roll for March and April of 1864, recorded him as absent, sick in Officer's Hospital in Memphis, Tennessee. He resigned May 13, 1864, in Snake Gap Creek, Georgia. Jeremiah Files' name appeared on the Returns as follows: September and October 1863, Present, on duty with company. Elected by company vote; November 1863, absent, on scout by order of Colonel Spencer; December 1863 and January 1864, Present; February 1864, Assigned to duty in Company A January 7, 1864, by Special Order No. 38; February 1864, Present numerically; March and April 1864, absent, sick in Memphis, Tennessee. A letter from Jeremiah was found in his military records and it stated the following: Headquarters, 1st Alabama Cavalry Volunteers, Memphis, Tennessee, dated March 10, 1864, Colonel, I hereby respectfully tender my resignation as 2nd

Lieutenant 1st Regiment Alabama Cavalry Volunteers. I am incompetent physically and mentally. I was appointed 2nd Lieutenant, 1st Alabama Cavalry September 25, 1863, by authority of Secretary of War, Brigadier General Dodge. I have never done any duty as an officer except as an officer of the guard a few times. I have never had command of a company, never anticipated for, or had in my possession any government property of any kind. I know I am incompetent and desire to quit the service as an officer, if my health will permit, I will endeavor to serve my country in a capacity where my services will benefit it. I have the honor to be very respectfully your obedient servant, Lieutenant Jeremiah F. Files, 1st Alabama Cavalry Volunteers. Another letter in Jeremiah's records stated the following: Headquarters Department, Army of the Tennessee, Huntsville, Alabama April 20, 1864, Special Order #79, Extract, IV. The following named officers, having tendered their resignations based on mental and physical incapacity , are hereby honorably discharged the service of the United States with condition they shall receive no final payments until they have satisfied the Pay Department that they are not indebted to the government: Jeremiah F. Files, 2nd Lieutenant, 1st Alabama Cavalry Volunteers. By order of Major General James B. McPherson; Sergeant W.T. Clark, Assistant Auditor General. There are other letters in his records but mostly illegible. One stated that Jeremiah assisted in the organization of the company and furnished a number of men. He was a strong Union man and willing to do anything to further the cause. However, he did not have much education and had never commanded a company before. He requested to be honorably discharged. Captain Sanford Tramel requested that the honorable discharge be given to Files as soon as possible. Jeremiah F. Files was relieved from duty and dropped from the rolls May 13, 1864, at Snake Gap Creek, Georgia.

Jeremiah F. Files was born June 2, 1836, in Blount County, Alabama and died April 14, 1901, in Beech Grove, Walker County, Alabama. He was the son of Jeremiah Benton Files, Jr. and his wife, Margaret "Peggy" Dunn. On February 1, 1856, Jeremiah married Rhoda E. Feltman in Walker County, Alabama. Rhoda was the daughter of Jacob Benjamin and Elvira Traywick Feltman. Children of Jeremiah F. and Rhoda E. Feltman Files were: Jeremiah Benjamin, born February 6, 1858, died August 22, 1881; James Dennison, born August 26, 1856, died 1863; John Thomas, born September 25, 1859, died February 1, 1942; Miranda Jane, born May 1, 1861, died December 27, 1938; Jerome Jasper, born March 7, 1866, died February 22, 1947; Kate Fargo, born February 1, 1868, died 1871; George E., born December 12, 1869, died November 23, 1943; Roscoe Conklin, born February 6, 1872; died December 21, 1959; Eli Logan, born February 6, 1874, died May 29, 1959; and Oliver Perry Files, born April 5, 1876, died January 31, 1962. Jeremiah F. Files' father, Jeremiah Benton Files, Jr., was born 1797 in Anderson County, South Carolina and died 1870 in Carbon Hill, Walker County, Alabama. His wife, Margaret "Peggy" Dunn, was born about 1799 in Greene County, Tennessee and died about 1870 in Fayette County, Alabama. Rhonda Elizabeth Feltman, Jeremiah F. Files' wife, was born April 22, 1837, and died December 29, 1892. Her father, Jacob Benjamin Feltman, was born August 27, 1799, in Newberry, South Carolina, and died February 5, 1879, in Carbon Hill, Walker County, Alabama. Jacob's wife, and Rhoda's mother, Elvira Traywick, was born August 22, 1813, in Carroll County, Georgia and died June 24, 1901, in Haleyville, Winston County, Alabama. Their children were: Isham Botener, born November 10, 1840, died July 1, 1888; Benjamin F., born November 12, 1842, died February 18, 1913; George Spencer, born 19 February 19, 1833, died April 13, 1919; Louvinia Elvira "Lovie", born April 3, 1846; Margaret, born about 1848; Helen C., born September 19, 1852, died about 1900; Samuel D., born September 26, 1856; died 1905; Henry Clay, born April 5, 1850, died April 5, 1850; Rhonda Elizabeth, born April 22, 1837, died December 29, 1892; and Sarah Melissa Feltman, born October 26, 1835, and died December 24, 1915.

Jeremiah F. Files' brothers-in-law, Isham B. and Benjamin F. Feltman both enlisted in Company L of the 1st Alabama Cavalry, USV on September 25, 1863 in Fayette County, Alabama. See Feltman brothers information above.

Southern Claim filed by Jeremiah Franklin Files.

In case No. 11312 of the Southern Claims Commission filed by Jeremiah Files, he states the following:

In Case No. 116312 of the Southern Claims Commission filed by Jeremiah Files, he states the following: "From April 1862 until June 1865 I spent my time between Fayette County, Alabama and the Union lines, and also in the Union lines... My business was a portion of the time recruiting for the Union Army. I crossed quite a number of times between April 1862 and March 1864 for the purpose of getting Union men out of the rebel lines and getting them into the Union lines. I then joined the Union Army at Glendale, Mississippi, I joined the First Regiment Alabama Cavalry Volunteers commanded by Colonel George E. Spencer and remained with the army until Nov. Following on the 24th day of November 1863, I left camp at Camp Davies, Mississippi with two other soldiers and came back to Fayette County, Alabama and got about fifty Union men and reached camp at Camp Davies taking the above mentioned number of Union men with me and reached there on the 13th day of December 1863. I then remained in the Union lines, until the summer of 1864. I then taken up the same occupation gathering Union men for the Union army and was so employed until the surrender. In the summer of 1865, I came back to my farm where I now reside.

I was threatened by every rebel that knew me with damage to my person and property. I was threatened to be hanged, shot, and even burned, all on account of my Union sentiments. I influenced about five hundred men to go in to the army...

I did not have any relatives in the rebel army except cousins. I had two brothers and two nephews, also two brothers in law and quite a number of cousins in the Union army....."

Southern Claim No: 11631, Date of Hearing: January 30, 1873.

Place of Residence: Fayette County, Kansas Post Office (Walker County, Alabama,) Age: 37 years

Place of Residence at Time of Incident/s: "My farm" on Wolf Creek in Fayette County

Remarks: He was threatened by the rebels with damage to his person and property – they threatened to hang him, shoot him and burn him. They took his property and even drove his wife and children away from home after taking all they had to subsist on. He enlisted 1863 in 1st Alabama Cavalry at Glendale, Mississippi; served part-time as 2nd Lieutenant and part-time as recruiter for the regiment. He influenced about 500 men to join Union army, including two brothers, two nephews, two brothers-in-law and a number of cousins.

Brief Description of Incident/s: On or about October 1, 1863, at Glendale, Mississippi, claimant furnished 1st Lieutenant [William P.] Gray – quartermaster of the 1st Alabama Cavalry – two horses and one saddle worth $285. Witnesses, Testifiers and Others: B.F. Felpman (Feltman), age 28, resident of Fayette County; witnessed incident at Glendale, Mississippi; J.J. Kinet?, resided in Decatur, Morgan County, Alabama in January 1872; Richard Panter, age 33, resident of Fayette County; witnessed incident at Glendale, Mississippi; Colonel George E. Spencer, resided in Washington, D.C., in January 1872; acquainted with claimant since 1862, when he came into Union lines "as a refugee from rebel lines"; J.V. Tiara, witnessed claimant's petition (1872); Jeremiah B. Tiara, witnessed claimant's petition (1872).

Files, Jesse - Jesse Files, also shown as James L. Files, enlisted in Company L of the 1st Alabama Cavalry, USV as a private on September 25, 1863, in Fayette County, Alabama for a period of 1 year. He was enrolled by Captain Tramel and was mustered in September 25, 1863, in Glendale, Mississippi. The Company Descriptive Book recorded him as being 44 years of age, 5'-10" tall, having a dark complexion, blue eyes, dark hair, born in Jefferson County, Alabama, and a farmer by occupation. The Muster-In Roll stated he was 39 years of age. The November and December 1863 Muster Roll recorded him as being absent with leave since November 20, 1863, by order of Lieutenant Colonel Dodds. The January and February 1864 Muster Roll recorded him as being absent, on recruiting service since November 20, 1863, by order of Colonel Spencer. He was also shown as being absent, recruiting in Alabama December 20, 1863, by order of Colonel Spencer. A note in his records stated the following: Mr. Pratt, please let the bearer Mr. Hunting look at the rolls of Company L of the 1st Alabama Cavalry. He has a badly mixed case that we are unable to unravel. Yours truly, O.B.D. On the same note, it stated: March 13, 1895, Mr. Douglas, will you please oblige him and Jones. G.M.P. The next note stated: Name Jesse Files has never been found on rolls of Company L. There was Jesse Files in company who was mustered out with company September 28, 1864, and a Jesse L. Files in the company who was killed in action at Jack's Creek, Tennessee, December 26, 1864. The only other man borne on rolls of company March and April 1864 whose Christian name is "Jesse", is Jesse W. Austin, who died March 3, 1864, in Overton Military Hospital in Memphis, Tennessee of measles. Respectfully H.D. He was mustered out September 28, 1864, in Rome, Georgia due to expiration of term of service. His name appeared on the Returns stating he died March 4, 1864, of disease in Memphis, Tennessee.

However, the next sentence stated he was discharged September 29, 1864, by reason of expiration of term of service.

There were some cards mixed up between the Jesse L. Files' records but Jesse Files, Jr. was killed in action at Jack's Creek, Chester County Tennessee on December 24, 1863. There was a one-day battle between Nathan Bedford Forrest's soldiers and the Union on December 23, 1863, at Jack's Creek, Tennessee. Jesse Files, Sr. was shown as being discharged September 20, 1864, but another card stated he died of disease March 4, 1864, in Memphis, Shelby County, Tennessee. See Jesse, Sr. above, and Jesse, Jr., below.

Jesse Files, Sr., was born about 1825 in Jefferson County, Alabama and died May 21, 1906, in Rushing, Stone County, Arkansas. He was buried in the Rushing Cemetery. He married Malvina Roby about 1844, and had the following children: John H.; Jesse L., Jr.; Thomas G.; Martha N.; Erastus M.; Margaret A.; Roland R.; and E.M.C. Files.

<u>Files, Jesse L., Jr.</u> - Jesse L. Files, Jr. enrolled in Company L of the 1st Alabama Cavalry, USV as a private on September 25, 1863, in Fayette County, Alabama for a term of 1 year. He was enrolled by Captain Tramel and was mustered in September 25, 1863, in Glendale, Mississippi. The Company Descriptive Book recorded him as being 18 years of age, 5'-10" tall, having a fair complexion, blue eyes, light hair, born in Fayette County, Alabama, and a farmer by occupation. The November and December 1863 Muster Roll recorded him as having been killed in action at Jack's Creek, Tennessee on December 24, 1863, however, this was the Jesse. A Notation in his records from the Adjutant General's Office of the War Department dated August 13, 1883, stated the following: Treated in Post Hospital in Corinth, Mississippi December 27, 1863, for gunshot wound and died December 27, 1863, of the gunshot wound.

<u>Files, John H.</u> - John H. Files, son of Jesse L. Files, Sr. and brother of Jesse L. Files, Jr., enlisted in Company L of the 1st Alabama Cavalry, USV as a private on September 25, 1863, in Fayette County, Alabama for a period of 1 year. He was enrolled by Captain Trammel, and was mustered in the same day in Glendale, Mississippi. The Company Descriptive Book recorded him as being 19 years of age, 5'-11" tall, having a fair complexion, blue eyes, light hair, born in Fayette County, Alabama, and a farmer by occupation. He was mustered out September 18, 1864 in Rome, Georgia due to expiration of term of service.

<u>Files, Thomas Benton</u> - The blood of patriots flowed deeply in the veins of Thomas Benton Files and his brother Jeremiah Franklin Files. Their great grandfather was Captain John Files, soldier of the American Revolution and hero in the Battle of Cowpens in South Carolina. Captain Files and his three sons served together with Colonel Andrew Pickens in the South Carolina Volunteers. One of those sons, Jeremiah Benton Files, moved south into what is now Blount County, Alabama about 1800.

Thomas Benton Files enlisted in Company A of the 1st Alabama Cavalry, USV as a private on March 23, 1863, in Glendale, Mississippi for a period of 1 year, and was mustered in March 24, 1863, in Glendale. He was promoted to Sergeant July 1, 1863, and was promoted to 1st Sergeant September 16, 1863. In April 1863, he was recorded as being absent, sick in the hospital but it did not state which hospital or where. According to descendant John Bush, Thomas B. Files served with the guides and scouts in March and April 1863. From April 15th to May 2nd, they were on a scouting expedition through Alabama. In May and June, he was with the group on a raid on Pikeville, Alabama and May 21st through the 27th, they had a raid on Fulton, Mississippi. June 5th through the 11th, they were on a raid on Tuscumbia, Alabama, and June 17th, through 23rd, another raid on Barnesville, Alabama. They were back in camp at Glendale, Mississippi from July through October. He was mustered out December 22, 1863, due to expiration of term of service.

Thomas Benton Files was born August 12, 1839, in Blount County, Alabama to Jeremiah Benton Files, Jr. and Margaret "Peggy" Dunn. Jeremiah was born 1797 in Anderson County, South Carolina and died 1870 in Carbon Hill, Walker County, Alabama. He was the son of Jeremiah Files and Abigail Montgomery. Jeremiah Benton Files married Margaret "Peggy" Dunn in 1818. Margaret was born 1799 in Green County, Tennessee, and died in 1870 in Fayette County, Alabama. Thomas B. Files married Martha Jane Feltman February 1, 1856 in Walker County, Alabama and died June 26,

1901, in Walker County, Alabama. Martha was the daughter of Jacob Benjamin Feltman and Elvira Trawick. Jacob was born August 27, 1799, in Newberry, South Carolina and died February 5, 1879, in Carbon Hill, Walker County, Alabama. Elvira Trawick was born August 22, 1813, in Carroll County, Georgia and died June 24, 1901, in Haleyville, Winston County, Alabama. They were married May 16, 1832, in Tuscaloosa, Alabama. Other children of Jeremiah and Margaret Dunn Files were: Jeremiah Franklin, born June 2, 1836, died March 1, 1905; Lucinda C., born 1820, died 1860; Jesse, born December 1, 1824, died May 21, 1906; Elizabeth Jane, born February 10, 1833, died, February 12, 1917; and William Tobias Files, born April 30, 1837. Children of Thomas Benton Files and Margaret "Peggy" Dunn were: Mary Frances, born April 3, 1857, died March 30, 1936; Pernini Elizabeth, born September 26, 1858, died February 10, 1933; Margaret "Peggy" Elvira, born October 20, 1863, died between 1901 and 1905; Etta Lucinda, born June 23, 1866; Helen Liza, born February 3, 1868, died before October 30, 1897; Eva Lucinda, born October 8, 1869, died March 1, 1969; Cornelia Matilda, born 27 May 1871; Lavona Martha, born October 16, 1874, died after 1940, and Jeremiah Franklin Files, born February 22, 1877, and died November 21, 1944. Thomas B. Files was buried in the McDade Cemetery in Walker County, Alabama.

Thomas Benton Files' daughter, Eva Lucinda Files, married James Patmon Cooner, son of James Carroll Cooner. Thomas Benton and James C. Cooner served together in the 1st Alabama Cavalry, USV. Eva Lucinda Files Cooner often told the story of the return of her father from the war. She was a post-war baby and her older sister told the story. They had all assumed their father was dead; the war had been over for several years. One day as they were playing outside the girls saw a man coming up the lane. Having been warned about men coming on the place where only women and girls were left, the children began to run for the house, but the older sister recognized her father from a distance and began to yell "Ma, it's Pa!" And indeed it was. He had walked home back to Walker County from Memphis, stopping to work along the way to earn traveling money. The family story is that he had been injured and spent some time in the hospital, but I've not been able to confirm that. Family information submitted by John Bush.

Descendant John Bush stated Thomas Benton Files' daughter, Eva Lucinda Files, married James Patmon Cooner, son of James Carroll Cooner. Thomas Benton and James C. Cooner served together in the 1st Alabama Cavalry, USV. Eva Lucinda Files Cooner often told the story of the return of her father from the war. (She was a post-war baby; her older sister told the story.) They had all assumed their father was dead; the war had been over for several years. One day as they were playing outside the girls saw a man coming up the lane. Having been warned about men coming on the place where only women and girls were left, the children began to run for the house, but the older sister recognized her father from a distance and began to yell "Ma, it's Pa!" And indeed it was. He had walked home back to Walker County from Memphis, stopping to work along the way to earn traveling money. The family story is that he had been injured and spent some time in the hospital, but I've not been able to confirm that.

Thomas Benton Files' Southern Claim: Claimant enlisted in the 1st Alabama Cavalry on the 23rd day of March 1863 and served for one year. His loyalty is satisfactorily established by the evidence. On the 15th of August he furnished a mule to the quartermaster of the Regiment which was used in the service of the army and for which the said quartermaster promised to pay him, but he never received any pay. We allow the sum of one hundred and twenty dollars.

To the Commissioners of Claims (under Act of 3rd March, 1871) Washington, D.C.: The petition of Thomas B. Files, respectfully represents:

That your petitioner is a resident of the County of Winston in the State of Alabama; that his post office address is Houston, Winston County in said State; and that at the time his claim and each item thereof as set forth accrued he was a soldier in the Union army; that he is the original owner of said claim; that he has never sold, assigned or transferred the same or any part thereof to any person; that no mortgage, bill of sale or other lien of like nature has at any time rested upon it, or any part thereof, nor has it been attached or taken in execution; that the same has not been paid by the United States or any of their officers or agents, nor have the United States any legal offset against the same or any part thereof; that he is the sole owner of the said claim, no other person being interested therein; that said claim does not contain any charge for property which was destroyed or stolen by the troops or other persons; that the rates or prices charged are reasonable and just, and do not exceed the market rate or price of like stores or property at the time and place stated; all of which your petitioner states of his own knowledge.

Your petitioner further states that he is now and was at the time the several items of his said claim accrued, as stated therein, a citizen of the United States; that he remained a loyal adherent to the cause and Government of the United States, during the war of 1861 &c; and was so loyal before and at the time of the taking or furnishing of the property for which this claim is made.

And your petitioner further represents, and of his own knowledge states, that on the 20th day of May, A.D. 1863, at Glendale, Mississippi in the State of Mississippi the following property or stores were furnished by your petitioner for the use of the army of the United States, and for which payment is claimed, viz: one mule, which said property or stores being of the kind, quantity, quality and value above stated was furnished to Lieutenant Smith belonging to the 1st Regiment of Alabama Cavalry Volunteers, Department of the United States Army, in the service of the United States, whose rank was Lieutenant of the 1st Regiment of Alabama Cavalry Volunteers acting as Lieutenant, who, as your petitioner has been informed and believes was stationed at Glendale under the command of Colonel George S. Spencer, who at that time had command of the United States forces in the District in which said property was furnished.

And your petitioner further represents that he has been informed and believes that the said stores or property was taken from your petitioner as above stated and removed to Glendale, Mississippi for the use of Company A of the 1st Regiment of Alabama Cavalry Volunteers; that at the taking of said property, or stores, no vouchers, receipt or other writing was given therefor by the person taking the same as aforesaid or received at any time by your petitioner. Your petitioner further states that the claim, within and above mentioned has never been presented to any officer or to Congress nor to any agent nor to any department of the government and no action has been had in regard to the same.

Your petitioner hereby constitutes and appoints Lewis & Fullerton Attorneys-at-Law, of Washington, D.C., his true and lawful attorneys with full power of substitution and association, to prosecute this his claim, and to receive a draft payable to the order of your petitioner for such amount as may be allowed, and to do all acts necessary and proper in the premises.

Your petitioner therefore prays that his said claim may be examined and considered under the provisions of the Act of Congress approved 3rd March 1871, dated this 30th day of June 1871. [signed] T.B. Files; Witnesses: [signed] Jacob Feltman and Isham Feltman.

State of Alabama, County of Walker, To wit: T.B. Files, being duly sworn deposes and says, that he is the petitioner named in the foregoing petition, and who signed the same; that the matters therein stated are true, of the deponent's own knowledge except as to those matters which are stated on information and belief, and as to those matters he believes them to be true; and deponent further says that he did not voluntarily serve in the Confederate army or navy, either as an officer, soldier, or sailor, or in any other capacity, at any time during the late rebellion; that he never voluntarily furnished any stores, supplies, or other material aid to said Confederate army or navy, or to the Confederate government, or to any officer, department or adherent of the same in support thereof, and that he never voluntarily accepted or exercised the functions of any office whatsoever under, or yielded voluntary support to, the said Confederate government. [signed] T.B. Files. Sworn to and subscribed before me this 30th day of June 1871. [signed] John Brown, Judge of Probate.

One mule ($150) That, as stated in the Petition referred to, the property in question was furnished by petitioner of Clear Creek, in the State of Alabama, for the use of a portion of the army of the United States, known as the 1st Alabama Cavalry Volunteers and commanded by Colonel George E. Spencer, and that the persons who took or received the property, or who authorized or directed it to be taken or furnished, were the following: Quartermaster Gray at Glendale, Mississippi. That the property was removed to Glendale, Mississippi and used for or by the 1st Alabama Cavalry volunteers; all this on or about the 15th day of August in the year 1863, as appears by the petition presented to the Commissioners. That the Claimant is unable to produce the witnesses hereafter to be named before the Commissioners at the city of Washington for and because of the following reasons, to wit: the claim is too small and claimant too poor to defray the expense of his witnesses to Washington, D.C. That, by the following named persons, the claimant expects to prove that, from the beginning hostilities against the United States to the end thereof, his sympathies were constantly with the cause of the United States; that he never, of his own free will and accord, did anything, or offered, or sought, or attempted to do anything, by word or deed, to injure said cause or retard its success, and that he was at all times ready and willing, when called upon, or if called upon, to aid and assist the cause of the Union, or its supports, so far as his means and power and the circumstances of the case permitted: Honorable Discharge.

That, by the following named persons, the Claimant expects to prove the taking or furnishing of the property for the use of the army of the United States:

John Shaw, of Walker County, Alabama and Jasper Whitley, of Fayette County, Alabama.

I left in February 1863 [from] home in the night and made my way in the night to Glendale, Mississippi and there I joined the Union army and remained inside of the Union lines until April, 1865 and then I came back to Fayette County, Alabama about the last day of April 1865.

I was arrested in the Winter of '64 at Laverne, Tennessee by General Forrest. I was kept under arrest two weeks; was taken to Corinth, Mississippi and there I made my escape and fell in with Colonel Fulmer's Cavalry and I went with them to Decatur, Alabama.

The Rebs taken one horse and ten or twelve head of cattle, 40 or 50 head of hogs and all of my household and kitchen furniture; 3 or 4 hundred bushels of corn and in fact everything I had and I never received any pay for it.

I was threatened by D.H. Whatley, a Rebel captain. He said he would hang me at some crossroads if he could get me, but never got me. I was molested and injured by the taking of my property.

I sympathized with the Union cause. My feelings and language was with the Union all the time. I exerted my influence and cast my vote on the side of the Union all the time and after the Ordinance of Secession was passed, I went with the Union and acted with the Union. I endorse every word in this question and I think my acts prove that I done all I could for the Union and its supporters. Signed Thomas B. Files; Attest: John Brown.

Testimony of Thomas B. Files, claimant, on facts: I furnished the mule. I was present and furnished one mule that is stated in my petition to the U.S. army and furnished said mule to Quartermaster Gray at Glendale, Mississippi. Quartermaster Gray was Quartermaster of the 1st Regiment of Alabama Cavalry Volunteers and was a soldier in the 1st Alabama Regiment of Volunteers and my family was in Alabama and my wife came to Glendale and rode my mule and the regiment was scarce of stock and Quartermaster Gray wanted my mule and said he would pay me a good price for the mule and I let him the mule and it was used by the regiment all the time that I was in the regiment. I never received any voucher or receipt for the mule. I never thought of any such thing. He said, Quartermaster Gray, would pay me for said mule and furnished the mule to Quartermaster Gray of the 1st Alabama Cavalry volunteers on or about the 15th day of August 1863 at Glendale, Mississippi. There was quite a lot of soldiers present when I furnished the mule. John Shaw, Jasper Whitley, Thomas Lowrimore and others were present at the time of the furnishing of said mule. The mule was in good work order about seven years old, very large, as large a mule as I ever seen at any time. It [was] worth I think at the time, one hundred and fifty dollars and I know that the mule was used for and by the 1st Alabama Cavalry Volunteers commanded by Col. George E. Spencer and I have never received any pay for said mule at all. [signed] Thomas B. Files, Attest: [signed] John Brown.

Testimony of John Shaw on facts, first being duly sworn deposes and says my name is John Shaw, my residence is Walker County, Alabama. My occupation a farmer. I was present at Glendale, Mississippi on or about the 15th day of August 1863 and saw Thomas B. Files furnish to Quartermaster Gray of the 1st Alabama Cavalry Volunteers one mule for the use of the U.S. army. Said Files was a soldier in said regiment and the Rebs had drove his wife off and she succeeded in getting to camps with one mule and Quartermaster Gray said he needed the mule very much and told claimant he would pay him a good price for the mule and claimant let him, Quartermaster Gray, have the mule. There was all of Company A of the 1st Alabama Cavalry present at the time; Jasper Whitley, Thomas Lowrimore, Andrew Studdard, and many others. There was no voucher or receipt given; none asked for. The mule was actively needed in the regiment. The regiment was encamped at Glendale, Mississippi and remained there for several months and said mule was used by said regiment as long as I was with the regiment and I know the mule was furnished for the use of the army of the United States. The mule was in very good order; was a very large mule; one of the largest size about 7 or 8 years old and I think it was worth one hundred and seventy-five dollars at the time furnished and I am satisfied there has been nothing paid for said mule. My age is 36 years. [signed] John Shaw, Attest: [signed] John Brown.

Testimony of Jasper Whitley on facts, first being duly sworn deposes and says my name is Jasper Whitley. My age is 32 years. My residence, Fayette County, Alabama. My occupation is that of a farmer. I was present at Glendale, Mississippi on or about the 15th day of August 1863 and saw Thomas B. file furnish Quartermaster Gray of the First Alabama Cavalry Volunteers one mule for the use of the U.S. army. Said Files was a soldier in the 1st Alabama Cavalry Volunteers and the Rebs had driven his family from Alabama and his wife came in to our camps at Glendale, Mississippi and she fetched the mule with her and our regiment was very scarce of stock and Quartermaster Gray said to Files that he wanted his mule and that he should be well paid for it and Files turned the mule over to him. I taken the mule to the wagon yard myself and it was kept and used by the regiment as long as I stayed in the army. I know said mule was furnished for the actual use and benefit of the U.S. army. There was no voucher or receipt given for the mule; nothing was said about any voucher. The regiment was stationed at Glendale, Mississippi at the time of the furnishing of said mule and remained there for several months. The regiment was commanded by General George E. Spencer. He was Colonel of the regiment at that time. I don't think that said Files has ever received any pay at all for the mule. The mule was a very large mule about 6 or 7 years old in good work order and worth at time furnished to the U.S. army two hundred dollars. I have never heard claimant say anything about the value of said mule. [signed x his mark] Jasper Whitley, Attest: [signed] John Brown.

State of Alabama, Walker County: I, John Brown, Commissioner to take testimony in cases pending before "The Commissioners of claims," now pending before them against the United States, and as Judge of Probate in and for the County of Madison and State of Alabama, do certify, that Thomas B. files, of Winston County, Alabama, the claimant in this cause, and as a witness, and John Shaw and Jasper Whitley, as witnesses, came before me at Kansas, Alabama, on the 31st day of January, A.D. 1875, the said witnesses to testify in behalf of Thomas B. Files, the claimant in this cause; that before said witnesses were examined they were each severally sworn by me to tell the truth, the whole truth, and nothing but the truth, relative to said claim; that the answers of each of said witnesses were taken down; that after the same were carefully read over to said witnesses, I caused each of them to subscribe his said deposition. And I further certify, that said depositions have not been out of my possession since they were so taken, nor have the same been in any way altered or changed.

Given under my and seal, this 31st day of January, A.D., 1875. [signed] John Brown, Special Commissioner

To all whom it may concern: Know ye, That Thomas B. Files, a Sergeant of Captain Frank O. Burdick's Company A, 1st Regiment of Alabama Cavalry Volunteers who was enrolled on the 23rd day of March one thousand eight hundred and sixty-three to serve one year of during the war, is hereby discharged from the service of the United States, this 21st day of December 1863, at Camp Davis by reason of term of enlistment expiring. (No objection to his being re-enlisted is known to exist).

Said Thomas B. Files was born in Blount County in the State of Alabama, is 24 years of age, 5 feet 9 ½ inches high, dark complexion, black eyes, black hair, and by occupation, when enrolled a farmer.

Given at Camp Davis, Mississippi, this 21st day of December 1863. [signed] George E. Spencer, Colonel 1st Alabama Cavalry. (Transcribed and submitted by Robin Sterling, condensed by author.) Thomas was allowed $120 for his mule. Family information submitted by descendant John Bush.

Finch, Francis M. - Francis M. Finch enlisted in Company B of the 1st Alabama Cavalry, USV as a private on July 14, 1863, in Glendale, Mississippi, for a period of 1 year. Another record stated he enlisted for a term of 3 years. He was enrolled by Captain Phillip A. Sternberg. The Regimental Descriptive Book recorded him as 29 years of age, 5'-8½" tall, having a dark complexion, dark eyes, dark hair, born in Spartanburg, South Carolina, and a farmer by occupation. He mustered in August 7, 1863, in Corinth, Mississippi. The September and October 1863, Muster Roll recorded him as a prisoner of war in the hands of the enemy from the Battle of Vincent's Crossroads near Bay Springs, Mississippi, on October 26, 1863. However, he was shown as present in November and December 1863. He mustered out January 22, 1864, in Memphis.

Finerty, Thomas W. - Thomas W. Finerty enlisted and mustered into Company K of the 1st Alabama Cavalry, USV as a Corporal on July 31, 1862, in Huntsville, Alabama. He was enrolled by

Captain Bankhead for a period of 3 years. The Regimental Descriptive Book recorded him as 36 years of age, 5'-7 3/8" tall, having a dark complexion, gray eyes, brown hair, born in Rockingham County, Virginia, and a farmer by occupation. Thomas Finerty was one of the early enlistees shipped to Nashville, Tennessee and merged with Company E of the 1st Middle Tennessee Cavalry, which later became the 5th Tennessee Cavalry. He died of measles on October 20, 1862, in Hospital #14, in Nashville, Davidson County, Tennessee. He kept the rank of corporal throughout his service. A letter to Captain Smith of the 1st Alabama from R. Henry Nevill, U.S.V. Surgeon in charge, dated October 20, 1862, from Hospital #14, in Nashville, informed Captain Smith of Thomas W. Finerty's death and stated he died of congestion of the lungs. Thomas W. Finerty was probably buried in the Nashville National Cemetery unless his body was claimed by his family and buried in a family cemetery in Alabama.

Thomas Wilson Finerty was born November 2, 1826, in Rockingham County, Virginia to James Finniter and Esther Wilson. Thomas married Mary Ann Parker, who was born September 22, 1834, in Morgan County, Alabama, and died 1878 in Morgan County. Two known children were Julia Frances Finerty and Tandy Walter Finerty. Tandy was born August 27, 1861, in Walker County, Alabama and died January 18, 1949, in Lewis County, Tennessee.

Finley, James - James Finley enlisted in Company H of the 1st Alabama Cavalry, USV on February 20, 1865, in Huntsville, Alabama, and was mustered in April 4, 1865, in Nashville, Tennessee. He was enrolled by Captain James W. DeVaney for a period of 3 years. The Muster and Descriptive Roll recorded him as being 19 years of age, 5'-11" tall, having a dark complexion, blue eyes, black hair, born in Hawkins County, Tennessee, and a farmer by occupation. The May and June 1865 Muster Roll recorded him as being absent without leave since June 27, 1865. However, he was recorded as being present on the July and August 1865 Muster Roll. He was mustered out October 20, 1865, in Huntsville, Alabama, owing the U.S. Government $15.25, with a note stating the following: Stop for 1 Colts Pistol retained under General Order #101, War Department. Stopped for 1 belt and plate, 1 pistol cartridge box, and one-half shelter tent cost. A Notation in his file from the Adjutant General's Office of the War Department dated December 13, 1886, stated the following: Application for certificate in lieu of list discharge. One certificate furnished.

Fish, O. - This probably should be Oliver Fishback as he was in Company F and was sick in the hospital August 8, 1865, in Carlinville, Illinois. Only one card was found for O. Fish which was filed at the end of the last roll of microfilm of the 1st Alabama Cavalry, USV records. It stated he enlisted in Company F of the 1st Alabama Cavalry, USV and was absent, sick in the US General Hospital, whereabouts not known at this time. See Oliver H. Fishback, below.

Fishback, Oliver H. - Oliver H. Fishback first enlisted in the Union Artillery 2nd Regiment, Illinois Light Artillery on March 4, 1862. He was discharged to accept promotion in Company D, Alabama 1st Cavalry Regiment on February 15, 1864, for a period of 3 years, and was mustered in March 19, 1864. He was promoted to full 2nd Lieutenant and appointed by the Secretary of War, Brigadier General G. M. Dodge, January 1, 1864, Left Wing, 16th Army Corps. He was promoted from Sergeant, of Company B, 2nd Illinois Light Artillery. The January and February 1865 Muster Roll stated he had pay due as company commander since August 31, 1864. The organization was mustered out October 20 1865, at Huntsville, Alabama; however, Fishback was recorded as being absent, sick in Carlinville, Illinois since August 18, 1865, and was not issued a discharge at muster out of organization. He was later issued a discharge by Captain W.H. Barnett of Huntsville, Alabama by order of the War Department. His name appeared on the Returns as follows: June 1864, on detached service by Special Order #61, Headquarters U.S. Forces in Rome, Georgia; July 1864, present, transferred to Company F from Company L since July 25, 1864; January to February 1865, absent, on duty with dismounted men by Special Order #3; March and April 1865, on special duty commanding Company M; August to September 1865, absent without leave since August 1865. However, a letter from Fishback dated July 55, 1865, stated the following: I have the honor to respectfully request a leave of absence for (20) twenty days to visit my parents in Carlinville, Illinois for the following reasons: (1) I have been in service over four years; (2) I have never been absent without leave, have never had a leave of absence; (3) My people are sick and I have not visited them in over four years. (4) I am the only son and my presence is very necessary now at home; (5) Business of the utmost importance demands my immediate presence. Hoping, Lieutenant, that this meets your favorable consideration. I have the honor to be your obedient servant, Oliver H. Fishback. Oliver H. Fishback was born August 17, 1841, in Fayette County, Kentucky to Sheriff William Harrison Fishback and his wife, Margaret Elizabeth Black, who were married October 1, 1839, in Huntsville, Madison County, Alabama. Oliver Fishback died September 16, 1866, in Carlinville, Macoupin County, Illinois and is buried in the Carlinville City Cemetery in Macoupin County, Illinois.

Fisher, Pleasant P. - Pleasant P.A. Fisher enlisted in Company E of the 1st Alabama Cavalry, USV as a private on March 3, 1863, in Glendale, Mississippi, and was enrolled the same day in Corinth, Mississippi. The January and February 1964 Muster Roll recorded him as being absent, on detached service as teamster in Vicksburg, Mississippi in Quartermaster Department since January 25, 1864. He was mustered out March 18, 1863, in Memphis, Tennessee due to expiration of term of service.

Fisher, Thomas J. - Thomas J. Fisher enlisted in Company E of the 1st Alabama Cavalry, USV as a private on March 2, 1863, in Glendale, Mississippi for a period of 1 year, and was mustered in March 31, 1863 in Corinth, Mississippi. He was reported to have deserted December 10, 1863, near Corinth, and joined the 6th Tennessee Cavalry. On December 26, 1864, Fisher returned to Camp Davies, Mississippi from desertion. He transferred to the 6th Tennessee Cavalry in Memphis, Tennessee on February 1, 1864.

Fitzpatrick, John C. - John C. Fitzpatrick enlisted in Company M of the 1st Alabama Cavalry, USV as a private on December 8, 1863, in Camp Davies, Mississippi for a period of 3 years. He was enrolled by Captain Lomax, and mustered in December 29, 1863, in Corinth, Mississippi. The Company Descriptive Book recorded him as 17 years of age, 5'-4" tall, having a fair complexion, blue eyes, auburn hair, born in Itawamba County, Mississippi, and a farmer my occupation. The March and April 1864 Muster Roll recorded him as being absent, sick in the Cumberland U.A.A. Hospital in Nashville, Tennessee. It also stated he was due a bounty of $300. The May and June Muster Roll recorded him as being present. The November and December Muster Roll recorded him as being absent, deserted November 11, 1864, from Rome, Georgia with 1 Smith Carbine, 1 Remington Revolver, and accoutrements.

Flanagin, Andrew Pink - Andrew Pink Flanagin, also shown as Flannigan, enlisted in Company G of the 1st Alabama Cavalry, USV as a private on April 24, 1864, in Mooresville, Alabama for a period of 3 years. He was enrolled by Lieutenant Cobleigh, and was mustered in the same day in Rome, Georgia. The Muster and Descriptive Roll recorded him as 18 years of age, 5'-10" tall, having a light complexion, blue eyes, light hair, born in DeKalb County, Alabama, and a farmer by occupation. He was mustered out October 20, 1865, owing the U.S. Government $8.25 for losing 1 halter, 1 curb bridle, 1 mess pan and 1 camp kettle.

Biography of Andrew Pink Flanagin
By Lewis Flanagin ©2012

Andrew Pink Flanagin, also known as A. P. Flanagin, was born on May 14, 1847, in Wills Valley, DeKalb County, Alabama. He was the only son and second of three children born to James M. Flanagin, a Primitive Baptist preacher, and Abigail Wilson Flanagin. He was raised by his parents in Wills Valley about six miles from Van Buren and near Hendrixville. His neighbors there included Josh Graves, Bill Graves, Alex Graves, George Gilbreath, John Milwee, Hiram Smith, and James Roden.

In 1861, A. P. moved to a farm near his uncle, Thomas Wilson, about 15 miles northeast of Jasper in Walker County, Alabama. His neighbors there included Bill Watts, Jim Abbott, and Cafe Abbott. He lived in Walker County about a year and then returned to DeKalb County in 1862.

Andrew Pink Flanagin enlisted on April 24, 1864, in Mooresville, Alabama, as a Private in Company G of the 1st Regiment of the Alabama Cavalry in the Union Army under Lieutenant E. J.

Cobley, Orderly Sergeant Samuel Byers, and Colonel George E. Spencer. Others in his company included George W. Gilbreth, his bunkmate, William Fagan, Jefferson W. "Bill" Kirkland, Franklin Walker, John Brown, Nathan Grace, and Yerby Fretwell. In May 1864, while on picket at Kennesaw Mountain in the State of Georgia, he contracted a disease of the eyes (referred to as "red sore eyes") from exposure. He was subsequently seen by the regimental doctor. His eyes continued to give him trouble ever since. His company also camped at Marietta and Rome, Georgia. All of his company had the chills and fever in the summer (July or August) of 1865 in Decatur, Alabama. He was discharged at Huntsville, Alabama, on October 20, 1865.

After the war, A. P. went to Larkinsville in Jackson County, Alabama, where he married Sarah Elizabeth Sanders on June 3, 1866. He lived next door to Samuel C. Carmen, his brother-in-law, who had married his older sister, Mary Liza Flanagin. He was also a neighbor to David Zachariah Gold, his other brother-in-law, who had married his younger sister, Sarah Elizabeth Flanagin. A. P. and his wife, Sarah, had their first child and only daughter, M. E. Flanagin, in about 1868 in Alabama. They lived in Larkinsville near Scottsboro, Alabama, for five years and then moved to Orizaba in Tippah County, Mississippi, in about 1869. Their first two sons were born in Mississippi: Samuel David Flanagin on November 7, 1871, and William Thomas Flanagin on January 5, 1876. A. P. continued farming while he lived in Mississippi. His neighboring farmers in Orizaba included Pink Ashley, Harp Steward, Sam Steward, Sam Snell, Bob Snell, Young Cox, Henry Smith, William Foote, and David Pride. A. P. and his family lived in Orizaba for about eight years.

In about 1877, A. P. and his family came to Texas and settled about 14 miles southwest of Goliad in Goliad County, Texas. His third son and last child, Andrew Jackson Flanagin, was born on March 1, 1878, in Texas. His neighbors in Goliad included George Sanders, Jack Sanders, Bill New, Jake New, Joe Burgess, Cyrus Lucas, and H. Rollins. A. P. lived in Goliad for about three years and then moved to Paint Rock in Concho County, Texas, in March 1880. While he lived in Paint Rock, he followed freighting. His neighbors in Paint Rock included George Kemp, Newt Kemp, Cas. Guller, J. E. House, W. T. Melton, and D. A. Edmiston. In about 1886, A. P. moved to Fredonia in Mason County, Texas, and lived there for the remainder of his life. In the medical reports in his pension files, he is described as 5 feet, 10 inches tall, with a fair complexion, light hair, and blue eyes. The records of the Mason County M. Bevin Eckert Memorial Library in Mason County, Texas, list him as a school trustee for the Oak Groves School, No. 30, in 1890. He died January 12, 1899, in Fredonia, and he is buried in Wagram Cemetery in Mason County, Texas.

Flint, Mortimer R. - Mortimer R. Flint, also listed as M.K. Flint, enrolled in Company E of the 1st Alabama Cavalry, USV on March 18, 1863, for a period of 1 year. He was mustered in March 18, 1863, and promoted to Captain after Captain Erasmus D. Chandler was killed in action at the Battle of Vincent's Crossroads near Bay Springs, Mississippi. Flint was promoted from 1st Lieutenant of Company D of the 10th Missouri Volunteer Cavalry. The March 1864 through December 1864 Muster Rolls recorded him as being absent, on detached service as A.A. Inspector General Mounted Troops of Cavalry Left Wing, 16th Army Corps since April 20, 1864, by Special Order #34, by order of Brigadier General G.M. Dodge. Mortimer R. Flint's name appeared on a November 1864 Return of the 4th Division of the 15th Army Corps, In the Field near Slater's Mill, Georgia November 30, 1864, Assistant Aide-De Camp. His name was also recorded on the November and December 1864 Muster Roll , Station, Savannah, Georgia, Aide-De Camp, 4th Division 15th Army Corps per Special Order #7. His name appeared on the Returns as follows: November 1863, present, commanding company. Appointed by Brigadier General G.M. Dodge, reported for duty November 28, 1863; February 1864, present numerically; March, present; April 1864, A.A.I.G.; June to September 1864, on detached service as Inspector of cavalry, Left Wing, 16th Army Corps; October to December 1864, Acting Aide-De Camp to Brigadier General Corse commanding 4th Division, 15th Army Corps; January 1865, mustered out January 18, 1865, by reason of expiration of term of service. A note in his file stated, "No final pay until he presents proper indebtedness from the War Department.

Colville Examiner - Saturday, September 5, 1931
CAPT. M. R. FLINT PASSES; WELL-KNOWN ORCHARDIST

Captain M. R. Flint, 95, for many years a resident near Meyers Falls, died in a Tacoma hospital late Friday of last week, following a brief illness. He was a widely known Civil War veteran. He moved to Tacoma 16 years ago.

Captain Flint was born August 21, 1836, at Porter, New York, and graduated from Wilson Collegiate Institute near that city. He then turned his attention the merchandising business and accompanied his father to Salem, Missouri, where he was operating a store of his own when the Civil War started. He organized the first Union reserve regiment at Salem and was commissioned captain of the reserve regiment.

When the war was concluded, Captain Flint was mustered out of the service on January 18, 1865. He sold surplus army stocks for the government, engaged in private merchandising, started a bank in Illinois, worked on a Fargo, North Dakota, newspaper and acted as receiver for a big factory in Minneapolis before coming to Stevens county. He was always a doer.

Captain Flint's residence in Stevens County was on a 320-acre ranch of Meyers Falls. It was widely known as the "Flint Orchard," and under his direction it received many improvements. It had a water system connected with the lake, and in addition to the apple orchard there were 500 cherry trees. The big Bing cherries from this place made the name of Flint known to all cherry fanciers.

In 1916 Captain Flint traded this place, through O. N. Bell, and moved to Tacoma, and the next year A. J. Lee purchased the ranch and has owned it since then.

Captain Flint was a member of the Military Order of the Loyal Legion. In 1924 he served as commander of the order. He was a member of the Custer Corps. Despite his age, he was enrolled as a member of the Young Men's Business club of Tacoma on May 26, 1930. He observed his 95th birthday anniversary August 21st, as the guest of honor of the club.

He is survived by his second wife, Alice; a son, Chester, of Tacoma; two daughters, Mrs. G. E. Brewer of Meyers Falls and Mrs. Abe Howell of Colville; a sister, Mrs. Ben Steward of Columbus, Kansas, and three grandchildren, including Flint Howell of Colville. Those attending the funeral service from here were Mr. and Mrs. Brewer, Mrs. Abe Howell and Mr. and Mrs. Flint (Cappy) Howell.

Mortimer R. Flint died August 28, 1931, in Tacoma, Pierce County, Washington and was buried in the Highland Cemetery in Colville, Stevens County, Washington.

Flippo, Francis Marion - Francis Marion Flippo, also shown as Flippor, enlisted in Company H of the 1st Alabama Cavalry, USV as a private on April 20, 1865, in Huntsville, Alabama for a term of 3 years. He was enrolled by Captain James W. DeVaney, and was mustered in May 20, 1865, in Nashville, Tennessee. The Muster and Descriptive Roll recorded him as 18 years of age, 5'-8" tall, having a fair complexion, blue eyes, light hair, born in Jackson County, Alabama, and a farmer by occupation. He was mustered out October 20, 1865, in Huntsville, Alabama owing the U.S. Government $4.75 for ½ of a shelter tent lost. His Muster-Out Roll stated he was due a bounty of $100.

Francis Marion Flippo was born March 23, 1846, in Jackson County, Alabama to Henry Sandville "Sandy" Flippo and Susannah "Susan" Nipper, who were married February 23, 1842, in Madison County, Alabama. On May 25, 1874, Francis Flippo married Martha Jane "Frankie" Williams, in Jackson County, Alabama. Martha Jane was born September 11, 1856, in Jackson County, Alabama and died October 4, 1943, in Jackson County, Alabama. She was the daughter of John Williams and Margaret Carolyn Garden, who married February 9, 1852, in Trenton, Jackson County, Alabama. Francis and Martha Flippo had the following children: William Lewis, born October 7, 1876, died March 29, 1966; John Henry, born September 1, 1888, died May 1973; Dollie Minnie Mae, born February 12, 1890, died August 1977; Pearl Mae, born October 1894; and a male infant born November 29, 1882, and died November 30, 1882. Francis M. Flippo died August 27, 1910, in Jackson County, Alabama and was buried in the Webb Cemetery near Trenton, Jackson County, Georgia.

Floyd, John A. - John A. Floyd, also shown as Floid, enlisted in Company C of the 1st Alabama Cavalry, USV as a private on July 10, 1863, in Glendale, Mississippi for a period of 1 year. He was enrolled by Captain John Latty, and was mustered in August 15, 1863, in Corinth, Mississippi. The Company Descriptive Book recorded him as 26 years of age, 5'-7" tall, having a dark complexion, gray eyes, black hair, born in Henderson County, Tennessee, and a farmer by occupation. He was recorded as being single. The January and February 1864 Muster Roll stated John A. Floyd was admitted as a patient to Adams U.S.A. General Hospital in Memphis, Tennessee on January 20, 1864. He was discharged July 27, 1864, in Rome, Georgia due to expiration of term of service.

Floyd, William D. - William D. Floyd enlisted in Company A of the 1st Alabama Cavalry, USV as a sergeant on January 23, 1864, in Camp Davies, Mississippi for a period of 3 years. He was enrolled by Lieutenant Hinds and was mustered in February 5, 1864, in Memphis, Tennessee. He was appointed Sergeant February 5, 1864. The Muster and Descriptive Roll recorded Floyd as 23 years of age, 6'-1" tall, having a fair complexion, gray eyes, dark hair, born in Murray County, Georgia, and a farmer by occupation. The July through October 1864 Muster Rolls recorded him as being absent, on recruiting service in Alabama since August 7, 1864. The July and August 1865 Field and Staff Muster Roll stated he was promoted from sergeant of Company C to date from August 1, 1865, by Special Order #29, Headquarters Regiment. William D. Floyd's name appeared on the Company Muster- Out Roll for Company A stating he was promoted to Regimental Commissary Sergeant and transferred to regimental staff rolls August 30, 1865. He was mustered out October 20, 1865, in Huntsville, Alabama. He was due a bounty of $300, and his Muster-Out Roll stated he was paid $180 of the bounty and due $120, to make up the $300 bounty.

A letter found in Floyd's records stated the following: Headquarters, 1st Alabama Cavalry Volunteers, Decatur, Alabama, September 11, 1865. General, I have the desire to call to your attention the case of W.D. Floyd, Commissary Sergeant of this regiment. On the 29th of July 1864, General Howard issued an order for Lieutenant Emerick, 1st Alabama Cavalry, and five enlisted men to proceed to Decatur, Alabama for the purpose of recruiting for the regiment. As was our usual way of recruiting the Lieutenant sent some of the men into the country for the purpose of inducing the men to leave their homes in the mountains and come enlist in our regiment. Sergeant Floyd was from the fact of his being one of our best men and a splendid recruiting sergeant was sent into the country bordering on Mississippi. While there in the regular and legitimate discharge of his duty, his horse gave out and he was compelled to leave because the Rebels had found out he was in there and knew almost his exact locality. Being thus circumstanced he captured from a Confederate soldier a horse which he, Sergeant Floyd, rode into out lines and turned over at Decatur to Lieutenant Dublin. While at home recently on a regular permission to visit his family the Sergeant was arrested by Sabun Thomas, a Justice of the Peace in Itawamba County, Mississippi. On a warrant sworn to by Steven Duncan charged with stealing the horse I have above spoken of. At first the parties were going to take him out of his house and kill him, then they started with him to jail when his friend compelled the Justice to place him under a bond, which he (The Justice) did of $500 binding him to appear at the next term of court to be held in Itawamba County, Mississippi. I have quite a number of men in my regiment from that locality. The citizens there swear they will never let them live there again. Sergeant Floyd's case is only the commencement of what the Rebel officers, civil and citizens will do in regard to my men _____ General, who are men who have served their country honestly and faithfully to be arrested by every one horse Justice in the country and placed under bond for capturing horses from Rebels in the Rebel Army simply by leaving their homes to enlist in the Federal Army. Hoping you will cause the bond to be destroyed or held of no effect. I am, General, very Respectfully your most obedient servant, F.S. Cramer, Major 1st Alabama Cavalry, Commanding Regiment. Another letter stated the following:

The State of Mississippi, Itawamba County, Personally appeared before me Eli Phillips, Clerk of the Probate Court of said county, E.B. Hawkins, Clerk of the Circuit Court, who on oath said that sometime during the month of November, last, that J.L. Finley of said county handed him some papers which were very much soiled and mutilated, that said Finley told affiant that the same papers were sent up by William Bedford, an acting Justice of the Peace in and for said county, to be filed in the Circuit Clerk's Office. Affiant says that owing to the soiled and mutilated condition of these papers and the informal manner in which they were brought into his office they were not filed but thrown into a lot of other loose papers – That one of these papers was said to be Floyd's bond for his appearance of the next term of the Circuit Court of said county. Affiant further says that since receiving Major General Woods' order for said bond that he has searched diligently and repeatedly for the same but has been unable to find it and said affiant says he believe the same is entirely lost. Signed E. Hawkins, Circuit Court. Sworn to and subscribed before me this the 30th Day of January 1966. Eli Phillips.

Camp 1st Alabama Cavalry, Decatur, Alabama, September 10, 1865 – I George M. Emerick, 1st Lieutenant of Company A, Alabama Cavalry do certify that Sergeant William D. Floyd was one of the five enlisted men detailed in Special Field Order #82, Headquarters, Department of the Army of Tennessee, and with me sent inside the Confederate lines to recruit for the 1st Regiment Alabama Cavalry Volunteers. While in the county his horse broke down and he was compelled to press another which he turned over to the Quartermaster at Decatur after coming back. Coming home a short time after he was arrested, by the citizens and compelled to enter into a bond of $500 for his appearance in court to answer to the charge of horse stealing. The soldier, Sergeant William D. Floyd, has been and still is one of the best soldiers in the regiment, has never been given to plundering, but is a high minded exemplary man and I am satisfied took this animal for the use of the government. George W. Emerick, Lieutenant 1st Alabama Cavalry.

Okolona, Mississippi, October 27, 1865: M.T. Stafford, 1st Lieutenant and Adjutant, 108 U.S.C. – I have the honor to submit the following report as the result of my investigation as per Special Order #21 dated Headquarters, 108 U.S.C. Okolona, Mississippi, October 27, 1865. On the 11th Day of October 1865 I started for Itawamba County, Mississippi through Chickamauga, Richmond, and Fulton. Whilst in route I ascertained that the parties implicated in placing Sergeant William Floyd under $500 bond were residing in Guntown. The road being in a bad condition, and the distance being farther from Fulton than from Okolona, I returned to Okolona where I arrived on October 14, 1865. Being taken with the chills and fever I was unable to start again until October 24, 1865. I reached Guntown on the eve of the 24th, on the 25th I found Saban Thomas, formerly Justice of the Peace of Guntown and obtained true copies of the affidavit of S.P. Dancer, the warrant and the bond herewith enclosed. After obtaining the papers, I made some further investigation in regard to the general character of Sergeant William Floyd which was bad. He has been at home quite a number of times before and after his arrest and has never been troubled (with the exception of his arrest.) S.P. Dancer is living in Tishomingo County. There being no more that I could rely upon as true and thinking I had investigated the case as far as possible, I returned to Okolona October 27, 1865. I have the honor to be sir, Very Respectfully your Obedient Servant, Charles M. Chase, Captain, 108 U.S.C.

Fonsh, James - (Name probably misspelled.) Only one card was found for James Fonsh which was filed at the end of the last roll of microfilm of the 1st Alabama Cavalry, USV records. It recorded him as having enlisted in Company L, stating he was on detached service in September 1864. No further information relative to this soldier was found.*

Ford, J.M. - Only one card was found for a J.M. Ford which was filed at the end of the last roll of microfilm of the 1st Alabama Cavalry, USV records. It recorded him as a private in Company M, stating he enlisted in the 1st Alabama Cavalry December 25, 1863. No further information relative to this soldier was found.*

Ford, James N. Calloway - James N. Callaway Ford enlisted in Company F of the 1st Alabama Cavalry, USV as a private on November 25, 1863, in Camp Davies, Mississippi for a period of 1 year. He was enrolled by W.H. Cheney, and mustered in February 24, 1864, in Memphis, Tennessee. The Company Descriptive Book recorded James as 35 years of age, 5'-10" tall, having a light complexion, gray eyes, dark hair, born in Monroe County, Georgia, and a farmer by occupation. The January and February 1864 Muster Roll, which was in with John A. Ford's records, recorded him as being absent, sick in the hospital in Memphis, Tennessee. The December 31, 1863, through June 30, 1864, Muster Roll, which was also mixed in with John Ford's records, stated he was sick at Louisville, Kentucky. The July and August 1864 Muster Roll stated he was absent, sick in Louisville, Kentucky since he returned. The September and October 1864 Muster Roll recorded him as present. The November and December 1864 Muster Roll recorded James as being absent, sick in Nashville, Tennessee since November 6, 1864. The January through August 1865 Muster Rolls recorded him as absent, sick in Nashville, Tennessee since November 6, 1864. James N. Ford's name was on the January and February 1864 Hospital Muster Roll for Washington U.S.A. General Hospital in Memphis, Tennessee stating he had been a patient since February 14, 1864. His name was also on the November 1864 through February 1865 Hospital Muster Rolls for U.S.A. General Hospital in Madison, Indiana. The March and April 1865

Madison U.S.A. General Hospital Muster Roll recorded James N. Ford as being absent without leave. It also stated he was paid $32 for November and December 1864, and $32 for January and February 1865. His name appeared on the Returns as follows: February and March 1864, absent, sick in hospital in Memphis, Tennessee; April 1864, returned from absent sick. Absent, sick April 10, 1864, at Mooresville, Alabama; July 1864 to August 1864, absent, sick at Nashville, Tennessee since April 30, 1864; April 1865 to September 1865, absent, sick in U.S. General Hospital. No discharge was issued to James at the muster out of the organization October 20, 1865, in Huntsville, Alabama due to him still being in the hospital in Nashville. On the back of this same muster roll it stated "Hospital in Madison, Indiana for March and April 1865 reports him absent without leave. Another Muster-Out Roll for James H. Ford from Indianapolis, Indiana stated he mustered out May 26, 1865, had drawn $10.50 for clothing while in Madison U.S.A. General Hospital and had been paid by Major Phillips for November and December 1864 and January and February 1865; Mustered Out under Special Order of the War Department May 3, 1865. His diagnosis for being in the hospital in Louisville, Kentucky was recorded as Intermittent fever. A note in his file stated he was transferred to Barracks Number 1, in Louisville, Kentucky on July 26, 1864. A Notation in James N. Ford's file from the Adjutant General's office of the War Department dated November 20, 1909, stated the following: The records of the above named soldier, James N. Ford, was mustered out of service June 12, 1865, are on an individual muster roll of that date, and that so much of said roll as shows that he was discharged to date May 26, 1865, is erroneous. NOTE: Records on James A. Ford and John H. Ford are all mixed up together. Anyone wishing to request military records on either soldier, need to request both files.

Ford, John A. - John A. Ford, also shown as John H. Ford, enlisted in Company F of the 1st Alabama Cavalry, USV as a private on November 25, 1863, in Camp Davies, Mississippi, and was mustered in February 24, 1864, in Memphis, Tennessee. The Muster and Descriptive Roll recorded him as 25 years of age, 5'-11" tall, having a light complexion, gray eyes, dark hair, born in Harris County, Georgia, and a farmer by occupation. The December 31, 1863, through August 1864 Muster Rolls recorded John absent, sick in Louisville, Kentucky. The September and October 1864 Muster Roll stated John A. Ford died June 10, 1864, of chronic diarrhea in Chattanooga, Tennessee. The November 1864 through April 1865 Muster Rolls recorded John A. Ford as absent, sick in Nashville, Tennessee since May 1, 1864. The May and June 1865 Muster Roll stated he was absent, sick in Nashville, Tennessee since November 6, 1864. The July and August 1865 Muster Roll stated he was absent, sick in Nashville since May 1, 1864. The Company Muster-Out Roll stated the following: Sick in hospital in Nashville, Tennessee since May 1, 1864, assigned to duty from 1 year organization of 1st Alabama Cavalry July 25, 1864, by order of Colonel Spencer. No discharge furnished on muster out of organization. A Casualty Sheet for John A. Ford stated he died of fever September 17, 1864, in Chattanooga, Tennessee. A Notation in John's file, except with the name of James N. Ford from the Adjutant General's office of the War Department dated November 20, 1909, stated the following: The records of the above named soldier, James N. Ford, was mustered out of service June 12, 1865, are on an individual muster roll of that date, and that so much of said roll as shows that he was discharged to date May 26, 1865, is erroneous. John A. Ford is buried in the Chattanooga National Cemetery in Chattanooga, Hamilton County, Alabama.

Ford, Joseph Jordan - Joseph Jordan Ford enlisted in Company H of the 1st Alabama Cavalry, USV on October 18, 1863, in Glendale, Mississippi for a term of 1 year, and was mustered in December 18, 1863, at Camp Davies, Mississippi. He was immediately appointed Captain by Brigadier General Dodge. Another muster roll stated Ford mustered in July 11, 1863. Another one stated "Joined for duty and enrolled July 11, 1863." The January and February 1864 Muster Roll stated the following: Full pay and allowances due from the 11th Day of July to the date of going on duty the 29th of February except absence of twenty days under Special Order Number 4, Headquarters, 11th Army Corps. Joseph Ford's name appeared on the Returns as follows: September 1863 to December 1863, Present commanding company; January 1864, on leave of absence by order of General S.A. Hurlbut. October 1864, absent on detached service witnessing payment of Detachment of Discharged men; November 1864, term of service expired, mustered out November 2, 1864. He was temporarily attached from Corporal, Company L, 15th Illinois Cavalry. The Individual Muster Roll recorded him as mustering out November 3, 1864, and stated, "This officer to receive no final pay until he presents the proper certificates of non-indebtedness from the War Department. A note in his file stated the following: This officer has served in the same grade during his term and now he has no command. A letter in Ford's file requesting a leave of absence stated: Headquarters H Company, 1st Alabama Cavalry Volunteers, Camp Davies, Mississippi, December 21, 1863. Captain, I would respectfully renew the application for the leave of absence forwarded during the month of November. The application was returned with permission to apply again at the end of twenty days. I have not been absent from my command on leave of any kind whatever during the two years I have been connected with the service. Both Lieutenants are present for duty with the company. I have the honor to be, Captain, Very Respectfully your obedient servant, Joseph Ford, Captain commanding Company H, 1st U.S. Cavalry Alabama Volunteers. Another note found in his records state that he was granted his leave. It is dated 4 January 1864, Head-Quarters 16th Army Corps, Memphis, Tennessee and states: Twenty days, is hereby granted to the following named Commissioned Officer, Captain Joseph Ford, 1st Alabama Cavalry, with permission to proceed beyond the limits of the Department of the Tennessee. By order of Major General S. A. Hurlbut, and signed by T.C. Harris, Assistant Adjutant General.

Captain Joseph Jordan Ford was born July 26, 1832, in Madison, Jefferson County, Indiana, to George W. Ford and Mary Ann Miller, who were married December 24, 1829, in Jefferson County, Indiana. Joseph married Eliza Jane Jones, daughter of Lewis and Mary Brown Jones. Eliza was born July 16, 1842, in Crawford County, Illinois, and died June 26, 1909. Joseph Ford died November 26, 1934. He was over 102 years of age, in Flat Rock, Honey Creek Township, Crawford County, Illinois and was buried in Jones Cemetery in Crawford County, Illinois. Children of Joseph and Eliza Ford were: Mary Etta, born July 19, 1861, died November 28, 1937; Martha Elizabeth, born June 22, 1863, died July 2, 1863; Lewis W., Louisa, born June 29, 1864, died February 7, 1918; Dorothy Catherine, born August 22, 1869; John W., born December 25, 1871, died September 19, 1872 Laura Lavina, born about 1872, died February 25, 1930; Amy Louisa, born January 26, 1877, died February 27, 1931; Minnie, born December 1879, died February 27, 1931; Eva Emma, born December 12, 1880, died August 1960; and William John Ford, born about 1882, died 1907.

Ford, Joseph Madison - Joseph Madison Ford enlisted in Company M of the 1st Alabama Cavalry, USV as a private on December 25, 1863, in Camp Davies, Mississippi for a period of 3 years. He was enrolled by Captain Lomax, and mustered in the same day at Corinth, Mississippi. The Company Descriptive Book recorded him as 19 years of age, 5'-7" tall, having a dark complexion, hazel eyes, dark hair, born in Henry County, Georgia, and a farmer by occupation. The January and February 1864 Muster Roll recorded him as being absent, sick in hospital in Memphis, Tennessee since January 25, 1864. He was recorded as present in March and April 1864, however, the May 1864 through August 1865 Muster Rolls recorded him as absent, sick in the hospital in Louisville, Kentucky since June 16, 1864. His name appeared on a hospital muster rolls for the Smallpox U.S.A. General Hospital in Memphis, Tennessee from January through June 1864 stating he was admitted to the hospital September 25, 1864. His name appeared on another muster roll for the Totten U.S.A. General Hospital in Louisville, Kentucky for July and August 1864. He was discharged June 16, 1865, at Camp Chase, Ohio by reason of General Order #77 of the War Department. When he was discharged, he owed the U.S.A. Government $19.06 for losing 1 carbine swing and swivel, 1 carbine cartridge box, 1 curb bridle, 2 saddle blankets, and 1 halter strap. He was shown as being due a bounty of $300. He was transferred to the Veteran's Reserve Corps. Nature of disability was: Youthfulness, feeble constitution, and chronic diarrhea. The Hospital Record stated Joseph M. Ford was single and listed his nearest relative as E.W. Ford of Baccus, Marion County, Alabama, and that he was admitted to the hospital in Nashville July 7, 1864. He was transferred to Jeffersonville, Indiana September 24, 1864.

Joseph M. Ford was born April 28, 1845, in Henry County, Georgia to Elijah Walker Ford and his wife, Elvi Purse, who were married August 15, 1844, in Henry County, Georgia. Joseph married Mary Elizabeth Hicks on December 9, 1858. Mary Elizabeth was born August 11, 1843, in Tennessee, and died October 15, 1887, in Tishomingo County, Mississippi. Joseph had the following children and some of them may have belonged to Calista Jane: John B., born June 3, 1869, died May 20, 1942; Mary M.; Sarah F. Ford; Florence L. Ford, born June 25, 1876, died May 9, 1955; Arvilla Ford; James M. Calaway Ford, born June 16, 1881, died December 21, 1955; and Austin Phillip Ford, born May 21,

1883, and died May 15, 1967. Joseph married next, Calista Jane Mills Higginbottom, born January 18, 1855. Joseph Madison Ford died November 28, 1920, in Tishomingo County, Mississippi and is buried in the Chapel Hill Cemetery in Tishomingo County. This cemetery is located just north of Burnsville, Mississippi.

Ford, Michael D. - Michael D. Ford enlisted in Company G of the 1st Alabama Cavalry, USV as a private on July 11, 1863, in Glendale, Mississippi for a period of 1 year and was mustered in the same day in Corinth, Mississippi. He was 17 years old when he enlisted. His name appeared on the Returns for July 1863 and stated he enlisted July 8, 1863, at Glendale. He was mustered out November 26, 1863, in Memphis, Tennessee.

Ford, Richmond Richard - Richmond Richard Ford enlisted and mustered into Company K of the 1st Alabama Cavalry, USV as a saddler on December 13, 1863, in Camp Davies, Mississippi. He was enrolled by Lieutenant Hornback. Ford traveled 300 miles, probably by horseback, from his home in Randolph County, Alabama to Camp Davies, Mississippi, to enlist in the Union Army. The Company Descriptive Book recorded Ford as 25 years of age, 6'-1" tall, light complexion, gray eyes, brown hair, born in DeKalb County, Georgia, and was a saddler by occupation. The November and December 1864 Muster Roll recorded him as being absent, on secret service in Alabama November 10, 1864. The December 31, 1864, through April 30, 1865, Muster Roll recorded him as being absent, on secret service in Randolph County, Alabama since November 10, 1864. Ford's name appeared on the Returns stating he was the Regimental Saddler in June 1865. There was a note in his file which stated: Cairo, Illinois, April 6, 1864, Requisition of Sergeant R. Ford, Company K, 1st Alabama Cavalry, USV; 9 stragglers and 1 paroled prisoner, from Cairo, Illinois to Nashville, Tennessee, Nature of Service: Transportation furnished to stragglers under General Orders 49, Department of the Tennessee.

Richmond Richard Ford was born about 1838 in DeKalb County, Alabama to William and Mary A. Ford. Other children of William and Mary were: Rebecca, Sarah, Elizabeth, Nancy, Frances, Terza, and Gracie C. Ford. Richmond married Sarah Ann Strain, daughter of James Strain, and Elizabeth Esther Huff. Richmond and Elizabeth had at least 2 children: Elizabeth and Arminta B. Ford. Richmond died May 1, 1877, in Randolph County, Alabama and is buried in the Liberty Grove Congregational Methodist Church Cemetery near Wedowee, Randolph County, Alabama. On March 8, 1901, someone ordered a tombstone for him from Vermont Marble Company.

Ford, Thomas - Thomas Ford enrolled in Company F of the 1st Alabama Cavalry, USV as a private on May 15, 1863, in Memphis, Tennessee for a period of 1 year. He was enrolled by Lieutenant Hinds and was mustered in August 13, 1863. The Company Descriptive Book recorded Thomas as 23 years of age, 5'-10" tall, having a fair complexion, dark eyes, dark hair, born in City, New York (probably New York City, New York) and a seaman by occupation. The September and October 1863 Muster Roll recorded him as being absent, supposed to have been taken prisoner of war in October 26, 1863, which would have been the Battle of Vincent's Crossroads, near Bay Springs, Mississippi. The November and December 1863 through October 1864 Muster Rolls recorded him as absent, missing in action since October 26, 1863, it also listed him as a Corporal. The November and December 1864 recorded him as absent, sick in the hospital in Nashville, Tennessee since October 28, 1863. The January through April 1865 Muster Rolls recorded him as absent, sick in the hospital in Memphis, Tennessee, since October 26, 1863. The May and June 1865 Muster Roll recorded him as absent, sick at Louisville, Kentucky since October 26, 1863. The July and August 1865 Muster Roll stated Ford was still sick at Louisville, Kentucky from wounds received in the Battle of Vincent's Crossroads October 25, 1863. However, there was a muster roll in his records from the Cumberland U.S.A. General Hospital in Nashville, Tennessee dated July and August 1865, stating he had been admitted to that hospital. Thomas Ford was also listed on a DeCamp U.S.A. General Hospital Muster Roll, in David's Island, New York Harbor, dated September and October 1865 stating he was attached to the hospital October 13, 1865, as a patient. The November and December 1865 DeCamp U.S.A. General Muster Roll recorded him as being discharged November 7, 1865. Thomas Ford's name was listed on a Descriptive List of Deserters from Camp Douglas, Chicago, Illinois, May 7, 1864, stating he was taken prisoner of war from Vincent's Crossroads, Alabama October 26, 1863. Ford's name appeared on a

Company Muster-Out Roll stating that no discharge was furnished at muster out of organization. Discharged November 4, 1865, at DeCamp General Hospital in David's Island in New York Harbor, in accordance of War Department A.G.O. May 31, 1866, because of loss of right leg by amputation at middle third of tibia. Disability total. Fit to reenlist in V.R.C. Exchanged prisoner of war April 5, 1865. His name appeared on a Descriptive List of Deserters recording him as taken prisoner of war October 26, 1863, at Vincent's Crossroads, Alabama. He escaped from there soon after and was with the Army at New Orleans, and deserted from there. He was arrested March 3, 1864, received at Headquarters Garrison at Camp Douglas, Chicago, Illinois April 30, 1864. The headquarters of his regiment on April 18, 1864, was at Alabama, he should be forwarded via Nashville to Decatur, Alabama. A letter in Ford's records from the Office of Provost Marshall, Third District Illinois, March 2, 1864, to Lieutenant Colonel James Oakes, 4th US Cavalry, Springfield, Illinois; Colonel, I have the honor of reporting that I have under arrest on suspicion of being a deserter, a man giving his name as Martin Mahar, but whose real name is probably Thomas Ford. He is 5'-9½" high (in his boots) about 22 years of age, brown hair, blue eyes, fair complexion. Says he is a native of Perth Amboy, New Jersey. There were found upon him two papers as follows, Office Provost Marshall, Barrancas, January 15, 1864. Thomas Ford, 1st Alabama Cavalry, to Fort Pickens. Signed Salmon Dutton, Captain, 7th Vermont Volunteers, Provost Marshall. Also: Defenses New Orleans, Office Provost Marshall, Number 48, Bayonne Street, New Orleans, January 31, 1864. Guards and Patrol will pay will pay bearer Private Thomas North 1st Alabama Cavalry until 9 A.M. January 31st. Signed B. Warren, Captain A.A. Provost Marshall. The letter continued; He finally stated to me that he found these papers on a steamboat. Afterwards he said he was employed on a schooner (of which he can't recall the name) going from New Orleans to Pensacola after coal in November 1863, that he was captured by the Rebels and taken to Cahaba Prison, Alabama, 20 miles he says from Selma, that he escaped from there along with one, Samuel Johnson, who he says does belong to the 1st Alabama Cavalry, while he was confined there, one Thomas North was also a prisoner; and that he obtained these papers from him. He wears a breast pin, a silver figure. Denies that he is or has been in the service. I should add to his description that he limps. I am, Colonel, Very Respectfully, Your obedient servant, Colonel _____, Captain and Provost Marshall, 3rd District Illinois. Attached to this letter was a note stating; Office A.A.P.M.G. Illinois, Springfield, March 7, 1864; Respectfully forwarded to the Provost Marshall General for instructions as for proper disposition to be made of this man. The circumstances seem suspicious but the records of this office furnish no means of identifying Mahar as a deserter. Signed, James Oakes, Lieutenant Colonel, 4th U.S. Cavalry, A.A.P.M.G., Illinois. A note in his file stated: Respectfully request a special transfer to his home in New York City, New York. The next note stated: Respectfully approved and forwarded. This man has been a prisoner twenty (20) months in Andersonville Prison, Georgia, having lost his leg from exposure, and not sufficiently reconned from the inhuman treatment while a prisoner of war. (Signature illegible.) Thomas Ford was given a Certificate of Disability for Discharge. In the discharge he stated he suffered in Rebel prisons in Andersonville, Georgia and Cahaba Prison in Alabama. The discharge was issued to him November 4, 1865, at DeCamp General Hospital in David's Island, New York Harbor. A Prisoner of War Record in his files stated he was captured October 26, 1863 at Bay Springs, Mississippi, confined at Andersonville, Georgia and admitted to the hospital at Andersonville on September 15, 1864, with Scorbutus. Another prisoner of war record stated he was admitted to the hospital at Andersonville Prison on April 13, 1865.

Ford, William Green - William Green Ford enlisted in Company M of the 1st Alabama Cavalry, USV as a private on September 14, 1863, in Chewalla, Tennessee for a period of 3 years. He was enrolled by Captain Lomax. The Company Descriptive Roll recorded him as 39 years of age, 5'-10" tall, having a fair complexion, dark eyes, dark hair, born in Hardeman County, Tennessee, and a farmer by occupation. He was reported as having deserted on October 28, 1863, from Glendale, Mississippi, and was never mustered in. His name appeared on the Returns as follows: November 1863, absent without leave October 22, 1863. [William Ford could very well have deserted, but several soldiers were reported as having deserted around October 26, 1863, from the Glendale, Mississippi area when in fact they had been captured by the enemy at the Battle of Vincent's Crossroads, Mississippi. If any descendant wanted to verify this, they need to order his pension records, provided he or his widow filed for one.]

William Green Ford was born about 1827 in Hardeman County, Tennessee, and married Jane Penn on May 7, 1845, in Limestone County, Alabama. Some children of William and Jane were: William P.; John J.; Sarah E.; and Richard S. Ford. Jane Penn was born February 26, 1827, and was the daughter of Stephen Chandler Penn and his wife Henrietta Esther "Hattie" Day, who were married November 11, 1819, in Hawkins County, Tennessee. All three of Stephen and Hattie Penn's sons served in the 1st Alabama Cavalry. Their other children were: Pleasant; Richard William; Nancy J.; Elizabeth; Matilda; and Mary "Polly" Penn. See the Penn brothers for additional information on the Penn family.

Forest, Israel - Only one card was found for Israel Forest which was filed at the end of the last roll of microfilm of the 1st Alabama Cavalry, USV records. It recorded him as having enlisted in Company D of the 1st Alabama Cavalry, USV but was discharged for a disability at Glendale, Mississippi on April 5, 1863. No further information relative to this soldier was found.*

Forest, Thomas - Only one card was found for Thomas Forest which was filed at the end of the last roll of microfilm of the 1st Alabama Cavalry, USV records It recorded him as being in Company F, stating he was absent with leave in November 1863 in Alabama. No further information relative to this soldier was found.*

Forman, Elijah - Elijah Forman enlisted in Company B of the 1st Alabama Cavalry, USV as a private on January 18, 1863, in Glendale, Mississippi for a period of 1 year. He was enrolled by Captain Phillip A. Sternberg and was mustered in January 22, 1863, in Corinth, Mississippi. The Regimental Descriptive Book recorded him as 23 years of age, 5'-10" tall, having a dark complexion, blue eyes, dark hair, born in Marshall County, Alabama, and a farmer by occupation. The Company Muster-Out Roll recorded him as 33 years of age. His Casualty Sheet was certified by Henry Y. Summer, Captain Commanding Company. It was signed by Isaac C. Dowling, Clerk. A Notation was found from the Adjutant General's Office of the War Department, dated June 18, 1874, which stated: Died June 4, 1863, at Glendale, Mississippi of Valvular disease of the heart.

Forrester, John T. - John T. Forrester, also shown as Forrister, enlisted in Company M of the 1st Alabama Cavalry, USV as a private on September 6, 1863, at Chewalla, Tennessee for a period of 3 years. He was enrolled by Captain Lomax, and was mustered in the same day in Corinth, Mississippi. The Company Descriptive Book recorded Forrester as being 16 years of age, 5'-6" tall, light complexion, blue eyes, light hair, born in Tishomingo County, Mississippi, and a farmer by occupation. The November and December 1863 Muster Roll recorded him as being absent, on detached service as a nurse in the U.S.A. Post Hospital in Corinth, Mississippi November 22, 1863. The March and April 1864 Muster Roll recorded him as absent, sick in Cumberland U.S.A. Hospital in Nashville, Tennessee. The May and June 1864 Hospital Muster Roll from Adams U.S.A. General Hospital in Memphis, Tennessee stated he returned to duty June 20, 1864. The November and December 1864 Muster Roll reported him as absent, deserted November 11, 1864, from quarters at Rome, Georgia with Smith Carbine, Remington revolver and accoutrements.

Forrester, John - One card was found for a John Forrester which was filed at the end of the last roll of microfilm of the 1st Alabama Cavalry, USV Muster Rolls. It recorded him as a private in Company L, and stated he was absent, on detached service as nurse in hospital in Memphis, Tennessee in January 1864. Could be the same John Forrester, above, but it shows him in a different company. No further information relative to this soldier was found.*

Forsythe, Thomas J. - Thomas J. Forsythe, name appears also as T.J. Forsythe, enlisted in Company I of the 1st Alabama Cavalry, USV as a private on July 21, 1862, in Huntsville, Alabama for the duration of the war. He was enrolled by Captain Bankhead and was mustered in August 18, 1862, in Huntsville. Thomas was one of the early enlistees who shipped to Nashville, Tennessee and merged with the 1st Middle Tennessee Cavalry which later became the 5th Tennessee Cavalry, US. He was assigned to Company D of the 1st Middle Tennessee Cavalry, and was recorded on their Company

Muster Roll on November 30, 1862. The Company Descriptive Book recorded him as 30 years of age, 5'-11" tall, having a dark complexion, blue eyes, dark hair, born in Habersham County, Georgia, and a farmer by occupation. The November and December 1862 Muster Roll for the 1st Middle Tennessee Cavalry, recorded him as absent with leave with wagon train at Nashville, Tennessee since November 27, 1862. He was listed on the Returns as being absent on courier post in January 1863 in Readyville, Tennessee. The December 31, 1862, through June 30, 1863, Muster Roll recorded him as missing in action April 28, 1863, from the Battle of Day's Gap in Alabama. No further information in his records.

Fortner, William D. - William D. Fortner enlisted in Company H of the 1st Alabama Cavalry, USV as a private on September 13, 1963, in Glendale, Mississippi for a period of 1 year. The March and April 1864 Muster Roll recorded him as a Bugler. His name appeared on the Returns as follows: September to December 1864, on daily duty as company cook; February 1864, on daily duty as Company Bugler; April 1864, on daily duty as Company Bugler; July to August 1864, on daily duty as Company Bugler. He mustered out September 29, 1864, due to expiration of term of service.

Foster, John - John Foster enlisted and mustered into Company K of the 1st Alabama Cavalry, USV as a private on December 13, 1863, at Camp Davies, Mississippi for a period of 3 years. He was enrolled by Lieutenant Hornback after traveling 250 miles from Chattanooga, Tennessee to Camp Davies, Mississippi to enlist in the Union Army. The Company Descriptive Book recorded him as 21 years of age, 5'-7" tall, having a light complexion, blue eyes, brown hair, born in Washington County, Illinois, and a farmer by occupation. The January and February 1864 Muster Roll stated he absent, on detached service as a teamster in Vicksburg, Mississippi in General Sherman's Expedition since January 24, 1864, by order of General Grierson. He was mustered out July 19, 1865, in Nashville, Tennessee.

Foster, Samuel M. - Samuel M. Foster enlisted in Company D of the 1st Alabama Cavalry, USV as a private on May 20, 1864, in Decatur, Alabama for a period of 3 years. He was enrolled by Lieutenant Pease, and was mustered in June 16, 1864, in Decatur. The Muster and Descriptive Roll recorded him as 18 years of age, 6' tall, having a light complexion, blue eyes, light hair, born in Calhoun County, Alabama, and a farmer by occupation. He was mustered out October 20, 1865, in Huntsville, Alabama, owing the U.S. Government $1.30 for losing 1 cartridge box, and was shown as being due a bounty of $100.

Foulkes, Harrison - See Harrison Fulks.

Foust, John M. - John M. Foust, also shown as Forest, enlisted in Captain Tramel's Company L of the 1st Alabama Cavalry, USV as a private on September 25, 1863, in Fayette County, Alabama at age 21, for a period of 1 year, and was mustered in the same day in Glendale, Mississippi. His enlistment muster roll recorded him as being detached as a scout for General Dodge on October 20, 1863, by order of Major Fairfield, Commanding Sergeant. John's name appeared on the Returns and stated he was missing in action October 26, 1863, from the Battle of Vincent's Crossroads, near Bay Springs, Mississippi. It also recorded him as gained from missing in action on November 1, 1863. He was discharged September 29, 1864, from Rome, Georgia after having served as a scout, which was an extremely dangerous job, all during his service.

Fowler, Israel - Israel Fowler enlisted in Company D of the 1st Alabama Cavalry, USV as a private on May 31, 1863, in Glendale, Mississippi for a period of 1 year. He was enrolled by Lieutenant John A. Snelling. The Company Descriptive book recorded Israel as 19 years of age, 5'-9" tall, having a dark complexion, dark eyes, dark hair, born in Marion County, Alabama, and a farmer by occupation. His name was shown on a Return as L. Fowler and was filed at the end of the last roll of microfilm of the 1st Alabama Cavalry, USV Records. It recorded him as being in Company D, stating he was enrolled May 31, 1863, at Glendale, Mississippi, so it is definitely Israel Fowler. His May and June 1863 Muster Roll recorded him as being absent, sent to general hospital with insanity. The July and August 1863 Muster Roll stated Fowler died of disease in the hospital in Corinth, Mississippi on July 28, 1863.

There was a Notation in his file from the Adjutant General's office of the War Department dated October 11, 1887, which stated: The records of this office afford no further information as to date, place or cause of death than is stated on company rolls. His name appeared on the Returns as follows: June 1863, Prisoner of war, supposed to have been taken prisoner on June 17th; and July 1863, absent, sick in Corinth, Mississippi April 17th; August 1863, died in hospital July 28th at Glendale, Mississippi. (Previous record stated he died in the hospital in Corinth, however, Corinth was about 10-20 miles from Glendale. A form signed by Jude H. Shurtleff dated August 1, 1863; stated Fowler died July 28, 1863, in the Post Hospital at Corinth, Mississippi. He is buried in Grave Number A-2190, in the Corinth National Cemetery.

Fowler, James - James Fowler enlisted and mustered into Company H of the 1st Alabama Cavalry, USV as a private on September 13, 1863, in Glendale, Mississippi, at age 18 for a period of 1 year. He was mustered out September 29, 1864, from Rome, Georgia due to expiration of term of service. When he mustered out, he owed the U.S. Government thirty-three cents due to losing 1 unpainted haversack.

James was born January 15, 1848, and died April 17, 1927. He as buried in the County Line Cemetery in Creal Springs, Williamson County, Illinois.

Fowler, L. - See Israel Fowler, above.

Fowler, Samuel Barney - Samuel Barney Fowler enlisted and mustered into Company E of the 1st Alabama Cavalry, USV as a private on October 4, 1864, in Rome, Georgia for a period of 3 years. He was enrolled by Lieutenant Hunter. The Muster and Descriptive Roll recorded him as 25 years of age, 5'-6" tall, having a light complexion, gray eyes, light hair, born in DeKalb County, Georgia, and a farmer by occupation. He was promoted from private to corporal on October 20, 1864. He was mustered out October 20, 1865, in Huntsville, Alabama. Samuel first enlisted in Company H of the 7th Alabama Cavalry, CSA, and later enlisted Sample Battery of Artillery, CSA in June 1863, when he then enlisted in the 1st Alabama Cavalry Union Army in October.

Samuel died in 1916 and was buried in the Valley Grove Primitive Baptist Church Cemetery in Foster's Crossroad in Randolph County, Alabama. He was a brother to William Fowler, below.

Fowler, William - William Fowler, brother to Samuel, above, enlisted in Company D of the 1st Alabama Cavalry, USV on May 3, 1863, in Glendale, Mississippi. He was enlisted by Captain James A. Snelling. The Company Descriptive Book recorded him as 18 years of age, 5'-8" tall, having a dark complexion, dark eyes, dark hair, born in Marion County, Alabama, and a farmer by occupation. The May and June Muster roll recorded him as being absent, sent to the general hospital with insanity. His name appeared on the Returns for June 1863, stating he was a prisoner of war, supposed to be in the hands of the enemy since June 17, 1863. The July and August 1863 Muster Roll recorded him as having died of disease July 4, 1863, at Corinth, Mississippi. His Record of Death and Interment stated he died of imbecility caused by masturbation. This form stated he died July 4, 1863, in the Military Hospital at Corinth, Mississippi.

Fowler, William N. - William N. Fowler enlisted in Company E of the 1st Alabama Cavalry, USV on March 1, 1863, at Corinth, Mississippi, and was mustered in the same day at Glendale, Mississippi. He was reported to have deserted from Glendale, Mississippi on May 1, 1863, and no more information was found in his files.

Southern Claim No: 10017, Date of Hearing: February 4, 1873, Place of Residence: Fayette County, at or near Handy. Occupation: Blacksmith, Length of Residence in Fayette County: "Always resided in Fayette County before and after war.", Age: 55 Years, Place of Residence at Time of Incidents:

Same Remarks: He was postmaster at Handy Post Office when the war broke out. After refusing to take the Confederate Oath, he was arrested by Rebel Colonel Jenkins and kept in prison for several days; the Post Office equipment was moved to Mr. Garrison's house. He was arrested twice more during the war and held for six weeks one time and for 13 days another time. He aided Union men to escape the Rebels and Rebel conscription officers. Two of his nephews served in 1st Alabama Cavalry.

Brief Description of Incident/s: On April 15, 1865, a mare valued at $200 was seized by order of Colonel Crosdon during General Wilson's raid. The horse was bridled and saddled and tied to a gate at the residence of Lewis Idson in Fayette County when it was taken.

Witnesses, Testifiers and Others: H.L. Bolton, age 37, resident of Fayette County; acquainted with claimant for 17 years; lived 1½ miles from him during war; served in the Union army and was assisted by claimant on a "recruiting expedition" in the spring of 1864.

William Hisaw, witnessed incident at the Idson farm.

Mary Idson, age 54, wife of Lewis Idson; witnessed "Yankees" taking claimant's horse".

R.G. Johnson, age 46, resident of Fayette County; acquainted with claimant for 20 years; lived three miles from him during war; Union soldier William Lawrence, witnessed claimant's petition (1871).

Nathaniel Nellums (Nelms), age 64, witnessed incident at the Idson farm.

Frambers, Samuel C. - Only one card was found for Samuel C. Frambers which was filed at the end of the last roll of microfilm of the 1st Alabama Cavalry, USV records. It recorded him as a private in Company A, stating he was reported to have deserted from Memphis, Tennessee on February 4, 1864. No further information relative to this soldier was found.*

Franks, James M. - James M. Franks enlisted in Company K of the 1st Alabama Cavalry, USV on December 15, 1862, at Glendale, Mississippi at age 23 for a period of one year. He was mustered in December 31, 1862, at Corinth, Mississippi. He died of measles on February 5, 1863, at Corinth, Mississippi. His death notice stated he was 23 years old, 5' 10" tall, had a light complexion, hazel eyes, dark hair and was a farmer by occupation. It stated he had never been paid and his clothing allowance was never settled. He had been advanced $33.50 for clothing. It stated he died the 5th Day of February 1863, "Death by Measles". The Death Certificate was signed by Capt. Frank C. Burdick. An Inventory of the Effects of James M. Franks stated he had no effects. It stated he died at the General Hospital in Corinth, Mississippi. His certificate of death was signed by Captain Frank C. Burdick.

James Franks was born about 1840 in Marion County, Alabama to Lemuel Franks and Hulda Jane Gann. A marriage record for James was not found, and it is thought he was single when he joined the 1st Alabama Cavalry and therefore died single. He was one of four brothers who joined the 1st Alabama Cavalry; Jeremiah, Peter and William Franks.

Franks, Peter - Peter Franks, also listed as Frankes, enlisted in Company K of the 1st Alabama Cavalry, USV as a private on December 15, 1862, in Glendale, Mississippi for a period of 1 year, and mustered in December 31, 1862, in Corinth, Mississippi. The January and February 1863 Muster Roll recorded him as absent with leave due to being sick. He was recorded as being present in March and April 1863. He was mustered out December 22, 1863, at age 19 from Memphis, Tennessee due to expiration of term of service.

Franklin, R.J. - Only one card was found for R.J. Franklin which was filed at the end of the last roll of microfilm of the 1st Alabama Cavalry, USV records It recorded him as being a private in Company I of the 1st Alabama Cavalry, USV, and was absent with leave in September 1863. No further information relative to this soldier was found.*

Franks, Jeremiah "Jerry" - Jeremiah Franks enlisted in Company K of the 1st Alabama Cavalry, USV as a private on December 15, 1862, at Glendale, Mississippi for one year. He was mustered in December 31, 1862, at Corinth, Mississippi. The January and February 1863 Muster Roll stated he was absent, sick in the hospital in Corinth, however, he was present in March and April 1863. He was mustered out December 22, 1863, in Memphis, Tennessee with $53.79 having been advanced him for his Clothing Allowance. A Muster and Descriptive Roll showed Jeremiah to have been 18 years of age, 5'-7" tall, having a dark complexion, dark eyes, dark hair, born Marion County, Alabama, and a farmer by occupation. Jeremiah reenlisted on February 1, 1864, in Memphis, Tennessee for three years, and mustered in March 10, 1864. He received no bounty. The January and February 1865 muster roll stated he was absent and had been sick in the USA General Hospital in Savannah, Georgia since January 23, 1865. He was mustered out of service on October 20, 1865, with the rest of the regiment.

Jeremiah was born about 1844 in Marion County, Alabama to Lemuel Franks and Hulda Jane Gann. Lemuel was born about 1795 in North Carolina and died 1858 in Marion County, Alabama. Hulda Jane was born about 1810 in Bradley County, Tennessee and died 1860 in Marion County, Alabama. Jeremiah married Nancy Cagle about 1867, daughter of Samuel and Esther Johnson Cagle, who married May 30, 1843, probably in Paulding County, Georgia. Children of Jeremiah "Jerry" and Nancy were: Addie, Amie, Rheney, James Lemuel, born 1868, died 1917; Janey, born 1874; Elizabeth, "Bettie", born July 14, 1879,

Jeremiah was the brother of James, Peter and William Franks, all members of the 1st Alabama Cavalry, USV. He is buried in the Keys Cemetery in Itawamba County, Mississippi.

Franks, Peter F. - Peter Franks enlisted in Company K of the 1st Alabama Cavalry, USV December 15, 1862, at Glendale, Mississippi at the age of nineteen, for a period of one year, and was mustered in December 31, 1862, at Corinth, Mississippi. The January and February 1863 Muster Roll listed him as being absent with leave due to being sick. It also showed him to be in Company A, rather than K. He was shown as present in March and April. He was mustered out on December 22, 1863, at Memphis, Tennessee, still listed as being in Company A.

Peter F. Franks was born in March 1840 in Pikeville, Marion County, Alabama to Lemuel Franks and Huldah Jane Gann. On January 26, 1864, Peter married Julia Ann "July" Pace, daughter of William Pace and Mary Ann Pollard, who were married February 28, 1847, in Georgia. Children of Peter and Judy were: Sarah J., born about 1868; Thomas Jefferson, born March 1874, died in 1904; William N., born August 1875, died February 1941; Henry Lee, born December 17, 1877, died January 16, 1968; James Morrow, born January 5, 1880, died September 12, 1947; and an infant son, born and died October 12, 1888. July died April 17, 1896, in Itawamba County, Mississippi, and Peter married Nancy Belle Gregory on September 29, 1897, in Itawamba County, Mississippi. Nancy died November 15, 1909, and Peter F. Franks died April 5, 1910, in Itawamba County, Mississippi where he is buried in the Keyes Cemetery.

Franks, William M. - William Franks enlisted with Company A of the First Alabama Calvary of the United States Army on December 15, 1862, at Glendale, Mississippi, along with his brothers, James, Peter and Jeremiah. His tenure of service was one year. He was mustered into service on December 31, 1862, at Corinth, Mississippi. He was listed as present on all muster rolls during his tenure. During November of 1863, he was listed as in detached service at the refugee camp at Corinth, Mississippi and was entered on the mustered-out roll dated December 22, 1863, at Memphis, Tennessee. His military medical records show that he was treated from February 27 to March 31, 1863, for Rubeola and From April 8 to April 17, 1863, for pneumonia at the General Hospital in Corinth, Mississippi. Earlier on February 2, 1863, William's older brother James, died in the army hospital at Corinth.

For the first few months of service, the First Alabama Cavalry was headquartered at Glendale, Mississippi. They were largely engaged in successful scouting and foraging expeditions in northern Mississippi and Alabama owing to their acquaintance with the area. In early May of 1863, Brigadier General Grenville M. Dodge in a report to Major General Stephen A. Hurlbut praised the First Alabama Cavalry for bravely charging Colonel Phillip D. Roddy's Confederates at Bear Creek with unloaded muskets. Colonel Florence M. Cornyn, who had been closer to the Alabamians in their baptism of fire than his Brigadier General, was less complimentary in his report: "I ordered a charge by the First Alabama Cavalry, which I am sorry to say, was not obeyed with the alacrity it should have been. After charging to within short musket-range of the enemy, they halted for a cause I cannot account for, and the enemy escaped into the woods..." What Cornyn probably couldn't understand was that when these men came into musket-range of the Rebel forces and could see the enemy face to face, it came home to them that they weren't fighting some unknown enemy but friends, neighbors and in many cases members of their own families.

Two companies of the First Alabama Cavalry were attached to Colonel Abel D. Streight in his famous charge across Alabama against Confederate General Nathan Bedford Forest which ended in a battle near Gadsden, Alabama. In October, 1863 the First Alabama under the command of Colonel George E. Spencer, a force of about 650 men, was ordered to move out of Corinth toward Columbiana, Alabama. It's objective was to destroy the railroad from Line Station to Elyton. However, about 40 miles out of Glendale at Jones' Crossroads (present-day Red Bay, Alabama), the regiment was attacked by 2000 Confederates.

During the remainder of 1863 the main body of the First Alabama Cavalry remained in the Memphis, Tennessee area recuperating. From time to time, a regiment, a picked patrol or a company of this unit was sent out on reconnaissance expeditions, sometimes skirmishing with Confederate cavalry patrols.

After leaving the United States service in late 1863, William went back to Marion County, Alabama, where his wife and young son, James W. were living. His brother-in-law, sister and nephew had all died during the war (Enoch, Sarah Franks and James W. Cooksey). He took in his two nieces, Sarah and Cynthia Cooksey. Times were hard in Marion County during this time as people were starving. He took his family, along with his two Cooksey nieces, traveled to Memphis, Tennessee and boarded a river boat for Cairo, Illinois. Aboard the river boat, Sarah Cooksey became ill with smallpox and died. During the middle of the night the authorities came on a "dead boat" and took her body away. Cynthia Cooksey, her sister, always hoped that they buried her or dumped her in the river, but rumor was that they burned her body to keep the disease from spreading. William Franks continued to raise Cynthia Cooksey as his own child until she married Floyd Washington Wigginton on January 3, 1875, in McNairy County, Tennessee. (The Wiggintons moved to Itawamba County, Mississippi along with the Franks and lived in Itawamba County until 1908 when they moved to Norman, Oklahoma. The Wiggintons later moved on to central Texas where they lived out their lives. Cynthia Cooksey Wigginton along with her husband Floyd W. are buried in Dyess Grove Cemetery near Temple, Texas).

About 1862, William M. Franks married Margaret Caroline McGowen (one descendant stated her last name was Cooksey, but she may have been married previously). Margaret was born about 1843 in Marion County, Alabama and died in 1909 in Itawamba County, Mississippi. Children of William and Margaret Franks were: James William, born January 26, 1863, died February 29, 1940; Nancy E., born about 1866; Laura Jane, born September 28, 1869, died January 16, 1908; Sarah J., born about 1871; Thomas W., born about 1872; and Samuel Mansfield Franks, born February 8, 1880, and died August 11, 1946. William also married Nancy Jane Varnell. He was the son of Lemuel Franks and his wife, Huldah Jane Gann.

William Franks and his family lived in or near Cairo, Illinois for four years and about 1868 moved back to Marion County, Alabama where he lived for about two years. He then moved his family to McNairy County, Tennessee where his other brothers' families were living. In June 1863, the US Army escorted about 300 Unionists to Illinois on June 20, 1863, because of the Confederate Home Guard burning their homes, barns, crops, etc. and murdering them. After the war was over, many of them remained in Marion County and surrounding counties in Illinois, and are buried there. William and his family may have some of these people who desperately needed protection. The Franks brothers were familiar with the McNairy County area being that they were stationed in nearby Corinth, Mississippi during the Civil War. The Franks families continued to live in McNairy County, Tennessee until about 1879, when they moved to Itawamba County, Mississippi. He died December 27, 1911, in Itawamba County, Mississippi.

William M. Franks Civil War Pension

William M. Franks Civil War pension records state he was sick in General Hospital in Corinth, Mississippi February 28, 1863. The medical records show him treated February 27 to March 31, 1863, for rubella and from April 8th to 17th, 1863 he was treated for pneumonia and returned to duty.

On October 3, 1890, William Franks signed a Declaration For Invalid Pension stating he was 48 years old, a resident of Ballardsville in Itawamba County, Mississippi and that he was unable to earn a support by manual labor by reason of Rheumatism. He signed with his mark and it was witnessed by H.T. Gillentine and Floyd Wigginton.

An undated affidavit by Floyd Wigginton, aged 49 years and O.F. Wigginton, aged 24 years, stated they were personally acquainted with Wm. Franks and that they had been since 1900. They stated he was afflicted with the following disabilities: Rheumatism and having been associated with the said claimant know that he has been incapacitated for manual labor, there being many things _____ to his avocation that of a farmer that he cannot do Viz chopping firewood. In fact all that he can do approaching a full days work is plowing the ___ and chest being affected more than the lower limbs and they further state that as to ___average of manual labor on the farm they think it impossible for him to do more than one third as much as an able bodied man can do and their reason of knowing the above is having been associated with the claimant Wm. Franks. Signed Floyd x Wigginton and O.J. x Wigginton. Witnessed by E.H. Gray and J.D. Bradley

A Medical Affidavit dated July 1, 1891, states William Franks of Ballardsville, Mississippi was disabled with Rheumatism. He makes the following statement upon which he bases his claim: I have had Rheumatism for the last four or five years. It is in my right knee and ankle. Knee is swelled now and generally swelled. I can't walk much as it makes my knee and ankle swell up and pain me. The doctor states: Upon examination we find the following objective conditions: Pulse rate, 92; respiration, 20; temperature, 100; height 5' 9"; weight, 160 pounds; age 48 years. Right knee swollen one inch larger than the other. There is a puff and some tenderness just above and to the inside of Patella. Complains when Patella is moved a little ____. Nothing wrong about action of heart except to rapid today. He is feverish probably from Malaria as his tongue has white coat. Skin yellow which is evidently high colored by otherwise healthy. He cannot have this feverish excitement often with a weight of 160 pounds that he has Rheumatism today and possibly may have it occasionally as he says. There is no swelling of heart. Atrophy as any distortion of the ankle. No other disability found. He is entitled to ¼ rating for the disability caused by Rheumatism of knee. Signed J.W. Greely.

An undated General Affidavit signed by H.H. Murphy of Ballardsville in Itawamba County, Mississippi states: I have known William Franks about four years. I have saw the said William Franks suffering with rheumatism so that he could not get about and I think said William Franks is disabled from manual labor about one half of the time and said William Franks has been disabled for manual labor ever since I knew him. Signed H.H. Murphy

Another undated General Affidavit signed by W.W. Bradley states: I, W.W. Bradley, a resident of Ballardsville, in the county of Itawamba and State of Mississippi, aged 29 years on oath deposes and says in relation to the pension claim of William Franks, Company A, 1st Alabama Volunteers: I have known William Franks about 15 years and have lived a close neighbor to him a good portion of the time and I have saw said William Franks suffering with Rheumatism so that he was totally disabled for manual labor and I think said William Franks is disabled for manual labor about one half of his time and said William Franks has been disabled for about five years to my knowing. Signed W.W. Bradley

The following is an affidavit by Christopher C. Roller about Franks when he applied for a pension:

General Affidavit - State of Tennessee, County of Wayne

In the matter of Nancy Jane Varnell nee Franks whom I am informed is an applicant for a pension War of 1861-5. Personally came before me a acting Justice of the peace in and for aforesaid County and State, Christopher C. Roller citizen of the County of Wayne, State of Tennessee, reputable and entitled to credit, and who, being duly sworn, declare in relation to aforesaid case as follows: That he is 58 years of age, (and resides at Martins Mills) that was marked through. That he had so resided for 14 years, has known her personally for about 15 years. That he was also personally acquainted with her former and late husband William Franks. he states that he was captured in Wayne or Hardin County Tennessee (being on or near the line between the two counties) on the 27th day of May 1864, that at that time he was a discharged soldier. That on the same day the same command of Rebel also captured the said William Franks in the same neighborhood. That he and said Wm. Franks were taken together to Andersonville Georgia and there put in prison together and remained there together about three months. That the said William Frank was taken sick in that prison and became very bad off and was taken out of prison to the Rebel Hospital connected with the prison. That he helped to take said William Franks to the Hospital and went with him as far as the prison gate and he has never seen or heard of him since that time. That said Franks was then dangerously sick and he is perfectly satisfied that he died in that Hospital within a short time after he was taken there. Witness state that he and said

Franks were put in Andersonville Prison about the June 27, 1864. He states that he resides in Wayne County, Tennessee and his address is at Martin's Mill Wayne County Tennessee and that he is about 58 years of age. That he was formerly a private in Company B 1st Alabama Cavalry Regiment. He further declares that he has no interest in said case, and is not concerned in its prosecution, and is not related to said applicant.

W.J. Martin, Signature of Affiants: Christopher Roller (his X mark), J.R.B. Copeland

A Declaration for Pension dated May 1, 1907, in Itawamba County, Mississippi states Will Franks was 66 years of age and a resident of Dorsey. He stated he was 5' 9" tall, had dark complexion, black eyes, black hair and his occupation was a farmer. He stated he lived in Illinois for four years when he was two years old, ten years in Tennessee and lived in Itawamba County, Mississippi the remainder of the time. He gave his pension certificate number as 692.257. He signed his affidavit with his mark: W. M. x Franks, and W.W. Bradley and J.M. Spradling witnessed it. William died December 27, 1911 in Itawamba County, Mississippi.

Freehour, W.H. - See William N. Freshour.

Freeman, Benjamin Franklin -Benjamin F. Freeman enlisted in Company B of the 1st Alabama Cavalry, USV as a private on March 18, 1864, in Decatur, Alabama for a period of 3 years. He was enrolled by Lieutenant Judy, and was mustered in April 13, 1864, in Decatur, Alabama. The Muster and Descriptive Roll recorded him as 18 years of age, 5'-7" tall, having a fair complexion, blue eyes, light hair, born in Cherokee County, Georgia, and a farmer by occupation. The January and February 1865 Muster Roll stated he was sent to the hospital from Sister's Ferry, Georgia. The March through August 1865 Muster Rolls recorded him as absent, left sick in the hospital in Savannah, Georgia February 3, 1865. His Muster-Out Roll stated he was not issued a discharge at muster out of organization due to being in the hospital in Savannah, Georgia since February 3, 1865. Benjamin Freeman's name appeared on a Hospital Muster Roll for the USA General Hospital in Savannah, Georgia as a patient since February 27, 1865. The March and April 1865 Hospital Muster Roll stated he was returned to duty March 27, 1865. His name also appeared on a Hospital Muster Roll for the Foster USA General Hospital in New Berne, North Carolina. The May and June 1865 Hospital Muster Roll recorded him as a patient in Sickel USA General Hospital in Alexandria, Virginia as having been attached as a patient on June 15, 1865. He was listed as being in Hospital Number 2131, being admitted June 15, 1865, from the field with a Post Office address of Benagin, Walker County, Alabama, and diagnosed with chronic diarrhea. He was discharged August 11, 1865.

Benjamin Franklin Freeman was born November 1, 1847, in Cherokee County, Georgia to Benjamin Benajah Freeman and his wife Susannah McCarter who married February 2, 1830, in Franklin County, Georgia. Benjamin F. Freeman married Elizabeth Jane Harvell in 1866 in Fayetteville, Lincoln County, Tennessee. Children of Benjamin and Elizabeth Jane were: Mary Anna, born 1834, died 1890; John F., born January 18, 1835, died August 8, 1912; George, born 1837, died 1860; Susan V., born January 14, 1840, died September 6, 1881; Hiram, born 1843, died, 1860; Henry V., born December 13, 1844, died April 30, 1884; Benjamin Franklin, born November 1, 1847, died October 28, 1911; Frederick, born March 14, 1850, died April 15, 1922; and Serepta, born May 4, 1865, died in October 1927. Benjamin F. Freeman died October 28, 1911, in Houston, Texas County, Missouri and was buried in the Houston Cemetery, in Texas County, Missouri.

Freeman, John - John Freeman (could possibly be the John Freeman, below) enlisted in Company I of the 1st Alabama Cavalry, USV as a private on November 1, 1863, in Glendale, Mississippi. He was reported to have deserted from Camp Davies, Mississippi on December 17, 1863. No further information relative to this soldier was found.*

Freeman, John F. - Only two cards were found for John Freeman which were filed at the end of the last roll of microfilm of the 1st Alabama Cavalry, USV records which stated he enlisted in Company I of the 1st Alabama Cavalry, USV on October 10, 1863, in Glendale, Mississippi as a private. He was enrolled by Lieutenant Snelling for a period of 3 years. The Returns stated he enlisted November 1, 1863. The Company Descriptive Roll recorded him as 27 years of age, 5'-11" tall, having a light complexion, gray eyes, auburn hair, born in Cherokee County, Georgia, and a farmer by occupation. He was enrolled by Lieutenant Snelling for a period of 3 years. His name appeared on the Returns stating he deserted December 17, 1863, from Camp Davies, Mississippi. No further information relative to this soldier was found.*

John F. Freeman was born January 8, 1835, in Cherokee County, Georgia to Benajah Freeman and Susannah McCarter. John married Frances, "Frankie" Sandlin, daughter of Jonathan "Junk" Sandlin and Nancy Vest, who were married April 9, 1833, in Morgan County, Alabama. Children of John and Frankie were: George W., born September 18, 1867, died December 8, 1838; Malinda Lynn, born September 1869, died June 1931; Benjamin "Bert", born February 20, 1871, died March 1, 1936; Jonathan Asbery, born February 26, 1873, died August 1962; Dennis, born 1876; Sarah Jane, born May 22, 1877, died November 8, 1948; and Thomas M. "Fiddling Tom" Freeman, born February 2, 1884, died February 16, 1952. A second tombstone placed on John Freeman's grave mistakenly lists his service as being in the 1st Alabama Cavalry CSA. John's wife, Frances "Frankie" died January 28, 1923. John died August 8, 1912, and was buried at the site of the alter of the original Antioch Church Cemetery in Bug Tussle near Bremen, Cullman County, Alabama. John had given four acres of his land for the church to be built upon. Family information submitted by J.D. Weeks.

Freeman, Robert D. - Robert D. Freeman enlisted in Company F of the 1st Alabama Cavalry, USV as a private on June 5, 1863, in Corinth, Mississippi for a period of 1 year, and was mustered in August 13, 1863, in Corinth. He was enrolled by Lieutenant Hinds The Company Descriptive Book recorded him as 44 years of age, 5'-11" tall, having a dark complexion, dark eyes, brown hair, born in Choctaw County, Mississippi, and a doctor by occupation. The July and August 1863 Muster Roll recorded him as absent, sick near Glendale, Mississippi. His name appeared on the Returns for September 1863 as follows: Died September 29, 1863, in Regimental Hospital in Glendale, Mississippi. He died of a disease contracted in service.

French, - Only one card was found for a soldier with the last name as French, no first name listed. It was filed at the end of the last roll of microfilm of the 1st Alabama Cavalry, USV records. It recorded him as being in Company A, stating he was on detached service as a guide in October 1864. Many times the guides and spies were not actually enlisted in the regiment. No further information relative to this soldier was found.*

Freshour, Samuel C. - Samuel C. Freshour enlisted in Company A of the 1st Alabama Cavalry, USV on December 26, 1863, in Camp Davies, Mississippi for a period of 3 years. He was enrolled by Lieutenant Hinds, and mustered in February 5, 1864, in Memphis, Tennessee. The Muster and Descriptive Roll recorded him as 22 years of age, 6'-2" tall, having a fair complexion, blue eyes, light hair, born in Walker County, Alabama, and a farmer by occupation. He was reported to have deserted February 4, 1864, in Memphis, Tennessee, owing the U.S. Government $17.16 for taking 1 pistol, saber belt and accoutrements, complete.

Freshour, William N. - William N. Freshour enlisted in Company E of the 1st Alabama Cavalry, USV as a private on March 1, 1863, in Corinth, Mississippi for a period of 1 year. He mustered in March 13, 1863, in Glendale, Mississippi at age 18. He was reported to have deserted June 1, 1863, in Glendale, Mississippi. The Returns stated he deserted May 4, 1863, from Glendale, Mississippi.

Fretwell, Erby - Erby Fretwell, also listed as Fortwell, enlisted in Company G of the 1st Alabama Cavalry, USV on March 21, 1864, in Decatur, Alabama as a private for a period of 3 years. He was enrolled by Lieutenant Pease, and mustered in April 13, 1864, in Decatur. The Muster and Descriptive Roll records him as 38 years of age, 5'-7" tall, having a fair complexion, gray eyes, dark hair, born in Winston County, Alabama, and a farmer by occupation. He was promoted to a Corporal on May 1, 1864. He was mustered out October 20, 1865, in Huntsville, Alabama, owing the U.S. Government fifty-five cents for losing 1 wiper and thong, and 1 screwdriver. His Muster-Out roll stated he was due a bounty of $300.

Erby Fretwell was born May 21, 1827, in Winston County, Alabama to Yerby Fretwell and was a brother to William W. Fretwell, below. Erby married Amanda J. Aikens in December 1850. Amanda was born January 22, 1836, and died October 3, 1917. Erby and Amanda had the following children: William Sylvester, born September 1852, died October 14, 1928; Elizabeth F., born June 9, 1859, died December 25, 1898; Kanzada, born August 11, 1862, died May 2, 1896; Ervin Lawson, November 13, 1865, died March 22, 1950; Emma, born January 3, 1870, died November 22, 1895; and Edward Thomas Fretwell, born March 1873. Erby Fretwell died January 7, 1911, in Lawrence County, Alabama, and was buried in the Old Town Creek Cemetery, in Lawrence County, Alabama.

Fretwell, William Washington - William Washington Fretwell enlisted in Company G of the 1st Alabama Cavalry, USV as a private on March 21, 1864, in Decatur, Alabama for a period of 3 years. He was enrolled by Lieutenant Pease, and mustered in April 13, 1864, in Decatur. The Muster and Descriptive Roll recorded him as 42 years of age, 5'-6" tall, having a fair complexion, blue eyes, dark hair, born in Blount County, Alabama, and a farmer by occupation. The July and August 1864 Muster Roll recorded him as absent with leave. He was mustered out October 20, 1865, in Huntsville, Alabama owing the U.S. Government $6.75 for losing 1 halter, 1 curb bridle, 1 cap box, and 1 mess pan. He was due a bounty of $300.

William W. Fretwell was born about 1822 in Blount County, Alabama to Yerby Fretwell, and was a brother to Erby Fretwell, above. He married Emaline "Emma" Abilene, about 1844 and had the following children: Mary Elizabeth; Levi G.; William; Alabert James; Narcissis; Martha J.; Tabitha S., and Maggie Fretwell. William died January 7, 1911 in Lawrence County, Alabama

Frost, Christopher S. - Christopher S. Frost enlisted in Company H of the 1st Alabama Cavalry, USV on October 18, 1864, in Rome, Georgia for a period of 3 years. He was enrolled by Captain James W. DeVaney. The Muster-In Roll stated he was mustered-in October 16, 1865, in Huntsville, Alabama which might indicate he re-enlisted at that time. The March and April 1865 Muster Roll stated he had not been mustered in at that time. The Muster and Descriptive Roll recorded him as 18 years of age, 6' tall, having a fair complexion, blue eyes, light hair, born in Walker County, Alabama, and a farmer by occupation. It also stated he was absent, sick at Jeffersonville, Indiana at the time. The Jeffersonville U.S.A. General Hospital Muster Roll recorded him as being admitted December 15, 1864. The hospital was listed as hospital #11300, records Christopher's age as 17, single, records the person closest to him as Edward Frost in Sheffield, Walker County, Alabama. He was sent to Jeffersonville from Hospital #14, in Nashville, Tennessee. The January and February 1865 Muster Roll recorded him as still being present in the Jeffersonville Hospital, and diagnosed with intermittent fever. He mustered out October 20, 1865, in Huntsville, Alabama, owing the U.S. Government $36.75 stating he was paid $32 while a patient in the hospital at Jeffersonville, Indiana, and also for losing 1 shelter tent. He is buried in the West Corona-Frost Cemetery, Walker County, Alabama

Froshour, Samuel C. - See Samuel C. Freshour above.

Fry, J.H. - Only one card was found for J.H. Fry which was filed at the end of the last roll of microfilm of the 1st Alabama Cavalry, USV records. His name appeared on the Returns for September 1864 and recorded him as a Private in Company L. It stated he was discharged September 29, 1864, in Rome, Georgia due to expiration of term of service. No further information relative to this soldier was found.*

Fry, Thomas W. - Thomas W. Fry enlisted in Company L of the 1st Alabama Cavalry, USV as a private on September 25, 1863, in Fayette County, Alabama for a period of 1 year. He was enrolled by Captain Sanford Tramel, and was mustered in the same day in Glendale, Mississippi. The Muster and Descriptive Roll recorded him as 20 years of age, 6' tall, having a fair complexion, gray eyes, dark hair, born in Forsythe County, Georgia, and a farmer by occupation. The Company Muster Roll for September 25 to October 31, 1863, recorded him as being absent with leave. The November and December 1863 Muster Roll stated he returned from missing in action December 1, 1863. His name appeared on the Returns which stated the following: October 1863, absent with leave; November 1863, absent, left sick in Alabama by order of Colonel Spencer; December 1863, returned from desertion

December 2, 1863. He was mustered out September 28, 1864, from Rome, Georgia by reason of expiration of term of service.

Thomas W. Fry was born April 4, 1843, in Forsythe County, Georgia to William A. Fry and Margaret Denning, who were married August 25, 1835, in Lumpkin County, Georgia. Thomas married Mary Laissa Ingle on February 15, 1863, in Winston County, Alabama. Thomas died March 17, 1926, Pittsburg County, Oklahoma and is buried in the Blanco Cemetery in Pittsburg County, Oklahoma. His sister, Sarah Fry, married Murray Ingle who also served in this regiment. Family information submitted by Nancy Fry.

Fulks, Harrison - Harrison Fulks, also spelled as Foulks Foulkes, enlisted in Company B of the 1st Alabama Cavalry, USV as a private on September 10, 1863, in Stevenson, Alabama for a period of 1 year. His description was given as 44 years of age, 5'-6" tall, having a fair complexion, blue eyes, light hair, born in Caswell County, North Carolina, and a farmer by occupation. A Record of Death and Interment stated Harrison Foulks died of chronic diarrhea on November 18, 1863, in the Cumberland USA General Hospital in Nashville, Tennessee. It listed his Grave Number as 5575, but did not say where. Most of the Union soldiers, who died in Nashville, were buried in the City Cemetery and reinterred in the Nashville National Cemetery in Nashville, Davidson County, Tennessee. There was a Harrison Fulks who enlisted in Company B of the 1st Tennessee and Alabama Independent Vidette Cavalry, USV as a Bugler and died November 20, 1863, in Nashville, Tennessee. He was 44 years of age, and is probably the same Harrison Fulks who enlisted in the 1st Alabama Cavalry, USV. Many of the soldiers in the Vidette Cavalry, went on to serve in the 1st Alabama Cavalry, USV, but while his name was shown as having enlisted in the 1st Alabama Cavalry, USV, it may have been an error on the clerks part. One record in his file stated he enlisted in Company B of the 2nd Alabama while another stated he enlisted in Company B of the 1st Alabama Cavalry, and died November 20, 1863 in the Cumberland Hospital in Nashville, Tennessee.

Funderburk, Christopher C. - Christopher C. Funderburk enlisted and mustered into Company K of the 1st Alabama Cavalry, USV as a corporal on July 24, 1863, in Huntsville, Alabama for a period of 3 years. He was enrolled by Captain Bankhead. The Regimental Descriptive Book recorded him as 25 years of age, 5'-11" tall, having a dark complexion, dark eyes, dark hair, born in Rome, Floyd County, Georgia, and a farmer by occupation. Christopher was one of the early enlistees sent to Nashville, Tennessee, and merged with Company E of the 1st Middle Tennessee Cavalry, US, which later became the 5th Tennessee Cavalry. He was sent to Winston County, Alabama for recruiting and recorded as being absent and never heard from again since August 13, 1862. However, the May and June 1864 Muster Roll recorded him as having died while a prisoner of war February 21, 1864. His name appeared on a Company Muster-Out Roll dated July 19, 1865, and stated the following: Sent on recruiting service August 13, 1862, to be absent 21 days; Dropped as deserter October 1, 1862; Reported to company at Palmyra, Tennessee April 11, 1863; Captured May 3, 1863, by Rebels near Rome, Georgia, not heard from since, prisoner of war. No discharge furnished. He died February 21, 1864, while a prisoner of war in the hands of the enemy.

Furth, Elmore - Only one card was found for Elmore Furth which was filed at the end of the last roll of microfilm of the 1st Alabama Cavalry, USV records. It recorded him as a private in Company E, and was Hospital Muster Roll for Gayoso USA General Hospital in Memphis, Tennessee for January and February 1864, stating he was a patient. No further information relative to this soldier was found.*

- G -

Gaddy, Calvin M. - Calvin M. Gaddy enlisted in Company F of the 1st Alabama Cavalry, USV as a private on December 8, 1862, in Chewalla, Tennessee at age 28 for a period of 1 year, and was mustered in the same day in Corinth, Mississippi. A Company Muster Roll recorded him as absent from February 28, 1863, through June 1863, sick in hospital in Corinth, Mississippi. His name appeared on the Returns as follows: March 1863, Absent, sick; April 1863, Absent with leave; May 1863, Absent without leave, to be dropped as deserter after date; December 1863, Loss December 16,

1863, due to expiration of term of service. He was discharged December 16, 1863, in Memphis, Tennessee due to expiration of term of service. Another card stated he mustered out December 17, 1863.

Gaddy, Stephen H. - Stephen H. Gaddy enlisted in Company E of the 1st Alabama Cavalry, USV as a private on December 8, 1862, in Chewalla, Tennessee for a period of 1 year, and was mustered in the same day in Corinth, Mississippi. His name appeared on the Returns stating that from March to November 1863, he was on duty as an orderly in the Regimental Headquarters. The July and August 1863 Muster Roll recorded him as being on mounted or daily duty in Regimental Headquarters. He was mustered out December 17, 1863, in Memphis, Tennessee due to expiration of term of service.

Gadsey, Robert - See Robert Godsey.

Gaff, William T. - See William T. Goof.

Gaggers, G.W. – (May be Jaggers) Only one card was found for G.W. Gaggers which was filed at the end of the last roll of microfilm of the 1st Alabama Cavalry, USV records. His name appeared on the Returns for December 1863 and recorded him as being in Company D, stating he enlisted in the 1st Alabama Cavalry, USV on December 10, 1863, as an artificer. No further information relative to this soldier was found.*

Gaha, William C. - See William C. McGaha.

Gailey, David J. - David J. Gailey enlisted in Company A of the 1st Alabama Cavalry, USV as a private on September 8, 1862, in Iuka, Mississippi for a period of 1 year, and was mustered in October 1, 1862, in Corinth, Mississippi. The Company Descriptive book recorded him as 24 years of age, 5'-5½" tall, having a light complexion, gray eyes, light hair, born in Habersham County, Georgia, and a farmer by occupation. The November 1862 through June 1863 Muster Rolls recorded him as absent, sick in the hospital in Corinth, Mississippi. The November and December 1862 Muster Roll recorded him as a corporal and he held that rank until he was discharged. A Hospital Muster Roll for Washington U.S.A. General Hospital in Memphis, Tennessee recorded him as being a patient, being admitted June 26, 1863. He was discharged September 16, 1863, from Corinth, Mississippi due to expiration of term of service.

Gaines, Charles W. - Charles W. Gaines enlisted as a private in Company H of the 1st Alabama Cavalry, USV as a private on December 20, 1864, in Rome, Georgia for a period of 3 years. He was enrolled by Captain James W. DeVaney, and was mustered in February 13, 1865, in Nashville, Tennessee. He was paid a bounty of $100, and his enlistment was credited to Ripley, Chautauqua County, New York The Muster and Descriptive Roll recorded him as 28 years of age, 5'-3" tall, having a fair complexion, gray eyes, light hair, born in Gwinnett County, Georgia, and a saddler by occupation. Gaines died of smallpox March 8, 1865, in the Post Hospital in Huntsville, Alabama.

Gaines, Ralph - Only one card was found for Ralph Gaines which was filed at the end of the last roll of microfilm of the 1st Alabama Cavalry, USV records. His name appeared on the Returns for March 1863, stating he was in Company E of the 1st Alabama Cavalry, USV and was absent, sick. No further information relative to this soldier was found.*

Galbraith, John - Only one card was found for John Galbraith which was filed at the end of the last roll of microfilm of the 1st Alabama Cavalry, USV records. It recorded him as a private in Company C. The November and December 1865 Muster Roll recorded him as being absent, sick in General Hospital #2 in Louisville, Kentucky. No further information relative to this soldier was found.*

Gallion, John - Only one card was found for John Gallion which was filed at the end of the last roll of microfilm of the 1st Alabama Cavalry, USV records. It recorded him as a private in Company H, and stated he was absent, sick in the Smallpox U.S.A. Hospital in Memphis, Tennessee on March 28, 1864. No further records relative to this soldier were found.*

Galloway, Jason C. - Only three cards were found for Jason C. Galloway which were filed at the end of the last roll of microfilm of the 1st Alabama Cavalry, USV records. They recorded him as a private in Company B. The September and October 1863 Muster Roll recorded him as absent, sick in General Field Hospital in Stevenson, Alabama. The November and December 1863 Muster Roll recorded him as a patient in the U.S.A. General Hospital in Evansville, Indiana. He was also recorded as being sick in the U.S.A. General Hospital in Evansville, Indiana, Crittenden U.S.A. General Hospital, Branch E, in Louisville, Kentucky where he was admitted February 10, 1864. His name appeared on the March and April Hospital Muster Roll for the Smallpox USA General Hospital in Memphis, Tennessee, where he was admitted March 28, 1864. No further information relative to this soldier was found.*

Gammill, Joseph E. - Joseph E. Gammill, also listed as G. Gammville, enlisted in Company F of the 1st Alabama Cavalry, USV as a Commissary Sergeant on May 23, 1863, in Corinth, Mississippi for a period of 1 year. He was enrolled by Captain Pierce and was mustered in August 13, 1863, in Corinth, Mississippi. The Company Descriptive Book recorded him as 32 years of age, 5'-7" tall, having a fair complexion, blue eyes, brown hair, born in Pickens County, Alabama, and a farmer by occupation. The July and August 1863 Muster Roll recorded him as absent, on furlough for thirty days. The September and October 1863 Muster Roll recorded him as a private, and stated he was absent, without leave since October 1, 1863. His name appeared on the Returns for September 1863, stating he deserted September 24, 1863, while on furlough.

Gammonville, G. - Only one card was found for G. Gammonville which was filed at the end of the last roll of microfilm of the 1st Alabama Cavalry, USV records. It stated he was a sergeant in Company F of the 1st Alabama Cavalry, USV and deserted while on furlough September 24, 1863.

Gann, David - Also spelled David Ganns. Only one card was found for David Gann which was filed at the end of the last roll of microfilm of the 1st Alabama Cavalry, USV records. It recorded him as a private in Company A, stating he transferred to Company B in the 1st Alabama Cavalry March 1, 1863, at Glendale, Mississippi. He may have been temporarily attached from one of the northern regiments. No further information relative to this soldier was found.*

Gann, G.W. - Only one card was found for G.W. Gann which was filed at the end of the last roll of microfilm of the 1st Alabama Cavalry, USV records. It recorded him as a hospital nurse in Company F, in September 1863. No further information relative to this soldier was found.*

Gann, Newton E. - Newton E. Gann enlisted in Company F of the 1st Alabama Cavalry, USV as a private on June 29, 1863, in Corinth, Mississippi for a period of 1 year. He was enrolled by Captain Pierce and was mustered in August 13, 1863, in Corinth. The Descriptive Roll recorded Gann as 27 years of age, 5'-9" tall, having a light complexion, gray eyes, brown hair, born in McNairy County, Tennessee, and a farmer by occupation. The September 1863 through December 1864 Muster Rolls recorded him as absent, sick at Corinth, Mississippi. In November and December 1863, his name appeared on the Hospital Muster Roll for the U.S.A. Post Hospital in Corinth, Mississippi. The January through April 30, 1864, Muster Rolls recorded him as absent, sick at Memphis, Tennessee. Newton E. Gann's name appeared on the Returns as follows: December 1863, absent, sick at Corinth, Mississippi; January 1864, absent, sick in hospital in Memphis, Tennessee; February 1864, died of disease in Memphis, Tennessee February 11, 1864; April 1864, died of smallpox February 11, 1864, in the Smallpox Hospital in Memphis, Tennessee. He was recorded as having deserted September 20, 1863, from Glendale, Mississippi, however, he was probably in a hospital and the clerk was not aware of where he was. Newton E, Gann is buried in Section B, Grave #1381 in the Memphis National Cemetery in Memphis, Shelby County, Tennessee.

<u>**Gann, Smith William**</u> - Smith William Gann enlisted in Company F of the 1st Alabama Cavalry, USV as a private on November 25, 1863, at Camp Davies, Mississippi for a period of 1 year. He was enrolled by Lieutenant W.H. Chaney and mustered in October 17, 1864, at Rome, Georgia. The Company Descriptive Book recorded him as 23 years of age, 5'-9½" tall, having a light complexion, gray eyes, light hair, born in Marion County, Alabama, and a farmer by occupation. The January and February 1864 Muster Roll recorded him as absent, sick in Memphis, Tennessee. The April 30, 1864, Muster Roll recorded him as absent, sick in Nashville, Tennessee. The December 31, 1863, through June 30, 1864, Muster Roll recorded him as absent, sick at Rome, Georgia. He returned from the hospital in Rome, Georgia on August 20, 1864, and was mustered out December 17, 1864, due to being on the march from Atlanta to Savannah, Georgia. Gann was listed on the Adams U.S.A. General Hospital in Memphis, Tennessee as having been admitted February 17, 1864, as a patient. Smith supposedly was thrown from his horse while in the army and hit his head. He stated he was in a charge when his horse fell over a stump and threw him off. He struck the back of his head and mashed in his skull. (This is according to his widow's pension claim) It pressed on his brain and caused him to have seizures which continued until his death. He was born about 1840 in Hamilton, Marion County, Alabama and died May 24, 1879, in Lamar County, Alabama. Smith Gann stated he had "layed out" in the woods to keep out of Rebel service. He is buried in the Old Campground Cemetery which is between Guin and Sulligent, Alabama It is just over the Marion County, Alabama line in Lamar County, Alabama. His mother, Rachael Miller Gann, is also buried there along with several other family members.

Smith W. Gann was the son of Thomas Jefferson Gann and Rachel Louisa Miller, who was the daughter of Nathaniel Miller, Sr. and his wife, Margaret Newton. His father, Thomas Jefferson Gann served in Company K of the 5th Alabama Cavalry, CSA during the Civil War and died or was killed about 1865 during the war.

Smith W. Gann first married Winnie "Puss" Ford, who died February 15, 1862, near Pikeville, Marion County, Alabama. He and Winnie had one child who was stillborn. Winnie was a sister of the wife of George F. Motes, who was also a soldier in the 1st Alabama Cavalry, USV. George was an affiant for Smith W. Gann's 2nd wife, Mary, in her request for pension. Smith married 2nd to Mary Ann "Welch" Waters, born June 15, 1833, in Georgia and died March 11, 1934. She was the daughter of John S. and Elizabeth Welch. They were married by Nathaniel Miller, who was his grandfather on his mother's side.

She had been married to Samuel Leroy Waters who fought for the Confederacy and died in Virginia while in service. Mary and Leroy had one child who died at birth and was not named. Mary Ann's parents moved from Georgia to Fayette County, Alabama when Mary was three-weeks old.

Children of Smith & Mary Gann were: John Thomas, born January 6, 1867, died in May 1893; William J., born January 13, 1869, died 1940; James H., born July 5, 1872, died 1961; George Henry, born February 7, 1874, died August 2, 1947; Elam Nathaniel, born July 5, 1876, died February 4, 1956; and Rachael Elizabeth Gann, born February 6, 1879, died 1973.

Another descendant submitted the following information on the children of Smith and Mary Gann, which is different from the above: John Thomas, born January 6, 1867, died January 1938; William Joshua, born January 13, 1869, died 1940; James Franklin, born July 5, 1872, died November 26, 1939; George Henry, born February 7, 1874, died August 2, 1947;Elam Nathaniel, born July 5, 1877, died February 4, 1956; Rachel Elizabeth Gann, born February 6, 1879, died before 1973. They possibly had a daughter named Martha Jane Gann.

In a General Affidavit by Matilda Moats, age 71, a resident of Pikeville in Marion County, Alabama stated that she was present at the birth of the following named children of Smith W. and Ann Gann in the capacity of Midwife on the dates hereinafter mentioned as follows: George Henry Gann on the 7th day of February 1873; Elam Nathaniel Gann, on the 9th of July 1875; and Rachael Elizabeth Gann on the 6th day of February 1879. She stated the children were born in Marion County, Alabama. The affidavit was witnessed by C.C. Chaffin and William H. McCollough.

An undated Physician's Affidavit signed by W.L. Walton, M.D., a resident of Marion County, Alabama, stated, "I certify that I examined Smith W. Gann twice in 1875. On the second examination I found a depression of the Parietal bone of the Head, caused by a fall from his horse whilst in the Federal Army, so he stated, the pressure of which on the brain caused epileptic fits which incapacitated him from labor at all if he was to do himself justice. I also certify that I have been a practitioner of medicine for forty years – did not treat Soldier but only examined him.

A Declaration for Original Pension of a Widow dated July 14, 188?, signed by Mary A. Gann, stated she lived 6 miles from Webster, Alabama. She also stated: "I am the widow of Smith W. Gann who served during the late War of the Rebellion under the name of Smith W. Gann as a Private in Co. F, 1st Alabama Cav. and who was honorably discharged from the service and who died of Epilepsy on the 24th day of May 1879 at home in Marion County, Alabama." She stated she was without other means of support than her daily labor; that she was married under the name of Mary A. Waters to said Smith W. Gann on the 18th day of December 1865 by Nathaniel Miller at Wm. West's in Marion County, Alabama, and that both had been previously married; her husband died May 6, 1865, and Smith's wife died February 15, 1862; that the following are the names and dates of birth of all his legitimate children who are under sixteen years of age at the present time: John Thomas Gann, born January 6, 1867; William J. Gann, born January 13, 1869; James H. Gann, born July 4, 1872; George H. Gann, born February 4, 1874; Elan N. Gann, born July 5, 1876, and Rachael E. Gann, born February 6, 1879. She stated there were no children from a former marriage.

In a Declaration for Original Pension of a Widow, dated July 14, 1890, Mary A. Gann, age 49, a resident of Lamar County, 5 miles from Guin in Marion County, Alabama, and witnessed by William J. Kirk and A.C. Kirk. Mary stated she was a widow of Smith W. Gann who served during the late War of the Rebellion under the name of Smith W. Gann as a Private in Company F of the 1st Alabama Cavalry, and who was honorably discharged from the service and who died of Epilepsy on May 24, 1879 at home in Marion County, Alabama. She stated she was without other means of support than her daily labor, that she was married under the name of Mary A. Waters to said Smith Gann on December 18, 1865 by Nathaniel Miller at William West's in Marion County, and that neither she nor her husband had previously been married and that they had no children of their own and that she had remained a widow. She listed his children who were under the age of sixteen as: John Thomas Gann, born January 6, 1867; William J. (Jesse), born January 13, 1869; James H.,, born July 4, 1872; George H. (Henry), born February 4, 1874; Elam N. (Nathaniel), born July 5, 1876; and Rachel E. (Elizabeth) Gann, born February 6, 1879.

A Declaration For Children Under Sixteen Years of Age dated November 10, 1890, was completed by John A. Shaw, (who was married Smith W. Gann's sister, Melvina Abigail Gann). He stated he was 37 years old and a resident of Marion County, Alabama. He stated he was the legal guardian of the legitimate children of Smith W. Gann

An General Affidavit dated March 2, 1896, signed by William J. Kirk, age 53, a resident of Sizemore, in Lamar County, Alabama, and James F. Kirk, age 45, a resident of Guin in Marion County, Alabama, both attested to the names of Smith W. Gann's children and wife, Mary.

A Deposition dated September 14, 1896, (Case of Mary Ann Miller, No. 276,963) (sic) (see later about her marriage to Miller) stated: On this 14th day of September 1896 at Guin, County of Marion, State of Alabama, before me, J.B. Goodlett, a Special Examiner of the Pension Office, personally appeared Mary Ann Miller, who, being by me first duly sworn to answer truly all interrogatories propounded to her during this Special Examination of aforesaid pension claim, deposes and says: "I am 59 years old, no occupation, P.O. as above. I am the identical Mary Ann Miller who is an applicant for pension as the widow of Smith W. Gann who was a soldier in Company F, 1st Alabama Volunteer Cavalry. He was never in any other Regiment. He was never in the Confederate service. I do not know the dates of his enlistment and discharge. He died May 24, 1879, of fits (seizures). He died with a fit (seizure) on him. No sir, there was nothing else the matter with him. He was sitting at the table eating supper and when he got up from the table I saw the fit coming on him and found a ____ for him and called Mr. William Shaw and his brother John Shaw and they took him and laid him on the bed and he died in a very few minutes. He had had another fit that day in the afternoon. Mr. Gann and I were married December 14, 1865m by Squire Nathaniel Miller. (Nathaniel Miller was Smith Gann's grandfather on his mother's side of the family.) We had a license and were regularly married. We lived together as husband and wife up to his death. I remained a widow two years when I married Newton Miller. We were married June 7, 1881. He had a license and Bud Nesmith, now dead, married us. The court house at Hamilton was burned and the records were all destroyed. I know I was a widow two years. The children and I finished the crop Mr. Gann had in when he died, and we made and gathered one more and made another when Mr. Miller and I were married. Sarah Ann and Jane Nesmith were the only persons present when we were married. The ceremony was performed in Mrs. M...'s house. Mr. Gann and I had both been married before. My first husband was named Samuel Waters. He was killed during the war while in the Confederate Army. Mr. Gann's first wife was named Winnie Ford, she died before Mr. Gann and I were married. She did not have any children. I had six children by Mr. Gann. These are all living and are the only children we each had except one by his first wife which was born dead. The names and dates of birth of these children are as follows: John Thomas, born January 6, 1867; William J., born January 13, 1869; James H., Born July 5, 1871; George H., born February 7, 1874; Elam N.,, born July 5, 1876; and Rachel E. Gann, born February 6, 1879. There is no record of the births of these children's births public or private. I had a midwife with me at the births of these children. Betty Smith with John, and Rachel, his grandmother, was with me when William J. was born. Mrs. Smith was with me when George H. was born and Mrs. Matilda Moates was with me when the last three were born. Mrs. Smith and Mrs. Moates are dead. Mrs. Gann lives near Guin. Mrs. Louisa Gann was present when William and James were born. Mrs. Susan Moats was present when John Thomas was born, Mrs. D... Lockhart was present when the last three were born. There was no one else now living who was present when these children were born. These children left me and went and lived with relatives. Mr. John A. Shaw was appointed their guardian and has Rachel E. and George H. Address of James H. is Gold Mine, Marion County, Alabama.

Question: By whom can you prove that these children were with you until you re-married and that they are still living?

Answer: William J. Shaw, John A. Shaw, Sarah A. Murphy, Mary Jane Nesmith, Mrs. D. Lockhart and plenty of others. They also know about Mr. Gann and I were never divorced and that I remained a widow until I married Mr. Miller.

Question: By whom can you prove the date and cause of Mr. Gann's death"

Answer: There was no doctor present. He had consulted Dr. Walton, Dr. Martin, and Dr. Elliott at different times. Dr. Walton is dead. Dr. Martin lives at Vernon, Kentucky, Dr. Martin at Hamilton and Dr. Elliott at C... Station, Alabama. Mr. Shaw took him to Dr. Martin about a month before his death. He was the last doctor who examined him that I know of. Mr. William J. Shaw, John A. Shaw, and William Markham, Sarah E. Shaw and Melvina A. Shaw were present when he died. His mother, Rachel Gann, was present and they can all tell you the cause of his death.

Question: What was the cause of his having fits?

Answer: He was thrown from a horse while in the army so he told me. I do not remember when or where this happened. He said he was in a charge and his horse fell over a stump and threw him off. He struck on the back part of his head and mashed the skull in. It pressed on his brain and caused him to have fits. I have often seen and felt the dented place in his skull. It was round and about the size of a half dollar. He had some fits before he come out of the army. I never saw him have one until the second day after we were married. I knew of his having them before that though. He had them all along every month until he died. No sir none of the rest of his family ever had fits that I know of. He said he never had any fits until after he was thrown from his horse.

Question: By whom can you prove that Mr. Gann was injured as you state and that he never had fits prior to that time.

Answer: George Moates of Booneville, Mississippi was in the army with him. I do not know of anyone else now living who was in the army with him. Wm... might know something of it. Mr. G.T. Akers, at Guin, Alabama, J.W. Boseman and Mr. .... All knew him well and ever since the war and can tell you of his condition both before and since discharge.

Question: Would any of these men know it? (List...)

Answer: Mr. Fontaine might. William M. McLarty and Robert M. McLarty might to. They were in his company and lived here before the war and awhile afterwards. Sam And... also used to live here. I do not know any of the others. Witnesses were W.H. Matthews and W.J. Shaw. It was signed by Mary Ann Miller with her mark.

Sworn to and subscribed before me this 14 day of September 1896 and I certify that the contents were fully made known to deponent before signing. Signed by J.B. Goodlett, Special Examiner

Deposition dated January 5, 1898 (Case of Mary A. Gann, No. 486,407)

On the 5th day of January 1898, at Bay Village, County of Cross, State of Arkansas, George F. Motes stated: (sic) My age is 55 years. Residence and P.O. address at present, Bay Village, Cross County, Arkansas, I am a Farmer.

I know Mary A. Gann well. She was a sister of my first wife. No, Gann married my 1st wife's sister and Mary A. Gann was his second wife. Smith W. Gann was the soldier in this case. I knew his first wife. She was called Puss. Her maiden name was Ford. She died in Marion County, Alabama about 1862. I helped bury her. She died near Pikeville, Marion County, Alabama. Smith W. Gann and Puss never had any children living. Smith W. Gann remarried after the war. She was a widow woman when he married her. I do not now remember what had been her maiden name nor what was her first husband's name. I left there the first year after the surrender and Smith W. Gann had just been married before I left. I have never been about them to say anything. I had seen Smith W. Gann often times. I knew nothing about what children Smith W. Gann had when he died nor about any remarriages of his widow.

I became acquainted with Smith W. Gann at his father's house near Pikeville, Marion County, Alabama in 1860. We had enlisted in Company F, 1st Alabama Cavalry, Colonel Spencer, Captain Pearce and Lieutenant Jerome J. Hinds at Camp Davies near Corinth, Mississippi. It was in the fall of 1863. We were discharged at Mouth of Savannah River in South Carolina. We were in service about fifteen months and were discharged in 1864. (George F. Motes and Smith W. Gann were both discharged on December 17, 1864.) I was Regimental Blacksmith, Gann was a lift Private. Part of the time I bunked and messed with Gann, but a part of the time I was out on detached service. I was well acquainted with Gann before our service. Lived about two miles from him. Gann and myself layed out in the woods together to keep out of Rebel service before our service. Gann was a big fat stout man before service. Yes, we were examined by doctors two or three times when enlisted.

I could not tell you really what sickness he had in service. He had rheumatism while he was in service. It was in his knees as I recollect it now. I never saw him in hospital. I was not at hospital when he was there that I remember. I do not remember any particular place he was affected with rheumatism. I never made any examination of him in service. I was generally not quartered with the regiment and was not at sick call. I have no recollection of him suffering from anything except like rheumatism while he was in service. We were mustered out at the same time. We went to New York, New York, where we were paid off. Went by ship to New York and we came home from New York City to Marion County, Alabama. He was suffering badly from rheumatism at the time we were discharged and all the way home. We stayed at Decatur, Alabama. Two or three weeks because I and he had rheumatism. He was not down, he was complaining all the time. He could go, but it seemed he could not hold out. He complained of rheumatism in his knees and legs. I never heard any other part of his body. He said he was sick and complained more of his knees than anything else.

A Deposition dated March 2, 1898 (Case of John A. Shaw, Guardian, No. 486.407)

On this 2nd day of March 1898 at Dime Box, County of Lee, State of Alabama, before me, G.S. Arnold, a Special Examiner of the Pension Office, personally appeared William A. McLarty, who being by me first duly sworn to answer truly all interrogatories propounded to him during this Special Examination of aforesaid pension claim, deposes and says: My age is 65 years. Occupation Merchant and Postmaster. Residence and P.O. as above. During the late war I served as Commissary Sergeant in Company F, 1st Alabama Cavalry. I enlisted in 1862 and served 12 months. I cannot recall date of discharge. Yes, I recall Smith Gann as a member of my company. He served as a private. He enlisted some time in 1863 and was still with the company when I left. I had known him some 5 or 6 years before the war. We were living in Marion County, Alabama at the time. We were neighbors and I saw him quite often. He was a stout able bodied man at that time. I cannot at this time recall that I ever heard of his receiving an injury or contracting any disability in the service. I recall that he had the measles at Memphis, Tennessee. Cannot fix the date. It was soon after he joined. I do not recall whether the measles left any permanent disability. I cannot recall that he was in the hospital at any time except when he had the measles. I cannot recall how long he was laid up with the measles. Yes, it seems to me that he was thrown from his horse at some time or other while in the service but I am not sure. I saw him first after muster out in 1867. This was at the old home in Alabama. I was no longer living there but went there on a visit. I saw him at his home and was with him two or three days. He then had epileptic fits and I asked him what caused them and he said it was due to exposure in the army. If he spoke of any accident causing the fits I do not recollect it. I saw him have one of those fits on that visit. He had no fits before he entered the army and I have no idea what caused those spells. That was the only time I saw him after the service and did not know he was dead. He might have been thrown from his horse as that was quite a common occurrence. I do not think he ever knocked a hole in his head at any time during his service. Yes, he was complaining of rheumatism while in the service, had it in his knees, was not in the hospital with it but complained at different times and was some times excused for duty on that account. His habits were good. I am not related and have no interest. I am recorded correctly. Signed William McLarty, Deponent

A Deposition dated October 6, 1898 by William N. Roberson who stated he was 67 years old and his post office address was Norman, Lamar County, Alabama. He enlisted in Company F of the 1st Alabama Cavalry at Corinth, Mississippi about June or July 1863, served 12 months and was mustered out in June or July 1864 in Memphis, Tennessee. He stated he and Smith Gann were in two fights together and the first one was at Bear Creek in Mississippi in the fall or winter of 1863, and the whole regiment was in the fight with Roddy's company. He stated they charged on the bridge on Bear Creek. He stated the second fight was at Benson (Vincent's) Cross Roads right on the line between Alabama and Mississippi. He did not know what epilepsy was and didn't know of Smith Gann being afflicted with it.

Roberson stated he did not remember who Gann's mess mates were but thought one was an Ellis and he didn't remember his first name but he was half Indian. (There was an Isaac R. Ellis and a Lorenzo D. Ellis in Company F with Gann.)

A letter to Honorable H. Clay Evans, commissioner of Pensions, dated November 28, 1898, signed by Charles D. Sloan, Special Examiner at Huntsville, Alabama states: "Sir: In claim No. 486,407 of John A. Shaw of Guin, Marion County, Alabama as guardian of the minor children of Smith W. Gann, deceased, Private Company F of the 1st Alabama Volunteer Cavalry, I have the honor with the return of all the papers to submit the following report. The claim was filed under the Act of July 14, 1862, and is based upon soldier's death from "desias" (fits) alleged result of an injury to his head incurred by being thrown from a horse in service. The papers were set to me to obtain the deposition of W.N. Robinson of Norman, Lamar County, Alabama as to origin, see his reply to Bureau letter. This deposition accompanies this report but it does not change the status of the case. In my opinion the claim may have merit but it lacks evidence of incurrence. It is recommended that the A and NS Division be called upon for the address of Stanford Johnson, Orderly Sergeant of soldier's Company with a view of obtaining his deposition as to origin. It might be proper also to obtain the depositions of Samuel Audition and Enoch F. Tucker upon the same point, see their replies to letters Special Examiner Ragsdale's report. The claim should then be further examined at Guin, Marion County, Alabama for better evidence, if practicable of the dates of birth of children, their post-office addresses over their own signatures, correct dates of widow's remarriage and soldier's death and whether child Rachel E. was born before or after soldier's death. See… approved by the Chief of the Board of Review of October 23, 1896. Very Respectfully, Chas. D. Sloan, Special Examiner

(Comment at bottom of letter written and signed by U.J.V. Rev., Dec. 10, 1898 – "Note: The District of which Marion County, Alabama is a part is now vacant and the last paragraph of Spl. Ex. Sloan's summary cannot be complied with at the present time.")

Letter dated December 23, 1898, from John A. Shaw, Guardian of Minor Children, to Commissioner of Pensions. "Sir: Enclosed find the names and Post Office of Elam N. Gann and Rachel E. Gann. Elam N. Gann P.O. is Waco, Franklin County, Alabama. He can't sign his name. Here is Rachel E. Gann's own signature in her own hand writing."

(Comment: Mr. Shaw has hand-written this letter on letterhead stationery which states: "John A. Shaw & Co., Livery and Feed Stable.")

Mary Ann Miller signed a Deposition dated December 4, 1931, stating she was 98 years old and a resident of Marion County, Alabama. She stated "The first husband to whom I was married to name was Sam Waters, married some time before the Civil War, the date of which I do not remember. He was killed in action during the second year of the Civil War to the best of my memory. The second husband I was married to was Smith W. Gann, about the year 1867, I do not remember the exact date. His death was May 24, 1875. The third husband I was married to was Newton Miller, some time in the month of July 1882. His death was August 31, 1888. Newton Miller did not serve in the Navy, Marine, or Army of the United States. I have lived with my son, J.T. Gann continually since the death of my last husband, Newton Miller. To all of which I state to the best of my knowledge and memory."

Mary Ann Welch married Newton "Newt" Miller, Sr. who was much younger than she was. Her father did not want them to marry because Newt was so much younger than Mary. Mary and Newt had two children, a girl whose name was not given and a son, Newton, Jr.

Deposition dated December 4, 1931, by J.T. Gann stated he was 65 years old, a resident of Marion County, Alabama and that although he was the son of the claimant, he was present at the marriage of her to Newton Miller in the summer of 1882, at the home of Mr. and Mrs. Bud Nesmith in Guin, Alabama. He stated they were deceased and he was unable to obtain statements from them.

Martha Ann Stanford signed a Deposition dated February 1932, at Guin, Marion County, Alabama stating she was 59 years old and the wife of James Stanford, a farmer. She stated she had resided there all of her life. She was talking about Mary A. Miller and stated: "I am acquainted with the claimant, Mary A. Miller, and I have known her practically all my life. I was not personally acquainted with the soldier, Smith W. Gann, but just heard of him, although I remember the fact that he died here in this neighborhood when I was about 7 years of age, as my mother and father went to his burial. Claimant continued to live in this neighborhood from the time soldier died until she married again which was to Newton Miller. My father, Martin Nesmith, married the claimant and Newton Miller, and although I was not present at the wedding I was in the house at the time. They married in my father's house, and it seems to me it was sometime during the Summer of 1882, about July, and this coming July, 1932 it will have been 50 years since that marriage was solemnized. My brother is now 53 years of age, and he was about six months old when soldier, Smith W. Gann, died, and he had been dead about 3 years when claimant married Newton Miller.

The claimant's marriage to Newton Miller was dissolved by death of Newton Miller. Although I was not present when he died, nor did I attend his burial, I know that he died. I heard of his sickness that resulted in his death. I don't think Newton Miller lived more than 3 or 4 years after his marriage to the claimant, and I am more inclined to believe he did not live but three years after marriage to the claimant, and he and claimant were married in July, and he died during the month of August.

Following the death of Newton Miller I continued to see the claimant off and on until about 10 years ago. She lived with her children and I saw them off and on. I don't believe I have seen the claimant in about 10 years, now, although I know that she is living within a mile of me at the time." (There were a few questions and answers with this letter but the information would be a repetition of previous answers.)

Mary Gann Miller's son, Newton E. Miller, stated in a Deposition dated February 4, 1932, that he was 49 years of age, his occupation was sawmilling, his Post Office Address was Guin, Alabama, he was born in Marion County, Alabama and lived there all of his life. He stated the claimant, Mary A Miller, was his mother and his father was Newton Miller, and that he did not remember his father at all because he had been told that his father died about five months before he was born. He stated he made his home with the claimant until he was 18 and then he went to "railroading". Elizabeth Gann signed a Deposition February 4, 1932, stating she was 63 years old and the wife of John Thomas Gann, who was disabled for work and their Post Office Address was Guin, Alabama.

Mary A. Miller signed another Deposition dated February 4, 1932, stating she was 98 years old, and that she was born in Georgia and her parents moved from Georgia to Fayette County, Alabama when she was three weeks old. She stated her husband, Smith William Gann, died close to Guin in Marion County, Alabama and died in her arms. She stated her father was John S. Welch and her mother was Elizabeth Welch but she didn't remember her maiden name. Mary stated in her Deposition that her first husband, Samuel Leroy Waters, was killed in action in Virginia during the War between the States while he was in the Southern Army. She stated a Mr. Pryor who was in the same company with her husband wrote her a letter in which he said that her husband had been killed in action and that he helped to bury him. Mary also stated she was out in the field working when her husband, Newt Miller, died, and when she went back to the house, she found him dead. She stated she had two children by him but the first one, an unnamed female, died at birth, and the other child was a male named Newt Miller. She went on to say her husband, Newt Miller, died the last day of August and her son, Newt Miller, was born the 15th of October following the death of his father.

John T. Gann signed a Deposition but it was the same information previously given by the claimant. Witnesses were: Sigmon Williams and J.N. Barton; Elum N. Gann.

In a letter to the Director of Pensions in Washington, DC, dated February 8, 1932, C.R. Raum, Field Examiner stated: "In the event this claim is allowed it will be necessary to have a guardian appointed, as claimant is physically and mentally incapable of taking care of her own financial affairs. She did not know the difference between a one-dollar bill and a twenty-dollar bill. He stated he made a discreet inquiry and failed to learn of anything detrimental to the character and reputation of the claimant, or that there was any indication of a possible forfeiture of title to pension on account of her manner of living since the death of soldier in 1879. He stated he believed that Mrs. Elizabeth Gann, wife of John Thomas Gann, of Guin, Alabama would be a proper person to act as guardian for the claimant, as she was able to read and write."

On March 2, 1932, W.H. Cantrell, Judge of Probate of Marion County, Alabama stated: "Letters of Guardianship over the estate of Mrs. Mary A. Miller, a person of unsound mind, of the age of 99 years, are hereby granted to D.C. Holloway who has duly qualified and given bond as required by law, and is authorized to discharge all the functions attached to said Guardianship."

This is the rest of this sad story: Forty-two years after Mary A. Gann Miller first applied for a Widow's Civil War Pension, a check for $5,733.17 of accrued money from the pension was paid to Mary one month before her 99th Birthday, and she died less than two years later at the age of 100. She was receiving a pension check for $40 per month when she died. Had this pitiful lady been awarded this pension in a timely manner, she would have been able to live out her life in luxury, as this final check for almost $6,000 was a fortune at the time it was received.

Ganns, David F. - David F. Ganns, also shown as David F. Gann, enlisted in Company K of the 1st Alabama Cavalry, USV as a private on December 11, 1862, in Glendale, Mississippi, and was mustered in December 31, 1862, in Corinth, Mississippi. The January and February 1863 Muster Roll recorded him as absent with leave, sick. The March and April 1863 Muster Roll stated he died of measles at home April 12, 1863. Another muster roll stated he died at home near camp of measles. The Descriptive Roll recorded him as 19 years of age, 5'-5" tall, having a dark complexion, hazel eyes, dark hair, born in Marion County, Alabama, and a farmer by occupation. The name David F. Ganions appeared in the records of David F. Ganns; however, it stated he died April 12, 1863, at Corinth, Mississippi, which is when David F. Ganns died. Clerk probably misspelled the last name. The Inventory of Effects recorded David's place of death as Glendale, Mississippi.

Ganns, David J. - David J. Ganns, also shown as Gans, enlisted in Company K on January 6, 1863, and was absent, sick near camp at his house. He was enrolled by Captain Phillip A. Sternberg for a period of 1 year. The Company Descriptive Book recorded David J. Gans as 35 years of age, 5'9" tall, having a light complexion, blue eyes, light hair, born in Newell, Tennessee, and a farmer by occupation. (There was a Newell in Gibson County, Tennessee and a Newell Station in Sevierville, Tennessee. It did not state which county.) He was later reassigned to Company A. There was a David Gans in Company B and on the March and April 1863 Muster Roll, he was recorded as being absent, sick at home in Alabama. The May through August 1863, Muster Rolls stated Gans was absent, sick in Alabama. He was recorded as present on the September and October 1863 Muster Roll. A Muster -Out Roll stated he was absent without leave on November 30, 1863, however, a Notation from the Record and Pension Office of the War Department stated: "Honorable discharge furnished October 17, 1872, by Commanding General Department South, to date January 6, 1864, date of expiration of term of service. His name appeared on the returns as follows: March to July 1863, absent, sick at home in Alabama since March 8, 1863; August and September 1863, absent, sick in Alabama April 2, 1863; November 1863, absent with leave since November 15, 1863, in Corinth, Mississippi; January 1864, absent with leave. The November and December 1863 Muster Roll recorded him as being absent, sick in the Refugee Camp at Corinth, Mississippi since November 15, 1863.

Garden, Samuel - See Samuel J. Gordon.

Gardner, Charles - Charles Gardner enlisted in Company F of the 1st Alabama Cavalry, USV as a private on May 25, 1863, in Memphis, Tennessee for a period of 1 year. He was also recorded as a

Bugler. He was enrolled by Lieutenant Hinds, and was mustered in August 7, 1863, in Corinth, Mississippi. The Company Descriptive Book recorded him as 25 years of age, born in Bourbon County, Kentucky, and a butcher by occupation. No further information was shown on the form. The September and October 1863 Muster Roll recorded him as a Bugler. The November and December 1863 Muster roll recorded him as absent, in confinement at Corinth, Mississippi. In April 1864 he was recorded as absent without leave. He was discharged July 27, 1864, in Rome, Georgia due to expiration of term of service. He owed the U.S. Government $12 due to losing 1 Remington revolver, and owed the sutler $9.25.

Gardner, James - Only one card was found for James Gardner which was filed at the end of the last roll of microfilm of the 1st Alabama Cavalry, USV records. It recorded him as a private in Company I, and was reported to have deserted October 24, 1863, from Winston County, Alabama. No further information relative to this soldier was found.*

Gardner, John - John Gardner enlisted in Company I of the 1st Alabama Cavalry, USV as a private at Glendale, Mississippi for a period of 3 years. He was enrolled by Lieutenant Snelling, and was mustered in October 1, 1863, in Camp Davies, Mississippi. The Company Descriptive Book recorded him as 25 years of age, 5'-10" tall, having a light complexion, gray eyes, sandy hair, born in Winston County, Alabama, and a farmer by occupation. The January and February 1864 Muster Roll recorded him as absent, sick in the Overton U.S.A. Hospital in Memphis, Tennessee since January 20, 1864. He was reported to have deserted on October 24, 1863, but rejoined his company November 10, 1863, at Camp Davies, Mississippi. In April 1864 he was recorded as the company cook. He mustered out July 19, 1865, in Nashville, Tennessee.

John Gardner was a brother to William Henry Gardner, below, and was born in May 1842, in Winston County, Alabama to Samuel James Gardner, Sr. and his wife, Nancy Forsythe, who were married November 15, 1832, in Carnesville, Franklin County, Georgia. John married Nancy Jane Young September 11, 1863, in Jones Chapel, Cullman County, Alabama, and they had the following children: Andrew; Martha L.; John Wesley; Mary E.; Mira D.; and Gaby A. Gardner. John died June 4, 1912 in Winston County, Alabama, and was buried in the Dodd Memorial Cemetery in Lynn, Winston County, Alabama

Gardner, John Quincy Adams - John Quincy Adams Gardner enlisted in Company E of the 1st Alabama Cavalry, USV on February 1, 1863, at Corinth, Mississippi for one year and was mustered in February 9, 1863, at Corinth. He was promoted to orderly sergeant from private on February 28, 1863. He reenlisted September 25, 1863, for another year at Corinth, Mississippi and was promoted to 2nd Lieutenant from Orderly Sergeant at the age of 37. The Company Muster Roll for May and June 1864 stated John was entitled to $10 per month as Company Commander from April 20, 1863, through June 30, 1863. He was mustered in as 2nd Lieutenant by Lieutenant Meager to rank from September 25, 1863, at Camp Davies. In June 1864 he was shown as being absent, commanding the company at Decatur, Alabama. On September 28, 1864, he was mustered out for expiration of term of service. Muster-Out Roll stated: This officer to receive no pay until his accounts are adjusted with Government and pay due as commanding company to date – it being impossible for him to be mustered out sooner.

John Q. A. Gardner was born December 8, 1828, in Selma, Dallas County, Alabama to John G. Gardner and Lucy Allen Melton, who were married about 1827. John Gardner married Mariah Emmaline Bobo on May 3, 1848, in Fayette County, Alabama. Mariah was born March 15, 1824, in Spartanburg County, South Carolina and died June 12, 1906, in Campbell, Dunklin County, Missouri. She was the daughter of Tillman Bobo and Beulah Yarbrough. John and Mariah had the following children: Alice E., born June 20, 1849, died June 23, 1909; Hiram A., born June 8, 1851, died December 3, 1919; America Ann, born October 13, 1853, died August 28, 1875; Winfield Scott, born August 28, 1856, died October 21, 1936; William Lewis, born October 13, 1858, died July 10, 1863; and John Franklin Gardner, born April 18, 1861, and died June 2, 1933. Other children of John G. and Lucy Melton Gardner were: Garth D.; Elvy E.; Lucy Caroline; Welty Jane; and Rebecca Clary Gardner. John Q. A. Gardner died June 15, 1911 in Campbell, Dunklin County, Missouri and he Mariah are buried in the Woodlawn Cemetery in Campbell, Dunklin County, Missouri. John Q.A. Gardner's name was listed in the 1890 Dunklin County, Missouri Veterans' Census.

<u>Gardner, William Henry</u> - William Henry Gardner enlisted in Company I of the 1st Alabama Cavalry, USV as a private on November 15, 1863, in Camp Davies, Mississippi for a period of 3 years. He was enrolled by Lieutenant Snelling. The Company Descriptive Book recorded Gardner as 23 years of age, 5'-10½" tall, having a light complexion, blue eyes, dark hair, born in Winston County, Alabama, and a farmer by occupation. He was appointed Corporal December 1, 1863, by Colonel Spencer. Another muster roll stated he was appointed colonel by Lieutenant Colonel Dodds. He was mustered out July 19, 1865, in Nashville, Tennessee.

William Henry Gardner was a brother to John Gardner, above, and was born April 18, 1839, in Winston County, Alabama to Samuel James Gardner, Sr. and Nancy Forsythe, who were married November 15, 1832, in Carnesville, Franklin County, Georgia. Nancy Forsythe Gardner was born in 1816 in Georgia and died April 18, 1916 in Walker County, Alabama. William Henry Gardner married Susannah Elizabeth Gutherie, daughter of Calvin and Rhoda Cooper Gutherie on December 9, 1865, in Nesmith, Cullman County, Alabama. Children of William and Susannah Gardner were: Franklin; Patrick Dayton; Clarenda; Newton; Samuel Henderson; Rhoda; John; Mary Matilda; Marion Damascus; David Pressley; Matthew Luke; James J.; and Melia A. Gardner. William Henry Gardner died April 12, 1916, in Winston County, Alabama, and was buried in the hickory Grove Cemetery in Winston County.

The Heritage of Winston County (page 143) reported Gardner, along with his brother John "served in the Civil War" together with Calvin Guthrie who later became father-in-law to William H. Gardner. Seems most of the Guthrie/Guthreys from that era were Unionists. This paragraph submitted by Robin Sterling.

<u>Gargis, Meredith</u> - Meridith Gargis, also recorded as Meridith Goggiss enlisted in Company E of the 1st Alabama Cavalry, USV as a private on March 1, 1863, in Glendale, Mississippi for a period of 1 year, and mustered in March 6, 1863, in Corinth, Mississippi. The July and August 1863 Muster Roll recorded him as having deserted in July 1863. No further information relative to this soldier was found.

<u>Garrett, Dorsey</u> - Only two cards were found for Dorsey Garrett which as filed at the end of the last roll of microfilm of the 1st Alabama Cavalry, USV records. They recorded him as enlisting in Company D. His name appeared on the Returns for October 1863 recording him as absent, sick in Alabama October 20, 1863. According to the March and April 1864 Muster Roll, he was in the Webster U.S.A. General Hospital in Memphis, Tennessee where he was admitted March 5, 1864. No further information relative to this soldier was found.*

<u>Garrett, James</u> - Only one card was found for James Garrett which was filed at the end of the last roll of microfilm of the 1st Alabama Cavalry, USV records. It recorded him as a private in Company H and stated he was absent, sick in Alabama October 20, 1863. He was an ambulance driver in March and April 1864. No further information relative to this soldier was found.*

<u>Gay, Jonathan</u> - Jonathan Gay enlisted in Company B of the 1st Alabama Cavalry, USV as a private on April 10, 1864, in Decatur, Alabama for a period of 3 years. He was enrolled by Lieutenant Judy, and was mustered in April 13, 1864, in Decatur. The Muster and Descriptive Roll recorded him as 25 years of age, 5'-10" tall, having a dark complexion, gray eyes, dark hair, born in Morgan County, Alabama, and a farmer by occupation. The Company Descriptive Roll stated he was born in Limestone County, Alabama. He was appointed corporal August 1, 1864. He was promoted to sergeant from corporal on June 1, 1865. His name appeared on the Returns dated July and August 1865 which stated he was absent, sick in Huntsville, Alabama July 28, 1865. He was mustered out October 20, 1865, in Huntsville, Alabama.

Jonathan Gay was born August 13, 1839, in Limestone or Morgan County, Alabama, to William Gay and Emily Lindsay. His brother, William R. Gay, below, also served in this regiment. Jonathan married Elizabeth Ann Simms on February 23, 1860, in Blount County, Alabama, and had the following children: Sarah Ann; Louisa Jane; John William, Hattie; Beryan; Daniel M.; Mary S.; and Cully Gay. Jonathan died September 19, 1911, in Cullman County, Alabama, and was buried in the Hopewell Cemetery in Cullman County, Alabama.

Gay, William R. - William R. Gay enlisted and mustered into. Company I of the 1st Alabama Cavalry, USV on July 1, 1862, in Huntsville, Alabama for a period of 3 years. He was enrolled by Captain Bankhead. He was with the early enlistees who were immediately shipped to Nashville, Tennessee where they were merged with the 1st Middle Tennessee Cavalry, which later became the 5th Tennessee Cavalry. William was with Company D of the 1st Middle Tennessee Cavalry, US. The Company Descriptive Book recorded him as 24 years of age, 5'-11" tall, having a light complexion, and light hair. In January 1863, he was absent, as courier at Readyville, Tennessee January 27, 1863. A Company Muster Roll from December 31, 1862, through June 30, 1863, recorded him as absent, sick in hospital in Murfreesboro, Tennessee from June 24, 1863. The July and August 1863 Muster Roll recorded him as present, back in Company I of the 1st Alabama Cavalry, USV. The June 30 to October 31, 1863, Muster Roll recorded him as absent, missing in action from Vincent's Crossroads near Bay Springs, Mississippi, but rejoined company November 1, 1863 in Glendale, Mississippi. William R. Gay's name appeared on the Returns as follows: April 1864, absent with leave; June 1864, absent at Decatur, Alabama since May 1, 1864; September 1864, absent on furlough; October 1864, absent without leave from September 29, 1864. He was appointed from Corporal to 1st Sergeant on January 1, 1864, by Lieutenant Colonel Dodds. The March and April 1864 Muster Roll recorded him as absent with leave from April 15, 1864, by order of General Dodge. He was mustered out July 19, 1865, from Huntsville, Alabama.

William R. Gay was born November 11, 1833, in Somerville, Morgan County, Alabama to William Gay and Emily Lindsay. He married Sarah Eliza Truitt on January 30, 1861, in Winston County, Alabama. William R. and Sarah Truitt Gay had at least 2 children; William Franklin, born October 28, 1861; and James Isaac Gay, born April 12, 1866. See Jonathan Gay, above for parents and other family information.

Gaylor, Robert - Robert Gaylor, also spelled Guyler and Gayler, enlisted and mustered into Company M of the 1st Alabama Cavalry, USV as a private on September 5, 1864, in Rome, Georgia. He was enrolled by Captain Lomax for a period of 3 years. The Muster and Descriptive Roll recorded him as 18 years of age, 5'-8" tall, having a fair complexion, blue eyes, light hair, born in Cherokee County, Alabama, and a farmer by occupation. He was shown as being due a bounty of $300. The November and December 1864 Muster Roll recorded him as being attached to Foster U.S.A. General Hospital in Durham Station, New Bern, Craven County, North Carolina as a nurse. The March and April 1865 Muster Roll also recorded him as being absent, on duty in the hospital in Durham's Station, North Carolina since March 20, 1865. He was mustered out October 20, 1865, in Huntsville, Alabama owing the U.S. Government $8.91 for losing 1 carbine swing and swivel, 1 carbine cartridge box, 1 saber belt and plate, 1 cap pouch, pick, curry comb, halter strap, and 2 spurs and straps. He was paid a bounty of $100. Gaylor's name appeared on the Returns as follows: October 1864, absent with leave, recruiting since October 5, 1864; March to May 1865, absent, nurse in hospital since March 20, 1865; June 1865, returned June 1, 1865, from absent on duty.

Gean, John - John Gean, also spelled Jean in some military records, enlisted in Company F of the 1st Alabama Cavalry, USV as a private on July 6, 1863, in Corinth, Mississippi for a period of 1 year. He was enrolled by Captain Pierce, and mustered in August 13, 1863, in Corinth. The Company Descriptive Book recorded him as 29 years of age, 5'-9" tall, having a light complexion, gray eyes, brown hair, born in Clinton County, Tennessee, and a farmer by occupation. He was recorded as having deserted September 20, 1863, in Glendale, Mississippi. No further information relative to this soldier was found. John, Wiley and William Gean all enlisted the same day in the same place, and all of them were reported to have deserted September 20, 1863.

John Gean was a brother to Wiley and William Gean, below, and they were sons of James Thomas Gean and Nancy Warren, who married in 1830 in Tennessee. James was born 1798 in North Carolina and died after 1851 in Tennessee. Nancy Warren Gean was born May 29, 1814, in Lincoln

County, Tennessee, and died in January 1860 in Wayne County, Tennessee. Nancy Warren was the daughter of William R. and Sarah Warren John H. Gean was born January 12, 1835, in Wayne County, Tennessee, Descriptive Roll stated he was born in Clinton County, Tennessee, and died in 1900. Other children of James and Nancy Gean besides John, Wiley and William, were: Nancy; Mary E.; Martha B.; Thomas P.; Elisha Hardy; and Sarah Jane Gean.

Gean, Wiley Frederick - Wiley Frederick Gean, also spelled Jean, enlisted in Company F of the 1st Alabama Cavalry, USV as a private on July 6, 1863, in Corinth, Mississippi for a period of 1 year. He was enrolled by Captain Pierce and was mustered in August 13, 1863, in Corinth. The Company Descriptive Book records Wiley as 27 years of age, 5'10" tall, having a light complexion, blue eyes, light brown hair, born in Loudon County, Alabama, should be Tennessee, and a farmer by occupation. The September and October 1863 Muster Roll recorded him as having deserted September 20, 1863, from Glendale, Mississippi. Wiley, John and William Gean all enlisted the same day in the same place, and were all three reported to have deserted September 20, 1863, from Glendale, Mississippi.

Wiley Frederick Gean was born in March 1841 in Loudon County, Tennessee. See family information for John Gean, above. The census records state Wiley was a Cooper by trade.

Gean, William Robert - William Robert Gean, also spelled Guin and Jean enlisted in Company F of the 1st Alabama Cavalry, USV as a private on July 6, 1863, in Corinth, Mississippi for a period of 1 year. He was enrolled by Captain W.F. Pierce, and was mustered in August 13, 1863, in Corinth. The Company Descriptive Book recorded William as 25 years of age, 5'-9" tall, having a light complexion, gray eyes, brown hair, born in Clinton County, Tennessee, and was a farmer by occupation. William's name appeared on the Returns as follows: July 1864, absent, sick in the general hospital in Nashville, Tennessee. He was reported to have deserted September 20, 1863, from Glendale Mississippi, with brothers Wiley and John Gean.

William Gean was born January 12, 1836, in Chilton County, Tennessee, and died in 1880. He married Sarah E., last name unknown, about 1857, in Waynesboro, Wayne County, Tennessee, and they had the following children: John Hargus; James T.; Jasper M., and Martha Gean. He enlisted with his brothers, John and Wiley on the same day and they were all three reported to have deserted the same day.

Gear, J.J. - Only one card was found for J.J. Gear which was filed at the end of the last roll of microfilm of the 1st Alabama Cavalry, USV records. It recorded him as being in Company F, 1st Alabama Cavalry, USV stating he was absent, on daily duty as a nurse at Corinth, Mississippi in July 1863. No further information relative to this soldier was found.*

Gentry, John L. - John L. Gentry enlisted in Company C of the 1st Alabama Cavalry, USV as private on December 15, 1862, in Corinth, Mississippi for a term of 1 year. Another muster roll stated he enlisted December 1, 1862. He was enrolled by Captain John Latty, and was mustered in December 22, 1862, in Corinth, Mississippi. The Regimental Descriptive Book recorded him as 26 years of ate, 5'-10" tall, having a fair complexion, brown eyes, dark hair, born in Shelby County, Alabama, and a farmer by occupation. The May and June 1863 Muster Roll stated John L. Gentry died June 3, 1863, in quarters in camp at Glendale, Mississippi.

Gerrings, D. - Only one card was found for D. Gerrings which was filed at the end of the last roll of microfilm of the 1st Alabama Cavalry, USV records. It recorded him as a private and stated he was absent, sick in Memphis, Tennessee in April 1864. No further information relative to this soldier was found.*

Gewin, Rasey - See Rasey Guin.

Ghoaff, William T. - See William T. Goof.

Ghist, William Harrison - See William Harrison Gist.

Gibbs, Anderson - Anderson Gibbs enlisted and mustered into Company H of the 1st Alabama Cavalry, USV as a private on October 17, 1863, in Glendale, Mississippi for a period of 1 year. Gibbs' name appeared on the Returns as follows: December 1863, on daily duty as nurse; March and April 1864, absent, sick in hospital in Memphis, Tennessee. He was mustered out at age 45 on October 24, 1864, in Rome, Georgia due to expiration of term of service. At the time he mustered out, he owed the U.S. Government $2.45 for losing 1 thong and brush wiper and one painted blanket.

Gibbs, John W. - John W. Gibbs enlisted in Company H of the 1st Alabama Cavalry, USV as a private on May 1, 1865, in Huntsville, Alabama for a period of 3 years. He was enrolled by Captain James W. DeVaney, and was mustered in May 20, 1865, in Nashville, Tennessee. The Muster and Descriptive Roll recorded him as 18 years of age, 5'-7" tall, having a dark complexion, blue eyes, black hair, born in Cherokee County, Georgia, and a farmer by occupation. He was appointed Sergeant on July 15, 1865, when Charles Bodkin was reduced to ranks. John W. Gibbs was able to sign his Enlistment Forms. He was mustered out October 20, 1865, in Huntsville, Alabama with the rest of the organization.

Gibson, Jackson E. - Jackson E. Gibson enlisted in Company C of the 1st Alabama Cavalry, USV as a private on February 10, 1863, in Corinth, Mississippi, for a period of 1 year. He was enrolled by D.R. Adams, and mustered in February 18, 1863, in Corinth, Mississippi. The Company Descriptive Roll recorded him as 23 years of age, 5'-11" tall, dark complexion, blue eyes, dark hair, born in Gilmore County, Georgia, married, and a farmer by occupation. He was discharged March 26, 1864, due to expiration of term of service. However, the Muster-Out Roll stated he was mustered out February 10, 1864.

Gibson, John - Only one card was found for John Gibson which was filed at the end of the last roll of microfilm of the 1st Alabama Cavalry, USV records. He enlisted in Company K of the 1st Alabama Cavalry, USV as a private on November 22, 1863, in Camp Davies, Mississippi. No further information relative to this soldier was found.*

Gibson, John H. - John H. Gibson enlisted in Company C of the 1st Alabama Cavalry, USV as a private on December 6, 1862, in Corinth, Mississippi for a period of 1 year. He was enrolled by Captain John Latty, and was mustered in December 22, 1862, in Corinth. The Regimental Descriptive Book recorded him as 28 years of age, 5'-3" tall, having a fair complexion, blue eyes, dark hair, born in Simpson County, Mississippi, and a farmer by occupation. The May and June 1863 Muster Roll stated he died May 26, 1863, in the Regimental Hospital in Glendale, Mississippi.

Gibson, M. - Only one card was found for M. Gibson which was filed at the end of the last roll of microfilm of the 1st Alabama Cavalry, USV records. It recorded him as a being in Company L, stating he enlisted on October 15, 1863, in Glendale, Mississippi as a private. No further information relative to this soldier was found.*

Gibson, Richard Byrd - Richard Byrd Gipson enlisted in Company I of the 1st Alabama Cavalry, USV as a private on August 26, 1862, in Huntsville, Alabama for a period of 3 years. He was enrolled by Lieutenant Abbott and was mustered in the same day in Nashville, Tennessee. He was with the group of early enlistees who were immediately shipped to Nashville, Tennessee and merged with the 1st Middle Tennessee Cavalry, which later became the 5th Tennessee Cavalry. Richard was with Company I of the 1st Middle Tennessee Cavalry, US. His horse and equipment were furnished by the US Government. The Company Descriptive Book recorded him as 21 years of age, 5'-10¼" tall, having a light complexion, blue eyes, light hair, born in Morgan County, Alabama, and a farmer by occupation. His name appeared on the Returns as follows: January and February 1863, absent, on courier service January 27, 1863, in Readyville, Tennessee; December 1863, he was the Company Clerk; April 1864, he was the Company Clerk; April 1864, he was Company Clerk; October 1864, Richard was on duty as an ambulance driver for Regimental Surgeon; January 1865, he was on duty at

Regimental Headquarters; February 1865, he was a clerk in the adjutant's office; March and April 1865, Richard was Regimental Clerk, and in May 1865, he was on duty at Regimental Headquarters. The December 31, 1862, through June 30, 1863, recorded him as being in Company D of the 1st Middle Tennessee Cavalry. From June 30, through October 31, 1863, he was recorded as being in Company I of the 1st Alabama Cavalry, USV. Richard mustered out July 19, 1865, in Nashville, Tennessee.

Richard Gibson was born January 30, 1841, to James W. Gibson and Mary Day and the grandson of John Gibson and of David Day, Jr. He had several cousins and other relatives in the 1st Alabama Cavalry, USV. After the war he returned to his home and married Emily Day, who was born January 13, 1846, in Basham's Gap in Morgan County, Alabama, and died 18 January 18, 1930 in Morgan County, Alabama. Emily was the daughter of Richard Byrd Day, born November 25, 1799, in Hawkins County, Tennessee, and died July 1, 1878, in Morgan County, Alabama who married Elizabeth Penn on July 1, 1820 in Lawrence County, Alabama. Emily was born September 22, 1802, in North Carolina, and died October 16, 1854, in Morgan County, Alabama. Richard and Emily Day Gibson had the following children: Adren Lutisha; James Luther; William Byrd; Mary Emily; Simeon Blake; John Walker; Robert Everett; Richard Lewis; and Maye Gibson. Another descendant stated they only had 7 children. Richard Byrd Gibson died June 21, 1925 at age 84, and was buried in the Evergreen Cemetery in Morgan County, Alabama.

Gibson, William R. - Only one card was found for William R. Gibson which was filed at the end of the last roll of microfilm of the 1st Alabama Cavalry, USV records. It recorded him as being a private in Company D, stating he was absent, sick in Refugee Camp November 5, 1863. No further information relative to this soldier was found.*

Gilbreth, George W. - George W. Gilbreth, also spelled Gilbreath, enlisted in Company G of the 1st Alabama Cavalry, USV as a private on April 24, 1864, in Mooresville, Alabama for a period of 3 years. He was enrolled by Captain Cobleigh and was mustered in the same day in Rome, Georgia. When George signed his name to his Enlistment Forms, he signed it George W. Gilbreth. The Muster and Descriptive Roll recorded him as 18 years of age, 5'-8" tall, having a fair complexion, blue eyes, auburn hair, born in DeKalb County, Georgia, and a farmer by occupation. In September 1864, he was on duty as company cook. He was mustered out October 20, 1865, in Huntsville, Alabama owing the U.S. Government $11.05 due to losing 1 halter, 1 curb bridle, 1 surcingle, 1 saber belt and plate. George had previously served in the 1st Tennessee and Alabama Independent Vidette Cavalry, US.

George W. Gilbreth was born June 5, 1884, in DeKalb County, Alabama to William Baxter Gilbreth and Hayes. He married Nancy Ann Owens, who was born September 28, 1846 and died February 14, 1926. George died February 20, 1923, in DeKalb County, Alabama and he and his wife, Nancy, are buried in the Providence Hill Church Cemetery in Lathamville, DeKalb County, Alabama.

Gilbreth, James M. - James M. Gilbreth, also spelled James A. Gilbraith, and James N. Gilbraith, enrolled in Company H of the 1st Alabama Cavalry, USV as a private on March 1, 1865, in Stevenson, Alabama, for a period of 3 years. He was enrolled by Captain James W. DeVaney and was mustered in April 5, 1865, in Nashville, Tennessee. The Muster and Descriptive Roll recorded him as 30 years of age, 6'-1½" tall, having a light complexion, blue eyes, dark hair, born in Jefferson County, Tennessee, and a farmer by occupation. He mustered out October 20, 1865, in Huntsville, Alabama, and was paid a bounty of $100.

Gilliam, David Calvin - David Calvin Gilliam, also spelled Gillim, enlisted in Company A of the 1st Alabama Cavalry, USV as a private on January 23, 1864, in Camp Davies, Mississippi for a period of 3 years. He was enrolled by Lieutenant Hinds and was mustered in February 5, 1864, in Memphis, Tennessee. The Muster and Descriptive Roll recorded him as 19 years of age, 5'-6" tall, having a fair complexion, gray eyes, dark hair, born in Fayette County, Alabama, and a farmer by occupation. A Company Muster Roll dated February 29, 1864, recorded him as absent, sick in General Hospital in Memphis, Tennessee. David's name appeared on the January and February 1864 Gayoso U.S.A. General Hospital in Memphis, Tennessee as a patient. He was still shown as being in Gayoso Hospital on the March and April 1864 Muster Roll but stated he returned to duty. His name appeared on the

Returns as follows: February 1864, absent, sick in hospital in Memphis, Tennessee since February 14, 1864; March 1865, Orderly at Brigade Headquarters; April 1865, absent, with Brigade Headquarters The January and February 1865 Muster Roll recorded him as absent, on detached service at Headquarters, 3rd Brigade. He was mustered out October 20, 1865, in Huntsville, Alabama owing the U.S. Government $2.15, due to losing 1 saber belt complete. He was paid a bounty of $180, and was shown as being due another $120, to total the $300 bounty he was due. He also owed the U.S. Government $17.01 for his clothing allowance.

David Calvin Gilliam was born January 13, 1844, in Fayette County, Alabama to Peter Gilliam and Mary A. "Polly" Loftis. David married Mary Adeline Lindsey on July 31, 1865, in Fayette County, Alabama. Polly Loftis was the daughter of Levi and Judah Lindsey. Mary was born May 20, 1844, in Alabama and died June 12, 1919, in Quanah, Hardeman County, Texas. Children from this marriage were: Jay Hugh, born November 8, 1870, died April 15, 1948; Roland "Rolly" Gains, born September 1866, died in 1910; Leander Alexander, born August 23, 1868, died April 2, 1945; Hiram Roscoe, born January 25, 1873, died February 11, 1938; Izore, born November 11, 1875, died February 19, 1943; and John Luther Gilliam, born July 18, 1878, and died after 1930. After the war ended, Gilliam moved to Texas, and when the land opened up in Oklahoma, he moved to the old Greer County and settled in Pleasant Hill. David Calvin Gilliam was a devoted father, and helped to develop his community. He was instrumental in establishing the small school. He lived in a half dug-out until a house could be built. The breaking of the new land, establishing a new home, and the way of living, made life a very difficult adjustment to living. David died August 15, 1916, in Harmon, Greer County, Oklahoma, and was buried in the Pleasant Hill Cemetery which he helped establish.

Ginn, Benjamin F. - Benjamin F. Ginn enlisted in Company G of the 1st Alabama Cavalry, USV on February 20, 1863, in Chewalla, Tennessee for a period of 1 year, and was mustered in February 20, 1863, in Corinth, Mississippi. The July and August 1863 Muster Roll recorded him as absent, on sick leave since August 25, 1863. A Notation in his file from the Adjutant General's Office dated January 16, 1888, stated "See also Company A, 7th Tennessee Cavalry." His name appeared on the Returns as follows: August 1863, absent, sick in Pocahontas, Tennessee, on Surgeon's Certificate since August 25, 1863; October 1863, absent, sick in Memphis, Tennessee; November 1863, Company Cook. A note at the bottom of the Return stated, "Also appears as Benjamin F. Guin. He was mustered out November 26, 1863, in Memphis, Tennessee.

Gird, W.F. - Only one card was found for W.F. Gird which was filed at the end of the last roll of microfilm of the 1st Alabama Cavalry, USV records. It recorded him as enlisting in Company F, stating he was captured and taken prisoner of war in November 1863. No further information relative to this soldier was found.*

Gist, Sidney C. - Sidney C. Gist enlisted in Company C of the 1st Alabama Cavalry, USV as a private on January 1, 1863, in Chewalla, Tennessee for a period of 1 year. He was enrolled by Captain Pierce and mustered in March 13, 1863, in Corinth, Mississippi. The Company Descriptive Roll only recorded him as 25 years of age, and no other information. He was reported as having deserted March 18, 1863, from Glendale, Mississippi. A Company Muster Roll dated to June 30, 1863, reported Gist as absent without leave since April 25, 1863. Another muster roll stated he deserted April 5, 1863. His name appeared on the Returns stating he deserted May 1, 1863, from Glendale, Mississippi. His name appeared on another Return stating he deserted July 2, 1863.

Gist, William Harrison - William Harrison Gist, spelled Ghist in military records but family stated it should be Gist, enlisted in Company A of Captain Frank C. Burdick's Company of the 1st Alabama Cavalry, USV as a private on September 8, 1862, at Iuka, Mississippi, for a period of 1 year, and was mustered in October 1, 1862, in Corinth, Mississippi. The Regimental Descriptive Book recorded him as 18 years of age, 5'-8" tall, having a dark complexion, hazel eyes, dark hair, born in Marion County, Alabama, and a farmer by occupation. He mustered out September 16, 1863, in Corinth, Mississippi due to expiration of term of service.

William H. Gist was born January 16, 1844, in Marion County, Alabama. He married Malissa

Elizabeth East on March 22, 1864, in Franklin County, Alabama. They were married by Rev. Carrol Patterson. Malissa was born March 12, 1846, in Rome, Floyd County, Georgia, and died March 16, 1923, in Killen, Lauderdale County, Alabama. Children of William and Malissa were: William Newton; Thomas; Andrew Jackson; James Walker; Christopher Columbus; Joanna E.; Mary Etta; and Mattie Lou Gist. William H. Gist died April 28, 1914, in Killen, Lauderdale County, Alabama, and he and his wife were both buried in the Harrison Cemetery in Killen, Lauderdale County, Alabama.

Glasgow, William Balis - William Balis Glasgow, also spelled Glascoe, first enlisted in Company E of the 1st Alabama Cavalry, USV on March 6, 1863, at Glendale or Tishomingo County, Mississippi for a period of 1 year. He mustered in the same day in Glendale, Mississippi. He was reported to have deserted April 25, 1863, from Glendale, Mississippi. His name appeared on the Returns as follows: April 1863, absent with leave at Corinth, Mississippi; June 1863, deserted May 3, 1863, from Glendale, Mississippi. William Glasgow then re-enlisted in Company A of the 1st Alabama Cavalry, USV as a private on December 26, 1863, at Camp Davies, Mississippi for a period of 3 years. He was enrolled by Lieutenant Hinds and was mustered in February 5, 1864, in Memphis, Tennessee. The Muster and Descriptive Roll recorded him as 22 years of age, 5'-11" tall, having a dark complexion, black eyes, black hair, born in Marion County, Alabama, and a farmer by occupation. The March and April 1864 Muster Roll recorded him as being absent, in confinement at Athens, Alabama. Glasgow's name appeared on the Returns as follows: February 1864, on duty as a teamster; March 1864, on duty as a teamster; April 1864, absent, in arrest in prison; October 1864, on duty as a wagoner; November 1864, on duty as a Regimental Teamster; August 1865, on duty as a teamster. September 1865, on duty as a Regimental Teamster. A letter found in Glasgow's file stated the following: Charges and Specifications against Private William Glasgow, Company A, 1st Regiment Alabama Cavalry Volunteers – Charge: Desertion. Specification: In this that Private William Glasgow of Company A, 1st Alabama Volunteer Cavalry, did on or about the 16th day of April 1864, desert his company and regiment and attempt to pass the lines into the enemy's country taking with him arms and ammunition the property of the United States, all this at or near Mooresville, Alabama on the day above specified. Signed: J.J. Hinds, Captain 1st Alabama Cavalry commanding Company A. Camp Mooresville, Alabama, April 20, 1864. Witnesses: Sergeant John A. Hogan, Sergeant George W. Benson, and Sergeant Anderson Looney, all of Company A, 1st Alabama Cavalry Volunteers. A note from a Captain and Judge Advocate stated the general court martial had been dissolved. He mustered out October 20, 1865, in Huntsville, Alabama owing the U.S. Government $5.47 due to losing 1 saber belt complete, 1 sling and swivel, and 1 carbine cartridge box. He was paid a bounty of $180 and stated he was still due $120 to make the complete bounty of $300.

William Glasgow was born March 10, 1851, in Marion County, Alabama to William H. and Nancy Jane Wright Glasgow. William married several times and had several children. Different descendants have different wives, dates of marriage and children, so the following is what the majority of them sent. He first married Julia Ann Adams on April 29, 1866, in Alcorn County, Mississippi. Julia was born March 15, 1847, in Old Tishomingo County, Mississippi and died February 10, 1872, in Choctaw County, Mississippi. Children of William and Julia were: Samuel; Calvin C.; and Unity S. Glasgow. He married next Tina Lou Hale, who was shown with a marriage date of 1882 and also 1892. According to the birth dates of the children, it appears the 1892 date would be closer to correct. Children of William and Tina Lou were: John Henry Dennis; George Ward; Jacob Nash; Artie Leona; William Riley; Vertie Mae; and Earlie Ray Glasgow. Due to the confusion among descendants about wives and children, this is all that will be listed. William Balis Glasgow died November 8, 1925, in Comanche County, Oklahoma and was buried in the Faxon Cemetery in Comanche.

Glass, Elisha - Elisha Glass enlisted in Company G of the 1st Alabama Cavalry, USV as a private on March 23, 1864, in Decatur, Alabama for a period of 3 years. It stated he mustered in October 16, 1865, but above that, it stated he mustered the same day he enlisted in Huntsville, Alabama. He was enrolled by Lieutenant Pease. The Muster and Descriptive Roll recorded him as 19 years of age, 5'-10" tall, having a fair complexion, gray eyes, dark hair, born in Marion County, Alabama, and a farmer by occupation. It also stated he was due a bounty of $300. Elisha's name appeared on the Returns as follows: July 1864, Absent, sick at Chattanooga, Tennessee since May 22,

1864; September 1864, Absent, sick in hospital in Resaca, Georgia since May 25th; October 1864, Absent, sick in hospital in Decatur, Alabama May 1, 1864; November 1864 to January 1865, Absent, sick. February 1865 to May 1865, Absent, sick in hospital in Kingston, Georgia June 1, 1864; June 1865, absent, sick in hospital in Kingston, Georgia May 22, 1864. Elisha Glass was able to sign all of his Enlistment Forms. He was mustered out October 20, 1865, in Huntsville, Alabama owing the U.S. Government $10 due to losing 1 saber belt and plate, 1 carbine cartridge box, 1 cap pouch, 1 thong and wiper, and 1 screwdriver.

Gleen, J. - Only two cards were found for J. Gleen which were filed at the end of the last roll of microfilm of the 1st Alabama Cavalry, USV records. It recorded him as enlisting in Company B of the 1st Alabama Cavalry, USV as a private. A Casualty Sheet stated he J. Gleen died of disease on March 9, 1864, in Richmond Virginia.

Glenn, George W. - Only one card was found for George W. Glenn which was filed at the end of the last roll of microfilm of the 1st Alabama Cavalry, USV records. The Return for January to March 1864 stated he was a private in Company I, and was absent, sick in the hospital in Memphis, Tennessee from January 20, 1864. No further information relative to this soldier was found.*

Glenn, James F. - James F. Glenn enlisted in Company B of the 1st Alabama Cavalry, USV as a private on January 13, 1863, in Glendale, Mississippi for a period of 1 year. He was enrolled by Phillip A. Sternberg and was mustered in January 22, 1863, in Corinth, Mississippi. The Regimental Descriptive Book recorded him as 47 years of age, 5'-8" tall, having a light complexion, blue eyes, light hair, born in Lawrence County, South Carolina, and a farmer by occupation. On the March and April 1863 Muster Roll it recorded him as absent, sick in the hospital in Jackson, Tennessee. The May and June 1863 Muster Roll stated he was absent with leave to take his family North. The US Army escorted about 300 Unionists to Marion County, Illinois in June 1863 for their protection. The Confederate Home Guard were burning their homes, barns, crops, abusing and sometimes killing some of them. The July and August 1863 Muster Roll stated they were still in Illinois where James died August 10, 1863, in Perry County, Illinois. James F. Glenn's name appeared on the Returns as follows: February and March 1863, absent, sick in hospital in Corinth, Mississippi with measles since February 20, 1863; April 1863, Absent at Jackson, Tennessee since March 28, 1863; June, July and August 1863, absent with leave to take family North; August 10, 1863, died. The two oldest sons of James F. and Mary Mitchell Glenn also served in the First Alabama Cavalry. See James H. Glenn and Matthew H. Glenn, below.

Pension #42932, Mary Glenn, Perry County, Illinois applied July 14, 1862. Her age was 40 and she was a resident of Jackson County, Illinois. James enlisted January 14, 1863, for one year at Glendale, Mississippi, was in service for 7 months, and died at Perry County, Illinois August 10, 1863, due to chronic diarrhea contracted in service. They were married June 10, 1846, in Laurens, County South Carolina by Jefferson Sullins, Justice of the Peace, that she was Mary Mitchell. She states that the following children are under age 16 and live in Jackson County, Illinois: David, born July 29, 1851; Eusley H., born June 12, 1857; Russell P., born June 11, 1860; and Mary J. Glenn; born January 4, 1863. Mary states that James was ill and he had no absence or furlough but was sent north by order of Colonel John Morrow to recover his health and that from the time of leaving his regiment he grew worse of the disease of Chronic Diarrhea until he died August 10, 1863. Mathew H. Glenn testified that he knew James and Mary for 15 years.

In the "Claim for Widow's Pension", It is stated that the soldiers together with about 300 other parties, mostly families of the Union men in Alabama, who had joined the Union Army and convalescent union soldiers were ordered to go to Illinois by Colonel Morrow, who at that time had command at that point. James F. Glenn, then very sick with chronic diarrhea, was among the number. No written leaves or furloughs were given. The sick and convalescent soldiers were ordered to return to their regiments as soon as they were able. One of these affiants (Milner) was detailed to take charge of the company and both swear the soldier died with chronic diarrhea August 10, 1863. Pension admitted June 22, 1866, at $8.00 per month, commencing August 10th 1863. It is stated that James went out in the country and got a house for his family to live in when he got to Illinois.

(In June 1863, the US Army escorted over 300 people, including sick and convalescing Union soldiers, their families, and other Union families whose husbands were off fighting in the 1st Alabama Cavalry, USV and the wives and children were being harassed by the Confederate Home Guard. After the war, many of the families remained in Illinois, Indiana, and other surrounding counties, and the husbands joined them. Some later returned to Alabama but most of them remained and are buried there.)

On November 16, 1869, in Marion County, Alabama Nancy Innon and Sarah Mitchell make statement that they have been intimately acquainted with Mary Glenn for at least 20 years, have lived most of that time neighbors to her, that they were acquainted with her children and their ages were from their knowledge the fact that they were present at the time of the births of the children and have been intimate with them nearly all the time since their birth and also that we have noticed the Bible record of their ages, which corresponds with the statements given above. Matthew H. Glenn also signed this paper. Taken from James F. Glenn's Civil War Records.

James F. Glenn was born about 1816 in Laurens County, South Carolina and married Mary Jane "Polly" Mitchell on June 10, 1846, in Laurens County. Mary Jane was born May 15, 1825, in Laurens County, South Carolina and died May 15, 1896, in Marion County, Alabama. She was buried at Mt. Zion Cemetery on County Highway 25. Mary Jane Mitchell was the daughter of John Taylor Mitchell and his wife, Nancy "Anny" Culbertson, who were married in October 1805. Children of James and Mary Jane Glenn were: William, born 1843; Matthew Haston, born September 2, 1947, died March 9, 1929; David, born July 29, 1851; Ensley Howard, born June 12, 1857; Russell Pelham, born June 11, 1860, died September 22, 1873; and Mary Jane Glenn, born January 4, 1863, and died in 1949.

<u>Glenn, James H.</u> - James H. Glenn, son of James H. Glenn, above, and brother of William Glenn, below, enlisted in Company B of the 1st Alabama Cavalry, USV December 15, 1862, in Glendale, Mississippi for a period of 1 year. He was enrolled by Lieutenant Frank C. Burdick and was mustered in December 31, 1863, in Corinth, Mississippi. The Regimental Descriptive Book recorded him as 19 years of age, 5'-8" tall, having a light complexion, gray eyes, light hair, born in Laurens County, South Carolina, and a farmer by occupation. The May 1863 through December 1863 Muster Rolls recorded him as absent, on detached service as secret scout for Colonel Morrell. A company muster roll dated February 6, 1864, stated he was absent, a prisoner of war in Belle Island, Virginia. His Prisoner of War Record stated he was captured August 11, 1863, in West Tennessee, confined at Richmond, Virginia September 26, 1863, admitted to Hospital #21 in Richmond, Virginia February 24, 1864, where he died March 9, 1864, of chronic diarrhea in the Confederate military prison hospital. He is buried in the Richmond National Cemetery in Richmond, Virginia.

<u>Glenn, John W.F.</u> - John W.F. Glenn enlisted and mustered into Company I of the 1st Alabama Cavalry, USV as a private on December 21, 1863, in Camp Davies, Mississippi for a term of 3 years. He was enrolled by Lieutenant Snelling. The company Descriptive Book records him as 20 years of age, 5'-8" tall, having a light complexion, blue eyes, light hair, and a farmer by occupation. The January through April 1864 Muster Rolls recorded him as absent, sick in Adams U.S.A. General Hospital in Memphis, Tennessee since January 20, 1864. He was transferred to Overton U.S.A. General Hospital in Memphis on March 21, 1864. The May and June 1864 Muster Roll recorded him as absent, sick in the hospital in St. Louis, Missouri. His name appeared on a Company Muster-Out Roll stating he died January 20, 1864, of phthisis pulmonalis, consumption of the lungs, at Jefferson Barracks U.S. General Hospital in St. Louis, Missouri. A Certificate for Government Undertaker was found in his files and stated that John W.F. Glenn died June 11, 1864, in Ward "T" at Jefferson Barracks in St. Louis, Missouri. It was signed by M.F. Randolph, Surgeon USA in Charge. The List of Effects for John W.F. Glenn recorded him as having 1 great coat, 1 hat, 1 cap, 1 pair of cotton drawers, 1 pair of boots, 1 pair of stockings, 1 pair of trowsers, 1 flannel shirt, 2 wool blankets, and 1 silver watch. John W.F. Glenn was buried in Section 8, Site 8131 in the Jefferson Barracks Cemetery in St. Louis, Missouri.

<u>Glenn, Matthew Haston</u> - Matthew Haston Glenn, also spelled Matthew Hasten Glenn, enlisted in Company B of the 1st Alabama Cavalry, USV as a private on January 13, 1863, in Glendale,

Mississippi for a period of 1 year. He was enlisted by Captain Phillip A. Sternberg, and mustered in January 22, 1863, in Corinth, Mississippi. The March and April 1863 Muster Roll recorded him as absent, sick in the hospital in Corinth, Mississippi since March 26, 1863. He was mustered out January 22, 1864, in Memphis, Tennessee.

Matthew H. Glenn was born September 2, 1847, in Laurens County, South Carolina to James F. Glenn and Mary "Polly" Mitchell. He was the brother of James F. Glenn, who along with their father served in the 1st Alabama Cavalry, USV. Matthew married Elizabeth Palmer, born May 29, 1845, in Marion County, Alabama, and died February 23, 1923, in Marion County, Alabama. (Elizabeth was a sister to John M. Palmer who married Mary M. Brown. John is the son of Joseph M. and Permelia Brown Palmer. Mary was the daughter of William M. and Susan Tice Brown.) Children of Matthew and Elizabeth were: Mary Ann, born July 31, 1870, died August 29, 1943, and James Joseph Glenn, born May 15, 1872. Matthew died March 9, 1929 in Marion County, Alabama and was buried in the Bethany Baptist Church Cemetery in Marion County, Alabama along with his wife and two children.

Glover, Silas J. - Silas J. Glover, brother of William Thomas Glover, below, enlisted in Company D of the 1st Alabama Cavalry, USV as a private on May 20, 1864, in Decatur, Alabama for a period of 3 years. He was enrolled by Lieutenant Pease and was mustered in June 16, 1864, in Decatur, Alabama. The Muster and Descriptive Roll recorded him as 24 years of age, 5'-9" tall, having a light complexion, blue eyes, dark hair, born in Jefferson County, Alabama and a farmer by occupation. He mustered out October 20, 1865, in Huntsville, Alabama owing the US Government $15.50 for losing 1 revolver.

Silas was born about 1840 in Jefferson County, Alabama to Richard W. Glover and his wife, Martha "Patsey" Wood. Silas married Mary Ann E. Reid November 14, 1865, in Jefferson County, Alabama. Mary was the daughter of Daniel Reid and Tabitha James, who were married September 1, 1833, in Jefferson County, Alabama. Children of Silas and Tabitha were: Nancy Catherine, born December 1866, died August 23, 1914; Richard Daniel, born February 3, 1867, died November 9, 1947; James Harvey, born February 11, 1871, died January 14, 1972; and John Thomas Glover, born about 1875. Silas J. Glover died sometime before 1880.

Glover, William - William Glover enlisted in Company G of the 1st Alabama Cavalry, USV as a private on March 10, 1864, in Decatur, Alabama for a period of 3 years. He was enrolled by Lieutenant Pease, and was mustered in April 13, 1864, in Decatur. The Muster and Descriptive Roll recorded him as 21 years of age, 5'-7" tall, having a dark complexion, black eyes, dark hair, born in Montgomery County, Alabama and a farmer by occupation. He was promoted from private to corporal on May 1, 1864. He was reported to have deserted November 17, 1864, from Atlanta, Georgia with 1 Colt Revolver and accoutrements. His name was recorded on the Descriptive List of Deserters from Thunderbolt, Georgia December 27, 1864, stating he deserted from the camp with side arms.

Glover, William Thomas - William Thomas Glover, brother of Silas J. Glover, above, enlisted in Company D of the 1st Alabama Cavalry, USV as a private on May 20, 1864, in Decatur, Alabama for a period of 3 years. He was enrolled by Lieutenant Pease and was mustered in June 16, 1864, in Decatur. The Muster and Descriptive Roll recorded him as 22 years of age, 5'-8" tall, having a dark complexion, black eyes, black hair, born in Jefferson County, Alabama, and a farmer by occupation. He was appointed corporal from private on December 1, 1864, by order of Colonel Spencer. He was mustered out October 20, 1865, in Huntsville, Alabama owing the U.S. Government $1.80 for losing 1 curry comb and 1 surcingle.

William Thomas Glover was born in July 1843, in Jefferson County, Alabama to Richard W. Glover and Martha "Patsey" Wood. William Thomas married first Elizabeth Brooks on February 26, 1861, in Jefferson County, Alabama. Elizabeth was the daughter of William and Icy Mullins Brooks. William T. and Elizabeth had the following children: William Silas; John W.; Martha Ellen; James E.; Richard W.; Isabella; Thomas J. and Robert M. Glover. William married second, Lucinda Elizabeth Campbell, and third, Malinda J. Sullivan. William Thomas Glover died November 30, 1921, in Glover's Bend, Jefferson County, Alabama and was buried in the Oak Grove Cemetery

<u>Goad, James</u> - There was one muster roll for James Goad, also spelled Goode, mixed in with John M. Goode's records that stated James Goode enlisted in Company K of the 1st Alabama Cavalry, USV, and that he died in Nashville, Tennessee March 3, 1863. He was buried in Grave E-0850 in Nashville National Cemetery in Nashville, Davidson County, Tennessee.

<u>Goad, William A.</u> - William A. Goad, also shown as William A. Good, enlisted as a private in Company F, 1st Alabama Cavalry, USV at Bridgeport, Alabama on January 29, 1864. He was described as being 29 years old, with dark complexion, black hair & eyes, standing 6'-1" tall, and a farmer by occupation. He had previously been mustered into the Confederate Army in February of 1862, probably involuntarily. He was discharged in September of the same year for medical disability. His name appeared on the Returns for April 1865 stating he had been captured and taken prisoner of war. His enlistment in the Union forces was likely the best of 2 evils, for like many men of North Alabama, he probably did not want to be a part of the rebellion against his country. He also served in Company H of the 1st Tennessee and Alabama Independent Vidette Cavalry, US.

William was born in 1829 in Greene County, Indiana to Hiram Goad and Eliza Nicholson. Eliza was living with sons James and William, but without Hiram, in Murray County, Georgia at the time of the 1850 census, near her Nicholson relatives. Hiram joined her sometime after the census and they had 2 daughters born in the 1850's. One of these daughters, as Eliza Goad Watts, filed a Cherokee claim in 1907, claiming Cherokee blood thru her mother's side. Eliza Nicholson Goad is said to have been a descendant of Isaac Nicholson and his Cherokee wife, Betsy Walking stick. My mother, the great granddaughter of William A Goad, told me her grandmother, Elsie Goad, who had married Rowlen Tidwell, was Cherokee. She also told me how the Goad name was spelled, though in many of the war records it seems to have been spelled 'Good'.

In 1856, William was living in Benton, now Calhoun County, Alabama where he married Elizabeth Jackson, daughter of Clark William Jackson and Jane Creasy Reynolds. The Jackson's likely had some Cherokee blood, as Elizabeth Jackson Goad's youngest son, John N. Romine, claimed both Indian and White as his race on his WW I Draft Registration.

In 1860, William A Goad purchased a land grant from the federal government for 160 acres in Walker County, Alabama and moved his wife and children there. He was listed as a farmer in both of his Civil War enlistment records. His wife's sister, Margaretta Jackson Bailey, also moved her family to Walker County. It is said that when the Civil War broke out, Margaretta went back to Calhoun County and brought their parents back with her to Walker County, where they lived the rest of their lives.

William and Elizabeth Goad had four children, the eldest of whom was my great grandmother, Elsie Goad Tidwell. The second eldest was William A Goad, Jr. who was said by his mother to have been 'helpless from birth' and her reason for seeking a pension. The third child was Nancy Jane and the fourth, Wilborn Dallas. Dallas, born in December of 1864 after William was executed by the Confederate Home Guard.

William A Goad was said by his widow in her 1886 Pension application to have been on leave from the Alabama & Tennessee Independent Vidette Cavalry in March of 1864 to move his family to safety behind Union lines. He was captured, in uniform, by the Confederate Home Guard and held for 6 months at the Jasper, Alabama jail. According to the sworn testimonies of James Stanley Abbott, a fellow prisoner, and George Ary, who was in charge of the Jasper jail at the time, William was taken from the jail on the 10th of September 1864 by the order of Captain Goodwin to South Lowell, which is a little north of Jasper, where he was blindfolded, shot and buried. In another sworn affidavit, Simeon Coven stated he was present when Goad was buried and was about a mile away and heard the shot that killed him.

Elizabeth Jackson Goad said in her pension application that after her husband had been executed, the Confederate Home Guard came to her home and destroyed everything she owned, cutting her featherbeds and scattering the feathers into the wind. She stated that when he was captured she feared for the lives of her children, and so destroyed his military papers. The pension application dragged on for 5 years as effort was made to prove that his leave was valid; he was listed on the final muster records of the Alabama & Tennessee Vidette as having deserted, but in another record he was

327

listed as a prisoner of war by the 1st Regiment of the Alabama Cavalry, the Vidette having disbanded while he was in the Jasper Jail. Finally, in 1993, the pension was denied based on her remarriage, after Congressman Joe Wheeler introduced a House of Representatives bill seeking a review of her pension application. Perhaps he was instrumental in having William A Goad's body reinterred after the war at Corinth National Cemetery in Alcorn County, Mississippi.

I visited his grave at Corinth in 2008 to pay homage to the man who gave his life for our country. I am proud to be his great, great granddaughter. Submitted by Dorothy Duke Rhodes.

Godfrey, George Lucious - George Lucious Godfrey enlisted in the 1st Alabama Cavalry, USV as Major and was mustered in October 18, 1863, in Glendale, Mississippi for a period of 1 year. He was promoted from 1st Lieutenant and adjutant of the 2nd Iowa Infantry Volunteers, by Special Order #2, Left Wing, 16th Army Corps dated October 18, 1863, in Corinth, Mississippi. The Field and Staff Muster Roll for May and June 1864, recorded him as a Lieutenant Colonel, stating he was promoted from Major May 8, 1864. On May 9, 1864, he was mustered out in the field at Resaca, Georgia for promotion to Vice Lieutenant Colonel for a period of 3 years. A.J. Dodds resigned May 2, 1864. Relieved from duty May 9, 1864. The July and August 1864 Muster Roll recorded him as absent, on detached service collecting absent enlisted men of the regiment by order of Major General John A. Logan by Special Order 79, headquarters, Department of the Tennessee July 26, 1864. The January and February 1865 Muster Roll recorded him as absent, in charge of stores in Savannah, Georgia S.F.O. #12, Headquarters, 3rd Cavalry Division, January 19, 1865. The May and June 1865 Muster Roll recorded him as being on leave of absence, Special Order 46, Headquarters, Department of the Cumberland, June 17, 1865. The July and August 1865 Field and Staff Muster Roll recorded Godfrey as absent, on leave of absence, awaiting resignation papers, Special order 64, Department of the Cumberland, June 17, 1865. He was mustered out October 20, 1865, in Huntsville, Alabama. On June 15, 1865, George Lucious Godfrey requested a leave of absence of twenty days due to sickness in his family which required his immediate attention, stating he had been in military service four years and had but one short leave.

From *The History of Polk County, Iowa*

At this point the record of this gallant and brave soldier drops out of the record of Iowa patriots. When Sherman's forces had got well into the South, a regiment of brave Union men was formed in Alabama, and Adjutant Godfrey was assigned to it as lieutenant-colonel and subsequently promoted to colonel. They were a noble body of men, who not only took their own lives in their hands, but also staked that of their own kith and kin at home, and all the prosperity, they possessed. The incendiary torch, and the assassin's knife or shot-gun wreaked a rapid vengeance on all these noble patriots left behind them.

The regiment operated with Sherman's army through the Carolinas. Col. Godfrey was selected to bear important dispatches from Gen. Sherman to the rebel General Johnson, after Lee's surrender.

Arriving at Wade Hampton's headquarters, that General refused to permit him to pass through his lines to Johnson's army headquarters. "All right," replied Col. Godfrey, "I will return and report the matter to Gen. Sherman." Hampton offered to send the dispatches to Johnson, but he failed to catch the Colonel in that way. "My orders were to deliver the dispatches to Gen. Hampton," said Colonel Godfrey; "I propose to do so."

He then called an adjutant to accompany the Colonel to Johnson's headquarters, but the Colonel fell back on his dignity and army etiquette, and refused to accept any officer below his own rank as escort. A staff officer was finally sent with him. He also was the bearer of the dispatches from Gen. Grant to Gen. Johnson, proposing the place of meeting between the two generals for the arrangements of the final surrender of the Confederate army and the Confederacy, and he was present at the consultation.

When the Confederacy "busted" he was near Raleigh, North Carolina. Wade Hampton, who had occupied that city, moved out and sent word to Col. Godfrey that he might enter the city and protect the government and its citizens. The Colonel selecting a few of his staff officers and several line officers, started in advance of the column, at the solicitation of the governor of the State, mayor of the city, and prominent citizens, to prepare the way and also to hoist the stars and stripes over the State house. As they were riding through the streets they were fired upon by a band of desperadoes, who had broken loose from Hampton's army. Col. Godfrey gave the order to catch the devils if they could, but they all escaped except one, and when the regiment entered the State house yard, the assassin was swinging from the limb of a tree.

Entering the State house, the Colonel found the janitor, an antiquated negro, who was nearly white with fright: "Uncle Sam," said the Colonel, "Where are the flags?" "I dunno, massa, 'spects deys all toted off," replied the negro. "The Yanks are here," said the Colonel," the rebs are all gone, and we want the flags; hunt them up." "Well," said the negro, I reckon you'll find suthin' in dat ar' box," pointing to a long narrow box. "Well, open it quick," said the Colonel. The old negro hustled about, with a broad grin on his face, opened the box, and enclosed therein were twenty-one Union flags, which had been captured, and several tattered and torn rebel flags. The Union flags were, by the Colonel, quickly spread along the fence about the State house to greet the Union column.

It was while at Raleigh the preparations were made for the march to Washington for the grand review. The Colonel's regiment cared more for home and friends than the review and desired to return to Huntsville, Alabama, and be mustered out at once. They had received tidings of friends assassinated, homes burned, and they were anxious to know the worst, and gather together their scattered families. Gen. Sherman protested against the movement as a dangerous one, as the march would be through the enemy's country, through which the Union army had just passed.

The Colonel determined to go with the men who had served so nobly and faithfully, and the regiment marched across the country to Huntsville without molestation. There they were paroled and sent to their homes, and the Colonel was mustered out October 26, 1865. He, therefore, was not present at the grand review at Washington; failed to receive his brevet-brigadier-general's commission, and little silver star as a badge of honor and promotion.

Col. Godfrey was wounded at Ft. Donelson, February 14th, 1862. At the battle of Corinth he received special mention for his coolness and bravery; one horse was shot dead under him, and a second, a favorite animal, was knocked down. The Colonel left him lying flat on the earth, supposing he was a dead equine, but what was his surprise soon after, as he was passing along the line encouraging his men, to see his pet horse following him.

George Godfrey was born on the 4th of November, 1833, in Orleans County, Vermont. In the fall of 1855, he came to Iowa, stopping at Dubuque, where he engaged in school teaching, and in 1859 took up his permanent residence in Des Moines. He began his law studies with Judge C. C. Cole and was admitted to the bar just before the War of the Rebellion began. In May, 1861, he enlisted in Company D, of the famous Second Iowa Volunteer Infantry and in December was promoted to second lieutenant and in June, 1862, became first lieutenant and adjutant of the regiment. He served with distinction in the great battles of Fort Donelson and Shiloh, and marching to Corinth with Grant's army he bore a conspicuous part in the two days' desperate battle in that famous town, having two horses shot under him. When the First Alabama Cavalry was organized from Union men Captain Godfrey was commissioned major, in 1863, and was soon after promoted to lieutenant-colonel. In this regiment he served with distinction in Sherman's famous march to the sea. At the close of the war he was mustered out with his regiment at Huntsville, Alabama. Before his return to Iowa Colonel Godfrey was elected a member of the House of the Eleventh General Assembly on the Republican ticket. In the spring of 1866 he completed his law course at the State University at Iowa City and began the practice of his profession. He served as city solicitor and assistant United States District Attorney for several years. In 1876 he was one of the presidential electors chosen by the Republicans. In 1870 he was appointed receiver of the United States Land Office at Des Moines. In 1882, upon the creation of the Utah Commission, Colonel Godfrey was appointed a member. The object of the Commission was the suppression of polygamy in the Territory. The Commission consisted of five members appointed by the President, was non-partisan and had supervision of all elections. The membership was changed from time to time, with the exception of Colonel Godfrey who served during three administrations and was for four years president of the Commission. When the Commission was established to superintend the erection of monuments on the battle-field of Shiloh, Governor Shaw appointed Colonel Godfrey one of the members. In 1903 he was appointed surveyor of the port of Des Moines. Col. George Lucious Godfrey is buried in the Woodland Cemetery, Des Moines, Iowa. From The History of Polk County,

Iowa. George L. Godfrey died April 24, 1915. He first married Carrie L., last name unknown, born December 20, 1845, died September 28, 1879. He married next Ella Fisher, born May 12, 1856, died November 19, 1935.

Godsey, John J. - John J. Godsey enlisted in Company D of the 1st Alabama Cavalry, USV as a private on May 4, 1864, in Decatur, Alabama for a period of 3 years. He was enrolled by Lieutenant Ewing and was mustered in May 4, 1864, in Rome, Georgia. The Muster and Descriptive Roll recorded him as 18 years of age, 6' tall, having a light complexion, blue eyes, broth hair, born in Morgan County, Alabama, and a farmer by occupation. The November and December 1864 Godsey was promoted to Corporal November 1, 1864, by order of Colonel Spencer at Rome, Georgia. On July 28, 1864, he transferred from Company D to Company A in Rome, Georgia. He was mustered out October 20, 1865, from Huntsville, Alabama.

According to descendants, John J. Godsey was the brother of Robert A. Godsey, below. He was born June 18, 1845, in Morgan County, Alabama to Augustus Woolridge Godsey and Judith E. Alderson who were married October 22, 1838, in Powhatan, Powhatan County, Virginia. John J. Godsey married Margaret Frances Hood, daughter of William Wilson Hood and Elizabeth Isabel Lindsey who were married June 29, 1841, in Tuscaloosa, Alabama. John and Margaret were married about 1866 and had, at least, the following children: William, died February 22, 1925; James Robert, born December 5, 1867; and Augustus Godsey, born March 10, 1865 and died April 24, 1941. John J. Godsey died in 1935, and is buried in the Friendship Cemetery in Haleyville, Winston County, Alabama.

Godsey, Robert Asa - Robert Asa Godsey enlisted in Company D of the 1st Alabama Cavalry, USV on February 15, 1863, in Glendale, Mississippi for a period of 1 year. He was enrolled by Lieutenant Wesley Williams and was mustered in the same day in Camp Davies, Mississippi. The Regimental Descriptive Book recorded him as 22 years of age, 5'-11" tall, having a dark complexion, dark eyes, dark hair, born in Morgan County, Alabama, and a farmer by occupation. His name appeared on the Company Muster Roll to April 30, 1863, stating he was absent, hurt in a skirmish and supposed to be taken prisoner of war in the hands of the enemy. The May and June 1863 Muster Roll also recorded him as absent, taken prisoner of war while on the Tuscumbia Raid. The July and August 1863 Muster Roll recorded him as absent, captured by the enemy April 25, 1863. The September and October Muster Roll recorded him as present. The November and December 1863 Muster Roll recorded him as having deserted November 26, 1863, from Camp Davies, Mississippi, owing the U.S. Government $47.85 for taking the arms and equipment. A Notation in his file from the Adjutant General's Office of the War Department stated the following: Application for the removal of the charge of desertion and for an honorable discharge has been denied. His name appeared on the Returns as follows: March 1863, absent, prisoner of war, captured on scout February 26, 1863; June 1863, Absent, supposed to be taken prisoner; Absent with leave June 1, 1863; July 1863, Absent without leave; August 1863, Absent on secret service; November 1863, Absent, prisoner of war since October 26, 1863, which would have been the Battle of Vincent's Crossroads near Bay Springs, Mississippi.

Robert Asa Godsey was the brother of John J. Godsey, above. He was born June 15, 1841, in Morgan County, Alabama to Augustus Woolridge Godsey and Judith E. Alderson. Other children of Augustus and Judith were: John J., born June 18, 1845; Mary V., born 1829; Catherine Booker, born November 18, 1830; William R., born July 16, 1832; Martha, born January 1, 1843; and Elizabeth Amelia Godsey, born August 7, 1847. Robert died March 16, 1911, in Winston County, Alabama, and is buried in the Friendship Primitive Baptist Church Cemetery near Ashridge, in Winston County, Alabama.

The Winston New Era, March 3, 1911

A Good Man Gone. On last Saturday night, Mr. R.A. Godsey, one of our oldest and best citizens departed this life and his spirit went to dwell with the redeemed on heaven's peaceful shore. He had suffered for several months with indigestion and bore his afflictions patiently. He was a member of the Primitive Baptist Church and was prominent in its counsels. He was the father of a large family of boys who are now good and noble citizens with families of their own, and a large host of other relatives with whom the Era force mourns his departure from the state of earthly existence, and with whom we rejoice in the assurance that he wears a faithful servants crown in the paradise above. He was about 71 years old and will be greatly missed by our people. He was buried at Friendship near Ashridge, Monday.

Godwin, Henry K. - Henry K. Godwin, also listed as Goodwin, enlisted in Company K of the 1st Alabama Cavalry, USV as a private on August 25, 1862, in Huntsville, Alabama for a period of 3 years. He was enrolled by Lieutenant Millard and mustered in November 1, 1862, in Nashville, Tennessee. The Company Descriptive Book recorded him as 25 years of age, 5'-8" tall, having a dark complexion, black eyes, black hair, born in Cass County, Georgia and a farmer by occupation. Godwin was in the early group of enlistees who were immediately shipped to Nashville and merged with the 1st Middle Tennessee Cavalry, which later became the 5th Tennessee Cavalry. He was recorded as being in Companies E and F of the 1st Middle Tennessee Cavalry on the November and December 1862 Muster Roll. A notation on his July and August 1863 Muster Roll stated he had always done duty in Captain Smith's Company by order of Colonel Stokes. His name was listed on the Returns as follows: January and February 1863, absent on January 27, 1863, on courier post, probably in Readyville, Tennessee; October 1863, absent at Bay Springs (Mississippi), October 26, 1863, sent to Memphis, Tennessee; November 1863, absent, sick in Memphis, Tennessee November 29, 1863, wounded at Vincent's Crossroads; December 1863, loss December 9, 1863, Memphis, Tennessee, died from wound received at Vincent's Crossroads October 26, 1863. The June 30, 1863 through October 31, 1863, Muster Roll recorded him as being back in Company K of the 1st Alabama Cavalry, USV, and as being in Colonel Spencer's raid on Vincent's Crossroads where he was wounded in battle October 26, 1863, when he was wounded in the right arm, which was amputated. Henry K. Godwin died in Overton U.S.A. General Hospital in Memphis, Shelby County, Tennessee, December 9, 1863, of gangrene. The Overton Hospital Inventory of Effects of Private Henry K. Godwin recorded him as having 1 hat, 1 blouse, 1 flannel sack coat, and 2 pairs of trowsers. He was due a bounty of $100.

Henry K. Godwin was born about 1836 in Cass County, Georgia and was the son of James A.J. Godwin, Sr. and his wife, Ann Knowling, who were married October 13, 1832, in Fayette County, Georgia. Cass County, Georgia is since defunct and the name was changed to Bartow County. Henry was the brother of Samuel J. Godwin, below, who also served in Company K of the 1st Alabama Cavalry, USV. On October 18, 1859, Henry married Catherine Storie in Marshall County, Alabama. Catherine died February 4, 1915, in Venus, Texas. Most of Venus is in Ellis County, Texas, but some of it is in Johnson County. Henry K. Godwin died of gangrene on December 9, 1863, due to a gunshot wound to the right arm during the Battle of Vincent's Crossroads near Bay Springs, Mississippi. He died in Overton Hospital in Memphis, Shelby County, Tennessee, and was buried in Grave #1382 in the Memphis National Cemetery.

Godwin, James A. - See James A. Goodwin.

Godwin, Samuel J. - Samuel J. Godwin, brother of Henry K. Godwin, above, enlisted in Company K of the 1st Alabama Cavalry, USV as a private on August 25, 1862, in Huntsville, Alabama for a period of 3 years. He was enrolled by Lieutenant Millard and was mustered in September 25, 1862, in Company F of the 1st Middle Tennessee Cavalry, US in Nashville, Tennessee. Like his brother, Henry K., and possibly James A. Godwin, he was one of the early enlistees who were immediately shipped to Nashville, Tennessee where they were merged with the 1st Middle Tennessee Cavalry, which was later the 5th Tennessee Cavalry. The Company Descriptive Roll recorded Samuel as 24 years of age, 5'-9" tall, having a light complexion, blue eyes, auburn hair, born in Cass County, Georgia, and a farmer by occupation. In January and February 1863 he was recorded as being absent on Courier Post January 27, 1863, probably in Readyville, Tennessee. He was always on duty in Captain Smith's Company by order of Colonel Stokes, as was his brother, Henry. On April 30, 1863, Samuel was recorded as missing in action from Crooked Creek, Alabama. The June 30, 1863, to October 31, 1863, Muster Roll recorded him as being absent, missing in action at the Battle of Vincent's Crossroads near Bay Springs, Mississippi. On December 4, 1863, Samuel was returned to Camp Davies, Mississippi from missing in action at Vincent's Crossroads.   The January and February 1864 Muster roll recorded him as absent, on detached service as teamster on General Sherman's Expedition in Vicksburg, Mississippi since January 24, 1864, by order of General Grierson. The March and April 1864 Muster Roll recorded him as absent, prisoner of war since March 21, 1864. He was captured by the enemy in Arkansas, near Memphis, Tennessee on March 21, 1864.

Samuel J. Godwin was born December 14, 1838, in Cass County, Georgia. Cass County is since defunct and the name was changed to Bartow County, Georgia See Henry K. Godwin, above, for parents. Samuel married Martha Elizabeth Golden, who was born December 24, 1867, and died November 12, 1958.

Goff, William T. - William T. Goff, also listed as William T. Ghoaff, enlisted in Company A of the 1st Alabama Cavalry, USV as a private on August 1, 1864, in Rome, Georgia for a term of 1 year. He was enrolled by Captain Pierce or Hinds and was mustered in October 20, 1864, in Rome, Georgia. The Company Descriptive Book recorded him as being 18 years of age, 5'-8" tall, having hazel eyes, brown hair, born in Lawrence County, Alabama, and a farmer by occupation. The July and August 1863 Muster Roll recorded him as being confined in Post Guard House. The September through December 1863 Muster Rolls recorded him as being absent, in confinement at Corinth, Mississippi. The January and February 1864 Muster Roll recorded him as being absent, with Lieutenant Streight, A.A.Q.M., 16th Army Corps. From December 1863 through June 1864, he was in arrest at Rome, Georgia. The September and October 1864 Muster roll showed him to have been absent, prisoner of war since October 1, 1864, in Rome, Georgia. The Muster-Out Roll stated he was still a prisoner of war through October 20, 1865, and was not issued a discharge at muster out of organization. His name appeared on the Returns as follows: December 1863, absent, in confinement in Corinth, Mississippi; January and February 1864, absent, teamster in Quartermaster Department in Vicksburg, Mississippi since January 25, 1864; July 1864, absent, in arrest in Rome, Georgia; October 1864, absent, sick in General Hospital; The July and August 1865 Muster Roll recorded him as absent, captured September 11, 1864, from Rome, Georgia and not heard from since. November 1864 to March 1865, absent, prisoner of war since October 26, 1863. This would have been at the Battle of Vincent's Crossroads near Bay Springs, Mississippi. His name appeared on the Returns as follows: September 1864, Loss September 25, 1864, from Rome, Georgia. Supposed to have been killed. October 1864, absent, supposed to be sick in General Hospital, no name of hospital or city given. January to September 1865, absent, prisoner of war in the hands of the enemy. No discharge was furnished at muster out of organization and he had never been paid.

Goggiss, Meredith - See Meredith Gargis.

Going, Doctor - Doctor Going, also spelled Goins and Goings, and Goyans, enlisted in Company D of the 1st Alabama Cavalry, USV as a private on March 15, 1863, in Glendale, Mississippi for a period of 1 year. He was enrolled by W. Williams and was mustered in March 26, 1863, in Corinth, Mississippi. The Regimental Descriptive Book recorded him as 44 years of age, 6'-2" tall, having a dark complexion, blue eyes, dark hair, born in Pittsylvania County, Virginia, and a farmer by occupation. The May and June 1863 Muster Roll recorded him as a sergeant. However, the November and December 1863 Muster Roll stated he had been reduced to ranks from sergeant December 3, 1863. The Individual Muster-Out Roll recorded him as mustered out May 18, 1864, in Cairo, Illinois due to expiration of term of service. He had never received any bounty. Doctor Going's name appeared on the Returns as follows: January 1864, absent, at Refugee Camp in Memphis, Tennessee. March 1864, absent, sick in hospital in Memphis, Tennessee.

Good, William A. - Only one card was found for William A. Good, also listed as William A. Goad, probably the same William A. Good, below, which was filed at the end of the last roll of microfilm of the 1st Alabama Cavalry, USV records. It recorded him as enlisting in Company F, was captured and taken prisoner of war in April 1865. No further information relative to this soldier was found.*

Good, James - See James Goad.

Good, William A. - See William A. Goad.

Goode, John McKinly - John McKinly Goode (also listed as John McKinley Goode but descendant Ron Goode stated his middle name was spelled McKinly in the old family Bible) was enlisted and mustered into Company K of the 1st Alabama Cavalry, USV as a private in Huntsville, Alabama for a period of 3 years. He was enrolled by Lieutenant Millard. The Regimental Descriptive Book recorded him as 30 years of age, 5'-10½" tall, having a light complexion, blue eyes, brown hair, born in Lauderdale County, Alabama, and a farmer by occupation. John was one of the early enlistees shipped to Nashville, Tennessee where they were merged with Company E of the 1st Middle Tennessee Cavalry, which later became the 5th Tennessee Cavalry. The January and February 1864 Muster Roll recorded him as absent, on detached service as teamster in General Sherman's Expedition since January 24, 1864, by order of General Grierson. The March and April 1864 Muster roll stated he died of smallpox March 3, 1864, near Vicksburg, Mississippi while on detached service as a teamster. John's name appeared on the Returns as follows: October 1862, on duty as company cook; January and February 1863, absent on courier post January 27, 1863, probably in Readyville, Tennessee; January and February 1864, absent in Vicksburg, Mississippi January 24, 1864; March 1864, loss March 3rd, died of smallpox while on detached service as teamster near Vicksburg, Mississippi in General Sherman's Mississippi Campaign. He was captured during the Battle of Day's Gap in Alabama May 1, 1863, confined at Richmond, Virginia May 9, 1863, and paroled May 14, 1863, at City Point, Virginia, reported at Camp Parole, Maryland May 16, 1863, sent to C.C.O. May 19, 1863, and sent back to regiment on June 9, 1863.

John McKinly Goode was born June 11, 1832, in Lauderdale County, Alabama to Milton Goode and his wife, Letty R. Lentz. John had a brother, James, who is most likely the James Goode, above, who also served in this regiment. John married Rhoda Lentz October 27, 1856, in Limestone County, Alabama. Rhoda was born February 2, 1827, and died June 16, 1877, and was the daughter of Benjamin L. Lentz and Mary "Polly" Jackson, who married July 20, 1822, in Limestone County, Alabama. Children of John and Rhoda were: Christopher Columbus, born August 15, 1857; died September 2, 1926; Marion C.; Letty A.; and John Thomas Goode, born February 27, 1861. John M. Goode died March 3, 1864, near Vicksburg, Warren County, Mississippi.

Civil War Service - John McKinly Goode, 1862-1864, Huntsville, Madison, Alabama, USA

The American Civil War was a terrible time in America, not only dividing the nation, but also many families over whether the union was to be preserved or not. Pvt. John McKinly Goode came from such a place and family. Limestone County, in Northern Alabama had very strong unionist sympathies among many of its inhabitants, and so divided many a family dinner table. While John, and many others like him from this area, chose to join the Union Army, his brother William took up the cause of the South, fighting for the confederacy.

John McKinly Goode, at the age of 30, enlisted at the rank of Private in Company K., 1st Regiment Alabama Cavalry USV on August 22nd, 1862. Mustering in at Huntsville, Alabama with many of his friends, neighbors and relatives, they signed on for a three year enlistment. This regiment is the only organization of Union troops from Alabama for which the National Archives has separate compiled service records, with the exception of those organizations designated as US Colored Troops. These men of the 1st Cavalry not only fought in the Civil War, but fought for what they believed in. Many of the men in the 1st Cavalry lived in Northwest Alabama and did not approve of the secession. However, living in the South, they were unable to speak out against it. These men had to travel long distances to avoid being captured by Confederate soldiers, and branded as traitors to join the Union Army. Many stated their grandfathers fought too hard and suffered too much fighting for this country in the Revolutionary War, and they certainly couldn't fight against the same country they fought, suffered and in some instances, died for. They could not fire on "Old Glory", the Flag of their forefathers. John McKinly Goode's thoughts may have been for his great grandfather, who was a

Major during the Revolutionary War and his grandfather's and uncles who had fought England for the Union a second time in the War of 1812.

There are 24 document records on file in the National Archives pertaining to Private John M. Goode. The records lack much detail of the specific events the regiment were involved in; however we do know that it was attached to the XVI Corps in various divisions until November 1864, when it became part of the XV Corps. During this time, its duties mostly consisted of scouting, raiding, reconnaissance, flank guard, and providing screening to the infantry while on the march. In one such event, in May of 1863 John was captured at the Battle of Days Gap at Sand Mountain Alabama. This battle was the first battle in the infamous running skirmishes and engagements between Union Colonel Abel D. Streight and Confederate General Nathan Bedford Forrest that took place from April 30, thru May 3rd 1863. Union Colonel Abel D. Streight led a provisional brigade on a raid to cut the Western & Atlantic Railroad that supplied General Braxton Bragg's Confederate army in Middle Tennessee. From Nashville, Tennessee, Streight's command traveled to Eastport, Mississippi, and then proceeded east to Tuscumbia, Alabama, in conjunction with another Union force commanded by Brigadier General Grenville Dodge. On April 26, 1863, Streight's men left Tuscumbia and marched southeast, their initial movements screened by Dodge's troops. On April 30, Confederate Brigadier General Nathan Bedford Forrest's brigade caught up with Streight's expedition and attacked its rearguard at Day's Gap on Sand Mountain. The Federals repulsed this attack and continued their march to avoid further delay and envelopment. Thus began a running series of skirmishes and engagements at Crooked Creek (April 30), Hog Mountain (April 30), Blountsville (May 1), Black Creek/Gadsden (May 2), and Blount's Plantation (May 2). Forrest finally surrounded the exhausted Union soldiers near Rome, Georgia, where he forced their surrender on May 3rd. Pages 19 thru 22 of John's service records document this event and his subsequent release from capture in a prisoner exchange on June 9th, 1863, in Richmond, Virginia. According to page 12 of John's service record we know that in January and February 1864, he was on detached assignment to General William T. Sherman's expedition through Jackson, Mississippi. It was during this time period when John became ill and was struck down near Vicksburg, Mississippi, where there he died as a result of contracting small pox disease March 3rd, 1864. There are several pages in his service records that record his death of the disease.

William Richard Goode, the younger brother who fought for the Confederacy, was much more fortunate than John, as he made it through the war and lived a long and productive life.

Another sad and odd occurrence was that John M Goode's widow, Rhoda Goode was now a widow for the second time due to a soldier's life. Her first husband, James S Gower was a veteran of the Mexican American war of 1848 and died as a result of the disabling wounds he received during that war soon after his return. Family information submitted by Ron Goode, a Civil War historical researcher. John McKinly Goode is his 1st cousin 4X removed.

Goodwin, James A. - James A. Goodwin, also spelled Godwin, enlisted in Company C of the 1st Alabama Cavalry, USV. The first Hospital Muster Roll was for the U.S.A. General Field Hospital in Stevenson, Alabama for September and October 1863, and recorded him as James W. Goodwin. The November and December 1863 Muster Roll recorded him on a Hospital Muster Roll, No. 2, U.S.A. General Hospital, (Branch No. 10,) Louisville, Kentucky, stating his pay was due from enlistment. He was recorded as being a corporal. The next muster roll listed his name as James A. Goodwin, and appeared on Hospital Muster Roll No. 2 Eruptive U.S.A. General Hospital, Louisville, Kentucky, dated January and February 1864. The next muster roll was for the same hospital, dated March and April 1864, recoding his name as James A. Goodwin.

Goof, William T. - William T. Goof, also appears as William T. Goop, Gaff, and other spellings. The name could be Good. He enlisted in Company F of the 1st Alabama Cavalry, USV as a private on June 30, 1863, in Corinth, Mississippi for a period of 1 year. He was enrolled by Captain Pierce and was mustered in July 1, 1863, in Corinth. The Company Descriptive Book recorded him as 18 years of age, 5'-8" tall, having hazel eyes, brown hair, born in Lawrence County, Alabama, and a farmer by occupation. The July and August 1863 Muster Roll recorded him as being in confinement in Post Guard House. The September 1863 through December 1863 Muster Rolls recorded him as being absent, in confinement in Corinth, Mississippi. The December 1863 through June 1864 Muster Roll recorded him as absent, in arrest at Rome, Georgia. The January and February 1864 Muster Roll recorded him as being absent, with Lieutenant Streight, A.A. Quartermaster, 16th Army Corps. The April 30, 1864 Muster Roll recorded him as present. The September through August 1865 Muster Rolls recorded him as absent, prisoner of war since October 1, 1864, in Rome, Georgia. The Muster -Out Roll stated the following: Prisoner of war since October 1, 1864. Assigned to duty from one-year organization of 1st Alabama Cavalry July 25, 1864, by order of Colonel Spencer. Captured at Rome, Georgia, not mustered out at muster out of organization. A note in his file stated: Stop pay for one Remington Army Pistol, clothing account never settled, clothing allowance due from enlistment. Due sutler, $2.35. William T. Goof's name appeared on the Returns as follows: December 1863, absent in confinement at Corinth, Mississippi; January and February 1864, absent, teamster in Quartermaster's Department in Vicksburg, Mississippi since January 25, 1864; July 1864; absent, in arrest at Rome, Georgia. Discharged, term of service expired July 27, 1864 in Rome, Georgia. (This is contrary to other records.); October 1864, absent in general hospital; November 1864 to March 1865, absent, prisoner of war; June to September 1865, absent, prisoner of war since October 26, 1863. (This would have been about 4 months after he enlisted and would have been when the Battle of Vincent's Crossroads near Bay Springs, Mississippi was fought.

Gordon, Samuel J. - Samuel J. Gordon enlisted in Company B of the 1st Alabama Cavalry, USV as a private on March 10, 1864, in Decatur, Alabama for a period of 3 years. He was enrolled by Lieutenant Judy and was mustered in March 27, 1864, in Decatur. The Muster and Descriptive Roll recorded him as 22 years of age, 6'-2" tall, having a fair complexion, gray eyes, light hair, born in Morgan County, Alabama, and a farmer by occupation. The November and December 1864 Muster Roll recorded him as absent, wounded in action November 23, 1864, at Oconee River, Georgia and sent to hospital. Died December 17, 1864, at Beaufort, South Carolina from wounds received in the Battle of Balls Ferry, Georgia November 23, 1864. Another muster roll stated he died in Hilton Head, South Carolina from wounds received in action. Gordon's name appeared on the Returns for January 1865, stating he died of wounds received in action January 1865 in Beaufort, South Carolina. He was buried Lot No. 21, Grave #867, in Beaufort County, South Carolina. Gordon was reinterred in Grave #6346, Beaufort National Cemetery, in Beaufort, South Carolina and a Confederate tombstone was erroneously erected on his grave. After advising the Veterans Administration about this error, they asked for the pension records to prove he was in fact a Union soldier. The certified documents were obtained from the National Archives and provided to the VA, but to date they have failed to replace the tombstone for this loyal citizen soldier who has been buried under false colors for over one-hundred and fifty years.

In the pension records of Samuel J. Gordon, his mother submitted a "Father, Mother, or Orphan Brother's Application for Army Pension", stated on November 26, 1865, that she was Caroline M. Gordon, aged 56 years, living in Morgan Co., AL, and was the mother of Samuel J. Gordon, deceased, who was a Sergeant in Company B of the 1st Regiment of Alabama Cavalry Volunteers, and that he died in Hilton Head, South Carolina on or about December 27, 1864, from wounds received in battle at Balls Ferry, Georgia. She further declared that she was entirely dependant on him and that he left no widow, minor child under sixteen years of age, or any other person who would be entitled to his pension. She listed her address as the Wagon Road leading from Decatur, Alabama to Moulton, about 20 miles from the county seat of Morgan County, Alabama. She signed her name as Caroline M. Gordon. Pension records stated cause of Gordon's death was listed as "Prostration from amputation of right leg, amputation before admission."

Sarah L. Russell and S.A. Langston signed an "Evidence of Dependence" Form stating they had known Caroline M. Gordon for fifteen years and knew her to be the mother of Samuel J. Gordon, and that her husband, also named Samuel J. Gordon, died near Decatur, Alabama on or about February 5, 1842. They also stated they knew Caroline M. Gordon had been dependant on her son for the past ten years and that while in the United States Army, he sent her about one hundred dollars in sums of $10, $20, and $30. They stated her son had worked on their small farm and supported her by his labor, paid the taxes and kept her in clothing. The "Claim for Mother's Pension" stated the Surgeon General's report stated the soldier was admitted to Division No. 1 General Hospital in Beaufort, South Carolina on Dec. 20, 1864, from field for treatment for shell wound received in action necessitating amputation of right leg, upper third, and he died December 27, 1864, at that hospital of amputation of right thigh. The claimant stated she was 56 years of age, was poor, having no means of support except a dower interest in 200 acres of poor mountain land worth about 75 cents per acre, Her pension, No 169.709 was approved June 9, 1869, in the amount of $8 per month, commencing December 28, 1864.

Gordon, W. - Only one card was found for W. Gordon which was filed at the end of the last roll of microfilm of the 1st Alabama Cavalry, USV records. It was a Prisoner of War Record and recorded him as a private in Company L, which stated he was captured October 25, 1863, and taken prisoner of war from the Battle of Vincent's Crossroads near Bay Springs, Mississippi. He was confined at Richmond, Virginia, and was mustered out November 2, 1863, in Mobile, Alabama. No further information relative to this soldier was found.*

Gorley, Samuel - Only one card was found for Samuel Gorley which was filed at the end of the last roll of microfilm of the 1st Alabama Cavalry, USV records. It recorded him as a private in Company K, stating he enlisted in the 1st Alabama Cavalry, USV November 22, 1863, in Camp Davies, Mississippi. This was recorded on a Return. No further information relative to this soldier was found.*

Gortney, Lorenzo M. - Lorenzo M. Gortney enlisted in Company C of the 1st Alabama Cavalry, USV as private on January 29, 1863, in Corinth, Mississippi for a period of 1 year. He was enrolled by Captain John Latty and was mustered in February 5, 1863, in Corinth. The Regimental Descriptive Book recorded Gortney as 25 years of age, 5'-8½" tall, having a fair complexion, blue eyes, light hair, born in Franklin County, Georgia, and a farmer by occupation. The September and October 1863 Muster roll recorded him as absent, taken prisoner of war. The November and December 1863 Muster Roll recorded him as being present. Gortney's name appeared on the Returns as follows: July 1863, on duty as company cook; October 1863, absent, in the hands of the enemy since October 26, 1863, which would have been during the Battle of Vincent's Crossroads near Bay Springs, Mississippi; November 1863, returned from being prisoner of war November 2, 1863, to Glendale, Mississippi. He was mustered out January 31, 1864, in Memphis, Tennessee.

Gortney, Marion - This is possibly the Lorenzo M. Gortney, above. Only one card was found for Marion Gortney which was filed at the end of the last roll of microfilm of the 1st Alabama Cavalry, USV records. It recorded him as a private in Company C, stating he was on duty as a cook August 20, 1863, and on duty as the company cook September 11, 1863. No further information relative to this soldier was found.*

Goss, Allen L. - Allen L. Goss enlisted in Company H of the 1st Alabama Cavalry, USV as a private on March 20, 1865, in Stevenson, Alabama for a period of 3 years. Goss was enrolled by Captain James W. DeVaney, and was mustered in April 5, 1865, in Nashville, Tennessee. DeVaney was previously a Sergeant Major in the 30th Illinois Infantry. The Muster and Descriptive Roll recorded him as 34 years of age, 5'-8½" tall, having a dark complexion, black eyes, black hair, born in Gwinnett County, Georgia, and a farmer by occupation. He was mustered out October 20, 1865, in Huntsville, Alabama and paid a bounty of $100.

Gown, N. - Only one card was found for N. Gown which was filed at the end of the last roll of microfilm of the 1st Alabama Cavalry, USV records. It recorded him as being in Company F, stating he was absent, sick in March 1864. No further information relative to this soldier was found.*

Grace, Nathan P. - Nathan P. Grace enrolled in Company G of the 1st Alabama Cavalry, USV as a private on March 21, 1864, in Decatur, Alabama for a period of 3 years. He was enrolled by Lieutenant Pease and was mustered in April 13, 1864, in Decatur. The Muster and Descriptive Roll recorded him as 22 years of age, 5'-10" Tall, having a fair complexion, blue eyes, dark hair, born in Pike County, Georgia, and a farmer by occupation. He was promoted from private to Corporal May 1, 1864. He was mustered out October 20, 1865, in Huntsville, Alabama owing the U.S. Government $10 for losing 1 carbine retained under General Order 101, 1 wiper and thong, and 1 screwdriver.

Nathan Grace was born in May 1842 in Pike County, Georgia to John Grace, Sr. and Mary Polly Caldwell. Other children of John & Mary were: John, Jr.; Daniel, Richard Y.; Thomas; William and Solina Grace. The family moved from Georgia to Walker County, Alabama about 1859. Family information submitted by descendant James Grace.

Granger, Henry H. - Only one card was found for Henry H. Granger which was filed at the end of the last roll of microfilm of the 1st Alabama Cavalry, USV records. It recorded him as enlisting in Company M of the 1st Alabama Cavalry, USV in Camp Davies, Mississippi as a private. No further information relative to this soldier was found.*

Granger, William H. - William H. Granger enlisted in Company A of the 1st Alabama Cavalry, USV as a private on January 11, 1864, in Camp Davies, Mississippi for a period of 3 years. He was enrolled by Captain Lomax, and was mustered in February 5, 1864, in Memphis, Tennessee. The Company Muster and Descriptive Roll recorded him as 22 years of age, 5'-8" tall, having a fair complexion, blue eyes, light hair, born in Henry County, Tennessee, and a farmer by occupation. A Company Muster Roll dated February 29, 1864, recorded him as absent, on detached service in Company M by Regimental Order Number 47. He was transferred March 9, 1864, Memphis, Tennessee, per Regimental Order Number 50 to Company M to complete organization. Granger was transferred to Company M, 1st Alabama Cavalry, Regimental Order Number 50. The November and December 1864 Muster Roll recorded him as being promoted from Corporal to Sergeant December 1, 1864, for meritorious conduct in the field. He was recorded as being due a bounty of $300. He was mustered out October 20, 1865, in Huntsville, Alabama owing the U.S. Government $16.05 for losing 1 saddle blanket, 1 pistol, 1 screwdriver case, 1 screwdriver, 1 halter and strap, 1 saber belt and plate, 1 curb bridle, 1 horse brush and comb, 2 spurs and straps, 1 thong and brush wiper. He was due a bounty of $300, paid $180 and shown as being due $120 to make up the $300 bounty. Granger's name appeared on the Returns stating he had been absent on furlough since September 27, 1864.

Granville, James - Only one card was found for James Granville which was filed at the end of the last roll of microfilm of the 1st Alabama Cavalry, USV records, and stated he enlisted in Company F. It recorded him as absent, on furlough in August 1863. No further information relative to this soldier was found.*

Graves, Benjamin - Benjamin Graves enlisted and mustered into Company I of the 1st Alabama Cavalry, USV as a private on July 21, 1862, in Huntsville, Alabama. He was enrolled by Captain Bankhead for a period of 3 years. The Company Descriptive Book recorded him as 22 years of age, 5'-11½" tall, having a dark complexion, hazel eyes, dark hair, born in Monroe County, Tennessee, and a farmer by occupation. Graves was one of the first enlistees and they were immediately shipped to Nashville, Tennessee where they were merged with the 1st Middle Tennessee Cavalry, later became the 5th Tennessee Cavalry. He was assigned to Company D of the 1st Middle Tennessee Cavalry. The November and December 1862 Muster Roll recorded him as absent, sick in the hospital in Nashville, Tennessee since December 12, 1862. The March and April 1863 Muster Roll recorded him as being back in Company I of the 1st Alabama Cavalry, USV. He was appointed Corporal November 1, 1863, by order of Colonel Spencer. The March through June 1864 Muster Rolls recorded him as absent, sick in hospital in Nashville, Tennessee since April 3, 1864. The July and August 1864 Muster Roll recorded him as being present, however, the September through December 1864 Muster Rolls recorded him as absent, sick in hospital in Nashville, Tennessee since April 15, 1864. Graves' name appeared on the Returns as follows: December 1862, absent, sick since December 12, 1862, at Nashville, Tennessee; February 1863, absent on courier line, probably in Readyville, Tennessee; May 1863, on duty as a teamster; December 1863, on duty as stable guard; January and February 1864, on duty as stable guard; July 1864, absent, sick in Memphis, Tennessee; August 1864, absent, sick in hospital in Nashville, Tennessee since April 15, 1864; September 1864, absent, sick in hospital; October 1864, absent, sick in hospital in Nashville, Tennessee since April 15, 1864; January 1865, absent, prisoner of war since November 22, 1863; and February and March 1865, absent, sick in US General Hospital.

Benjamin Graves was private until November 1863 when he was appointed corporal by Lieutenant Dodds. No discharge given due to him being absent, sick in hospital in Nashville, Tennessee at time of muster out.

Graves, Ralph - Ralph Graves enlisted in Company E of the 1st Alabama Cavalry, USV as a private on January 1, 1863, in Corinth, Mississippi for a period of 1 year. He was enrolled by Captain Pierce and was mustered in March 13, 1863, at Corinth. His name was on the Descriptive List of Deserters stating he deserted May 1, 1863, from Glendale, Mississippi. However, the Company Muster Roll dated February 28, 1863, stated he was absent due to being sick. The March and April 1863 Muster Roll recorded him as being absent without leave. His name appeared on the Returns as follows: April 1863, absent with leave; May 1863, absent without leave to be dropped as deserter after date; June 1863, deserted May 1, 1863.

Gray, William Thomas - William Thomas Gray enlisted in Company F of the 1st Alabama Cavalry, USV as a Sergeant on June 30, 1863, in Corinth, Mississippi for a period of 1 year and was mustered in July 1, 1863, in Corinth. The Company Descriptive Book recorded him as 20 years of age, 5'-9" tall, having a dark complexion, blue eyes, dark hair, born in Fayette County, Tennessee, and a farmer by occupation. A Company Muster Roll dated April 30, 1864, recorded him as absent, sick in Memphis, Tennessee. He was mustered out in Rome, Georgia on July 27, 1864, due to expiration of term of service. William T. Gray's name appeared on a Hospital Muster Roll for Gayoso U.S.A. General Hospital in Memphis, Tennessee for March through June 1864, stating he was returned to duty on June 22, 1864.

Gray, William T. "Willis" - William T. "Willis" Gray enlisted in Field and Staff (F&S) as a Lieutenant on March 16, 1863, in Glendale, Mississippi, he as promoted from 2nd Master Sergeant of the 57th Illinois Volunteer Infantry. He was first mustered in October 1, 1861, in Chicago, Illinois, and was mustered out April 30, 1864, in Decatur, Alabama. He was appointed by order of General Dodge and mustered into service from March 16, 1863, in Glendale, Mississippi. He was assigned to duty by order of Brigadier General G.M. Dodge. His name appeared on the Returns as follows: March to June 1863, detached from 57th Illinois Infantry; October and November 1863, on duty with regiment; February 1864, absent, sick in Memphis, Tennessee, present numerically; March 1864, relieved from duty by expiration of term of service, not mustered out. A.G.O. announced as out of the service of the U.S. March 15, 1864. The reports and records of the regiment being irregular and conflicting. He will receive no final payment under this order until he shall have fully ratified the payment department that he is not indebted to the government and that he has not previously accepted or presented any discharge papers upon which final dues were paid. He was relieved from duty March 15, 1864, at age 35 due to expiration of term of service. A note in his file stated his accounts had not been settled with the government. The Officers' Casualty Sheet stated he resigned September 2, 1864. A Notation from the Adjutant General's Office of the War Department dated March 19, 1887, stated that Investigation fails to elicit further information. A note in William T. Gray's file stated: "Willis Gray, Scout, Company E, 1st Alabama Cavalry, no record of death or discharge on file.

Green, Elijah C. - Elijah C. Green enlisted in Company M of the 1st Alabama Cavalry, USV on December 16, 1863, in Camp Davies, Mississippi for a period of 3 years. He was enrolled by Captain Lomax and was mustered in December 29, 1863, in Corinth, Mississippi. The Company Descriptive Book recorded him as 17 years of age, 5'-11" tall, having a fair complexion, blue eyes, light hair, born in Marion County, Alabama, and a farmer by occupation. The January and February 1864 Muster Roll stated he was due a bounty of $300. The March and April 1864 Muster Roll recorded him as having deserted April 17, 1864, with a Remington revolver, belt and pistol cartridge pouch. His name appeared on the Descriptive List of Deserters in Mooresville, Alabama April 17, 1864. Another muster roll stated he deserted April 19, 1864, from Mooresville, Alabama.

Sgt. Jasper Newton Green - Including Lemuel and Peyton Burnett

Green, Jasper Newton - Jasper Newton Green was born December 8, 1831, in Marion County, Alabama to Elijah C. Green and Kizziah Kemp. On January 7, 1857, Jasper married Martha Jane Burnett, daughter of Lemuel Burnett and Matilda Cantrell. Children of Jasper and Martha Burnett were: Benjamin Franklin, born October 14, 1859, died December 26, 1953; Patience Kizziah, born July 10, 1862, died November 14, 1960; Frances Adeline, born November 22, 1865, died September 16, 1921; Mary Talitha, born December 20, 1857, died May 24, 1910; Elijah Sherman, born 1870; and Lemuel Grant Green, born July 20, 1873, died May 26, 1907. Other siblings of Jasper N. Green were: Patience Diana, born June 2, 1835, died November 27, 1916; Benjamin, born January 26, 1837, died October 1, 1862; Mary, born September 18, 1841, died October 1, 1856; Elizabeth, born November 15, 1843, died September 22, 1865; and Stephen Young Green, born December 3, 1847, died September 10, 1921. Jasper's wife, Martha Jane Burnett, was the daughter of the staunch Unionist, Lemuel Burnett and his wife, Matilda Cantrell. Lemuel was born February 2, 1812, and died January 6, 1881. Matilda Cantrell Burnett was born about 1819 and died January 21, 1857, in Warren County, Tennessee. Martha Jane Burnett's brother enlisted and mustered in to Company K of the 1st Alabama Cavalry, USV on December 1, 1863 at Camp Davies, Mississippi, probably went with his brother-in-law, Jasper N. Green, because Peyton also rode his horse 90 miles from Marion County, Alabama to Camp Davies. On March 21, 1864, Peyton was captured and taken prisoner of war in Arkansas, near Memphis, Tennessee. He was mustered out July 19, 1865, at Nashville, Tennessee. His Muster-Out Roll stated he was due $300 Bounty, and also entitled to pay for one horse brought into service at his enlistment. He kept himself mounted until June 15, 1865, when his horse failed for want of forage and was abandoned. The Company Descriptive Book recorded Peyton Burnett as 27 years of age, 5'-5" tall, having a light complexion, gray eyes, auburn hair, born in Spartanburg County, South Carolina, and a farmer by occupation.

Jasper Newton Green enlisted as a Private in Company K of the 1st Alabama Cavalry, USV on December 1, 1863, at Camp Davies, Mississippi for a period of 3 years. He rode his horse 90 miles from his home in Marion County, Alabama to Camp Davies, Mississippi to enlist in the Union Army. The Company Descriptive Book recorded him as 32 years of age, 5'-11" tall, having a light complexion, black eyes, black hair, born in Marion County, Alabama and a farmer by occupation. He was promoted to Sergeant January 1, 1864, by Colonel Spencer. On November 10, 1864, he was sick and sent to the hospital in Nashville, Tennessee. From November 10, 1864, to April 1865, Jasper was sick in the hospital in Chattanooga, Tennessee. He was mustered out July 19, 1865, in Nashville, Davidson County, Tennessee, being owed a Clothing Allowance of $17.96 and $300 for Bounty. He died February 18, 1905, in Marion County, Alabama at age 73 years, 2 months and 10 days, according to his tombstone. He was buried in the Old Green Cemetery near Brilliant in Marion County, Alabama. His wife, Martha, had died two years before on September 25, 1903, in Brilliant, Alabama.

Jasper Green was well liked by all of his Unionists neighbors. There were several children named after him by other Unionists.

Jasper's father-in-law, Lemuel Burnett, was knowingly a staunch Unionist, helping any other Unionist who needed help. However, he was captured by John Stout's "bandito association", but later released.

Green, John B. - John B. Green enlisted in Company H of the 1st Alabama Cavalry, USV on September 14, 1863, for a period of 1 year. The September and October 1863 Muster Roll recorded him as absent, supposed prisoner in the hands of the enemy. The November 1863 through October 1864 Muster Rolls recorded him as absent, prisoner of war since October 26, 1863, which would have been during the Battle of Vincent's Crossroads near Bay Springs, Mississippi. A Notation in his file from the Adjutant General's Office of the War Department dated December 22, 1773, stated he was discharged to date September 29, 1864, due to expiration of term of service. Another Notation in his file from the Adjutant General's Office of the War Department dated October 12, 1877, stated John B. Green was captured October 26, 1863, and held as prisoner of war until sometime after expiration of term of service. He is entitled to Commutation of rations from October 26, 1863, to September 29, 1864.

Green, John J. - John J. Green enlisted in Company D of the 1st Alabama Cavalry, USV as a private on February 15, 1863, in Glendale, Mississippi for a period of 1 year. He was enrolled by W.

Williams and was mustered in March 20, 1863, in Corinth, Mississippi. The Regimental Descriptive Book recorded him as 20 years of age, 5'-8" tall, having a light complexion, blue eyes, light hair, born in Franklin County, Alabama, and a farmer by occupation. The July and August 1863 Muster Roll recorded him as having died of disease July 25, 1863, in the Post Hospital in Glendale, Mississippi. John J. Green was buried in Grave A-2067 in the Corinth National Cemetery in Corinth, Alcorn County, Mississippi.

Green, Joseph Riley - Joseph Riley Green enlisted in Company K of the 1st Alabama Cavalry, USV as a private on November 14, 1862, in Corinth, Mississippi, and was mustered in December 30, 1862, in Corinth. He was later reassigned to Company A. Joseph was recorded as 50 years of age, 6'-1" tall, having a light complexion, gray eyes, dark hair, born in Montgomery County, North Carolina, and a farmer by occupation. The January and February 1863 Muster Roll recorded him as absent, sick in the hospital in Corinth, Mississippi. Joseph Green died of disease March 2, 1863, in Corinth, Mississippi. Captain Frank C. Burdick signed his Certificate of Death. The Record of Effects stated he did not have any effects. Joseph Riley Green was buried in Grave #A-100 in the Corinth National Cemetery, in Corinth, Alcorn County, Mississippi.

Joseph Riley Green was born February 1814 in Montgomery County, North Carolina to Gideon Green and Frances Brown. Joseph married Martha Frederick about 1834 in Marion County, Alabama. Martha was born April 22, 1816, in Rutherford County, Tennessee to Hezekiah Frederick and his wife, Ezilla Hobson, and died in June 1863 in Marion County, Alabama. Children of Joseph and Martha Frederick Green were: Margaret M.; Elletion Jasper; Joseph Newton; Martha; Absalom; James S.; John Frederick; Susan M.; Zilley A.; and "Babe" Green. One descendant stated Martha Frederick died November 26, 1862, while another descendant stated she died June 1, 1863.

Records for Joseph Riley Green contain guardianship papers for Susan M., and Joseph N. for father's pension, stating that widow, Martha died in June 1863. Original Pension of Minor Children", Susan M. Green, Richard W. Sessions, guardian, Jonesboro, Union, Illinois, Attorney James C. Smith, Joseph Green, Private County A., 1st Alabama Cavalry, November 14, 1862, death March 2, 1863, No widow's pension, Minor's Application filed June 2, 1864, Guardian Application March 25, 1864, death of widow, Martha Green is June 1863. A letter from Richard W. Sessions, June 18, 1870, states the minor heirs of Joseph Green, "they left here in 1867 and said they were going to Texas and that they would write but I have never heard from them since." Susan was the only child under age 16 on June 2, 1864. Union County, Illinois. In county court March term, 1864, Richard W. Sessions appointed guardian for Joseph N. Green, aged 20 years on the February 1, 1864, and Susan M. Green, aged 12 years on May 6, 1863.

Green, Robert - Robert Green enlisted in Company B of the 1st Alabama Cavalry, USV as a private on April 4, 1864, in Decatur, Alabama for a period of 3 years. He was enrolled by Lieutenant Judy, and was mustered in April 13, 1864, in Decatur. The Muster and Descriptive Roll recorded him as 20 years of age, 5'-8" tall, having a fair complexion, blue eyes, dark hair, born in Walker County, Alabama, and a farmer by occupation. Robert Green was reported to have deserted May 11, 1864, from near Chattanooga, Tennessee with horse and equipment, Smith Carbine, sling and swivel, cartridge box, cap pouch and pick, and waist belt and plate.

Green Samuel - Samuel Green enlisted and mustered into Company K of the 1st Alabama Cavalry, USV as a private on December 1, 1863, in Camp Davies, Mississippi for a period of 3 years. He was enrolled by Lieutenant Hornback. He traveled 90 miles from his home in Marion County, Alabama to Camp Davies, Mississippi to enlist in the Union Army. The Company Descriptive Book recorded him as 24 years of age, 5'-6" tall, having a dark complexion, blue eyes, brown hair, born in Marion County, Alabama, and a farmer by occupation. The March and April 1864 Muster Roll recorded him as absent, sick, sent to U.S.A. General Hospital in Nashville, Tennessee April 3, 1864. The May and June 1864 Muster Roll recorded him as absent, sick in the hospital in Decatur, Alabama. The July and August 1864 Muster Roll stated Samuel Green died July 7, 1864, in Decatur, Alabama of chronic diarrhea. His brother, Sergeant Green, also served in the 1st Alabama Cavalry, USV. Samuel Green was buried in Grave #3241, in the Corinth National Cemetery, in Corinth, Mississippi.

Green, Samuel - Samuel Green enlisted in Company M of the 1st Alabama Cavalry, USV on December 16, 1863, in Camp Davies, Mississippi for a period of 3 years. He was enrolled by Captain John Lomax, and was mustered in on December 29, 1863, in Corinth, Mississippi. The Company Descriptive Book recorded Samuel as 43 years of age, 6'-1" tall, having a dark complexion, hazel eyes, dark hair, born in Madison County, Alabama, and a farmer by occupation. The January and February Roll of this company recorded Samuel as having died in the Regimental Hospital in Memphis, Tennessee on February 29, 1864. Inventory of Effects by company commander reports that a Samuel Green of Company M, 1st Alabama Cavalry, US died in Regimental Hospital at Memphis, Tennessee February 29, 1864, of erysipelas, also known as "St. Anthony's Fire". The Inventory of Effects recorded Samuel as having 1 hat, 1 great coat, 1 uniform jacket, 2 pairs of cotton drawers, 2 flannel shirts, 1 pair of boots, 2 blankets and 1 rubber blanket.

Green, William - William Green enlisted in Company H of the 1st Alabama Cavalry, USV as a private on September 14, 1863, in Glendale, Mississippi, for a period of 1 year. He was recorded as a Saddler and 40 years of age. Another muster roll recorded his age as 46. He was mustered out September 29, 1864, at Rome, Georgia due to expiration of term of service. When he mustered out, he owed the U.S. Government $1.27 for losing one painted blanket. A record in his file stated he died February 25, 1864, in the Washington U.S.A. General Hospital in Memphis, Shelby County, Tennessee and was buried in Grave 1335 in the Memphis National Cemetery in Memphis, Tennessee. There was not a date listed on the Casualty Sheet for this soldier.

Green, William G.B. - William G.B. Green's name was listed at the end of the muster rolls of soldiers in the 1st Alabama Cavalry, USV. It stated he enlisted in Company M of the 1st Alabama Cavalry, USV on December 16, 1863 at Camp Davies, Mississippi for a period of 3 years, enrolled by Captain Lomax, but was rejected. The Company Descriptive Book recorded him as 20 years of age, 5'-10" tall, having a fair complexion, blue eyes, red hair, born in Marion County, Alabama, and a farmer by occupation. No further information relative to this soldier was found.*

Green, William R. - William R. Green enlisted in Company M of the 1st Alabama Cavalry, USV on September 9, 1863, at Chewalla, Tennessee for a period of 3 years. He was enrolled by Captain Lomax, and was mustered in December 29, 1863, in Corinth, Mississippi. The Company Descriptive Book recorded him as 38 years of age, 6'-2" tall, having a fair complexion, blue eyes, dark hair, born in Warren County, Tennessee, and a farmer by occupation. The January and February 1864 Muster Roll reported him to have deserted January 28, 1864, at LaGrange, Tennessee. Another muster roll stated he deserted from Camp Davies, Mississippi. The Descriptive List of Deserters stated he deserted perhaps to McNairy or Hardeman County in Tennessee. William R. Green deserted with Smith Carbine and Remington Revolver. A Notation in his records from the Record and Pension Office of the War Department dated August 3, 1893, stated the following: Application for the removal of the charge of desertion and for an honorable discharge has been denied.

Greenhaw, John - John Greenhaw enlisted in Company G of the 1st Alabama Cavalry, USV, and was temporarily attached from the 11th Illinois Cavalry to which organization he belonged.

Grey, Willis - A form at the end of the last roll of microfilm listing records of 1st Alabama Cavalry, USV soldiers stated Willis Gray served in E.

Griffin, Franklin - Franklin Griffin enlisted in Company H of the 1st Alabama Cavalry, USV as a private on October 29, 1864, in Rome, Georgia for a period of 3 years. He was enrolled by Captain James W. DeVaney. Franklin Griffin died of variola, also called smallpox, on February 10, 1865, in the Post Hospital in Huntsville, Alabama. He had not been mustered in. The Company Descriptive Book recorded him as 19 years of age, 5'-7½" tall, having a light complexion, blue eyes, dark hair, born in Spartanburg County, South Carolina, and a farmer by occupation.

Griffin, John - John Griffin enlisted and mustered into Company A of the 1st Alabama Cavalry, USV as a private on September 30, 1864, in Rome, Georgia for a period of 3 years. The Muster and Descriptive Roll recorded him as 18 years of age, 5'-10" tall, having a dark complexion, dark eyes, dark hair, born in Cherokee County, Alabama, and a farmer by occupation. He was shown as being due a bounty of $300. The May and June 1865 Muster Roll recorded him as having deserted April 15, 1865, from Lincolnton, North Carolina with complete equipment. A Notation in his records from the Record and Pension Division of the War Department dated July 27, 1889, stated: The charge of desertion of May 15, 1864, and April 25, 1865, are removed for error. The charge of desertion of May 15, 1865, is removed and he is discharged to date May 15, 1865, to complete his military record under the provisions of the Act of Congress approved March 2, 1889. Discharge Certificate furnished August 3, 1889, by the War Department.

Griffin, Rufus Marian - Rufus Marian Griffin enlisted and mustered into Company K of the 1st Alabama Cavalry, USV as a private on December 6, 1863, in Camp Davies, Mississippi for a period of 3 years. He was enrolled by Lieutenant Joseph Hornback. The Company Descriptive Book recorded him as 19 years of age, 6'-½" tall, having a dark complexion, gray eyes, auburn hair, born in Cherokee County, North Carolina, and a farmer by occupation. Rufus traveled 300 miles from his home in Randolph County, Alabama to Camp Davies, Mississippi, dodging the Confederates, to join the Union Army. He joined as a recruit. The November and December 1864 Muster Roll stated he was sent to Nashville sick, on November 10, 1864. The December 31, 1864, through April 30, 1865, Muster Roll stated he was still sick in Nashville, Tennessee. However, his name was recorded on the Returns as having been sick in the hospital in Chattanooga, Tennessee since November 10, 1864. Apparently he was in Nashville rather than Chattanooga. The May and June 1865 Muster Roll recorded him as present. He was mustered out July 19, 1865, in Nashville, Tennessee with a bounty of $300 due him.

Rufus Marian Griffin was born April 15, 1844, in Cherokee County, North Carolina to William and Talitha Wiggins Griffin. He married Maretta Jane Reeves, daughter of Archibald T. and Mary "Polly" Richardson Reeves. Maretta was born December 10, 1849, in Covington, Newton County, Georgia and died January 15, 1935, in National City, San Diego, California. Children of Rufus and Maretta were: Marietta "Mary" E.; William; Archibald "Archie" Joseph, born November 12, 1871, died October 4, 1948; Emma Arminda, born March 21, 1874, died March 11, 1955; Martha Jane, born May 29, 1876, died, July 2, 1955; Rufus Nathan, born April 10, 1878, died July 19, 1951; Oscar Franklin, born September 21, 1881, died September 18, 1939; and Charles Warner Griffin. Rufus Marian Griffin died June 8, 1936 in National City, San Diego County, California and was buried in the Greenwood Memorial Park Cemetery in San Diego, California. Family information submitted by Peggy Brown and John H. Griffin, Ph.D.

Griffin, William - Only one card was found for William Griffin which was filed at the end of the last roll of microfilm of the 1st Alabama Cavalry, USV records. It recorded him as being in Company E, stating he was in the U.S.A. General Hospital in Bridgeport, Alabama from April through June 1864, and was returned to duty June 18, 1864. No further information relative to this soldier was found.* According to the census records, William Griffin was born in North Carolina.

Griffith, Green L. - Only two cards were found for Green L. Griffith which were filed at the end of the last roll of microfilm of the 1st Alabama Cavalry, USV Records. A POW card recorded him as being in Company K stating Prisoner of War Records furnished no information. The other record stated he enlisted in Company L. No further information relative to this soldier was found.*

Grimes, William R. - William R. Grimes enlisted in Company K of the 1st Alabama Cavalry, USV as a private on February 23, 1864, in Memphis, Tennessee for a period of 3 years. He was enrolled by Lieutenant Files and was mustered in February 26, 1864, in Memphis. The Muster and Descriptive Roll recorded him as 18 years of age, 5'-8" tall, having a dark complexion, dark eyes, dark hair, born in Franklin County, Alabama, and a farmer by occupation. The March and April 1864 Muster Roll recorded him as absent, sick in the Hospital in Nashville, Tennessee since April 5, 1864. The July and August 1864 Muster Roll stated he was absent, sick in the U.S.A. General Hospital in Nashville,

Tennessee. The November and December 1864 Muster Roll recorded him as absent, sick in hospital in Louisville, Kentucky April 5, 1864. The January and February 1865 Muster Roll recorded him as sick in the hospital in Nashville, Tennessee. The March and April 1865 Muster Roll recorded him as present. William R. Grimes' name was recorded on the Hospital Muster Roll for the Brown U.S.A. Hospital in Louisville, Kentucky in Ward 10 from May through December 1864, and for the Cumberland U.S.A. General Hospital in Nashville, Tennessee for March and April 1865. His name appears on the Returns as follows: April 1864, absent, sick in general hospital in Memphis, Tennessee; September 1864, absent, sick in the hospital in Nashville, Tennessee; November and December 1864, absent, sick in the general hospital. William R. Grimes was mustered out October 20, 1865, in Huntsville, Alabama owing the U.S. Government $2.02 for losing 1 carbine sling and swivel. He was due a bounty of $300 and was paid $180 and shown as being due $120 for the bounty.

Grimmest, Francis C. - Francis C. Grimmest, also recorded as Grimm it, enlisted in Company I on July 21, 1862, in Huntsville, Alabama for a period of 3 years. He was enrolled by Captain Bankhead, and mustered into Captain Jones' Company in the 1st Alabama Cavalry, USV as a private on August 18, 1862, in Huntsville. The Company Descriptive Book recorded him as 25 years of age, 5'-9¾" tall, having a dark complexion, blue eyes, light hair, born in Walker County, Alabama, and a farmer by occupation. The November and December 1862 Muster Roll recorded him as absent with leave with wagon train in Nashville, Tennessee since December 27, 1862. In January 1863, he was absent, on courier post January 27, 1863, at Readyville, Tennessee. Grimmest was with the group of early enlistees immediately shipped to Nashville, Tennessee and merged with the 1st Middle Tennessee Cavalry, which later became the 5th Tennessee Cavalry, Francis C. Grimmest was merged with Company D of the 1st Middle Tennessee Cavalry. In July and August 1863, he was recorded as being back with the 1st Alabama Cavalry. The Company Muster Roll for June 30 through October 31, 1863, recorded him as missing in action October 26, 1863, from the Battle of Vincent's Crossroads near Bay Springs, Mississippi. He rejoined the company November 21, 1863. The September through December 1864 Muster Roll recorded him as absent without leave since September 4, 1864. A Prisoner of War Record stated Francis C. Grimmest was captured May 3, 1863, in Rome, Georgia, confined at Richmond, Virginia May 18, 1863, paroled at City Point, Virginia May 15, 1863, reported at Camp Parole, Maryland May 18, 1863, sent to Camp Chase, Ohio May 19, 1863. Grimmest was mustered out July 19, 1865, in Nashville, Tennessee.

Grinnell, James - Only one card was found for James Grinnell which was filed at the end of the last roll of microfilm of the 1st Alabama Cavalry, USV records. His name was listed on the Returns which recorded him in Company D of the 1st Middle Tennessee Cavalry, US. The first enlistees into the 1st Alabama Cavalry were immediately shipped to Nashville, Tennessee where they were merged with the 1st Middle Tennessee Cavalry, which later became the 5th Tennessee Cavalry. When they left Nashville, they were recorded as being back with the 1st Alabama Cavalry, USV. Apparently his records for the 1st Alabama Cavalry have been lost or misplaced. No further information relative to this soldier was found.*

Grines, William R. - Cards filed under William R. Grimes.

Grisham, Green Washington - Green Washington Grisham enlisted and mustered into Company K of the 1st Alabama Cavalry, USV as a private on August 22, 1862, in Huntsville, Alabama for a period of 3 years. He was enrolled by Lieutenant Millard. The Muster and Descriptive Roll recorded him as 18 years of age, 5'-9¼" tall, having a light complexion, blue eyes, brown hair, born in Limestone County, Alabama, and a farmer by occupation. Grisham was in the group of early enlistees immediately shipped to Nashville, Tennessee, and merged with the 1st Middle Tennessee Cavalry, which later became the 5th Tennessee Cavalry. He was merged with Company E of the 1st Middle Tennessee Cavalry. His name was recorded on the Returns for the 1st Middle Tennessee and stated: January 1863, absent, on courier post, probably in Readyville, Tennessee; February 1863, absent, on courier post; March 1864, absent, taken prisoner of war by the enemy in Arkansas, near Memphis, Tennessee on March 21, 1864; April 1864, absent, prisoner of war since March 21, 1864. He was appointed Corporal

January 1, 1864. The March and April 1864 Muster Roll recorded him as absent, prisoner of war since March 21, 1864. However, he was recorded as present on the May and June 1864 Muster Roll. He was mustered out July 19, 1865, in Nashville, Tennessee. His Muster-Out Roll recorded him as having a dislocated left elbow due to a fall from a horse when on the march in Georgia November 28, 1864. He was a private until January 1, 1864, when appointed Corporal by Colonel Spencer. A Prisoner of War Record stated Grisham was captured May 1, 1863, from Day's Gap, Alabama, sent from Nashville, Tennessee to Richmond, Virginia May 8, 1863, confined at Richmond, Virginia May 9, 1863, paroled at City Point, Virginia, reported at Camp Parole, Maryland May 16, 1863, sent to camp chase, Ohio May 19, 1863, reported there May 22, 1863, and sent to regiment June 9, 1863.

Green Washington Grisham was the son of Louis Cullen Grisham, born 1820, died 1853 and his wife Eliza Suzannah Speegle, born January 29, 1825, and died January 7, 1875. He was the grandson of Thomas Grisham of Duplin County, North Carolina who moved to Limestone County, Alabama in 1801. He was born December 9, 1843, in Athens, Alabama and died October 18, 1914, in Holland, Faulkner County, Arkansas. He was married January 29, 1868, to Georgia Ann Potete/Poteet, who was born September 6, 1852, and died September 5, 1924, and they had 12 children: Fressie, Arthur, Luther, Virgil, Simeon, Rosetta, Lewis Peale, Noble Ernest, Flora, Eva Pearl, Sarah, & Rualla. There is a Grisham/Gresham family reunion in Athens, Alabama on Memorial Day Week-end for the descendants of this Thomas Grisham. Family information submitted by Michael J. Woodruff.

Groves, Patterson - Patterson Groves enlisted in Company M of the 1st Alabama Cavalry, USV as a private on August 2, 1863, in Chewalla, Tennessee for a period of 3 years. He was enrolled by Captain Lomax and was mustered in December 29, 1863, in Corinth, Mississippi. The Company Descriptive Book recorded him as 27 years of age, 6' tall, having a dark complexion, blue eyes, brown hair, born in Madison County, Tennessee, and a farmer by occupation. The January and February 1864 Muster Roll stated he was due a bounty of $300. The March and April 1865 Muster Roll recorded him as absent, prisoner of war since March 10, 1865, which was when the Battle of Monroe's Crossroads was fought. He was mustered out as a Sergeant on June 12, 1865, in Camp Chase, Ohio by reason of General Order 77 of the War Department. The Muster-Out Roll stated he owed the U.S. Government $2.46 for transportation. It also stated the following: Received notice of discharge at Camp Chase, Ohio June 13, 1865, by General Order Number 77 of the War Department but the clothing account and the amount of payment not_____. Patterson Groves' name appeared on the Muster Roll of Paroled Prisoners at Camp Chase, Ohio dated January and February 1865, stating he was captured March 10, 1865, from Solomon Grove, North Carolina. A Prisoner of War Record in his file stated he was captured at Bentonville, North Carolina March 10, 1865, brought from Raleigh North Carolina March 28, 1865, paroled at Boulware and Cox's Wharf, Virginia, March 30, 1865, returned (to regiment) April 9, 1865.

Guess, William C. "Mack" - William C. "Mack" Guess enlisted in Company B of the 1st Alabama Cavalry, USV as a private on March 29, 1864, in Decatur, Alabama for a period of 3 years. He was enrolled by Lieutenant Judy and was mustered in April 13, 1864. The Muster and Descriptive Roll recorded him as 18 years of age, 5'-11" tall, having a fair complexion, dark eyes, dark hair, born in Marion County, Alabama, and a farmer by occupation. Another Descriptive Roll recorded him as 16 years of age and born in Limestone County, Alabama. He was actually born August 24, 1846, in Fayette County, Alabama. He was mustered out October 20, 1865, in Huntsville, Alabama. His Muster-Out Roll recorded his age as 48, which was inaccurate since he was only 18 when he enlisted. His name appeared on a Hospital Muster Roll for 2nd Division U.S.A. Field Hospital in Rome, Georgia, stating he was attached to the hospital August 15, 1864.

William C. "Mack" Guess was born October 24, 1846, in Glen Allen, Fayette County, Alabama and was the son of Elijah Martin Guess and Talitha Whitehead. He married Laura Jane Biggers November 5, 1869, in Fayette County, Alabama. Laura was born in January 1851, and died December 8, 1920, in Ridgely, Lake County, Tennessee. She was the daughter of J.A. Biggers. Children of William and Laura were: Joseph Lute, born July 1872, died 1947; William Shirley, born May 1876 Daniel Mack, born November 18, 1877, A. Delmer, born February 20 1880, died December 1966; James Arthur, born May 7, 1882; and Andrew Frank Guess, born November 1886. After the war,

William moved to Hardin County, Tennessee and later Ridgely in Lake County, Tennessee where he died April 29, 1922. Laura died December 8, 1920. She and William are buried in Madie Cemetery near Ridgely, Tennessee.

Guice, Enoch M. - See Enoch M. Guyse.

Guice, James P. - James P. Guice enrolled in Company G of the 1st Alabama Cavalry, USV as a private on March 2, 1864, in Decatur, Alabama for a period of 3 years. He was enrolled by Lieutenant Pease and was mustered in April 13, 1864, in Decatur. The Muster and Descriptive Roll recorded him as 30 years of age, 5'-7" tall, having fair complexion, blue eyes, dark hair, born in Franklin County, Alabama, and a farmer by occupation. He was appointed Corporal July 1, 1865, by Special Order 31, Regimental Headquarters. He was mustered out October 20, 1865, in Huntsville, Alabama owing the U.S. Government $30 for losing 1 Smith Carbine. He also lost 1 surcingle.

Guins in the Civil War

Asa, Jason, Levi and Rasey Guin were brothers and children of Levi and Nancy Guin. Levi also had sons who served in the Confederacy. Michael Guin was the son of Levi's brother, Asa Guin, and cousins of Asa, Jason, Levi and Rasey. Asa Guin, Sr. also had sons who served in the Confederacy, so one can imagine the hostilities in these Guin families.

Guin, Asa - Asa Guin enrolled in Company A of the 1st Alabama Cavalry, USV as a private on January 23, 1864, in Camp Davies, Mississippi for a period of 3 years. He was enrolled by Lieutenant Hinds and was mustered in February 5, 1864, in Memphis, Tennessee. The Company Muster and Descriptive Roll recorded him as 28 years of age, 5'-11" tall, having a dark complexion, gray eyes, black hair, born in Anson County, North Carolina, and a farmer by occupation. Another Descriptive Roll stated he was born in Fayette County, Alabama. A Company Muster Roll dated February 29, 1864, recorded Asa as absent, sick in General Hospital in Memphis, Tennessee. The May and June 1864 Muster Roll recorded him as having deserted May 15, 1864, from Snake Creek Gap, Georgia with Carbine and accoutrements complete. He was recorded as having owed the U.S. Government $27.18 for taking the Smith Carbine and accoutrements. His name appeared on a Hospital Muster Roll for Overton U.S.A. General Hospital in Memphis, Tennessee dated January and February 1864 but did not give the day he was admitted.

Levi and Nancy Guin had four sons who enlisted in the 1st Alabama Cavalry, USV: Asa, Jason, Levi, and Rasey "Ras" Guin. Their daughter, Margaret "Peggy" Guin married Jeremiah F. Shaw, Sr., who served in Company A of the 43rd Alabama Infantry Volunteers, CSA. He also served in Company J. and was a Private. He filed for a pension because of kidney problems, stating he owned "one little house and lot of about 1/4 of an acre, a gun valued at $10.00, and household & kitchen furniture valued at $25.00. It was signed by John A. Shaw, Jeremiah's son. It also stated he served in Company H of the 10th Alabama Regiment, enlisting July 1, 1862, in Tuscumbia, Alabama. Margaret "Peggy" Guin and Jeremiah F. Shaw were married throughout the Civil War and one can imagine the tension between the families who had such different views. (Jeremiah F. Shaw and Margaret "Peggy" Guin Shaw were the great-great grandparents of the author.)

Guin, Jason - Jason Guin enlisted in Company A of the 1st Alabama Cavalry, USV as a private on January 23, 1864, in Camp Davies, Mississippi for a period of 3 years. He was enrolled by Lieutenant Hinds and mustered in February 5, 1864, in Memphis, Tennessee. The Company Descriptive Book recorded him as 32 years of age, 6' tall, having a dark complexion, black eyes, black hair, born in Anson County, North Carolina, and a farmer by occupation. He was promoted from private to sergeant on February 5, 1864; however, he was reduced to ranks December 30, 1864. The March 1864 through April 1865 Muster Rolls recorded him as absent, on recruiting service in Decatur, Alabama with Major Shurtliff since April 17, 1864. The May and June 1865 Muster Roll recorded him as absent, missing in action, however, he was present in July and August 1865. His name appeared on the Returns for June 1865 stating he was missing in action since March 10, 1865, which was the date of the Battle of Monroe's Crossroads. Jason Guin was mustered out October 20, 1865, owing the U.S. Government $10.15 for losing one pistol and one saber belt complete. He was sergeant from January 23, 1864, to when reduced to ranks by order of Colonel Spencer in Savannah, Georgia, retained one pistol, stoppages for one saber belt complete. Jason Guin was able to sign his Enlistment Forms.

Jason Guin was born April 14, 1821, in Anson County, North Carolina but stated he was only 32 when he enlisted in the Union army. He was conscripted into the Confederate army. He escaped to Union lines on the underground slave railway, which he had helped set up. He was first a civilian scout, carrying messages between various Union generals and E. Woolsey Peck of Tuscaloosa, Alabama, leader of the Unionist Cabal. While on a scouting mission he was cornered at E. Woolsey Peck's home but escaped, swimming the Warrior River on his horse, while bullets were flying about him. After the war, Jason was shot twice from ambush, attacked by overwhelming numbers and left for dead. He would have died but for the loyalty of a Negro who lived on his farm. Jason served several terms as sheriff in Sanford/Lamar County, Alabama.

Another similar story written by J. Foy Guin on October 3, 1962, to Mrs. Callahan, contained additional information about Jason's escape from Peck's home in Tuscaloosa, "He is said to have spent that night with his uncle in the Samantha area, knowing full well that since his uncle was a slave holder and a secessionist, the Confederates would not search for him there. As the story further goes, my grandfather Jason spent two additional nights in Tuscaloosa County, moving slowly to the north, before he got out of the county and went back to the Union Army over the underground slave route." (Callahan, Vol. II, p. 29)

It is very difficult to try to comprehend the impact of the Civil War on this family and how they dealt with their "friends" and "neighbors" after such an attack. We know very little about what the wives and children of Jason and his brothers Asa, Rasey and Levi were experiencing during the war when they were living in communities where they were considered traitors and spies. One can only imagine the level of fear they must have experienced on a daily basis just wondering when the stress of the war might become an impetus for their neighbors to become violent toward them.

To further compound the problem for Jason and Sarah, her father was a Captain in the CSA Home Guard and her brothers were soldiers in the CSA. Also, Jason's son, William Luke, was a CSA soldier. (Smith, p. 69) Jason went into battle knowing full well that he could have killed or been killed by his own son, three of his brothers (Bartley, Michael or James), or his in-laws. How would these family members ever be able to put this extreme situation behind them?

Jason Guin came to northwest Alabama in the period of 1831-32 as a boy, the third child of Levi and Nancy Guin of Anson County, North Carolina. The Guins, drawn by land and opportunity, caravanned their possessions and seven children westward to the recent settlements of Levi's brothers (Asa and Jeremiah) in Tuscaloosa County near the Sipsey River. Gilbert and Bartley were in their teens. Jason was ten or eleven; and Calvin, Mary, Margaret "Peggy" and Abigail were younger still.

The family quest was soon fruitful. On December 3, 1832, Levi made his first public land purchase in Alabama, a forty-acre tract just north of Newtonville in Fayette County. By mid-1835, he had increased the holding threefold with adjoining land. And some six months later, Jason (not yet fifteen) squared the family's quarter section with his own first land purchase.

From this start, the Levi Guin family continued to expand in number and acquire more land nearby and from the remote wilderness area that is now Lamar County. By the mid-1840s, five more sons and three daughters-in-law had been added to the family. In 1833, Jeremiah became the first family member born in Alabama, and James became the youngest a decade later. In between, Asa, Levi (young Levi) and Razy arrived in alphabetical order.

According to family lore, Jason was a shoemaker and leather worker for much of his early life, selling and bartering his wares for goods and farm labor within the communities where he lived and purchased land – later, passing down the craft to his first-born daughter and son.

Jason began his own family about 1845, marrying Frances of the Howell Gilliam family on a nearby farm - people that had also moved west from Anson County, North Carolina. By the 1850 Census, Jason and Frances had three children: Nancy Rachel, William Luke and Mary Jane. Following Mary Jane's birth, Frances may have soon taken ill for she and Jason had no more children before her premature death June 10, 1857.

Somehow, Jason's stoic plight with three small children attracted the attention, and eventually the affections of Sarah Ann Kirkland, eldest offspring of Jehu Chaney Kirkland and Permelia Chappell. The Kirklands were active in the affairs of the Newtonville community; and from 1855-57, Sarah's father (a lawyer and Democrat) represented Fayette County in the Alabama legislature. On Jason's birthday the following Spring, April 14, 1858, he and Sarah (born September 7, 1834) were married in her father's home near Newtonville, family attending. Justice of the Peace, Jeptha Branyon, officiated the simple, mid-week service. The secession – anti-secession acrimony that eventually enveloped the Guins, the Kirklands and other Fayette families, was not yet a dominant theme in their community. Family ties and reason still prevailed, but not for very long.

At the outset of the Civil War, Jason was forty years old - expected, but not required to serve. Yet by War's end, both his and Sarah's families were decimated by it. Sarah's father and younger brothers (James, Anderson and William) all joined the Confederate cause. James and Anderson both died due to battle action. William Luke, Jason's own teenage son, also risked his life for the Confederacy. Several Guin cousins and their sons served in CSA units from Tuscaloosa County: Asa died of fever; his eldest son, Azariah, was permanently crippled; and another son, Isaiah, died at seventeen. Most of the Guins in Fayette and Marion Counties opposed secession and tried to remain apart from it, but to no avail. Under persistent harassment from ardent secessionists, Jason moved his family northwest of the Luxapallila, nearer other kin. Then in late January 1864, he, his cousin Michael and younger bothers: Asa, Levi, and Razy made their way to Ft. Davis (Camp Davies, Mississippi) in northeast Mississippi to join the Union Army. All five were officially "mustered in" at Memphis on February 5, 1864.

Within a month, Michael died of smallpox; and soon thereafter, Levi perished of pneumonia. Jason might have suffered a similar fate, but was promptly detached, as Sergeant, "to recruiting duty in Alabama" – most likely a euphemism for scouting and courier duties. Asa and Razy soon fled Memphis and the 1st Alabama Cavalry for healthier precincts. By the end of 1864, Jason was assigned to a regular combat unit and ordered "reduced to ranks" - the 1st Alabama was being redeployed eastward to help escort and cover General Sherman's left flank on his final push from Atlanta to the sea. Jason was held prisoner for a period of time following his regiment's fierce engagement with CSA forces at Monroe's Crossroads, North Carolina on March 10, 1865. But when eventually released, he rejoined the remnants of his unit and remained on active duty until finally "mustered out" at Huntsville, Alabama on October 20, 1865.

On the Fayette home front, acts of terror by extremists mounted. In separate 1864 incidents, Jason's father and eldest brother, Gilbert, were barbarically slaughtered by renegade elements of the "home guard" - reprisal for their un-quailing opposition to secession and the War. The State authorized several measures in an effort to protect the citizenry, but only War's end and men returning to work and families prompted the gradual restoration of order.

Following the War, Jason returned home to begin rebuilding the life of his family and community in western Fayette County; and there was much to be done. Within months, he was appointed and began serving as Trustee of the Bethabra School along with neighbors: G. W. Allen and William W. Waldrop, to provide education in Township 16, Range 14 to students over six and under 21 years of age. In December 1866, the teacher Mr. Charles Graham reported to them that there were 39 students attending – including five from Township 16, Range 13.

Somewhat later when the Reconstruction Legislature approved the creation of what is now Lamar County, then Jones County; Jason played an important role in its formation and the ultimate restoration of local civil government. A Unionist and Republican, he was initially appointed as a County Commissioner and later served as the first elected Sheriff. In other positions of public trust, he served on Road Review Committees, the Board of the Vernon Institute, as Tax-book Examiner and Special Deputy U.S. Marshal.

In 1869, Jason purchased a 240-acre farm one mile south of the County Seat from Abner Pennington, fellow-veteran of the 1st Alabama Cavalry, US Volunteers. It included a house and quarter section from an 1825 U.S. land patent to Wiley Duke, probably the same one who married Eleanor, daughter of Col. William Metcalfe, in the mid-1820s and later moved to Yalobusha County, Mississippi. Constructed of hand-hewn timbers, the substantial house was most likely constructed by Duke in the 1825-32 timeframe. Enlarged and preserved, it became the Guin family's home-place. All of Jason's children lived there, and a number were born there. It was a refuge for both Jason and Sarah in their remaining days. Still owned and occupied by descendants in 2003, the "Guin Place" is a County landmark and rich source of early-day legends.

Jason Guin died suddenly on December 18, 1878, near Caledonia, Mississippi. Taking crops to market, he was walking after his teams and simply fell lifeless to the road.

Dr. Martin W. Morton, family physician and longtime neighbor, stated that reports of the incident and Jason's general condition indicated apoplexy (stroke). Sarah would live another 25 years until May 4, 1903, farming and rearing children for most of those years. Both she and Jason lie at rest in the old Odd Fellows section of the Vernon Cemetery near their home, their side-by-side graves are marked by monuments: his replacing the broken IOOF original, and hers the original inscribed obelisk. The following brief notes provide information on Jason's children (numbers 1-3, submitted by Frances Gilliam):

1. <u>Nancy Rachel</u> - "Aunt Nan" (1846-1932) learned to make shoes as a child, and later became a dressmaker and mothers' helper. She helped care for generations of family children over some seventy years, but never married. She was buried in the Vernon Cemetery near where she lived for so many years; but by the fall of 1996 her grave was unmarked.

2. <u>William Luke</u> (1848-ca.1892) also learned to make shoes as a child, served in the Confederate Cavalry (26th Alabama) during his teens, and later served as Lamar County Sheriff in early adulthood. Family tradition holds that Luke pursued medical training and may have practiced briefly in Vernon before moving elsewhere in the 1870's for greater professional opportunity. At the time, he was yet unmarried and left no property. He is known to have visited Vernon on at least one subsequent occasion as reported by *The Lamar News* of Thursday, March 31, 1887: "Dr. W.L. Guin of St. Joseph, Missouri, Formerly a citizen and also Sheriff of this County, is visiting relatives and many friends in this place."

3. <u>Mary Jane</u> (1850-after 1930) married James W. H. Redding, a Choctaw County, Mississippi farmer and widower with children, March 29, 1883. Later, they had three daughters of their own: Hattie (or Hallie) M.; Ella L.; and Eula R. Redding. Eula married Archie L. Manning, a blacksmith, of Drew, Sunflower County, Mississippi, April 9, 1911. Eula and Archie had two daughters: Mary Anna and Ruth E. Redding.

4. <u>Alonzo L.</u> (1859-1896) was a teacher, Sulligent Postmaster and merchant (Guin/Smith General Store). In 1880, he married Dorothy Chambliss, and they had five children surviving to adulthood: Howard Kirkland; Birdie (Hill); Carl; Walter; and Gertrude (Hill)- all orphaned to Guin kin when Alonzo was shot and killed in 1896 by his business partner, and Dorothy died some 18 months later. The three boys soon went to Texas to join their uncles Emmett and Lucious. The two girls remained in Sulligent with their aunt Jala, each to later marry brothers of the Hill family there. Alonzo and Dorothy are buried in the Sulligent Cemetery with an infant son interred earlier in 1891 – she absent a headstone.

5. <u>William R.</u> (1860-1904) married Fannie Townley of Townley, Walker County, Alabama in 1893. They initially made their home in Vernon, but later immigrated to Texas where he was appointed and served as Postmaster in Bosque County. There is no record of children.

6. <u>John Robert</u> (1862-1933) was a teacher in Vernon, Guin and Belgreen, Alabama; and served many years as Franklin County's Superintendent of Education. For a period, he also held a judicial appointment there as U. S. Commissioner. In 1889, John married Ida Guyton of Vernon, and they had three children surviving to adulthood: J. (Junius) Foy; Edna Lucille (Thompson); and Rena Marie (Ezzell). John and Ida are buried in the Old Belgreen Cemetery with other family members.

7. <u>Jason Levi</u> (1864-1925) immigrated to Arkansas, returning a widower in late 1890's to farm the Guin home-place. Married Louella Johnson in 1891 and reared: John Berton; Emmett L; and Mattie Lou (Lefstead). Later, he married Mrs. Molly (Andrews) Honnoll to father Ruby (McManus) and Rama (Card). Jason Levi was buried in the Vernon Cemetery; but by the fall of 1996, his grave was unmarked.

8. <u>Lucious Colfax</u> - "Bud" (1867-1936) was the twin of Lura and never married. He worked on farms/ranches in Texas and Arizona.

9. <u>Lura</u> (1867-1869), twin of Lucious, died very young.

10. <u>Jala</u> (1869-1931) was a teacher and in 1889 married Lee S. Metcalfe, a Lamar County farmer, Sheriff and Tax Assessor. They first lived in Vernon several years, later settling in Sulligent nearer their farm at Pharos. In 1911, following the earlier path of her Guin/Kirkland kinsmen, Jala and Lee immigrated to Wingate, Runnels County, Texas to farm with their surviving sons: Wiley L.; Jason S.; and Rayburn A. At the Onset of WWI when their sons began reporting to military service, Jala and Lee decided to resettle farther west up on the plains – selecting the Wilson community of Lynn County Lee continued farming for a time despite drought and labor shortages, but soon gave it up to open a grocery store at nearby Southland, Garza County. Jala and Lee are buried in the City of Lubbock Cemetery.

11. <u>Emmett Jehu</u> (1871-1947) immigrated to Texas and in 1893 married Lelia L. Gayle. They had three surviving children: Rama, Ava and Isaac Fay ("Rube"). As a widower, he married Lula Belle Mitchell in 1912. They had seven children: Lucille Allene, Edra Emmett, Frances Belle, Nan Marie, Mary Louise, John Preston and Terril Dale. Emmett owned/operated a general store in Wingate, Texas until 1922, and later worked as a cotton buyer and mill manager in the lower Rio Grande Valley at San Juan. He is buried in the Donna Cemetery, Hidalgo County, Texas.

12. <u>Hattie</u> (1873-1885) died at age 12.

13. <u>Emma</u> (1875-1903) was a teacher and married Emmett Champion on December 18, 1901. She died prematurely, only 54 weeks later - in January 1903, the same year her mother and grandmother Kirkland expired. Emma was buried in the Vernon Cemetery near the home where she was born; but by the fall of 1996, her grave was unmarked. Family information compiled and submitted by Rayburn A. Metcalfe. See sources he used in Bibliography.

<u>Guin, Levi</u> - Levi Guin enlisted in Company A of the 1st Alabama Cavalry, USV as a private on January 23, 1864, in Camp Davies, Mississippi for a period of 3 years. He was enrolled by Lieutenant Hinds and was mustered in February, 1864, in Memphis, Tennessee. The Muster and Descriptive Roll recorded him as 27 years of age, 5'-7" tall, having a dark complexion, gray eyes, black hair, born in Fayette County, Alabama, and a farmer by occupation. The March and April 1864 Muster Roll recorded him as absent, sick in Gayoso U.S.A. General Hospital in Memphis, Tennessee. The Gayoso Hospital Muster Roll for January and February 1864 stated he was returned to duty on February 26, 1864. His name appeared on the Returns stating he died of measles on April 7, 1864. A Notation in his file from the Adjutant General's Office of the War Department dated April 2, 1868, stated he died April 7, 1864, at Gayoso General Hospital in Memphis, Tennessee of pneumonia. Levi was able to sign his name to all of his Enlistment Forms.

Levi was born about 1834 in Fayette County, Alabama to Levi Guin and Nancy Daniels, some say her last name was Poole. He was a brother to Michael and Rasey, below, and Asa and Jason, above. He married Ruby Ann "Beuly" Yarborough about 1857 and had 2 children, Amanda and Lucinda. Levi died April 7, 1864, in Memphis, Shelby County, Tennessee and was buried in Grave B-1362, in the Memphis National Cemetery in Memphis, Tennessee.

<u>Guin, Michael</u> - Michael Guin enlisted in Company M of the 1st Alabama Cavalry, USV as a private on December 16, 1863, in Camp Davies, Mississippi for a period of 3 years. He was enrolled by Captain Lomax and mustered in December 29, 1863, in Corinth, Mississippi. The Company Descriptive book recorded him as 34 years of age, 6'-2" tall, having a fair complexion, blue eyes, dark hair, born in Tuscaloosa County, Alabama, and a farmer by occupation. Michael Guin was born about 1830 in Tuscaloosa County, Alabama to Asa and Mary Guin. Michael married Eliza Sue Howell on December 4, 1853, in Fayette County, Alabama, and they were married by Jack Rushing, Licensed Minister. The document to solemnize the marriage was issued December 1, 1853, by John C. Moore, Judge of Probate. The marriage took place in the home of G. (George) Traweck. The name Eliza was not short for Elizabeth. They had the following children: Rhoda "Babe", born September 2, 1854, died March 14, 1896; Sarah A., born January 3, 1856, died June 19, 1938; Adaline L., born December 21, 1857, died February 12, 1902; Eli B., born April 5, 1859, died November 27, 1910; Zimeriah "Zimri" R., born June 28, 1861, died 1933; and Angeline Guin, born December 2, 1862, died August 22, 1899. Michael Guin died March 22, 1864, of smallpox in Memphis, Shelby County, Tennessee and was buried in Grave B, Plot 1372 in the Memphis National Cemetery. Submitted by Janie Spencer from her book,

Guin, Rasey Poe "Ras" - Rasey Poe "Ras" Guin enlisted in Company A of the 1st Alabama Cavalry, USV as a private on January 23, 1864, in Camp Davies, Mississippi for a period of 3 years. He was enrolled by Lieutenant Hinds, and was mustered in February 5, 1864, in Memphis, Tennessee. The Company Muster and Descriptive Roll recorded him as 24 years of age, 5'-10" tall, having a dark complexion, gray eyes, black hair, born in Fayette County, Alabama, and a farmer by occupation. The February 29, 1864, Muster Roll recorded him as having deserted from Memphis, Tennessee on February 26, 1864. At the time the company mustered out October 20, 1864, he owed the U.S. Government $42.65 for 1 Carbine pistol, 1 saber belt with accoutrements complete.

Rasey Poe "Ras" Guin was born February 6, 1840, and was the 12th child of Levi and Nancy Guin. Rasey married Victoria Yarborough about 1861. Victoria was born in March 1842, and died after 1920. They had the following children: Terrell A., born January 18, 1862; Lively R., born January 1867; Mary Delia, born December 1869; Bedford Colfax, born February 25, 1873, died December 31, 1960; John L., born October 20, 1875, died January 6, 1962; Walter L., born September 1878, and Almus Bascom Guin, born December 1881 and died February 27, 1962. Victoria was born in March 1842, and died February 1, 1912, in Lamar County, Alabama. Rasey Poe Guin died March 11, 1912, in Millport, Lamar County, Alabama.

Guin, Gilbert Deason - Gilbert Deason Guin was born about 1817 in North Carolina and died in July 1864. He had four brothers, Jason, Levi, Asa, and Rasey Guin, as well as one first cousin, Michael Guin, who served in the 1st Alabama Cavalry, USV. He had numerous relatives in the Confederacy including some of his other brothers. While Gilbert was exempt from serving in the Civil War due to him holding the position of Justice of the Peace in Fayette County, Alabama. (By the authority of the Governor of the State of AL, G. D. Guin was classified as having an "exemption from military services" for the time period of 1861-1865 because he was the Justice of the Peace for Fayette Co., AL.)

The story of his horrific death, because of his family's participation in the Union Army, needs to be told. The following story was recalled and written in 1946 by an unidentified person named McDaniel who was the child of Nancy Guin McDaniel and a grandchild of Gilbert Guin. It would seem likely that McDaniel was probably a grandson in that some men will use their surname like a given name.

"Gilbert was murdered by a Confederate Army troop called the Dog Cavalry during the Civil War. This troop was led by an officer known as "Old Dog John Wilson." One story is that Gilbert was plowing in the field of his farm when he was abducted by the Home Guard. Another is that he was on his way to Columbus to take supplies to the soldiers. Gilbert had given "Old Dog" a thrashing just a few days prior to this.

Gilbert was found hanging from the limb of a dogwood tree, about six miles west of his home, near the old McGee graveyard in Lamar County. He was found by his wife who was accompanied by female neighbors, all of whom were on horseback. They had been roaming the woods and swamps for several days looking for Gilbert. He was located, as most dead carcasses were in those days, by the flight of buzzards. He had been dis-emboweled, his throat cut, and an iron wedge was driven down his throat. What was left by the buzzards was buried in old McGee graveyard which was near by.

Gilbert was opposed to Secession and he and his brothers, being Irish frontiersmen, were ready to die fighting against any measure they thought unjust or tyrannical towards themselves and their neighbors.

On the other hand, the Dog Cavalry had orders to bring those mountaineers into the Confederate Army, by the superior officers, at any cost, and to make bad matters worse, they were compelled to forage for their food, horses, and clothing while carrying out these orders. Under the circumstances trouble and bloodshed was inevitable." (Callahan, Volume II, pages 5-6.)

Frances Abigail Stewart Corley, the daughter of Margaret and granddaughter of Gilbert said, "Gilbert Guin was plowing when a man named Wilson (bushwhacker) came and took him with them." (Callahan, Volume II, page 6.) It was told that he was drug into the woods from his field behind Wilson's horse.

J. Foy Guin wrote on page 3 of his September 29, 1961, letter to Marguerite Callahan, "I remember my grandmother's stories about Captain John Wilson. According to other traditions of other families, Wilson operated as far North as Marion County. He had been an officer or a Captain of a Confederate Home Guard company, and he and his command turned guerilla. In all northwesterly Alabama, all the way from Tuscaloosa to the Tennessee River, where the Union Army held a line during most of the Civil War, the habit of Confederate Home Guard companies to turn guerillas and outlaw was not particularly unusual. The inspiration for such an action grew out of the situation itself."

Gilbert's grandchild, McDaniel, said he was buried at the McGee Family Graveyard near the location where he died. Rayburn Metcalfe said in a January 16, 2005 email, "There is some confusion about the burial place for Gilbert D. Guin. When he was slaughtered and hung in July 1864 some six miles west of his home, he was buried in a nearby family burial place called the McGee Cemetery because the land had been donated by a McGee family member. Since then, it has been renamed and possibly expanded as Walnut Grove Cemetery."

Members of the Lamar County Genealogical Society did an inscription of Walnut Grove Cemetery on March 20, 2003. They recorded his tombstone as saying only, "G. D. Guin – Killed 1865". His probate court documents indicated that he died in 1864; therefore, there appears to be an error on his tombstone. To get to the cemetery take Highway 17 south from Vernon, Alabama to County Road 22 that is also called Walnut Grove Road.

The atrocity committed by the CSA Home Guard in the death of Gilbert was truly unimaginable. To further compound the agony and anguish of this family, Gilbert and Jemima had a son, John Calvin, who was a Private in the CSA. Gilbert died because of his Unionists beliefs. Was his son truly for secession and committed to preserve the honor of the South, or was he forced to serve in order to avoid the same fate as his father? Additionally, Gilbert's brother, Bartley, was a soldier in the CSA Home Guard that was assigned to Fayette County. He was not, however, in the same Company of "Old Dog" Wilson. Two of Bartley's sons died as CSA soldiers in the 26th Alabama Infantry. It is impossible to comprehend what the family dynamics in this situation might have been.

Gundney - Only one card was found for a Gundney, no first name or initial listed. It was filed at the end of the last roll of microfilm of the 1st Alabama Cavalry, USV records. It was on a Return and recorded him as a private in Company F, stating he was absent, sick in March 1864. No further information relative to this soldier was found.*

Gunn, Simeon - Simeon Gunn enlisted in Company C of the 1st Alabama Cavalry, USV as a private on December 1, 1862, in Corinth, Mississippi for a period of one year. He was enrolled by Captain John Latty and was mustered in December 22, 1862, in Corinth. The Company Descriptive Book recorded him as 23 years of age, 5'-11" tall, having a dark complexion, brown eyes, dark hair, born in Bedford County, Tennessee, and a farmer by occupation. He was mustered out in Memphis, Tennessee on December 17, 1863, due to expiration of term of service.

Gurley, Charles A. - Charles A. Gurley enlisted in Company L of the 1st Alabama Cavalry, USV as a private on September 25, 1863, in Fayette County, Alabama for a period of 1 year. He was enrolled by Captain Tramel and was mustered in the same day in Glendale, Mississippi. The Company Muster Roll for September 25, 1863, through October 31, 1863, recorded him as absent with leave. The November and December 1863 Muster Roll recorded him as having returned from missing in action December 25, 1863, to be stopped on account of ordnance lost and owing the U.S. Government twenty-four cents. Charles Gurley's name appeared on the Returns as follows: April 1864, absent, sick in Nashville, Tennessee. He was mustered out September 28, 1864, in Rome, Georgia at age 32, due to expiration of term of service.

Guthery, Isaac - Isaac Guthery, also spelled Guthrie and Guthrey, enlisted and mustered into Company I of the 1st Alabama Cavalry, USV as a private on July 21, 1862, in Huntsville, Alabama for a period of 3 years. He was enrolled by Captain Bankhead and was mustered in The Company Descriptive Book recorded him as 29 years of age, 5'-7¼" tall, having a light complexion, blue eyes, light hair, born in Walker County, Alabama, and a farmer by occupation. The November and December 1862 Muster Roll recorded him as absent with leave with organization at Nashville, Tennessee since December 27, 1862. Isaac Guthery was one of the early enlistees immediately shipped to Nashville and merged with the 1st Middle Tennessee Cavalry, when later became the 5th Tennessee Cavalry. He was assigned to Company D of the 1st Middle Tennessee Cavalry, US. The December 31, 1862, through June 30, 1863, Muster Roll recorded him as absent, missing in action May 2, 1863, at Cedar Bluff, Alabama. His name appeared on the Returns for December 1862, stating absent on detached service with "train", probably wagon train, since December 27, 1862, also in January 1863, he was absent, on detached service as courier at Readyville, Tennessee January 27, 1863. A Prisoner of War Record in his records stated "Place, date and circumstances of capture not shown. Admitted to hospital at Andersonville, Georgia August 21, 1864, (9270) where he died September 8, 1864, of Scorbutus. There was a Notation in his records from the Adjutant General's Office of the War Department dated September 30, 1875, which stated Isaac Guthery died of Scorbutus on September 8, 1864, at Andersonville Prison in Georgia while a prisoner of war in the hands of the enemy. He was buried in Grave #8147 in Andersonville National Cemetery in Andersonville, Sumter County, Georgia.

Guthery, Jacob J. - See Jacob J. Guthry.

Guthery, James - See James Guthrey.

Guthery, John - John Guthery, also spelled Guthrie, enlisted in Company I of the 1st Alabama Cavalry, USV as a private on August 1, 1863, in Shelbyville, Tennessee for a period of 3 years. He was enrolled by Lieutenant Snelling. The Company Descriptive Book recorded him as 18 years of age, 5'-6" tall, having a light complexion, gray eyes, and sandy hair. The rest of it was incomplete. The June 30, to October 31, 1863, Muster Roll recorded him as missing in action October 26, 1863, from the Battle of Vincent's Crossroads near Bay Springs, Mississippi. His name appeared on the Company Muster-Out Roll dated July 19, 1865, from Nashville, Tennessee, stating he died at home in Alabama, but date was not known.

Guthery, Marion M. - Marion M. Guthery, also spelled Guthrie and Guttery, enlisted and mustered into Company I of the 1st Alabama Cavalry, USV on August 1, 1863, in Shelbyville, Tennessee for a period of 3 years. He was enrolled by Lieutenant Snelling. The Company Muster Roll recorded him as 19 years of age, 5'-7" tall, having a dark complexion, gray eyes, and dark hair. Place of birth and occupation were not completed. The June 30, through October 31, 1863, recorded him as missing in action October 26, 1863, from the Battle of Vincent's Crossroads, near Bay Springs, Mississippi. The May and June 1864 Muster Roll stated he was missing in action October 26, 1863, captured and sent by the enemy to Baltimore, Maryland. He died of bronchitis April 20, 1864. The Muster-Out Roll dated September 28, 1864, from Rome, Georgia stated he died at Baltimore, Maryland, absent, entire entry except rank "absent" cancelled on roll by line. His name appeared on the Returns as being in 3rd Regiment of the Tennessee Cavalry, enlisting August 1, 1863. There is a Marion M. Guthrey buried in Section A, Grave #334, in Loudon Park Cemetery in Baltimore, Maryland, according to Darlene Rudicelle, Program Assistant at the Baltimore National Cemetery. His body may have been moved or the cemetery may have changed names over the years. A Prisoner of War Record in his files is almost illegible as it has ink splattered on it, but stated Marion M. Guthery was captured at Jones Crossroads on October _, 1863, admitted to hospital at Richmond, Virginia in March due to bronchitis, paroled at City Point, Virginia April 16, 1864, admitted to West's Building U.S. Army General Hospital in Baltimore Maryland April 18, 1864, where he died April 20, 1864.

Guthery, William - William Guthery was enrolled in Captain Jones' Company of the 1st Alabama Cavalry, USV on August 18, 1862, in Huntsville, Alabama. He was one of the first enlistees who were immediately shipped to Nashville, Tennessee where they were merged with the 1st Middle Tennessee Cavalry, which later became the 5th Tennessee Cavalry. William was attached to Company D of the 1st Middle Tennessee Cavalry, U.S. On November 30, 1862, he was listed as being absent, sick in hospital November 12th, in Nashville, Tennessee. However, he was listed as present for the next muster roll. By July and August 1863, he was back with Company I of the 1st Alabama Cavalry, USV. The Company Descriptive Book recorded William as 19 years of age, 5'-11¾" tall, having light complexion, hazel eyes, light hair, born in Cherokee County, Alabama, and a farmer by occupation. Guthery re-enlisted on July 21, 1862, in Huntsville, Alabama for 3 years. He was enrolled by Captain H.C. Bankhead. He appeared on the Returns as a Stable Guard in December 1863 and January 1864. In October 1864, he had been absent without leave since September 29, 1864. He was mustered out on July 31, 1865, at Nashville, Tennessee with a $100 bounty due him from the U.S. Government. During the last six months of the war, he was one of the body guards of General Sherman and was said to have ridden a Bay horse No. 487329. He was chosen because of his excellent marksmanship and ability to ride any type of horse. During the last six months of the war, he was one of the body guards of General Sherman and was said to have ridden a Bay horse No. 487329. He was chosen because of his excellent marksmanship and ability to ride any type of horse.

William Guthery was born February 4, 1843, in Cherokee County, Alabama. He was the 5th child of David Guthery and Mary Ann Crone. William married Martha Beatrice Speegle on November 8, 1866, in what is now Cullman County, Alabama. He died June 12, 1912, and was buried in the Brushy Creek Cemetery in Cullman County, Alabama. Martha was born July 19, 1844, in Winston County, Alabama and died December 16, 1910, in Cullman County, Alabama. Martha Beatrice Speegle was the 11th child of David Speegle and Winifred Cranford. She had eighteen brothers and sisters and seven half brothers and sisters.

William was always willing to learn. He learned from anyone who could teach him what he wanted to learn and from his children that he kept in school. He had a good voice and learned most of the songs in the old hymn book. It had no musical notes. They sang by long meter and short meter.

After he and Martha were married, they lived in his father, David's cabin. David moved to what was known as the Jackson place, the 80 acres west of this being the homestead. As the family increased, William and Martha moved into the big house, as it was called and the 20' by 20' cabin became the kitchen. They lived the remainder of their lives at this location. William bought more land from time to time until he had enough to gave each of his sons, 80 acres.

William and Martha had 16 children. Margaret Melsena, born August 17, 1867; Benjamin Franklin, born July 31, 1868; King David, b. August 21, 1869; Rhoda Ann Francis, born November 5, 1870; William Henderson, born May 26, 1872; Martha Darinda, born May 19, 1873; John McDaniel, born September 12, 1874; Lorenza Jackson, born December 7, 1875; Jerusha Adeline, born December 22, 1876; Thomas Richard, born July 31, 1878; Elsberry Houston, born July 18, 1879; Naomia Winford, born September 25, 1880; Mikel Elcana, born November 2, 1881; Mary Magdalene, born May 17, 1883; Marilla Beatrice born August 2, 1885; and Chesley Emanuel Licagus Guthery, born September 8, 1887.

Mr. Richard H. May of Washington, D.C. gives the following information about the pension record of William Guthery: "William Guthery's pension file is about an inch thick. In it besides the original application and supporting papers, are reapplications at various times as a result of more liberalized pension laws or his increasing disability. His pension was evidently increased from time to time, the last just before his death. As to his death, a deposition in the pension file by R.H. Beard, M.D., County health officer for Cullman County, states that he died at 3:30 a.m. June 1, 1912, aged 69 years, 3 mo and 29 days, from pneumonia. He was a farmer, a widower, pensioner, had no children under 16, and was born in Alabama." Family information by Lem Guthery

<u>Guthery, William E.</u> - William E. Guthery enlisted in Company L of the 1st Alabama Cavalry, USV as a private on September 25, 1863, in Fayette County, Alabama for a period of 1 year. He was enrolled by Captain Tramel, and was mustered in the same day in Glendale, Mississippi. He was recorded as age 17. He was recorded as missing in action from Vincent's Crossroads, Mississippi on October 26, 1863. His name was recorded on the Small Pox U.S.A. General Hospital in Memphis, Tennessee for January and February 1864, stating he was sick and admitted to the hospital January 27, 1864. He was returned to the regiment March 15, 1864. He was discharged September 28, 1864, in Rome, Georgia due to expiration of term of service. He reenlisted April 24, 1865 in Huntsville, Alabama and was mustered in May 20, 1865, in Nashville, Tennessee. The Muster and Descriptive Roll recorded him as 17 years of age, 6'-½" tall, having a fair complexion, blue eyes, light hair, born in Walker

County, Alabama, and a farmer by occupation. He was mustered out October 20, 1865, in Huntsville, Alabama. There was a Company Descriptive Roll in the records of William E. Guthery for a William Guttry stating he was 35 years of age, 6' tall, having a fair complexion, gray eyes, red hair, born in Alabama, and a farmer by occupation. It stated he enlisted September 25, 1863, in Fayette County, Alabama by Captain Tramel for a period of 1 year and was discharged February 10, 1864. However, William E. Guthery was recorded as 17 years of age when he enlisted. Either this is a different William Guthery or the age is incorrect.) William E. Guthery's name appeared on the Returns as follows: January 1864, absent, sick in Memhis, Tennessee; March 1864, absent, sick in Memphis, Tennessee; April 1864, absent, in Nashville, Tennessee; September 1864, absent, on furlough. William E. Guthery died in 1919 in Lynn, Winston County, Alabama and was buried in the New Hope Baptist Church Cemetery, near Haleyville, in Marion County, Alabama.

Guthrey, David - David Guthery, also shown as Daniel Guthery, enlisted in Company B of the 1st Alabama Cavalry, USV as a private on March 16, 1864, in Decatur, Alabama for a period of 3 years. He was enrolled by Lieutenant Judy. The Company Descriptive Book recorded him as 23 years of age, 5'-9" tall, having a fair complexion, gray eyes, dark hair, born in Cherokee County, Alabama, and a farmer by occupation. The Company Muster Roll dated April 30, 1864, recorded him as absent, left sick in U.S. General Hospital in Decatur, Alabama April 17, 1864. David Guthrey was still recorded as being sick in the hospital in Decatur, Alabama on October 20, 1865, when the organization was mustered out and was not issued a discharge. David Guthrey, also listed as Daniel Guthery, enlisted in Company B of the 1st Alabama Cavalry, USV as a private on March 16, 1864, in Decatur, Alabama.

David Guthrey was born February 24, 1841, in Cherokee County, Alabama and was the brother of William and James and they were the sons of David Guthrey, born January 7, 1811, died April 23, 1893, and his wife, Mary Ann Crone, born April 16, 1818, and died April 13, 1892. David and Mary were married October 24, 1833. Descendants state that David, Jr. was killed April 25, 1864. In 1864, Cynthia Jane Milligan Guthery, wrote a letter to Washington, D.C. from Newburgh, Warrick County, Indiana, requesting a pension from David's service in the Civil War. The letter is filed with David's Pension records. She stated that she was the wife of David Guthery when he was killed in the war and gave their date of marriage and the birth and death of their only child. In 1870 she wrote another letter from Gibson County, Indiana. Also in this file are sworn statements by James Milligan, F.M. Halbrooks, Nancy Milligan and Dorcas Ann Halbrook, each one stating that this person, Cynthia Jane Guthery was who she claimed to be and that they were present when she married David in Winston County, Alabama.

Guthrey, James - James Guthrey, also spelled James Guthery, enlisted in Company B of the 1st Alabama Cavalry, USV as a private on March 16, 1864, in Decatur, Alabama for a period of 3 years. He was enrolled by Lieutenant Judy, and was mustered in March 27, 1864, in Decatur. His enlistment was credited to Decatur, Morgan County, Alabama The Company Descriptive Book recorded him as 18 years of age, 5'-10" tall, having a fair complexion, gray eyes, light hair, born in Cherokee County, Alabama, and a farmer by occupation. The April 1864 though August 1865 Company Muster Rolls recorded him as absent, left sick in the hospital in Decatur, Alabama since April 17, 1864. A Notation from the Adjutant General's Office of the War Department dated September 30, 1875, stated the following: "The Notation of September 13, 1867, showing this man died September 8, 1864, at Andersonville, Georgia is hereby cancelled. Investigation fails to elicit further information." (That was actually Isaac Guthrey who died September 8, 1864, in Andersonville Prison.) There was no discharge issued James when the organization was mustered out October 20, 1865, in Huntsville, Alabama, due to the fact he was still in the hospital. There was a Casualty Sheet for James Guthrey stating he died in 1865. The next record in his file stated there was no record of death on file for James Guthrey, and that his name was not borne on the Roll of Honor for Decatur, Alabama (Corinth).

James was the brother to William and David Guthery who also served in this regiment. They were sons of David Guthrey and Mary Ann Crone. According to descendant Lem Guthrey, James died of measles in a Decatur hospital April 21, 1864, one month after he enlisted. Another descendant stated that David Guthery, besides being a farmer, kept a large number of horses at all times. During the Civil War, all his horses were taken by the Confederate army, except one old mare that was blind in one eye. All of David's sons who were old enough fought in the Union army. William, the fifth son, was General Sherman's body guard for the last six months of the war.

Guthrie, Calvin - Calvin Gutherie enlisted in Company I of the 1st Alabama Cavalry, USV as a private on October 17, 1863, in Glendale, Mississippi, and died of disease at Cumberland U.S.A. General Hospital in Nashville, Tennessee. His widow was recorded as Rhoda Guttery and stated she lived at Basham's Gap Alabama.

Calvin Guthrie was born about 1823 in Tennessee to John and Elizabeth Guthrie. Calvin married Rhoda Cooper February 17, 1845, in Walker County, Alabama and had the following children: Susannah Elizabeth, born June 12, 1848, died 1905; Alice, born May 8, 1850, died July 4, 1925; John, born September 28, 1852, died July 22, 1927; Levi, born October 16, 1855, died July 26, 1951; Winford, born September 9, 1858; Reuben, born 18 December 18, 1860; and Nancy Jane Guthrie, born May 23, 1863, died May 18, 1936. Calvin Guthrie died April 20, 1864, in Nashville, Davidson County, Tennessee, and was buried in Grave H-9834 of the Nashville National Cemetery. Submitted by Treva Hood from the Cullman County, Alabama Heritage Book.

Guthrie, G.W. - G.W. Guthrie enlisted in Company D of the 1st Alabama Cavalry, USV as a private. His name appeared on the Returns as follows: September 1864, on detached service as orderly with General Dodge; January to March 1865, detached in north Alabama with Major Shurtliff; April 1865, on detached service with Captain Lomax. No further information relative to this soldier was found.*

Guthrie, George W. - George W. Guthrey, also shown as Guthrie, enlisted and mustered into Company H of the 1st Alabama Cavalry, USV as a private on October 10, 1863, in Glendale, Mississippi for a period of 1 year. The September and October 1863 Muster Roll recorded him as absent, supposed prisoner of war in the hands of the enemy since October 26, 1863. Probably from the Battle of Vincent's Crossroads which was fought on that date. The muster rolls through October 1864 record him as absent, a prisoner of war since October 26, 1863. His name appeared on the Returns for October 1864 stating he was sick in the hospital. No further information was located on this soldier.

Guthrie, Henry - Henry Gutherie, also shown as Henry Guttery, had two cards in the records for the 1st Alabama Cavalry, USV which were found at the end of the last roll of microfilm of the 1st Alabama Cavalry, USV Muster Rolls. They were both Returns and one stated he enlisted in Company F as a private on November 11, 1864, in Rome, Georgia. The other one stated Henry Guttery died of disease November 30, 1864, in the field in Georgia. No further information relative to this soldier was located.

Guthrie, Lemon - Leman Gutherie, also spelled Guthery, enlisted in Company B of the 1st Alabama Cavalry, USV as a private on February 4, 1864, in Pulaski, Tennessee for a period of 3 years. He was enrolled by Lieutenant Judy, and was mustered in March 27, 1864, in Decatur, Alabama. The Muster and Descriptive Roll recorded him as 28 years of age, 5'-11" tall, having a fair complexion, blue eyes, dark hair, born in Walker County, Alabama, and a farmer by occupation. His enlistment was credited to Pulaski, Giles County, Tennessee. The April 30, 1864, Muster Roll recorded him as a corporal. The September through February 1865 Muster Roll recorded him as being absent, on furlough for 15 days commencing September 22, 1864. Since that date he has been absent without leave. The March and April 1865 Muster Roll recorded him as absent without leave. The May and June 1865 Muster Roll recorded him as present, was with Lieutenant Major Shurtliff in Stevenson, Alabama when marked absent without leave. He was mustered out October 20, 1865, in Huntsville, Alabama. Gutherie was appointed corporal March 28, 1864.

Leman Guthrie was born January 10, 1835, in Walker County, Alabama and was the son of Daniel Guthrie. He married Christina Baker, daughter of Peter Baker and Christina Speegle. Leman died November 29, 1912, in Gravelton, Wayne County, Missouri. He is buried at Whitener Cemetery, in Marquand, Madison County, Missouri. His gravestone is inscribed, "Our bodies lie in the dust but our names will live forever.

Guthrie, Robert Franklin - Robert Franklin Guthrie, also listed as Robert L. Guthrie, enlisted in Company B of the 1st Alabama Cavalry, USV as a private on March 27, 1863, in Glendale, Mississippi for a period of 1 year. He was enrolled by Captain Henry J. Sumner The Company Descriptive Book recorded him as 29 years of age, 5'-4" tall, having a dark complexion, blue eyes, dark hair, born in Hall County, Georgia, and a farmer by occupation. He was mustered out January 22, 1864, in Memphis, Tennessee.

Robert Franklin Guttery was the father of William "Will" Guthrie. Robert was born July 1, 1831, in Walker County, Alabama. He was the son of Reverend Johnson Guttery and Mary Wilson. Robert Guttery married Gracie Frances Nesmith December 16, 1852, in Jasper, Walker County, Alabama. Gracie Nesmith was the daughter of William Nesmith and Martha "Patsy" O'Rear. Robert claimed this marriage record existed in a family Bible. The Court House in Walker County burned and records were destroyed by fire. Robert and Gracie Guttery are known to have had 9 children: Mary Ann, Johnson, Orlena, Alexander, William "Will", Lieuticia F., Sarah E., John H. and Nancy Jane. Robert F. Guttery received a land patent on the first day of December, 1859. He received 39.88 acres of land in Walker County, Alabama (certificate # 28305). Due to an illness, which he claimed he received during his time in the military, Robert F. Guttery eventually lost the use of his sight. The date of his death is unknown but Robert F. Guttery is buried at the Second Creek Cemetery, Second Creek, Lawrence County, Tennessee. Family information submitted by Layne Holley.

Guthrie, Seborn - Seborn Guthrie, also shown as Gutherie, enlisted in Company B of the 1st Alabama Cavalry, USV on February 6, 1864, in Pulaski, Tennessee for a period of 3 years. He was enrolled by Lieutenant Judy, and was mustered in March 27, 1864, in Decatur, Alabama. The Muster and Descriptive Roll recorded him as 18 years of age, 5'-6" tall, having a dark complexion, blue eyes, dark hair, born in Walker County, Alabama, and a farmer by occupation. He was mustered out October 20, 1865, in Huntsville, Alabama owing the U.S. Government $3.09 for losing a halter and bridle. His Muster Out Record stated he was due a bounty of $300.

Guthrie, William B. - William B. Guthrie enlisted in Company B of the 1st Alabama Cavalry, USV as a private on February 4, 1864, in Pulaski, Tennessee for a period of 3 years. He was enlisted by Lieutenant Judy, and was mustered in March 27, 1864, in Decatur, Alabama. The Company Descriptive Book recorded him as 38 years of age, 6'-2" tall, having a fair complexion, blue eyes, dark hair, born in Pall County, Georgia. His enlistment was credited to Pulaski, Giles County, Tennessee. The April 30, 1864, Muster Roll recorded him as a Sergeant. Guthrie was promoted to Sergeant on March 28, 1864, The September 1864 through April 1865 Muster Rolls recorded him as absent, on furlough for 15 days commencing September 22, 1864, since without leave. The May and June 1865 Muster Roll recorded him as present and stated he had been on detached service with Major Shurtliff in Stevenson, Alabama when marked absent without leave. Guthrie was mustered out October 20, 1865, in Huntsville, Alabama.

Guthry, B. - Only one card was found for B. Guthry which was a Return and was filed at the end of the last roll of microfilm of the 1st Alabama Cavalry, USV records. It recorded him as being Company B, and stated he was absent, sick in U.S. General Hospital on February 2, 1865. No further information relative to this soldier was found.*

Guthry, Jacob J. - Jacob J. Guthry, also shown as A.J. and Andrew J. Guthery, enlisted in Company D of the 1st Alabama Cavalry, USV as a private on May 1, 1864, in Decatur, Alabama for a period of 3 years. He was enrolled by Lieutenant Pease, and was mustered in June 16, 1864, in Decatur. The Muster and Descriptive Roll recorded him as 22 years of age, 6" tall, having a light complexion, blue eyes, light hair, born in Walker County, Alabama, and a farmer by occupation. Guthry's name appeared on the Returns as follows: July to October 1864, on duty as company cook; March to May 1865, absent, prisoner of war March 10, 1865; June 1865, Camp Chase, Ohio, by General Order No. 77, War Department 1865. The March and April 1865 Muster Roll recorded him as a prisoner of war, taken March 10, 1865, which was the date of the battle of Monroe's Crossroads. He was captured at

Solomon Grove, near Fayetteville, North Carolina. He was paroled at Aiken's Landing, NY March 30, 1865, reported to Camp Chase, Ohio April 5, 1865. He was furloughed April 9, 1865, for 30 days, returned May 9, 1865, reported to his regiment May 23, 1865, and mustered out at Camp Chase, Ohio June 13, 1865. A letter found in Guthry's records from the Assistant Quartermaster's Office, Railroad Transportation Department, Louisville, Kentucky, dated May 6, 1865, stated the following: I have the honor of notifying you that I have furnished Andrew J. Guthry, Company D, 1st Regiment Alabama Cavalry with transportation from this city to Columbus, Ohio, cost $5.27, to be deducted from his pay. Very Respectively, J.R. _____, Captain and Assistant Quartermaster.

Guthry, John Willis - John Willis Guthry enlisted in Company D of the 1st Alabama Cavalry, USV as a private on May 1, 1864, in Decatur, Alabama for a period of 3 years. He was enrolled by Lieutenant Pease, and was mustered in June 16, 1864, in Decatur. The Muster and Descriptive Roll recorded him as 28 years of age, 5'-8" tall, having a light complexion, blue eyes, light hair, born in Pontotoc County, Mississippi, and a farmer by occupation. The July and August 1864 Muster Roll recorded him as absent, on detached duty by Major General Dodge. The September and October Muster Roll recorded him as present, and the November 1864 through February 1865 Muster Rolls recorded him as absent, on detached duty by order of Major General Dodge. Guthry's name appeared on the Returns as follows: July 1864, he was an orderly for Major Shurtliff; October 1864, detached orderly to General Dodge; November and December 1864, on detached service. He was mustered out October 20, 1865, in Huntsville, Alabama owing the U.S. Government $10.55 for losing 1 shelter tent, 1 pair spurs and straps. He was shown as being owed a bounty of $100. Guthry's name appeared on the Returns of the 3rd Tennessee Cavalry showing he enlisted August 1, 1863, in Shelbyville, Tennessee. John originally enlisted in Company A, 22nd Alabama Infantry, CSA.

John Willis Guthry was the first mayor of Townley, Alabama. He was born February 24, 1838, in Pontotoc County, Mississippi, to Johnson Guttery and Mary Willis Guttery. Johnson Guttery was born March 12, 1806, in Georgia, and married November 24, 1824. Johnson Guttery was a son of William Guttery, born in 1775 in South Carolina, and Hannah Johnson. Johnson Guttery died May 23, 1876, in Walker County, Alabama. He was a Primitive Baptist Minister who preached in Alabama, Tennessee, and Mississippi. John Willis Guttery enlisted in the Confederate Army, 22nd Alabama Regiment, Company A, on September 30, 1861, at Jasper, Alabama. Three of his brothers enlisted in the 1st Alabama Cavalry on September 25, 1863: Benjamin, Robert, and Henry Guttery. John quit the Confederate Army in February, 1864. He enlisted in the 1st Alabama Cavalry USV on May 1, 1864, at Decatur, Alabama, at age 26. He was mustered out on October 20, 1865. John married Sarah Elizabeth Boshell who was born June 8, 1844, and died February 6, 1921. John died June 20, 1926. Both are interred in the Boshell Cemetery, Townley Alabama. The name on their grave marker is "Guthrie". His father's and grandfather's name was "Guttery". Family information submitted by Craig Burton, Jr.

Guttery, Benjamin F. - Benjamin F. Guttery enlisted and mustered into Company L of the 1st Alabama Cavalry, USV on September 25, 1863, in Fayette County, Alabama for a period of 1 year. He was enrolled by Captain Tramel. Guttery was recorded as present for each month he was in service, and the Company Descriptive Book was not completed. He was discharged September 28, 1864, in Rome, Georgia due to expiration of term of service. He was paid in full by Major Holt of Nashville, Tennessee.

Benjamin Franklin Guttery was born May 27, 1834, in Old Coffeeville, Yalabusha County, Mississippi. He was the son of Mary Willis and Johnson Guttery, March 12, 1806, in Georgia, and married November 24, 1824. Johnson Guttery was the son of William Guttery, born in 1775 in South Carolina, and Hannah Johnson. Johnson Guttery died May 23, 1876, and is buried in Townley, Boshell Graveyard, Walker County, Alabama. He was a Primitive Baptist Minister. William Guttery died July 7, 1825. In November 1857, Benjamin married Elizabeth Nesmith, born March 27, 1836, in Lynn, Winston County, Alabama. She died April 8, 1934, in Tennessee. Their children were: Martha Ann, born September 1858; Malinda Maniza, born 1863; Mary Elizabeth, born 1865; William Johnson, born October 1, 1866, died October 21, 1899; John Newton, born January 20, 1868, died April 7, 1950; Ariminta, born 1870; Benjamin Franklin, born 1872; Robert Martin, born April 3, 1875, died July 6,

1905. Benjamin, Sr. died December 10, 1920 in Five Points, Lawrence County, Tennessee and is buried in Second Creek Cemetery in Five Points, Lawrence County, Tennessee.

On July 30, 1920, Benjamin filed a Declaration for Pension in Lawrence County, Tennessee. He was 86 years old. Records state that he requires the regular personal aid and attendance of another person on account of the following disabilities: "Old age and his mind is no good, can't take care of himself and has to be watched all the time".

Affidavit to Origin of Disability (sic)

"Andrew D. Mitchell of Thorn Hill, County of Marion, State of Alabama, age 41, Sgt. in Co. L, 1st Regiment Alabama Cavalry Volunteers, states the following: (sic) "On or about 15 or 20th day(s) of June, 1864, while in the line of duty, and without fault or improper conduct on his part, at or near Kingston, State of Georgia said soldier was taken with chronic diarrhea and was sent back to Chattanooga, Tennessee to convalescent camps and I was sent with him and he was verry weak and I was also weak with the same complaint and when we got there we found it was on the bank of the river in a low nasty sickly looking place and we left there just as quick as we could get away and went back to the front for we thoat we would get worse or perhaps dye if we staide there. I never new B.F. Guttery untill we jainde the Army he was sound boddied so far as nowed."

Department of the Interior, Bureau of Pension: "January 11, 1889, respectfully returned to the Surgeon General USA for a further search of the records showing the nature of the disabilities for which the within named soldier was treated in General Hospital and convalescent camp at Chattanooga, Tennessee from April to August 1864." Benjamin Guttery's Death Certificate states he died from "infirmities of old age". (Submitted by descendant, Kathryn Heilman)

Guttery, Henry - Henry Guttery enlisted and mustered into Company L of the 1st Alabama Cavalry, USV on September 25, 1863, at Fayette County, Alabama for a period of one year. He was enlisted by Captain Tramel. The Company Muster Roll from September 25, 1863, to October 31, 1863, listed him as being absent, sick in hospital. However, the other muster rolls show him to be present. In April 1864, Henry was a company clerk. In October 1864, he was an orderly for Captain Trammel. The Company Muster Roll for September and October 1864 stated he enrolled in Glendale, Mississippi. Guttery was discharged September 28, 1864, at Rome, Georgia for reason of expiration of term of service. The Muster and Descriptive Roll dated October 17, 1864, in Rome, Georgia showed Henry Guttery to have been 22 years of age, 5'-10" tall, having a fair complexion, blue eyes, light hair, born in Walker County, Alabama, and a farmer by occupation. It also stated he reenlisted and mustered in September 29, 1864, for a period of 3 years in Rome, Georgia and was due $300 for bounty. Henry was shown as having been mustered out October 20, 1865, in Huntsville, Alabama at age 22. His Muster-Out Roll stated he was due $100 for bounty. It also stated Henry Guttery died of disease in hospital at Savannah, Dawson County, Georgia, on December 9, 1864. A Notation from the Adjutant General's Office of the War Department dated January 26, 1885, stated Henry Guttery died in Regimental Hospital on December 9, 1864, of Inflammation of the Lungs. Henry's Casualty Sheet states he was originally interred in the Beaufort National Cemetery in Beaufort, Beaufort County, South Carolina, the bodies in which cemetery were originally buried at various places in and about Georgia and South Carolina. A note in Henry's records stated the following: Returns of Diseased Soldiers, 4th Quarter 1864, shows Henry Guttery, Company F died December 9, 1864, near Savannah, Georgia, of fever. Name not born on Company F Doctor's Book. Other Regimental and Company L Records furnish no evidence of death.

Henry Guttery was born about 1842 in Walker County, Alabama. Most descendants think he was the son of Johnson and Mary Wilson Guttery, who were married November 24, 1824, in Walker County, Alabama, because he and his sister, Nancy, were listed as the two youngest children in Johnson and Mary's household in 1850, while their oldest child was Sarah. However, after Henry died in the Civil War, Sarah Guttery filed for a pension stating Henry was her only son. She also stated Nancy was her daughter. A Deposition she signed in March 1885 stated she was 78 years old, never married and only had the two children. She also stated she didn't know who their father was, however, she told later who the fathers were or Henry and Nancy. She stated Henry supported her by working on her father's farm for four years before he enlisted in the 1st Alabama Cavalry, USV, but received no pay for his labor, only support for what he did on the farm. Her father was a poor man and was happy for Henry to work on the farm and support his mother. Another descendant stated Henry Caywood was Henry Guttery's father and George Dallyrimple was Nancy Guttery's father. She stated she had not seen Henry's father since before Henry was born, and that he had died several years ago in Mississippi. She stated it had been at least 37 years since she had seen Nancy's father. Henry's mother stated she had worked at hard labor in the fields since Henry had died. She also stated her father was a loyal Union man and the "rebels came to hang him for his loyalty during the war, ran him off and took all of his horses and meat, leaving him only one yoke of cattle and his land. Sarah went on to say that the Yankee soldiers used to come to their house wanting something to eat and she and her sister would carry victuals to them in the woods where they were hiding out. She stated Henry never married or left any children, and he only had 7 hogs. After the war, Sarah's mother gave her a mule and while she was trying to make a crop, the horse which she traded for the mule, was taken for rent of the land. Her mother later gave her a cow which she sold. Sarah stated she was never married or lived with anyone else as wife since Henry was born. She was asked in a pension affidavit how she had made a living and she stated: I hired out a heap, hoeing, picking corn, weaving and coloring blue for people, spinning and nursing the sick. (Before there was modern laundry detergents with brighteners, there was a substance called "blue", which was added to the final rinse water on washday, and it supposedly whitened the clothes. This is probably what Sarah was talking about when she said "coloring blue".) Other children of Johnson and Mary Guttery besides Sarah were: William M.; Ann; Robert F.; Benjamin Franklin (Benjamin also served in the 1st Alabama Cavalry, USV); Elizabeth; John Willis; Mary Jane; and Francis Guttery.

<u>Guttery, Robert Franklin</u> - Robert Franklin Guttery enlisted in Company L of the 1st Alabama Cavalry, USV as a private on September 25, 1863, at Fayette County, Alabama for a period of one year. He was enrolled by Captain Tramel and was mustered in the same day at Glendale, Mississippi. He was discharged September 28, 1864, at Rome, Georgia by reason of expiration of term of service. He was paid in full by Major Holt of Nashville, Tennessee. While Robert's Descriptive Roll was blank, his Muster-Out Roll stated he was 32 years of age.

Robert Franklin Guttery was the father of William "Will" Guthrie. Robert was born July 1, 1831, in Walker County, Alabama. He was the son of Reverend Johnson Guttery and Mary Wilson who were married November 24, 1824. Robert Guttery married Gracie Frances Nesmith December 16, 1852, in Jasper, Walker County, Alabama. Gracie Nesmith was the daughter of William Nesmith and Martha "Patsy" O'Rear. Robert claimed this marriage record existed in a family Bible. The Court House in Walker County burned and records were destroyed by fire. Robert and Gracie Guttery are known to have had 9 children: Mary Ann, born October 10, 1853; Johnson, born January 2, 1856; Orlena born, March 9, 1859; Alexander, born April 4, 1860; William "Will", born May 8, 1862, died November 14, 1937; Lieuticia F., born June 6, 1864; Sarah E., born March 29, 1867; John H., born April 30, 1870 and Nancy Jane Guttery, born November 14, 1873.

Robert F. Guttery received a land patent on the first day of December, 1859. He received 39.88 acres of land in Walker County, Alabama (certificate # 28305). He was a Private in Company L, First Alabama Cavalry, United States Volunteers, during the Civil War. Due to an illness, which he claimed he received during his time in the military, Robert F. Guttery eventually lost the use of his sight. The date of his death is unknown but Robert F. Guttery is buried at the Second Creek Cemetery, Second Creek, Lawrence County, Tennessee.

A Colt revolver has been identified as the one issued to Robert Guttery. It is in the possession of a private collector. Family information submitted by Layne Holley and Glenda McWhirter Todd.

<u>Guttery, William</u> - (This was actually William Carroll Guttery) William Guttery enlisted in Company L of the 1st Alabama Cavalry, USV as a private on September 25, 1863, in Fayette County, Alabama for a period of one year. He was mustered in the same day in Glendale, Mississippi. One muster roll incorrectly listed his age as 17, when it was actually 35 and was corrected on another muster roll. The November and December 1863 Muster Roll stated he had returned from missing in action December 25, 1863, and while it did not state what happened, it is possible he was captured or

wounded at the Battle of Vincent's Crossroads on October 26, 1863. He was discharged February 10, 1864, for a disability by General Hurlburt, 16ᵗʰ Army Corps. William Guttery's name appeared on a Muster Roll dated September 28, 1864, in Rome, Georgia, listing him as being 35 years of age, and stated he was discharged on Surgeon's Certificate of Disability, February 10, 1864 by order of Major General Hurlburt. The Certificate of Disability for William Guttery was issued to him by Captain Sanford Trammel at Camp Davies, Mississippi, on June 6, 1864. It stated: I certify that I have carefully examined Private William Guttery of Captain S. Trammel's Company, and find him incapable of performing the duties of a soldier because of Phthisis Pulmonalis, (otherwise known as consumption of the lungs or tuberculosis), Of both lungs which existed before entering the service. He is not able for duty in the Invalid Corps. William is buried in the Guthrie Cemetery, near Townley, in Walker County, Alabama. Died in 1902.

Guttery, William E. - See William E. Guthery.

Guttry, Jacob J. - See Jacob J. or A.J. Guthry.

Guttry, John W. - See John W. Guthry.

Guyse, Enoch, M. - Enoch M. Guyse, also spelled Guice, enrolled in Company M of the 1ˢᵗ Alabama Cavalry, USV as a private on November 29, 1863, in Camp Davies, Mississippi for a period of 3 years. He was enrolled by Lieutenant Cobleigh and was mustered in December 29, 1863, in Corinth, Mississippi. The January and February 1864 Muster Roll listed Enoch Guyse as a corporal. The March and April Muster Roll listed him as being absent, wounded since March 10, 1865, which was the horrific Battle of Monroe's Crossroads near Fayetteville, North Carolina. The May and June 1865 Muster Roll stated Enoch M. Guyse died in the U.S. General Hospital in Willett's Point, New York on April 17, 1865, by reason of gunshot wound to chest and left knee from wounds received in battle. The name C.M. Gice appeared on a Hospital Muster Roll from Grant U.S.A. General Hospital in Willett's Point in New York Harbor stating he was attached to the hospital on March 30, 1865, and died there April 17, 1865, from wounds received at the Battle of Monroe's Crossroads in North Carolina. The Company Descriptive Book listed Enoch M. Guyse as having been 42 years of age, 5'-6" tall, having a light complexion, blue eyes, light hair, born in Buncombe County, North Carolina, and a farmer by occupation. Enoch's record of Death and Interment spelled his name Gice, and stated his residence before enlisting was Fayetteville, Alabama. It also stated he was single but listed his widow as Jane Gice, who was living in Nashville, Tennessee, at the time. On the 1850 McNairy County, Tennessee Census, Enoch was listed as a Baptist Clergy, and on the 1860 Hardeman County, Tennessee Census, it listed him as a United Baptist Minister.

Guyce, James P. – See James P. Guice.

Guyse, George Washington - George W. Guyse enlisted in Company L of the 1st Alabama Cavalry, USV on September 25, 1863 in Fayette County, Alabama for a period of one year. He was enrolled by Captain Trammel, and mustered in the same day at Glendale, Mississippi. George W. Guyse's name appeared on the Returns as being left sick in Alabama in November 1863, by order of Colonel Spencer. The Company Muster Roll for September 25, to October 31, 1863, listed him as being absent with leave, but the November and December 1863 Muster Roll listed him as being present. The same muster roll stated his pay was to be stopped for lost ordnance for which he was charged 53 cents. It stated he had returned from missing in action on December 25, 1863. (He may have been captured during the Battle of Vincent's Crossroads which occurred October 26, 1863.) George was mustered out September 18, 1864, at Rome, Georgia by reason of expiration of term of service.

George W. Guyse was born February 1846 in Fayette County, Alabama, married Malinda Cummins December 17, 1861 in Winston County, Alabama and had the following children: John, born October 10, 1862; Peter, born May 8, 1864; William J., born February 17, 1867; George P., born June 5, 1872 and Emma Guyse, born October 11, 1874. George died September 24, 1903 of Bright's disease. Family information submitted by Lester Guyse. George Washington Guyse is buried at Oak Hill Cemetery in St. Florian in Lauderdale County, Alabama. Submitted by Tim Guyse.

Explanations of Some Records in Roster

An asterisk at the end of any of the military records indicates that record was found in the Miscellaneous Card Extracts located at the end of Roll #10, Microcopy 276, Compiled Service Records of First Regiment Alabama Cavalry Volunteers. There are also some miscellaneous papers which include POW Records, letters concerning destruction of property by Rebels, Returns, and various medical records, etc. These records are all filed in one packet of information at the National Archives in Washington, DC.

****

The first enlistees into the 1st Alabama Cavalry, USV were immediately shipped to Nashville, Tennessee, some in boxcars, where they were merged with the 1st Middle Tennessee Cavalry, US, which later became the 5th Tennessee Cavalry, US. When they went back to Alabama, they were recorded as being in the 1st Alabama Cavalry, USV. However, some of the ones from the 1st Alabama Cavalry, who died in or around Nashville, were buried with "TENN" on their tombstones rather than "ALA". Anyone with a 1st Alabama Cavalry, USV ancestor buried in Nashville, Davidson County, Tennessee, needs to check the Tennessee records as well as the Alabama Records.

****

The roster of soldiers is in alphabetical order; therefore the book is not indexed. However, there are many other surnames listed in the pension records and Southern Claims under the names of different soldiers. Some of it may include the maiden names of spouses. Names of children and other family members are also listed in some of the pension records. It is surprising how many of these soldiers and their families are connected in some way as many of them married into the families of other 1st Alabama Cavalry, USV soldiers.

****

Any derivative of a surname should be checked as many names were spelled as they sounded. Some of them, like Guthrie, were spelled several different ways.

****

In 2009, during her research, the author found that the names of about eleven of the 1st Alabama Cavalry, USV soldiers had been recorded as belonging to the CSA and buried in Confederate Circle at Mt. Olivet Cemetery in Nashville, Tennessee. This error was due to the government undertaker not showing if they were Union or Confederate and apparently since they were from Alabama, he, like many others, assumed they were Confederates. These names and their dates of death were published in the *Nashville Union Newspaper*. In 1977, a member of UDC, [United Daughters of the Confederacy] wanting to help spruce up the cemetery, added these names from the newspaper to the Mt. Olivet Cemetery Records. This was confirmed by the Roll of Honor and brought to the attention of the cemetery staff. These names are scheduled to be stricken from their records due to the diligent work of a member of Friends of Metro Archives who has been researching this for almost two years. The names of the soldiers recorded as buried in Mt. Olivet Cemetery in Nashville, are as follows: William Bowlin, James H. Downum, Calvin Guthrie, Thomas Huey, Isaac R. Perrett, John B. Pitts, Jeremiah Russell, Daniel Sharpton, Henry C. Sinyard, John W. Stokes, and John B. West. These soldiers are buried in the Nashville National Cemetery, some in unmarked graves.

Civil War Military Hospitals in Nashville, Tennessee

Post Hospital - Cherry Street Baptist Church was used as the post hospital and contained 125 beds. Most Nashville Churches were seized by the military during the occupation.

Hospital No. 1 – The Third Presbyterian Church, situated at the corner of Mulberry and College Streets, stood south of the College Hill Armory. Along with the armory, it was used as Hospital No. 1. There was an adjoining one-story building and these three structures had a bed capacity of 650. The Primitive Baptist Church on College Street was used by the Federal army in conjunction with Hospital No. 1 and contained 60 beds.

A Federal style townhouse located on a corner lot on College Hill, was used in connection with Hospital No. 1.

Also used in connection with Hospital No. 1 was a College Hill Federal style two-story house.

Hospital No. 2 - Housing for the president and other staff of the University of Nashville was used by the Federal army as a part of Hospital No. 2. Lindsley Hall was used both by the Confederate and Federal armies as a military hospital. As a Federal hospital it contained 200 beds and was reserved for officers.

Hospital No. 3 – The Jones Hotel on the east side of the Public Square, and a pair of Federal-style townhouses which later became part of the Jones Hotel, were used as a part of Hospital No. 3.

The Ensley Building, perhaps the most handsome commercial structure in town, was on the south side of the Public Square and was used in connection with Hospital No. 3. It contained 200 hospital beds.

The elegant Federal-style house at 77 Broad Street was used in connection with Hospital No. 3 and contained 250 beds.

Hospital No. 8 – The First Presbyterian Church was used as part of Hospital No. 8 and contained 206 beds.

The four-story Masonic Hall on Spring Street, across from the First Presbyterian Church, was also used as a part of Hospital No. 8, and contained 368 beds.

The Cumberland Presbyterian Church on the corner of Cumberland Alley and Summer Street, was also used as part of Hospital No. 8 and contained 41 beds.

Hospital No. 14 – The Nashville Female Academy was taken over by the Federal Army and used as Hospital No. 14. It was also used as headquarters for the provost marshal and as a shelter for the refugees.

Hospital No. 15 – The First Baptist Church of Nashville was used in connection with Hospital No. 15.

Hynes School, on the corner of Line and Summer Streets, was used as Hospital No. 15 for the treatment of men who had venereal disease, and contained 140 beds.

Hospital No. 16 – A large three-story commercial structure on College Street, between Broad and Spring, was used in connection with Hospital No. 16, and contained 375 beds. This was a "colored" hospital.

Hospital No. 19 - The Watson House Hotel, a four-story building, was on Market Street south of the Public Square and was used in connection with Hospital No. 19.

The Morris and Stratton wholesale grocers building at 14 Market Street, near Clark Street, was used as part of Hospital No. 19, and contained 300 beds.

The French Building at the corner of Clark and Market Streets was also used in connection with Hospital No. 19.

Large buildings on Broad, College, and Cherry Streets were also seized during the war to be used as hospitals.

General Sherman used the George W. Cunningham house on High Street, a beautiful, elegant Renaissance-Revival dwelling, as his headquarters. Other Federal Commanders also used the house as their headquarters were: Don Carlos Buell, William S. Rosecrans, Ulysses S. Grant, and George H. Thomas.

The Federal Army would have probably used the unfinished Maxwell House Hotel as a hospital but apparently deemed it too dangerous. They did take it over and used it as a prison for captured Confederates until September 29, 1863, when a staircase collapsed as prisoners were being moved down it, killing four or five men and injuring seventy-five others. The hotel was finally completed in 1869.

There was a Nashville Venereal Disease Hospital but it was used for prostitutes. With the coming of 70,00 troops to occupy Nashville, prostitution grew and venereal disease was rampant in the army. The military tried to control it by eliminating the chief source. The prostitutes were rounded up and shipped north by river. When Louisville and Cincinnati refused to accept the "cargo", the women were returned to Nashville where they forced them to register, pay a license fee, submit to weekly health examinations, and stay clean. The disease was controlled but not entirely eliminated.

The above information was taken from James A. Hoobler's wonderful and interesting book, *Cities Under the Gun*, Images of Occupied Nashville and Chattanooga. There are pictures of all of these hospitals in his book with the exception of Hospital #14, and it is from the collection of the author.

Hospital No. 14 in Nashville, Davidson County, Tennessee, formerly the Nashville Female Academy

BIBLIOGRAPHY FOR *UNIONIST IN THE HEART OF DIXIE*
Volume I

"*A Civil War Diary*" by Mary Katherine Sproul, taken from the History of Fentress County, Tennessee.

Roster and military records: Microfilm of military records from National Archives in Washington, DC.

"Confederate Outlaw: Champ Ferguson and the Civil War in Appalachia, by Brian Dallas McKnight.

"First Alabama Cavalry, USA-Homage to Patriotism", by Glenda McWhirter Todd

Civil War National Park Service Battle Summaries

"The History and Debates of the Convention of the People of Alabama", William R. Smith, Montgomery, AL: White, Pfister, & Co., 1861. Library of Congress

The Files Family of Alabama: A Family of Patriots: Moss, Bobby Gilmer:

The Patriots of Cowpens, (3rd Printing) Scotia Press, 1994, p.100-101.

Revolutionary Soldiers in Alabama, p. 39.

Umphrey, Don. Southerners in Blue, Dallas: Quarry Press, 2002. Pgs. 97 & 158, Umphrey, p. 97.

New York Times article dated April 16, 1864

Richard J. Sommers, ed., Vignettes of Military History, Volume III (Carlisle Barracks, Pa.: US Army Military History Institute, February 1982), Vignette No. 177, contributed by Lieutenant Colonel Gerald C. Brown, drawn from William W. Cluett, History of the 57th Regiment, Illinois Volunteer Infantry. From the US Army War College.

The Civil War Dictionary – Mark M. Boatner Thomas Benton Files - Revolutionary Soldiers in Alabama, p. 39:

George Davis' Southern Claims Commission File (Claim #6090)

Letter from James B. Bell to Henry Bell, April 27, 1861

Sources used by Peter J. Gossett for his story "Free States Civil War Events and the Jasper Raid:

Jason Guin sources by Rayburn A. Metcalfe: Family and public records, *The Guin and Related Families* by Marguerite T. Callahan, *The Guin Family* by Mary Davis Elmore, *Lamar County Alabama* and genealogies by Rose Marie Smith and *The Heritage of Lamar County, Alabama, Vol. 38.*

Guin: Janie Spencer provided most of the Guin information from her books on *Guins of Northwest Alabama*, Volumes I and II.

The story about the murder of Gilbert Guin was recalled and written in 1946 by an unidentified person named McDaniel who was the child of Nancy Guin McDaniel and a grandchild of Gilbert Guin. Also, Frances Abigail Stewart Corley, the daughter of Margaret and granddaughter of Gilbert said, "Gilbert Guin was plowing when a man named Wilson (bushwhacker) came and took him with them."

(Callahan, Vol. II, p. 6) It was also stated that Gilbert's wife, Jemima wrote the story in her daily journal that she was keeping.

George Davis' Southern Claims Commission File (Claim #6090)

The Civil War Dictionary – Mark M. Boatner

"A Brief History of Winston County, Alabama" by Judge John Bennett Weaver

"Sons of Solomon" by John Lucian West

National Soldiers and Sailors System

Reminiscences of the Civil War, John Brown Gordon, 1832-1904, Electronic Edition

Military Structure by Dave Frederick

Nashville Daily Union Newspaper

Union pension records from the National Archives in Washington, DC

Cities Under the Gun, Images of Occupied Nashville and Chattanooga, by James A. Hoobler

Jasper Allison

Henry Alvis

William M. Amerson

Willis Barton

Hamilton Bates
See better picture of Hamilton Bates below

John Baughn

William Beasley

James Newton Blancit

Jessie Blankenship

Robert A. Boyd

James L. Brooks
See picture of James & Family below

Frank C. Burdick

John R. Campbell

Erasmus D. Chandler

Peter Richard Clement

William R. Crocker

Captain Ozro Dodds

Major Micajah Fairfield

Thought to be Andrew Pink Flanagan

Andrew Pink Flanagan

John Freeman

William G. Glasgow

Union Soldiers killed in Battle

General Ulysses S. Grant

General Ulysses S. Grant

Green Washington Grisham

Jason Guin

Asa & Rasey Guin

George Washington Curtis

William Wallace Davis

Enos Day

George Dickenson

Drury and Matilda Baggett

Charles F. Barker

Hamilton S. Bates

Thomas & Martha Jane Barnes

Gun issued to Robert F. Guttery During War

This is the sight where the Battle of Hog Mountain took place

Frederick Hicks Baughn & Family

Henry & Sarah Baughn & Family

Peyton Baughn

Peyton Baughn

William M. Beasley

James L. Brooks & Family

Burning of Columbia, South Carolina

Made in the USA
Lexington, KY
10 September 2017